Special Edition

Using
Sybase
System XI™

Special Edition

USING

SYBASE

SYSTEM XI™

Written by Peter Hazlehurst

Special Edition Using Sybase System XI

Library of Congress Catalog No.: 95-71472

ISBN: 0-7897-0087-5

98 97 96   6 5 4 3 2 1

Interpretation of the printing code: the rightmost double-digit number is the year of the book's printing; the rightmost single-digit number, the number of the book's printing. For example, a printing code of 96-1 shows that the first printing of the book occurred in 1996.

Credits

PRESIDENT
Roland Elgey

PUBLISHER
Joseph B. Wikert

PUBLISHING MANAGER
Fred Slone

SENIOR TITLE MANAGER
Bryan Gambrel

EDITORIAL SERVICES DIRECTOR
Elizabeth Keaffaber

MANAGING EDITOR
Sandy Doell

DIRECTOR OF MARKETING
Lynn E. Zingraf

ACQUISITIONS EDITOR
Al Valvano

PRODUCTION EDITOR
Thomas Cirtin

COPY EDITOR
Jan Loveland

PRODUCT MARKETING MANAGER
Kim Margolius

ASSISTANT PRODUCT MARKETING MANAGER
Christy M. Miller

STRATEGIC MARKETING MANAGER
Barry Pruett

TECHNICAL EDITOR
Ramesh Chandak

TECHNICAL SUPPORT SPECIALIST
Nadeem Muhammed

ACQUISITIONS COORDINATOR
Carmen Krikorian

SOFTWARE RELATIONS COORDINATOR
Patty J. Brooks

EDITORIAL ASSISTANT
Andrea Duvall

BOOK DESIGNER
Ruth Harvey

COVER DESIGNER
Dan Armstrong

PRODUCTION TEAM
Stephen Adams
Kevin Cliburn
Linda Cox
Maribeth Echard
Jessica Ford
Amy Gornik
Daniel Harris
Kay Hoskin
Casey Price
Laura Robbins
Bobbi Satterfield
Paul Wilson

INDEXER
Brad Herriman

Composed in *Century Old Style* and *ITC Franklin Gothic* by Que Corporation.

About the Author

Peter Hazlehurst was born in Oxford, England, in 1972. At a very young age, he moved to Australia with his parents and settled in Canberra, the national capital. Peter was educated at an Anglican private boys school—Canberra Grammar School—during which time he learned a little bit about computers on the school library's Apple IIe. Peter graduated from high school in October 1990 and decided to take a year off before going on to university.

During the year off, Peter took a job as a data entry officer for a government department, the Australian Quarantine and Inspection Service (AQIS). This was definitely what was known as mindless work, and was not a particularly stimulating introduction into the world of computers. Peter met the local guru, Kevin Mayes, during this time, and it was Kevin who gave Peter the chance to try programming. After a few months of working on some mainframe software, Peter took a class in SQLWindows and was introduced to client/server programming.

For two years, Peter worked for the Australian Quarantine and Inspection Service, writing and working on various systems that brought AQIS out of the mainframe world and into the client/server domain. In time, Peter entered university and began studying for a law degree. In the summer of 1992, Peter went to the Gupta Developer's Conference where he met one of the founders of a new company, Phoenix International.

Peter joined Phoenix in March of 1993 as its first employee and was responsible for much of the initial design and development of the Phoenix Banking System. The Phoenix Banking System is a retail banking system that manages all of a bank's operational needs, from opening a new deposit account to processing real-time ATM transactions and all the nightly updates. Phoenix's technology is based on two key products: SQLWindows from Centura Software Corporation and Sybase System XI. Phoenix's banking software is in production in over 25 institutions worldwide with another 30 banks committed to installing Phoenix over the next year and a half.

In July of 1996, Phoenix became a public company trading on NASDAQ (PHXX) with a successful IPO. Phoenix now has over 110 employees and is growing very rapidly.

Peter has been a guest speaker at the last three developer conferences held by Centura Software Corporation, talking on such subjects as "Object-Oriented Programming," "Very Large Application Design and Development," and "Multi-Language Software Design." Peter is also a certified Centura software developer and SQLBase certified DBA. Peter has been a contributing author of two other books for Que Corporation: *Special Edition Using Gupta SQLWindows* and *Special Edition Using Microsoft SQL Server 6.5*.

Peter can be reached for comments and questions electronically via the Internet at **phazlehurst@phoenixint.com** or via CompuServe at **73114,3145**.

Acknowledgments

There are many, many people to thank when writing a book, and it is often difficult to make sure that everyone is recognized in the appropriate order. Therefore, without further preamble, I will thank the following people in no particular order—I assure you!

To start, I'd like to thank Wendy. She put up with me for the whole process and endured late, late nights that I spent writing my book without considering coming to bed or going out to play. I know she's had a lot on her plate lately, and it took a considerable amount of patience to put up with me and my insomnia.

I'd especially like to pay homage to the great people at Que, particularly my acquisitions editor, Al Valvano. Al's a tireless editor who finds absolutely no fun in picking on me for slightly late chapters. Also at Que, thanks to Tom Cirtin, my production editor. Tom turned my gibberish and somewhat nonsensical verbiage into a readable tome that may even find its way onto a few mantles. I'd also like to mention Jeff Riley, my production editor on *Special Edition Using Microsoft SQL Server 6.5*. He's a great guy and helped convince Que to keep me in the stables as a regular author. Also, thanks to all the formatters and copy editors who are definitely the late-night kings and queens of Que!

Professionally, thanks to my peers at Phoenix for cutting me just a little bit of slack on the days when I was recovering from a horrible all-night chapter writing session! The Phoenix people are the best people I've ever worked with, and I'm extremely grateful that I can have the opportunity to spend time thinking about things with them. Thanks to JN for giving me lots of guidance and advice, and for convincing me not to quit just before the IPO!

On the personal front, I'd like to say hello to my Dad. While not quite being up to his par in terms of eclecticism of subject matter, I hope that the book will be a tough read (as were his numerous tomes on political history). Also thanks to my Mum for her continual, transatlantic calls and support. She's really an angel, and so said the church—congratulations on your ordination!

Thanks to my adoptive parents for their time and support during the last year. It's been quite traumatic, and it's really nice to have somewhere to turn to as a place of last resort.

Thanks again to everyone for all your help and support during this tiring writing process. Four months (give or take) to pull together a manuscript like this is pretty amazing, and I couldn't have done it without all of your help.

We'd Like to Hear from You!

As part of our continuing effort to produce books of the highest possible quality, Que would like to hear your comments. To stay competitive, we *really* want you, as a computer book reader and user, to let us know what you like or dislike most about this book or other Que products.

You can mail comments, ideas, or suggestions for improving future editions to the address below, or send us a fax at (317) 581-4663. For the online inclined, Macmillan Computer Publishing has a forum on CompuServe (type **GO QUEBOOKS** at any prompt) through which our staff and authors are available for questions and comments. The address of our Internet site is **http://www.mcp.com** (World Wide Web).

In addition to exploring our forum, please feel free to contact me personally to discuss your opinions of this book: I'm **74671,3710** on CompuServe, and I'm **avalvano@que.mcp.com** on the Internet.

Thanks in advance—your comments will help us to continue publishing the best books available on computer topics in today's market.

Al Valvano
Acquisitions Editor
Que Corporation
201 W. 103rd Street
Indianapolis, Indiana 46290
USA

N O T E Although we cannot provide general technical support, we're happy to help you resolve problems you encounter related to our books, disks, or other products. If you need such assistance, please contact our Tech Support department at 800-545-5914 ext. 3833.

To order other Que or Macmillan Computer Publishing books or products, please call our Customer Service department at 800-835-3202 ext. 666. ■

Contents at a Glance

Table of Contents

II | Using System XI

5   Understanding Databases, Devices, and Transaction Logs   113

IV   Advanced Features

Introduction

Welcome! I'm glad you chose to purchase this book, and I hope it will provide you with a comprehensive reference work for all your inquiries regarding Sybase System XI. I wrote this book to help myself document all the important features of System XI in one place. Sybase has some great documentation, but it's found in a lot of different manuals, and it's quite easy to get lost. With this book, I hope you are able to find just about everything you will ever need to know when using Sybase on a regular basis.

This chapter serves as a way for you to learn about the basics of SQL statement formatting and how SQL is shown throughout the text. There are many different preferences for formatting SQL statements, and I'm sure that what you see throughout this book will be at least a little bit different from what you are used to. ■

Understanding This Book

I have written about all of the more important elements of the Sybase toolset, so this book represents a fairly complete and diverse text. There's much to be learned about Sybase from this book; however, if you don't have the correct expectations, traversing its many chapters might be a bit daunting. This book is divided into five major parts, as follows:

■ Part I, "Getting Started," is an introduction to the book and to Sybase System XI, and gives you an installation guide.

■ Part II, "Using System XI," includes a detailed discussion of all aspects of Transact-SQL. This part provides the foundation for your understanding of Sybase's technology.

■ Part III, "Application Programming," gives you a lot of tips and ideas for using Sybase with application programming languages, such as Visual Basic, Centura Team Developer, Delphi Client/Server 2.0, and PowerBuilder.

■ Part IV, "Advanced Features," introduces you to the advanced capabilities of Sybase, including data replication, server configuration and tuning, and backups and restores.

■ The appendixes give you some comparisons between Sybase and SQL Anywhere, another relational database from Sybase's Watcom group, as well as some suggestions for naming conventions.

Each of these parts are built on top of each other, and so reading from the start to the end of this book is definitely a plus. However, if you have a pretty good understanding of the fundamentals of relational databases and specifically Sybase, you should be able to jump around to various topics and use this book as more of a reference work than a straight tutorial.

Throughout this book, you will see references to Sybase, System XI, System 11, and so on. These all refer to the Sybase SQL Server that is running on your chosen hardware platform. You will be alerted if the word *server* refers to anything other than the database server. It *is* important that you pay attention to this distinction. Sybase's products are all described as *servers,* and this can get a little confusing. The following are the most common products that you will interact with:

■ **SQL Server**—This is the database that is actually doing all the processing of data and handling requests from clients.

■ **Backup Server**—This server is the tool that Sybase gives you to perform database backups and restores. Its presence is essentially unnoticed because you perform interaction with it through regular Transact-SQL commands.

■ **Monitor Server**—This is a server that usually resides in the same box as the SQL Server. It manages the statistics of the SQL Server so that you can perform analysis and tune the SQL Server more effectively.

There are some additional *servers* available in Sybase, including *Audit Server* and *Replication Server*, which you can find discussed in Chapter 21, "Managing and Monitoring Security," and Chapter 24, "Managing Data Replication."

This book contains many examples and code that I have found useful in my own development of a large number of applications that interact with Sybase as the target database. It is my belief that by reading through these examples and putting them to use in your environment, you will gain a better understanding of how to use Sybase. Obviously, everybody has an individual style when it comes to working with databases, and so I've tried to represent what I believe is a good generic style for application and database development. The tips provided should give you ideas that will spur your own thoughts on development, and hopefully lead to better programs and database designs for your users.

There are some obvious limits in this book. The primary one is size. Try as I might, Que wouldn't authorize a six volume set for this topic, and so I've had to be fairly concise in some chapters in order to keep the page count under 1,000 pages. What this means is that in some places, I suggest other reference works for more information. This is the Macy's approach to book writing! I let you know when there's a great work available that covers a particular topic in more detail, and give you details on how to access it. The advantage of this approach is that you can still use *this* book as your primary resource for Sybase, and it will help you delve further into topics that are covered by other writers. I'm not afraid to even point you back to Sybase's documentation in some circumstances—there are simply some issues that it documents very well, and there's no point in reinventing the wheel.

Understanding the Conventions Used in This Book

There are many different ways to write a book and even more ways to format one. The Que style is an excellent way of breaking up information into a readable form that is easy to digest. This book uses the Que style throughout, and in this section I tell you what you can expect.

The majority of application programs written these days enables you to use either a mouse or a keyboard to operate the program. When giving you steps for performing a particular task, I always indicate the appropriate keystroke combinations that perform the action. Hot keys or accelerators are designated by an underline. For example, if I instruct you to open a file using Microsoft Word, you see the following:

Choose File, Open.

To indicate a combination of keys to be pressed at the same time, the two keys are joined by a plus sign (+). For example, if I instruct you to paste a piece of text from the Clipboard into a Word document, you see the following:

Choose Edit, Paste, or press Ctrl+V.

The initial letters of the names of dialog boxes and windows and dialog box and window options are capitalized. For example, when saving a file in Microsoft Word, the dialog box that is used to specify the file name is as follows:

File Save

New terms and ideas are set in *italics* when introduced, and messages that appear on the screen are set in a monospaced font, as follows:

```
All source code and examples of code listings are presented in a monospaced font.
```

Tips are used to indicate some cool trick or a neat way to organize your code. Watch out for Tips, and use them in your day-to-day work because they'll generally save you time or offer you a unique solution to a problem.

N O T E Notes provide extra information relating to the particular topic being discussed in the body of the text. ■

CAUTION

Cautions are designed to alert you to dangerous actions or situations that could cause damage to your environment. You should pay particular attention to Cautions so that you avoid creating a problem at your site.

 TROUBLESHOOTING

Troubleshooting items present the most common or expected problems as a question. They offer you the most likely solution to the problem as an answer.

If there's more information on a particular topic found in another chapter, you will see a cross reference that indicates the relevant section and page.

▶ **See** "The Origins of System XI," **p. 18**

Reading SQL Syntax

Learning to read a SQL statement is just like learning to read any programming language. To effectively use Sybase, you need to have a mastery of SQL, so it's important that you understand how statements are going to be formatted in this book. The basic rules of SQL or constructs are as follows:

- Command names, options, or other words that must be typed in accurately are printed in a monospaced font. For example: `sp_configure`, `Create Table`, and `Create Index`.

- Optional values or variables are printed in italics. You should substitute an appropriate value for this variable when executing the command. For example: *Database_Name*, *Table_Name*, and *Object_Name*.

- For any text or commands that are placed within braces ({}), one of the options listed must be selected. The available options are separated by the mathematical OR character, a pipe (|). Make sure that you don't include the curly braces when you type your selection. For example:

```
{ 'PROCEED' | 'ABORT' | 'IGNORE' }
```

This means that you can either `"PROCEED"` or `"ABORT"` or `"IGNORE"`.

- Any text or commands that are placed within square brackets ([]) can be optionally ignored by the SQL statement. Make sure that you don't include the square braces when you type your selection. For example:

```
sp_helpdb [Database_Name]
```

  This means that the variable *Database_Name* can be optionally ignored and does not need to be provided to execute the system stored procedure sp_helpdb.

- Parentheses are meant to be typed as part of the statement or command.

- A comma between options indicates that you can choose as many values from the list as you want.

- Ellipsis points (…) after any section in parentheses indicates that the whole section may be repeated. For example, the Create Table statement can have many columns, and the ellipsis points show the variable number of columns:

```
Create Table Table_Name(
Column_Name1 Datatype[,
Column_Name2 Datatype, ...]
```

Knowing Where to Look in This Book

This book is broken down into five major parts, which organize the information into logical groups that make reading easier. Nobody is going to grade you or test you as to whether you read everything in every chapter. I expect that you will jump around through the chapters looking for information that meets your needs. Use the following sections as a road map to help you figure out where in the book you need to go.

Part I: Getting Started

This first part is designed to introduce all the basics of the book and to set up your expectations for the rest of the book. There's quite a bit of good general reading to be had, and it's a nice warm-up.

Chapter 1, "Understanding Client/Server," teaches you about the basics of client/server.

Chapter 2, "Introducing Sybase System XI," presents System XI and all the new features that it adds to the base of System 10. If you are a long time user of System 10, you should check out this chapter to find out what's new.

How do you install Sybase System XI? Chapter 3, "Installing Sybase," teaches you how to install on Windows NT. There are also some general pointers for installing on different UNIX platforms.

Part II: Using System XI

In Part II is a comprehensive discussion of all elements of Transact-SQL (Sybase's particular flavor of SQL) and how to get the most out of the database you are working on. This part comprises chapters that grow in complexity and difficulty.

If you are new to Sybase, start at Chapter 4, "Introducing Transact-SQL." You will learn the difference between Data Definition Language (DDL) and Data Manipulation Language (DML). By using DDL, you can create tables, indexes, and other database objects. Once you have created some objects, you will want to add data to them and manipulate the data—that's what DML is for.

In Chapter 5, "Understanding Databases, Devices, and Transaction Logs," you learn how to create the fundamental units or components of a Sybase System XI database, and it is the basis for all the future work described in the rest of the book.

Chapter 6, "Understanding Tables and Datatypes," serves as a discussion of the database table. With this chapter mastered, you have all the information you require to design tables for use in your database. In addition, you have an understanding of the best use for different datatypes available in Sybase.

In order to store data correctly, it is sometimes necessary to apply rules, such as "there will be no records with a current balance greater than $500." Chapter 7, "Using Rules, Defaults, and Triggers," introduces you to three different ways of enforcing data integrity in Sybase.

Chapter 8, "Understanding Indexes and Keys," helps you in the performance arena through the use of indexes. Indexes help the database perform less work when answering user queries. I highly recommend this chapter if you are looking for tips on how to better organize and index your data.

Views provide you, as a DBA and user of your database, with two key advantages: security and simplicity. Check out Chapter 9, "Working with Views," for details on how to improve both in your database.

One of the great features of Sybase is its advanced stored procedure language that is enabled through Transact-SQL. Chapter 10, "Understanding Stored Procedures," is the first of a series of chapters that introduce you to the advanced features of Transact-SQL, specifically through the use of stored procedures.

Chapter 11, "Understanding Transactions and Locking," helps you understand the effects of performing database transactions on the server. Chapter 11 also explains the different sorts of locking available in Sybase and how they impact the server when you use them.

To enable processing on the server without the need for embedded SQL in a language like C or COBOL, Sybase introduced *cursors* in System 10. Chapter 12, "Understanding and Using Cursors," teaches you all the fundamentals of how cursors are used and what their advantages and disadvantages are.

Chapter 13, "Using Advanced Stored Procedures and Triggers," is the final chapter in Part II. It brings together everything you have learned throughout this part and offers some advanced examples and topics for you to digest. There is something here to challenge just about every user of Sybase.

Part III: Application Programming

Part III is targeted at the application programmer who is working with Sybase. It covers all the basics from such low-level issues as connectivity to examples of coding in various popular programming languages, such as Centura Team Developer, Delphi Client/Server 2.0, PowerBuilder, and Visual Basic.

Chapter 14, "Understanding the Sybase Client Model (Client Library)," is devoted to an explanation of how Sybase communicates on the network through its proprietary communications technology, Client Library.

In Chapter 15, "Using Client/Server Application Programming Tools," I introduce you to four of the most commonly used client/server application development tools on the market today: Centura Software Corporation's Centura Builder, Sybase's PowerBuilder, Borland's Delphi, and Microsoft's Visual Basic. Each of these tools represents a different segment of the tools race. Consequently, this chapter is quite "review like," so you'll be able to determine which language makes sense for you.

Chapter 16, "Partitioning an Application," is focused on the process of moving different parts of an application onto different hardware and software platforms. The most common implementation of application partitioning is a three-tier scheme consisting of a client, a business server that has business objects in it, and a database server for data storage.

No book could be complete without a good discussion of third-party products available for Sybase. Chapter 17, "Using Third-Party Products," has a good review of many top performing products available on the market today. The review serves as a primer to the demonstration software that is on the CD-ROM: tools from such vendors as Platinum Technologies, Embarcadero Technologies, and Sylvain Faust, Inc.

Also in Part III is a subject that's going to be very popular with most of you—the Internet. Chapter 18, "Introducing the Internet," takes you from the basics of the Internet to the latest trends in current technologies. This chapter is designed to help you get a thorough understanding of what the Internet means and how it can be used in your organization.

If you've got data in your database and clients with an Internet connection and a Web browser hitting your marketing pages on the corporate Web server, then the only thing missing is a connection between your database and the Web server. For this chapter, "Database Publishing on The Internet," use your Web browser to go to **http://www.mcp.com/que**.

Part IV: Advanced Features

This is the part of the book where it really starts to get interesting. All of these chapters are designed to consolidate the printed documentation from Sybase and add some real-world examples showing how to use the advanced features of Sybase in your organization.

Chapter 19, "Managing Data Availability," gives you all the information you require to manage backups and database loads such that your servers and databases will be available for use by your customers for the maximum amount of time.

The Database Consistency Checker (DBCC) is a utility that most Sybase DBAs dread to run due to its relatively poor performance. However, you must get in the habit of running it every now and then, so it's important that you know what you are doing. Chapter 20, "Understanding the Joys, Secrets, and Mysteries of DBCC," teaches you everything you wanted to know about DBCC and then some things that you didn't!

Security is a major concern at most companies—and if it's not at your company, then it probably should be. Chapter 21, "Managing and Monitoring Security," is a discussion of many different aspects of security. Here you will discover everything from integrated security under Windows NT to tips on how to make your database server hard to steal!

In Chapter 22, "Managing and Monitoring Performance," you learn how to perform realistic statistical analysis using SQL Monitor and the *Monitor Server* and *Historical Server*.

System 10 had scores of options and configurations that applied at the server, the database, and even at the query level. In System XI, Sybase has gone even further and exposed many more options to enable you to configure and tune your server in ways that were previously impossible. Rely on Chapter 23, "Using Sybase's Configuration Options," to be your one-stop center full of detailed information on every option available to you.

The final chapter in Part IV, Chapter 24, "Managing Data Replication," is a detailed discussion of database replication using Sybase's *Replication Server*. In addition, this chapter looks at competing replication technologies from such companies as Centura and Intersolv.

Part V: Appendixes

This is the catchall part of the book. Anything that didn't quite make it as a chapter was placed here. You should find some useful information in this part of the book relating to such issues as:

- Suggested naming conventions for all of your database objects;
- The differences between System XI and Sybase's other product, SQL Anywhere;
- Some suggested light reading for when you can't sleep;
- Sources of additional help, such as CompuServe and Sybase's Web site.

This is quite a lengthy book that I hope covers much of what you need to know about Sybase. I hope that it serves as more than just a reference for you, and actually helps you get a lot more out of Sybase than you were before. I learned a lot while writing this book and was exposed to a lot of technologies that I normally wouldn't have had the opportunity to spend time on during my work day. I hope that you benefit from the knowledge that I pass on to you, and that this book is a valuable resource to you in the future.

Getting Started

Understanding Client/Server

This chapter serves as a basic unit of work that you can base your understanding of client/server technologies on. From here, you learn what client/server is, how it was developed, and how it evolved from earlier mainframe technologies. It is not intended that this be an all-encompassing discussion of all the elements of client/server computing; rather, it is an introductory chapter that will, hopefully, whet your appetite. ■

Introduction to client/server

This brief discussion explains the technologies involved in client/server and what they mean.

Learn the evolution of client/server

In this chapter, you see a quick summary of the evolution of technologies that lead to the development of client/server tools.

Discover the tiering of technologies

Client/server systems can have multiple layers of processing. This chapter shows you the basics of those technologies as an introduction to the rest of the book.

What Is Client/Server?

What is client/server? This is a topic that's been on the mind of many a writer in the last few years. Client/server is a somewhat nebulous term that describes a very general technology in which a given computing task is distributed in some fashion between more than one execution point. If everything in that last sentence seemed rather vague, I apologize. The problem is that client/server is so hard to nail down to mean any *one* thing that it's quite easy to overlook some of its capabilities.

Let's start by breaking down my definition; perhaps that will illustrate what I mean. First of all, what is meant by a *computing task*? A computing task is a particular function or operation that requires processing. For example, a computing task could be something like producing a list of all the customers at a bank with an ATM card or something much more mundane, such as drawing a graphical window on a display.

Furthering the definition, what is meant by *distributed?* A distributed task is a task that is performed in more than one place with different parts of the task being shared by several processing or executing engines.

At its greatest or largest implementation, an *execution point* could be something like a computer or cluster of computers working in parallel to share a task. On the other end of the spectrum, a processing or execution point could be something as small as a single thread on a single CPU of a PC.

With this range of possibilities, you can see how it becomes a little difficult to give a good definition on what client/server really is. Rather than debating the language of client/server any further, I'll give you a list of some client/server implementations to clarify what I'm trying to describe:

- Client/server is often used to describe a scenario involving a centralized database server (such as Sybase System XI) that is processing a large number of queries from clients that are typically personal computers (PCs). The distribution of processing is based on the fact that the database server will analyze and retrieve the appropriate data for the client, and the client is responsible for data presentation to the user.

- Client/server is used by Microsoft to describe the relationship between various operating system components in Windows NT and the kernel of the OS. In this sense, Microsoft is saying that the server is the kernel and it processes requests from clients, such as the Graphics Device Interface (GDI). In fact, it is the very use of client/server in Windows NT that provides it with its robustness. The kernel is basically crash-proof, and because everything else is a client of the kernel, if the other task crashes, the kernel is unscathed.

- Client/server is now just about universally used as the way of distributing e-mail on the LAN. Microsoft through Exchange Server, HP with its OpenMail, and Novell through GroupWise have all successfully implemented mail on a client/server basis.

Because of its nature as a distributed task metaphor, client/server lends itself well to Open Systems. Client/server is itself just a technology; however, because of widespread adoption of various standards, client/server has become a nearly universal way of communicating between disparate technologies. For example, Sybase has enabled client/server communication with legacy systems on IBM mainframes through its set of products called *Open Servers*. These servers act as a gateway and provide a transaction layer between the mainframe and the client computers on the LANs and WANs that the mainframe is now serving.

Client/server was the most talked about technology of the 1990s until Java and the Internet were taken up by the computer press. You owe it to yourself to find out more about client/server. Please refer to Appendix C, "Suggested Reading," for some books that provide you with additional background on client/server technologies.

Learning the Evolution of Client/Server

Client/server computing has evolved pretty rapidly over approximately the last eight years since the time when Oracle started becoming successful in the late 1980s. In that time, a number of things have changed. Primarily, the underlying technologies and the definition of what a server is, does, and is *supposed* to do have changed. For example, back then the primary servers where minicomputers and the clients were PCs with character mode interfaces and relatively slow CPUs. As such, the client/server phenomenon was still being designed by the MIS shops in most companies who retained a strong central control over the technology and its accessibility within a company. This was not much of an improvement (as far as the users were concerned) over the IMS databases and flat file systems of the mainframe, but it was the beginning of a new era of distributed computing within corporate organizations.

Over time, the server side of client/server has become much more accessible to the average user and small department or workgroup of a business. This pushing down of technology from the upper echelons of the MIS groups to the workers and business groups within a company has necessitated a simplification of the installation, maintenance, and general running of a client/server shop. Centura Software Corporation pioneered the workgroup database with an easily deployable database: SQLBase.

Other companies have recognized this market and have jumped in after Centura: Microsoft broke from Sybase to produce its BackOffice database server, Microsoft SQL Server; Oracle spun off some of its technology into a more accessible (and definitely easier to install) product called Oracle Workgroup 2000; and Sybase, through its acquisition of Powersoft (which had recently purchased Watcom), released SQL Anywhere 5.0 as its workgroup database in late 1995.

These workgroup databases have become successful and popular due to the success of application-serving, network-aware operating systems, such as Windows NT Advanced Server, UNIX, and Novell's NetWare. Without the acceptance of these new operating systems and the OS's easy manageability, client/server would never have jumped into the limelight so quickly or so pervasively.

As the capabilities of the operating systems that the servers ran on grew, so, too, did the capabilities of the database servers themselves. Originally designed to answer relatively straightforward queries, early database servers from Oracle, IBM, Sybase, and Informix were compliant to the so-called standard SQL89. This ANSI standard (published many years after most vendors succeeded in implementing its features) described basic DML and DDL constructs that would enable a client program (such as a Windows-based PC) to send a request to the server without having any knowledge of the physical storage of the data, which would result in the returning of the data that matched the criteria specified.

It was quickly evident that the basic queries of SQL89 were not going to be sufficient to enable advanced processing of data sets on the server. Each vendor then split off from the standard to develop its own form of stored procedures. Oracle's PL/SQL was very successful as were Sybase's Transact-SQL extensions. These language extensions to SQL enabled developers to start being more flexible in the way that data was processed. The burden of processing could be shared between the clients and the server more evenly depending on the processing needs of a given situation.

Understanding Fat Clients

The first generation of client/server applications were called *fat clients* because a lot of processing was performed on them. The database server acted as a central repository for the data, but lacked any stored-procedure type language to allow for server-based processing of the data. This meant that for any repetitive operations that needed to be performed, the client was responsible for a large part of the work. This was extremely inefficient.

For example, say you have 10,000 checking accounts in a banking application that need to have their balances adjusted and interest payments made to them. A fat client would request a list of accounts from the server that would be transmitted back across the network from the server to the client. As each row was returned to the client, additional SQL statements and processing would occur that originated from the client back to the server. There was a tremendous network cost in processing data in this fashion.

Fat clients are still in use today for applications that try to maintain database vendor independence. The goal of these applications is to not be tied to any particular database vendor's implementation of SQL or stored procedure extensions. It is far easier to program an application in such a language as PowerBuilder and use generic SQL statements to the server than it is to have a relatively simple application and port the stored procedures to various database vendors, such as Sybase, Informix, and Oracle. Fat clients typically require faster PCs to achieve reasonable performance because there is a large burden on the PC to perform its part of the distributed processing.

Fat client-based applications have scalability problems when the datasets and serial data processing (long running tasks that require processing of each row of a large table) requirements grow large "overnight."

Understanding Fat Servers

The antithesis of a fat client is a *fat server,* which has all the processing performed on it with no balance to the clients. The clients are simply used as a display medium. An excellent example of a fat server is a 3270 terminal on an IBM mainframe. The server (in this case, the mainframe) performs all (or *almost* all) functions in any given transaction with the exception of data presentation.

Fat servers have an advantage that you can consolidate all the processing power in one place, making the management of technology relatively straightforward. However, this is also their greatest disadvantage: Fat servers have scalability problems when you need to increase the number of concurrent users of the system. As the number of users grows, the demands on the server grow, too, necessitating ever larger servers.

Understanding Two-and-a-Half-Tier and Stored Procedures

Fat clients and fat servers are known as *two-tier* client/server application models. This is because the processing is either on the server or on the client with very little capability to balance the workload.

With the advent of stored procedures, it becomes possible to distribute the processing far more evenly between the clients and the server or servers. Stored procedures that are executed from client PCs run at the full speed of the server and thus take advantage of its performance. At the same time, if it is necessary to perform ad hoc analysis (something fat clients are good at), then you can still do processing at the PC.

Stored procedures enable you to place the business logic's execution on the server, yielding great performance while retaining the flexibility of an intelligent client application. This approach to the distribution of processing is known as *two-and-a-half-tier* client/server—the *half* refers to the fact that the business rules have been encapsulated as stored procedures on the server.

Using Three-Tier Client/Server for Application Serving

If you take the model of moving business logic into stored procedures and progress it further, it is natural that the stored procedures themselves could actually be moved to a separate server: an *Application Server.* This is *three-tier* client/server computing.

The first tier is the client. It is responsible for basic/rudimentary rules validation that can be performed on the client, data presentation and display, and query execution.

The second tier is the application server, which stores all the business rules for the application. A client requests a transaction from the application server and it is responsible for interfacing with the database server.

The third tier is the database server. It acts as a central repository for all application-specific data and for some vendor-specific implementations of business rules via stored procedures.

The key advantage of a third tier is the distribution of processing even further. Now dedicated number crunchers or computers tailored for a particular business function can be used to perform the third tier of processing, leaving the database to manage the data instead of using stored procedures. In addition, the third tier can manipulate data from multiple data sources without the need for the client to even know. From the client's perspective, it has only requested that a transaction be performed on the application server. The application server is then responsible for managing whatever resources it has (one or many databases of different types) to perform the transaction and return the appropriate information to the client.

Three-tier computing is coming into fashion right now because of the need to integrate legacy systems with client/server applications. Companies are using a three-tier architecture to solve the data access problems without the need for moving large amounts of data down to the relational databases on the client/server networks. The third tier abstracts the client from the data and from the business rules, which is a great advantage if the underlying data's form or storage changes, or if the way of using the data changes internally.

Understanding Peer-to-Peer Processing (*n* tier)

The final step in the evolution of the client/server technology is that of true *peer-to-peer* processing. In this model, every computer on the network has a contribution to make: All computers are both clients and servers.

Peer-to-peer models have some development to go before they are accepted into general use by the body of computing professionals, but with the rapid insurgence of the Internet and the diversity of computing resources coming online, it is really the logical next step. For more information about how to partition your application programs, see Chapter 16, "Partitioning an Application."

From Here...

In this chapter, you received a brief introduction to client/server technologies. I hope this chapter has set an appropriate level of expectation for the rest of the book. There's a lot to learn for just about everyone (I know I've picked up a lot from writing it), and this is just the beginning.

Introducing Sybase System XI

Sybase System XI is the latest release of Sybase Corporation's well-known database management system. Sybase originally was developed to run on high-end UNIX hardware. However, Sybase's current product runs on many different hardware platforms, from Intel's Pentium Pro to DEC's Alpha, and many different operating systems, from IBM's OS/2 Warp to SCO's SCO UNIX.

Sybase is a truly universal database designed to solve many problems with a common engine. Sybase's core products are designed with an open architecture that lends them to extension very easily. For example, when Sybase needed to address the database replication market, it created an Open Server, *Replication Server*, based on the core technologies already available on the product and delivered replication to the marketplace. In a similar way, Sybase scaled up to the high-end data warehouses with Sybase's IQ product.

This chapter is designed to introduce you to all the components of Sybase and to guide you through the history of Sybase Corporation. This chapter also serves as an introduction to the new features that Sybase has added to the database server since releasing Sybase System 10 in late 1993. ■

Origins of Sybase and System XI

Have you ever wondered what it took to build such a product as System XI? This section presents the history of Sybase and puts the evolution of System XI in context for you.

What's new?

Learn what has changed and what's new in System XI.

What makes a database server solution?

In this chapter, you'll learn all about the various components that make up Sybase System XI and how they work together as an integrated family.

The Origins of System XI

Sybase didn't just appear overnight. Well, maybe compared to IBM and HP it did, but in reality, Sybase has been a company that has grown from pretty humble origins in 1984 to a billion dollar company in 1996. A late starter in the field of client/server software, Sybase entered a market already dominated by the likes of Oracle, Informix, and Ingres. Oracle clearly had the lion's share of the market (as it continues to have) and had quite a well-established presence based on five years of being in the industry prior to the conception of Sybase.

Home Improvement

Sybase began at home—Bob's home that is. With the same startup gumption of such industry luminaries as Hewlett and Packard (of HP) and Steve Jobs and Steve Wozniak of Apple fame, Sybase's founders, Bob Epstein and Mark Hoffman, started the Sybase Corporation in the home. Within a year (1985) of opening its doors, the revenues of the fledgling Sybase had climbed to $1.5 million, and Sybase was right on track to enter the information age. However, Sybase was a typical startup company and was unprofitable for the first three years of its existence—all the money went into the research and development arm of the company.

By 1988, Sybase had settled into the routine of a company and had chosen a field to play in: that of the relational database. In 1988, Sybase released its first major product and the ancestor of System XI—a relational database that was designed to be used on a network. Microsoft was a relatively small player at the time compared to market leaders Ashton-Tate, whose product dBASE III+ was hugely popular. Bill Gates is often credited with great strategic vision. He saw Sybase's product and decided that it was a great match for Microsoft. Microsoft's and Sybase's strategic relationship centered around a database that Microsoft would jointly market for its up-and-coming operating system, OS/2. 1988 was also the year that Sybase reached profitability for the first time.

Introducing Open Server and Open Client

In 1989, Sybase announced the cornerstone of its technology today: the application programming interfaces (APIs), Open Client and Open Server. These two APIs provided Sybase with the basis for developing a suite of tools that enable connectivity between any sort of client device, such as a PC, Macintosh, or UNIX box, and any sort of data.

The Open Client interface resides on the client computers on a network and is used as an interface to Sybase's network transmission protocols known collectively as NetLibrary. Open Client is a generic interface that all programmers could write to without needing to know anything about the underlying network transport. NetLibrary is written directly for each particular flavor of low-level protocol, such as Microsoft TCP/IP and Novell's SPX. For more information on Open Client and its new incarnation, Client Library, see Chapter 14, "Understanding the Sybase Client Model (Client Library)."

Open Server is a technology that enables Sybase and other vendors to publish data in a consistent manner for communication with clients that subscribe to the Open Client APIs. The benefit of the Open Server interface is that it's documented for others to use. Open Servers don't need to be database-related at all. The beauty of the Open Client/Open Server architecture is that, provided the Server conforms to the basic tenets of the API, it can be just about anything. For example, I once worked on a system written by some very clever guys at Microsoft's Consulting Services (MCS) who had written an Open Server that parsed DOS commands! You could enter SQL at the DOS command line (within limits), and the parser would determine that it was really a request for the database and would send it on to the appropriate database server.

Other applications that Open Server is particularly good at are database gateways. The Open Server API makes it very easy to develop gateways between clients used to interface to relational databases and data that is not in an easily accessible format.

In 1990, Sybase started to round out its full service offerings by acquiring a reasonably sized consulting firm: SQL Solutions. This firm served as the basis of the new consulting arm of Sybase, which would be called Sybase World Wide Professional Services. Also in 1990, Sybase introduced its suite of products to interface with legacy mainframe (MVS)-based solutions to the Open Server network. These products enabled the corporate developer to finally be able to concentrate on the application, knowing that the data was readily accessible through gateways.

Part
I

Ch
2

Going Public and Growing Fast

By 1991, Sybase had established itself as one of the leading contenders in the client/server world. With a revenue base of just over $100 million, Sybase went public on the NASDAQ exchange. This public offering further capitalized the company, allowing for more rapid expansion and a greater focus on software engineering. Sybase continued its growth and was named one of Fortune magazine's top 10 fastest growing companies for the second year in a row.

Following a successful initial public offering (IPO), Sybase's revenue grew at a rate of over 60 percent for the next few years. Having built up a significant war chest, Sybase set out on the acquisition trail to fill out its product line. Sybase acquired several key technology companies, including Deft, Inc. in 1991 and Gain Technology, Inc. in 1992. The developer tools of these two companies rounded out Sybase's offerings and made Sybase a formidable tools vendor as well as a server solution provider. Gain's products served the basis of Sybase's multimedia group through a set of tools known collectively as Gain Momentum.

System 10 Out the Door

System 10 was introduced to the market in 1992 with a full-scale rollout to commercial customers in production form in January of 1994. System 10 marked Sybase's most ambitious development project and linked together a number of technologies under a single unifying banner of the System 10 architecture. System 10 was targeted and marketed as a true enterprise-scale database engine. With System 10, Sybase introduced a number of key technologies, including server-based cursors, advanced transaction processing, and database tuning capabilities. System 10 was clearly at the leading edge of technology until the arrival of Oracle 7 on a platform other than 35 mm slide.

With System 10 still undergoing the final stages of QA and certification, Sybase's revenue kept climbing and the company kept growing. Announcing $265 million in revenues for the fiscal year of 1992, Sybase was really starting to become a big player. In 1993, Sybase unveiled two new key technologies: OmniSQLGateway and Replication Server. The first product was an extension of the Open Server technology and was designed to promote seamless interfaces to distributed data—no matter what database or platform it resided on. The second product was also an Open Server, but in this case designed to distribute Sybase databases to other servers. Replication Server is a core component of the Sybase toolset and is discussed in quite some detail in Chapter 24, "Managing Data Replication."

1994 was the year of System 10. As many companies adopted System 10—either as new recruits to the Sybase model or as upgrades from existing Sybase 4.2 or 4.9.2 servers or upgrades from Microsoft SQL Server 4.2—Sybase continued to be successful. Its growing branding internationally accounted for some 33 percent of the company's revenue, and this focus on an international presence was welcomed by those companies using and reselling Sybase's products into the international community. Sybase still with bulging pockets bought three strategically important companies in 1994: Micro Decisionware, Inc., Expressway Technologies, and the OASIS Group.

The OASIS Group strengthened Sybase's consulting experience and with its home base in England provided good leverage into the strongly growing European market. Micro Decisionware's products were well known for their enterprise connectivity, and this enabled Sybase to release a new product dubbed Enterprise CONNECT. Expressway Technologies brought a new kind of technology to Sybase: data mining of very large database support. Expressway's tools served as the kernel for Sybase's forthcoming offering, Sybase IQ. Sybase IQ is a tool designed to help model and answer queries on very large datasets or data warehouses.

1994 also was the year of the breakup. The romance with Microsoft was over and the two companies agreed to disagree on what was right for client/server software and to develop their databases independently. This made for great press back then, and since that time, Microsoft and Sybase remarkably have produced database servers that seem to have basically the same features.

Microsoft (as was expected) tended to focus on the clients that work in smaller shops and on the glitzy stuff, especially with the SQL Server 6.5 release. Microsoft also pushed some new technologies into the core of SQL Server, such as the parallel table scan architecture, the read ahead manager, and the new (in 6.5) row level locking on inserts. Highly recommended reading on SQL Server comes from yours truly, Steve Wynkoop, and Bob Branchek in the form of another tome from Que: *Special Edition Using Microsoft SQL Server 6.5.*

Sybase headed to the hills or the high end of the development and applications world, concentrating on the development of System XI's performance enhancements. It will be interesting to see the way the products intertwine over the next few years, as developers and engineers from both Microsoft and Sybase talk to each other across the wall that their companies' managers have erected. I suspect that the core technology will stay pretty similar between both products and the add-ons are where the differences will show up.

The Great Buyout—Powersoft Corp.

In 1995, Sybase grew tired of being labeled a database company with no consistent development tools strategy. Its developer tools were fragmented and generally lacking in any direction. Determined not to lose ground to Oracle's new Developer 2000 and Informix's NewEra, Sybase did what it does best: It bought the leading client/server developer tool company, Powersoft Corporation. The acquisition of Powersoft, although being a very costly maneuver at over $1 billion, produced the world's seventh largest software company. Raising the bar on the revenue base to in excess of $820 million, Sybase now had over 4,500 employees and was truly grasping the client/server bull by the horns.

Powersoft became Sybase's tools division in 1996 and was charged with the development, marketing, and management of everything under the sun with the exception of the SQL Server on UNIX platforms (which is managed by the Enterprise Group). SQL Server on Windows NT, SQL Anywhere, PowerBuilder, and the Watcom group all fall under the wings of the tools division.

Sybase essentially dumped its Gain Momentum product and rolled the developers into a new group entitled the New Media Division. As a group charged with creating business out of the new multimedia world, NMD has been very successful in courting several big names, among them BellSouth, Singapore Telecom, and Time Warner Communications.

And Finally...System XI Ships!

After much fanfare and quite a bit of vaporware in 1995, Sybase finally delivered System XI into the hands of developers in February 1996. System 10 had taken a battering in the performance arena over the last few years, and Sybase spent considerable amounts of its engineering resources ensuring that System XI would not look quite so anemic. Indeed, System XI quickly has shown that a good dose of steroids and quite a bit of lateral thinking from the staff engineers in Sybase research and development can turn out a really quick server. Battling Oracle and Informix in the trade press, Sybase finally had some truly great numbers to talk about. System XI opens the new world of performance to Sybase's customers and is the best upgrade a developer could want.

System XI also is the most tested release of Sybase's core technology to leave the doors at Emeryville. Sybase introduced the controls and policies into the company's development methodology to be one of the first large software vendors to achieve ISO 9001 certification. Plagued by bugs in its early incarnations, System 10.0.0 has been often referred to as "Ten Point Uh Oh." Sybase could no longer allow this public opinion to continue and vigorously fought to improve quality in System XI. I'm pleased to report that its efforts were not in vain. System XI is quite easily the best upgrade I've ever done and is probably the cleanest piece of software that I have had the pleasure of installing in quite some time.

If you're interested in seeing Sybase's history in a chronology that's maintained and updated by the company, use a Web browser, such as Microsoft Internet Explorer 3, and go to **http://www.sybase.com/inc/corpinfo/sybmile.html**.

What's New in System XI?

 Well, finally you get to the good stuff! I'm going to give you a basic rundown of what you get by installing or upgrading to System XI. The following sections outline the major new features in System XI. Each of these topics is addressed in appropriate chapters throughout the rest of the book, and pointers to those chapters are provided below. There are a number of minor features in System XI that have been introduced that are not discussed below, however. These are pointed out in the following chapters and are easily identifiable as differences to System 10.

Improvements to Cache Management

Recognizing the need to have greater customization of memory caching in System XI, Sybase has changed the caching architecture to enable an administrator to split up the data cache. By splitting up the cache, the administrator then can choose to bind or lock a database or database object to the named cache area. This flexibility enables the administrator to force particular tables into RAM, and they will stay there. No longer do you need to guess how to keep a highly accessed table in memory; using named caches will force it to do so.

Binding particular objects—such as the *sysindexes* table and its index, the *syslogs* table, and the *tempdb* database—will yield substantial performance gains and is highly recommended. The *sysindexes* table is highly accessed because it stores all the key information and data trend statistics that change every time an operation adds, deletes, or modifies a row in a table. *Syslogs* gains from being placed in a named cache because of another new feature in System XI: memory pooling. Memory pools enable you to write data to devices with faster I/O due to larger I/O sizes. The typical write in pre-System XI databases was 2K. In System XI, it is possible to configure a 4K memory pool that Sybase then will use to write to the log device in 4K chunks. This provides very substantial performance gains because log writes are typically I/O bound, and most physical devices can perform larger I/O requests than System 10's 2K limit.

In addition to these system tables, you should consider placing any very highly accessed tables, such as primary key tables, in their own cached area.

> **CAUTION**
>
> Take care if you create many named caches that your default cache is not too small. Named caches in themselves will produce performance gains only if you still have enough memory left over in the default cache for normal processing. To investigate how much memory is actually being used in the cache, use the following DBCC command:
>
> ```
> DBCC TraceOn( 3604 )
>         go
>         DBCC MemUsage
>         go
>         DBCC TraceOff( 3604 )
>         go
> ```
>
> For a more detailed discussion on how to use DBCC effectively, see Chapter 20, "Understanding the Joys, Secrets, and Mysteries of DBCC."

Improvements to Data Storage Management

In addition to the improvements made in the memory caching schemes used by System XI, Sybase has made great strides toward supporting easier configuration of the actual data storage. Probably the most useful new feature of System XI is the new keyword, `max_rows_per_page`. If you specify this value when creating an object, such as a table or index, then Sybase will allow only the indicated number of rows per data page. For highly accessed tables, this greatly simplifies the management of the table required to force a single row per page. In the past, it was necessary to fake a wide row by adding columns of datatype char(250) not null to fill up as much of the 2K as was remaining to make a wide row, or alternately to "guestimate" the spacing using the `fillfactor` keyword. `Max_rows_per_page` is far more accurate and simpler to work with.

In addition to enabling you to customize the exact number of rows that you want to place in a data page, Sybase introduced the capability to partition a table in System XI. To understand the benefit of a partitioned table, it is necessary to understand the constraint that this feature was designed to solve: bulk inserts. When inserting records into a table, Sybase locks the data page until the transaction is committed. If the record is narrow, then other inserts into the table that occur concurrently will be blocked until the first insert is completed. For highly transactional tables (which have a lot of transactions hitting them in the form of inserts), this can represent a fairly significant amount of time that the inserting records will be waiting for the first insert to complete.

System XI provides a way to remove this limitation by enabling you to partition or break up the data storage of a given table's data. To achieve this, Sybase gives you the option of having a table span multiple physical devices via the underlying segments being placed across multiple drives. Using the new `alter table` keyword `partition`, you can specify the number of partitions to make. Sybase then looks at the structure of the segment and determines the number of devices that the segment spans. Based on the number of physical devices that you have and the number of partitions that you have requested for a given table, Sybase then splits the data evenly across the drives. This is managed completely internally to Sybase, and you will experience no difference in using these tables except for better performance.

N O T E The DBCC commands `dbcc checktable` and `dbcc checkdb` will report the number of pages consumed per database table partition when run on a partitioned table. ▪

Partitioning a table substantially improves insert performance because Sybase can write inserts in parallel to multiple areas on the drive. If you have read any of the advanced performance tuning guides written by the HP Performance center, they suggest a simulated approach to this for System 10 by creating logical volume groups using HP's UNIX to manage the partitions. Trust me, this wasn't such an easy thing to set up, and it was quite a bit of a pain to look after. Using System XI to make inserts parallel is going to produce quite substantial performance gains to those users who have access to multiple drives.

Part
I

Ch
2

Don't forget to make sure that if you have a large number of physical devices in your server, you have an appropriate number of SCSI cards controlling them. Many times you will try to sneak an extra ounce of performance from the server by striping or partitioning your data onto multiple drives, and forget that you need to also provide Sybase with a way to move the data to the drive as quickly as possible. I recommend trying to stay at most on four devices per SCSI channel/card.

Improvements to Transaction Log Management

The most significant change in the way the transaction logs are utilized in System XI comes from the new user logs. User logs are transaction log areas assigned to each and every user connection or process on the server. When a user connects, the user log is allocated for the user's work to be placed in. The default size of the user log cache is 2,048 bytes or 2K. The key advantage of having user logs is that it greatly reduces the contention on the main transaction log when there are many users. Like the partitioning of tables, user logs enable Sybase to manage multiple concurrent logging operations and achieve greater throughput in the logging process. As with just about every new feature in System XI, there's a way to tune the size of the user log cache: The system stored procedure `sp_configure` can set the size when used with the option `user log cache size`.

Sybase's user logs are written to the main transaction log in a "flushing" operation that is substantially quicker in operation than if a user process individually placed its transactions in the log. Flushing the logs can cause potential multi-user concerns due to the fact that a user may be attempting to lock a resource in another user's private user log. Sybase manages this and other locking processes using an internal locking architecture known as a *spinlock*. Using spinlocks, Sybase ensures that any locks are freed by user connections before the data is written to the main transaction log.

For those users who have substantial activity on the transaction log that causes it to fill up quickly, Sybase has introduced a new system catalog table, *syslogshold*. The purpose of this table is to enable you to query the server to figure out how much of the log is filled by a currently active transaction. The reason that this information is important is that Sybase cannot dump from the logs any data that has yet to be committed or rolled back. Using the information in this table, it also is possible to determine the last time Replication Server extracted data from the transaction log.

This is useful because, like an active transaction, data that remains unsent or unfetched by other servers participating in a replication process cannot be dumped. By having undumpable data in the transaction log, you greatly reduce the amount of log space available for legitimate transactions. See Chapter 5, "Understanding Databases, Devices, and Transaction Logs," for tips on how to take advantage of the new features of transaction logs available in Sybase System XI.

Performance Enhancements for Better Querying

Sybase has made a number of advances in the area of performance enhancements for queries. One of the key new options in your arsenal is the capability to configure when Sybase chooses to change a set of page locks on a table to a full table lock. In prior releases of Sybase, if the number of pages locked by any given transaction or query exceeded 200, then Sybase would convert the lock to a full table lock. The reason it did this was for performance: It required less memory to lock the whole table as opposed to keeping pointers for 200 page locks.

In System XI, you have two new options that can be set: `lock promotion HWM` and `lock promotion LWM`. *HWM* and *LWM* refer to High Water Mark and Low Water Mark, respectively, and enable you to configure the maximum and minimum number of pages that must be locked before a lock is escalated to a table lock. This can provide substantial performance gains on very large tables that were getting table locked unnecessarily by complex transactions and therefore disallowing other activity on the table.

Part

I

Ch

2

A further gain for an application designer creating products using System XI is the introduction of a new `Isolation Level`, 0. Isolation levels provide a way of forcing Sybase to manage the access to a table in particular ways to help deal with multi-user situations effectively. `Level 0` enables you to query data that has yet to be committed by other users. This process is known as *dirty reading* and refers to the fact that the underlying data may or may not be the actual data left in the system after all pending user transactions are either committed or rolled back. The primary advantage of accessing data in this way is for query and reporting systems that are unaffected by the statistical deviations caused by active transactions. This isolation level acquires no locks when reading data and is ideal for systems that are not performing any changes on the data.

▶ **See** "Understanding Isolation Levels," **p. 291**

CAUTION

Do not use `Isolation Level 0` when the data you are working on is being relied on for its accuracy. Unless the database and/or application programs are *read-only*, any data returned from a select at `Isolation Level 0` must be considered suspect and only valuable for trend analysis, not for actual data representation.

Sybase has made a number of enhancements to the core processing involved with subqueries. Commonly used by complex systems, subqueries involve the use of additional queries in the WHERE clause of a SQL statement to limit the number of rows returned in a main query. Sybase's performance was notoriously poor in prior releases, but based on early benchmarks from some customers, the performance of the new subquery manager is up to 300 percent faster.

The final improvement in the realm of query processing relates to direct updates. A direct or in-place update is one that occurs in the table without the need for deleting the original row and inserting the updated one. System XI eliminates a number of conditions that would force a deferred or indirect (delete and insert) update to have occurred. By making these changes, Sybase has greatly improved the performance of those applications that process a large number of updates to existing data because less work needs to be done by the server to manage the update, and the whole record does not need to be written to the log any more. The only data being written to the transaction log in a direct update is the changed columns' data before and after the update occurred.

Advances in Locking Architectures

System XI introduces a number of internal enhancements to the underlying locking architecture that Sybase uses to manage concurrency. Sybase manages table access through the use of *hash buckets* (private tables with 101 rows) that store tables being locked and pages on them and then in 1031 row hash tables for the addresses of the pages being locked. In order to be more efficient with multiple CPUs accessing shared resources, Sybase's internal locking system, known as a *spinlock*, is now used to manage access to these shared hash table resources when requests came from multiple server threads (or client queries). By using spinlocks, Sybase maintains better performance and multi-CPU access times than going directly to the hash tables and doing full scans.

Spinlocks are tunable in the way that they protect their underlying datasets. For example, the default spinlocks configured for System XI are for 20 rows per spinlock process on the table hash buckets and 100 rows per spinlock process on the page address hash table. Under some circumstances (especially with multiple CPUs), it may be necessary to alter the number of rows per spinlock to improve performance. See Chapter 23, "Using Sybase's Configuration Options," for a more advanced discussion on the configuration of spinlocks using the `table lock spinlock ratio`, `page lock spinlock ratio`, and `address lock spinlock ratio` configuration options.

N O T E   Single engine servers only have one spinlock per hash table because there is no need for serialization or lock management between competing CPUs accessing the hash tables. ■

The determination of a deadlock is a costly operation for the database server because of the need to process the lock tree in both directions looking for crossed over locks. In Sybase prior to System XI, this deadlock management occurred 500 milliseconds after a lock was detected when waiting for a resource. This often could lead to unnecessary work for the server when applications do use locking but are known to deadlock infrequently. In System XI, you can tune the number of milliseconds that Sybase will wait before performing a deadlock condition test. This is done through the new option in `sp_configure` known as `deadlock checking period`. You can find out more about the deadlock management process in Chapter 11, "Understanding Transactions and Locking."

An additional configuration added in System XI is that of `max engine freelocks`. This option controls the lock manager in the server. In prior releases, all locks were managed at a global level for all database engines running on the server. This new configuration enables each online engine to manage its own set of locked resources and to share from the global pool if and when it needs to. This substantially reduces the amount of locking contention that occurs in the lock manager when using multiple CPUs. See Chapter 23, "Using Sybase's Configuration Options," for more information on how the lock manager's configuration through `max engine freelocks` is used.

Understanding SMP Support with Multiple Network Engines (MNE)

Sybase has been known to have some limitations in its support for multiple CPUs and for *SMP* (symmetric multi-processing) technology due to some of the core limitations in its architecture. One of the primary problems with the architecture revolved around the way networking transactions were managed when multiple online engines were being used. Despite the fact that each online engine could (and usually did) reside on a separate CPU, all networking operations had to go through the primary CPU on the physical server. This is why in prior releases, Sybase used to recommend that you should configure $n-1$ online engines, where n referred to the number of CPUs in the box that was going to be running the database server. The one CPU always was being reserved for network management (listening on database threads and sending and receiving data and queries from clients).

Part
I
Ch
2

In System XI, this networking limitation has been removed, and as a result, substantial performance gains can be had. In addition, with the removal of this limit, the maximum number of client connections has been raised. When a client connects, it initially attaches to Engine 0 running on the primary CPU in the server. Then, the primary engine moves or migrates the client to the CPU/engine that has the least number of active client connections.

Backup Server Improvements

System XI is fully compatible with backups made in any version of System 10 and will automatically convert them to the System XI format when you load the database from the backup dump. The only exception to this rule is that the *master* database cannot be restored from a prior release, and that for databases from servers prior to System 10, additional processing must be performed prior to loading into System XI.

Part of this enhancement has been to add a new command, `online database`, that once issued enables users to connect to the database. This command must be issued after a load database has taken place in System XI and will require scripts to be modified to support this syntax. Because of this change, scripts also will no longer be required to place a database in `single-user` or `dbo-use only` mode during the load process. Sybase automatically takes a database offline during the load process, and this is why the `online database` command must be issued after the load is completed.

In addition, Backup Server has been improved to be less dependent on the particular device being used for backups and restores when used on UNIX platforms. This lack of dependence shows itself by the fact that Backup Server will automatically attempt to identify the particular tape device being used for a backup or restore and configure itself for optimal performance for the particular device. If the tape unit is not found in Backup Server's list of available and supported database tape devices, Backup Server then will look for a special configuration file, $SYBASE/tape_backup.cfg, where $SYBASE has been configured on your server to be the path to the Sybase root. If this file is not found, Sybase then will prompt you with a warning. If you receive the warning, you can perform a dump/backup with the new keyword, `init`, which tells Backup Server to attempt to determine the actual attributes of the device and then store them in the configuration file.

▶ **See** "Performing Backups," **p. 492**

VLDB and VLM Support

System XI has been designed to support the new 64-bit processors coming out of Digital (the Alpha), HP (PA-RISC 8000), and Sun (the UltraSparc). Each of these 64-bit processors adds a huge amount of addressability to the server's processor. On a 32-bit processor, the largest number that can be represented by the processor is 2^{32-1} or 4,294,967,295 (4G). What this means is that the most amount of RAM that could be in the physical box was limited to 4G. On most versions of UNIX, the largest amount of user process accessible RAM was 2G because the rest of the RAM was reserved for the UNIX kernel. With 64-bit processors, the amount of addressable RAM increases to 2^{64-1} bytes or 1.844674407371 * 10^{19}, or in simple terms—lots and lots more!

The advent of this greater memory support has enabled Sybase to support much greater databases in memory. This is the *very large memory* (VLM) support that Sybase adds with System XI.

System 10 was able to create databases of sizes greater than 4G because the database server addressed the data through database devices (which were physical files on the OS), and each of these could have been up to 2G (2^{31} bytes) in size. Sybase has a limit of 255 database devices, meaning that the largest physical database can be up to 500G. A maintenance release of System XI, release 11.1, will raise the number of devices to 32,767, meaning a theoretical maximum database size of hundreds of terabytes. This release is being developed in conjunction with Hewlett Packard (HP) as part of the Taming the Terabyte or VLDB project.

Understanding the Components of System XI

Sybase System XI is more than just a way to store data in a SQL compliant relational database. System XI is a family of products that work together to provide a full data-management system for you. In this section, I introduce you to the main components of the System XI family so that you can become familiar with the various servers that are in the Sybase product line. The availability of some of the servers below is limited, based on hardware and operating system platform. If you see a product that you need, and Sybase doesn't have a version for your platform, it's just a case of talking to the right people and submitting a good business case as to why it should be there. Sybase *is* in the business of porting to various platforms, but it depends on volume and demand.

Using Data Server

The Data Server, otherwise referred to throughout this book as either Sybase SQL Server, System XI or just plain Sybase, is the main component that controls all the data storage and user management. The Data Server is the central repository for all databases and is basically *the server*. The Data Server is multi-threaded and can handle multiple simultaneous requests from different clients on a network. You interact with and use the Data Server with just about every operation that you perform. All of the other servers listed below require that the Data Server be operational on the network.

Table 2.1 shows the availability of the Data Server on hardware and operating system platforms.

Table 2.1   Platform Availability for the Sybase System XI Data Server

Operating System	Hardware Platform
Microsoft Windows NT	Intel 486, Pentium, and Pentium Pro
Novell NetWare 3.1x	Intel 486, Pentium, and Pentium Pro
Novell NetWare 4.x	Intel 486, Pentium, and Pentium Pro
UNIX	Digital, HP, Data General, Unisys, Motorola, Sun, IBM, NCR/ AT&T, Silicon Graphics, Tandem, and others

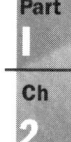

Part

I

Ch

2

For instructions on how to install the Data Server and how to get things up and running, see Chapter 3, "Installing Sybase."

Using Backup Server

The Backup Server is the Sybase tool/engine that performs backups and restores from the Data Server. In a normal environment, the Backup Server always is running while the Data Server is running, so that backups and restores can be performed at any time. The Backup Server also is responsible for performing data recovery in the event of a failure and, as such, is considered an integral extension to the base Data Server product.

The Backup Server is a device independent product in that it supports most major forms of media for backup and restore, including all forms of tape (including DLT and DDS), direct to hard disk, remote backups to other servers, devices, and magneto-optical devices. The Backup Server is available on the same platforms as the Data Server. See Table 2.1 for platform support lists.

Using Audit Server

In some environments it is necessary for compliance with internal and external corporate or institutional auditing to have a full listing of every transaction that occurred on the server. Audit Server is designed to perform this role for you. It works essentially as a transaction monitor sitting between the Data Server and the clients that are performing the operations. Audit Server monitors can monitor all users, something that most application driven security and audit trail types of products cannot do. In addition, Audit Server can be used to monitor third- party applications, such as report writers and ad hoc query tools.

Audit Server has its own database for recording events on the database server, and the data it contains has varying levels of audit detail available for querying and later storage on an offline media, such as tape (depending on the audit trail requirements you desire). Audit Server is considered an essential tool for those companies and institutions that have security concerns and want to perform detailed analysis of all activity (successful or otherwise) on the database.

N O T E Audit Server cannot only track and monitor every transaction that completes on the server and give you a list of what SQL was executed, and so on, it also can monitor failed transactions on the server. This way, you can monitor those users that are failing to perform actions due to security violations, such as a lack of granted permissions on database objects. Audit Server is a comprehensive auditing system that is very capable of monitoring all activity down to the lowest level, including that of the System Administrator. ■

Audit Server is available on the same platforms as the Data Server. See Table 2.1 for platform support lists.

Using Secure SQL Server

Sybase's Secure SQL Server is a product designed for very security-conscious institutions. It implements all the criteria required for a U.S. government certified B-1 secure environment. Compliant with what is known as the *Orange Book*, DOD 52.00.28-STD, Department of Defense Trusted Computer System Evaluation Criteria (TCSEC), Secure Server implements mandatory access control schemes to enforce the security that is available in the regular SQL Server.

Secure SQL Server also implements a row-level polyinstantiation (MLS) scheme that makes it possible to completely obscure the storage and existence of records in the database from the users. This means that it is possible in Secure SQL Server for two users to create a record with the same primary key information, such as a customer account; the only difference is the creator of the record. B-1 secure environments have the option of not informing users that records cannot be created due to the existence of a similar record in the system.

Secure SQL Server supports trusted users and the execution of trusted stored procedures and triggers. At this time, Secure SQL Server is available only on Sun and HP hardware. A version for Windows NT is anticipated in the near future. See Chapter 21, "Managing and Monitoring Security," for more information on how to use and take advantage of Sybase Secure SQL Server.

Using Replication Server

Sybase's Replication Server is a unique product that performs server-based data replication from one database server to another across a network. Replication enables you to distribute your data between servers for the benefits of data redundancy and also for balancing the loads on servers throughout a large network. Replication Server works by installing a process at the server level to read your database transaction log. As an action is committed and written to the log, Replication Server goes out across the network and applies the same transaction on the other database servers that are subscribing to the data. See Chapter 24, "Managing Data Replication," for more detailed examples and setup information for Replication Server.

Replication Server is available for all the same platforms as the Data Server. See Table 2.1 for platform support of Replication Server.

Using Sybase MPP

Sybase MPP (massive parallel processing) is the renamed version of Sybase Navigation Server. Sybase MPP is designed to facilitate the largest of the large databases and support. Sybase MPP supports massive databases in excess of 1 terabyte in size and supports hardware architectures with hundreds of CPUs that work in parallel to perform queries at optimum speed. The great advantage of Sybase MPP is that it looks like a regular Data Server and requires no additional coding to take advantage of its features and speed.

Part
I
Ch
2

Sybase MPP is a unique product that deserves attention from those of you who as customers have a lot of dollars to spend on a monster server and a lot of data to explore and manage. For an introductory white paper on Sybase MPP, check out **http://www.sybase.com/products/ system11/mppdata.html** on Sybase's Web Site. For more information on platform availability of Sybase MPP, contact your local Sybase representative.

Using Sybase IQ

Sybase IQ is the System XI component designed for data warehousing. It uses a proprietary binary data storage algorithm that speeds through data at up to 500 times the performance of the regular Sybase SQL Server.

Sybase IQ has integrated load capabilities to rapidly load data from a SQL Server to the IQ Server, and is designed to work hand-in-hand with an existing SQL Server installation.

Sybase IQ is currently available only for Sun hardware. For detailed information on Sybase IQ, go to **http://www.sybase.com/products/dataware/iqindex.html** on Sybase's Web Site.

From Here...

In this chapter, you were introduced to the origins of Sybase as a company and its products that form the System XI product suite. The development of Sybase is an excellent model for most companies: with an average of 60 percent growth per annum in revenues, Sybase has gone from strength to strength.

Also in this chapter you learned about all the new features of System XI and whetted your appetite for the good stuff that's covered in detail throughout the rest of the book. Finally, you learned the basics of the Sybase toolset and all the different servers that are available to you.

To plunge ahead, I suggest the following chapters for your review:

- See Chapter 3, "Installing Sybase," to get the goods installed so you can really put to use what you are learning in this book.
- See Chapter 4, "Introducing Transact-SQL," to learn all about Sybase's interpretation of the SQL standard.
- See Chapter 6, "Understanding Tables and Datatypes," for information on how to create tables and use datatypes to define columns.

- See Chapter 10, "Understanding Stored Procedures," for detailed instruction on how to work with advanced Transact-SQL statements and how to create procedural SQL code that you can use to emulate such languages as C or COBOL.

- See Chapter 14, "Understanding the Sybase Client Model (Client Library)," for a detailed discussion of the client side of using a Sybase database.

Installing Sybase

How to install Sybase System XI Server

A quick and easy-to-follow guide for installing Sybase System XI on Windows NT with some additional information for different UNIX vendors.

Installing and testing client connectivity

Getting a Client Library connection to work successfully can sometimes be tough. This section helps you understand all the elements of the installation process.

Starting Sybase

Some tips and tricks for getting the server running now that it's installed.

After buying Sybase and looking through some of the manuals, you probably are ready to get the installation going and the server up and running. The installation of Sybase is really not all that difficult, and with a little bit of planning and forethought, the installation will go quite smoothly.

The focus of this chapter is on getting you working with Sybase. For more information on how you actually *use* Sybase, you should look to the rest of this book for further guidance. ■

Installing the Server

Installing System XI is, thankfully, a lot more straightforward than installing System 10. In this chapter, I walk you through an installation of the System XI server on Windows NT 4.0. I've chosen the Windows NT installation as the best one for demonstrating a full installation because it is both the most obvious to understand and the most complete (in that it installs client connectivity at the same time).

In this chapter, I also point out some platform specific installation instructions and tips for various vendors' implementations of UNIX; however, the documentation from Sybase is really not that bad, so I suggest that you also refer to that before doing any installation. Typically, installing on UNIX has a few more "gotchas" than installing on Windows NT because of all the different vendor-specific features of each of the flavors of UNIX.

NOTE These instructions make the assumption that you already have installed the underlying operating system on the server that is going to be used, and that you have prepared hard disks and/or volumes for use by Sybase. If you have not prepared your environment for the installation, I recommend looking at the tips below in the section titled "Preparing for an Installation." ▪

Preparing for an Installation

There are a number of steps to perform, and issues to consider, before installing Sybase System XI on a server. The following checklist is designed to help you identify the major items that should be completed before you begin the installation:

■ Install all required hardware on the server.

Make sure that you've got all the drives, drive controller cards, network devices, tape drives, and so on, installed in the server before beginning the installation process.

■ Install the base operating system on the server.

Before beginning to install Sybase, the operating system must be installed. Also, make sure that any OS level mirroring and drive/volume partitioning has been installed and is working.

 TIP I highly recommend that you install Sybase on NTFS formatted partitions. NTFS provides substantial performance advantages and is far more reliable than FAT partitions.

■ Attempt to estimate the size of the database.

This will help you size the server correctly. (See Chapter 22, "Managing and Monitoring Performance," for more information on how to size a database.)

■ Gather `sp_configure` information from previous installations.

If this is an upgrade or you have other System 10 or System XI servers already installed, run `sp_configure` so that you can get an idea of the configuration options you set up on those servers.

- Make sure you know where your Customer Authorization String (CAS) is. Sybase uses a CAS to enable you to install the server and/or components.

 TIP Type the CAS into a text file and save it somewhere convenient, such as the root Sybase directory. You will need to enter the CAS each time you run the installation software, and copying and pasting from the text file will save you some time.

- Shut down any Sybase software already running.

  If this is an installation on a server that has other Sybase products on it, make sure that you shut them down first.

- Review any release bulletins that shipped with your version.

  Sybase publishes release bulletins that alert you to installation problems and other areas of concern with a particular release. Make sure that you carefully review the release bulletins that ships with your Sybase server before beginning the installation process. Specific release bulletin information also can be found on Sybase's Web site at **http://www.Sybase.com**, or you can go to Sybase's CompuServe forum: **GO SYBASE**.

- Decide on a name for the server and the location of the software.

  Before installing you should have a good idea what you want to name the server. Renaming a server can be a problematic operation because you need to modify many different configuration files.

  Make sure that you've decided on locations for the server's software to reside. Typically, you would want to place the database server binaries and operating system files on a single drive and then start placing data, such as the *master* database, on subsequent drives.

- Decide on the sorts of client protocols that you need to support.

  Most installations of Sybase support straight TCP/IP as the preferred client protocol; however, on some platforms, such as Windows NT and NetWare, you also can opt for protocols, such as Netbios, IPX/SPX, and Named Pipes.

- Decide on whether you intend to install the additional Sybase databases, *pubs2, pix2,* and *sybsyntax.*

  If you are considering installing these databases, you should change the default size of the *master* device from 21M to somewhere around 30M. This makes sure that you have enough room.

Part

I

Ch

3

Installing Sybase on Windows NT Server 4.0

The installation of Sybase on Windows NT is quite a lengthy process that involves a number of steps. The average installation should be completed in under an hour (unless you are creating very large disk devices), and if the installation seems to be hanging, you might want to consider shutting down the installation program through the Windows NT Task Manager. Perform the following steps to install Sybase:

1. Log on to the Windows NT machine with Administrator privileges. The System XI installation program will not work if you do not have the appropriate permissions to modify the System setup.

2. Insert the CD-ROM or other media into the appropriate drive.

3. To start the installation process, click the Start menu in Windows NT 4.0, and choose Settings, Control Panel. Figure 3.1 shows the Windows NT Desktop with the task bar at the bottom and the Start menu opened to access the Control Panel.

FIG. 3.1

The Windows NT 4.0 Desktop has a Start menu that is your home base from which you can launch programs, configure your desktop, and open program groups.

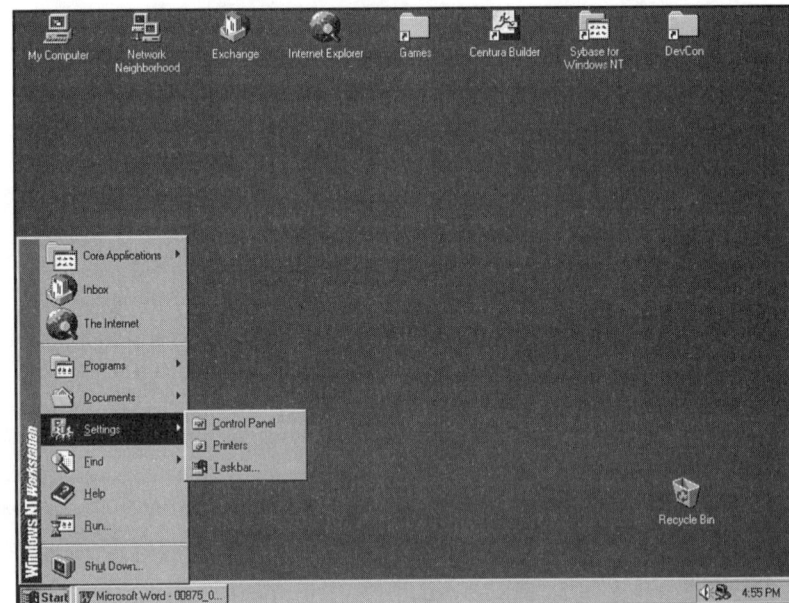

4. Once Control Panel has launched, double-click the Add/Remove Programs icon. In Figure 3.2, you can see the Control Panel list of applets that can be managed for this workstation.

FIG. 3.2

Control Panel consolidates all the configurations for a Windows NT machine. Use Control Panel anytime you want to review or change the settings of your server or workstation.

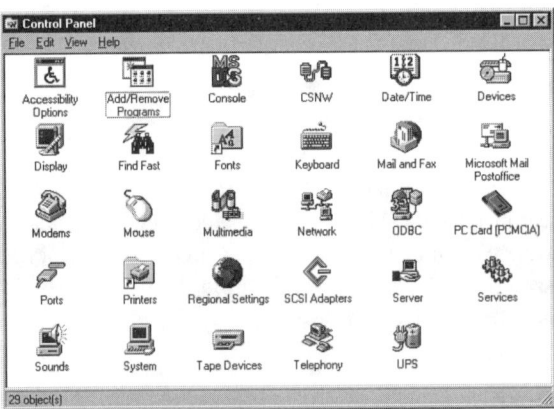

5. On the Add/Remove Programs Properties dialog box, click the Install button to run the Install Programs Wizard that comes with Windows NT (see Fig. 3.3).

FIG. 3.3

The Add/Remove Programs Properties dialog box is the central place for installing and removing software in Windows NT.

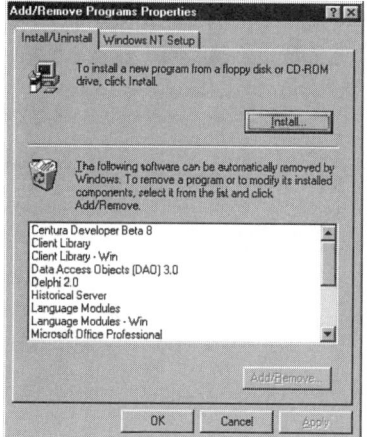

6. Click the Next button on the wizard, and Windows NT will search the floppy drives and CD-ROM drives attached to the computer to look for programs that will install software (typically named SETUP.EXE or INSTALL.EXE) and then will finish the wizard if it finds one. In Figure 3.4, you can see the completed wizard.

FIG. 3.4

The Add New Programs Wizard has found SETUP.EXE on the E: drive (a CD-ROM drive) and is about to launch it when the Finish button is pressed.

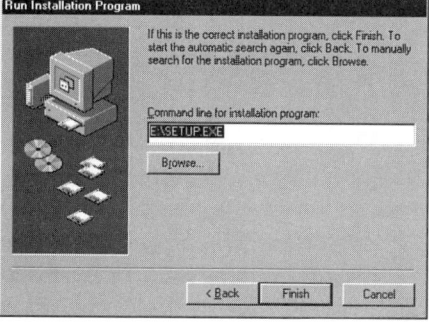

7. Click the Finish button to launch the Setup program for Sybase System XI. While the Setup program is loading, a banner is displayed, as shown in Figure 3.5.

8. Enter your Customer Authorization String (CAS) in the Welcome dialog box, and press the Continue button. In Figure 3.6, you can see the Welcome dialog box with a dummy or fake CAS entered.

FIG. 3.5

If the System XI Setup program startup banner is not displayed, you may have defective media.

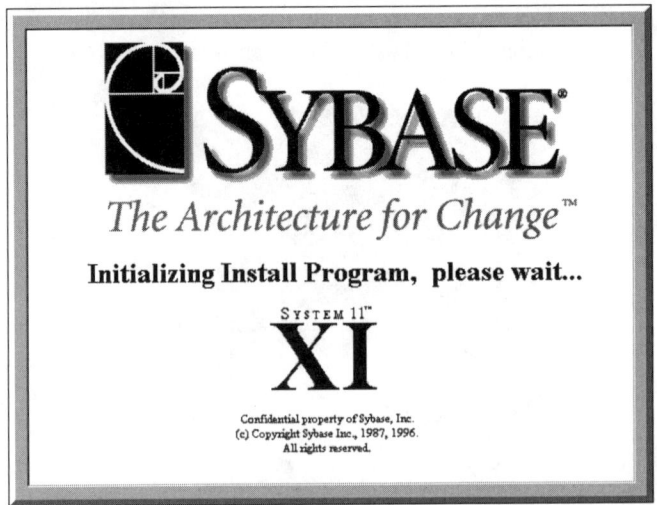

FIG. 3.6

Your CAS is typically a 34-character string and is specific to the piece of software you are installing from Sybase.

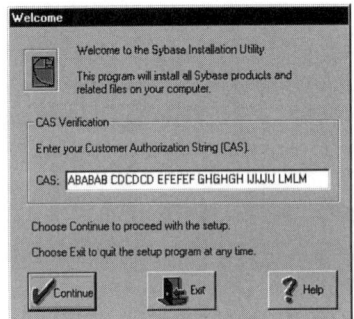

CAUTION

If you enter an invalid CAS, you will be warned and given a chance to retry it. The Authorization Failure! dialog box is shown in Figure 3.7. Under some circumstances, it is even possible to type in a CAS that's *incorrect,* but get past this authentication phase. In this case, you'll never know it, and I suppose you are registering somebody else's copy!

---

9. In the Product Set Selection dialog box, deselect the Windows Products (16-bit versions), unless you plan to run 16-bit applications from the server, and then click the Continue button (see Fig. 3.8).

FIG. 3.7

Entering an incorrect CAS happens to me about one in three times! Sybase's strings are hard to type correctly. Just hit the Resume button to retry.

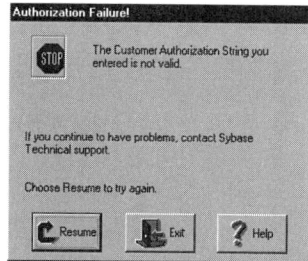

FIG. 3.8

The Product Set Selection dialog box enables you to install applications and tools for either 16-bit Windows (e.g., Windows 3.11) or 32-bit Windows (Windows 95, Windows NT) or both.

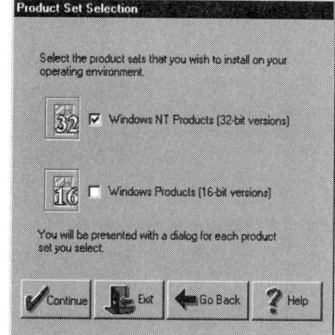

Part

I

Ch

3

N O T E If you are installing client connectivity under Windows 3.1 or Windows for Workgroups 3.11, the 32-bit selection is disabled. Furthermore, if you are installing client connectivity under Windows 95, the product set will indicate Windows 95 as opposed to Windows NT. For more information on Installing under Windows 95, see the section below, "Installing Client Library on Windows 95." ■

10. Using the Windows NT Product Selection Screen, as shown in Figure 3.9, you can choose the products that you want to install. Taking the default options will install the minimum functionality required to get Sybase up and running. If you do not want to customize the installation, please jump to Step 13.

  T I P For your first installation, you should take the defaults and see how everything is laid out on your drives. If you need additional functionality, you always can rerun the Setup program and add the pieces of software that you need.

11. To change the languages that are being installed for, click the Custom button that lines up with the Language Modules check box. By using the Custom Selection dialog box shown in Figure 3.10, you can select one or more languages for installation with the server. Press the Accept button when you are happy with your selections.

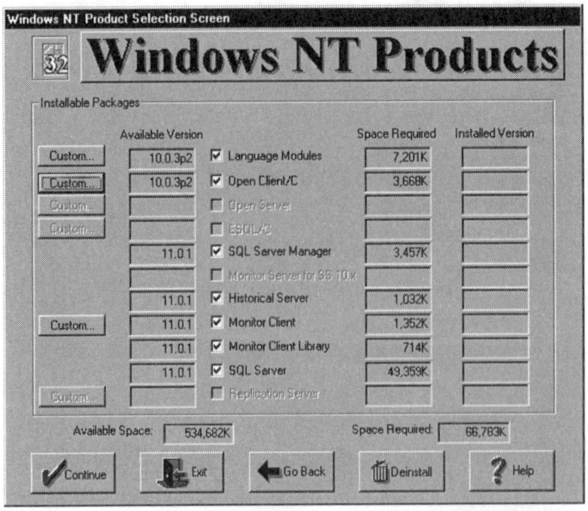

FIG. 3.9

The default options are selected on the Windows NT Product Selection Screen. Click any of the Custom buttons to alter the sub-components of a particular selection.

FIG. 3.10

In this installation, I'm installing French and German support along with the default US English. Note that for each language installed, additional disk space is consumed.

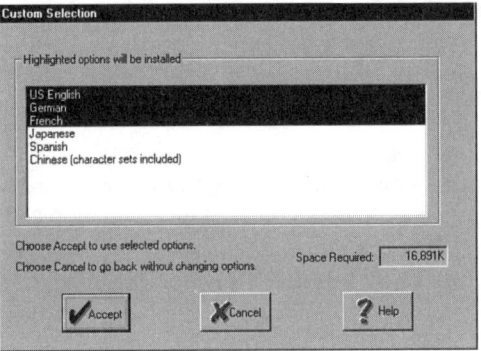

12. To change the client support for this installation, click the Custom button that lines up with the Open Client/C check box. You will be presented with the same dialog box shown in Figure 3.10; however, this time the options relate to client installation options. If you need to add support for additional networking protocols or want to add some sample applications written in C for use in application development, select those options now.

13. The Monitor Client also has a Custom button; however, these options seem to be very standard and always should be taken.

14. When you are satisfied with your selections on the Windows NT Product Selection Screen, click the Continue button, and the install program copies the files from the distribution media to the server's drives.

TIP Installing all the software at once can take a lot of time, depending on your hardware platform. Have some coffee, sit back, and enjoy the progress bars going from 0–100 percent!

15. The SQL.INI Dialog gives you the opportunity to modify the SQL.INI file (a configuration file used by clients connected to the Sybase server). Unless you are adding connections for other servers on your network, you can select the option Ignore for Now and press Continue because the default server configurations are added by the Setup program (see Fig. 3.11).

FIG. 3.11
From SQL.INI Dialog, you can select the option Run Sqledit to Edit Your SQL.INI to modify the file that Sybase is installing. Alternately, you can choose Import an Existing SQL.INI to import a file from another PC if you have one.

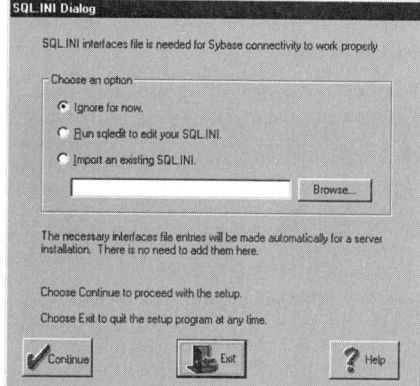

16. Use the SQL Server Configuration dialog box to specify the name of the SQL Server and the size and location of the *master* and *sybsystemprocs* devices. Note that the default SQL Server name is the name of the Windows NT machine itself (see Fig. 3.12).

FIG. 3.12
I recommend that you alter the size of the master device file to be at least 30M so that you have room to install the *pubs2* and *sybsyntax* databases.

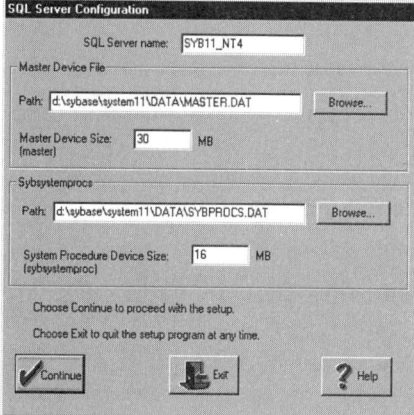

Part

I

Ch

3

17. When you are happy with your modifications to the SQL Server Configuration dialog box, press the Continue button and the Setup program will proceed to create the devices for you.

CAUTION

Creating the devices takes quite a lot of time—up to about 10 minutes, depending on your hardware and OS. Do not abort or shut down the Setup program at this time because you will leave the file system in a state that will require recovery.

---

18. After the successful installation of all the devices and the setup of the SQL Server, the Setup program also may require you to restart the computer so that all the changes can take effect. If you do not restart the computer at this point, you should not attempt to start the Sybase server. Restarting the computer will update the registry and environment so that applications can see the Sybase server (see Fig. 3.13).

FIG. 3.13
Successful completion of the installation of Sybase is indicated by the Installation Complete dialog box. Click the Finish button to exit from the Setup program.

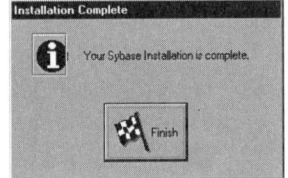

Understanding the Sybase Directories

During the installation of System XI, a large number of files was copied to your server's hard drive. In this section, you get an explanation of each of the directories so that you know what they are used for and where to find things.

After installing Sybase, the Setup program will have installed an environment variable called %Sybase%. This variable is the root directory where the Sybase installation was made, and by changing directories to it, you will be at the root of the Sybase files. By executing the following command, the machine would change directories to the Sybase root:

```
cd %Sybase%
```

All the directories shown in Table 3.1 are located off of the Sybase root.

 Variable names in Windows NT are not case sensitive, so you can type either %Sybase% or %SYBASE% or %sybase% and still get the same result.

Table 3.1   Sybase Directories and Their Uses Under Windows NT and Most UNIX Versions

Directory	Use
bin	This directory stores all the executables that are going to be used by the server and client programs.
Charsets	In this directory, Sybase places all the installed character sets that can be used by the server for storing data.
data	The data directory is where the physical device files are placed in a default installation. In an advanced installation these device files are probably on separate drives.
data\hs_data	hs_data is a subdirectory of the data directory in a default installation. Sybase uses this directory for storage of data used by the Historical Server.
Dll	This directory is used by clients connecting to the server. DLLs are used by Client Library to communicate across the network.
Help	These are help files, including release bulletins and Client Library documentation. Include C/C++ header files used by application developers writing programs that connect to Sybase.
Ini	This directory stores the SQL.INI file, which controls the list of available servers and protocols for the servers that a client can connect to. Use the SQLEDIT program to work with this file.
Init	This is a private directory for Sybase to log all its startup initialization.
Install	This is the primary installation directory. In this directory are scripts or batch files that can be used to launch the SQL Server. In addition, the *errorlog* is written to this directory.
Lib	These are lib files used by application developers writing programs that connect to Sybase.
Locales	This directory stores client specific locale information based on the languages you specify during the installation process.
Sample	The sample directory contains coding examples used by application programmers, and it also has a sample Historical Server script that creates views that can be used to monitor performance data on the server.
Scripts	The scripts directory has all the key script files used in conjunction with ISQL to build the server's primary databases and any additional databases that you want to install.
Upgrade	The upgrade directory has all the files that are needed to upgrade a pre-System XI database.

Part

I

Ch

3

Additional Information for Installing Sybase on UNIX

The Sybase installation on UNIX is quite similar to the installation on Windows NT with the major exception being that the installation is performed on a character mode terminal/console on the UNIX box itself. The steps involved for an installation are mostly the same and basically require four steps:

1. Install and configure the server with the appropriate hardware.
2. Initialize the physical disks, and install the operating system.
3. Transfer the software for the installation from the installation media (usually DAT) to the host UNIX machine.
4. Perform the installation of the Sybase binary software.

Each of these steps is documented in detail in the Sybase System XI Installation Supplement for your given UNIX platform. Some tips that you might want to consider when installing Sybase on UNIX are as follows:

- Dedicate the UNIX server to running Sybase. If you attempt to make a server multipurpose, you may have difficulties in tuning the server and getting optimal performance that are difficult to isolate to either Sybase or any of the other tasks running on the server.
- Contact your hardware vendor (such as Sun or HP), and find out where the Sybase performance/engineering center is. The Sybase center is where the hardware vendor and Sybase design and implement all the features of Sybase in an optimal fashion. By contacting the center, you will be able to get any tips that it has for installing Sybase in the best way.
- Do not create users on the UNIX box for your users that are going to have access to the Sybase database server—there's no need. Sybase users only require the capability to establish a TCP/IP connection to the database server; they do not need the ability to log on to the UNIX box. Granting logon access to the UNIX box is a security flaw that you should avoid.
- Maximize memory utilization for the Sybase System XI server by first calculating the amount of memory used by the operating system prior to loading Sybase; then allocate as much of the remainder as possible to Sybase using `sp_configure 'Memory'`. There's no need to have any free memory on the server (i.e., not allocated to Sybase) unless you plan to `Telnet` into the UNIX box for administrative purposes.
- Always utilize hardware or operating system level disk mirroring. Do not use Sybase's built-in mirroring because the performance is nowhere near as good.

Installing Client Connectivity

Previously you installed connectivity for the Windows NT machine to talk to the server on the same machine. This was 32-bit connectivity and was required so that you can administer the server on the same machine. In this section, you learn how to install connectivity under

Windows 3.1 and its closely related sibling, Windows for Workgroups 3.11, and also on Windows 95.

Installing Client Library on Windows 3.x

Windows 3.1, Windows 3.11, and Windows for Workgroups 3.11, collectively known as Windows 3.x, are straightforward installations. Using the same media as you installed the server from, follow these steps:

1. Using either Program Manager or File Manager, choose <u>F</u>ile, <u>R</u>un and type the drive letter and a colon followed by **setup.exe**. For example:

   ```
   e:setup.exe
   ```

2. By running Setup, you are launching the same program that was used earlier in this chapter to install the SQL Server. Follow the steps outlined above in the section titled "Installing Sybase on Windows NT Server 4.0" until you get to step 9.

3. On 16-bit Windows, you are presented with a smaller setup dialog box, offering you fewer selections, as shown in Figure 3.14. Modify any options that you want, and press the Continue button to copy the files to the computer.

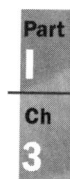

Part

I

Ch

3

FIG. 3.14

16-bit selections on the Windows Product Selection Screen enable you to change the languages being installed and to add communications protocols for whatever TCP/IP stack you are using.

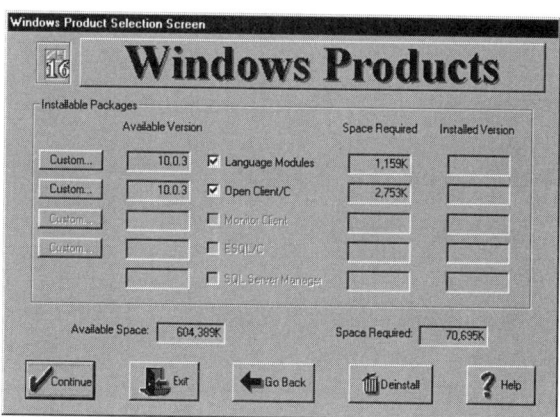

4. After the files are copied, you are given the opportunity to run SQLEDIT to configure your local SQL.INI file; please refer to the instructions below in the section titled "Using SQLEDIT."

Installing Client Library on Windows 95

Installation of Client Library under Windows 95 is identical to installing it under Windows NT, with the exception that you receive a modified Product Selection Screen from which you can choose installable software. On Windows 95, you have the option of installing the SQL Server Manager and the SQL Monitor Client. With these utilities, you can manage the SQL Server and monitor its performance.

Using SQL Server Manager is described throughout the book. For information on using SQL Monitor, please refer to Chapter 22, "Managing and Monitoring Performance."

Using SQLEDIT

SQLEDIT is Sybase's platform independent (well, it at least runs on Windows 3.x, Windows 95, and Windows NT) program designed to configure client connectivity. SQLEDIT works with a file that is stored in your INI directory off the Sybase root called SQL.INI.

You can edit SQL.INI by hand if you want, but it is far easier to use the graphical utility, and by using SQLEDIT, you can only then blame Sybase for any mistakes that might happen! SQLEDIT is a pretty simple program with one main window, as shown in Figure 3.15, and is logically organized.

FIG. 3.15

The SQLEDIT main user interface window is divided into regions. The left-hand side contains a list of known servers, while the right-hand side has connection setup information.

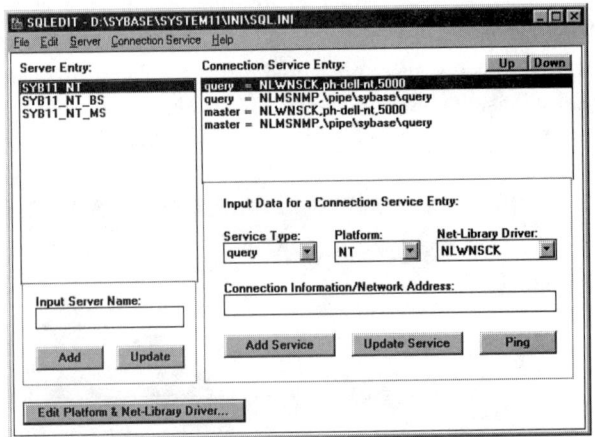

In the following sections, you create a server, add a master and query connection server entry, and ping the server to test connectivity.

 Don't forget to Save your work when you are happy with your SQLEDIT connection; it would be a real pain to lose everything after you get it working! To save in SQLEDIT, choose File, Save, or press Ctrl+S.

Adding a Server Using SQLEDIT To add a server using SQLEDIT, follow these steps:

1. Choose Server, New Server Entry, or press Ctrl+N.

2. Enter the name of the server in the Input Server Name field.

3. Press the Add button (or select Add Server Entry, Ctrl+A, from the Server menu) to add it to the list of available servers.

NOTE The difference between *master* and *query* server connections is that a master connection is used by the server itself when it starts up, and a query connection is used by any client that wants to connect to the server. ▪

Adding a Query Connection Using SQLEDIT   To add a query connection using SQLEDIT, follow these steps:

1. Choose Connection Service, New Service.
2. Select the Service type of query.
3. Choose the appropriate platform for the connection. For DOS connections, use DOS; for Windows 3.x connections, use Win3; and for Windows NT and Windows 95 connections, select NT.
4. Choose the appropriate Net-Library driver. The Net-Library driver controls what sort of communications you want to do with the server. The typically chosen values are either WDBWSKTC for a Windows Sockets TCP/IP compatible Windows 3.x connection, NLWNSCK for a Windows Sockets TCP/IP compatible Windows 95 or NT connection, or if you want to use Named Pipes, then the Net-Library driver would be either WNLNMP (Windows 3.x) or NLMSNP (Windows 95/NT).

N O T E   The list of TCP/IP stacks that are supported by Sybase is quite long. For a complete list of available Net-Library options, refer to the Sybase documentation. ■

5. Add the specifics of the connection in the Connection Information/Network Address field. For a TCP/IP connection, the specifics would be organized as `<host-name or IP address>,port`, for example:

   `205.160.254.1,5000`

   If you have a valid TCP/IP host-name configuration, use something like the following:

   `ph-dell-nt,5000`

   For a Named Pipes connection, enter the name of the pipe, for example:

   `\pipe\sybase\query.`

N O T E   When using Named Pipes on anything other than the server itself, you must precede the pipe name with a server name. For example, if you have a server named SPARKY, then the Sybase query pipe would be as follows: `\\SPARKY\pipe\sybase\query.` ■

6. Press the Add Service button (or choose Add Service, Connection Service) to add it to the list of available servers.

Testing the Connection   After adding your server and connection service to SQLEDIT, it is now necessary to test the connection. To do so, select the server and service connection you want to use, and press the Ping button. SQLEDIT then attempts to connect to the database across the network. Success or failure is indicated by a message that appears about 10 seconds after trying to connect to the database server.

If you fail to connect in this fashion, it's probably a good idea to consult the troubleshooting guide for connectivity that is supplied by Sybase.

Part

I

Ch

3

Starting Sybase

One of the neat features of Windows NT is that it has many different ways of doing the same thing or performing the same command. This is a flexibility that is unmatched by most other operating systems, and the key is the capability to start and stop services. Services in Windows NT can be the basic units of the operating system itself as well as anything external, such as Sybase System XI Server.

In Windows NT, there are three common ways of starting Sybase:

- You can use the Services Manager supplied by Sybase to start and stop various Sybase servers, such as the SQL Server, the Backup Server, and the Monitor Server.
- You can use the installed scripts in the %Sybase%\install directory. (Note that this is your typical option on UNIX.)
- You can use the Windows NT Control Panel Services dialog box.

In this section, you learn how to perform each of these options so that you can decide the best way of configuring your server.

Starting Sybase Using the Services Manager

Using the Services Manager is perhaps the easiest way of starting the server. To use the Services Manager, follow these steps:

1. From the Start menu in Windows NT, choose Programs, click Sybase for Windows NT, and click the Services Manager to start it (see Fig. 3.16).

FIG. 3.16
The Services Manager enables you to start any of the installed servers on this machine or on remote machines if you have configured them in your SQL.INI file.

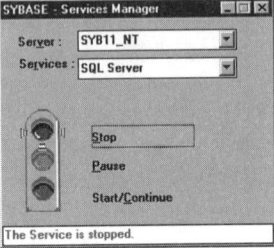

2. Select the Server you want to start from the Server combo box.
3. Select the service you want to start from the Services combo box.
4. Double-click the Start/Continue text or the green lamp from the stop light. Successful starting is indicated in the status line with the text The Service is running.

 TIP Always start up the Backup Server when you start the SQL Server so that if you need to do a backup at any time, you don't have to worry about whether the Backup Server has been started.

Starting Sybase Using the Install Scripts

The install scripts that are created are what the Services manager actually runs to start the server for you. By default, there are three different scripts in your %Sybase%\install directory. The following list shows the possible scripts where <ServerName> is the name you chose for your server at the time of installation:

- RUN_<ServerName>.bat—This starts the SQL Server.
- RUN_<ServerName>_BS.bat—This starts the Backup Server.
- RUN_<ServerName>_MS.bat—This starts the Monitor Server.

On UNIX, these same scripts will exist, but do not need to have a .bat extension on the files because they will be chmod changed so that they are executable. By running any of these batch files, you will start the required server. To run either of the batch files, simply change directories to %Sybase%\install and type the batch file name.

N O T E The Services Manager is not able to detect a running SQL Server if you start it by running these batch files directly, so it reports that the server is stopped even though it has been successfully started. To confirm a successful initialization of the server, you should try pinging the Server with SQLEDIT. ▩

Running one of these batch files in a command prompt window will lock that command prompt window open, and it will make that window the "console" to the server. When you view the starting of SQL Server, you will notice a lot of text flying by. This is normal, and is simply the startup information being written to the screen instead of directly to the errorlog file (that also can be found in the %Sybase%\install directory). If you close the window, you will shut down Sybase.

A better way to start a batch file such as this is to use the Start command in Windows NT. Using the Start command, you have the option of creating a new window for Sybase to live in, and you can have it minimized. For example, to start Sybase with high priority (meaning that it gets maximum CPU time) in a new window in the background, enter the following command:

```
start /high /min %Sybase%\install\run_<servername>.bat
```

Starting Sybase Using the Services in Control Panel

Sybase also can be started by using the Services option of the Control Panel. To start Sybase's Servers using Control Panel, follow these steps:

1. Start Control Panel and double-click the Services applet to run it (see Fig. 3.17).
2. Scroll down in the list to the Sybase entries, as shown in Figure 3.17, and then click the Start button. The Services applet attempts to start the Sybase server and shows you a status dialog box while it does so (see Fig. 3.18).
3. Select any of the other servers you want to start, and click Start for them, too. When you have finished starting the servers, click Close.

FIG. 3.17

The Services applet lists all the available services in Windows NT and indicates their current status and whether or not they have been configured to start automatically.

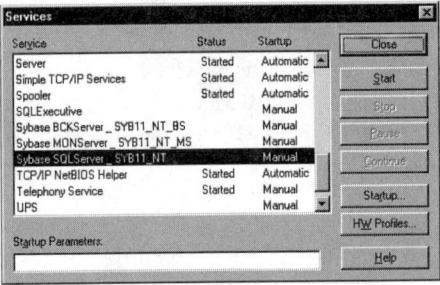

FIG. 3.18

The Service Control dialog box indicates that Windows NT is attempting to start a service.

One of the best features of the Services applet is that you can control the initial behavior of the Sybase servers when the Windows NT server is started. By clicking the Startup button, you can set a service to have a Startup Type of Automatic. This means that Sybase and its other servers can be started every time the Windows NT server is started without the need for a user to go in and manually start it with the Services Manager. Figure 3.19 shows the Service dialog box for the Sybase SQLServer named SYB11_NT.

FIG. 3.19

The Service dialog box enables you to start a particular service on an automatic basis. You also can specify the user that the service should log on as when it is started, though for Sybase, you typically would use the System Account.

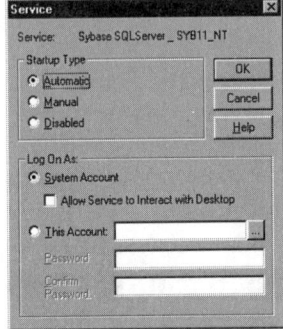

Checking to See if Sybase Is Running

There are a few different ways to determine if Sybase has started. If you started Sybase using the Services Manager, you can just start the Services Manager up again and look at the status of the server. If it says The Service is running, then you know that the server is up.

Alternatively, if you started the server using the install scripts, your best bet to test if the server is up is by using the SQLEDIT program and attempting to ping the server. If you can successfully ping the server, then it is up.

A third option is to use the Services applet in Control Panel. Simply start the Services applet, and scroll down to the Sybase services and look at the Status column. If it says `Started`, then the server is up.

Installing Optional Sybase Databases

Sybase ships with two databases that can be very useful for testing, training, and learning about Sybase: *pubs2,* which is a test database and is referred to a great deal in this book and in the Sybase documentation, and *sybsyntax,* which is a database that contains all the syntax for different Transact-SQL commands and enables you to get help from the server as to how to formulate a particular Transact-SQL statement.

Installing these databases is easy and is simply a function of running the scripts supplied by Sybase.

> **CAUTION**
>
> If you installed the *master* device with the default 21M size, I do not recommend that you install the *pubs2* and *sybsyntax* databases because you will not leave sufficient space in the *master* device for later use. Please reinstall Sybase or extend the *master* device's size. For help on extending a device size, see Chapter 5, "Understanding Databases, Devices, and Transaction Logs."

Part

I

Ch

3

The scripts are named as follows:

- `instpbs2`—This creates and installs the *pubs2* database.
- `instpix2`—This adds the special image data to the *pubs2* database. This data is not actually necessary for any of the examples in this book, but can be used to test the image storage capabilities of Sybase.
- `inssynsq`—This creates the *sybsyntax* database and adds syntax support for all Transact-SQL commands, system procedures, and SQL Server utilities.
- `inssyndb`—This adds support in the *sybsyntax* database for DB-Library routines and functions.

To run any of the scripts, follow these steps:

1. Open a command prompt in Windows NT.
2. Change directories to the Scripts directory off of the Sybase root:

   `cd %Sybase%\scripts`

3. Run ISQL to run the script:

   `isql -Usa -P -S<ServerName> -i<ScriptName>`

   For example, to install the *pubs2* database on a server named SYB11_NT, you would type:

   `isql -Usa -P -SSYB11_NT -iinstpbs2`

From Here...

In this chapter, you learned the steps involved in installing and starting the Sybase System XI server. In addition, you worked through the installation of the client connectivity software known as Client Library. With this information, you should be able to plan for and successfully deploy Sybase installations in your corporation or institution.

Please remember that the final word on installation specifics is the Sybase printed documentation. Quite often, Sybase will come out with revised versions of installation guides for particular hardware and operating system combinations. This book is accurate and a useful guide for a Windows NT installation, but you should refer to Sybase's documentation for the specifics on your particular platform if you install on UNIX.

From here, I think you would be served best by jumping to the following chapters:

- Chapter 5, "Understanding Databases, Devices, and Transaction Logs," contains information on how to create the base components of your server for your users to get tables created in.

- Chapter 6, "Understanding Tables and Datatypes," introduces the basic unit of data storage in Sybase: the table.

- See Chapter 10, "Understanding Stored Procedures," for detailed instruction on how to work with advanced Transact-SQL statements and how to create procedural SQL code that you can use to emulate a language like C or COBOL.

- See Chapter 19, "Managing Data Availability," for the steps involved in performing backups and restores of your new databases on your server.

Using System XI

CHAPTER 4

Introducing
Transact-SQL

Transact-SQL is Sybase's interpretation of the SQL standards created by the relational database community (as a result of Codd's work at IBM) as well as the ANSI standards committees that produced the SQL89 and SQL92 standards. Transact-SQL has a number of extensions to the standards beyond the base criteria as defined in the ANSI standards. In particular, Sybase's extensions are focused around their support for procedural logic in stored procedures and for advanced Data Manipulation Language (DML) extensions that enable joins in updates and deletes. More on the extensions can be found in the section, "Removing Data from a Table with Delete," later in this chapter.

This chapter's goal is to introduce you to the main components of SQL and to show you how Sybase's Transact-SQL is really a superset of the basics that SQL provides in its standards. This chapter serves as a good introduction for those of you who have had a limited involvement with SQL and want to get a feel for the rest of the book. ■

Working with Data Definition Language (DDL)

This chapter introduces you to all the important aspects of Transact-SQL related to creating and managing database objects such as tables and views.

Using Data Manipulation Language (DML)

Transact-SQL's syntax is explained for manipulating data by selecting, inserting, updating, or deleting from a table or view.

Introduction to Relational Theory

A brief discussion of how to *think* about your data and how to organize it in a slightly formal and normalized way.

Learn the intricacies of Transact-SQL

Understanding all the functions and command options in Transact-SQL can be difficult. This chapter shows you all that you need to know to be proficient in Sybase's flavor of SQL.

> **N O T E**   Almost all of the examples that you see in this chapter and throughout the rest of the book
> rely on the *pubs2* sample database that is supplied by Sybase to be installed. If you have
> not installed the database, please do so if you want to follow these examples exactly. ■

▶ **See** "Installing Optional Sybase Databases," **p. 51**

What Is SQL Anyway?

SQL (Structured Query Language) is a way of defining and making requests from a relational database in an abstract form. To put that another way, SQL provides a generic language that can be used to manage data in a relational database without knowing the underlying data structure.

SQL came from deep inside the research laboratories of IBM. It was a language proposed by Tedd Codd in his definitive paper, "Communications of the ACM," written in 1970. The design and definition came as a result of the work he was doing to try to eliminate a programmer's need to be concerned with the way data was stored. The goal was to provide an abstract language that would be interpreted by a database server that would then respond to the request with the appropriate information.

Working with Sets

SQL is a set-based language. This means that every operation is performed on a set of data, which can be a single row in a table or many rows. The point of set-based operations is that they logically occur at the same time to all of the records that fall within the set. Obviously, this is physically impossible. It is impossible to perform an operation on multiple records at the same time; however, logically all the records are affected at the same time.

For example, if you need to set every store's payment terms to be net 30, you might issue a single statement in Transact-SQL like this:

```
Update stores
Set     payterms = "Net 30"
```

The SQL Server will, in fact, process this request by sequentially doing the update on each row in the *stores* table. However, control will not return to you until they have all been updated. This is the notion of set processing. All records that match the criteria you specify are treated equally. For information on how to process records a row at a time and bypass Sybase's *set* processing see Chapter 12, "Understanding and Using Cursors."

Storing Data Abstractly

SQL has been designed so that the language used to query and work with data in the database does not have any particular reference to the actual location of the data. This is known as abstract data storage because you are abstracted, or made independent of, the data storage mechanism used by the server; and yet, you have full access to the stored data with a rich language.

SQL's goal of data storage abstraction offers a number of advantages to the user:

- Within some limits, an application that uses basic SQL is portable to different back-end servers such as Sybase, Oracle, or Informix, without any need for change.

- Application programmers no longer have to think about the way that the data is accessed or stored by the physical devices on which the server resides. This means that the database server vendor's implementation of data storage has shielded the programmer from needing to write data retrieval and management code.

- Application programmers have no need to implement locking or concurrency methods in code. The database server is responsible for managing data access by more than one user. This greatly reduces the chance for error introduced by the programmer who does not correctly access data.

- Data storage methods can change with different versions of the database server software without affecting client programs because the programs are unaware of the way the data is stored in the first place.

Writing SQL Statements

Another one of the benefits of SQL is that it is completely formless. This means that you can write the same SQL statement with different formatting and it will not affect the way the data is processed on the server. In Listing 4.1, you can see that different SQL statement formats do not affect the server.

Part

II

Ch

4

Listing 4.1 CHP04_01.SQL—SQL Can Be Written in Any Case or Formatting

```
/*
This script file shows that you can format the same
statement in SQL in many ways and yet get the same
result from the server. This is because SQL is a
formless language.
*/

/* Example 1 */
select stor_id, stor_name from stores
go

/* Example 2 */
select stor_id, stor_name
from stores
go

/* Example 3 */
select stor_id,
stor_name
from stores
go
```

continues

Listing 4.1 Continued

```
/* Example 4 */
Select
stor_id,
stor_name
From
stores
go

/* Example 5 */
Select Stor_Id, Stor_Name
From   Stores
Go
```

To make the SQL most easily readable by you, throughout this book I use the style shown in Example 5 in Listing 4.1, where each clause of the SQL statement is placed on its own line, and capitalization of the keywords has been performed.

TROUBLESHOOTING

I just ran the script in Error! Not a valid bookmark self-reference., and it gave me errors like "Invalid table name Stores" and "Invalid column name Stor_Id." The problem is that your database server or SQL Server has been installed with case sensitivity in the sort order. What this means is that you have configured SQL Server to treat pieces of text with consideration of their case, for example, "Hello World" is not the same as "hello world." Case sensitivity is an option that you can set up when configuring a SQL Server. A case sensitive server is slower at sorting results from queries than a case insensitive server because it has to consider the impact of the case of letters when sorting the data.

Unless you have a good reason for installing case sensitivity, I recommend that you turn it off. A case insensitive database does not care about the way you send database objects, such as table names and columns, to the database, and this makes it easier to work with because you don't have to think about how the tables and columns were actually named when they were created.

▶ **See** "Understanding Sort Orders," **p. 632**

Executing SQL Statements

In this chapter, you are going to need some way to actually work with the SQL statements that you see and the example listings that can be found on the CD ROM included with this book. Sybase provides isql, which is a fairly primitive tool for sending SQL to the server and is generally not recommended for day-to-day work—you will quickly get frustrated.

One of the first steps of setting up a Sybase environment is to choose a good tool for working with the database. I use a product called RapidSQL from Embarcadero Technologies, but there are plenty of other products on the market for interacting with the database. See Chapter 17,

"Using Third-Party Products," for a list and discussion of some of the more popular third party tools available for Sybase SQL Server.

Understanding SQL Identifiers

Sybase's particular implementation of SQL has some important limitations that you must be aware of. These limitations are related to the way that you can refer to or name objects in the database. Objects are identified by a name that can be up to 30 characters in length. The first character that is used to identify an object *must* be a character in the alphabetic character set that is currently installed on the server.

If you are using a double-byte or multi-byte character set such as Japanese, Chinese, or Cyrillic, you have a greater amount of flexibility with the first character used to identify the object, and you are not limited to the ASCII characters defined in US English.

Two symbols have special meaning in Sybase: @ and #. The @ symbol is used to reference a local variable in a stored procedure or command batch. The # symbol is used to declare a temporary table and must in fact be used as the first character of a temporary table's name. Avoid using these two characters when referencing objects so that you don't have problems with the server.

 When creating a temporary table that is going to live outside of *Tempdb,* make sure that you limit the length of the table name to 13 characters (including the pound [#] sign). This is because Sybase appends a special numerical suffix to guarantee their uniqueness in the database.

You cannot have spaces in your object names, and you cannot use any of the reserved words of SQL Server.

▶ **See** "Understanding Names You Can't Use," **p. 710**

 There's a system function called `Valid_Name( )` that will tell you if the name you are thinking about using for an object is acceptable or not. To use it, just follow this syntax example:

```
Select Valid_Name( "identifier" )
```

SQL Server returns a 0 (zero) if the name you want to use is invalid. If you get a 1 (one) back then everything's OK and the name is valid.

If you absolutely need to use a particular piece of text as a table name or object identifier, it is possible to get around the limits of the SQL identifiers used in Sybase by using the following command:

```
Set Quoted_Identifier On
```

Sybase then permits you to create an object with a normally invalid name provided that you place it within quotation marks. Note that an object named with quotation marks is limited to 28 characters because the two quotation marks count as characters in the object name, and you are still limited to 30 characters.

In Listing 4.2, you can see that it is possible to create tables using identifiers that would normally be unacceptable to SQL Server.

Part

II

Ch

4

Listing 4.2 CHP4_02.SQL—Creating Tables with Quoted Identifiers

```
/*
This script file shows you how to create tables
with invalid identifiers as their names.
*/

/*
This first table is invalid because the name of
the table is the word SELECT which is a Sybase
reserved word.
*/

Set Quoted_Identifier On
Go

Create Table "SELECT"
(Column1 Char(10))
Go

Set Quoted_Identifier Off
Go


/*
This second table is invalid because the name of
the table has invalid characters in the first position.
*/

Set Quoted_Identifier On
Go

Create Table "$%^Invalid$%^Characters"
(Column1 Char(10))
Go

Set Quoted_Identifier Off
Go
```

CAUTION

You are strongly cautioned to *not* use quoted identifiers to name your objects. If you do, you will not be able to use the object in a number of ways. The most unfortunate result of this naming convention is that if you forget to turn on Quoted_Identifier immediately prior to accessing an object, you will get a syntax error from the server because it is not expecting the quotation marks to be where an object name should be.

Limitations imposed by the use of quoted identifiers include the fact that you cannot pass quoted identifiers to system stored procedures. In addition the system utility BCP (Bulk Copy Program) cannot work with invalid object names. Finally, some application programming languages cannot handle invalid characters when referring to database objects.

Introducing Relational Theory

Relational theory is a subject that has consumed many database courses at the university level. Without attempting to reiterate the entire body of work available in many other sources, this section serves as a pointer to some of the basic elements of relational theory, so that you may have a better understanding of the whole application development process.

Most experienced developers will agree that a *database design* can make or break a project. Database design has as much impact on a successful application as the database or development tools used.

Before starting to develop your Sybase database, you must first get system requirements from the end user. Then use these requirements to analyze what data the database should contain and how it should be organized. Determining what data should be captured consists of defining your entities (or logical objects) needed for a system. Determining how the data should be contained in your database is a process called normalization.

Normalization is the act of defining your database tables in their most logical and broken-down form. Normalization is a key part of database analysis. Using normalization, you define primary keys that uniquely identify records in a table, and remove any duplicated data.

Codd defined three normal forms that lead to database normalization. (*Normal forms* are stages or steps an analyst would take to normalize a database.) Codd's "steps" or normal forms were logically named *first normal form* (1NF), *second normal form* (2NF), and *third normal form* (3NF).

Part

II

Ch

4

Codd was joined by Dr. R. Boyce to define the Boyce-Codd normal form (BCNF), which defined a further step sometimes needed in normalization. Finally, in 1977 and 1979, Dr. R. Fagin furthered the study of normalization by adding two more normal forms: *fourth normal form* (4NF) and *fifth normal form* (5NF).

This section helps you work with normal forms. You learn how to define them and how to use them with a simple stock broker database.

N O T E There are as many ways to design databases as there are to write programs. Your own personal database design methodology may differ slightly from the techniques discussed here. However, as with writing programs, there are pitfalls to avoid and techniques you can use to turn a mediocre or bad design into a good one.

Keep in mind that any good design methodology should be flexible enough to easily support additions to the design; it should help you organize your system so that you can deliver a quality job with a minimum amount of time.

In this section, you may notice that some design errors creep into the stock broker database you develop. These errors are introduced on purpose to show how the technique of database normalization can find database errors.

Although not used in this chapter, you'll probably find a CASE (Computer Aided Software Engineering) tool useful to help you design your database. Often such tools can make the monumental task of determining tables, columns, and relationships a little less complicated. ▩

Determining a Database's Tables and Columns

The first step in database analysis is to determine the tables you need and the columns contained in those tables. Let's assume that your users have given you the following very simple requirements:

- A system is needed to track securities sold through transactions called the Stock Broker system.
- The Stock Broker system should track the details about each transaction.
- The stocks involved in a transaction should also be tracked.

The first stage of a development project is generally the *analysis* phase. In the analysis phase of a project, the language you're using (PowerBuilder, C++, and so on.), the operating system (DOS, OS/2, Windows, and so on.), and the computer you're using (PC, Macintosh, Sun, and so on.) are not considered. When defining the tables and columns in the analysis phase, you should not worry about implementation, but rather on the current business activities and software requirements.

Finding the Entities (Tables)

The first step in analysis is finding all the entities in a system. (An *entity* is someone or something associated with a system.) In the Stock Broker system, you can easily define some entities. In Figure 4.1, I have identified a few entities that can be used in the Stock Broker system. Ultimately, each entity that is defined becomes a database table.

FIG. 4.1

By using graphical diagrams, it is easy to show all the entities that you identify during the analysis phase. (Note that the properties or attributes of the entities are also shown.)

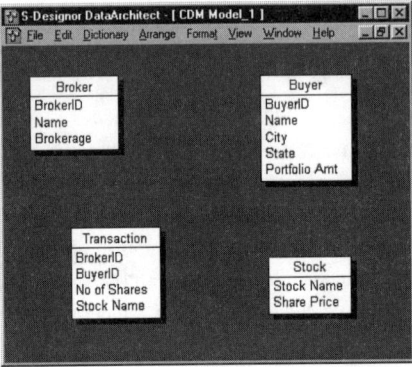

Determining Relationships

After determining the entities, you must decide how the entities relate to each other. This is done with *functions*. In other words, entities relate to each other by doing some action. To represent the relationship between two entities, you draw lines with words that describe the relationship between the entities. In Figure 4.2, the model has been expanded to show the relationships among the entities.

FIG. 4.2
By drawing lines between entities, I transformed the entity model into an entity-relationship model. The relationships (or lines) describe how the entities interact.

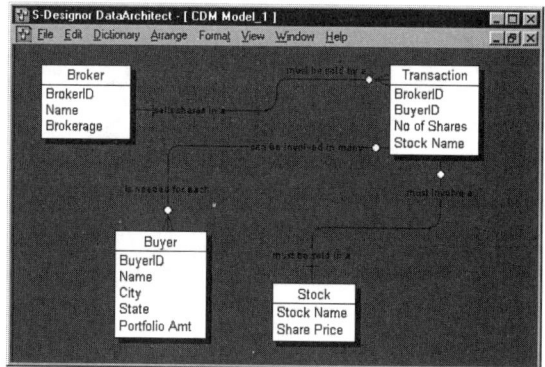

 Remember that functions are always verbs, and entities are nouns. Therefore, with a little bit of imagination, an entity-relationship diagram, like the one shown in Figure 4.2, should form simple sentences or phrases when read from entity to entity.

It is possible for two entities to have more than one relationship between them. However, it doesn't happen often. Be careful when defining two relationships between entities; it may mean that you don't have enough entities to appropriately model the data in the system. You shouldn't be afraid to draw more than one relationship when needed; you shouldn't feel forced to choose between two valid relationships. Just be aware that if you do have multiple relationships, the model may be unnecessarily complex and could be simplified.

Showing Cardinality

After you define the entities and relationships, you need to define *cardinality*, which describes the number of entities that can exist with another entity. To define cardinality, you have to ask yourself questions that describe the numbers of elements in the relationship between entities.

For example, how many stocks can be involved in each transaction? There can be only a single stock per transaction, however there can be multiple transactions for any given stock.

Thus, transactions and stocks have a one-to-many relationship, or a one-to-many cardinality. In a similar fashion, a broker can perform multiple transactions, but a transaction can only be performed by a single broker. In Figure 4.3, you can see that the cardinality is indicated by the various symbols on the lines joining the entities.

There is a set of cardinality characters used when creating entity-relationship diagrams. The following figures provide examples of the most commonly used cardinality characters or icons.

An example of a none-or-one to none-or-one relationship might be the relationship of buyers and sellers, as shown in Figure 4.3. A buyer and a seller may exist and they may or may not have a relationship of trading between each other. The circle indicates that the presence of the entity is optional.

Part
II

Ch
4

FIG. 4.3

The circle on either end of this relationship indicates that Entity 1 can have no (zero) or one corresponding instances of Entity 2.

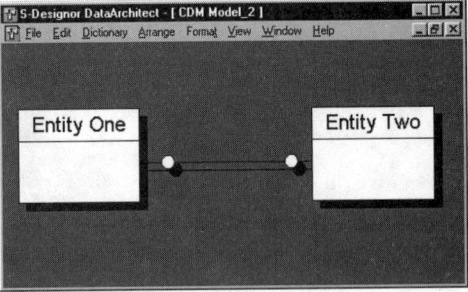

An example of a one to none-or-one relationship (see Fig. 4.4) might be that a buyer must have someone that he can purchase from, but a seller doesn't necessarily need someone to sell to. The bar indicates that the presence of the entity is mandatory.

FIG. 4.4

The straight line/bar on one end of this relationship indicates that Entity 1 can have one and only one corresponding instance of Entity 2.

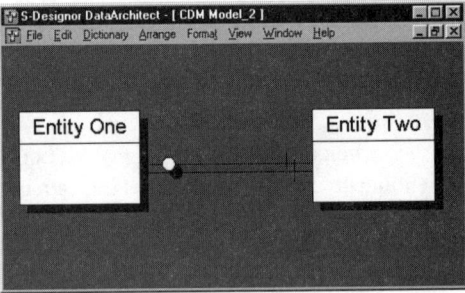

A seller may have one or more buyers and yet may have no sellers at all if the stock isn't desirable, as illustrated in Figure 4.5. The crow's foot indicates that many instances of the entity can be present if required.

FIG. 4.5

The addition of a triangle or crow's foot implies that many instances of Entity 2 can exist for a given instance of Entity 1.

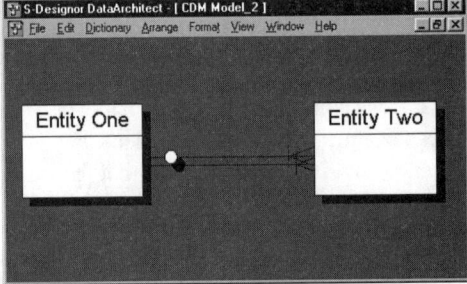

Adding Columns to Your Tables

Now you start thinking of your entities as tables, and come to the necessary but tedious task of adding columns to your table. The following questions will help you decide which columns you need to add to your table:

■ What are the different attributes of the entity that you want to track? *Attributes* are aspects about each *instance* or row of the table that tend to be constant. For example, an equity probably won't change its name or exchange; a broker probably won't change his or her address (at least not too often). Attributes include origin, color, size, effective date, and so on.

■ What are the different states of the entity that you want to track? *States* are aspects of each instance of the entity that tend to change, such as location, price, quantity, and obsolescence. For example, you probably will change the commission rate of an equity.

All columns must have corresponding datatypes. Datatypes are the method of storing the data. It is possible to store all data as text. However, this makes manipulation of the data difficult especially if you are trying to perform any kind of analysis. The common datatypes are text, number, and date-based. When you create a table, you specify the datatype of the columns as part of the create statement. See below in the section "Creating Objects in the Database" for more information on how to create tables.

Normalizing Your Database

So far, you have a database consisting of three tables. As it currently is designed, this database will be difficult to implement once development starts. You need to *normalize* the data. Normalizing consists of logically organizing the data on the table and making it easy to access.

Defining First Normal Form (1NF)   1st Normal Form (or 1NF) occurs when you have defined a column that can identify any row in your database table. This column is the primary key. It can be denoted with a (PK) added after the primary key column name.

1NF also is the phase where you determine which tables are *dependent* on other tables. Dependency occurs when you can't have a row on one table without having a related row on another table, making one table dependent on the other table. The column that is related to the other table is the foreign key.

N O T E   Often, you won't find any unique column that defines your table. This occurs when an entity can have duplicates. If that's the case, for design purposes, you must generate a number, Timestamp, and so on, to become the primary key. If you fail to uniquely identify each row on your database, both your database and your analysis will run into difficulties in areas that require tables to relate to each other. ■

1NF forces the analyst to determine an *atomic* identifier for each table. This means that each table must have one identifier that identifies the row. You are not allowed to have groups of information contained in several rows and related to each other in a single table. You are also not allowed to have a table without a primary key.

If dependencies between the tables are not defined by now, they should also be defined in 1NF via the use of foreign keys.

Defining Second Normal Form (2NF)   2NF deals with removing any repeating dependencies within a table and separating them in their own dependent tables. 2NF eliminates recurring information that is a subset of a table, creating a new dependent table based on the recurring columns.

2NF also eliminates many-to-many relationships. If you tried to implement a many-to-many relationship, you would need to use recurring information inside one or both of your tables. Instead, 2NF requires you to build an associative table to store all possible combinations of the two entities. This table is related to the other tables using a one-to-many relationship.

Defining Third Normal Form (3NF)   Although 2NF has removed the most glaring deficiencies of a data model, there are still problems to resolve. In the Transaction table, there is a great potential to duplicate repeat buyer data causing double data entry and making maintenance difficult. If the same buyer buys equities twice, his or her entire buyer information (name, address, phone) is repeated. Also, there's no way to leave comments about the buyer—there is no table available to do this.

If viewed from an entity standpoint, you can see that the buyer should not be part of the transaction entity. Third normal form (3NF) takes care of this. In 3NF, you remove any *non-dependent* information from tables. You could say that a buyer is not dependent on a single transaction. Rather, a transaction is dependent upon a buyer. A buyer could exist without being involved in a transaction.

Understanding Data Definition Language (DDL)

Data Definition Language (DDL) is the first component of Transact-SQL with which you should become familiar. DDL is the subset of the SQL language that describes the syntax and conventions used when creating and defining objects in the database. Database objects are the logical entities that Sybase uses to store data.

The most obvious and well-known database objects are tables. Tables are made up of `columns` that separate the components or fields of the table and help to describe the data. Tables can have 0 (zero), 1 or many `rows` in them that contain the data you are working with. Tables are usually "designed" by the database analyst or database administrator working on a particular project.

Other objects that you may or may not be familiar with are as follows:

- **Indexes**—Used to speed up access to data
- **Keys**—Used to document the nature of relationships between columns in multiple tables
- **Views**—Used to provide a *logical view* of one or more tables that are joined together
- **Rules**—Used to enforce integrity constraints on table data that is being added to a particular column
- **Defaults**—Used to add a default value to a column if no value is supplied when a record is added to a table
- **Stored procedures**—Used to enable procedural logic to be stored in the database for high speed execution on the server

- **Triggers**—Used to provide advanced conditional logic that executes when a table operation, such as an Insert, Update, or Delete, is performed
- **Temporary tables**—Used to store the results of queries that are going to be processed in another way by a second or subsequent query

Creating Objects in the Database

In this section, you learn the basics of creating objects. Fortunately, SQL is somewhat like English. Using SQL to create an object involves the command `Create`. SQL then has particular syntax conventions for the type of object you are creating.

Creating Tables   Tables are the primary data storage mechanism in SQL Server. They organize the data in terms of rows and columns much like a spreadsheet. The basic syntax of the `Create Table` statement is as follows:

```
Create Table Table_Name
(Column_Name DataType {Identity | NULL | NOT NULL }
[, ... ]
)
```

Using this statement, it is possible to create tables in a database of many different types. In Listing 4.3, you can see the syntax to create a table called *Stereo*. The *Stereo* table has a few different columns to illustrate the sorts of datatypes that can be used in a table.

Listing 4.3   CHP4_03.SQL—Creating a Simple Table

```
/*
This script file creates a sample table stereo
*/

Create Table Stereo
(Stereo_Id      Numeric(12,0) Identity,
 Brand_Name     Varchar(30),
 Price_Paid     Decimal(14,2),
 Date_Purchased SmallDatetime,
 No_Components  Tinyint,
 Comments       Text NULL)
Go
```

TIP   Using the underscore character to separate words in an object name makes it easier to read the name if you don't have the advantage of capitalization.

Tables can have up to 250 columns each of which must be validly named and of a valid datatype. Datatypes control the underlying structure that Sybase uses to store the data in the table.

The default behavior for a column in Sybase is to not permit NULL values or in other words to be NOT NULL. What this means is that if you don't supply a value for the column when you insert a record into a table, it will reject the insert because of the lack of a value for the column (you were implying that its value should be NULL). In Listing 4.3, the *Comments* column is defined NULL so that if you don't want to add a comment about the stereo you don't have to.

The *Stereo_Id* column is a special column of the datatype Identity. An Identity column has a property to which the SQL Server will automatically assign a value that is guaranteed to be unique. Identity columns are great for providing unique keys in database tables.

▶ **See** "Understanding the Identity Column," **p. 170**

The *Brand_Name* column is a Varchar(30), meaning that it can store up to 30 characters of variable data. The number in parentheses refers to the number of bytes of data that can be stored in the column. Essentially, you can place any piece of text that you want in this column.

The *Price_Paid* column is defined as a Decimal(14,2) so that it can store monetary amounts with a precision of up to 14 digits. Of these, two may be reserved for storing the scale of two decimal places (cents in U.S. currency).

The *Date_Purchased* column is a SmallDatetime column meaning that it can store date and time values. Sybase has an additional date datatype called Datetime. There are two key differences between SmallDatetime and Datetime: the range of dates that can be stored and the accuracy with which they are stored. For more information on the different Datetime options in Sybase, see Chapter 6, "Understanding Tables and Datatypes."

The *No_Components* column is defined as a Tinyint datatype. Tinyints can store values from 0 (zero) to 254. Because Sybase has a wide range of different numeric datatypes that can be used to store numbers, make sure that you choose the appropriate datatype for the situation.

Creating Indexes   Indexes are the means by which you as a database designer improve the performance of your system and access times of your users. Indexes are designed to complement a table and are used by the SQL Server to quickly gather information to respond to a user's query. Indexes contain summary data that represents the underlying table's data. They are generally much smaller than the table itself —making it quicker for the server to traverse the index looking for data than to scan the entire table. Indexes can also be used to enforce uniqueness in a table.

Creating indexes involves the same process as creating a table. Using the Create Index Transact-SQL command, you can create an index for a table. The basic syntax for Create Index is as follows:

```
Create [Unique] Index Index_Name
On Table_Name (Column_Name [, ... ])
```

In Listing 4.4, you can see the basics of creating an index that is designed to speed up access to the Stereo table if you need to find records by *Brand_Name*.

Listing 4.4   CHP4_04.SQL—Creating a Simple Index on Stereo

```
/*
This script file creates an index for the
sample table stereo
*/

Create Index Fk_Stereo
On Stereo( Brand_Name )
Go
```

TIP Prefix your index names with either Pk or Fk (for Primary key and Foreign key) to help make it easy to understand the intention of the index. A primary key index is an index on the columns that uniquely identifies the records in the table. A foreign key index is an index that is used to join between two tables to the second table's primary key. When you have two indexes of equal values, Sybase does an index merge, which is the quickest way of joining two tables. Refer to Chapter 8, "Understanding Indexes and Keys," for more information on using Indexes for performance.

By specifying multiple columns in the parentheses, you create a composite key. Composite keys are useful when you have more than one column that combined makes the record unique, such as a person's first name and last name.

Dropping Objects

After creating objects like tables and indexes in Sybase, it is important to know that you can get rid of them. Fortunately SQL provides a Drop statement that can be used to remove unwanted objects from the database. The principles of the Drop statement are very simple: use the Drop keyword followed by the type of object (such as Table, View, or Index) and then followed by the name of the object. The syntax is summarized as follows:

```
Drop Object_Type Object_Name
```

For example, to drop the *publishers* table, you would execute the following:

```
Drop Table publishers
Go
```

To drop an index such as the one you created earlier *Fk_Stereo* you would execute:

```
Drop Index Fk_Stereo
Go
```

TIP When you create an object in a Sybase database, Sybase actually adds your user name as a prefix or owner of the object. You can drop your own objects without needing to prefix the object with the owner name. If you want to drop another user's objects and you have appropriate authority to do so, you can prefix the object name with their user name. If, for example, the table *Stereo* had been created by the user *BlackThorne*, you would execute:

```
Drop Table BlackThorne.Stereo
Go
```

Part

II

Ch

4

Understanding Data Manipulation Language (DML)

When working with your Sybase database, you will most often use Data Manipulation Language (DML). You need to use DML every time you want to work with data that is stored in a table or is about to be stored in a table. DML contains all the core SQL statements that you use every day. These statements are broken into four types, as follows:

- **Select**—Used to retrieve data from a table or many tables
- **Insert**—Used to add data to a table
- **Update**—Used to modify the values of existing data in a table
- **Delete**—Used to remove data from a table

In addition to these four major DML commands, Sybase's Transact-SQL adds a few other commands, such as TRUNCATE TABLE, that are used to manipulate data. The TRUNCATE TABLE command is a special one because it performs the equivalent of a Delete of every record in a given table, without logging any of the activity to the transaction log. The purpose of TRUNCATE TABLE is to quickly remove all data from a table without having to wait for the logs to be written. By its very nature (without being logged), the TRUNCATE TABLE command cannot be rescinded and is thus a very dangerous command to use.

▶ **See** "Working with Transactions," **p. 293**

In this section, I discuss the four basic SQL statements and how to use them effectively. After reviewing and trying the samples shown here, you should be competent to handle all but the most complex of tasks using SQL.

Retrieving Data from a Table with Select

The Select statement is the tool with which you query the database. Using a Select statement you can retrieve a subset or the whole set of data that resides in one or more tables. The Select statement can take many forms, some of which I discuss below. When you execute a Select statement, the server finds all the records that match the criteria you specify and then returns them to you.

> **N O T E**   The Select statement has a couple of extensions in Transact-SQL. In a stored procedure or command batch, you can assign the values of a variable to be equal to that of a returned column using Select. For example:

```
Select @nTemp = Number1
From Table1
```

In addition, the Select statement can be used in a stored procedure or command batch to assign values to a variable. For example:

```
Select @nTemp = 35,
       @sTemp = 'Hello World'
```

There are so many possibilities of statements that can be constructed using the Select statement that many books exist on the topic alone. I highly recommend Joe Celko's excellent book,

Instant SQL Programming (Wrox Press, ISBN 1-874-41650-8). Celko is a frequent contributor to *DBMS* magazine and is, in my opinion, the acknowledged guru of the SQL language. As a further reference, take a look at Sams's worthy tome, *Teach Yourself SQL in 14 Days* (ISBN 0-672-30855-x).

Performing Simple Selects   The most basic syntax for the `Select` statement can be shown as follows:

```
Select Expression [, ...]
From   Table_Name
```

In this sense, an expression could be a column or list of columns, or it could be the result of a function. (See "Understanding Sybase System Functions" below.) By using this syntax, it is possible to retrieve all the records in a table. For example, say that you wanted a list of all the publishers and the state they were from in the *publishers* table, you would write the `Select` statement as follows:

```
Select pub_name, state
From   publishers
Go
```

The result of executing this statement would be this:

```
pub_name                                  state
----------------------------------------- -----
New Age Books                             MA
Binnet & Hardley                          DC
Algodata Infosystems                      CA
```

This result or *result set* is a list of all the records that matched the criteria you specified in the `Select` statement.

Using the Asterisk in a Select   If you don't want to specify which columns you want returned from a query, you can use the asterisk (*) to return every column. In the previous query, I asked for the publisher's name and state. In the following example, I will get every column by using the asterisk:

```
Select *
From   publishers
Go
```

The results from this query show the extra columns *pub_id* and *city*:

```
pub_id pub_name                                  city          state
------ ----------------------------------------- ------------- -----
0736   New Age Books                             Boston        MA
0877   Binnet & Hardley                          Washington    DC
1389   Algodata Infosystems                      Berkeley      CA
```

If you know that you want a particular column or set of columns but aren't sure about the rest of the data, you can use the asterisk to quickly get all the data. Sybase enables you to specify the columns that you know at the start of the expression list; then you use a comma followed by an asterisk to get a copy of all the columns in the table.

Part
II
Ch
4

This is a convenient way of getting data when you are unsure about all the columns in a table. It also helps when you have wide tables with lots of columns and you don't want to get buried in all the data. For example, say you want to get the name and the create date of all the tables in the system catalog table *sysobjects* but you aren't sure about the rest of the columns:

```
Select name, crdate, *
From    sysobjects
Go
```

Eliminating Duplicate Records with Distinct   If you perform a query on a set of data that produces the same results in repetition due to the underlying data, you can use the Distinct keyword to eliminate the duplicates. For example, the following query lists all the states in which authors live:

```
Select state
From    authors
Go
```

The results of this query are as follows:

```
state
-----
CA
CA
CA
CA
CA
KS
CA
CA
CA
CA
TN
OR
CA
MI
IN
CA
CA
CA
MD
CA
CA
UT
UT
```

As in English, if you wanted a distinct list of states that the authors live in, you would use the Distinct keyword to modify the results:

```
Select Distinct state
From    authors
Go
```

Using the Distinct clause returns the following:

```
state
-----
CA
IN
KS
MD
MI
OR
TN
UT
```

N O T E If you look at the two results of the states prior to and after using the Distinct keyword, you will notice that the data is sorted in the second result. This is because Sybase places each unique value that it finds in answer to the query into a temporary table prior to returning the results to the calling process. By placing the values in a temporary table, Sybase can quickly build a list of unique values (that are therefore distinct) to return. Sybase sorts the records alphabetically in the temporary table for performance reasons so that it doesn't have to scan the entire table to check for a duplicate value. ■

Specifying Record Criteria with the Where Clause The simple Select statement is not of much value if you have to retrieve every row from the table and process it locally on the client machine. SQL enables you to specify a Where clause, which is a set of conditions designed to qualify records for inclusion in the results that are returned to the user who executes the Select.

The basic premise of the Where clause is to construct conditions using standard operators such as =, != (not equal) and Like to find records. For example, to retrieve a list of all the authors that live in Utah you would execute:

```
Select  au_id, au_lname, au_fname
From    authors
Where   state = 'UT'
Go
```

```
au_id       au_lname                                       au_fname
---------   -------------------------------------------    --------------------
899-46-2035 Ringer                                         Anne
998-72-3567 Ringer                                         Albert
```

The complexity and range of possibilities in the Where clause is essentially unlimited. To apply more than one condition, you must use either an And or an Or. These operators enable multiple statements or expressions to be evaluated in the Where clause. For example, to find all those authors who live in California and have a last name starting with *D,* you would execute:

```
Select  au_id, au_lname, au_fname
From    authors
Where   state = 'CA'
And     au_lname Like 'G%'
Go
```

Part

II

Ch

4

```
au_id       au_lname                                      au_fname
----------  --------------------------------------------  -------------------
213-46-8915 Green                                         Marjorie
472-27-2349 Gringlesby                                    Burt
```

By using And, you are making the server apply both conditions to the table for a match before a record can be returned. By using Or, you can allow either condition to match for a record to be returned:

```
Select  au_id, au_lname, au_fname
From    authors
Where   state = 'CA'
Or      au_lname Like 'G%'
Go
```

```
au_id       au_lname                                      au_fname
----------  --------------------------------------------  -------------------
172-32-1176 White                                         Johnson
213-46-8915 Green                                         Marjorie
238-95-7766 Carson                                        Flagstaff
267-41-2394 O'Leary                                       Michael
274-80-9391 Straight                                      Dick
409-56-7008 Bennet                                        Abraham
427-17-2319 Dull                                          Ann
472-27-2349 Gringlesby                                    Burt
486-29-1786 Locksley                                      Chastity
527-72-3246 Greene                                        Morningstar
672-71-3249 Yokomoto                                      Akiko
724-08-9931 Stringer                                      Dirk
724-80-9391 MacFeather                                    Stearns
756-30-7391 Karsen                                        Livia
846-92-7186 Hunter                                        Sheryl
893-72-1158 McBadden                                      Heather
```

You can combine as many And/Or conditions that you want in order to specify the data to be returned. By using parentheses, you can specify multiple conditions that must be executed together or separately. The process of evaluating a SQL statement works very similarly to regular mathematical evaluation. Sybase will evaluate the statements with equal importance from left to right (or start to finish) in the Where clause, unless you indicate that certain statements should be evaluated together.

 Using parentheses is often not actually required, because Sybase will evaluate the query or expression correctly without its being based on Boolean algebraic rules. However, by using these rules, you can make it much easier for a reader to understand the meaning of a statement.

For example, in mathematics, if you wanted to add the values of A and B and then divide the results of the addition by C, you would express the formula like this:

```
(A + B) / C
```

Similarly in SQL, if you want to apply several conditions exclusively together, but then optionally with others, you can use parentheses to organize the logic for the Sybase query optimizer to resolve for you. For example, say you wanted to get a list of authors that either lived in California *and* had a last name starting with G *or* that lived in UT:

```
Select au_id, au_lname, au_fname
From    authors
Where   (state = 'CA'
And     au_lname Like 'G%')
Or      state = 'UT'
Go
```

```
au_id       au_lname                                  au_fname
----------  ----------------------------------------  --------------------
213-46-8915 Green                                     Marjorie
472-27-2349 Gringlesby                                Burt
899-46-2035 Ringer                                    Anne
998-72-3567 Ringer                                    Albert
```

In this way, the rules that you apply to records in the database can be very complex and have great flexibility in the way you retrieve data.

N O T E All this work with And and Or is what as known in the technical jungle as Boolean algebra. There are many good books and articles on how to resolve a problem in Boolean algebraic terms. ■

Using the In Keyword If you find yourself getting bogged down writing huge SQL statements with lots of Or conditions, then there's hope. The In keyword enables you to make a list of values that you would like to look for without the need for repeated Or conditions. For example, if you wanted to find all the authors that live in California, Washington state, and Maryland, you could execute this:

```
Select au_id, au_lname, au_fname
From    authors
Where   state = 'CA'
Or      state = 'WA'
Or      state = 'MD'
Go
```

```
au_id       au_lname                                  au_fname
----------  ----------------------------------------  --------------------
172-32-1176 White                                     Johnson
213-46-8915 Green                                     Marjorie
238-95-7766 Carson                                    Flagstaff
267-41-2394 O'Leary                                   Michael
274-80-9391 Straight                                  Dick
409-56-7008 Bennet                                    Abraham
427-17-2319 Dull                                      Ann
472-27-2349 Gringlesby                                Burt
486-29-1786 Locksley                                  Chastity
672-71-3249 Yokomoto                                  Akiko
724-08-9931 Stringer                                  Dirk
724-80-9391 MacFeather                                Stearns
756-30-7391 Karsen                                    Livia
```

```
807-91-6654 Panteley                        Sylvia
846-92-7186 Hunter                          Sheryl
893-72-1158 McBadden                        Heather
```

By using the In keyword it is possible to simplify the statement as follows and yield the same results:

```
Select au_id, au_lname, au_fname
From    authors
Where   state In ( 'CA', 'WA', 'MD' )
Go
```

To use the In keyword in an exclusionary fashion, you prefix it with the Not keyword. For example, to get a list of all the *other* authors that don't live in California, Washington state, and Maryland, you would execute:

```
Select au_id, au_lname, au_fname
From    authors
Where   state Not In ( 'CA', 'WA', 'MD' )
Go
```

```
au_id        au_lname                              au_fname
---------- ------------------------------------------ --------------------
341-22-1782 Smith                                 Meander
527-72-3246 Greene                                Morningstar
648-92-1872 Blotchet-Halls                        Reginald
712-45-1867 del Castillo                          Innes
722-51-5454 DeFrance                              Michel
899-46-2035 Ringer                                Anne
998-72-3567 Ringer                                Albert
```

Using Like for Partial Matches   By using the Like keyword in a Where clause, you can do text searching on columns that contain text data. The Like clause uses two different kinds of wild card characters that enable you to specify where the variable data can be in the text you are searching. The percent sign (%) means that one or many characters can be substituted at this position in the statement.

For example, if you want to search for all the publishers that have the word *New* as the first part of their title you would execute:

```
Select pub_name
From    publishers
Where   pub_name Like 'New%'
Go
```

```
pub_name
------------------------------------------
New Age Books
```

As you can see, the publisher, New Age Books, was found by this query because of the *New* in the name. If you want to be more specific and say that you want publishers that have a name starting in *B* and ending in *Y*, you would execute:

```
Select pub_name
From    publishers
```

```
Where   pub_name Like 'B%Y'
Go

pub_name
----------------------------------------
Binnet & Hardley
```

The second wild card that Sybase gives you is the underscore (_). The underscore tells Sybase to allow any *single* character to be in the position specified. For example, if you wanted to find all those authors whose third letter in their last name was the letter *I*, you would execute:

```
Select au_id, au_lname, au_fname
From   authors
Where  au_lname Like '__I%'
Go


au_id       au_lname                               au_fname
---------- ------------------------------------  --------------------
172-32-1176 White                                Johnson
341-22-1782 Smith                                Meander
472-27-2349 Gringlesby                           Burt
```

 T I P   You should avoid doing a Like with such text as '%hello%' to search for the characters *hello* anywhere in the text stream. By performing this kind of search, Sybase must perform a table scan, resulting in the processing and evaluation of every row in a given table for condition matching. The table scan is forced, because Sybase's query optimizer cannot use an index to find any of the records because the first characters could be variable.

For more information on Indexes and how to get better performance, refer to Chapter 8, "Understanding Indexes and Keys."

Part **II**

Ch **4**

Searching for Ranges of Data   Using SQL, it is possible to search for ranges of data. The tools of the trade are the *greater than* (>) and *less than* (<) signs and the Between keyword.

By using these options, it is possible to search the table for information that meets a range criteria. For example, to find all the titles with a price less than $10, you would execute:

```
Select title
From   titles
Where  price < 10
Go

title
----------------------------------
You Can Combat Computer Stress!
The Gourmet Microwave
Life Without Fear
Emotional Security: A New Algorithm
```

If you want to find the titles with a price less than or equal to $10, then you would use the following SQL:

```
Select title
From    titles
Where   price <= 10
Go
```

Using the *greater than* sign has the same but opposite effect of using the *less than* sign.

The Between keyword works by enabling you to specify the low and high values for a range of data. The Between keyword is inclusive, meaning that the values specified are themselves candidates for inclusion. For example, to get a list of titles that have a price between $15 and $20 you would execute:

```
Select title
From    titles
Where   price Between 15 And 20
Go
```

```
title
-------------------------------------------
The Busy Executive's Database Guide
Straight Talk About Computers
Silicon Valley Gastronomic Treats
Secrets of Silicon Valley
Prolonged Data Deprivation: Four Case Studies
```

Note that the previous query could have been written as follows:

```
Select title
From    titles
Where   price >= 15
And     price <= 20
Go
```

the Between keyword just makes it easier to read.

Sorting Data with Order By   After you have mastered getting the data you need with the Select statement, it is necessary to sort the data in an order that makes it easy to read and work with. SQL provides the Order By clause to enable you to sort the data in the way you want. The Order By clause permits you to either sort a result's data in ascending or descending order. Sorting in ascending order is implied by simply including the Order By clause. If you want to sort a result in descending order you must specify Desc in the column list.

For example, if you want to sort a list of stores by the store name in descending order, you would execute:

```
Select stor_name
From    stores
Order By stor_name Desc
Go
```

```
stor_name
-------------------------------------------
```

```
Thoreau Reading Discount Chain
News & Brews
Fricative Bookshop
Eric the Read Books
Doc-U-Mat: Quality Laundry and Books
Bookbeat
Barnum's
```

To sort the data in ascending order omit the Desc keyword.

If you have a function or expression in one of the columns and you want to sort the data by that column, then you must reproduce the function or expression in the Order By clause. A short cut to this is to assign a name to the column (see "Renaming Column Titles in Results" below) and then use that in the Order By clause. For example, to show the most profitable books you would execute:

```
Select title, "Earnings" = price * total_sales
From    titles
Where   price * total_sales > 75000
Order by "Earnings"
Go
```

```
title                                            Earnings
------------------------------------------------ --------------------
Prolonged Data Deprivation: Four Case Studies    81399.28
Straight Talk About Computers                    81859.05
The Busy Executive's Database Guide              81859.05
Secrets of Silicon Valley                        81900.00
Fifty Years in Buckingham Palace Kitchens        180397.20
But Is It User Friendly?                         201501.00
```

When performing Union operations (see "Using the Union Clause" below), you cannot refer to the column by name in the Order By clause. Instead you must refer to it by position. For example, in the following query you can see that the ordering is done by the first column in descending order:

```
Select title
From    titles
Where   price * total_sales > 100000

Union

Select pub_name
From    publishers
Order By 1 Desc
```

Part

II

Ch

4

CAUTION

Take care when performing ordering of data sets that are not ordered by an indexed column or columns. If there is no index that Sybase can use to sort the data, it must build a temporary table in which to place the sorted data prior to returning it to the client. This is a very costly operation and should be avoided.

Note that *all* descending sorts *require* temporary tables because Sybase can only create indexes in ascending order.

Working with More Than One Table   To further get value from the Select statement, it becomes necessary to combine data from multiple tables. To work with more than one table, you include the additional table in the From clause. When you combine data from more than one table, it is easy to get data that is the result of a Cartesian product. A Cartesian product occurs when there are records that are not joined between two tables in any unique manner. For example, if you combined the data from the *titles* and the *authors* table without specifying a join condition in the Where clause like this:

```
Select *
From    titles, authors
Go
```

you would end up with 414 records returned. This is because SQL Server will take each record from the *titles* table and return a row in the result set that has each of the records in the *authors* table. Since there are 18 records in the *titles* table and 23 records in the *authors* table, $18 \times 23 = 414$.

To clean up the query and return the data that you really want, don't forget to include an appropriate Where clause. In this particular case, you actually need to use the *titleauthor* table as well because each author could have many titles and this is a many-to-many relationship that requires an intermediary table like *titleauthor* to resolve the relationship:

```
Select au_lname, au_fname, title
From    titles t, authors a, titleauthor ta
Where   ta.au_id   = a.au_id
And     ta.title_id = t.title_id
Go
```

TIP   SQL enables you to use aliases or substitute names for tables. In the previous example, *t* serves as an alias for the table *titles*. The advantage of the alias is that other references to the *titles* table do not require the full text of the table name to be written out; the alias can be used instead.

Also, note that the SQL92 standard is to use the keyword As between the table and the alias name. Sybase's Transact-SQL *is not* compatible with the As keyword.

To avoid Cartesian products, you need to perform at least *N–1* joins where *N* corresponds to the number of tables in the From clause. So, if you wanted to get the publisher's name in your query above, you would need at least three joins:

```
Select au_lname, au_fname, title, pub_name
From    titles t, authors a, titleauthor ta, publishers p
Where   ta.au_id   = a.au_id
And     ta.title_id = t.title_id
And     p.pub_id = t.pub_id
Go
```

N O T E Using the asterisk (*) with multiple tables results in every column from each of the tables specified in the From clause being returned by the server. If you want to just get the columns from a particular table, you can prefix the asterisk (*) with the table name. For example, the following code will return all the columns from the *titles* table:

```
Select t.*
From    titles t, authors a, titleauthor ta, publishers p
Where   ta.au_id  = a.au_id
And     ta.title_id = t.title_id
And     p.pub_id = t.pub_id
Go
```

Renaming Column Titles in Results If you use functions or expressions in place of a column, you will not (by default) get a title or column header for the given column position. For example, if you wanted to get the Object_IDs for all the objects in the system catalog table *sysobjects*, you would execute the following:

```
Select Object_ID( name )
From   sysobjects
Go
```

```
- - - - - - - - - -
304004114
16003088
336004228
496004798
368004342
432004570
528004912
272004000
512004855
...
```

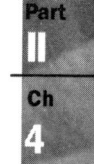

Notice that there is no column title. To correct this error, you can use specify a title for the column by preceding it with a quoted identifier and an equals sign. For example:

```
Select "Object Identity" = Object_Id( name )
From    sysobjects
Go
```

```
Object Identity
304004114
16003088
336004228
496004798
368004342
432004570
528004912
272004000
512004855
...
```

By renaming the column titles in a result, the output is often easier to read and understand.

Using the Union Clause   Suppose you have two dissimilar data sets and want to join them together for the purposes of providing a set of data that is a grouping of all the values. In this case, you can use the Union clause. The Union clause takes two result sets from two different queries and combines them into a single result for returning to the client. The important thing about using the Union clause is that the data in the columns in each of the Select statements that you are combining must have exactly the same datatypes.

For example, if you wanted to provide a consolidated list of names of titles, authors, and publishers in the system you would execute:

```
Select title
From    titles
Where   price * total_sales > 100000

Union

Select pub_name
From    publishers

Union

Select au_lname
From    authors
Where   au_lname Like 'D%'
Go


title
- - - - - - - - - - - - - - - - - - - - - - - - - - - - - - - - - - - - - - - - -
Algodata Infosystems
Binnet & Hardley
But Is It User Friendly?
DeFrance
del Castillo
Dull
Fifty Years in Buckingham Palace Kitchens
New Age Books
```

Did you notice that the results are sorted? I didn't specify an Order By clause, and yet Sybase sorted the data for me. This is because a regular Union works like the Distinct keyword in that it builds a unique list of values that meet the combined criteria of each of the unioned Select statements and then returns the data. This process is quite costly for the server because it needs to build a temporary table in which to store the data before returning it to the client.

By using a Union All statement, you are instructing Sybase to return *all* records that match the Select statements that you have specified, and to *not* eliminate any duplicate records. Union All is substantially quicker than a straight Union; however, the data may be less useful to you.

Working with Subqueries   For advanced searching, it is sometimes necessary to base a `Where` clause on the results of a `Select` from another table or tables. It is often possible to express these multiple table criteria by using join criteria, however sometimes it is not. When you can no longer express search criteria effectively or efficiently through joins, you need to rely on subqueries.

As their name implies, subqueries are an extension of SQL that enable you place a query inside another query. Using either the `In` keyword or the `Exists` keyword, you can evaluate the data returned from a second query in order to work with a `Where` clause of another query.

In the following simple example, say you want a list of authors that live in states where there are stores:

```
Select  au_lname
From    authors
Where   state in (Select state
                  From    stores)
Order by au_lname
Go
```

As you can see, you place all subqueries within parentheses. You can have as many subqueries in a main query as you need, but take care that you don't overuse them because they do require additional work for the sever to perform them.

Using Exists to Check for Existence   The `Exists` keyword enables you to check existence of a row in a second table for a subquery. Under some circumstances (such as when you have to check multiple columns), an existence check can be required instead of using the `In` keyword. For example, say you only want the authors that live in the states *and* the cities in which there are publishers:

```
Select  au_lname
From    authors a
Where   Exists (Select *
                From    publishers p
                Where   a.state = p.state
                And     a.city = p.city)
Order by au_lname
Go
```

Note that the `Exists` subquery is really an advanced join between the two tables *authors* and *publishers*.

Using Subqueries in the Column List   The most advanced use of a subquery is placing it in the column list to provide aggregate data in a result without the need for multiple queries. This sort of SQL is great for reports for which you need to process multiple layers of data by representing the master record on the same line as some of the detail records.

For example, say you wanted a list of authors that live in Utah and a sum of their current sales:

```
Select a.au_lname, t.title_id, t.title,
       "Quantity Sold" = ( Select Sum( qty )
                           From    salesdetail
                           Where   title_id = t.title_id )
```

Part

II

Ch

4

```
From    authors a,
        titles t,
        titleauthor ta
Where   a.state = 'UT'
And     a.au_id = ta.au_id
And     ta.title_id = t.title_id
Order by a.au_lname, t.title
Go


au_lname    title_id title                Quantity Sold
- - - - - - -  - - - - - - - -  - - - - - - - - - - - - - - - - - - - -  - - - - - - - - - - - -
Ringer      PS2091   Is Anger the Enemy?  2045
Ringer      PS2091   Is Anger the Enemy?  2045
Ringer      PS2106   Life Without Fear    111
Ringer      MC3021   The Gourmet Microwave 22246
```

 TIP It's easier to read a SQL statement when you put each clause and logical operation on a separate line. I'd suggest that you put each table on a separate line along with each Where clause condition that you are checking for.

Adding New Data to a Table with Insert

Now that you've learned about as much as you ever wanted to know about retrieving data from the database, it's probably important that you know how to get new data in there. The SQL statement Insert is used to add records to a table. In Transact-SQL, the basic structure of an Insert statement is as follows:

```
Insert [Into] Table_Name (Column_Name1 [, Column_Name2, ...])
Values (Value1 [, Value2, ...])
```

If you look at this syntax, you can see that it is necessary to match the number of columns in the column list with a value in the Values clause. By doing so, you are telling Sybase that you want to assign the specified value for the new row you are inserting.

N O T E The keyword Into is optional in the Insert statement, but can be included if you want to make your statements more *English-like* or readable. Into is required by some other vendors and is accepted by Transact-SQL for compatibility reasons. ■

For example, if you wanted to add a new record to the *publishers* table, you would execute:

```
Insert publishers( pub_id, pub_name, city, state )
Values ( '9999', 'QUE Corporation', 'Indianapolis', 'IN' )
Go
```

TROUBLESHOOTING

My inserts keep failing and I get an error, such as "Column XXX does not allow Null values." The problem is that you are not specifying a value for all the NOT NULL columns in the table in your Insert statement. Carefully review your table definition (use sp_help table_name to get Sybase to return the table definition to you) and identify all the columns that are NOT NULL. Make sure that you have mentioned all these columns in your Insert statement's column list, and that you have specified values for them in the Values clause.

Skipping the Column List   Transact-SQL permits you to skip the inclusion of a column list, provided that the columns in the Values clause exactly match those of the underlying table. You must also include every column in the correct order of the table into which you have inserted data. If you are in error because of not supplying all the columns or because of a column ordering problem, Sybase will reject the Insert.

For example, if you wanted to add a new store to the *stores* table and you knew the exact table layout, you could perform an Insert like this one:

```
Insert stores
Values( '9999', 'The QUE Bookstop', '1701 MCP Avenue',
        'Indianapolis', 'IN', 'USA', '37012', 'Net 120' )
Go
```

CAUTION

By not including the column list in an Insert, you are making yourself highly susceptible to problems caused by a change in the underlying table structure. If the column order changes in such a way as to make the Insert no longer valid, for example, a new NOT NULL numeric column is added between the *stor_id* and *stor_name* columns, this update will cease to function properly.

Omitting the Values Clause   In Transact-SQL, you can omit the Values clause if you replace it with a Select statement that has the same number of columns in its results as the number of columns specified in the Insert's column list. For example, if you want to double the number of publishers in the *publishers* table by giving them an additional *pub_id*, then execute the following:

```
Insert publishers( pub_id, pub_name, city, state )
Select '999' + Right( pub_id, 1 ), pub_name, city, state
From    publishers
Go
```

The resulting list of records now in *publishers* is:

```
Select *
From    publishers
Go
```

Part

II

Ch

4

```
pub_id pub_name                         city                  state
------ ------------------------------   --------------------  -----
0736   New Age Books                    Boston                MA
0877   Binnet & Hardley                 Washington            DC
1389   Algodata Infosystems             Berkeley              CA
9996   New Age Books                    Boston                MA
9997   Binnet & Hardley                 Washington            DC
9999   Algodata Infosystems             Berkeley              CA
```

 Using this method of inserting records into a table is very convenient when you have two databases on the server that need to be kept synchronized. Assume, for example, that you have a second database *pubsBackup* that also has a *publishers* table in it that you need to maintain. The following SQL demonstrates how to keep its data up-to-date and consistent with the *pubs2* database:

```
Delete pubsBackup..publishers
Go

Insert pubsBackup..publishers
Select *
From    pubs2..publishers
Go
```

> **CAUTION**
>
> Omitting the Values clause is a highly efficient method to use when copying data from one table to another. Take care however, that the Select statement that you use does not cause duplicate rows to be generated. Sybase will rollback the entire Insert statement if a single row violates a unique index.

Working with Select Into   Transact-SQL has one final method for adding records to a table: Select Into. This is a Transact-SQL extension to the base SQL standard and provides the most efficient method for copying data from one table to another because the operation is not logged to the transaction log. Because of the nature of a non-logged operation being performed on the database, Sybase requires that the database be placed in a special mode. To enable the use of the Select Into syntax, you must first perform the following steps:

```
Use master
Go
sp_dboption pubs2, 'Select Into', TRUE
Go
Use pubs2
Go
CheckPoint
Go
```
▶ **See** "Configuring and Managing Databases," **p. 662**

The syntax for the Select Into statement is as follows:

```
Select [column list]
Into    Target_Table_Name
From    Table_Name
[Where conditions]
```

If the table specified in *Target_Table_Name* already exists, then Sybase will copy the data directly into it, provided that the table structures match with *Table_Name*. If, on the other hand, *Target_Table_Name* has not been created, Sybase will create a copy of *Table_Name* using the basic column attributes. Sybase will not reproduce indexes or any other table characteristics of *Table_Name*.

If you want to create a new table, *authors2,* which is a copy of *authors*, this is all you need to do:

```
Select *
Into    authors2
From    authors
Go
```

 TIP If you need to create a duplicate table, and *don't* want to copy the data, here's a trick: In the Where clause, include a condition that can't possibly be true and thus will not find any records that match. For example, to create a table, *publishers2,* that has the same structure as *publishers* but doesn't copy the data, you would execute:

```
Select *
Into    publishers2
From    publishers
Where   0 = 1
Go
```

Modifying Data in a Table with Update

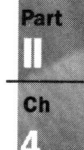

The Update statement is used to modify or change the value of a column or columns in a table. An Update's SQL syntax is structured to permit you to specify the columns being changed (and the new values you want to assign them), followed by a Where clause in which you can specify the criteria that a record must meet in order to be updated.

The simplified syntax of the Update statement is as follows:

```
Update Table_Name
Set    Column_Name = Expression
       [, ... ]
[Where  Expression(s)]
```

If a Where clause is omitted, then all records in the table are affected by the Update. A simple Update to change the last name of an author that got married and changed her name might be:

```
Update authors
Set    au_lname = 'Flagstaff'
Where  au_id = '238-95-7766'
Go
```

When an update fails to affect any rows (either because no rows are present in the table, or no rows match the Where clause criteria specified), you do not receive an error from Sybase. This is not an error condition, so if you need to know whether or not a record *was* modified, you must check the global system variable @@RowCount. In Listing 4.5, you can see that the previous Update on *authors* has been extended to add some error checking. This is the style of logic that you should copy and use in any stored procedure that you are working on.

Listing 4.5 CHP4_06.SQL—Using the Global Variables @@RowCount and @@Error to Check for Errors

```
/* Declare some local variables for working */
Declare @nRowCount Int,
        @nSQLError Int
/* Perform an update that will not actually
affect any rows */
Update authors
Set    au_lname = 'Terabyte-Tammi'
Where  au_id = '00000'

/* Now get the values of @@RowCount and @@Error
to see if anything broke during the last executed
statement */

Select @nRowCount = @@RowCount,
       @nSQLError = @@Error
/* Check for any SQL errors */
If @nSQLError != 0
Begin
    /* Perform a rollback for safety's sake */
    Rollback Tran
    Print 'A SQL error occurred: %1!', @nSQLError
End

/* Now check for any rows modified */
If @nRowCount = 0
Begin
    /* Perform a rollback for safety's sake */
    Rollback Tran
    Print 'No rows where updated!'
End
```

N O T E You should always use temporary variables, such as @nSQLError and @nRowCount in Listing 4.5, to cast or assign the values of @@Error and @@RowCount immediately after you perform an operation that requires error checking. Sybase continuously maintains the values of these variables after each operation in Transact-SQL, so if you perform a subsequent action that is successful, the variables will no longer indicate the error and you will have lost your opportunity to handle the error condition. ■

Because of the nature of set operations, you can change or assign the value of one column to another column, and in the same Update set the original column to a new value. For example, suppose you have a table, *Fruit,* and it has two columns: *Name1* and *Name2.* If you had a single row in the table with a value in *Name1* = Apples, your data set would look something like this:

```
Name1      Name2
- - - - - - - - - - - - - - -
Apples
```

In the following Update, I set *Name2* equal to the value in *Name1* and then assign a new value to *Name1*:

```
Update Fruit
Set     Name2 = Name1,
        Name1 = 'Oranges'
Go
```

With this Update your data would now look like this:

```
Name1       Name2
----------------
Oranges     Apples
```

As you can see, it's really not that hard to turn apples into oranges! But seriously, the power of sets and the flexibility of the Update statement enables you to construct very complex manipulations of data without the need for multiple updates. Obviously, the assignment Update could have been done in two operations as follows:

```
Update Fruit
Set     Name2 = Name1
Go
Update Fruit
Set     Name1 = 'Oranges'
Go
```

The cost in terms of performance is dramatic. Wherever possible, you want to combine the manipulation of multiple columns of a table in a single Update.

Removing Data from a Table with Delete

The Delete statement is used to remove data from a table. Care should be taken when using the Delete statement because data can be irrecoverably removed from the database requiring a restore from a backup tape, if it is inadvertently used.

The simplified syntax for a Delete statement is as follows:

```
Delete [from] {Table_Name | View_Name}
[Where Search_Conditions]
```

The from keyword is optional and is permitted for compatibility reasons with other vendors' implementations of SQL. The Delete statement applies the rules or search criteria specified in the Where clause and removes all the rows that match. For example, to remove all the stores in the state of California from the *stores* table, execute the following:

```
Delete Stores
Where   State = 'CA'
Go
```

If you don't supply a Where clause, Sybase will delete all the rows in the table. To delete all the stores no matter what state they were in, you would execute:

```
Delete Stores
Go
```

Part
II

Ch

4

The Delete statement in Transact-SQL has an additional From clause that is an extension over the basic SQL syntax. By using this extra From clause, you can specify criteria in external tables that must be matched before the Delete is performed. The complete syntax of the Delete statement in Transact-SQL is as follows:

```
Delete [from] {Table_Name | View_Name}
[From {Table_Name | View_Name}, {Table_Name2 | View_Name2} ...]
[Where Search_Conditions]
```

For example, say you only want to delete those stores that have authors in their state who get a royalty of 100 percent. The SQL that you would execute is as follows:

```
Delete Stores
From   Authors, Stores, TitleAuthor
Where  Stores.State = Authors.State
And    TitleAuthor.RoyaltyPer = 100
```

By using the additional From clause, you can greatly simplify complex Where clauses that have multiple sub-selects. The previous Delete could have been done as a regular Delete with a substantially more complex Where clause:

```
Delete Stores
Where  State In (
Select State
From   Authors
Where  Au_Id In (
Select Au_Id
From   TitleAuthor
Where  RoyaltyPer = 100 )
                    )
```

CAUTION

The additional From clause is definitely Sybase specific. By using it, you will be tying yourself to the Sybase database engine. If you are attempting to create an application that is cross platform and supports multiple database vendors, avoid using this Transact-SQL extension.

Understanding Sybase System Functions

The final section of Transact-SQL's DML commands that I cover in this chapter relates to system functions. System functions have been provided by Sybase to help you work with your data efficiently on the server without the need to send it to the client for more processing.

The system functions are broken into seven major areas, as follows:

- **System functions**—Used to obtain results from the Sybase server relating to such items as the object identifiers and validity of SQL Statements
- **Aggregate functions**—Used to accumulate and perform mathematical analysis on data, such as sums and averages
- **String functions**—Used to help you manipulate text data so that it can be searched for values, concatenated to other data, and so on

■ **Mathematical functions**—Used to provide mathematical analysis, such as Abs( ) that can be used to get an absolute value for a number and Log( ) that will return a logarithmic value for the supplied number to base *e*

■ **Text and image functions**—Used to manipulate text and image (binary) data stored in tables

■ **Datatype conversion functions**—Used to convert data between different datatypes for convenient evaluation

■ **Date functions**—Used to manipulate dates and do mathematical operations, such as adding a week to a given date

Individual functions are applied to columns or other functions that serve as *expressions*. When you execute a function, you can either have it stand alone with a simple Select statement, as follows:

```
Select GetDate( )
Go
```

```
- - - - - - - - - - - - - - - - - - - - - - - - - - -
May 13 1996 11:33:25:376PM
```

Or you can embed the function into a regular Select statement that involves columns, as follows:

```
Select "Years Old" = DateDiff( Year, pubdate, GetDate( ) ),
"Book Title" = RTrim( title )
From    titles
Order By pubdate
Go
```

```
Years Old   Book Title
- - - - - - - - - -   - - - - - - - - - - - - - - - - - - - - - - - - - - - - - - - - - - - - - - -
11          Fifty Years in Buckingham Palace Kitchens
11          The Gourmet Microwave
11          You Can Combat Computer Stress!
10          The Busy Executive's Database Guide
10          But Is It User Friendly?
9           Sushi, Anyone?
9           Secrets of Silicon Valley
9           Straight Talk About Computers
8           Cooking with Computers: Surreptitious Balance Sheets
8           Emotional Security: A New Algorithm
8           Prolonged Data Deprivation: Four Case Studies
7           Silicon Valley Gastronomic Treats
7           Is Anger the Enemy?
6           Life Without Fear
6           Computer Phobic and Non-Phobic Individuals: Behavior Variations
6           Onions, Leeks, and Garlic: Cooking Secrets of the Mediterranean
0           The Psychology of Computer Cooking
0           Net Etiquette
( 18 rows affected)
```

Using System Functions   Sybase's System functions are provided for a variety of different uses. Primarily designed to give you more information about a given object or thing, the most commonly used System functions are shown in Table 4.1.

Table 4.1   System Functions in Sybase System XI

Function Name	Description
Col_Name( )	Returns the name of a column in a table specified by offset column number
Col_Length( )	Returns the length of a column in a table specified
Data_Pgs( )	Returns the number of used data or index pages in a given table or index
DataLength( )	Returns the length (in bytes) of an expression
Db_Id( )	Returns the system-assigned identifier for the database specified
Db_Name( )	Returns the name of the database specified. If no database name is specified, then it returns the name of the database that's currently in use
Index_Col( )	Returns the name of the column in the index supplied at the column indicated
IsNull( )	Evaluates an expression and if it is equal to NULL, it returns the value of a second expression
Object_Id( )	Returns the system-assigned identifier for the object specified
Object_Name( )	Returns the name of an object given a system-assigned identifier
Proc_Role( )	Used when you write stored procedures to determine if the caller or executor of a stored procedure has sufficient privileges to run the procedure
Reserved_Pgs( )	Returns the number of pages allocated by Sybase to manage the data storage of the supplied table or index
RowCnt( )	Returns the approximate or estimated number of rows in a supplied table
Show_Role( )	Shows the role or roles (such as sa_role or sso_role) of the current user
Used_Pgs( )	Returns the total number of pages in use by a table or index
User( )	Returns the current user's user name
Valid_Name( )	Returns whether the supplied text is valid to be used as an object name in Sybase

Rather than go through each and every Sybase System Function's syntax for you here, I've decided that the best way that you can learn how the functions work is by looking at an example. In Listing 4.6, I have created a stored procedure, *procTableInfo,* that takes a single parameter of a table name, and uses many of System Functions to query the database for information and return it to you in a meaningful way. For more detailed information on each of these functions, please consult the Sybase documentation.

Listing 4.6 CHP4_05.SQL—Using Sybase's System Functions

```
/*
This script file creates a simple stored procedure
that reports the basic column information for a
supplied table.

In addition, it reports the amount of space consumed
by the table in the database.

The purpose of this script file is to demonstrate the
use of many of the Sybase System functions
*/

Create Procedure procTableInfo
        @psTableName varchar(30)
As
Print 'procTableInfo: Execution Begun'
/* Declare some working variables */
Declare @nCurrentColumn TinyInt,
        @nColumnLength  TinyInt,
        @nDataPages     Int,
        @sDataPages     Varchar(30),
        @nRowCount      Int,
        @sColumnName    Varchar(30),
        @sDBName        Varchar(30),
        @sUserName      Varchar(30),
        @sUserRoles     Varchar(30)

/* Get The Database Name */
Select @sDBName = Db_Name( )

/* Return the name of the DB */
Print 'Running in database %1!', @sDBName

/* Get User Information */
Select @sUserName = User_Name( ),
       @sUserRoles = Show_Role( )
/* Return User Information */
Print 'User: %1!, Privileges: %2!', @sUserName, @sUserRoles

/* Initialize the column counter */
Select @nCurrentColumn = 1
```

continues

Part

II

Ch

4

Listing 4.6 Continued

```
/* Get information about the first column */
Select @sColumnName = Col_Name( Object_Id( @psTableName ), @nCurrentColumn )
/* Print the Table Name Information */
Print 'Table: %1!', @psTableName


While @sColumnName != NULL
Begin
    Select @nColumnLength = Col_Length( @psTableName, @sColumnName )
    Print 'Column #: %1!, Name: %2!, Length: %3!', @nCurrentColumn,
    ➥@sColumnName, @nColumnLength
    /* Increment the column counter */
    Select @nCurrentColumn = @nCurrentColumn + 1

    /* Get information about the column */
    Select @sColumnName = Col_Name( Object_Id( @psTableName ), @nCurrentColumn )
End
/* Get basic Table Statistics */
Select @nDataPages = Data_Pgs( si.id, doampg),
    @nRowCount = RowCnt( doampg )
From    sysindexes si, sysobjects so
Where   so.id = si.id
And     so.name = @psTableName
And     indid in (0,1)

/* Print the Table Statistics */
Print '# of Data Pages: %1!, Approx # of Rows: %2!', @nDataPages, @nRowCount
Print 'procTableInfo: Execution Complete'
Return 0

Go
```

By running the stored procedure (after you've compiled it) on the table *authors,* you can get an idea of the power of the system functions. Here's the output from *procTableInfo*:

```
procTableInfo: Execution Begun
Running in database pubs2
User: dbo, Privileges: sa_role sso_role oper_role rep
Table: authors
Column #: 1, Name: au_id, Length: 11
Column #: 2, Name: au_lname, Length: 40
Column #: 3, Name: au_fname, Length: 20
Column #: 4, Name: phone, Length: 12
Column #: 5, Name: address, Length: 40
Column #: 6, Name: city, Length: 20
Column #: 7, Name: state, Length: 2
Column #: 8, Name: country, Length: 12
Column #: 9, Name: postalcode, Length: 10
# of Data Pages: 0, Approx # of Rows: 0
procTableInfo: Execution Complete
```

▶ **See** "Working with and Understanding Stored Procedures," **p. 256**.

Using Aggregate Functions   Sybase provides Aggregate functions to enable you to perform totaling and other forms of computation on data stored in the database. The most commonly used aggregate functions are shown in Table 4.2

Table 4.2   Sybase System XI Aggregate Functions

Function Name	Description
Avg( )	Returns the average of a numeric column or expression
Count( )	Returns a count of the records that match the criteria specified in a Select statement
Min( )	Returns the minimum value of a numeric column or expression
Max( )	Returns the maximum value of a numeric column or expression
Sum( )	Returns the sum or total value of a numeric column or expression

Some of the functions have limitations on what sorts of data they can be used with, as follows:

- The Avg( ) and Sum( ) functions can only be used when working with numeric columns (Int, SmallInt, TinyInt, Decimal, Numeric, Money, and Float).
- The Min( ) and Max( ) functions cannot be performed on columns or expressions that equate to bit datatypes.
- With the exception of the Count(*) function, none of the aggregate functions can be performed on Text or Image data columns or expressions.

  ▶ **See** "Choosing Datatypes for Your Data," **p. 149**

▶ **See** "Choosing Datatypes for Your Data," **p. 149**

Using the Min( ), Max( ), and Avg( ) Functions   The operation of each of the aggregate functions is essentially the same. To use them, perform a select statement that has a particular column or expression that you want to evaluate by aggregate rules. For example, to return the minimum, maximum, and average royalties paid to authors in the *roysched* table, you would execute:

```
Select Min( royalty ), Max( royalty ), Avg( royalty )
From   roysched
Go
```

```
---------- ---------- ----------
10          24          15
```

Working with Count( )   The Count( ) function is somewhat special in that it enables you to count the number of records that match the criteria you specify. In its simplest form, it can be used to count the number of records in a table. By using an asterisk (*) as the parameter to the function, Sybase will return a count of every element in the table. For example, to count the total number of sales in *salesdetail* you would execute:

```
Select Count( * )
From   sales
Go
```

```
- - - - - - - - - -
116
```

By combining the Count( ) function with the Group By clause, it is possible to get summary data returned from the database. For example, to total the number of books sold by title, you would execute:

```
Select title_id, "# of Sales" = Count( * )
From    salesdetail
Group by title_id
Go

title_id # of Sales
-------- ----------
BU1032   9
BU1111   7
BU2075   15
BU7832   7
MC2222   1
MC3021   15
PC1035   10
PC8888   6
PS1372   1
PS2091   3
PS2106   3
PS3333   5
PS7777   7
TC3218   5
TC4203   16
TC7777   6
```

N O T E Sybase ignores any values that are NULL when performing aggregate functions. So if you use the Count( ) function on a particular column in a table instead of using the asterisk, it will be possible to get different results. For example, if you count the number of records in *discounts* specifying the *lowqty* column you would get the following results:

```
Select Count( lowqty )
From    discounts
Go

- - - - -
2
```

If, however, you just executed Count(*), you would get the following results (showing the total number of rows in the table):

```
Select Count( * )
From    discounts
Go

- - - - -
4 ▪
```

Using Distinct with Aggregate Functions Transact-SQL enables you to use the Distinct keyword with aggregate functions like Count( ), Sum( ), and Avg( ) permit you to work with the distinct values in the column or expression. For example, if you wanted a count of the different titles that are in the *salesdetail* table, you would execute:

```
Select Count( Distinct title_id )
From   salesdetail
Go


----------
16
```

In a similar fashion, if you wanted to get the average of royalties being paid to authors who sell more than 5000 books, you would execute:

```
Select Avg( Distinct royalty )
From   roysched
Where  hirange > 10000
Go


----------
18
```

This is a different result from the non-distinct average:

```
Select Avg( Distinct royalty )
From   roysched
Where  hirange > 10000
Go


----------
17
```

Using String Functions   Sybase's string functions are provided to afford you the flexibility required to process string (Char and VarChar) data. These functions typically permit the manipulation of the data for common string concatenation and substringing. In Table 4.3, you can see a list of the string functions and their basic uses.

Table 4.3   Sybase's String Functions Used to Manipulate Char and Varchar Data

Function Name	Description
Ascii( )	Returns the numeric ASCII code for the first column in the text supplied to the function
Char( )	Returns a character represented by the number supplied to the function (the ASCII equivalent)
CharIndex( )	Returns the position in a given string of a second string that was being searched for
Char_Length( )	Returns the length in bytes of the string data or expression passed to the function

continues

Part

II

Ch

4

Table 4.3   Continued

Function Name	Description
Difference( )	Returns the difference (expressed as an integer) between two strings that are compared according to the logic of the Soundex algorithms
Lower( )	Returns a string that has had all capitalization removed from it and is all in lowercase letters
LTrim( )	Trims any leading blanks from a string or expression
PatIndex( )	Similar to CharIndex( ), PatIndex( ) returns the offset in String 2 of a piece of text being searched for (String 1)
Replicate( )	Repeats a string for a requested number of times
Reverse( )	Returns a string that has all the bytes reversed
Right( )	Returns the right-most number of characters from a string as specified by the function call
RTrim( )	Removes the trailing blanks from a string or expression
Soundex( )	Returns an integer that represents the Soundex equivalent of the supplied string
Space( )	Returns the specified number of spaces in a string
Str( )	Converts a number to a string with accuracy and precision as specified by the function call
Stuff( )	Inserts a string into another string at the place or offset specified by the function call
SubString( )	Returns a string extracted from another string at the offset and for the length requested in the function call
Upper( )	Returns a string in all uppercase letters

As you can see, there are quite a few different string functions available to you. Most of them are pretty important, so I've produced an example of each of them in action.

Using Ascii( )   The Ascii( ) function's syntax is as follows:

```
Ascii( Char_Expression )
```

Note that the Ascii( ) function only operates on the first character in the supplied text stream:

```
Select Ascii( 'Hello World' )
Go


---------
72
```

Using Char( )   The Char( ) function's syntax is as follows:

```
Char( Numeric_Expression )
```

Note that the Char( ) function relies on the supplied or installed and active character set in the server. If the requested character/numeric is in fact only the first portion or byte of a double-byte character, then the returned value could be undefined:

```
Select Char( 65 )
Go
```

```
- - - - - - - -
A
```

Using Str( )   As an extension of Char( ), Sybase provides the Str( ) function to convert numbers to strings with any required accuracy or level of truncation specified. The syntax for the use of the Str( ) function is as follows:

```
Str( Numeric_Expression [, Precision, Scale])
```

The *Precision*, if supplied, specifies the total number of characters, including a decimal point if necessary, that the numeric expression can be converted into. The *Scale* refers to the number of characters that can be placed to the right of the decimal point. For example:

```
Select Str( 123 ) + 'Hello'
Go
```

```
- - - - - - - -
123Hello
```

If the number after conversion does not fit into the *Precision* and *Scale* that you specify, Sybase will return a set of asterisks in place of the number. For example:

```
Select Str( 123.456, 2, 5 ) + 'Hello'
Go
```

```
- - - - - - -
**Hello
```

Using CharIndex( ) and PatIndex( )   The CharIndex( ) function is provided to help you search for the literal text of one string in another. The syntax for its use is as follows:

```
CharIndex( Char_Expression1, Char_Expression2 )
```

CharIndex( ) treats wild cards, such as the percent sign (%) and the underscore (_), as literals and does not treat them specially as normal wild cards as it does in the Like clause.

```
Select CharIndex( 'World', 'Hello World' )
Go
```

```
- - - - - - - -
7
```

PatIndex( ) permits the searching of wild-card pieces of text and actually forces you to wild card the search string. The syntax for PatIndex( ) is as follows:

```
PatIndex( Char_Expression1, Char_Expression2 )
```

To find all the system tables in the *sysobjects* table that have a fourth character between *f* and *i*, you would execute:

Part

II

Ch

4

```
Select  name
From    sysobjects
Where   PatIndex( 'sys[f-i]%', name) > 0
Go
```

```
- - - - - - - - - - - -
sysgams
sysindexes
syskeys
```

N O T E CharIndex( ) and PatIndex( ) differ in that CharIndex( ) cannot be used on
Text columns or data. You will get an error if you use CharIndex( ) on a Text
column. With PatIndex( ), you can perform any of the query extensions that the Like clause
permits. ▪

Using Char_Length( ) Char_Length( ) returns the length of string expressions. Its syntax is
as follows:

```
Char_Length( Char_Expression )
```

For example:

```
Select Char_Length( 'Hello World' )
Go
```

```
- - - - - - - - -
11
```

Using Soundex( ) Functions Sybase's sound related functions, Soundex( ) and
Difference( ), can be used for clever searching that looks for words that sound similar
when spoken by humans. The syntax for these functions is:

```
Select Soundex( Char_Expression )
Select Difference( Char_Expression1, Char_Expression2 )
```

To see how a word "sounds," use the following code:

```
Select Soundex( 'Hello World' )
Go
```

```
- - - - - - - - -
H400
```

To see the numeric difference between two phrases or words, use the following:

```
Select Difference( 'Hello World', 'Hello Wheeled' )
Go
Select Difference( 'Hello World', 'Hallow Wild' )
Go
Select Difference( 'Hello World', 'Windows 95' )
Go
- - - - - - - - -
4
- - - - - - - - -
4
- - - - - - -
0
```

The value returned from `Difference( )` represents how similar the two phrases or expressions are to each other. The value can range from 0 (zero) to 4 with 4 being a very close sounding similarity.

Using Upper( ) and Lower( ) to Manipulate String Cases   Sybase has two functions that allow for the easy conversion between cases of string expressions. Both functions take a single parameter of a string expression and return a modified result. For example:

```
Select Upper( 'Hello World' ), Lower( 'Hello World' )
Go


----------- -----------
HELLO WORLD hello world
```

Cleaning Up Strings with LTrim( ) and RTrim( )   Sybase has two useful functions, `LTrim( )` and `RTrim( )`, that enable you to remove excess spaces or blanks from string expressions. They are simple functions that take a single parameter of a string and return the cleaned up data string. It is often necessary to use `RTrim( )` when dealing with data returned from a `Char` column. Sybase pads `Char` data that is not as long as the full length of the column.

To show these functions at work, look at the following example:

```
/* This first example concatenates an exclamation
mark to the two strings so that you can see that
the spaces are really there!

Then using the trim functions, they are removed
*/
Select '!' + ' Hello World', 'Hello World ' + '!'
Go
Select '!' + LTrim( ' Hello World' ), RTrim( 'Hello World ' ) + '!'
Go
--
------------- -------------
! Hello World Hello World !
------------- -------------
!Hello World  Hello World!
```

Repeating Strings with Replicate( ) and Space( )   If you ever need to repeat a character string, rather than typing it in repetitiously, you should use the `Replicate( )` function. Likewise, if you need to add a number of spaces to a string, use the `Space( )` function. These functions make it easier for you to maintain your code without hand copied or typed spaces and replicated strings. For example:

```
Select Replicate( 'Hello', 2 ), Space( 10 ), Replicate( 'World', 2 )
Go
---------- ---------- ----------
HelloHello            WorldWorld
```

Getting Pieces of a String with SubString( ) and Right( )   Sybase enables you to either get a sub portion of a string using the `SubString( )` function or to get the right-most part of a string using the `Right( )` function. Unlike many databases, Sybase has no `Left( )` function, so you must use the `SubString( )` function with an origin of 1 to simulate the results from the `Left( )` function. For example:

Part

II

Ch

4

```
Select SubString( 'Hello World', 1, 5 ), Right( 'Hello World', 5 )
Go


----- -----
Hello World
```

Using Stuff( ) If you need to insert a string into another string at a given point, you can use the `Stuff( )` function. As its name implies, `Stuff( )` "stuffs" a string into another one. The syntax for `Stuff( )` is as follows:

```
Stuff( Char_Expression1, Numeric_Offset, Delete_Chars, Stuff_Expression )
```

To use stuff you would execute:

```
Select Stuff( 'He rld', 3, 1, 'llo Wo' )
Go


-----------
Hello World
```

If the starting position or numeric offset is greater than the length of the original expression, SQL Server will return a NULL string. If you do not want to remove any characters when you add your new expression to the existing one, you can set the number of characters to be deleted equal to 0 (zero).

Using Mathematical Functions System XI has a number of mathematical functions that can be performed on numeric expressions to provide advanced mathematical capabilities to your applications. Using mathematical functions in Sybase is straightforward because they all have the same basic syntax:

```
function_name( expression )
```

In Table 4.4, you can see a list of all the most commonly used mathematical functions that Sybase contains. These functions will be used by you on a day-to-day basis when performing mathematical analysis on the database's data.

Table 4.4 Sybase's Essential Mathematical Functions and Their Uses

Function Name	Description
Abs( )	Returns the absolute value of a number (i.e., a number without a sign)
Ceiling( )	Returns an integer that represents the number closest to and greater than the numeric expression specified
Exp( )	Returns the exponential value of a number or numeric expression specified. The accuracy or precision of the returned value depends on the CPU class of the server being used
Floor( )	The opposite of the Ceiling( ) function, Floor( ) returns the largest integer that is still less than the numeric expression specified
Log( )	Returns the natural logarithm of the numeric expression specified
Log10( )	Returns the base 10 logarithm of the numeric expression specified

Function Name	Description
Pi( )	Returns an approximation of the numeric construction known as Pi. The precision of the result will depend on the CPU class of the server.
Power( )	Returns a number based on a numeric expression supplied that has been raised to the power of a second numeric expression
Rand( )	Returns a random decimal number between 0 and 1
Round( )	Returns a rounded number with the requested level of precision
Sign( )	Returns +1 for a positive number, –1 for a negative number, and 0 for 0
Sqrt( )	Returns the square root of the supplied numeric expression

In addition to the numeric or mathematical functions described in Table 4.4, Sybase has a number of trigonometric functions that provide all the basic Sine, Cosine and Tangent manipulations on values represented in either radians or degrees. Trigonometric functions are typically used in systems that perform geometric analysis of data or on systems that work with spacial (geographic and region-based) data. The trigonometric functions available in Transact-SQL are ACos( ), ASin( ), ATan( ), ATn2( ), Cos( ), Cot( ), Degrees( ), Radians( ), Sin( ), and Tan( ). These trigonometric functions are very rarely used and therefore are not discussed in this text.

Part

II

Ch

4

Using Abs( ) and Sign( ) The Abs( ) and Sign( ) functions enable you to write some very generic *functional* stored procedures that can perform conditional logic based on the data passed into them. In the following example, you can see how the Sign( ) function reports the sign of a number:

```
Select Sign( 0 )
Go

Select Sign( 100.02 )
Go

Select Sign( -100.02 )
Go

- - - - - - - - - -
0

- - - - - - - - - -
1.00

- - - - - - - - - -
-1.00
```

In the following example, you can see that the absolute value function removes any sign from a number:

```
Select Abs( 0 )
Go
```

```
Select Abs( 100.02 )
Go

Select Abs( -100.02 )
Go


----------
0


----------
100.02


----------
100.02
```

Using Ceiling( ), Floor( ), and Round( )   The `Ceiling( )` and `Floor( )` functions are useful if you want to do integer-based math that is approximately accurate, based on a decimal value supplied. These two functions typically have use in financial systems that rely on the terms ceiling and floor when referring to such items as interest rates and margins. To use the `Ceiling( )` and `Floor( )` functions, you would execute something like this:

```
Select Ceiling( 134.393 ), Floor( 134.3393 )
Go


------- -------
135    134
```

If the `Ceiling( )` and `Floor( )` functions don't provide the sort of accuracy that you need for doing rounding of numbers, you can use the `Round( )` function. With the `Round( )` function, you can specify the number of digits of precision you require in the result. The following example illustrates the affects of rounding in Transact-SQL:

```
Select Round( 100.34983, 0 )
Go

Select Round( 100.34983, 1 )
Go

Select Round( 100.34983, 2 )
Go

Select Round( 100.34983, 3)
Go

Select Round( 100.34983, 4)
Go

Select Round( 100.34983, 5)
Go


---------
100.0


---------
100.3
```

```
- - - - - - - -
100.35

- - - - - - - -
100.35

- - - - - - - -
100.3498

- - - - - - - -
100.34983
```

Using Power( ) and Sqrt( ) With the trio of functions, Power( ), Exp( ) and Sqrt( ), it is possible to perform all the basic exponential mathematical analysis required by most systems. The following example demonstrates the use of each of these functions:

```
Select Power( 3, 4 )
Go

Select Sqrt( 16 )
Go

- - - - - - - - - - - -
81
```

```
- - - - - - - - - - - -
4.0
```

Using Pi( ) and Exp( ) In some systems that work with geometric data, it is necessary to take advantage of some mathematical constants, π and e. Sybase provides the Pi( ) and Exp( ) functions to enable you to work with these constants to the precision of your CPU. In the following example, you can see the execution of Pi( ) and Exp( ) on a Windows NT System XI server:

```
Select Pi( )
Go

Select Exp( 1 )
Go

- - - - - - - - - - - - - - - -
3.141592653589790

- - - - - - - - - - - - - - - -
2.71828182845905
```

Using Text and Image Functions The Text and Image functions provided by Sybase provide little support for anything other than basic referencing of data in the tables. Most of the access to these datatypes should be done through either the DB-Library or Client Library APIs, which provide a far richer interface to these datatypes. For more information on Client Library, see Chapter 14, "Understanding the Sybase Client Model (Client Library)." The list of functions is shown in Table 4.5.

Table 4.5 Text and Image Functions in Sybase System XI

Function Name	Description
PatIndex( )	Works the same as when used on regular string data and is used to find matching patterns of data in a text column
TextPtr( )	Returns a 16-byte pointer to the text data in the table
TextValid( )	Returns a status indicating whether a variable contains a valid pointer to a text column
Set TextSize( )	Enables you to configure the amount of data that should be returned from a text column

In normal use, you are unlikely to need any of the Text functions with the exception of PatIndex( ). The other functions are provided for your use by application tools vendors when implementing text support for 4Gls. For information on the PatIndex( ) function, see "Using String Functions" above.

Using Datatype Conversion Functions   Sybase has three functions available to convert datatypes. The most commonly used function, Convert( ), is a general purpose function that enables you to convert data between many different datatypes. Additionally, Sybase has two special conversion functions, IntToHex( ) and HexToInt( ), for working with hexadecimal numbers.

The IntToHex( ) and HexToInt( ) functions take a single number in either hexadecimal or regular decimal form and return the appropriately converted value to you. The importance of IntToHex( ) and HexToInt( ) is that they are hardware platform neutral. What this means is that if you convert a number to hexadecimal and back again using these functions, the result will be the same irrespective of whether you are running on a DEC Alpha or an IBM RS/6000. Platform conversion takes place because of the different implementations of hardware floating point mathematics and the underlying limitations of CPU architecture.

To illustrate the problem, look at the two conversions that are going to be performed on Sybase System XI on Windows NT running on an Intel Pentium processor:

```
Select HexToInt( '0x00000100' )
Go

Select Convert( Int, 0x00000100 )
Go
```

They *should* return the same value. However, here are the results:

```
- - - - - - - - - -
256


- - - - - - - - - -
65536
```

Clearly, these values are different. Welcome to the world of differences among CPUs!

N O T E Hexadecimal numbers are numbers that are represented in base 16. Hexadecimal numbers are common when writing application programs in assembler or other low-level programming languages; in addition, a large number of the constants that are used in the Windows API (Win16 and Win32) require hexadecimal-based constants.

Traditional decimal numbers are represented in base 10; the valid digits that can be used are 0-9. Base 16 implies that there are 16 valid digits, but as you know, there are in fact only ten (0-9). To work around this, the letters A-F (typically capitalized) are also used.

Hexadecimal numbers are normally indicated or designated by a prefix of 0x; however, if you see a character like an A in a number it is pretty safe bet that the number is really in Hex. For example: 0x123F is hexadecimal for 4671. ▨

It is only necessary to use the datatype conversion functions when Sybase doesn't implicitly convert a datatype for you. Implicit datatype conversion means that Sybase considers the datatypes so similar that it can (without prompting or function use) convert the data for you. The following list shows the groups of datatypes for which implicit conversion occurs:

- `Binary, VarBinary, TinyInt, SmallInt, Int, Decimal, Numeric, Real, Float, SmallMoney, Money`
- `Char, NChar, Varchar, VarcharN`
- `SmallDatetime, DateTime`

Despite the groups above, it is possible that you will receive truncation errors when implicitly converting between datatypes. For example, if you converted a `DateTime` that was storing accuracy of date and time down to the millisecond, you would lose information when it was converted to a `SmallDateTime`. Similarly if you convert from `Decimal` to `Numeric`, the precision and scale differ on each of the datatypes and you should expect truncation errors. In these cases, you can use the `Convert( )` function to remove any possibility of error.

If you need to do conversions between any other datatype pair, you must use the `Convert( )` function. The syntax for the `Convert( )` function is as follows:

```
Convert( New_Datatype, Expression [, Style] )
```

The *New_Datatype* keyword should be replaced with the required datatype to which you want the expression to be converted. The optional *Style* keyword is supplied so that if you are converting from a `DateTime` to a `Char` or `VarChar` format, you can apply a format mask to the data. As an example:

```
Select Convert( VarChar( 10 ), GetDate( ), 1 )
Go

----------
05/18/96
```

The list of available styles is shown in Table 4.6.

Part

II

Ch

4

Table 4.6   Styles That Can Be Used with the Convert( ) Function on a Date

Style Number	Example Output
0/100	month dd yyyy hh:miAMPM
1	mm/dd/yy
2	yy.mm.dd
3	dd/mm/yy
4	dd.mm.yy
5	dd-mm-yy
6	dd month yy
7	month dd, yy
8	hh:mi:ss
9/109	month dd yyyy hh:mi:ss:mmmAMPM
10	mm-dd-yy
11	yy/mm/dd
12	yymmdd
101	mm/dd/yyyy
102	yyyy.mm.dd
103	dd/mm/yyyy
104	dd.mm.yyyy
105	dd-mm-yyyy
106	dd month yyyy
107	month dd, yyyy
108	hh:mi:ss
110	mm-dd-yyyy
111	yyyy/mm/dd
112	yyyymmdd

Notice that the styles greater than 100 are the same as the other styles less than 100 with the exception that they display a four digit year.

TROUBLESHOOTING

I converted a number into a string and keep getting the message, `"Insufficient result space for explicit conversion of NUMERIC value 'XXXX.XXXX' to a CHAR field."` The problem is that the Char or VarChar datatype that you are attempting to convert the number into isn't big enough to store the converted number. You cannot convert such a number as 123.53 into a Char(3) because the number is too long when represented as a string.

Make sure that you have allocated enough space in the string to store the data.

▶ **See** "Choosing Datatypes for Your Data," **p. 149**

Using Date Functions   Sybase's date functions are provided largely to aid you in the working with dates. The primary date functions are listed in Table 4.7.

Table 4.7   Date Functions in Sybase System XI

Function Name	Description
GetDate( )	Returns the current system date and time of the server
DatePart( )	Returns to you a portion of a date in units you specify
DateName( )	Returns the name of the portion of a date specified
DateDiff( )	Returns to you the difference between two dates in the units (hours, minutes, seconds, and so on) that you desire
DateAdd( )	Adds a specified number of units (hours, minutes, seconds, and so on) to a given date

Part
II

Ch
4

All the date functions that take arguments of a unit of measurement (for the amount of a date) work with the following keywords:

- Millisecond
- Second
- Minute
- Hour
- Day
- Week
- Month
- Year

Using GetDate( )   To get the current date and time from the server, you can use the GetDate( ) date function. The GetDate( ) function takes no parameters and therefore its syntax is very straightforward. GetDate( ) will return you the full date, which you could then either format on the client program (using standard date formatting routines) or format to a desired style using the Convert( ) function described above in the section "Using Datatype Conversion Functions."

In the following example, you see the result of executing the GetDate( ) date function:

```
Select GetDate( )
Go


- - - - - - - - - - - - - - - - - - - - - - - - -
May 13 1996 11:21:15:026PM
```

Using DatePart( )   The DatePart( ) function works by extracting the required date component from the supplied expression. The expression can be either a column or the result of another function (or functions) that in turn returns a date. The syntax for DatePart( ) is as follows:

```
DatePart( Date_Component, Date_Expression )
```

For example, to get the current month of the system you would execute:

```
Select DatePart( Month, GetDate( ) )
Go


- - - - - - - - - -
5
```

Using DateName( )   The DateName( ) function works in a very similar manner to the DatePart( ) function by extracting the required date component and returning it in the native language of the installed Sybase from the supplied expression. The expression can be either a column or the result of another function (or functions) that returns a date. The syntax for DateName( ) is as follows:

```
DateName( Date_Component, Date_Expression )
```

For example, to get the name of the current month of the system you would execute:

```
Select DateName( Month, GetDate( ) )
Go


- - - - - - - - - -
May
```

Using DateDiff( )   The DateDiff( ) function is used when you need to compare two different dates or date expressions in a required number of date units. The syntax for DateDiff( ) is as follows:

```
DatePart( Date_Component, Starting_Date_Expression, Ending_Date_Expression )
```

For example, if you wanted to list the number of days since the creation of the tables in the system catalog table, you would execute:

```
Select name, crdate, DateDiff( Day, crdate, GetDate( ))
From    sysobjects
```

```
Order By crdate
Go
```

This would yield the following results:

```
name                             crdate
- - - - - - - - - - - - - - -    - - - - - - - - - - - - - - - - - - - - - - -    - - - - - - - - -
syskeys                          Jan  1 1900 12:00:00:000AM    35196
syslogs                          Jan  1 1900 12:00:00:000AM    35196
systypes                         Jan  1 1900 12:00:00:000AM    35196
sysusers                         Jan  1 1900 12:00:00:000AM    35196
sales                            May  6 1996  1:37:18:920AM    7
...
au_pix                           May  6 1996  1:37:18:920AM    7
blurbs                           May  6 1996  1:37:18:920AM    7
stores                           May  6 1996  1:37:18:920AM    7
titles                           May  6 1996  1:37:18:920AM    7
...
sysgams                          Jan  1 2000 12:00:00:000AM    -1328
```

N O T E   If the start date is actually greater than the ending date, you will end up with a negative number being returned from DateDiff( ), as shown above for the *sysgams* table. ■

Using DateAdd( )   DateAdd( ) enables you to perform arithmetic on date columns and expressions. The syntax for DateAdd( ) is similar to that of the other date functions and is as follows:

```
DateAdd( Date_Component, Quantity, Starting_Date_Expression )
```

For example, to add three hours to the current server time, execute the following:

```
Select DateAdd( Hour, 3, GetDate( ) )
Go
```

```
- - - - - - - - - - - - - - - - - - - - - - - - - - -
May 14 1996  3:03:40:196AM
```

TIP   To subtract a number of hours, days, or other date unit from a given date, supply a negative quantity to the DateAdd( ) function.

From Here...

In this chapter, you were introduced to the major elements of Transact-SQL. In addition, we explored the differences between Transact-SQL and the standards that have been proposed by ANSI in SQL89 and SQL92. This chapter should have helped you become comfortable with the basics of SQL and how to use it to work with data in your environment. However, there's so much more to show you. The whole of Part II, "Using System XI," is devoted to Transact-SQL, so you can randomly flick to pages anywhere in this section, and you will be certain to find something useful.

I highly recommend reviewing the following chapters for more information about Transact-SQL:

- See Chapter 5, "Understanding Databases, Devices, and Transaction Logs," and Chapter 6, "Understanding Tables and Datatypes," for information relating to DDL and the creation of database objects that you can use for later work.

- Chapter 7, "Using Rules, Defaults, and Triggers," provides instruction on enforcing some data integrity constraints on your tables.

- Review Chapter 8, "Understanding Indexes and Keys," for information on how to improve access times to the data that you place in the tables you create.

- See Chapter 10, "Understanding Stored Procedures," for an introduction to Transact-SQL's procedural extensions.

- Chapter 11, "Understanding Transactions and Locking," provides guidelines for how to use locking to maintain data integrity in a transaction.

- Consult Chapter 12, "Understanding and Using Cursors," for tips on using cursors to improve performance of your data-intensive operations.

Understanding Databases, Devices, and Transaction Logs

The storage of physical data in Sybase is controlled through the creation of data devices. *Data devices* are areas of disk that are preallocated for the use of Sybase. You need to preallocate the space so that other applications and tasks running on the same server don't consume the resources. Sybase can use devices for the storage of either data, logs, or dumps.

Databases are logical areas that Sybase reserves for the storage of tables and indexes. One or many databases can be created on a data device—provided the device is an appropriately large size.

Transaction logs are the work areas that Sybase uses to manage the transactions performed by client processes. The transaction logs are used to store the information required by Sybase to roll back a transaction if a client process issues a Rollback Transaction.

▶ **See** "Undoing a Transaction with Rollback Tran,"
p. 294

Creating and using data devices

Sybase uses devices to store and manage data; this chapter introduces you to them.

How to create and manage databases

Creating and working with databases can be a chore. SQL Server Manager makes it easy to create and manage databases in Sybase on a local or remote server.

Learn about database segments

Sybase organizes data in segments that may span multiple devices. By using segments, you get better performance on your server and have more manageable data.

Learn all you ever needed (or wanted) to know about Tempdb

Tempdb is Sybase's work area. Tempdb is a special database that Sybase uses to store results from queries prior to returning them to a client.

Dump devices are used to unload or back up a database. They can be disk or tape based and are used as export areas. ■

▶ **See** "Performing Backups," **p. 492**

Working with Devices

Devices are the physical files that Sybase creates on disk for storing databases and logs. Devices must be created before databases can be created. A device can be of two types: database (used for storing databases) and dump (used for storing transaction logs). Strictly speaking a device does not refer to a particular physical disk device. On some operating systems such as HP-UX, you can create logical volumes that span multiple physical disks but present themselves to the user/operating system as a single disk. In this case, a Sybase device is simply an area on the logical volume reserved to be used by Sybase databases and dumps.

Devices can store more than one database or transaction log in them; however, you often can get better performance with a single database per device, because each device is managed by a single I/O thread from the operating system. A database can span multiple devices if it needs to grow, and this can be an optimizing method due to striped physical disk access over multiple drives.

When you first install Sybase, a single device, the *master* device is created for you. In this *master* data device, Sybase installs the *master* and *tempdb* databases and any of the optional databases that you chose at installation time. For more information on the installation process, refer to Chapter 3, "Installing Sybase."

Creating Devices

You can create a disk device in Sybase in two ways: graphically or through Transact-SQL. The graphical method is performed by using Sybase SQL Server Manager. The Transact-SQL method is performed using the `Disk Init` command. Both methods are discussed in the following sections. If you do not have access to Sybase SQL Server Manager because of platform considerations (you don't have a Windows 95 or Windows NT machine) you should refer to the section titled "Using Disk Init."

Using Sybase SQL Server Manager   Sybase SQL Server Manager is a versatile tool that permits DBAs to perform most of the administrative functions of Sybase without requiring knowledge of the often-cryptic Transact-SQL commands required. However, Sybase SQL Server Manager does not permit an automated installation or "scripted" installation procedure. For this, you will need to use Transact-SQL.

To use Sybase SQL Server Manager to create a device, follow these steps:

1. Start Sybase SQL Server Manager from the Sybase for Windows NT or Sybase for Windows group in Program Manager. Figure 5.1 shows Sybase SQL Server Manager just after it has been started.

FIG. 5.1

In the left pane of SSM, you can see the available servers. Note that no server is selected or active and that the toolbar is disabled.

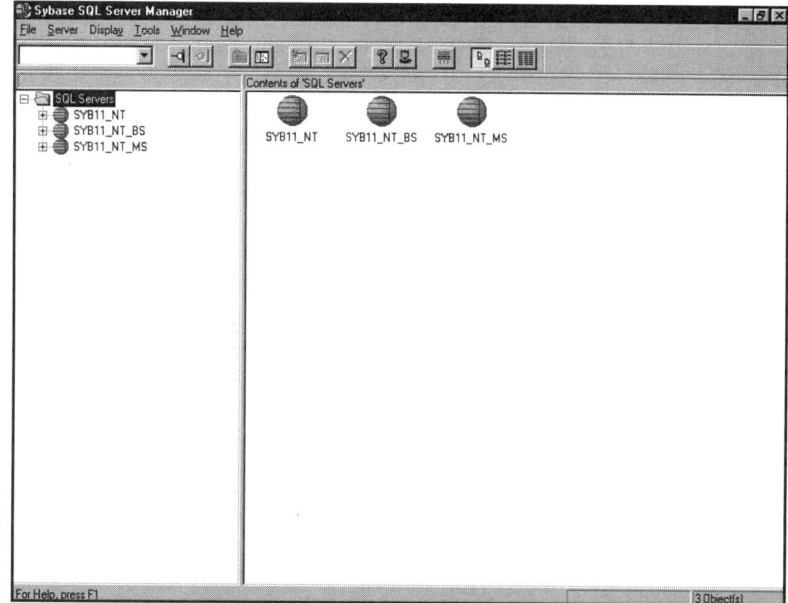

2. Select the server that's going to be managed by clicking it. When you do, a dialog box is displayed asking you to log on or connect to the server. In Figure 5.2, you can see the Sybase SQL Server Manager Connect dialog box being used to connect to the server SYB11_NT.

FIG. 5.2

The SSM Connect dialog box requires that you enter a valid logon and password to manage the server.

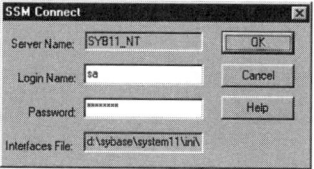

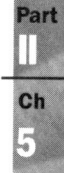

N O T E The Interfaces file field on the Sybase SQL Server Manager Connect dialog box is used to specify the SQL.INI file or Interfaces file that will be used to locate the server that you are connecting to. The Interfaces file is a text file that contains logical names of the servers (such as SYB11_NT) and the associated protocols and addresses used to get to or communicate with the server. You can edit the Interfaces file by using SQLEdit, which is described in Chapter 3, "Installing Sybase." ▓

After connecting to the server, you will notice that there is a lightning bolt in the server icon and that the right pane of the Sybase SQL Server Manager has changed to show the available options for the server. In Figure 5.3, you can see the Sybase SQL Server Manager after connecting.

FIG. 5.3

The SSM after successful connection and expansion of some of the tree on the left pane shows the available options that can be managed in SYB11_NT.

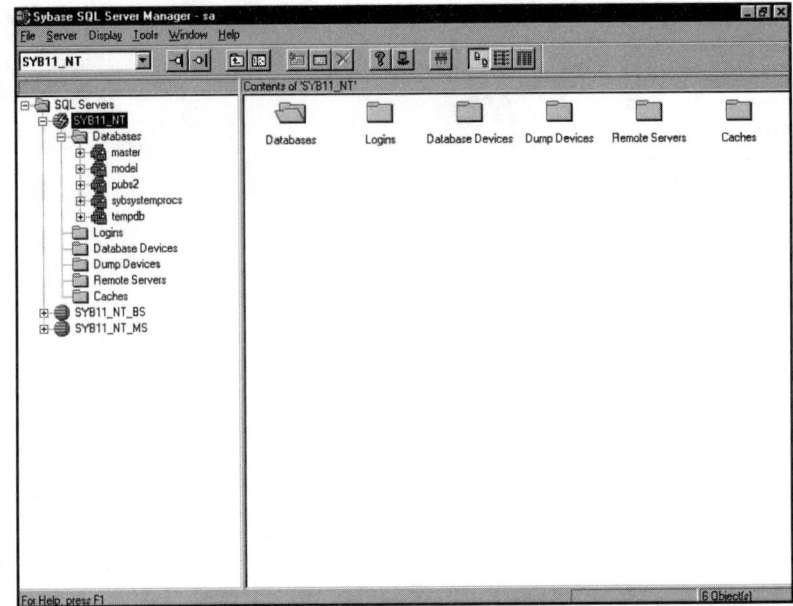

3. Choose Server, Create, and select Device to display the Sybase SQL Server Manager Create Database Device dialog box shown in Figure 5.4.

FIG. 5.4

The SSM Create Database Device dialog box enables you to specify all the options required for the creation of the device.

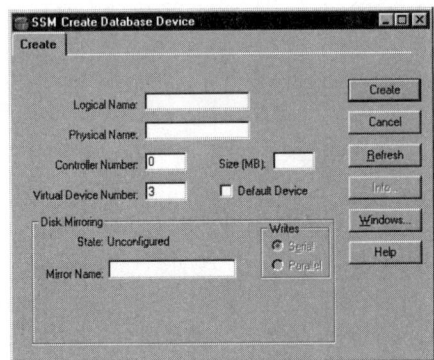

 TIP In Sybase SQL Server Manager, it is possible to complete the same task in many ways. Sybase SQL Server Manager treats all things as objects. In the toolbar, you will notice the button with a flash on it (see Fig. 5.5). By clicking this button, you will be shown an appropriate Create dialog box based on whatever object (database, device, table, index, and so on) is currently in the right pane of the Sybase SQL Server Manager.

Another way of creating an object is to right-click in the right-hand pane and select Create ObjectType from the context menu that is displayed.

FIG. 5.5

The Create button enables you to create an object, such as a database, device, or table, without needing to find the correct menu option.

4. Enter the name of the logical device that you want to create in the Logical Name field (see Fig. 5.4).

5. Enter the physical name that should be used for the device, making sure that the physical location is on the correct volume or storage area that you want to use. Note that the physical name of the device may have semantic requirements based on the hardware platform that you are installing to.

   For example, on Windows NT, you should enter a fully qualified path name like `D:\Devices\MyDevice.Dat`. On most forms of UNIX, you would enter something like `/vdev1/MyDev.Dat`.

6. Enter the size of the device in megabytes and decide whether you want it to be a default device. A default device is one that is shared by all databases that need to expand and don't specify which device they need to expand on to.

N O T E Do not modify the Controller Number field unless you are instructed to by Sybase Technical Support. This controller number refers to the physical device controller that is used to control the device on the server. By leaving it 0 (zero), Sybase enables the underlying operating system to determine the correct controller that should be used.

There should also be no need to modify the Virtual Device Number field. Sybase assigns the device numbers in sequence (up to 255) for you and will place the next available number in the field automatically. ■

7. Click the Create button to physically create the device. The process of creating a device can take a long time depending on the device's size and the underlying operating system. Be patient and wait for success or failure to be indicated by the Sybase SQL Server Manager. (It took about three minutes to create a small device of only 2M, but your times may vary depending on the hardware being used for the server and the drives.)

After creating the device, the dialog box changes to indicate the successful device creation and to enable you to view more information about the device. Figure 5.6 shows the modified dialog box for a new device that has just been created called *MyDevice*. Note the additional tabs that have been enabled to allow you to get more information about the use of the device. For information on the Disk Mirroring and Writes options, see the section titled "Using Device Options."

FIG. 5.6

The SSM Database Device dialog box shows the current information about a database device. You can access this dialog box at any time by double-clicking a device in the right pane of the SSM.

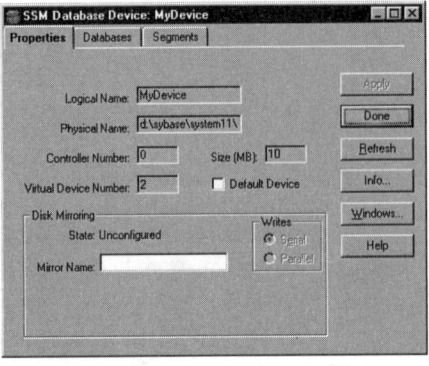

After you close the Sybase SQL Server Manager Database Device dialog box by pressing the Done button, you will notice that the new device has been added to the list of devices available on the database server. In Figure 5.7, you can see that the new device, *MyDevice,* has been added to the list and that its unused space (in megabytes) is NULL or empty indicating that there are no databases using the device.

FIG. 5.7

SSM has a variety of views of objects. Here you can see the Database Devices in a Details view. The Details view shows all relevant information about the objects being displayed.

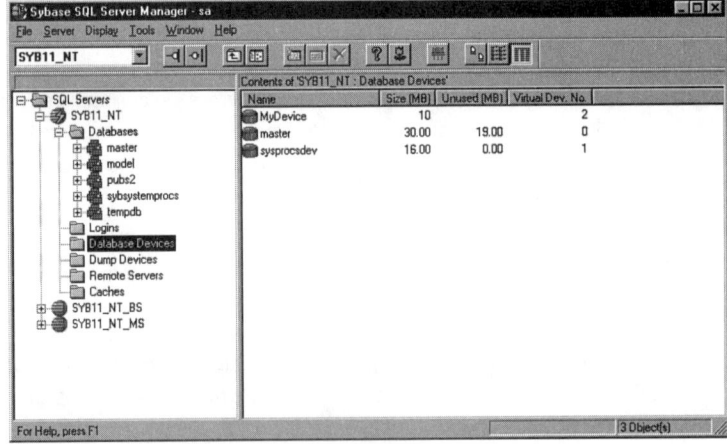

N O T E   Sybase on Windows NT creates a physical file on the drive when the device is created. If you are using Windows NT's NT File System (NTFS), the operating system will return control to the application (Sybase SQL Server Manager) immediately after executing the create command because of the way NTFS represents files to calling programs. Don't be concerned if you were used to seeing device creation take a long time on FAT or OS/2 HPFS and now it's suddenly very quick. This is one of the blessings of NT's new file system. ■

CAUTION

After creating a data device, it is very important that you dump or back up the *master* database because Sybase stores configuration information about the devices in the *master* database. In the event of a device failure, you need to make sure that the backup of your *master* database has all the correct and up-to-date information about the devices stored in it.

If you don't back up the *master* database and a failure occurs on the *master* database or device, you will have to reconstruct the device information by hand. Consult the Sybase emergency recovery documentation for detailed instruction on how to rebuild the device information in the *master* database.

Using Disk Init Disk Init is the SQL equivalent of creating a device through Sybase SQL Server Manager. In fact, Sybase SQL Server Manager's graphical front end is actually just creating the right Disk Init command to be sent to the server. The syntax for the use of Disk Init is as follows:

```
Disk Init
Name = 'Logical_Name',
Physname = 'Physical_Name',
Vdevno = Virtual_Device_Number,
Size = Number_Of_2k_Blocks
[, Vstart = Virtual_Address,
CntrlType = Controller_Number]
[, Contiguous] (Open VMS Only)
```

The options for the Transact-SQL command Disk Init are as follows:

- Logical_Name—This is any valid Sybase identifier. A shorter name is probably preferable because it has to be used each time a database is created.

- *Physical_Name*—This is the full path and file name of the file to be used on the operating system to store the data. I suggest adding an extension of .dat to the file name so that it is easy to identify that this is a data device used by Sybase.

- *Virtual_Device_Number*—This is the unique system identifier for the device. It can range from 0 to 255, where 0 is reserved for the master database.

- *Number_Of_2k_Blocks*—This is how a device is sized. The minimum value is 512 (meaning 1M), the maximum value is 1,048,576 (meaning a 2G device).

- *Virtual_Address*—This parameter controls the virtual paging of the data device and how Sybase accesses it. *This parameter should be used only when you're working with Sybase Technical Support.*

- *Controller_Number*—This parameter controls the physical device controller that will be used for the device. *This parameter should be used only when you're working with Sybase Technical Support.*

- Contiguous—Use this on OpenVMS to force the database file to be created on contiguous blocks of the underlying physical disk. This improves performance dramatically.

The following SQL statement creates the same data device that was created earlier using the Sybase SQL Server Manager:

Part
II

Ch
5

```
Disk init
Name = 'MyDevice',
Physname = 'D:\Sybase\System11\DATA\MyDevice.DAT',
Vdevno = 2,
Size = 5000
```

> **CAUTION**
>
> There are two common problems that occur when creating devices: You don't have enough physical disk space to create them and you don't have the appropriate permissions on the underlying operating system.
>
> To avoid the first problem, make sure that you accurately calculate the amount of space being consumed on the physical device and that there's room enough for it.
>
> To avoid the second problem, make sure that the user who logged on to the operating system to run the Sybase executables has permissions to create devices. Otherwise, the user will get errors when attempting to create the device.

Using Device Options

You should consider two important device options when creating devices in Sybase: *mirroring* and *default devices*. Both options are important to mission-critical environments where downtime needs to be minimized.

Mirroring   *Mirroring* is used to provide an absolute copy of the database (usually) on a different physical device so that if a hardware failure occurs on the primary device, the database can be switched over to run on the mirror device. Sybase performs mirroring by installing a mirror-handling "user" on the server. This user is listed as `spid 3` "MIRROR HANDLER" in the system processes, which you can list by running the system procedure `sp_who`. Mirroring is a continuous operation and provides maximum redundancy in the event of a failure.

Mirroring can be performed at two levels within Sybase: either by the underlying operating system or by Sybase itself. More information on mirroring the operating system can be found in the documentation that accompanies the operating system you are running on. In most cases, the operating system's implementation of mirroring will provide better performance and options—such as various different implementations of redundant arrays of inexpensive drives (RAID)—than Sybase. There are six levels of RAID (levels 0 to 5) that can be implemented, and they provide different methods of distributing physical data (and its copies) across multiple drives. See Appendix E, "Redundant Array of Inexpensive Disks (RAID)," for more information about RAID.

Furthermore, with many operating systems it's possible to mirror whole drives, thereby protecting all devices that reside on the drive.

Sybase's mirroring works by creating an additional device on the specified disk and then using the mirror handler to copy every transaction that the device receives to the mirror device.

Using Sybase SQL Server Manager to Mirror a Device   To enable mirroring on a device by using Sybase SQL Server Manager, follow these steps:

1. Start Sybase SQL Server Manager, select the server that's going to be managed, and then select Database Devices from the left pane and double-click the device that you want to manage. The Sybase SQL Server Manager Database Device dialog box appears (refer to Fig. 5.6).

2. In the Disk Mirroring group box, enter the name of the Mirror device. This should be the physical name of the mirror that is going to be stored somewhere on a physical device. I suggest using the same name as the main physical device and adding an extension of `.mir` to the file name so that it is easy to identify that this is a mirror device used by Sybase.

3. Indicate whether you want the writes to the mirrored device to be in serial or in parallel. Serial writes provide more redundancy for the primary device because they are verified first before initiating the mirrored devices write. However, serial writes take more time because the server has to wait for confirmation on one device before writing to the second. This option has an effect only when working with an operating system that supports Asynchronous I/O (or the capability to post multiple requests to the underlying disk subsystem in parallel without needing to wait for a response from any of them).

4. Click the Apply button to create the mirror device and start mirroring the primary data device.

After creating the device, the dialog box will change to add some new fields through which you can disable the physical or mirror devices permanently or temporarily. These new fields can be seen in Figure 5.8.

Part

II

Ch

5

FIG. 5.8

The SSM Database Device dialog box after adding a mirror to a device enables you to take a device offline in the event of a failure.

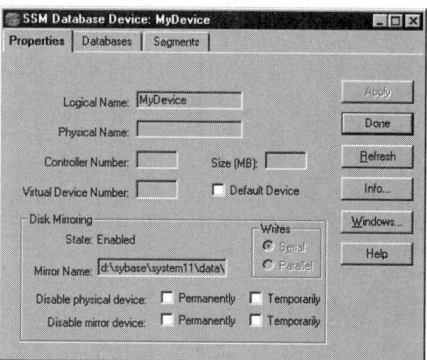

You would disable a device temporarily if a physical failure occurred and you needed to switch over to the other device to swap out the physical device. By disabling a device permanently, you are instructing Sybase to remove the mirror and return (or free) the space allocated by Sybase back to the operating system.

> **N O T E** There appear to be bugs in the version of the Sybase SQL Server Manager that I was using when running on Windows NT. The nature of the bugs is that when you display the Sybase SQL Server Manager Database Device dialog box, it does not correctly pick up the information about the device. If you look closely at Figure 5.8, you will notice that some of the fields are blank; this is an example of the bug. The version (obtained from the About box) that I was using is SQL Server Manager/11.0.1/P/PC/Win32/1/February 8, 1996. If you experience similar problems, contact Sybase Technical Support. ■

CAUTION

On some operating systems, such as Windows NT, Sybase does not remove the physical device that was created on the server when you elect to disable a device permanently. In this situation, the database server is notified that the device is no longer in use, but the physical device file is not removed.

Take care that you don't over commit the amount of allocated space because you assumed that the device would be deleted or removed for you. Go to a command shell and physically delete the device file before attempting to add another device.

Using the Disk Mirror Command Mirroring can also be done by using Transact-SQL. The Disk Mirror command's syntax is as follows:

```
Disk Mirror
Name = 'Logical_Name',
Mirror = 'Physical_Name'
[, Writes = {Serial | Noserial }]
```

The options for the Transact-SQL command Disk Mirror are as follows:

- *logical_name*—This is the name of the device that will be mirrored.
- *physical_name*—This is the full file name of the mirror device.
- Writes—This enables you to specify whether you should write in serial or parallel to the mirror device. This option is supported only on operating systems that support asynchronous I/O.

The following example shows how to mirror the *MyDevice* physical data device created earlier:

```
Disk Mirror
Name = 'MyDevice',
Mirror = 'D:\Sybase\System11\DATA\MyDevice.Mir'
```

Default Devices Default devices are used by Sybase when the Create Database command isn't accompanied by a specific device that it should be placed on. Many devices can be specified as default. Sybase will use them alphabetically until each device is filled.

To make a device a default device, select the Default Device check box on the Sybase SQL Server Manager Database Devices dialog box (see Fig. 5.6), and apply the changes by pressing the Apply button.

Alternately, you can use the `sp_diskdefault` system-stored procedure. The syntax for `sp_diskdefault` is as follows:

```
sp_diskdefault Device_Name, {DefaultOn | DefaultOff}
```

The options for the system stored procedure `sp_diskdefault` are:

- *Device_Name*—This is the logical device name that's being made default (or not). If your device name has special characters, you may need to enclose the device name in single quotes so that Sybase will recognize it.
- *DefaultOn*—This tells Sybase to make this a default device.
- *DefaultOff*—This tells Sybase to make this a non-default device.

In the following example, the device *MyDevice* is made a default device:

```
sp_diskdefault MyDevice, defaulton
```

Viewing Information on Devices

There are two ways to find information about the devices that are now installed/active on a Sybase: by using Sybase SQL Server Manager or by using the system-stored procedure `sp_helpdevice`. By now, you should be pretty familiar with using Sybase SQL Server Manager to find information, so this section concentrates on `sp_helpdevice`.

The syntax for `sp_helpdevice` is as follows:

```
sp_helpdevice [logical_name]
```

logical_name is the name of the device that's to be inspected. If no device is specified, `sp_helpdevice` will report information on all the devices on the server.

The following example shows the output and use of `sp_helpdevice` to view all the devices on the server:

```
sp_helpdevice
Go

device_name     physical_name
description
status cntrltype device_number low        high
- - - - - - - - - - - - - - - - - - - - - - - - - - - - - - - - - - - - - - -
master       master.dat
special, default disk, physical disk, 30.00 MB
3      0         0             0        15359

MyDevice     d:\sybase\system11\data\MyDevice.Dat
special, MIRROR ENABLED, mirror = 'd:\sybase\system11\data\MyDevice.Mir',
serial writes, reads mirrored, physical disk, 10.00 MB
738    0         2             33554432   33559551

sysprocsdev d:\sybase\system11\DATA\SYBPROCS.DAT
special, physical disk, 16.00 MB
2      0         1             16777216   16785407
```

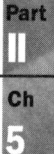

Part

II

Ch

5

```
tapedump1    \\.\TAPE0
tape,        625 MB, dump device
16     3       0              0            20000

tapedump2    \\.\TAPE1
tape,        625 MB, dump device
16     3       0              0            20000
```

Creating Dump Devices

Dump devices are special devices that Sybase uses to perform backups and to *dump* (clear out) the transaction logs on databases. By default, Sybase creates dump devices for the use of backups and log clearing. Three types of dump devices can be created, based on the medium that's being used to write the data to:

- **Disk**—A disk device can be a local disk device area or a network disk device that's used for dumping data from the database to in the form of a backup. If the device is on the network, make sure that the server that's running Sybase can access the network share the device is placed on.

- **Tape**—A tape dump device is used to back up a database directly to a tape device attached to the local computer. It isn't possible to dump to a tape attached to a remote computer.

- **NULL**—This is the special device that's used to dump the transaction logs of a database so that they're freed for more transactions to be posted against the server. Performing a dump to a NULL device removes log entries from the database/log without adding data to the device itself. The NULL device is named DISKDUMP and is added to the system automatically when Sybase is created. You can't manually add a NULL device to an existing Sybase.

On some particular hardware platforms, there are additional dump device options such as magneto-optical drives and a new hook in the Backup Server enables you to write an application that will manage the dump data. More information on backups and dumps can be found in Chapter 19, "Managing Data Availability."

There are two ways to add a dump device to the system: through Sybase SQL Server Manager, or by using the system-stored procedure sp_adddumpdevice. The following two sections show you how to use both methods.

Using Sybase SQL Server Manager to Add a Dump Device   Using Sybase SQL Server Manager to add a dump device removes the burden on the DBA to remember the syntax required for the system-stored procedures that must be executed to perform the task.

To add a dump device by using Sybase SQL Server Manager, follow these steps:

1. Launch Sybase SQL Server Manager. Connect to the server that you want to manage, and then open the folder in the left pane titled Dump Devices.

2. Choose Server, Create, and select Dump Device; this will cause the Sybase SQL Server Manager Create Dump Device dialog box to appear (see Fig. 5.9).

FIG. 5.9

The SSM Create Dump Device dialog box enables you to specify the name and location of a new dump device that you are adding to the Sybase server.

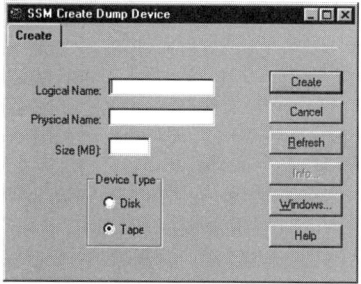

3. Give the dump device a logical name and then a physical name that represents the actual location of the device. If you are setting up a disk-based dump device, you must give a full file name. A tape-based dump device requires only a path to the mounted tape volume.

4. If you chose a tape device, enter the maximum data storage capacity of the tape drive in the Size field that is enabled for you.

5. Click the Create button to have Sybase create the dump device.

Using sp_addumpdevice   Sybase's system-stored procedure sp_addumpdevice is used to add dump devices to the system. The syntax for sp_addumpdevice is as follows:

```
sp_addumpdevice {'disk' | 'tape'},
Logical_Name,
Physical_Name,
TapeSize
```

The options for the system-stored procedure sp_addumpdevice are as follows:

- *Logical_Name*—This is the logical name of the device that's going to be used for backups/dumps.

- *Physical_Name*—This is the physical name of the device that's going to be used for the dump. For a 'disk' dump device, specify the full path of the output file that should be created. For a 'tape' device on Windows NT, reference the locally attached tape device by using Windows NT's Universal Naming Convention (UNC)—for example, "\\.\tape0".

- *TapeSize*—Specify the size of the tape device's capacity in megabytes. It is recommended that you specify a size that is slightly less than the maximum storage capacity of the tape unit so that Sybase has room for its own internal headers. This parameter does not need to be included for disk-based dump devices.

The following example adds a disk-based dump device to Sybase:

```
sp_addumpdevice 'disk',
'DiskBackup',
'D:\Sybase\system11\Data\DISKBACKUP.BKP'
```

Part
II

Ch
5

The following example adds a remote disk-based dump device on the network based Windows NT server *MainFileServer*:

```
sp_addumpdevice 'disk',
'NetworkBackup',
'\\MainFileServer\Data\NETBACKUP.BKP'
```

The following example adds a tape dump device to Sybase on Windows NT:

```
sp_addumpdevice 'tape',
'TapeBackup',
'\\.\Tape0',
625
```

Dropping Devices

System XI provides two ways to drop a device: by using Sybase SQL Server Manager or by using the system-stored procedure sp_dropdevice. Dropping a device completely deallocates the disk space associated with the device and frees the space up for other uses by the operating system or server.

If a device is not in use anymore or is not correctly sized, it may be necessary to drop it so that it can be appropriately resized or so the disk space can be given back to the operating system for other uses. Use the methods described in this section to drop the device.

Using Sybase SQL Server Manager to Remove Devices   Sybase SQL Server Manager provides a simple interface to the removal of database devices and is a convenient tool for managing large enterprises where lots of servers are involved. The DBA no longer has to know all the physical layouts of the server's devices because they are represented graphically by Sybase SQL Server Manager.

> **CAUTION**
>
> For some reason, the drop device feature of Sybase SQL Server Manager defaults to not removing the device file physically from the hard drive, nor does it give you an option to tell it to do so. Consequently, using Sybase SQL Server Manager to remove a disk device won't actually make any disk space available for use on the server. You must go to a command prompt or to File Manager and manually delete the file.
>
> If you're deleting a device to free up some allocated disk space on the server, you're probably better off using sp_dropdevice and specifying DelFile.

To use Sybase SQL Server Manager to remove a database device, follow these steps:

1. In the Sybase SQL Server Manager screen, select the server from which you want to remove the device, connect to it, and then select the Devices folder from the left pane.

2. Click the device that you want to remove.

3. Choose Database-Device, Delete and answer Yes to the message asking you if want to delete the device (see Fig. 5.10).

FIG. 5.10

This is your last chance to avoid deleting or removing a device. If you are unsure whether you really want it removed, click No.

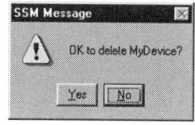

If you try to delete a device that is in use by a database, Sybase will stop you and give you a warning (see Fig. 5.11) so that you cannot accidentally delete a device that has a database on it.

FIG. 5.11

Sybase alerts you to the fact that you can't delete a device that is in use by a database. Drop the database or databases before trying to drop the device.

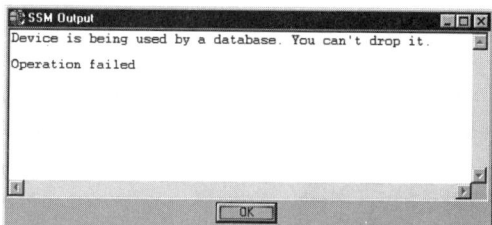

Using sp_dropdevice   The system-stored procedure `sp_dropdevice` is provided for dropping devices from Sybase. The syntax for `sp_dropdevice` is

```
sp_dropdevice logical_name[, DelFile]
```

The options for the system-stored procedure `sp_dropdevice` are as follows:

- *logical_name*—This is the name of the device to be removed.

- *DelFile*—If `DelFile` is included, the physical file that was created on the server will also be removed.

An error will occur if this procedure is run against a device that has databases in it. The databases must be dropped before the device can be deleted.

Part

II

Ch

5

Working with Databases and Transaction Logs

Databases are logical entities in which Sybase places tables and indexes. A database exists on one or many database devices; correspondingly, a database device can have one or many databases on it.

Every database has a transaction log that belongs or is associated with it. The transaction log is a place that Sybase writes all the database transactions to before writing them to the database. The transaction log is used to hold "open" transactions (transactions started with a `Begin Tran` statement) until they're "closed" (`Committed` or Rolled Back). By default, the transaction log is placed on the same database device as the database; however, better performance can be achieved by creating two devices—one for the log and one for the database itself.

Sybase can logically maintain up to 32,767 databases on a single server. However, it's more likely that the server will run out of disk, memory, and CPU resources before this limit is ever reached. A database can be up to 1T (terabyte) in size and can have as many as 32 device *fragments* (that is, placements on database devices).

Given that a physical disk will unlikely be greater than 10G (gigabytes) in size, it would seem to be impossible to get a database much bigger than 320G with System XI (which would suggest that Sybase should increase the number of device fragments permitted). However, a database device actually can be mapped to multiple physical devices, provided some form of software- or hardware-based striping is in use.

Striping involves splitting up a single logical device into several portions that span several physical devices. The intent of striping is to present to the operating system a single "file" despite the fact that it is actually (physically) several files on several physical devices. Striping is highly recommended because it provides substantial performance gains due to multiple physical disk drives being used for a single database device. When used with RAID, striping also provides an extra level of data integrity in case of a media failure. See Appendix E, "Redundant Array of Inexpensive Disks (RAID)," for more information.

Understanding the Special System Databases

When Sybase is installed, several special databases are created for use by the server. These are what is known as system databases. These system databases are used by the server under various circumstances as described below:

- *master*—The *master* database is the custodian of all the server-wide configuration parameters used by the System XI server. In the *master* database are all the system catalog tables that contain information describing the things that are referenced at a server level, such as devices, databases, and logons.

- *model*—The *model* database is the database that is copied when a new database is created with Create Database. In the *model* database are all the basic tables that will be added (along with their associated indexes and data) to the newly created database. If you want to have a particular table in every one of your new databases, add it to the model database. By adding elements to the *model* database, you are increasing the minimum size for all databases on the server from that point forward. Take care not to arbitrarily add every table to the *model* database.

- *sybsystemprocs*—The *sybsystemprocs* database is where Sybase stores all the text and code that underlies all the system-stored procedures that start with sp_. By adding a stored procedure to the *sybsystemprocs* database, it becomes globally accessible from all the other databases on the server without the need to qualify the procedure with a database name.

- *tempdb*—The *tempdb* database is where Sybase performs all temporary calculations and data sorting prior to returning results to a client. In addition, you can place tables in there for super fast performance due to the fact that *tempdb* operations are not logged.

Creating Databases and Transaction Logs

The process of creating a database causes Sybase to copy the *model* database to the new database name. This process copies all the items in the model database's catalog. If you want to have custom default tables and objects in every database created on a server, add them to the model just like you would add them to any database.

You can take two approaches to create a database and transaction log: You can use either Sybase SQL Server Manager or the Create Database command.

Using Sybase SQL Server Manager to Create Databases and Transaction Logs   To create a database using Sybase SQL Server Manager, follow these steps:

1. Launch Sybase SQL Server Manager and connect to the server on which you are going to create the database.
2. Choose Server, Create, and select Database to display the Sybase SQL Server Manager Create Database dialog box, as shown in Figure 5.12.

FIG. 5.12

The SSM Create Database dialog box gives you all the options necessary to create a database without needing to resort to Transact-SQL.

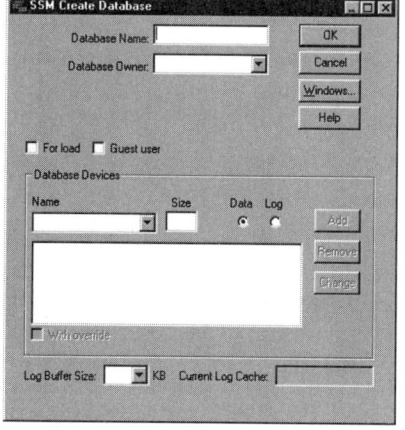

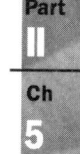

Part

II

Ch

5

3. Enter a name for the database.
4. Select an owner of the database. (Typically set this to the System Administrator, sa)
5. Indicate whether you want the database created For Load or not. A database created with the For Load option cannot be accessed by a user until a restore has been completed from either tape or disk.
6. Indicate whether you want to allow a guest user to have access to this database. Unless you have a specific reason for adding this user, I recommend against it. This is a basic security problem that is covered in more depth in Chapter 21, "Managing and Monitoring Security."
7. Select the data device on which you want the first fragment of the database created, and enter the size of the database fragment on that device (make sure that you have selected

the Data radio button). Press the Add button to add the device fragment to the fragment list. If you need to use additional devices for more fragments of the database, enter them now.

8. Select the Log radio button and allocate space on a device for the transaction logs to be placed on. Note that if you are going to use the same device as the database, you must check the With Override check box to force Sybase to place the database and logs on the same device.

9. Select the required Log Buffer Size in kilobytes. By default, this will be 2K until you resize the Log Buffer.

10. Click the OK button to create the database.

Using Create Database to Create Databases and Transaction Logs The Create Database command is the Transact-SQL method to creating a database. The syntax for Create Database is as follows:

```
Create Database Database_Name
      [On {Default | Database_Device} [= size]
      [, Database_Device [= size]]...]
      [Log On Log_Device [= size]
      [,Log_Device[= size]]...]
      [With Override]
      [For Load]
```

The options for the Transact-SQL command Create Database are as follows:

- *database_name*—This is the name of the database to be created. The database name must comply with the standard rules for naming objects.

- *database_device*—This is the device or list of devices that this database is to be created on and how much disk space, in megabytes, is to be reserved on each. If Default is specified, Sybase will choose the next free default database device to use.

- *log_device*—The Log On parameter is where the log device is specified. Like the database device, it's possible to specify more than one device to be used for the logging of the database being created.

- With Override—This option is required when you create the database and transaction log on the same device.

- *For Load*—This parameter disallows user access until a Load or restore operation has been completed on the database.

The following example creates a 3M database called *MyDatabase* on *MyDevice* with a 2M log on the same device. Note that you have to use the With Override because the database and logs are on the same device.

```
Create Database MyDatabase
      On MyDevice = 3
      Log On MyDevice = 2
```

```
        With Override
        For Load
    Go
```

Viewing Information on Databases and Logs

By opening the Databases folder on the required server, in Sybase SQL Server Manager you can see a high-level list of the details of the databases on the server. Figure 5.13 shows the Sybase SQL Server Manager's database list in the Details view mode.

FIG. 5.13

The list view of databases on the server SYB11_NT shows all the basic details, including owner, size, and free space.

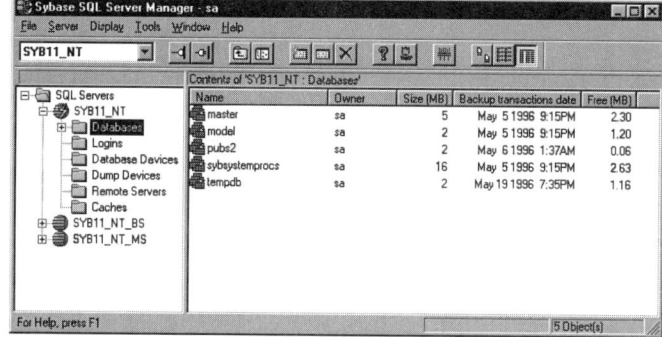

To view this information in Transact-SQL, use the system-stored procedure `sp_helpdb`. The syntax for `sp_helpdb` is

```
sp_helpdb Database_Name
```

If a `Database_Name` is supplied, `sp_helpdb` reports information about that database; otherwise, it reports information about all the databases on the server.

The following example shows the use of `sp_helpdb` for all the databases on the server. The information provided shows only the total size of the database and any options in effect:

```
sp_helpdb
Go

name            db_size  owner dbid created      status
-------------------------------------------------------------------
master          5.0 MB sa    1    Jan 01, 1900 no options set
model           2.0 MB sa    3    Jan 01, 1900 no options set
pubs2           2.0 MB sa    5    May 06, 1996 select into/bulkcopy
sybsystemprocs 16.0 MB sa    4    May 05, 1996 trunc log on chkpt
tempdb          2.0 MB sa    2    May 19, 1996 select into/bulkcopy
```

In the following example, a database is supplied, and more detailed information, including device fragment information, is returned from Sybase. Make sure that you do a `use database_name` prior to running the `sp_helpdb` system stored procedure, so that you get the device fragment information:

```
Use pubs2
Go
```

Part
II

Ch
5

```
sp_helpdb pubs2
Go

name            db_size owner dbid created      status
------------------------------------------------------------------
pubs2           2.0 MB sa    5    May 06, 1996 select into/bulkcopy

device_fragments   size    usage            free kbytes
------------------  ------- ---------------- ----------
master             2.0 MB   data and log        64

device             segment
------------------------------------------------
master             default
master             logsegment
master             system
```

TIP The segment information is displayed only if you're executing `sp_helpdb` from the database that you're inspecting.

Increasing the Size of the Database and Transaction Log

Sybase enables the size of a database to be resized in case its space is consumed by user data. In the same way, transaction logs can be increased in size if they get full too quickly and require excessive dumping.

Using Sybase SQL Server Manager to Extend a Database To increase the size of a database or transaction log by using Sybase SQL Server Manager, follow these steps:

1. Run Sybase SQL Server Manager, connect to the required server, and click the database that you want to manage.

2. Choose Database, Properties, which displays the Sybase SQL Server Manager Database Properties dialog box for the selected database (see Fig. 5.14).

FIG. 5.14
Using the SSM Database Properties dialog box, you can extend a database. Notice the highlighted 1M extension to the *pubs2* database here.

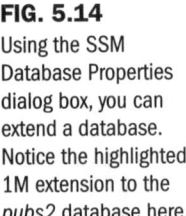
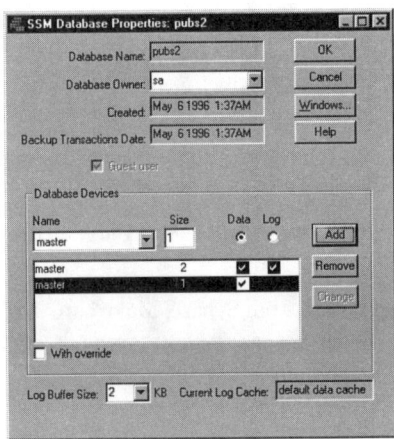

3. Select the device that you want to extend the database into and indicate the amount of space you want to grab from the device.

4. Press the Add button to finalize the additional device fragment.

   Repeat Steps 3 and 4 for as many new device extensions that you require.

5. Press the OK button to get Sybase to extend the database or transaction log on to the specified additional devices.

Using Alter Database to Extend a Database   Transact-SQL provides the `Alter Database` command to enable a database to be extended. Transaction logs are also extended by using the `Alter Database` command; however, after the database is extended, the system-stored procedure `sp_logdevice` is used to specify that the extension to the database is actually for transaction log use.

The syntax for `Alter Database` is as follows:

```
Alter Database Database_Name
    [On {Default | Database_Device} [= size]
    [, Database_Device [= size]]...]
    [With Override]
    [For Load]
```

The options for the Transact-SQL command `Alter Database` are as follows:

- *Database_Name*—This is the name of the database that's being extended.

- *Database_Device*—This is one or more database devices and the size (in megabytes) to be allocated to the database.

- `On Default`—If Default is specified, Sybase will allocate the requested space to the first free database device or devices that have enough space to meet the request.

- `With Override`—This option is required when you create the database and transaction log on the same device.

- `For Load`—This parameter disallows user access until a `Load` or restore operation has been completed on the database.

In the following example, *MyDatabase* is extended by 5M on the *MyDevice* database device:

```
Alter Database MyDatabase
    On MyDevice = 5
Go
```

In the following example, *MyDatabase* is extended by a further 5M, and the logs are placed on the extended portion:

```
Alter Database MyDatabase
    On MyDevice = 5
Go
sp_logdevice MyDatabase, MyDevice
Go
```

Part

II

Ch

5

N O T E   Note that in the last example, the system-stored procedure sp_logdevice was used to move the logs onto the extended database fragment. This is because the Alter Database command has no provision for a Log On clause like the Create Database command. ■

Dropping a Database

Dropping a database frees up any space that it consumed on any database devices, and removes any objects that it contained. Dropping a database isn't reversible, so be careful; a restore will be required to recover the database.

N O T E   Remember the difference between dropping a database and dumping one. Dropping a database drops all the tables and indexes and removes the logical area on the database device reserved for the database. Dumping a database creates a backup of the database's data on a disk or tape. ■

User accounts that have their default database as the database that's being dropped will have their default database changed to *master*. Only the System Administrator (sa) or the database owner (dbo) can drop a database. The master, model, and tempdb databases can't be dropped by any user account. Also, any databases that are participating in replication or have active users can't be dropped until the replication is suspended or until the users have disconnected from the database.

Using Sybase SQL Server Manager to Drop a Database   To use Sybase SQL Server Manager to drop a database, follow these steps:

1. Run Sybase SQL Server Manager, connect to the server, and select the database you want to drop.
2. Choose Database, Delete. This displays a warning (see Fig. 5.15).

FIG. 5.15
By answering Yes to this message, you will delete a database. Make sure that you really intended to delete this database before continuing.

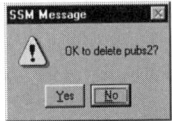

3. Answer Yes to delete the database.

Using Drop Database to Drop a Database   The syntax for the Drop Database command in Transact-SQL is as follows:

```
Drop Database Database_Name, [Database_Name]
```

Database_Name is the name of the database or databases that need to be dropped.

Databases in all "states" (including Active, Damaged, Suspect, Offline, or Not recovered) can be dropped by using the `Drop Database` command. A database that's still in Recovery status must be dropped by using the system-stored procedure `sp_dbremove`.

Understanding Database Space Management and Segments

Segments are logical groups of disk devices (or portions of devices) on which database objects are placed. Database segments are created in a database, which, in turn, can be placed on a particular database disk device. The advantage of segments is that individual objects, such as tables and indexes, can then be explicitly placed in a segment, allowing for greater performance.

Typically, two segments would be created for a database that spans two disk devices. These segments would then be used in such a way that all the tables with non-clustered indexes would be created on one segment and the non-clustered indexes would be created on the other segment. *Non-clustered indexes* are indexes that are binary search trees of the data. This has a tremendous performance advantage because the reading and writing of the data and index pages can execute concurrently on two physical devices rather than run serially.

▶ **See** "Creating Indexes," **p. 206**

Segments are also good for allowing the text and image data associated with a database table to be stored on a separate physical device, and for splitting large tables across separate physical devices.

 T I P Better performance and far easier management is provided by splitting the database devices themselves across multiple disks at the operating system or hardware level by the use of RAID, rather than by using segments.

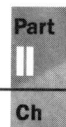
Part
II

Ch
5

Using Default Segments

When a new database is created, three default segments are created for it. The System segment houses all the system tables and their indexes. The Logsegment stores the transaction log for the database. The Default segment stores any user-created objects, unless they're explicitly moved or placed on a different segment.

Creating Segments

You add segments by using the system-stored procedure `sp_addsegment` or by using Sybase SQL Server Manager. It is often convenient to use Sybase SQL Server Manager to work with segments because you can easily visualize which objects are contained on the segment and what the relationships between segments and objects are.

Using Sybase SQL Server Manager to Create a Segment   To use Sybase SQL Server Manager to create a segment, follow these steps:

1. Run Sybase SQL Server Manager, connect to the server, and select the database that you want to create a segment in.

2. Select the Segments folder in the left pane to get a list of the currently created segments (see Fig. 5.16).

FIG. 5.16

The list of segments in the right pane of SSM shows you what has been created and how much free space is available in each of the segments.

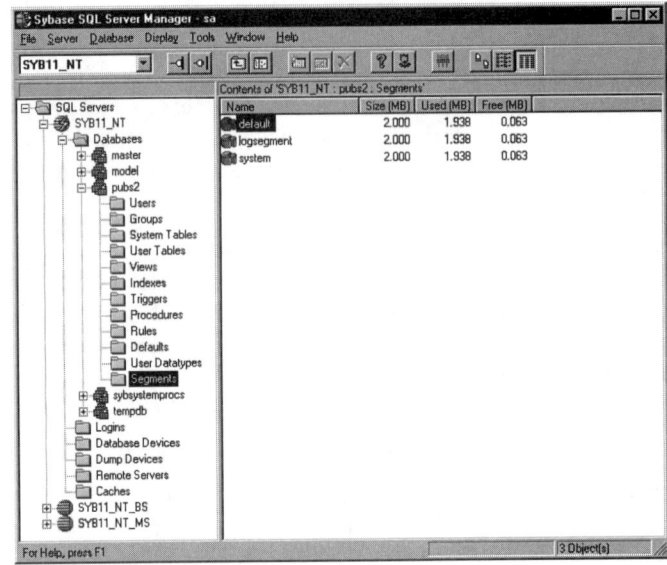

3. Choose Database, Create, and select Segment to display the Sybase SQL Server Manager Create Segment dialog box (see Fig. 5.17).

FIG. 5.17

The SSM Create Segment dialog box enables you to create a segment on any of the database devices on which the active database has been placed.

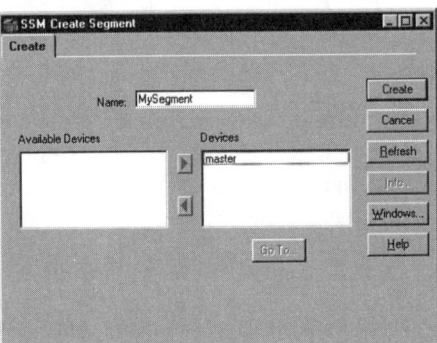

4. Enter the name of the segment and select the device on which you want it to be placed.

5. Click the Create button to create the segment. Doing so will enable two additional tabs on the dialog box that will enable you to inspect extra information about the use of the segment.

To view the information or objects that are stored on a particular segment, use the Sybase SQL Server Manager Segment dialog box and click the Contains tab (see Fig. 5.18).

FIG. 5.18

The Contains tab lists all of the tables and indexes that are placed on a given segment. In this example of the *pubs2* database's Default segment, you can see quite a lot of different objects on the segment.

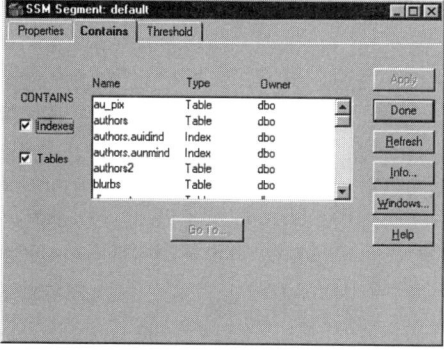

Using sp_addsegment to Create a Segment

The syntax for sp_addsegment is as follows:

```
sp_addsegment Segment_Name, Database_Device
```

The options for the system-stored procedure sp_addsegment are as follows:

- *segment_name*—The name of the segment that's being added.
- *database_device*—The name of the database device that this segment should be placed on.

The following example creates a segment on the database device MyDevice:

```
sp_addsegment seg_MyDevice1, MyDevice
Go
```

TIP

If you want to extend the DEFAULT segment, you must enclose default in quotation marks because default is a reserved word. For example:

```
sp_extendsegment 'default', NewDevice
Go
```

Using Segments

After segments are created on a database, you can place an object on those segments in two ways. Both Create Table and Create Index have an On Segment option that enables a table or index to be created on a particular segment.

▶ **See** "Creating and Managing Tables," **p. 144**

Sybase also provides a system-stored procedure, sp_placeobject, that directs the server to place any new data for a table onto a new segment. You would need to use this for tables that you want to partially load on one segment and then switch over to another segment. Executing sp_placeobject doesn't move any previously existing data allocations to the new segment; all it does is cause any future allocations to occur on the requested new segment.

Part
II

Ch
5

The syntax for `sp_placeobject` is as follows:

```
sp_placeobject Segment_Name, Object_Name
```

The options for the system-stored procedure `sp_placeobject` are as follows:

- *segment_name*—This is the name of the segment that the object should be placed on.
- *object_name*—This is the object that's to be moved. The object can be a fully qualified table column if the column's data type is `Image` or `Text`. Because Sybase doesn't store `Image` or `Text` data in the same data pages as the rest of the table data, these column types can be placed on their own segment. This provides substantially better performance. Image or Text data should be placed with `sp_placeobject` before table population to ensure that all rows' data is stored in the correct segments.

The following example makes all further data allocations for the table authors on the new segment seg_data2:

```
sp_placeobject seg_data2, authors
Go
```

The following example moves the logo column from the *pub_info* table to a new segment for image data:

```
sp_placeobject seg_ImageData, 'pub_info.logo'
Go
```

Viewing Information on Segments

You have already seen how to get information on segments using Sybase SQL Server Manager. To find out information about segments using Transact-SQL, you need to use the system stored procedure `sp_helpsegment`. The syntax for `sp_helpsegment` is as follows:

```
sp_helpsegment [Segment_Name]
```

If you don't supply a `Segment_Name`, you get a list of all the segments in the database that you are currently using. In the following example, you can see a list of all the segments in the *pubs2* database:

```
sp_helpsegment
Go

segment name                                status
------ ------------------------------ ------
0      system                               0
1      default                              1
2      logsegment                           0
3      MySegment                            0
```

 The Status column returned from `sp_helpsegment` indicates whether a particular segment is defined as a "Default" segment or not. A "Default" segment is where an object will be placed if you don't specify the particular segment using the On keyword in a Create statement.

By specifying the segment that you want to inquire on, you can get more details about the contents of the segment. For example, to list the objects in the default segment, you would execute:

```
sp_helpsegment 'default'
Go
```

```
segment name                                 status
------ -----------------------------  ------
1       default                              1

device                          size                    free_pages
----------------------------  ----------------------  ----------
master                          2.0MB                   32

table_name                      index_name              indid
----------------------------  ----------------------------  ----
au_pix                          au_pix                  0
au_pix                          tau_pix                 255
authors                         auidind                 1
authors                         aunmind                 2
...
titles                          titleidind              1
titles                          titleind                2
```

 T I P Make sure that you enclose any segment names that are Sybase-reserved words (such as `default`) in quotation marks so that Sybase knows that you want to use it as a name instead of as the reserved word.

▶ **See** "Understanding Names You Can't Use," **p. 710**

Dropping Segments

 Part
II

Ch
5

Dropping segments removes them from the database devices that they reside on. A segment can't be dropped if it contains any database objects; those objects need to be dropped first. A segment can be removed using either Sybase SQL Server Manager or Transact-SQL. Refer to the section above titled "Dropping a Database" for instructions on how to drop a database.

▶ **See** "Creating and Managing Tables," **p. 144**

▶ **See** "Removing Indexes," **p. 220**

Using Sybase SQL Server Manager to Drop a Segment   To drop a segment in Sybase SQL Server Manager, follow these steps:

1. Launch Sybase SQL Server Manager and connect to the server that has the database you want to work with.

2. Select the database you want to work with and go to the Segments folder.

3. In the right pane, select the segment that you want to remove and choose Segment, Delete.

4. Answer Yes to the question about whether you want to delete the segment, and it will be removed.

Using sp_dropsegment to Remove a Segment   Segments are dropped by executing the system-stored procedure `sp_dropsegment`. The syntax for `sp_dropsegment` is as follows:

```
sp_dropsegment segment_name[, device_name]
```

- *segment_name*—This is the name of the segment that's to be dropped.

- *device_name*—This is the database device from which the segment should be removed. If no database device is specified, the segment is dropped from all the devices that it spans. If, however, a database device name *is* specified, the segment is removed only from that device.

Understanding Tempdb

Tempdb is a special database that's used by Sybase to handle any "dynamic" SQL requests from users. *Tempdb* is a workspace for Sybase to use when it needs a temporary place for calculations, aggregations, and sorting operations. *Tempdb* is used for:

- Creating temporary tables for sorting data;

- Holding temporary tables created by users and stored procedures;

- Storing the data that matches any server cursors that are opened by a user process.

One key advantage to using *Tempdb* is that its activity isn't logged. This means that any DML activity done on `Tempdb` temporary tables are much faster than normal disk devices. This is a double-edged sword, however, because if Sybase is brought down at any time, all the information in *Tempdb* is lost. Take care not to rely on *Tempdb* without having application code that can restart itself in the event of a server shutdown.

Adjusting the Size of Tempdb

The default size of *Tempdb* when Sybase is installed is 2M. For most production environments, this size will be insufficient for *Tempdb*. If the environment is highly active with large queries or lots of requests for queries, I recommend that *Tempdb* be extended.

Tempdb is created in the master device by default and can be expanded in that device, or it can be moved so that it spans multiple database devices. To increase the size of *Tempdb*, follow the same steps for resizing any other database as outlined in the section "Increasing the Size of the Database and Transaction Log."

Improving the Performance of Tempdb

There are a number of steps that can be taken to improve the performance of systems that are reliant on *Tempdb*. The primary methods that should be used are the following:

- Ensuring that *Tempdb* is large enough to handle the most complex user requests. If *Tempdb* runs out of space, it will abort the transaction and rollback any pending activity.

- Ensuring that *Tempdb* is placed in an appropriate disk volume such that it will get parallel writes while being accessed (independently of the other databases).

- Using a private data cache for *Tempdb* to improve performance through larger I/O block writes and also through guaranteed memory allocation.

Sizing Tempdb   In order to get optimal performance from *Tempdb*, it is important that you create it to be large enough to satisfy all your user requests. To help in the estimating of the required size of *Tempdb* it is good to consider the following elements:

- Estimate the number of pages consumed by the average user query and multiply this by the number of users that you expect. Use the set statistics I/O option to get accurate statistics of how many data pages are consumed by a query.
- Estimate the number of stored procedures that you think are in use at any one time, and multiply this by the number of pages that you think will be required for resolving data that needs to be sent to the client.
- Add a 20–25 percent fudge factor to your calculations to help with miscalculation.

Placing Tempdb   It is critical that you place *Tempdb* on the fastest disks that you have. *Tempdb* is accessed constantly by just about every process on the server and its performance alone can make huge differences to the overall performance of the server. After you are comfortable that *Tempdb* is large enough for your normal operations, you should set about providing the best location for *Tempdb* to live in.

Your best (and most pricey) option is to purchase *solid state disks* or *silicon disks*. These are physical devices that can be added to most operating systems and look like regular magnetic drives to the OS. However, they are actually RAM chips placed together for super fast performance. Placing *Tempdb* on a silicon disk will give you at least an order of magnitude greater performance simply due to the fact that writing to and reading from RAM is about 10 times quicker than the same operations on magnetic storage devices.

If money is an important criterion in your performance analysis, here are a few tips that might help out without breaking the bank:

- Make sure that *Tempdb* is on its own physical device separated from all other databases on the server.
- Make sure that the *Tempdb* database device is not mirrored. Even the fastest mirroring incurs a slight performance cost. Mirroring *Tempdb* serves no purpose because the data in the database is transient anyway, and Sybase will re-create the *Tempdb* database each and every time the server is restarted.
- Do not allow *Tempdb* to span multiple physical disks. Disk spanning causes performance problems when reading and writing temporary tables. It is better to allocate contiguous disk space for *Tempdb* to live in.
- Experiment with using different file systems for storing the *Tempdb* database's device. On most UNIX systems, the recommended option is to use raw disk partitions for Sybase with asynchronous I/O. However, it has been shown that using regular UNIX file system partitions can improve performance with *Tempdb*. HP is actually recommending to some customers to use their new Journaling File System (JFS) for databases.

Part
II

Ch
5

Using a Private Cache   In System XI, you have the option of partitioning the global user memory cache in such a way that you can explicitly place objects and/or databases in pieces of memory without other objects affecting the cache. This is what is known as a Named or Private Cache. By using a Private Cache, you are helping to keep cached data pages used by *Tempdb* in memory without having them fall out of the cache due to other operations. You also improve general memory performance because the I/O is written to multiple memory caches with multiple threads instead of to a singularly managed cache.

For more information on how to bind *Tempdb* to its own cache, see Chapter 22, "Managing and Monitoring Performance."

From Here...

In this chapter, you learned all about devices, databases, and segments. This chapter provided you with information on how to create all the fundamentals for your server. To further develop your Sybase and application programming knowledge, look at the following chapters:

- Chapter 6, "Understanding Tables and Datatypes," shows how you can create tables in the databases and segments created in this chapter.
- Chapter 8, "Understanding Indexes and Keys," explains how to place the new indexes you create on the new index segments that you created in this chapter.
- Chapter 19, "Managing Data Availability," tells you how to use the dump devices for backups and restores.
- Chapter 23, "Using Sybase's Configuration Options," explains how to further configure Sybase and your databases for better performance.

Understanding Tables and Datatypes

Data-processing systems involve the storage, processing, and retrieval of information. You must define where data will be stored before it can be processed and retrieved. All units of information, from characters to the logical definition of the entire database, can be defined through SQL Server components.

In this chapter, you learn all about data structures called tables and how these tables can be used to store and organize your data. Tables are the basic element or object in all relational databases and are something that you will become very familiar with quickly as you work through this chapter and the rest of the book. ▪

Create and manage tables on your databases

In this chapter, you learn all the steps you need to take to create a table to store and organize the data you are managing.

Using and understanding datatypes

There are many different datatypes available for use in Sybase. Knowing the correct datatype for the storage of data will be paramount to optimizing the data storage of your database.

Partitioning tables

Using table partitioning can have a big impact on the performance of your application system, especially for large databases. This chapter introduces the partitioned tables to you and helps you work with them on your data.

Creating and Managing Tables

Data in a relational database, such as Sybase System XI, is stored in tables that are two-dimensional arrays. The columns and rows of a table are already familiar to database users and are effectively the same as the common spreadsheet that you may have used, such as Microsoft Excel. Tables were chosen as the logical structure for storing data because of their familiarity to users and ease of use for retrieving, displaying, and manipulating data.

In System XI, you can either create a table using the Transact-SQL command Create Table or you can use Sybase SQL Server Manager to guide you through the process. Most people will use Transact-SQL to create tables because it offers a convenient and reusable (via a script) way of doing table definition; however, using Sybase SQL Server Manager is a viable option if you are a little lacking in confidence with the Transact-SQL syntax.

Using Sybase SQL Server Manager to Create a Table

To make use of Sybase SQL Server Manager to create a table, follow these steps:

1. Launch Sybase SQL Server Manager and log on to the data server that you want to work with.

2. Select the Database in the left pane and open the User Tables folder in the explorer (see Fig. 6.1).

FIG. 6.1
The explorer in SSM makes it easy for you to navigate to the database object that you want to work with. Here, you can see a detail view of all the user tables in the *pubs2* database.

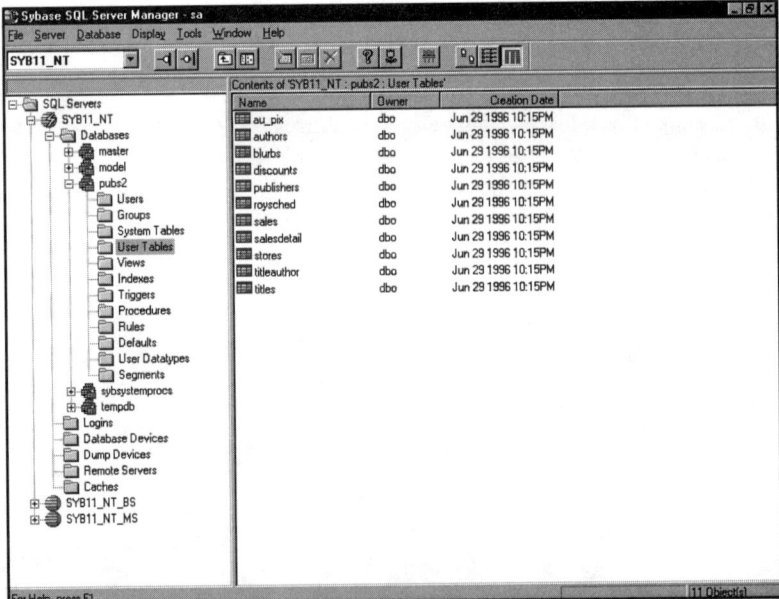

3. Choose Database, Create, and select Table to display the Sybase SQL Server Manager Create Table dialog box (see Fig. 6.2).

FIG. 6.2

The SSM Create Table dialog box makes it easy to access the advanced functionality offered in System XI's Create Table statement. A particularly nice feature is that the Cache Strategy can easily be picked via check boxes at the bottom of the dialog box.

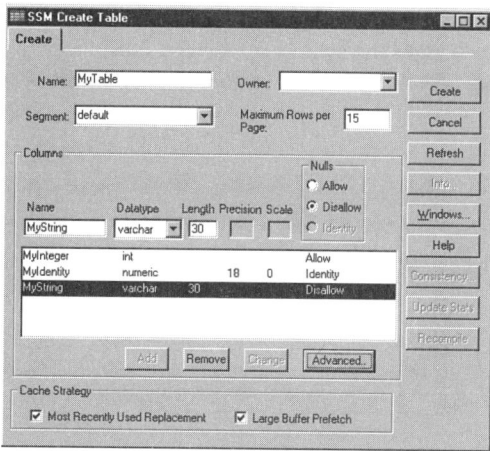

4. Give the table a name by entering it in the Name field.

5. If you want to place the table on a particular database segment, select it from the Segment combo box, or just leave it blank to have the table created on the default segment for the database.

6. Next you need to name the columns that you want to add, select a datatype, and click the Add button.

7. To specify advanced properties for the table column, click the Advanced button to display the Column dialog box (see Fig. 6.3).

FIG. 6.3

The Column Properties dialog box of SSM makes it easy to bind defaults and rules and add Check Constraints to a table's column. Add any of the options that you want, and click OK.

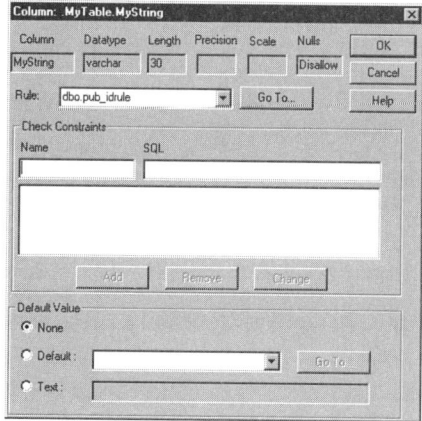

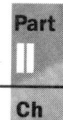

Part

II

Ch

6

8. After you are happy with all the columns (and their properties) that you are going to add to the table, choose the cache strategy that you want to use.

9. Click the Create button to actually create the table. After creating the table, Sybase SQL Server Manager changes the style of the Create Table dialog box shown in Figure 6.2 to include additional tabs that provide you access to all the other properties of the table (see Fig. 6.4).

FIG. 6.4

The new SSM Table dialog box gives you access to many different properties of a table. Click any of the tabs at the top of the dialog box to change the property being displayed.

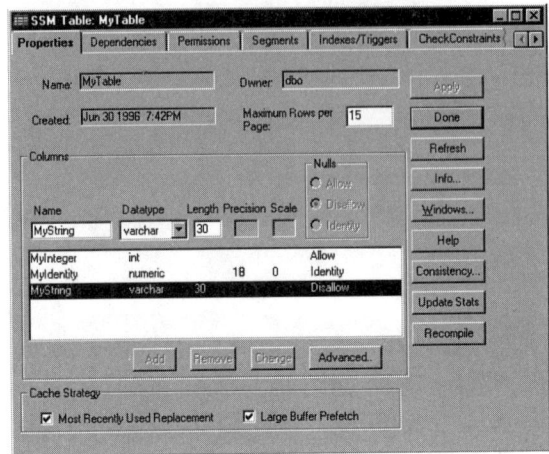

Using Transact-SQL to Create a Table

You can create Sybase System XI database tables with the Create Table Transact-SQL statement. Theoretically, you can create up to 2 billion tables in each database; in reality, anything over a few thousand tables makes for a pretty unusable database. The major part of the creation of a table is the definition of the datatypes for columns. The syntax for Create Table is as follows:

```
Create Table Table_Name
(Column_Name Datatype [Not Null | Null] Identity [Constraint]
[, Column_Name Datatype [Not Null | Null] Identity [Constraint] ...)
[Table Based Referential Integrity, e.g. Primary and Foreign Keys]
[With Max_Rows_Per_Page = X]
[On Segment_Name]
```

The options or values for the Transact-SQL command Create Table are as follows:

- *Table_Name*—Any valid SQL identifier can be used for the name of the object, up to 30 characters in length.

- *Column_Name*—The name of one or many columns should be entered here. Standard naming rules apply for all database objects, and the names for the columns must be unique on the table.

    ▶ **See** "Understanding Names You Can't Use," **p. 710**

- *Datatype*—Any system or user-defined datatype can be used to define the characteristics of the column that you are adding.

■ Not Null | Null—A nullable column enables you to omit specifying a value for it when inserting or updating the data in a row. A column defined Not Null must have a value in it at all times.

■ Identity—Identity columns have a special property in that the server assigns numeric values to them for you and they are guaranteed to be unique. More information can be found below in the section titled "Using the Identity Datatype."

■ Constraint—Column level constraints include rules and hand code constraints. For a complete discussion of how to work with constraints on columns, see Chapter 7, "Using Rules, Defaults, and Triggers."

■ Table Based RI—This section of the Create Table statement is designed to enable you to place referential integrity constraints that apply at the relationship level between tables. This kind of RI is also known as primary key and foreign key relationship and is discussed in great detail in Chapter 8, "Understanding Indexes and Keys."

 ■ With Max_Rows_Per_Page = X—This is a new feature of System XI, and it enables you to explicitly limit the number of records that will be placed on a particular page in the table. With this feature, you no longer have to fumble around with allocating free space on clustered indexes and such to force a single row per page (and implicitly create a row-level-locking database table).

■ On Segment_Name—Use this option to move the table's data to live or reside on another data segment other than the database's default segment. The typical use of this feature is not for tables, but to use the On Segment_Name parameter of a Create Index statement to move the non-clustered indexes onto a separate segment from the data—yielding substantial performance benefits.

Optionally, you can enter the database in which the table is created, as well as an owner of the table. You'll find it more convenient to define the current database in which you're working first with a Use Database_Name Transact-SQL command. After you define your current database with the USE command, all subsequent commands are performed within the database specified with the USE command.

 TIP When you create a logon account to the Sybase database server, you can specify a default database that the account will be connected to. Take advantage of this default database to make it easy and quick to logon to a database and get working.

Part
II

Ch
6

If you don't enter the name of the owner of an object (such as a table) when you create a table, you'll be its owner. Often, tables are created from the System Administrator's (sa) account, to restrict subsequent access to the tables.

The owner of the database in which the table is defined is automatically granted the Create Table permission, which enables the creation of tables. The database owner or sa can grant Create Table permission to other users so that they can create tables in the database. You don't have to grant permission to create temporary tables in a database.

By creating segments on different physical disks, you speed up access to table data because the underlying operating system and disk subsystems can perform a large part of the data transfer from two physical disks simultaneously. Each drive gets an individual I/O thread from the OS and therefore works in parallel. Sets of data located on a single physical disk must be accessed serially due to the fact that only a single I/O thread can physically read from the disk drive.

▶ **See** "Creating Segments," **p. 135**

Creating Temporary Tables

Creating a temporary table is a useful technique that you should know how to take advantage of. Temporary tables are created exactly the same way as real tables except that you prefix them with a pound sign (#) in the name. A temporary table is created in the *tempdb* database and has a great advantage in that operations performed on it aren't logged. This means that they are highly efficient for performance reasons. There are some caveats with temporary tables, however:

- A temporary table can be accessed only by the session in which it was created.
- A temporary table is automatically dropped when the session in which it was created ends.
- You can't use more than 13 characters, including the pound sign, to name a local temporary table because Sybase uses the remaining 17 characters available in the 30-character limit for the object name to add unique information that will guarantee that two users don't create the same named table twice at the same time.

Note that if you *do* use more than 13 characters for the name of a temporary table, Sybase will truncate the name and then apply the 17 digits to make the table name unique. Furthermore, if you don't have a long enough table name (i.e., it's shorter than 13 characters), Sybase will add underscore characters (_) to bring the length of the name up to 13 characters.

N O T E   Constraints can be defined for temporary tables, but foreign key constraints are not enforced. ■

You can use temporary tables to store sets of data that need to be operated on before permanently storing. For example, you can combine the results of the data from multiple data sets into a temporary table, and then access the combined data in the temporary table throughout your session. With this technique, temporary tables are often used for reporting systems that are trying to bring together very complex data sets that require more than the permitted 16 tables in a join.

Data that has already been combined in a temporary table can be accessed faster than data that must be dynamically accessed from multiple tables. A temporary table that combines the results of two tables is faster to access because Sybase doesn't need to reference the database tables to retrieve the information.

You might also find it convenient to use a temporary table to make a set of data available to a stored procedure that's invoked from another procedure. You'll find it easier to make data available to another procedure within a temporary table rather than pass data as a set of parameters. For more information on how to work with stored procedures effectively, see Chapter 10, "Understanding Stored Procedures."

N O T E One thing that's often overlooked by DBAs and programmers that use temporary tables to solve a problem of temporary data is that real tables can also be created in the *tempdb* database and then accessed by multiple users in different sessions. Operations that write to *tempdb* are optimized for performance due to the lack of database logging. ■

CAUTION

Using *tempdb* for anything valuable or data-dependent is very unwise. In its very name, you can see its nature—that of a temporary storage area. Sybase does not log or monitor any activity in *tempdb*, so if the server goes down, *tempdb* is not recoverable. *Tempdb* is rebuilt each time the server starts, and should be considered a transient entity to all applications that use it for performance reasons.

Choosing Datatypes for Your Data

The major part of defining a table is specifying the datatypes for the columns of the tables. Transact-SQL enables you to use several different datatypes, including those for the storage of characters, numbers, and bit patterns. You can also define your own datatypes for use in stored procedures, tables, and other work that you'll be doing with the database tables.

You must define at least one column for a table, and you can define up to 250 columns. You're also limited to a maximum row length of 1,962 bytes; this may seem less than the 2K (2,048 bytes) width of a data page, but the difference is due to header information that is stored in the database and is used to manage the allocation of the data on the table.

 T I P You can use image or text datatypes to get around the 1,962-byte limit for rows. Columns that are defined by using the image and text datatypes are stored outside the table and can store more than two billion bytes of data.

You should be careful to follow the rules for relational database design whenever feasible, however, to ensure the optimum response time and use of your SQL Server engine.

Tables are created by using a unit of measure called an *extent*. When you create a new table, the allocation of space for the table is initially set at one extent—which is eight pages, each of which is 2K in size. When the table fills the space in the already allocated extents, additional extents are automatically implemented up to the space allocated to the overall database size.

Part

II

Ch

6

You can use the system-stored procedure sp_spaceused to obtain a report on the space allocated to a table.

The *datatype* is the first characteristic you define for the column of a table. The datatype of a column controls the type of information that can be stored within the column. Define the datatype by following the column name with a keyword that may also require some parameters. After you define the datatype of a table column, it's stored as a permanent characteristic and can't be changed. To redefine a column's datatype, you would need to create a new table and then move the data from one table to the other using Transact-SQL's Insert statement that was populated by a Select.

You can also use datatypes to define other data-storage structures, such as parameters and local variables. Parameters and local variables are storage structures defined in RAM rather than on disk. You're limited to a subset of the datatypes for the definitions of parameters and variables.

▶ **See** "Using Parameters to Procedures," **p. 256**

The next sections of this chapter review each of the different system-defined datatypes that you can use in the definition of your SQL Server tables and stored procedures.

Understanding the Different String Datatypes

You'll frequently use character or string *datatypes* to define table columns or other storage structures. Character datatypes enable the storage of a wider variety of symbols than numeric datatypes. Character datatypes enable you to store letters, numeric symbols, and special characters, such as ? and >. You enter character data in either single or double quotation marks (' or ") when loading it into a storage area, such as the column of a table.

Understanding the Char Datatype   The Char datatype is the first type of character datatypes that you can use. When you store data in a Char datatype, each symbol or character stored uses one byte. The number in parentheses specifies the size of storage for all sets of characters. For example, if you define a table column as the datatype Char(15), each value of the column is 15 bytes in size and can store 15 characters. If you enter fewer than 15 characters, SQL Server adds blanks/spaces after the last specified character until the 15 characters are consumed. In this sense, Char columns are the same as fixed length columns in other systems. Sybase will always ensure that Char columns occupy the same amount of space throughout a table.

You can define a Char(n) datatype to contain up to a maximum of 255 characters. Remember, the column value always contains the specified number of characters. SQL Server automatically adds spaces to the end of a value to fill the defined length of space.

 If you are using either Centura's SQLWindows or Team Builder, you will want to define a Char or Varchar column with a maximum length of 254 characters. This limitation is imposed by both SQLWindows and Team Builder being processed through Centura's internal SQL/API, which has a limit of 254 characters for string datatypes.

N O T E An interesting effect is observed in Sybase if a column is defined char and allowed to be null. In this case, Sybase does not know what sort of data you are going to store in the column and thus cannot guarantee that each column will even have a value in it. Because of these limitations, Sybase will treat the column as a varchar and will not gain the benefits of a fixed-length datatype. ■

The primary advantage of a Char datatype is that it makes the space consumed by a table absolutely calculable with no inaccuracy. The capability to calculate the space used by a table can be very important, especially in very large systems where the difference of a few bytes can equate to megabytes of data savings.

Using the Varchar Datatype   You can use the Varchar datatype to store a variable-length string of up to 255 characters. Unlike the Char datatype, the storage space used varies according to the number of characters stored in each column value of rows of the table.

For example, if you define the table column as Varchar(15), a maximum of 15 characters can be stored in the corresponding column of each table row. However, spaces aren't added to the end of the column value until the size of each column is 15 bytes. You can use a Varchar to save space if the values stored in a column are variable in size. You can also specify a Varchar datatype using the keyword Char Varying.

Using Character Datatypes   In the following examples, a table is created with two columns defined as Char and Varchar datatypes. The inserted row stores only two characters in each column of the row. The first column is padded with three spaces so that it occupies five bytes of storage. The second column of the row isn't padded and occupies only two bytes of storage to store the two characters. The retrieval of the row in the example displays each column value identically, masking the underlying storage difference.

```
/* First create the table */
Create Table String_Example
(Char1 Char(5),
 Char2 Varchar(5))
Go

/* Now insert a record into the table */
Insert Into String_Example
Values( 'AB', 'CD' )
Go

/* Now select from the Table */
Select *
From   String_Example
Go

Char1 Char2
----- -----
AB    CD
```

In the following example, a row is inserted into the table that contains column values that are longer by one character than the maximum length of the datatypes of the table columns. The Select statement in the example shows that the column values of the inserted row were

Part II

Ch 6

truncated, or cut off, and contain only the first five characters of the column values. Note that you will not receive a message that the truncation occurs when a row is inserted.

```
Insert Into String_Example
Values( 'abcdef', 'abcdef' )
Go

Select *
From    String_Example

Char1 Char2
----- -----
AB    CD
abcde abcde
```

TROUBLESHOOTING

Every time that I enter the name of a long department into the department column of a table, the department name is cut off at the end. Why? When a table column is defined using the Char or Varchar datatype, the maximum length is specified for all values that are later inserted into the column. SQL Server will automatically truncate (cut off) all characters that are longer than the maximum length that was defined. SQL Server doesn't notify you that the truncation is being performed.

I've created several reports that I produce with code in my application. On some columns, the values line up fine, but on others, they aren't lined up. What's causing the problem? When you use Char datatypes, the fields are padded with extra spaces to fill the entire defined space for the column. These columns should appear fine on your report, depending on how you've read the values from SQL Server. If the extra spaces in the field are the problem, either use a trim statement in your query or store the data as a Varchar.

Understanding the Different Numeric Datatypes

In Sybase System XI, you have several different numeric datatypes available for use when defining a column:

- Integers
- Floating point numbers
- Monetary numbers

Using Integer Datatypes

Integer datatypes are the first of several datatypes that you can use to define storage objects for numbers. Integer datatypes enable you to store whole numbers. You can directly perform arithmetic operations on Integer datatypes without using functions. Numbers stored in Integer datatypes always occupy the same amount of storage space, regardless of the number of digits within the allowable ranges for each Integer datatype within the guidelines of the datatype's individual precision.

Using Int or Integer Int (or Integer) is the first of three Integer datatypes. You can store negative and positive whole numbers within the range of $-(2^{31})$ to 2^{31}—approximately 4.3 billion numbers. The range is –2,147,483,648 to 2,147,483,647. Each value that's stored in an int datatype is stored in four bytes, using 31 bits for the size or magnitude and one bit for the sign.

Using Smallint Smallint is the second Integer datatype. You can store whole numbers within the range –32,768 to 32,767. Each value that's stored in a Smallint datatype occupies two bytes and is stored as 15 bits for the magnitude and one bit for the sign.

Using Tinyint You can store only whole positive numbers in a storage structure defined as Tinyint within the range 0 to 255. Each value stored as a Tinyint occupies one byte.

The following example shows the creation of a table with three columns. The columns are defined as the Int, Smallint, and Tinyint datatypes. A single row is inserted into the Number_Example table with values within the acceptable range for storage of each datatype. select is subsequently used to retrieve the row.

```
/* First create the table */
Create Table Number_Example
(Int1 Int,
 Int2 Smallint,
 Int3 Tinyint)
Go

/* Now insert a record into the table */
Insert Into Number_Example
Values( 400000000, 32767, 255 )
Go

/* Select the data back from the table */
Select *
From   Number_Example
Go

Int1         Int2    Int3
----------- ------- ----
400000000   32767   255
```

Enforcing Value Ranges Sybase System XI automatically enforces the insertion of values within the range of each datatype. In the following two examples, values are inserted into columns that are defined as Smallint and Tinyint, although the values are outside the range of acceptable values.

The column values are specified in the Values clause of the Insert statement in the same order in which the columns were defined in the table. Sybase returns an error message that describes the reason for the failed row insertion: The attempted insertion of a value is outside the allowable range for the datatype.

```
/* First attempt to insert an oversized value into
   the Smallint Column */
Insert Into Number_Example
Values( 1, 32768, 1 )
Go
```

Part
II

Ch
6

```
Arithmetic overflow during implicit conversion of INT value '32768'
to a SMALLINT field .

/* Now try to insert an oversized value into
   the Tinyint Column */
Insert Into Number_Example
Values( 1, 1, 256 )
Go

Arithmetic overflow during implicit conversion of INT value '256'
to a TINYINT field .
```

T I P You can use a `Tinyint` or `Smallint` column to store integer values in one-quarter or one-half the storage space used for storing integer values in an `Int` datatype. These are especially useful as flags, status indicators, and so forth.

Using Floating Point Datatypes

Floating point datatypes are the second group of several numeric datatypes you can use to define storage structures, such as table columns. Unlike the `Integer` datatypes, floating point datatypes can store decimal numbers.

Unfortunately, some of the floating point datatypes are subject to the rounding error. The storage of a value in a `Numeric` datatype that's subject to the rounding error is accurate only to the number of digits of precision that's specified. For example, if the number of digits of precision is 15, a number that's larger than 15 digits can be stored, but the digits beyond 15 may inaccurately represent the initial number inserted into the storage. Also, the number may inaccurately return results of computations that involve floating point datatypes. The rounding error affects a number's least-significant digits—the ones at the far right. You can accurately store numbers within the number of digits of precision available in floating point datatype.

N O T E Sybase describes datatypes, such as the floating point datatypes, as *approximate numeric datatypes* because values stored in them can be represented only within the limitations of the storage mechanism. You should avoid performing comparisons (such as in a `Where` clause) of data that's stored in approximate datatypes because a loaded value that's larger than the number of digits of precision is altered by the rounding effect during storage. ▪

Using the Real Datatype The first of the floating point datatypes is `Real`, which is stored in four bytes. You can store positive or negative decimal numbers in the `Real` datatype with up to seven digits of precision. You can store numbers in a column defined as `Real` within the range of 3.4E–38 to 3.4E+38.

The range of values and representation is actually platform-dependent. The `Real` datatype stored on each of the several computer hardware systems that a Sybase version was written for varied in the range of allowable characters and the actual representation of characters due to different CPUs. For example, the range of decimal numbers stored by OpenVMS on Digital's VAX computers is 0.29E –38 to –1.7E+38.

Remember that data stored in floating point datatypes, which is moved between different Windows NT hardware platforms with different processor architectures, such as DEC Alpha, Intel Pentium Pro, and Motorola PowerPC, may require conversion to compensate for different representations and ranges of values.

Using the Float Datatype   The second of the floating point datatypes is Float, which is stored in eight bytes if a value for (*n*), the precision, is omitted. A Float column is either defined with parentheses surrounding a precision value (similar to the way you define a Char(n) column) or the parentheses can be omitted. You can store positive or negative decimal numbers in the Float datatype with as many as 15 digits of precision. You can store numbers in a column defined as Float within the range of 1.7E–308 to 1.7E+308.

If you specify a value for *n* within the range of 1 to 7, you're actually defining a Real datatype. If you specify a value within the range of 8 to 15, the datatype has the identical characteristics as if *n* were omitted.

In the following example, a table is created with two columns defined as Real and Float. A single row is added with identical numbers that are subsequently added to each column of the table. The retrieval of the row from the table shows that the number stored in the real column was stored accurately to only seven digits, the maximum number of digits of precision for a Real datatype. The same eleven-digit number was stored correctly in the column defined with the datatype Float because Float allows up to 15 digits to be stored accurately.

```
/* First Create the table */
Create Table Precision_Example
(Num1 Real,
 Num2 Float)
Go

/* Now insert a record into the table */
Insert Into Precision_Example
Values( 4000000.1234, 4000000.1234 )
Go

/* Now select from the table */
Select *
From    Precision_Example
Go

Num1                    Num2
------------------- ---------------------
4000000.0           4000000.1234
```

Using the Decimal[(p[, s])] and Numeric[(p[, s])] Datatypes   You can use either the name Decimal or Numeric to select a datatype that, unlike Float or Real, allows the exact storage of decimal numbers. The scale and digits of precision are specified in the arguments *p* and *s*. You can store values within the range 10^{38-1} through -10^{38} using two to 17 bytes for storage.

Use *p* to define the total number of digits that can be stored to the left and right of the decimal point. Use *s* to define the number of digits to the right of the decimal point that must be equal to or less than the value of *p*. If you omit a value for *p*, it defaults to 18; the default of *s* is 0. Table 6.1 shows the number of bytes that are allocated for the specified precision (value of *p*).

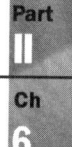

Part

II

Ch

6

Table 6.1   Number of Bytes Allocated for Decimal/Numeric Datatypes

Bytes Allocated	Precision
2	1–2
3	3–4
4	5–7
5	8–9
6	10–12
7	13–14
8	15–16
9	17–19
10	20–21
11	22–24
12	25–26
13	27–28
14	29–31
15	32–33
16	34–36
17	37–38

The following example shows the storage and subsequent retrieval of a single row stored with the columns of a table defined as numeric/decimal datatypes. This example shows the default precision and scale and an explicit precision and scale being displayed.

```
/* First create the table */
Create Table Definition_Example
(Num1 Decimal,
 Num2 Numeric(7,6))
Go

/* Now insert a record into the table */
Insert Into Definition_Example
Values (123456789123456789,1.123456)
Go

/* Now select from the table */
Select *
From   Definition_Example
Go

Num1                      Num2
----------------------    ----------
123456789123456789        1.123456
```

N O T E The maximum precision permitted in the `numeric`/`decimal` datatypes is 28 unless you start Sybase from the command line and change the precision. Use the command `sqlservr` with the option `/p`, which has the following syntax:

```
sqlservr [/dmaster_device_path][/pprecision_level]
```

For example, the following command starts Sybase with a maximum precision of 38:

```
sqlservr /dg:\sql60\data\master.dat /p38.
```

If no value is specified after the precision qualifier `/p`, the precision for the `numeric`/`decimal` datatype is set to the maximum of 38.

Understanding Monetary Datatypes

Sybase permits the storage of monetary values in special columns of type `Money` and `Smallmoney`. These datatypes were provided prior to the availability of the absolute `Decimal` and `Numeric` datatypes, and are not used that often in new application programs because they lack the flexibility required in storing monetary values for some currencies where precision greater than four digits of accuracy is required.

Using the Money Datatype   The `Money` datatype stores monetary values. Data values stored in the `Money` datatype are stored as an integer portion and a decimal-fraction portion in two four-byte integers. The range of values that you can store in the `Money` datatype is from −922,337,203,685,477.5808 to 922,337,203,685,477.5807. The accuracy of a value stored in the `Money` datatype is to the ten-thousandth of a monetary unit. Some front-end tools display values stored in the `Money` datatype rounded to the nearest cent.

Using the Smallmoney Datatype   The `Smallmoney` datatype stores a range of monetary values that's more limited than the `money` datatype. The values you can store in the `Smallmoney` datatype range from −214,748.3648 to 214,748.3647. Data values stored in the `Smallmoney` datatype are stored as an integer portion and a decimal-fraction portion in four bytes. Like values stored in a table column defined by using the `Money` datatype, some front-end tools display values stored in the `Smallmoney` datatype rounded to the nearest cent.

When you add values to a table column defined as `Money` or `Smallmoney`, you must precede the most significant digit with a dollar sign ($) or a sign of the defined monetary unit.

In the following example, a table is created with two columns that are defined using the `Money` and `Smallmoney` datatypes. In the first `Insert` statements, values are incorrectly added because they aren't preceded with a dollar sign. A `Select` statement shows that the values displayed are identical to those that were stored.

```
/* First Create the table */
Create Table Monetary_Table
(Money1 Money,
 Money2 Smallmoney)
Go

/* Now insert some data */
Insert Into Monetary_Table
Values( 16051.3455, 16051.3455 )
Go
```

Part

II

Ch

6

```
/* Now get the data from the table */
Select * From Monetary_Table
Money1                          Money2
-------------------------       -------------------------
16,051.35                       16,051.35
```

In a continuation of the same example, a three-digit monetary value is added to both table columns, followed by a value that's outside the storage bounds for the datatype on the computer architecture.

```
Insert Into Monetary_Table
Values( $123, $123 )
Go
Insert Into Monetary_Table
Values( 1232922337203685477, 214748.3647 )
Go

Arithmetic overflow during implicit conversion of NUMERIC value
'1232922337203685477' to a MONEY field .
```

The integer value 1232922337203685477 is out of the range of machine representation, which is four bytes.

Understanding the Different Date/Time Datatypes

The Datetime and Smalldatetime datatypes store a combination of the date and time. You'll find it more convenient to store dates and times in one of the date and time datatypes rather than a datatype such a Char or Varchar. If you store data in one of these datatypes, you can easily display them because Sybase automatically formats them in a familiar form. You can also use specialized date and time functions to manipulate values stored in this manner.

If you store date and time in char or varchar (or if you store time in Numeric datatypes), date and time values aren't automatically formatted in conventional ways when they're displayed.

Using the Datetime Datatype   Datetime is the first type of date and time datatype that you can use to define storage structures, such as table columns. In the Datetime datatype, you can store dates and times from AD 1/1/1753 to AD 12/31/9999.

The total storage of a Datetime datatype value is eight bytes. Sybase uses the first four bytes to store the number of days after or before the base date of January 1, 1900. Values that are stored as negative numbers represent dates before the base date; positive numbers represent dates since the base date. Time is stored in the second four bytes as the number of milliseconds after midnight.

N O T E   Datetime values are stored to an accuracy of 1/300th of a second (3.33 milliseconds) with values rounded downward. For example, values of one, two, and three milliseconds are stored as zero milliseconds; the values of four through six milliseconds are stored as three milliseconds.

When you retrieve values stored in Datetime, the default format for display is MMM DD YYYY hh:mmAM/PM—for example, Sep 23 1949 11:14PM. You must enclose Datetime values in single quotation marks when they're used in an Insert or any other statement. You can enter either the date or time portion first because Sybase can recognize each portion and store the value correctly.

You can use upper- or lowercase characters for the date and one or more spaces between the month, day, and year when you enter Datetime values. If you enter time without a date, the default date is January 1, 1900. If you enter the date without the time, the default time is 12:00AM. If you omit the date and the time, the default value entered is January 1, 1900 12:00 AM.

You can enter the date in several ways. Each is recognized and stored correctly by Sybase. You can enter the date in an alphabetic format, using either an abbreviation for the month or the full name of the month. You can use or omit a comma between the day and year.

If you omit the century part of the year, decades that are less than 50 are represented as 20 and those that are 50 or more are entered as 19. For example, if you insert the year 49, the complete year stored is 2049. If you enter the year as 94, the complete year stored is 1994. You must explicitly enter the century if you want a century different from the default. You must supply the century if the day is omitted from the date value. When you enter a date without a day, the default entry is the first day of the month.

 TIP In order to protect yourself from future nightmares due to conversion to a four-digit year in the year 2000, I highly recommend that you always reference years in four digits internally to your application programs. Despite that user's requests for two-digit displays, take care to store things in the code with four digits.

The Set option Dateformat isn't used if you specify the month of the year in alphabetic format. If you installed Sybase System XI with the US_English Language option, the default order for the display of Datetime values is month, day, and year. You can change the default order for the display of the date portion of a Datetime value using the Set Dateformat command.

▶ **See** "Configuring and Managing Queries," **p. xxx [Ch 24]**

p. xxx [Ch 24]

You can enter dates several ways, including the following examples:

- Sep 23 1949
- SEP 23 1949
- September 23 1949
- sep 1949 23
- 1949 sep 23
- 1949 23 sep
- 23 sep 1949

Part

II

Ch

6

The numeric format for Datetime values permits the use of slashes (/), hyphens (-), and periods (.) as separators between the different time units. When you use the numeric format with a Datetime value, you must specify the month, day, and year of the date portion of the value.

In the numeric format, enter a separator between the month, day, and year entered in the order defined for Dateformat. If you enter the values for a Datetime datatype that's in the incorrect order, the month, day, or year will be misinterpreted and stored incorrectly. If you enter the information in the incorrect order, you may also receive an error message that tells you the date is out of range.

The following is an example of several entries for the numeric form of the date portion of a Datetime datatype value with Set Dateformat defined as month, day, and year and the language as US_English:

- 6/24/71
- 06/24/71
- 6-24-1971
- 6.24.1971
- 06.24.71

The last of the possible formats for the date portion of a Datetime datatype value is unseparated four-, six-, or eight-digit values or a Time value without a Date value portion. The Dateformat controlled through Set Dateformat doesn't affect Datetime datatype values referenced as the unseparated digit format.

If you enter a six- or eight-digit unseparated value, it's always interpreted in the order of year, month, and day. The month and day are always interpreted as two digits each. Four unseparated digit values are interpreted as the year, with the century and the month and day default to the first month and the first day of that month. Table 6.2 lists the possible interpretations of unseparated digit Datetime datatype values:

Table 6.2   Interpretation of Unseparated Digit Dates for Datetime Datatypes

Digits	Equivalent Representation in Alphabetic Format
710624	June 24, 1971
19710624	June 24, 1971
1971	January 1, 1971
71	Not valid
"	January 1, 1900 12:00AM

TROUBLESHOOTING

I omitted the entry of a value for a table column that was defined as the `Datetime` **datatype when I added a new row. When I subsequently displayed the new row, the entry for the column defined as** `Datetime` **was January 1, 1900, and 12 midnight.** When you inserted the new row, you must have used empty single quotation marks ('') as a value for the `Datetime` column, mistakenly thinking that it would result in a `Null` entry. When two single quotation marks are used with no characters inserted between them as the value for either of the date and time datatypes, the entry January 1, 1900, and 12 midnight is always inserted by Sybase.

You must enter the time with the time units in the following order: hours, minutes, seconds, and milliseconds. You must have a colon as a separator between multiple time units to enable a set of digits to be recognized as a time rather than a date value. You can use AM or PM, specified in upper- or lowercase, to specify before or after midnight.

You can precede milliseconds with a period or a colon, which affects the interpretation of the millisecond unit. A period followed by a single digit specifies tenths of a second; two digits are interpreted as hundredths of a second; three digits are interpreted as thousandths of a second. A colon specifies that the following digits will be interpreted as thousandths of a second. Table 6.3 shows several possible interpretations of the time portion of a `Datetime` datatype value.

Table 6.3 Datetime Datatype Values

Time	Interpretation
11:21	11 hours and 21 minutes after midnight
11:21:15:871	11 hours, 21 minutes, 15 seconds, and 871 thousandths of a second AM
11:21:15.8	11 hours, 21 minutes, 15 seconds, and eight tenths of a second AM
6am	Six AM
7 PM	Seven PM
05:21:15:500 AM	Five hours, 21 minutes, 15 seconds, and 500 milliseconds after midnight

Using the Smalldatetime Datatype `Smalldatetime` is the second of the date and time datatypes you can use to define storage structures (such as table columns). In the `Smalldatetime` datatype, you can store dates and times from AD 1/1/1900 to AD 6/6/2079.

The total storage of a `Smalldatetime` datatype value is four bytes. Sybase uses two bytes to store the number of days after the base date of January 1, 1900. Time is stored in the other two bytes as the number of minutes after midnight. The accuracy of the `Smalldatetime` datatype is one minute. You can use `Smalldatetime` to store values that are within its more limited range and lesser precision when compared to `Datetime`.

Part
II

Ch
6

TIP By using the Smalldatetime datatype, you will save 50 percent of the data space required over a Datetime column.

In the following example, one column is defined by using the Datetime datatype, and the second column is defined using the Smalldatetime datatype. After the table is created, a minimum value is inserted into each column of a single row for the respective datatypes.

```
/* Create the table first */
Create Table Date_Table
(Date1 Datetime,
 Date2 Smalldatetime)
Go

/* Now insert a record */
Insert Into Date_Table
Values( 'Jan 1 1753', 'Jan 1 1900' )
Go

/* Now fetch the record from the database */
Select *
From    Date_Table
Go
```

```
Date1                        Date2
--------------------------   --------------------------
Jan 1 1753 12:00AM           Jan 1 1900 12:00AM
```

In the following example, successive Insert statements insert a date that's beyond both the range of the columns defined by using the Smalldatetime and the range of Datetime datatypes. An error is returned as a result of both Insert statements.

```
Insert Into Date_Table
Values( 'May 19 1994', 'Jun 7 2079' )
Go

Arithmetic overflow during implicit conversion of VARCHAR value
'Jun 7 2079' to a SMALLDATETIME field .
```

In the preceding example, the conversion of char to Smalldatetime resulted in a Smalldatetime value out of range:

```
Insert Into Date_Table
Values ('Jan 1 10000','May 19 1994')
Go

Syntax error during implicit conversion of VARCHAR value
'Jan 1 10000' to a DATETIME field.
```

The example shows a syntax error converting Datetime from a character string.

Using Specialized Datatypes in System XI

Transact-SQL contains a set of specialized datatypes for data storage. Most of the time you'll store data in more conventional datatypes, such as Integer, floating point, and Character. You can store dates and times in the Datetime or Smalldatetime datatypes.

Although you'll probably find that you can use the Integer, floating point, Character, and date/time datatype formats for storing 90 percent of your data, in some cases you'll probably need a custom solution.

In these cases, you can use one or more of the specialized datatypes. For example, you may need to store only data that can be represented as true or false, yes or no. Because this is a binary condition, you may decide to create a custom datatype. As another example, you may need to store sets of data in a column that's larger than the 255-character limitation of the conventional character datatypes. Several additional datatypes are available to enable you to choose the best datatype for storing your information.

Using the Bit Datatype   You can use the Bit datatype to store information that can be represented in only two states. A Bit datatype is stored in a single bit; as a result, only two possible patterns can be stored—0 or 1. If you enter any other value than 0 or 1 in a data-storage structure, such as a table column, 1 is stored. You can't define the Bit datatype to allow Null entries.

 TIP   Although it is not explicitly stated in the Sybase documentation, the Bit datatype corresponds to the Boolean datatype in other relational databases and programming languages.

You can also use a single byte to define up to eight different bit columns of a table by using the Bit datatype. The amount of space allocated for one or more bits is a single byte, and the Bit columns don't have to be contiguous. If you define nine columns of a table using the Bit datatype, two bytes are used for the total of nine Bit datatypes.

Using the Timestamp Datatype   If you define a column of a table using the Timestamp datatype, a counter value is automatically added to the Timestamp column whenever you insert a new row or update an existing row. You can't explicitly enter a value into the column defined as a Timestamp. A uniformly increasing counter value can be implicitly inserted only into a Timestamp column by Sybase.

The counter value inserted by Sybase into a Timestamp column specifies the sequence of operations that Sybase has performed. Values entered into a Timestamp column are stored in a Varbinary(8) format, not a Datetime or Smalldatetime format—so the notion of Timestamp is really a bit of a misnomer. Null values are permitted in a Timestamp column by default. A Timestamp value isn't a date and time, but it's always unique within the table and database; it does however represent a mathematically precise version of the current time that an operation occurred on a row in a table. You can define only a single column of a table as a Timestamp.

Part

II

Ch

6

N O T E Timestamps are often used to ensure that a row can be uniquely identified. If you're updating columns in a row, it's a common practice to specify the Timestamp field in the Where clause of your Update statement. This makes sure that you update only one row of the table. You can be assured of the uniqueness of the value because the server will maintain and update it any time you insert or update a row.

Timestamps are also used—again, as part of the Where clause—to prevent two people from updating the same row. Because the Timestamp is updated automatically whenever an update is made to the row, you can be sure that you're not going to overwrite someone else's information. If someone else updates a row that you're now working on, when they save their update, the row's Timestamp will be *updated*, no longer matching your copy. When you issue the Update command to save your changes, the Where clause will not find any rows because it can't find the specific row that you retrieved. Timestamps are excellent, server-maintained ways to make sure that you have a unique row identifier. ■

If you define a column with the column name Timestamp and don't specify a datatype, the column is defined using the Timestamp datatype.

Using the Binary Datatype You can use the Binary datatype to store bit patterns that consist of up to 255 bytes. Use the integer specified in parentheses to define the length of all bit patterns from one to 255 bytes. You must specify the size of a binary column to be at least one byte, but you can store a bit pattern of all zeroes.

You must enter the first binary value preceded with 0x (which in most programming languages indicates that a hexadecimal number is going to follow). You can enter binary data using the characters 0 through 9 and A through F. For example, enter the value A0 by preceding it with 0x, like this: 0xA0. If you enter values greater than the length that you defined, the values are truncated. Values are also padded with zeroes after the least significant digit.

A column defined as Binary(1) can store up to the maximum value of FF. In the following example, a table is defined with two columns with the datatypes Binary(1) and Binary(2). Three Insert statements are used to enter successive pairs of values of 0, 1, FF, and FFF in both columns.

```
/* First Create The Table */
Create Table Binary_Table
(x Binary(1),
 y Binary(2))
Go

/* Now insert values into the table */
Insert Into Binary_Table
values( 0x0, 0x0 )
Go
Insert Into Binary_Table
Values( 0x1, 0x1 )
Go
Insert Into Binary_Table
Values( 0xFF, 0xFF )
Go
```

```
Insert Into Binary_Table
Values( 0xFFF, 0xFFF )
Go

/* Now select from the table */
Select *
From   Binary_Table
Go

x    y
---- ------
0x00 0x0000
0x01 0x0100
0xff 0xff00
0x0f 0x0fff
```

Using the Varbinary Datatype   You can use the Varbinary datatype to store bit patterns that consist of *up to 255 bytes*. You use the integer specified in parentheses to define the maximum length of all bit patterns from one to 255 bytes. You must specify the size of a binary column to be at least one byte, but you can store a bit pattern of all zeroes.

Unlike the Binary datatype, Varbinary datatype storage is limited to just enough space for the length of the actual value. Like the Binary datatype, you must enter the first binary value preceded with 0x. You can enter binary data using the characters 0 through 9 and A through F. If you enter values that are greater than the maximum length you defined, the values are truncated.

In the following example, a table is defined with two columns with the Varbinary(1) and Varbinary(2) datatypes. Three Insert statements are used to enter successive pairs of values of 0, 1, FF, and FFF in both columns.

```
/* First create the table */
Create Table Varbinary_Table
(x Varbinary(1),
 y Varbinary(2))
Go

/* Now insert some data */
Insert Into Varbinary_Table
values( 0x0, 0x0 )
Go
Insert Into Varbinary_Table
Values( 0x1, 0x1 )
Go
Insert Into Varbinary_Table
Values( 0xFF, 0xFF )
Go
Insert Into Varbinary_Table
Values( 0xFFF, 0xFFF )
Go

/* Now select from the table */
Select *
From   Varbinary_Table
Go
```

Part
II

Ch
6

```
x     y
----  ------
0x00  0x00
0x01  0x01
0xff  0xff
0x0f  0x0fff
```

Unlike the values entered into a table in which the columns are defined as `binary(1)` and `binary(2)`, the values are stored in only the amount of space that's required. Values are truncated if they're greater than the maximum space defined when the table is created.

Understanding the Different Text and Image/BLOB Datatypes

You can use the `Text` and `Image` datatypes to store large amounts of character or binary data. You can store more than 2 billion data bytes in either a `Text` or `Image` datatype. It's wasteful to preallocate space for text or image datatypes to any significant extent, so only a portion of the space is preallocated. The remaining space is dynamically allocated. The minimum space allocated for a `Text` or `Image` column that is not defined as nullable is a full 2K page. Therefore, unless you have a real reason or you know for sure that every column you are working with needs to be defined as `Not Null`, I recommend that you define the column as `Null`.

N O T E The `Text` and `Image` datatypes are really synonymous. You can store binary information in `Text` columns and you can store string or character information in `Image` columns. Generally speaking, I use `Text` columns universally; however, in future versions of Sybase, expect to see the differences between these two datatypes become more obvious as Sybase adds support for various other datatypes, such as video and geographic data. ▪

Using the Text Datatype Use a `Text` datatype for storing large amounts of text. The characters stored in a text field are typically characters that can be output directly to a display device, such as a monitor window or a printer. You can store from one to 2,147,483,647 bytes of data in a `Text` datatype.

Your data is stored in fixed-length strings of characters in an initially allocated 2K (2,048 bytes) unit. Additional 2K units are dynamically added and are linked together. The 2K data pages are logically—but not necessarily physically—contiguous. If you use an `Insert` statement to insert data into a column defined as `Text`, you must enclose the data within single quotation marks.

Using the Image Datatype You can use the `Image` datatype to store large bit patterns from one to 2,147,483,647 bytes in length. For example, you can store employee photos, pictures for a catalog, or drawings in a single column value of a table row. Typically, the data stored in an image column isn't directly entered with an `Insert` statement.

Your data is stored in fixed-length byte strings in an initially allocated 2K (2,048 bytes) unit. Additional 2K units are dynamically added and are linked together like the pages for a text column. The 2K data pages are logically—but not necessarily physically—contiguous.

Using Text and Image Datatypes Values that are stored as either `Text` or `Image` datatypes are displayed just as other columns are when you use a `Select` statement. The number of bytes displayed is limited by the global value `@@Textsize`, which has a default value of 32K. You can specify the Null characteristic for Text or Image columns. A Null for a Text or Image column of a table doesn't allocate any 2K pages of storage, unless an Update is performed on a row containing the Null value.

In the following example, two table columns are defined using image and text. Values are inserted into each column of a single row using an Insert statement. The row is then retrieved from the table with a Select statement.

```
/* First Create the table */
Create Table Imagetext_Table
(Image1 image,
 Text1 text)
Go

/* Now insert some data */
Insert Into Imagetext_Table
Values( '123456789aczx+=\', '12345678aczx+=' )
Go

/* Now select the data that was inserted */
Select *
From   Imagetext_Table
Go
```

```
Image1                                              Text1
- - - - - - - - - - - - - - - - - - - - - - - - - - - - - - - - - - - - - - -
0x31323334353637383961637a782b3d5c     12345678aczx+=
```

Data in a column defined as an Image datatype isn't translated from its ASCII representation automatically when it's displayed with a Select statement. Data stored in a column defined as the Text datatype is automatically translated to ASCII characters when the data is output with a Select statement.

Understanding the Restrictions on Text and Image Columns   You'll encounter several restrictions on the use of data stored in Text and Image datatypes. You can define only table columns using the Text or Image datatypes. You can't define other storage structures (such as local variables or parameters) as Text or Image datatypes.

The amount of data that can be stored in a Text or Image table column makes each datatype unsuitable for use or manipulation in many Transact-SQL statements. This is simply because the amount of data that would have to be manipulated is too great. You can't specify a table column in an Order By, Group By, or Compute clause that's a Text or Image datatype. Sybase won't try to sort or group a table's rows using a column that can contain more than 4 billion bytes of data because too much data would have to be moved around and too large a space would have to be allocated in which to order the rows.

You also can't use a Text or Image column in a Union unless it's a Union All. You can't use a subquery that returns data values from a Text or Image datatype. You also can't use a Text or Image column in a Where or Having clause, unless the comparison operator Like is used. You can't specify Distinct followed by a table column that's defined as a Text or Image datatype.

Part
II

Ch
6

Finally, you can't create an index or a `primary` or `foreign` key that's defined using a table column that you've defined as an `Image` or `Text` datatype.

Creating Your Own User-Defined Datatypes

You can define your own datatype, which can then be used as a datatype for a storage structure, such as a table column. You always define a user-defined datatype as one of the existing system datatypes. A user-defined datatype enables you to define a datatype that can contain a length specification, if necessary, and a `null` characteristic.

You can use a descriptive name for the user-defined datatype that describes the type of data that it contains. You can create user-defined datatypes either by using Sybase SQL Server Manager or through the Transact-SQL command `sp_addtype`.

Using sp_addtype to Create a User-Defined Datatype   You can define a user-defined datatype with the system-stored procedure `sp_addtype`. The syntax for `sp_addtype` is as follows:

```
sp_addtype User_Defined_Datatype_Name, System_Datatype, Not Null | null |
Identity
```

`User_Defined_Datatype_Name` is a name that you want to give the datatype and `System_Datatype` is the real Sybase datatype that it is going to use for storing the data.

After you define a user-defined datatype, you can use it to specify the datatype of a storage structure, such as a table column. You can use the system procedure `sp_help` to display a user-defined datatype. You can create and then bind defaults and rules to user-defined datatypes. You bind rules and defaults to user-defined datatypes with the same procedures used for system datatypes `sp_bindefault` and `sp_bindrule`.

In the following example, a user-defined datatype is created by using `sp_addtype`. The characteristics are displayed with `sp_help`.

```
sp_addtype Customer_Name, 'Char(15)', Null
Go
sp_help Customer_Name
Go


------------------------------------------------------------
Type added.
Type_name        Storage_type    Length Prec Scale Nulls
Default_name     Rule_name       Identity
------------------------------------------------------------
Customer_Name    char                15              1
                                      0
```

Using Sybase SQL Server Manager to Create a User-Defined Datatype   To use Sybase SQL Server Manager to create a user-defined datatype, follow these steps:

1. Launch Sybase SQL Server Manager and log on to the appropriate server.
2. Select the database that you are going to manage in the left pane of the explorer.

3. Click the User Datatypes folder in the left pane of the explorer to get a list of all the user-defined datatypes currently created on the server (see Fig. 6.5).

FIG. 6.5

The SSM explorer view of the system catalog shows all the user-defined datatypes in the *pubs2* database. Note that you can also see the underlying datatype that is being used in the last column on the right.

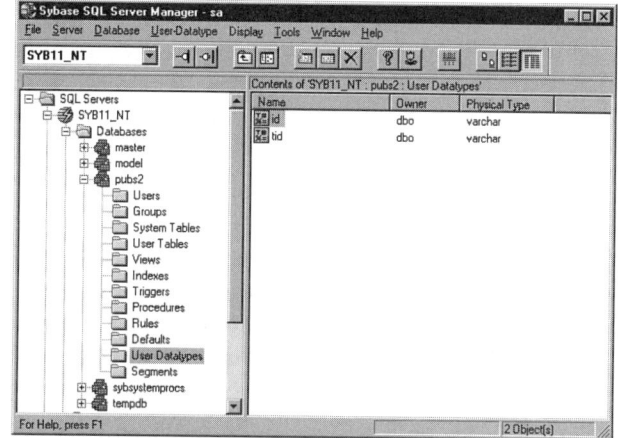

4. Choose <u>D</u>atabase, Crea<u>t</u>e, and select <u>U</u>ser Datatype to display the Sybase SQL Server Manager Create User Datatype dialog box (see Fig. 6.6).

FIG. 6.6

The SSM Create User Datatype dialog box prompts you through the process of creating the type by enabling you to enter a name for the type and then assigning its properties.

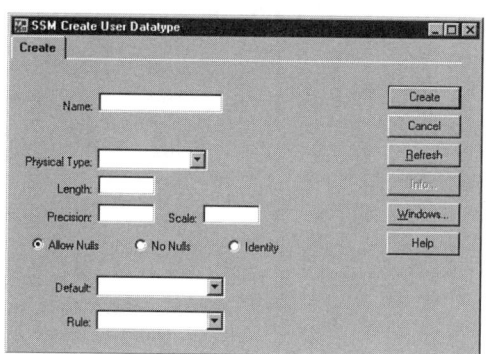

5. Enter a name for the datatype.
6. Select the properties that you want to apply for this datatype, and choose any predefined Defaults or Rules that you also want to use for the datatype.
7. Click the Create button to add the type. Doing so modifies the dialog box to include a new tab page that enables you see dependencies of the datatype.

Dropping User-Defined Datatypes   You can use the system procedure `sp_droptype` to remove a user-defined datatype. The procedure uses the following syntax:

```
sp_droptype User_Defined_Datatype_Name
```

Part
II

Ch
6

You can't drop a user-defined datatype if one or more tables have a column that's defined using it. You can drop the user-defined datatype only if it isn't in use by any tables. In the following example, a user-defined datatype can't be dropped until you first drop the sole table in which a column is defined using the user-defined datatype.

It is also possible to use Sybase SQL Server Manager to drop a user-defined datatype. To drop a type using Sybase SQL Server Manager, navigate the explorer until you find the type that you want to remove and right-click it. This displays a context menu from which you can select Delete.

Understanding the Identity Column

In addition to defining the datatype of a column to allow or disallow nulls, you can define a column with the property of Identity. When you add rows to the table, you omit entering a value for the column defined with the Identity property. The value for the identity column is automatically entered by adding the increment value to the column value of the last row.

In the following example, the second column is defined with the property Identity. After two rows are added to the table, a subsequent retrieval of the table rows shows that the identity column values were generated by the Identity mechanism.

```
/* First create the table */
Create Table Identity_Table
(Name Char(15),
 Row_Number Numeric(12,0) Identity Not Null)
Go

/* Insert some data */
Insert Into Identity_Table( Name )
Values( 'Bob Smith' )
Insert Into Identity_Table( Name )
Values( 'Mary Jones' )
Go

/* Select the data */
Select *
From    Identity_Table
Go

Name              Row_Number
--------------- -----------
Bob Smith         1
Mary Jones        2
```

You can assign the Identity property only to a column that's defined with the datatypes Numeric(p,0)—but not if the column permits Nulls. Only a single column of a table can be defined with the property Identity. The Identity property doesn't guarantee that rows will be unique (but they almost always will be). You must establish a unique index on the identity column to guarantee unique table rows.

Partitioning Tables

The object of the game of being a DBA is to try to deliver the most reliable data storage system that you can to your users. In addition to this requirement, your users have come to require that you will make access to that data timely and rapid. What does this mean? It means that basically, it's your job to make the database go quickly, be reliable, and have optimal performance.

One of the key requirements of an optimally performing system is that transaction time in OLTP (On-Line Transaction Processing) systems be short. To achieve this goal, there are many programmer steps that can be taken to reduce the amount of time from the moment a transaction is begun until it is either committed or rolled back. As a DBA, you are responsible for making sure that the database has a structure that is going to be conducive to good performance, and as such, table design plays a key role in achieving that goal.

Sybase has traditionally been a relatively good performer in terms of the capability to handle large numbers of simultaneous database requests. In a project that I've been working on recently, a System 10 database server was processing a bank's overnight routines including reports in about 4.5 hours. System XI—with a little tweaking on the server side, but no changes to the application or stored procedures themselves—took over 100 minutes off of that time on the same hardware! This was just a software upgrade by Sybase and it saved over 37 percent. You might argue that all we have to do as application developers is take advantage of additional performance gains delivered by your software vendors, such as Sybase, and by buying bigger hardware from such companies as Sun, HP, and IBM.

Unfortunately, this is a naive assumption—eventually, budgetary and technological constraints will get in the way of building a bigger and faster system. It's at this point that you have to start getting smart about how your system works, and you have to optimize your application to take full advantage of all the capabilities of the underlying or supporting software and hardware that are available to you.

System XI's performance improvements are numerous, but one particular feature—*table partitioning*—is critical to the support of very highly transactional systems. The principle of table partitioning is built around the requirement to split the physical data of a table to separate physical locations on separate physical devices so that parallel reads and (most importantly) writes can be executed by the server.

Part

II

Ch

6

Understanding Table Partitions

Partitioned tables are really designed to address the specific problem of page contention during the execution of multiple concurrent `Insert` transactions on a table. Why is there a problem in the first place? To understand the nature of the problem, it is necessary to understand first how data is managed in Sybase's table structures and how they are managed on the physical disks.

In typical database tables that are not indexed with a clustered index, all new records that are inserted into the database are simply added to the next free database page in the table. This doesn't sound too much like a problem until you consider that Sybase is a page-level locking database, so a single insert will in fact stop any other inserts until it has either been committed or rolled back. This is the contention that the database designers at Sybase were trying to alleviate.

Generally speaking, people coded around this problem quite effectively by either minimizing the length or duration of a transaction in the first place or by taking advantage of placing a clustered index on the table. Clustered indexes tend to solve this contention problem (provided that the clustering is based on an appropriately distinct set of data elements) by forcing Sybase to place data rows in the physically accurate or correct order of the index.

Why does this help? Because typically, two concurrent inserts differ by some value that is usually in the key. This difference will be normally responsible for the inserts going to different places in the clustered index, and thereby moving the inserted rows into different places on the database.

So what are table partitions? They are a way in Sybase that you can split up the data in a table across physical devices and ensure an equal distribution of data across those devices.

How does partitioning work? Partitioning relies on a feature of Sybase that should be already familiar to you—database segments. By using segments, you can specify where the database is placed and how it will grow onto separate physical disks and/or devices on your database server. Segment construction and manipulation is discussed in full in Chapter 5, "Understanding Databases, Devices, and Transaction Logs." If you have any need for clarification on how to use segments or how they interact with your database, please see Chapter 5.

The convenient trick about partitioning a table is that you get to define the number of partitions that you want the table to occupy and then based on the segments that the database spans, the server will create equally sized data areas on each segment and split the data up across those segments. This may seem a little hard to grasp, so let's try an example to see how this partitioning works.

Say that you have a database that spans two data segments named *DataSegment1* and *DataSegment2*. Say, then, that you have a table that you want to partition in halves. The database server will create two equally sized sets of data pages for the data in the table and split them across both of the segments *DataSegment1* and *DataSegment2*. Then, if two concurrent inserts are executed by two users of the system, each will be placed independently of each other on *DataSegment1* and *DataSegment2*.

You can partition a table more times than you have segments available. In this case, Sybase splits the data up into the number of partitions that you request and evenly divides these partitions among the underlying segments. For example, say that you partitioned the table six times: Sybase would create three partitions that would alternate with partitions 1, 3, and 5 on *DataSegment1* and partitions 2, 4, and 6 on *DataSegment2*.

NOTE Simulating table partitioning has always been available as an option to the savvy database administrator. It was always possible to physically split up a database across multiple segments and, therefore, physical devices if you designed the database correctly. The major problem with this is that there was no scientific way to guarantee how much data would be on each disk and how the data would be split across the drives. Sybase's new table partitioning is designed to fix the lack of science and place a measurable way of addressing this issue in your hands.

Another option that dramatically improves overall database performance (not limited to just individual tables) in both reads *and* writes is available on some operating systems that allow the operating system to define the logical representation of the disk in chunks that are split across multiple devices. In this approach, you are doing your own partitioning, but at a significantly lower (and therefore generally faster) level than the application program—Sybase System XI.

On HP hardware, this capability to redefine the disk areas is done through the logical volume manager. I have seen performance improvements in the order of 30–50 percent on existing systems—with absolutely no application changes—by simply redefining the way the data is stored. At HP, there's a super guru who spends all day optimizing hardware and the HP-UX operating system for performance: Bill Allen. If you ever have any doubts about how to tune a system, talk to your local HP support person, and have him contact Bill on your behalf.

Bill has done the world a great favor by documenting a large number of his findings in a Microsoft Word document that can be found on the Sybase OpenLine CompuServe forum in the SQL Server/SA section. The file name is PTUHPUX.DOC. For more information on using Sybase's CompuServe support forums, please see Appendix D, "Knowing Where to Go for More Help." ▪

Creating Table Partitions

In this section, you learn how to partition a table using both Sybase SQL Server Manager and Transact-SQL. Before you attempt to partition the tables, make sure that you have multiple devices (preferably on multiple disks) created. In Figure 6.7, you can see that there are two new database devices, *Device1* and *Device2,* that I have just created to be the basis of my table partitions.

After establishing that you have a valid set of devices available for use with the database, you will need to extend the database onto those devices so that the disk areas are made available for use by the tables and objects in the database. Now that you have extended the database onto those devices, you will need to make sure that you have created two segments that are taking advantage of these new devices for storing data (see Fig. 6.8).

Part

II

Ch

6

FIG. 6.7

The Database Devices view of the explorer in SSM lists all the available devices on the server and how much free space exists in each of them.

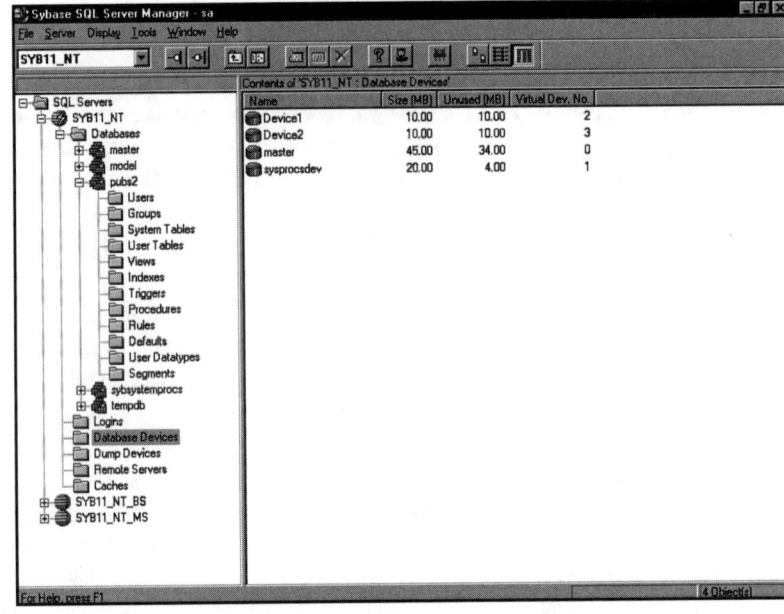

FIG. 6.8

This database Segments view of the *pubs2* database shows that there are now two additional segments available for use to the database: DataSegment1 and DataSegment2. These two new data segments are in turn mapped to the new database devices that were created earlier.

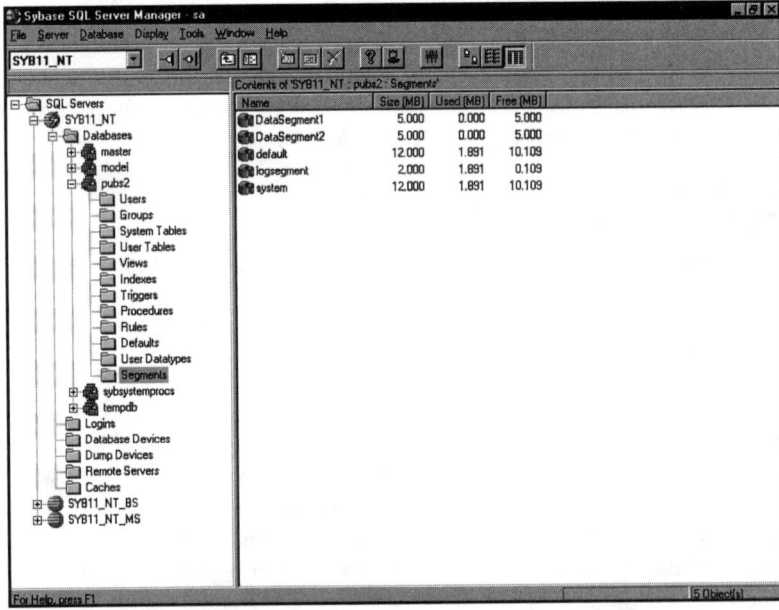

Partitioning a Table Using Sybase SQL Server Manager   Partitioning a table involves several steps, but can be performed easily using Sybase SQL Server Manager. To partition a table, follow these steps:

1. Launch Sybase SQL Server Manager and log on to the server that you are going to work on.

2. Select the database that has the table you want to partition in the explorer, and navigate the explorer until you get the table.

3. Double-click the table (or choose <u>P</u>roperties, Ta<u>b</u>le) to display the Sybase SQL Server Manager Table dialog box.

4. Select the Partition tab to display the partitioning properties for the table (see Fig. 6.9).

FIG. 6.9

The SSM Table properties dialog box enables you to modify and work with any of the table's properties. The Partition tab displays any partitions that exist on the table, and also enables you to explicitly add partitions to the table.

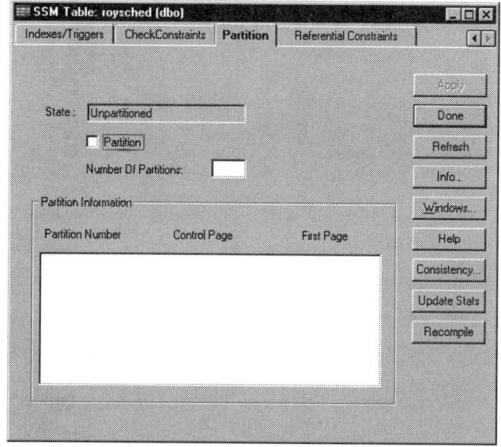

5. Check the Partition check box, and enter the number of partitions that you want to create in the Number Of Partitions field.

6. Click the Apply button to make the partitions.

Adding partitions to the table will change the display of the dialog box to be more of an informative way of understanding how the partitions have been allocated on the database. In Figure 6.10, you can see the *roysched* table after it has been split into four equally sized partitions.

Partitioning a Table Using Transact-SQL   The syntax for partitioning a table in Transact-SQL is really quite straightforward and an extension of the existing `Alter Table` statement:

```
Alter Table Table_Name Partition Number_Of_Partitions
```

Table_Name is the name of the table that you want to partition and *Number_Of_Partitions* is the number of partitions that you want the server to create for the data storage.

For example, if you wanted to partition the *discounts* table in the *pubs2* database into four partitions, you would execute:

```
Alter Table discounts Partition 4
Go
```

Part

II

Ch

6

FIG. 6.10

After partitioning a table, you can see how Sybase split the data across different pages in the lower part of the dialog box titled Partition Information.

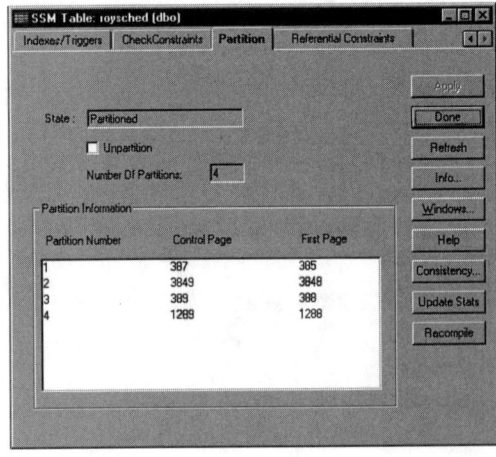

N O T E   You cannot partition a table that has a clustered index. If you attempt to do so, you will receive an error. For example, if you were to try to partition the *authors* table in the *pubs2* database, you might execute the following:

```
Alter Table authors Partition 4
Go
```

```
Cannot partition table 'authors' because it has a clustered index.
```

For more information on the limitations of a partitioned table, please see the section later in this chapter, "Understanding the Limitations of Table Partitioning." ■

Getting Information about Partitioned Objects

There are two ways of getting information about tables that are partitioned in the database: Use Sybase SQL Server Manager and use system-stored procedures in Transact-SQL. Sybase SQL Server Manager has already been demonstrated earlier when you partitioned the *roysched* table.

There are two system-stored procedures that provide valuable information about an object that can be partitioned: sp_help and sp_helpartition.

The system-stored procedure sp_help is a universal object definition procedure that will report any partitions on an object. The syntax for sp_help is as follows:

```
sp_help Object_Name
```

Object_Name refers to the object that you want to find information about. For example, to review the information available on the *discounts* table that you partitioned earlier, you would execute:

```
sp_help discounts
Go
```

```
Name        Owner Type
---------   ----- ----------
discounts dbo    user table
Data_located_on_segment       When_created
---------------------------   --------------------------
default                       Jun 29 1996 10:15:58:126PM
Column_name   Type      Length Prec Scale Nulls Default Rule Identity
-----------   -------   ------ ---- ----- ----- ------- ---- --------
discounttype  varchar     40                0                        0
stor_id       char         4                1                        0
lowqty        smallint     2                1                        0
highqty       smallint     2                1                        0
discount      float        8                0                        0
Object does not have any indexes.
keytype   object         related_object     object_keys related_keys
-------   -------------  -----------------  ---------------------------
foreign   discounts  stores                 stor_id, *, *, *, *, *, *, *
                                            stor_id, *, *, *, *, *, *, *
primary   discounts  -- none --             discounttype, stor_id, *, *, *,
                                            *, *, *, *, *, *, *, *, *, *, *

partitionid   firstpage controlpage
-----------   --------- -----------
          1         489         490
          2        3841        3842
          3         376         377
          4        1281        1282
```

The important additional information is shown at the end of the sp_help procedure's output under the titles *partitionid*, *firstpage*, and *controlpage*.

TIP You can review the information that's stored in each of the data pages described in the partition information by using the undocumented DBCC command DBCC Page. You can find more information about using all the undocumented features of DBCC in Chapter 20, "Understanding the Joys, Secrets, and Mysteries of DBCC."

 The partition information is really the output from the new (in System XI) system-stored procedure, sp_helpartition. The syntax for sp_helpartition is the same as that of sp_help, and it takes a single parameter of the object name that you want to inquire on. For example, to explicitly get the information about the partitions that were created on the *roysched* table, you would execute:

```
sp_helpartition roysched
Go

partitionid   firstpage controlpage
-----------   --------- -----------
          1         385         387
          2        3848        3849
          3         388         389
          4        1288        1289
```

Part

II

Ch

6

Understanding the Limitations of Table Partitioning

Table partitioning isn't a true cure for all your performance ills, and should not be the only technique that you try to help improve the speed of your application. Performance tuning and monitoring is discussed in detail in Chapter 22, "Managing and Monitoring Performance," and is worth reading as a good comprehensive discussion on all issues relating to performance.

Table partitioning has some limitations that you should be aware of:

- You can't partition a table that has a clustered index on it—this would be in direct conflict with the needs of the clustered index to store the data in the absolute order of the index.

- You can't use the highly optimized table delete command of Transact-SQL—Truncate Table.

- You can't actually even drop a table until it has been unpartitioned.

- You can't use the system-stored procedure sp_placeobject to move a table onto another segment because the partitioning is already responsible for spreading the data on the table's segments.

- You can't alter the number of partitions. However, you can unpartition the table first and then repartition it.

- Any tables with long data of either Text or Image datatypes will be able to be partitioned; however, the Text and/or Image data will be stored in separate disk areas of sequentially allocated segmented disk space.

- If a particular partition runs out of space on the segment, Sybase will automatically use a page from another segment. However, this causes substantial performance problems because Sybase maintains a mapping record in the originally attempted segment to the new page and may also cause pages to be on the same physical device.

- Indexes cannot be partitioned, so there may still be performance and data insert contention due to inserts into the index itself.

> **N O T E**   To unpartition a table, you use the Alter Table command with a new option of Unpartition. The syntax for the Unpartition command is as follows:
>
> Alter Table *Table_Name* Unpartition
>
> *Table_Name* is the name of the table that you want to unpartition. ■

From Here...

In this chapter, you learned how to create and manage database tables. The process of creating a table involves the selection of the appropriate datatypes for your table columns and then the application of logical constraints to those columns. You learned to create, drop, and list the characteristics of a table using Transact-SQL syntax and the Sybase SQL Server Manager.

For further discussion about topics mentioned in this chapter, see the following chapters:

- Chapter 4, "Introducing Transact-SQL," teaches you how to use Transact-SQL syntax to retrieve the data that you've stored in table columns.

- Chapter 7, "Using Rules, Defaults, and Triggers," teaches you how to create and bind rules and defaults to user-defined datatypes and table columns.

- Chapter 8, "Understanding Indexes and Keys," provides information on how to create and use keys and indexes and how to constrain rows and columns to unique values.

- Chapter 10, "Understanding Stored Procedures," teaches you how to define storage structures, such as parameters and local variables, by using system variables. You also learn how to reference global variables.

- Chapter 23, "Using Sybase's Configuration Options," shows you how to use query options to control the display of data through Set command options.

Part

II

Ch

6

Using Rules, Defaults, and Triggers

Sybase has a number of ways that you can enforce and manage the integrity of data that is stored in your tables. In this chapter, you learn how to use the most common ways to make sure that the data in a table is the data that you want in the table.

Rules are used to help define the valid values that can be inserted into a column when a record is added to a table. Defaults are used to help you catch a situation in which a programmer fails to supply a value for a column (during an Insert), and you want a Default value to be inserted into the database.

Triggers are a method that Sybase provides to the application programmer and database analyst to ensure data integrity. Triggers are very useful for those databases that are going to be accessed from a multitude of different applications because they enable business rules to be enforced by the database instead of relying on the application software. ■

How to manage data integrity through rules, defaults, and triggers

Sybase provides several different ways to manage your data. This chapter introduces you to the key data management objects and methods.

How to review and manage the rules, defaults, and triggers on your database

Sybase provides a number of system-stored procedures that can be used to view information on triggers.

Examples and tips for writing your own rules, defaults, and triggers

Practical examples show you how to write each of the data integrity objects, which you can use on your own server.

Understanding Rules

Rules are provided by Sybase to enhance the checking of data that is entered into a column when you Insert or Update a record in a table. The advantage of a rule is that you can have a basic table column defined as something like Char(12) and then apply advanced checks to ensure that the data entered is formatted in a particular way that you specify.

Creating Rules

To create a rule in the database, you use the Create Rule Transact-SQL command. You also can use Sybase SQL Server Manager to create rules, but it doesn't save you any time doing it that way, so there's no point documenting its use here.

The syntax for Create Rule is as follows:

```
Create Rule Rule_Name
As Rule_Expression
```

Rule_Name is a valid Sybase object identifier and *Rule_Expression* is an expression that correctly defines the rule's values.

A *Rule_Expression* is a set of Transact-SQL commands that defines the values of a passed-in argument. Remembering that a rule is evaluated per column, you would most likely name the argument either a generic name, such as @sRuleArgument, or if you know specifically the column that a rule is being bound for, you could name the argument the same as a column. If this all seems a little confusing, perhaps have a look at the example below, which is designed to create a rule that validates social security formatting:

```
Create Rule Rule_SSN_Format
As @sSSNField Like   "[0-9][0-9][0-9]-[0-9][0-9]-[0-9][0-9][0-9][0-9]"
Go
```

TIP To simplify the identification of rules, it's a good idea to prefix a rule's name with Rule.

The name of the argument really doesn't make any difference, provided that you prefix it with an @ sign. The logic of the *Rule_Expression* can be anything that you would use in a Where clause of a regular SQL statement.

An example of a rule that validates that only people with certain color eyes are added to a table might be the following:

```
Create Rule Rule_Eye_Color
As @Color In ( 'Green', 'Blue', 'Brown' )
Go
```

Applying Rules to Columns

Creating a rule just defines the object in the database. It has no value until it is applied to a column in a table. The process of applying a rule is known as *binding* the rule to the column. To bind a rule to a column, you use the system stored procedure `sp_bindrule`. The syntax for `sp_bindrule` is as follows:

```
sp_bindrule Rule_Name, Object_Name
```

Rule_Name is the name of the rule created earlier and *Object_Name* is a fully qualified column (including the table name separated by a period). For example, to bind the rule created earlier, `Rule_Eye_Color`, to the column *Eyes* in the table *body*, you would execute:

```
sp_bindrule Rule_Eye_Color, "body.Eyes"
Go
```

To remove a rule that is bound to a column, you use the system stored procedure `sp_unbindrule`. The syntax for `sp_unbindrule` is as follows:

```
sp_unbindrule Object_Name
```

For example, to unbind the rule bound to the *Eyes* column, you would execute:

```
sp_unbindrule "body.Eyes"
Go
```

N O T E You can only have one rule per column, so if you have complex statements or conditions that need to be tested, you may be better off using a `trigger`. ■

Getting Information on Rules

There are two easy ways that you can get information describing the views in the database. You can use Sybase SQL Server Manager's Rule browser or you can execute `sp_help` on a particular table to see if it has any rules associated with it.

Using Sybase SQL Server Manager to Examine Rules   To use Sybase SQL Server Manager to view rules, follow these steps:

1. Run Sybase SQL Server Manager from the Sybase System XI group.
2. Log on to the server, and open the database that you want to manage.
3. Select the Rules folder in the left pane, and you get a list of rules that are currently created in the database (see Fig. 7.1).
4. Double-click the rule that you want to review to display the Sybase SQL Server Manager Rule dialog box (see Fig. 7.2).
5. To modify or review the columns and tables that are bound to the rule, click the Bindings tab (see Fig. 7.3).

Part

II

Ch

7

FIG. 7.1
SSM provides a convenient detailed view of the rules that are created on the database. In the right pane, you can identify the create date and the owner of the rule.

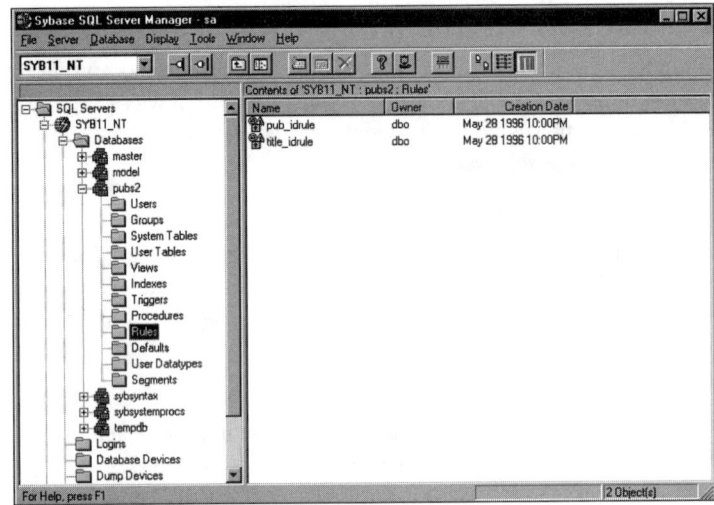

FIG. 7.2
The SSM Rule dialog box enables you to review and modify the text in the rule. (In addition, by clicking the Dependencies tab, you can see which objects this rule depends on.)

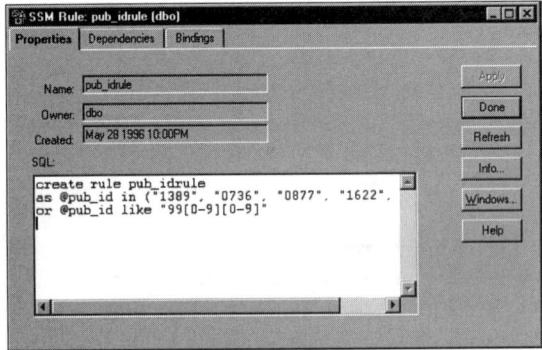

FIG. 7.3
The Bindings tab provides an easy method to manage the way the rule is bound to a particular column. To bind the rule to a column, move the required column from the Available Objects list to the Bound Objects list, and click Apply.

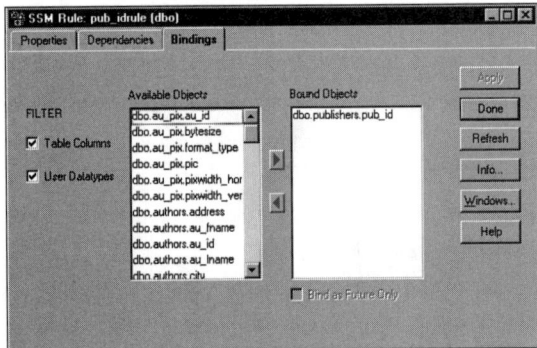

Using sp_help to Examine Rules The system stored procedure `sp_help` is your universal way to find out information about an object. When you execute it on a table that has a rule, you see that indicated in the far right column. For example, if you executed `sp_help` on the *publishers* table, you would see that there is a rule, `pub_idrule`, bound to the `pub_id` column:

```
sp_help publishers
Go


Name        Owner Type
---------- ----- ----------
publishers dbo   user table
Data_located_on_segment         When_created
---------------------------- --------------------------
default                         May 28 1996 10:00:27:930PM
Column_name    Type           Length Prec Scale Nulls Default_name
  Rule_name       Identity
---------------------------- ------------------------------------------------
pub_id         char                   4              0
  pub_idrule            0
pub_name       varchar               40              1
                      0
city           varchar               20              1
                      0
state          char                   2              1
                      0
...
Object is not partitioned.
```

Revoking or Dropping Rules

To remove a rule from the database, you execute the Drop Rule command in Transact-SQL. The syntax for Drop Rule is as follows:

```
Drop Rule Rule_Name
```

For example, to drop the rule created earlier, you would execute:

```
Drop Rule Rule_Eye_Color
Go
```

N O T E You cannot drop a rule that is bound to a column. You must unbind the rule from any columns first. ▨

Understanding Defaults

Defaults are provided in Sybase to help you handle inserts that are executed by your users that don't include all the columns for a table. Defaults are particularly useful when you need to add a column to an existing table and don't have the capability to modify all applications that use the table to make sure that they supply an appropriate value for the column.

Defaults and rules behave very similarly. You create a default on the database, and then bind it to a particular column just like you bind rules to columns.

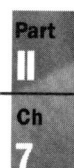

Part
II

Ch

7

Creating Defaults

Creating a default is almost always done by using the `Create Default` Transact-SQL command. You can create defaults using Sybase SQL Server Manager, but there's no particular advantage to doing so because it requires that you still enter basically the same information. The syntax for `Create Default` is as follows:

```
Create Default Default_Name
As Expression
```

Default_Name is a valid Sybase identifier that is used to identify the Default you are creating, and *Expression* is a constant of any datatype. For example, to create a default date, such as "Christmas," you would execute the following:

```
Create Default Def_Christmas
As '12-25-1996'
Go
```

To create a default, such as "Zero" (which is useful for binding to numeric columns), you would execute the following:

```
Create Default Def_Zero
As 0
Go
```

Applying Defaults to Columns

Binding a `Default` to a column is almost the same process as binding a `Rule` to a column: you use the system stored procedure `sp_bindefault`. The syntax for `sp_bindefault` is as follows:

```
sp_bindefault Default_Name, Object_Name
```

For example, to bind "Zero" to the table *Account* on the column *Balance,* execute the following:

```
sp_bindefault Def_Zero, "Account.Balance"
Go
```

To undo or remove a default from a column, you use the system-stored procedure `sp_unbindefault`. The syntax for `sp_unbindefault` is as follows:

```
sp_unbindefault Object_Name
```

For example, to unbind the "Zero" `Default`, execute the following:

```
sp_unbindefault Def_Zero
Go
```

Getting Information on Defaults

Retrieving information on defaults is essentially the same process used for rules: you can use the system stored procedure `sp_help` to show you if any Defaults exist on a particular table, or you can use Sybase SQL Server Manager. To use Sybase SQL Server Manager to find out information about Defaults, follow these steps:

1. Run Sybase SQL Server Manager from the Sybase System XI group.

2. Log in to the server and open the database that you want to manage.

3. Select the Defaults folder in the left pane, and you get a list of defaults that are currently created in the database (see Fig. 7.4).

FIG. 7.4
In this view, Sybase SQL Server Manager shows you each default created on the database, who created the default, and when it was created.

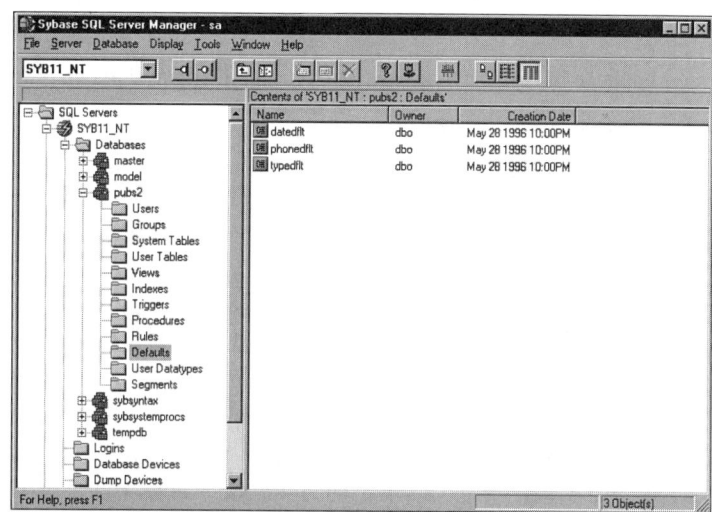

4. Double-click the rule that you want to review to display the Sybase SQL Server Manager Default dialog box, which is identical to the Rules dialog box except its title (see Fig. 7.2).

5. To modify or review the columns and tables that are bound to the rule, click the Bindings tab.

Revoking or Dropping Defaults

To remove a default from the database, you execute the `Drop Default` command in Transact-SQL. The syntax for `Drop Default` is as follows:

```
Drop Default Default_Name
```

For example, to drop the default created earlier, you would execute the following:

```
Drop Default Def_Zero
Go
```

N O T E You cannot drop a default that is bound to a column. You must unbind the default from any columns first. ■

Part
II

Ch
7

Understanding Triggers

A *trigger* is a special type of stored procedure that is executed by Sybase automatically when a particular table modification, such as an Update, is actually applied (or "hits") by the Sybase server on a given table. The most common use of a trigger is to enforce business rules in the database. Triggers are used when the standard constraints or table-based *Declarative Referential Integrities* (DRI) are not adequate. If a DRI constraint is enforced by Sybase, then the trigger will not be executed because it was not needed.

Triggers have a very low impact on the performance of the server and often are used to enhance applications that have to do a lot of cascading operations on other tables and rows.

▶ **See** "Defining Keys," **p. 221**

In Sybase System 10, Sybase added ANSI compliant DRI statements that can be used in the Create Table statement. The sorts of rules that can be enforced by them are relatively complex; however, it makes the understanding of the table creation quite difficult.

Besides the inability to perform complex business rule analysis based on values that are supplied when a trigger is executed, DRI has one important limitation: the current implementation does not permit referencing values in other databases. Although this may seem a relatively insignificant problem, it has a substantial impact on those people trying to write distributed applications that may need to check data constraints or values on other databases and servers.

Within a trigger, there are some limitations and they are described below. In general, unless you intend to move your application to another ANSI-compatible, SQL92 database platform (which ensures DRI compliance), you will be best served by the use of triggers over constraints or DRI because the triggers offer more functionality than DRI offers. However, there is a performance cost for both DRI and triggers. My recommendation is to run a test or quality assurance (QA) environment with triggers or DRI enabled, but for production systems, to remove them. This way, you get to find all the flaws in QA, but get the performance gains in production.

 TIP To provide a good level of recovery for your applications, you always should maintain an offline copy of your stored procedures, triggers, table definitions, and overall structure of the server-side of your Sybase application. This information can be used to reload the server in case of any problems.

Creating Triggers

It is possible to create a trigger both using Sybase SQL Server Manager and using the Transact-SQL statement Create Trigger. Using Sybase SQL Server Manager to create a trigger is not done often because it doesn't really save you any time or buy you anything.

Creating a trigger using Transact-SQL is much like declaring a stored procedure, and it has a similar syntax, as follows:

```
Create Trigger Trigger_Name
On Table_Name
For {Insert, Update, Delete}
As Sql_Statement
```

The options for the Transact-SQL command `Create Trigger` are as follows:

- *Trigger_Name*—The name of the trigger must conform to standard Sybase naming conventions.

- `Insert`, `Update`, `Delete`—With these keywords, the trigger's scope is defined. This determines which actions initiate the trigger.

- *Sql_Statement*—A trigger can contain any number of SQL statements in Transact-SQL, provided they are enclosed in valid `Begin` and `End` delimiters. Limitations on the SQL statements permitted in a trigger are described in the next section.

N O T E When a trigger is executed, a special table is created by Sybase into which the data that caused the trigger to execute is placed. The table is either `Inserted` for `Insert` and `Update` operations or `Deleted` for `Delete` and `Update` operations. Because triggers execute after an operation, the rows in the `Inserted` table are always a duplicate of one or more records in the trigger's base table. Make sure that a correct join identifies all the characteristics of the record being affected in the trigger table so that data is not accidentally modified by the trigger itself. (See the following examples to get an idea of how to construct a trigger.) ▨

Examining Limitations of Triggers

Sybase has some limitations on the types of SQL statements that can be executed while performing the actions of a trigger. The majority of these limitations are because the SQL cannot be rolled back (or inside a transaction), which may need to occur if the `Update`, `Insert`, or `Delete` that caused the trigger to execute in the first place also is rolled back.

The following is a list of Transact-SQL statements that are not permitted in the body text of a trigger; Sybase will reject the compilation and storing of a trigger with these statements:

- All database and object creation statements: `Create Database`, `Table`, `Index`, `Procedure`, `Default`, `Rule`, `Trigger`, and `View`

- All `Drop` statements

- Database object modification statements: `Alter Table` and `Alter Database`

- `Truncate Table`

N O T E `Delete` triggers are not executed when a `Truncate` operation is initiated on a table. Because the `Truncate` operation is not logged, there is no chance for the trigger to be run. However, permission to perform a `Truncate` is limited to the table owner and to the system administrator `sa`—and it cannot be transferred, making it unlikely for this event to happen unnecessarily. ▨

- Object permissions: `Grant` and `Revoke`
- `Update Statistics`
- `Reconfigure`
- Database load operations: `Load Database` and `Load Transaction`
- All physical disk modification statements: `Disk...`
- Temporary table creation: either explicit through `Create Table` or implicit through `Select Into`

Additionally, the following are limitations that should be clearly understood:

- A trigger cannot be created on a view, but only on the base table or tables that the view was created on.
- Any `Set` operations that change the environment, although valid, are in effect only for the life of the trigger. All values return to their previous states once the trigger has finished execution.
- Manipulating binary large object (BLOB) columns of datatype `Text` or `Image`, whether logged or not by the database, will not cause a trigger to be executed.
- `Select` statements that return result sets from a trigger are not advised because of the very special handling of result sets that would be required by the client application code (whether in a stored procedure or not). Take care to make sure that all `Select` operations read their values into locally defined variables available in the trigger.

> **CAUTION**
>
> Sybase will not warn you if you create a trigger on a table that already has a trigger. Instead, Sybase simply replaces the existing trigger with the new one. Take care that you don't accidentally lose a trigger by overwriting it with another one.

Using Triggers

In this section, several types of triggers are created for use. These examples aren't very sophisticated, but should give you ideas on how you might implement triggers in your own environment.

Triggers are *fired* or *executed* whenever a particular event occurs. In the following sections, you see the different events that can cause a trigger to be executed and some idea of what you may want to do on those events.

Using Insert and Update Triggers   `Insert` and `Update` triggers are particularly useful because they can enforce referential integrity constraints and make sure that your data is not invalid before it ever enters the table. Typically, `Insert` and `Update` triggers are used to verify that the data on the columns being monitored by the trigger meets the criteria required. Triggers are used when the criteria for verification are more complex than what can be represented in a declarative referential integrity constraint.

In Listing 7.1, the trigger is executed whenever a record is inserted into the *sales* table or when it is modified. If the order date does not occur during the first 15 days of the month, the record is rejected.

Listing 7.1 CHP07_01.SQL—Simple Trigger to Stop a Record from Being Inserted

```
/*
   This is a simple trigger that
   monitors inserts into the sales
   table
*/
Create Trigger Tri_Ins_Sales
On     sales
For    Insert, Update
As

/* declare local variables needed */
Declare     @nDayOfMonth      tinyint

/* Find the information about the record inserted */
Select @nDayOfMonth = DatePart( Day, I.Date )
From   sales s, Inserted I
Where  s.stor_id = I.stor_id
And    s.ord_num = I.ord_num

/* Now test rejection criteria and return an error if necessary */
If @nDayOfMonth > 15
Begin
      /* Note: Always Rollback first; you can never be sure what
      kind of error processing a client may do that may force locks
      to be held for unnecessary amounts of time */
      Rollback Tran

      /* Raise an error so that front-end applications can track down
         problems if they occur */
      Raiserror 20100 'Orders must be placed before the 15th of the month'
End
   Go
```

N O T E Notice the way the Inserted table is referred to in the previous join. This *logical* table is created specially by Sybase to enable you to reference information in the record being modified. Using an alias I (as shown) makes it easy to reference the table in the join criteria specified in the Where clause. ■

If you were to try to Insert a record that violated the trigger, you would execute something like the following:

```
Insert sales( stor_id, ord_num, date )
Values    ( '5023', 'Blah Order', '6/19/1996' )
Go
```

Part

II

Ch

7

```
- - - - - - - - - - - - - - - - - - - - - - - - - - - - - - - - - - - - - - - - -
Orders must be placed before the 15th of the month
```

Using Delete Triggers   Delete triggers typically are used for two reasons. The first reason is to prevent deleting records that will have data integrity problems if they indeed are deleted (for example, they are used as foreign keys to other tables). The second reason for a Delete trigger (which is really an extension of the first reason) is to perform a cascading delete operation that deletes children records of a master record, such as deleting all the order items from a master sales record.

In Listing 7.2, the trigger is executed whenever a user attempts to delete a record from the *stores* table. If there are sales at that store, then the request is denied.

Listing 7.2   CHP07_02.SQL—Using a Delete Trigger to Stop Invalid Deletes

```
/*
    Trigger to demonstrate the use of the Delete
    option when creating and working Triggers
*/

Create Trigger Tri_Del_Stores
On     stores
For    Delete
As

/* First check the number of rows modified and disallow
anybody from deleting more than one store at a time */
If @@RowCount > 1
Begin
    Rollback Tran
    Raiserror 20101 'You can only delete one store at a time.'
End

/* declare a temp var to store the store
that is being deleted */
Declare @sStorID char(4)

/* now get the value of the author being nuked */
Select @sStorID = D.stor_id
From   stores s, Deleted D
Where  s.stor_id = D.stor_id

If exists (Select *
        From   sales
        Where  stor_id = @sStorID )
Begin
    Rollback Tran
    Raiserror 20102 'This store cannot be deleted because there are still
sales valid in the sales table.'
End
 Go
```

Use `Raiserror` as an easy way to send the calling process or user detailed and specific information about the error to the calling process or user.

Using Nested Triggers

Triggers can be nested up to 16 layers deep. However, if it is not desirable to have nested trigger operations, Sybase can be configured to disallow them. Use the nested triggers option of `sp_configure` to toggle this option.

▶ **See** "Configuring and Managing Servers," **p. 635**

Triggers become nested when, during execution of one trigger, it modifies another table on which there is another trigger—which is therefore executed.

 You can check your nesting level at any time by inspecting the value in `@@NestLevel`. The value will be between zero and 16.

Sybase cannot detect nesting that causes an infinite loop during the creation of a trigger until the situation occurs at execution time. An infinite loop could be caused by having a trigger, `Trigger_A` on `Table_A`, that executes on an update of `Table_A`, causing an update on `Table_B`. `Table_B` has a similar trigger, `Trigger_B`, that is executed on an update and causes an update of `Table_A`. Thus, if a user updates either table, then the two triggers would keeping executing each other indefinitely. If Sybase detects such an occurrence, it shuts down or cancels the trigger.

N O T E If a trigger causes an additional modification of the table from which it was executed, it does not cause itself to be executed recursively. Sybase has no support for *re-entrant* or *recursive* stored procedures or triggers in the current version. ■

For example, suppose you have two triggers: one on the *sales* table and one on the *stores* table. The two triggers are defined in Listing 7.3.

Listing 7.3   CHP07_03.SQL—Creating Two Nested Triggers

```
/*
   These two triggers are used to demonstrate
   nesting in trigger execution
*/

/* First trigger deletes stores if the sales are deleted */
Create  Trigger Tri_Del_Sales
On      sales
For     Delete
As
```

continues

Part

II

Ch

7

Listing 7.3   Continued

```
/* Announce the trigger being executed */
Print "Delete trigger on the sales table is executing..."

/* declare a temp var to store the store
that is being deleted */
Declare @sStorID char(4)

/* now get the value of the store being deleted */
Select  @sStorID = stor_id
From    Deleted            /* Deleted is a fake table created
                              by Sybase to hold the values of
                              records deleted */

Group By stor_id

/* Now delete the store record */
Print "Deleting store %1!", @sStorID


Delete  stores
Where   stor_id = @sStorID
Go

/* Second trigger deletes discounts if a store is deleted */
Create  Trigger Tri_Del_Stores
On      stores
For     Delete
As

/* Announce the trigger being executed */
Print "Delete trigger on the Stores table is executing..."

/* declare a temp var to store the store
that is being deleted */
Declare @sStorID char(4)

/* now get the value of the store being deleted */
Select  @sStorID = stor_id
From    Deleted            /* Deleted is a fake table created
                              by Sybase to hold the values of
                              records deleted */

Group By stor_id

If @@rowcount = 0
Begin
        Print "No Rows affected on the stores table"
        Return
End

/* Now delete the store record */
Print "Deleting discounts for store %1!", @sStorID


Delete  discounts
Where   stor_id = @sStorID
  Go
```

If a `Delete` is executed on the *sales* table, the trigger is executed on the *sales* table, which in turn causes a trigger to execute on the *stores* table.

```
Delete From sales
Where stor_id = '8042'
Go


-------------------------------------------------
Delete trigger on the sales table is executing...
Deleting store 8042
Delete trigger on the Stores table is executing...
Deleting discounts for store 8042
```

TIP Triggers and DRI don't typically work together very well. I recommend that, wherever possible, you implement either triggers or DRI.

Handling Rollbacks in Triggers

Because triggers mainly are used to ensure data and referential integrity, they must be prepared to handle errors. When an error occurs, you typically will perform a rollback to return the data to its original state. Triggers can handle two types of rollbacks—transaction rollbacks and trigger rollbacks—as follows:

- `Rollback Transaction`—When your trigger uses the `Rollback Transaction` statement after an error occurs, the entire transaction (including anything that was executed prior to the trigger itself being fired) is rolled back, and any statements in the calling program that follow the rollback will not be executed. You would use this sort of rollback when you are writing a trigger that you expect to be called from many different situations and you don't want other invalid operations to continue to be executed.

- `Rollback Trigger`—When your trigger uses the `Rollback Trigger` statement after an error occurs, the rollback affects only the data modification that caused the trigger to fire. Any statements in the calling program that follow the rollback will still be executed.

Displaying Trigger Information

If you need to view the behavior that is being enforced on a table due to a trigger, you must display the information that describes the triggers (if any) that a table owns. There are a number of ways of obtaining information about a trigger that is on any given table. In this section, the two most common—using Sybase SQL Server Manager and the system procedures `sp_help` and `sp_depends`—are demonstrated.

Using Sybase SQL Server Manager to Review Triggers   There are two ways to view information about a trigger using the Sybase SQL Server Manager. The first way is to perform the following steps:

1. Run Sybase SQL Server Manager from the Sybase System XI group.
2. Log in to the server and open the database that you want to manage.

3. Select the Triggers folder in the left pane, and you get a list of triggers that currently are created in the database (see Fig. 7.5).

FIG. 7.5
The details view of the SSM shows you a list of triggers that exist for the *pubs2* database and the tables they are created on.

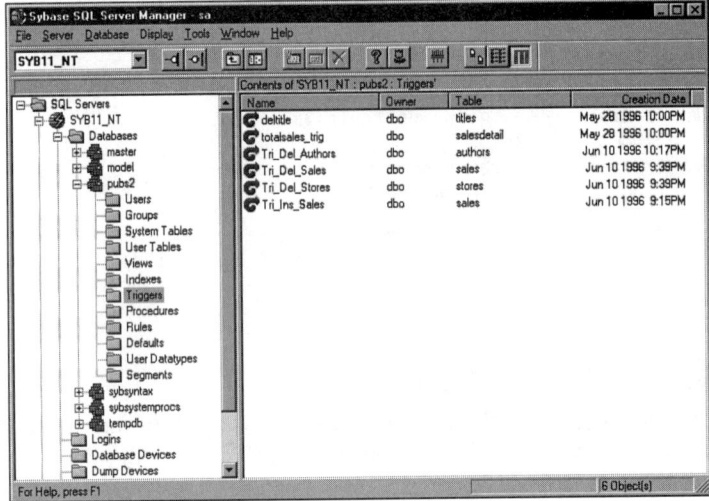

4. Double-click the trigger that you want to review to display the Sybase SQL Server Manager Trigger dialog box (see Fig. 7.6).

FIG. 7.6
The SSM Trigger dialog box enables you to review and modify the text in the trigger. (In addition, by clicking the Dependencies tab, you can see which objects this trigger depends on.)

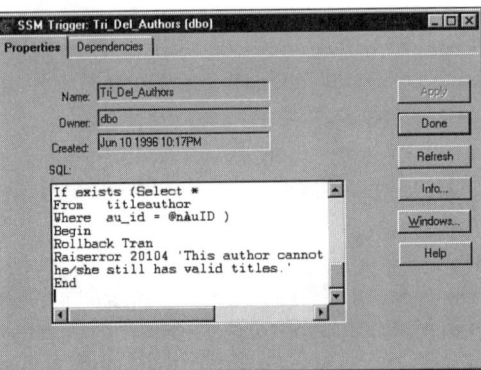

The other way to review trigger information involves examining the table that has (or may have) a trigger on it and clicking the Indexes/Triggers tab (see Fig. 7.7).

Using sp_help, sp_depends, and sp_helptext   The system stored procedures—sp_help, sp_depends, and sp_helptext—provide valuable information in determining if a trigger exists, what it references, and what its actual text or source code looks like. In Listing 7.4, a trigger is created that you will examine with different system stored procedures below.

FIG. 7.7

The Indexes/Triggers tab of the SSM Table dialog box lists all the indexes and triggers that belong to the table. To review an individual trigger, select the trigger in the list and click the Go To button.

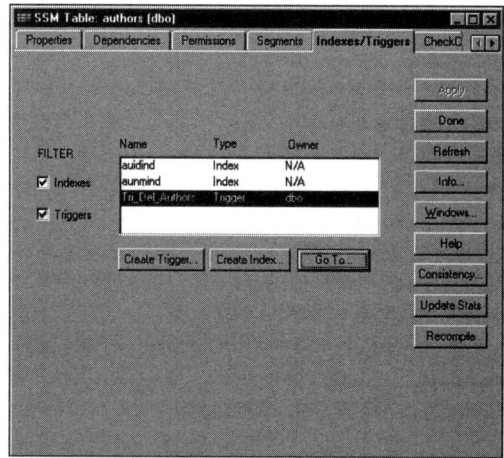

Listing 7.4   CHP07_04.SQL—Working Trigger that Stops Deletes from the Authors Table

```
/* create a basic trigger to stop anyone deleting an
author that still has records titleauthor table */

Create Trigger Tri_Del_Authors
On     authors
For    Delete
As

/* First check the number of rows modified and disallow
anybody from removing more than one author at a time */
If @@RowCount > 1
Begin
     Rollback Tran
     Raiserror 20103 'You can only delete one author at a time.'
End

/* declare a temp var to store the author
that is being deleted */
Declare     @nAuID id

/* now get the value of the author being deleted */
Select @nAuID = D.au_id
From   authors A, Deleted D     /* Deleted is a fake/logical table created
                                   by Sybase to hold the values of
                                   records deleted */

Where A.au_id = D.au_id

If exists (Select *
           From   titleauthor
           Where  au_id = @nAuID )
```

Part

II

Ch

7

continues

Listing 7.4   Continued

```
Begin
     Rollback Tran
     Raiserror 20104 'This author cannot be deleted because he/she still has
valid titles.'
End
 Go
```

Using sp_help   The system-stored procedure `sp_help` is a generic procedure that reports information about any object in the database. The following syntax can be used:

```
sp_help [Object_Name]
```

If the *Object_Name* is omitted, Sybase will report information on all user objects found in the *sysobjects* system catalog table.

By using `sp_help`, you can determine who created a trigger and when it was created. The following is an example of the output from `sp_help` when used on the trigger created in Listing 7.4, `Tri_Del_Authors`:

```
sp_help Tri_Del_Authors
Go

Name             Owner Type
---------------- ----- -------
Tri_Del_Authors dbo    trigger
Data_located_on_segment        When_created
------------------------------ --------------------------
not applicable                 Jun 10 1996 10:17:11:443PM
```

Using sp_depends   The system stored procedure `sp_depends` returns a database object's dependencies, such as tables, views, and stored procedures. The syntax is as follows:

```
sp_depends Object_Name
```

After adding the trigger shown in Listing 7.4, if you want to see an example of the output from `sp_depends`, execute the following:

```
sp_depends authors
Go

In the current database the specified object is referenced by the following:
name                                           type
---------------------------------------------- ----------------
dbo.reptq2                                     stored procedure
dbo.titleview                                  view
dbo.Tri_Del_Authors                            trigger
```

Using sp_helptext   User defined objects, such as rules, defaults, views, stored procedures, and triggers, store their text in the system catalog table, *syscomments*. This table is not the most easy to read, so the sp_helptext procedure is provided to enable easier access. The syntax for `sp_helptext` is as follows:

`sp_helptext` *Object_Name*

Dropping Triggers

There are a number of reasons that you might want to remove triggers from a table or tables. For example, you might be moving into a production environment and you want to remove any triggers that were put in place to enforce good quality assurance but that were costing performance. Or, you might simply want to drop a trigger so that you can replace it with a newer version. To drop a trigger, use the following syntax:

`Drop Trigger` *Trigger_Name*`[,`*Trigger_Name…*`]`

Dropping a trigger is not necessary if a new trigger is to be created that will replace the existing one. Note also that by dropping a table, all of its child-related objects, such as triggers, also are dropped. The following example drops the trigger created in Listing 7.4:

```
Drop Trigger Tri_Del_Authors
Go
```

From Here...

In this chapter, you learned about the values of rules, defaults, and triggers and how they can be applied to enforce referential integrity in your application. In addition, you learned that triggers can be nested and that they can be used to provide more complex business rule validation than `Constraints` that can be defined during table creation. Take advantage of rules to enforce per column integrity checks, and use defaults to catch any missed columns in an `Insert`.

Look at the following chapters for more information that may be useful in helping you write effective triggers:

- Chapter 8, "Understanding Indexes and Keys," discusses how to enforce integrity constraints through table-based declarative referential integrity and unique indexes.

- Chapter 10, "Understanding Stored Procedures," is an introductory chapter on working with Sybase's Transact-SQL language to create stored procedures and triggers.

- Chapter 13, "Using Advanced Stored Procedures and Triggers," provides advanced examples and information on how to create stored procedures that you can execute as triggers.

Part
II

Ch
7

Understanding Indexes and Keys

One of the most important responsibilities of a database designer is to correctly define a database table for optimal performance. Sybase's basic table design doesn't specifically define how data is to be accessed or stored physically, beyond data-type constraints and any referential constraints placed on a column or columns designated as `Primary Key`. Instead, Sybase provides a mechanism of indexes or keys to a table that help the program optimize responses to queries.

Without an index, Sybase must *table scan*, or read every row in a table, before it can know the answer to any given query. In large tables, this is obviously an expensive option for the server to take. Indexes provide a way for Sybase to organize pointers to the required data. An index in a database works the same way as an index in a reference book. Like a book index, an index in a database is a list of "important" values that contain references to pages in the database table that contain the information that matches the index value. This enables the database to read from a (usually) smaller list of index pages that will in turn point to the data that will answer any given request. ∎

Defining Indexes

Indexes are Sybase's internal method of organizing the access to data in a table in such a way that it can be retrieved in an optimal fashion. *Optimal*, in this case, refers to the quickest way. Sybase indexes are collections of unique values in a given table: their corresponding list of pointers to the pages of data where those values are physically represented in a table.

At a high level, indexes are a shorthand way for the database to record information that it's storing in tables. Indexes are just another kind of object in the database and have storage needs like tables. Just as tables require pages of data in which to store their rows, indexes require pages to store their summary data in. The advantage of an index is that it generally reduces the number of I/Os required to reach any given piece of data in a table.

When you create an index in Sybase, you tell the database to scan the table, gather the discrete values in the particular column or columns being indexed, and then write a list of data pages (and row identifiers) to the index page that match the value being indexed. This enables the server to scan a list of index pages before choosing to scan the whole table for matching data.

Sybase provides no interface to interact with the indexes. They are a transparent entity that Sybase uses by itself to determine the best way of retrieving data from the database. The presence of an index and the data it contains are known to Sybase and not to the application or program that is requesting data.

Understanding the Types of Indexes

When you index data, there are a couple of things you can do. If, for example, you want to index or optimize the access to a table based on a column, you would simply create an index on that column. That is the simplest form of an index. One obvious example might be the last name of an employee.

If, however, you need to create an index on a table that has multiple columns that describe the record you want to find (for example, the last name *and* the first name of the employee), you would create a *composite* index, *composed* of the unique values of each of the items.

Sybase also permits the creation of a *unique* index. An index that is unique ensures that all the data or rows added to the underlying table have unique values. This feature enables you to enforce data integrity or uniqueness in Sybase's data.

In terms of data storage, Sybase has two different types of indexes that you can create: `clustered` and `non-clustered`. These different types of indexes control the way the summary data that the index stores is structured. At the most basic level, both index types are B-tree based. A B-tree index seeks to sort or index data in a tree structure, based on unique values for the data. The structure involves a root page of data that has the high-level splits of the data. For example, say you have a data set consisting of the following cities:

```
Unsorted Data
-------------
Canberra
Sydney
```

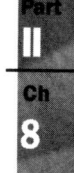

```
Melbourne
Albuquerque
Coonabarrabran
New York
Washington
Brisbane
Portland
Charles City
Orlando
Minneapolis
San Francisco
Port Douglas
```

If you wanted to index this data by the name of the city, a B-tree index would build a root page that contained as many unique values as fit (remember Sybase's implementation will be a 2K page minus a little bit of space needed for index header information) that clearly describe the coming data. Usually, this means that the index will have the first distinct value in alphabetical order. For example, the following might be the data that was stored in the root page:

```
Large Root Page
- - - - - - - - - - - - -
Albuquerque
Canberra
Melbourne
New York
Orlando
Port Douglas
San Francisco
Washington
```

Note that if there wasn't much room in the root page, the database server would reduce the values so that it broke down the available data into groups of the alphabet, such as:

```
Small Root Page
- - - - - - - - - - - - -
Albuquerque
Melbourne
Port Douglas
San Francisco
```

In this way, the database is responsible for balancing the load in the root page. The idea is that it maximizes the utilization at the root so that the minimum number of I/Os are required to find a record.

After the root page are one or many branch pages. Like the root page, branch pages are required to split up the data until you get to the lowest page of the index, which is known as the leaf page. The leaf page contains a pointer to the data itself in the table. In the last example, if you consider the data, a branch page for Albuquerque might contain the following elements:

```
Branch Page
- - - - - - - - - - - - -
Brisbane
Canberra
Charles City
Coonabarrabran
```

The purpose of the B-tree is to define a unique list of values that ultimately describes the location of the data. Remember that in the table, there may actually be multiple records from `Canberra`. For example, the following values may actually be in the leaf pages previously described by the branch page:

```
Leaf Page
- - - - - - - - - - - - - - - - - - - -
Brisbane        (0x1232142)
Brisbane        (0x1232145)
Brisbane        (0x1232163)
Brisbane        (0x1232190)
Brisbane        (0x1232242)
Brisbane        (0x1232432)
Brisbane        (0x1232525)
Brisbane        (0x1233366)
Canberra        (0x1232142)
Canberra        (0x1232145)
Canberra        (0x1232163)
Canberra        (0x1232190)
Canberra        (0x1232242)
Canberra        (0x1232432)
Canberra        (0x1232525)
Canberra        (0x1233366)
...
```

Note that in the above leaf pages, the number in parentheses is an example of a *pointer* to the actual data page. The purpose of the index is to speed up access to the table; it is quicker to find a record from a distinct list of values that the index contains than it is to scan the entire table from top to bottom (*table scanning*).

Using Clustered Indexes   A `clustered index` is a special index that minimizes the number of branch pages. In fact, a `clustered index` sorts the data in the table in the exact same order as the index. The advantage of a `clustered index` is that maximum performance is achieved when retrieving a record by the index. If you need to find an account record in a listing of customer accounts, a `clustered index` on it will have the fewest number of I/Os; once the index has been scanned through the primary or root page and the branch page, you will be sitting right on the record.

Obviously, there are a few limitations of clustered indexes:

- You can only have one per table. If you think about it, this makes sense. There's only one way to physically store the data. If it's in the order of the `clustered index`, then the data is stored that way and can't be rearranged without creating an additional table.

- `Clustered indexes` take a lot of disk space to create. Because they have to reorganize the data in a table, creating a clustered index requires about 120 percent of free space available, compared to the space consumed by the table data in the database while the creation is performed.

- `Clustered indexes` perform a lot of I/O if you are adding records in the middle of a table that already has a lot of data in it. If you anticipate adding new data to a table, make sure that you configure a large amount of free space per data page on the tables for which you create `clustered` indexes; otherwise, you will incur a performance penalty.

`Clustered indexes` are almost always quicker to use to find data than `non-clustered indexes` because the data page is right on the leaf of the index. In addition, you can get substantial performance improvements when you use a `clustered index` on tables from which you expect to retrieve ranges of data. Because the data is stored in order, fetching a range of data is simply the act of reading contiguous pages from the index. `Non-clustered indexes` do not guarantee or influence the storage of the underlying table data; as such, they may cause performance penalties when retrieving range-based data because you have no way of knowing whether the data is stored contiguously in the underlying table or not. Nine times out of ten, you will find that the data is stored in the order that it was placed or inserted into the table, with little regard for the way the `nonclustered index` was created. Take as an example a need to retrieve a range of data, such as an alphabetical list of customers with last names between *F* and *K*. If you were using a `nonclustered index`, Sybase would be required to jump around on the physical disk because the index is not in the same order as the data.

Using NonClustered Indexes   `Nonclustered Indexes` store their data independently from the underlying table data; therefore, there can be more than one of them per table. You can create up to 249 different `nonclustered indexes` per table if you want to.

Each `nonclustered index` is a straight B-tree designed to speed up table access by reducing the number of I/Os required to find a data record in the underlying database table being indexed.

A `nonclustered index` is the default; if you don't specify that an index be clustered at creation time, Sybase will create it nonclustered.

Because a `nonclustered index` does not influence the table's data storage, the recommended procedure is to create the index itself on a different segment than the table. This will give you substantial performance improvements if the segments are placed on different physical devices because the I/Os performed to the underlying table and the index can be performed in parallel.

▶ **See** "Creating Segments," **p. 114**

Why Index Data?

The primary reason for indexing data is to improve data access times. The difference between finding a record on an indexed column and on an unindexed column can be very dramatic. However, there are some caveats that you should be aware of before arbitrarily indexing every column in a table:

- Indexes take up a lot of space or disk storage. It is possible to consume more space in the database with indexes than with the data itself. Take care that you balance the needs of performance with your data storage requirements.

- Indexes will slow down `Inserts`, `Updates`, and `Deletes` if you are modifying indexed data columns. This occurs because the database not only has to update the underlying data table, but also has to modify the index data, which are kept up to date. However, this cost will be easily recouped when you consider the benefits that you get during the retrieval of data from the database table.

- Creating indexes takes a lot of time.

- Indexes only provide value where a lot of different values are listed in the columns being indexed, a feature known as *cardinality*. If the table column has a low number of distinct values, then it has a high cardinality and is a bad choice for indexing because the number of branch pages would be severely limited. In other words, you will end up with as many leaf pages in the index as you would data pages in the underlying table. For example, there's usually no point in indexing such a column as *sex,* which only has two values: *male* and *female.*

- You cannot place indexes on columns that have datatypes of bit, image, or text because Sybase has no way of understanding the underlying data or knowing the boundaries of the column. An indexed *key value* can only be 249 bytes wide, which makes it impossible to use for image or text data that are at least 2K in size.

Despite these cautions, I urge you to create appropriate indexes for the most commonly accessed data. For example, if you have a historical database table that has data stored by account number and also has a record create date column, I recommend adding a *composite* index on the combination of the data columns. This will enable you to do sorting and searching based on the historical data as well as just by the account number.

You should consider indexing all columns that are commonly used for queries (for example, in the Where clause) and all columns that are used for sorting. This will enable Sybase to optimize its access to the data for you. In addition, you should look to index those columns that are used when joining between two or more tables. Once indexed, these columns will enable Sybase to perform an index merge to find the data, which is the quickest way of joining two tables.

Creating Indexes

Sybase has two methods of creating indexes: a graphical method provided in Sybase SQL Server Manager and a Transact-SQL command, using the Create Index statement. Only the table's owner can create an index on a table. It is often easier to use Sybase SQL Server Manager to create an index because you don't have to remember the syntax of the SQL statement involved in the Create function. However, if you ever need to run any kind of automated installation of a database, you will need to know the Transact-SQL commands required so that you can place them in a script file that can be run against the database you are creating.

Creating an Index with Sybase SQL Server Manager   To create a simple index using Sybase SQL Server Manager, follow these steps:

1. Run Sybase SQL Server Manager from the Sybase for Windows NT folder in the Start menu. Connect to the server and select the database to which you want to add an index.

2. Open or click the Indexes folder in the left pane of Sybase SQL Server Manager to display a list of currently created indexes on the database. In Figure 8.1, you can see a list of indexes on the *pubs2* database created by Sybase on installation of the server.

FIG. 8.1

The list (or details view) of SSM provides good information to help you understand all the indexes currently created on your database.

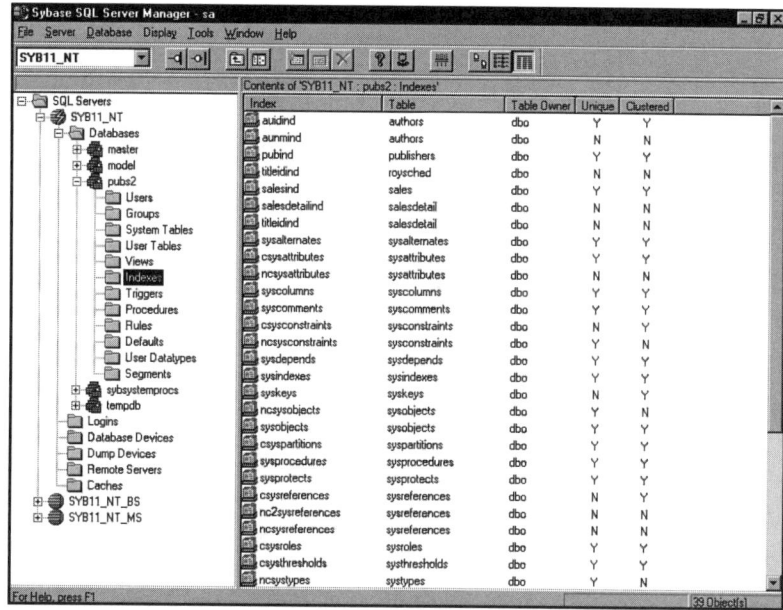

3. Right-click the right pane of the Sybase SQL Server Manager or click the Indexes folder itself and select Create Index. This will open the Sybase SQL Server Manager Create Index dialog box that you can see in Figure 8.2.

4. Enter a name for the index that you want to create.

 TIP Prefixing index names with *pk* for primary key or *fk* for foreign key makes it easier to identify the index type without having to inspect its properties.

5. Select the segment on which you want the index created. For better performance in a `nonclustered index`, select a segment other than that where the table is located. Sybase will give you twice the I/O performance because an additional thread will be allocated to all reads and writes from the index, especially if it is located on a different physical drive.

6. Select the table you want to index in the table combo box—as you do so, the list of Available Columns will be filled, giving you a list from which to select.

7. Select the column, or columns if you are creating a *composite* index, that you are indexing from the Available Columns list; click the right-facing arrow to move the selected column to the Indexed Columns list.

8. Check the Primary Key check box if you want Sybase to automatically set the required fields for a Primary Key field (unique values).

9. Click the Create button to create the index.

FIG. 8.2

The SSM Create Index dialog box provides all the options you will need to create any type of index without ever needing to know the correct Transact-SQL syntax.

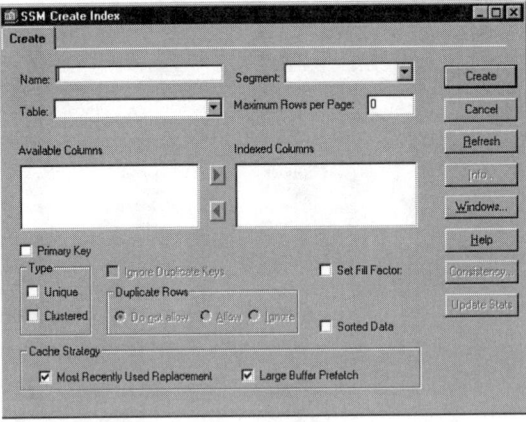

After creating the index, an additional tab, Segments, will be available (see Fig. 8.3). In addition to adding an extra tab, Sybase SQL Server Manager's Index properties dialog box has a few extra buttons enabled: Consistency and Update Stats. These buttons are provided to help you manage the index.

FIG. 8.3

The segments tab of the SSM Index dialog box enables you to see how the index uses segments of the database for storage.

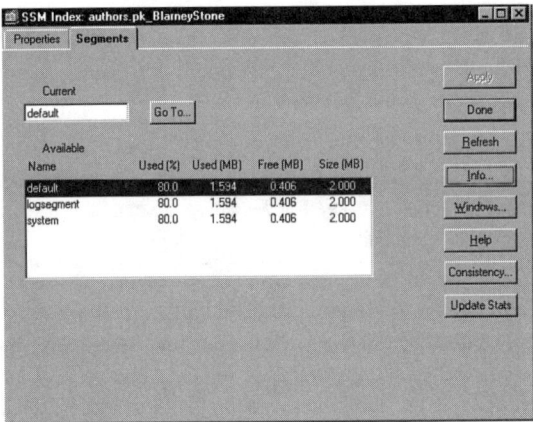

Clicking the Consistency button will take you to the Consistency Check dialog box for the selected index, as shown in Figure 8.4. This dialog box's options provide you with the capability to perform database consistency checks on the index without needing to remember the syntax for the DBCC commands.

For example, to do a full analysis of the index, select the Index Allocations radio button and then check the Full Report Type option. By checking the Fix problems check box, you would be instructing Sybase to correct any errors that were found. In Figure 8.5, you can see a sample of what Sybase SQL Server Manager returns after checking an index.

FIG. 8.4

The Consistency Check dialog box gives you easy access to the DBCC options that are appropriate for an index.

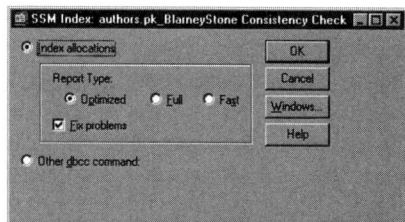

FIG. 8.5

The output from a Consistency Check can be quite lengthy. Here's an example of a quick check on a very small index. Notice that the database was placed in Single User mode to run this command.

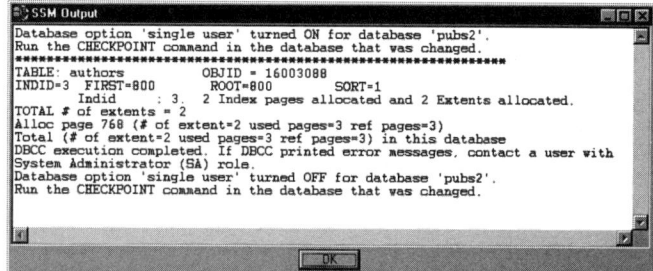

> **N O T E** A number of advanced options weren't discussed in this section. They are explained in detail in the following section. ■

Creating an Index with Create Index   The command Create Index in Transact-SQL is used by the Sybase SQL Server Manager to perform the index creation: creation occurs when the Create button is clicked in the Sybase SQL Server Manager Indexes dialog box. The syntax for Create Index is as follows:

```
Create [Unique] [Clustered | Nonclustered] Index Index_Name
On [[database.]owner.]table_name (Column_Name [, Column_Name]...)
[With
      [FillFactor | Max_Rows_Per_Page = x]
      [[,] Ignore_Dup_Key]
      [[,] Sorted_Data]
      [[,] {Ignore_Dup_Row | Allow_Dup_Row}]]
[On Segment_Name]
```

The options for the Transact-SQL command Create Index are as follows:

■ *Unique*—If an index is created as unique, Sybase disallows duplicate values in the index and therefore stops a client from inserting a record into the base table. This is the most common use of an index to enforce integrity on a table. Unique indexes can't be created on tables that have duplicate values in the columns being indexed—the duplicate data must be removed first. If enabled, the Ignore_Dup_Key option (described later) allows Updates that modify index keys to complete, even if the new index key values become duplicates. The duplicate values will be rolled back and the transaction will continue; no error will be generated.

■ *Clustered*—A clustered index is a special index that forces Sybase to store the table data in the exact order of the index. Using a clustered index to physically store the data in the table in a particular way can greatly improve access performance to the table. Data requested from tables that are scanned repeatedly by the index key value can be found very quickly because Sybase knows that the data for the index page is right next to it. Any further values are guaranteed to be in the following data pages.

If Clustered isn't specified in the Create Index statement, the index is assumed to be Nonclustered. There can be only one clustered index per table because the data can be in only one physical order.

> **CAUTION**
>
> Specifying a segment for a clustered index to be placed upon will actually move the table data too. Be careful using the On *segment_name* keyword when creating a clustered index. You must have approximately 120 percent space free on the target segment for the clustered index and data; otherwise, the segment's free space will be filled and a new segment will need to be created. Sybase won't warn you before index creation that the segment space is inadequate because it has no way of knowing or accurately estimating the size required for the index.

■ *Nonclustered*—This is the default index type and means that Sybase will create an index whose pages of index data contain pointers to the actual pages of table data in the database. You can create up to 249 nonclustered indexes in a table.

■ *Index_Name*—An index name must be unique by table; that is, the same index name can be given to two indexes, provided that they're indexing different base tables in the database. Index names must follow standard Sybase naming conventions for objects.

> ▶ **See** "Understanding Names You Can't Use," **p. 710**

■ *Table_Name*—This is the name of the table that is being indexed.

■ *Column_Name*—This is the column that's being indexed. If more than one column is placed here, a composite or compound index is created. Multiple columns should be separated by spaces. You can specify up to 16 columns to create a composite key; however, the maximum width of the data types being combined is 256 bytes.

■ *FillFactor* = *x*—Specifying a FillFactor on an index tells Sybase how to "pack" the index data into the index data pages. FillFactor tells Sybase to preserve space on the index data page for other similar rows that are expected for the same index keys or similar index key values.

Specifying a FillFactor for frequently inserted database tables can improve performance because Sybase won't have to split data onto separate data pages when the index information is too different to fit on a single page. Page splitting is a costly operation (in terms of I/O) and should be avoided if possible. The value of the FillFactor refers to the percentage of free space that should be preserved on each index page.

A small `FillFactor` is useful for creating indexes for tables that don't have their complete dataset yet. For example, if you know that a table is going to have many more values than it does now, and if you want Sybase to preallocate space in the index pages for those values so that it won't need to page split, specify a low `FillFactor` of about 10. A page split occurs when the index fills up so that no further values will fit in the current 2K data page. As a result, Sybase *splits* the page in two and puts references to the newly created page in the original page.

A high `FillFactor` will force more frequent page splits because Sybase will have no room on the index page to add an additional value when a new record is inserted into the table. A `FillFactor` of 100 will force Sybase to completely fill the index pages. This option is good for highly concurrent, read-only tables. It's extremely bad, however, for tables that are inserted or updated frequently; every insert will cause a page split, and, if key values are updated, many of the updates will also cause page splits.

If no `FillFactor` is specified, the server default (usually 0) is used. To change the server default, use the system stored procedure `sp_configure`.

▶ **See** "Server Options Explained," **p. 639**

Be careful when specifying a `FillFactor` for a `clustered` index— it will directly affect the amount of space required for the storage of the table data. It is important to note that a `clustered` index is bound to a table because the physical order of the table data is mapped to the order of the `clustered` index. This means that a `FillFactor` on the index will space each data page of the table apart from the others according to the value requested. This idiosyncrasy can consume substantial amounts of disk space if the `FillFactor` is sparse.

N O T E When creating an index on a table without data, specifying a `FillFactor` has no effect because Sybase has no way of correctly placing the data in the index. For tables that have dynamic datasets that need to be indexed with an index specifying a `FillFactor`, you should rebuild indexes periodically to make sure that Sybase is actually populating the index pages correctly.

■ *Max_Rows_Per_Page* = *x*: Sybase deserves credit for recognizing the complexity and pain involved in estimating the correct `FillFactor` required to ensure page density in an index or table because they added the new option `Max_Rows_Per_Page` to simplify matters. As its name implies, this option enables you to define exactly how many rows will be stored on each index page. By specifying a low value in this configuration option, you will reduce the amount of locking contention on the index page because each user will be pushed on to a different page. However, it is possible that a lock will more quickly escalate to a table lock if you update multiple records in a single update because the number of pages affected will be greater. For more information on configuring lock escalation thresholds, see Chapter 23, "Using Sybase's Configuration Options."

The default value for this option is 0 (zero), which means that Sybase will manage the table as it has in the past in Sybase System 10. If you want to change the rows per page limit after the table has been created, you can use the system-stored procedure `sp_relimit`.

CAUTION

The maximum number of rows per page that you can set is 256, which would imply that if you got all the rows on the physical page, then the index row size would be less than eight bytes because a page is 2K in size. This is somewhat unlikely to be the case, and by specifying such a high number, you will force Sybase to do a page split and thereby incur performance penalties. Make sure that the value you suggest for Max_Rows_Per_Page is realistic, given the underlying table data that are being indexed.

- *Ignore_Dup_Key*—When SQL is executed, this option controls Sybase's tendency to cause duplicate records to exist in a table with a unique index defined on it. By default, Sybase will always reject a duplicate record and return an error. This option enables you to get Sybase to continue processing as though this isn't an error condition.

    This configuration option can be useful in highly accessed tables where the general trend of the data is more important than the actual specifics. It shouldn't be used for tables in which each individual record is important, however, unless application code is providing appropriate referential constraints to the data.

    If multiple records are affected by an update or insert statement, and the statement causes some records to create duplicates, the statement will be allowed to continue. Those records that created duplicates will be rolled back with no error returned.

CAUTION

When enabling Ignore_Dup_Key, be careful that you don't lose required data due to the occurrence of unwanted updates. If Ignore_Dup_Key is enabled for a unique index and an update is done to data that causes duplicate records to exist, not only will the duplicates be rejected by the update, but the original records will also be removed. This is because of the way Sybase performs updates—by deleting the record and then reinserting it. The reinsertion of the record will fail due to the duplicity of the record, so neither the original record nor the updated record will exist.

- *Sorted_Data*—Sybase uses the Sorted_Data keyword to speed up index creation for clustered indexes. By specifying Sorted_Data, you're saying that the data to be indexed is already physically sorted in the order of the index. Sybase will verify that the order is indeed correct during index creation by checking that each indexed item is greater than the previous item. If any item isn't found to be sorted, Sybase will report an error and abort index creation. If this option isn't specified, Sybase will sort the data for you as it would do normally.

    Using the Sorted_Data keyword greatly reduces the amount of time and space required to create a clustered index. The time is reduced because Sybase doesn't spend any time ordering the data; the required space is reduced because Sybase no longer needs to create a temporary workspace to place the sorted values before creating the index.

■ `Ignore_Dup_Row`—This option is for creating a non-unique clustered index. If enabled at index creation time on a table with duplicate data in it, Sybase will

- Create the index;
- Delete the duplicate values;
- Return an error message to the calling process indicating the failure. At this point, the calling process should initiate a `Rollback` to restore the data.

If data is inserted into or updated in the table after the index is created, Sybase will

- Accept any non-duplicate values;
- Delete the duplicate values, and in so doing, possibly delete the original record, if a duplicate occurs during an update;
- Return an error message to the calling process, indicating the failure. At this point, the calling process should initiate a `Rollback` to restore the data.

▶ **See** "Undoing a Transaction with Rollback Tran," **p. 294**

N O T E Using `Ignore_Dup_Row` has no effect on `nonclustered` indexes. Sybase internally assigns identifiers to the records being indexed and doesn't have to manage the physical order of the data according to the clustering. ■

■ `Allow_Dup_Row`—This option can't be set on an index that's allowed to `Ignore_Dup_Row`. It controls behavior for inserting or updating records in a non-unique clustered index. If `Allow_Dup_Row` is enabled, no errors are returned and no data is affected if multiple duplicate records are created in a clustered index.

■ `On Segment_Name`—Specifying a segment on which the index can reside allows the placement of an index on a different segment of the data. This will improve performance of `nonclustered` indexes because multiple I/O handlers can be used to read and write from the index and from data segments concurrently.

Clustered indexes that have a segment name specified will move the data that's being indexed, as well as moving the index to the indicated segment.

Understanding Statistics

The value of an index for helping Sybase resolve a query largely depends on how accurately the index's data reflects the actual data in the database. Sybase maintains heuristic or trend statistics on the indexed data to help it choose the appropriate index that will yield the least number of I/Os to get to the actual table data. When available, clustered indexes will almost always be chosen as a valid key over `nonclustered` indexes. Clustered indexes are favored because no physical I/O is necessary after the data is found in the index because the data is on the same page.

Sybase's statistics-gathering engine is on an as-needed basis; its statistics are maintained only when an index is being built or the statistics on those indexes are forced to be updated by the `Update Statistics` statement. Sybase doesn't maintain statistics on the fly purely for performance reasons.

Part II

Ch

8

The additional overhead of maintaining the statistics dynamically generally isn't considered advantageous to fetching the data because on average, it will consume more resources than would have been saved by the additional data. Sybase's statistics indicate trends in the data and don't necessarily represent every key data element. These trends are reviewed by Sybase to determine the best index to use.

An important exception to the benefits of dynamic index statistic management would be an index created on a table with no data in it. Sybase has no way of knowing what the trends in the data are and, as a result, makes very basic assumptions of normal distribution. These assumptions are often very wrong after a number of records are added to the table; thus, Sybase will perform a table scan even though there's an appropriate index. In this situation, perform an Update Statistics on the table, and the index's distribution information will be updated.

Updating Statistics with Sybase SQL Server Manager   To use Sybase SQL Server Manager to Update Statistics on a table or an index, follow these steps:

1. Launch Sybase SQL Server Manager and select the server, database, and table or index that you want to update.
2. Right-click the table or index, and from the context menu, choose <u>U</u>pdate Statistics to perform the Update Statistics command. Sybase SQL Server Manager will give you a message when the Update Statistics function has been completed.

TIP   By updating the statistics on a table, you will update the statistics for all the indexes, not just for a particular index. This can save you the effort of identifying each index that requires an update.

Using Update Statistics   The Update Statistics statement is used to update the index statistics on a table or index. The syntax for Update Statistics is as follows:

```
UPDATE STATISTICS [[database.]owner.]Table_Name [Index_Name]
```

- ■ *Table_Name*—This is the name of the table that the index resides on. If no index is specified, all the indexes on the table are updated at the same time.
- ■ *Index_Name*—This is the name of the index having its statistics updated.

N O T E   Performing an Update Statistics on a database table can affect the plan that a stored procedure has generated for accessing data. Because stored procedures are compiled and stored in the procedure cache when they're first executed, they can store invalid access paths to data based on the index statistics at the time the procedure was first run. To force a stored procedure to refresh its access path, use the system-stored procedure sp_recompile and pass the table that was updated as a parameter. For example, sp_recompile authors will force all the procedures that use the authors table to be recompiled the next time they're executed. ■

Demonstrating Index Benefits

It is possible to show the way an index is being used by using the configurable option statistics io. In Listing 8.1, you can see the execution of a simple select, with the results being the last names of the authors as expected plus some statistical information.

Listing 8.1 CHP08_01.SQL—Using statistics io

```
/*
  This script demonstrates the use of
  statistics io.
*/
Set statistics io On
Go

Select au_lname
From   authors
Order By au_id
Go

au_lname
----------------------------------------
White
Green
Carson
O'Leary
Straight
Smith
Bennet
Dull
Gringlesby
Locksley
Greene
Blotchet-Halls
Yokomoto
del Castillo
DeFrance
Stringer
MacFeather
Karsen
Panteley
Hunter
McBadden
Ringer
Ringer

Table: authors  scan count 1,  logical reads: 1,  physical reads: 0

Total writes for this command: 0
```

The values that are returned from the statistics io command are as follows:

- **Scan count**—This is the number of times that the server searched or traversed an index or table.
- **Logical reads**—This is the number of pages that were read from memory or from the cache.
- **Physical reads**—This is the number of pages that were read from disk.
- **Total writes**—This is the number of writes that Sybase performed to answer your query.

Ideally, you would have all logical reads and no physical reads; what this would mean in simple terms is that all the data you were working with would be in the cache.

In Listing 8.2, a new table, *authors2,* is created and the data populated from the *authors* table. However, this time there are no indexes.

Listing 8.2   CHP08_02.SQL—Creating a Duplicate Table, authors2, without Indexes

```
/*
  Create a duplicate of the authors
  table for showing the benefits
  of indexing.
*/
Create Table authors2(
    au_id       id              NOT NULL,
    au_lname    varchar(40)     NOT NULL,
    au_fname    varchar(20)     NOT NULL,
    phone       char(12)        NOT NULL,
    address     varchar(40)         NULL,
    city        varchar(20)         NULL,
    state       char(2)             NULL,
    country     varchar(12)         NULL,
    postalcode  char(10)            NULL)
Go

Insert Into authors2
Select * From authors

Go
```

The same Select statement is run on the *authors2* table (the same data returned), and these are the statistics io results:

```
Table: authors2  scan count 1,  logical reads: 1,  physical reads: 0
Table: Worktable1   scan count 0,  logical reads: 28,  physical reads: 0
Total writes for this command: 0
```

You will notice that the absence of an index forced Sybase to create a work table, *Worktable1,* into which it placed the data from the *authors2* table in the correct order. Sybase then read the data from *Worktable1* back to the client in a table scan of the new table. The number of read pages went from 1 to 29 and a temporary table was created. Clearly, the fact that the number of reads increased by a factor of 29 shows the benefits of the index. In a similar fashion, you will see great advantages to indexing your data when you have to perform Where clause searching.

TROUBLESHOOTING

I have a client with a large table: 200+ columns and 3 Million rows. The client runs a query that runs for hours with no data returned. The most likely problem is that the query is not retrieving data based on an index. Using ISQL, run the query with SHOWPLAN turned on. If you see in any of the steps the phrase Table Scan, this means that Sybase did not find a suitable index with which to answer your query. You have two options: either reformulate your query so that it takes advantage of existing indexes or add an additional index to help the query. Be forewarned, however, that adding an index on a table with 3 million rows will take a great deal of time and should only be done during a non-production-critical time.

Forcing the Use of a Particular Index

If Sybase fails to pick an index that you know should provide better performance than the index it automatically chose, you can force the use of a different index by specifying it in the From clause. To force an index, use the *optimizer hints* section of the Select statement's syntax. In simplified syntax, here's a Select statement:

```
Select ...
From    Table_Name (n) /* optimizer hints are placed after the table */
...
```

For more information on the syntax of Select statements, see Chapter 4, "Introducing Transact-SQL."

The number in parentheses following the table name tells Sybase to use the index specified by the numeric *n*. If *n* equals 0, Sybase will table scan. If *n* equals 1, Sybase will use the clustered index if one is in the table. The other values of *n* are determined by the number of indexes on the table.

In Listing 8.3, you can see the way you force Sybase to use the optimizer hints when selecting from the *authors* table:

Listing 8.3 CHP08_03.SQL—Using Different Optimizer Hints to Force the Use of an Index

```
/* Turn on statistics io, so that the results can be seen. */
set statistics io on
Go

/* Basic Select with no hints to show the optimizer
   choosing the clustered index */
Select au_id, au_fname
```

continues

Listing 8.3 Continued

```
From    authors
Where   au_id between '172-32-1176' and '238-95-7766'
Order By au_id
Go

/* Force a table scan */
Select au_id, au_fname
From    authors (0)
Where   au_id between '172-32-1176' and '238-95-7766'
Order By au_id
Go

/* Force the clustered index. */
Select au_id, au_fname
From    authors (1)
Where   au_id between '172-32-1176' and '238-95-7766'
Order By au_id
Go

/* Force the first alternate index. */
Select au_id, au_fname
From    authors (2)
Where   au_id between '172-32-1176' and '238-95-7766'
Order By au_id
Go
```

The results of the script are shown here, and you can clearly see its different effects on the work that Sybase needed to perform:

```
Total writes for this command: 0
au_id        au_fname
---------- --------------------
172-32-1176 Johnson
213-46-8915 Marjorie
238-95-7766 Cheryl
Table: authors  scan count 1,  logical reads: 1,  physical reads: 0
Total writes for this command: 0
au_id        au_fname
---------- --------------------
172-32-1176 Johnson
213-46-8915 Marjorie
238-95-7766 Cheryl
Table: authors  scan count 1,  logical reads: 1,  physical reads: 0
Total writes for this command: 0
au_id        au_fname
---------- --------------------
172-32-1176 Johnson
213-46-8915 Marjorie
238-95-7766 Cheryl
Table: authors  scan count 1,  logical reads: 2,  physical reads: 0
Total writes for this command: 0
au_id        au_fname
---------- --------------------
172-32-1176 Johnson
```

```
213-46-8915 Marjorie
238-95-7766 Cheryl
Table: authors  scan count 1,  logical reads: 2,  physical reads: 0
Table: Worktable1   scan count 0,  logical reads: 8,  physical reads: 0
Total writes for this command: 0
```

CAUTION

The effects of forcing an index are clearly shown in these examples. The last example shows an extremely expensive option being forced on the server. You can cause major performance problems by forcing index use, so I generally *do not* recommend that you force alternate indexes to be used.

Forcing index selection in a query is also dangerous if the application code is left unchanged and the indexes are changed or rebuilt. Changing the indexes may cause severe performance degradation due to the forcing of indexes that no longer provide optimal performance.

If you must resort to index forcing and believe that the optimizer should have chosen a different index, it's recommended that you call Sybase or your local support provider and log a bug with the query optimizer.

Getting Information on Indexes

Sybase has two ways to show information about indexes. The graphical method is via Sybase SQL Server Manager's Index Manager; the Transact-SQL way is via the system-stored procedure `sp_helpindex` and the ODBC-stored procedure `sp_statistics`.

Sybase SQL Server Manager's Index Manager has been discussed in detail in previous sections in this chapter. Please refer to the section "Using Sybase SQL Server Manager to Update Statistics" to get instructions on how to view the statistics associated with an index.

Using sp_helpindex   The system-stored procedure `sp_helpindex` has been provided to get information about indexes. The syntax for the procedure's use is

```
sp_helpindex Table_Name
```

`Table_Name` should be replaced with an unqualified table name. If the table you want to inquire on isn't in the current database, you must change to the required database before executing this procedure.

`sp_helpindex` will return the first eight indexes that are found on a database table. In the following example, `sp_helpindex` shows all the indexes on the authors table:

```
sp_helpindex authors
Go

index_name index_description                      index_keys
index_max_rows_per_page
- - - - - - - - - - - - - - - - - - - - - - - - - - - - - - - - - - - - - - - -
auidind    clustered, unique located on default  au_id
0
aunmind    nonclustered located on default       au_lname, au_fname
0
```

Using sp_statistics   `sp_statistics` is a special stored procedure that has been created to help Sybase "publish" information for the ODBC interface to the database. Sybase created this stored procedure so that an ODBC driver could retrieve all the relevant information about an index from a single call to the database. The information returned can be gathered in a number of other ways; however, it's often convenient to use `sp_statistics` to summarize all the relevant information on a particular table. The syntax for `sp_statistics` is as follows:

```
sp_statistics Table_Name [, Table_Owner] [, Table_Qualifier]
    [, Index_Name] [, Is_Unique]
```

The options for the system-stored procedure `sp_statistics` are as follows:

- *Table_Name*—This is the name of the table that you require the index information on.
- *Table_Owner*—This is the owner of the table.
- *Table_Qualifier*—This is the name of the database in which the table resides.
- *Index_Name*—This is the specific index being requested.
- *Is_Unique*—If this parameter is set to `'Y'`, Sybase will return only unique indexes on the table.

 Most stored procedures have many kinds of parameters. To save time, you can indicate a particular one by placing an @ sign in front of the parameter name, rather than specify all the parameters, For example:

```
sp_statistics authors, @is_unique = 'Y'
Go
```

Removing Indexes

Sybase has two ways of dropping indexes on a table. The graphical way can be performed by using Sybase SQL Server Manager. The Transact-SQL way is by using the SQL statement `Drop Index`.

Using Sybase SQL Server Manager to Drop an Index   To use Sybase SQL Server Manager to drop an index, follow these steps:

1. Launch Sybase SQL Server Manager, connect to the server, and select the database and indexes folder in the left pane of Sybase SQL Server Manager.
2. In the right pane of the Sybase SQL Server Manager, select the index you want to drop and choose Index, Delete. A message box appears asking for confirmation in case you accidentally picked the option prior to dropping the index (see Fig. 8.6).
3. Click the Yes button to drop the index.

FIG. 8.6

This SSM Message is the last chance you get to abort the dropping of the index. You cannot undo a dropped index without rebuilding it.

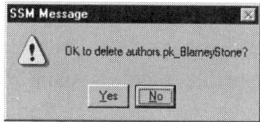

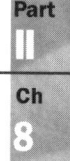

Using the Drop Index Command   To remove an index using Transact-SQL, use the Drop Index statement. The syntax for Drop Index is as follows:

```
Drop Index [owner.]Table_Name.Index_Name
[, [owner.]Table_Name.Index_Name...]
```

The options for the Transact-SQL command Drop Index are as follows:

- *Table_Name*—The name of the table that the index resides on. If the user running Drop Index is the Database Owner (DBO) or System Administrator (SA) and the table isn't owned by that user, *Table_Name* can be prefixed by the *owner* of the table.

- *Index_Name*—The name of the index to be removed. You can remove multiple indexes by indicating them in the same statement, separated by commas.

The following example drops the *barny* index on the *authors* table:

```
Drop Index authors.barny
Go
```

No output is generated after executing this command.

Defining Keys

Keys and indexes are often synonymous in databases; however, in Sybase, a slight difference exists between them. In Sybase, keys can be defined on tables and then can be used as referential integrity constraints in the same fashion as the ANSI standard for SQL.

A *primary key* is a unique column or set of columns that defines the rows in the database table. In this sense, a primary key performs the same integrity role as a unique index on a table, except that notionally, Sybase allows only one primary key to be defined for a table; on the other hand, there can be many unique indexes. Primary keys enforce uniqueness by creating a unique index on the table on which they're placed.

Foreign keys are columns in a table that correspond to primary keys in other tables. The relationship of a primary key to a foreign key defines the domain of values permissible in the foreign key. The domain of values is equivalent to a distinct list of values in the corresponding primary key. This foreign key domain integrity is a useful way of enforcing referential integrity between associated sets of columns. Foreign keys don't create indexes on the table when the key is created.

Primary and foreign keys in Sybase offer much of the functionality that previously had to be coded with triggers in prior versions of Sybase. In versions of Sybase prior to System 10, primary and foreign keys weren't much more than documentation and were useful to third-party programs that needed to know key information about a table. To find out more about the documenting system-stored procedures `sp_primarykey`, `sp_foreignkey`, and `sp_commonkey`, see a following section "Using Keys for Documentation." In Sybase, keys provide needed functionality and should be used as a referential integrity enforcer.

Adding Primary and Foreign Keys

In Sybase, you can add primary and foreign keys in two ways. The graphical method is performed by using Sybase SQL Server Manager. The command-line method is done by using the Transact-SQL command `Alter Table...Add Constraint`, or by specifying `Primary/Foreign Key` in the `Create Table` statement.

Using Sybase SQL Server Manager to Add Primary and Foreign Keys   To use Sybase SQL Server Manager to add a primary key, follow these steps:

1. Launch Sybase SQL Server Manager, connect to the server, and select the database and tables folder in the left pane of the Sybase SQL Server Manager.

2. Select the table that you want to add a key for in the right pane, and choose Table, Properties. This will display the Sybase SQL Server Manager Table dialog box on which you should scroll the tabs until the Referential Constraints tab is visible, as shown in Figure 8.7.

FIG. 8.7
The Referential Constraints tab of the SSM Table dialog box enables you to create and manage primary and foreign keys.

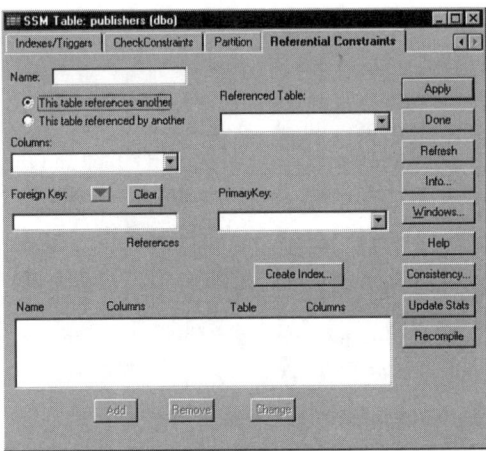

3. If you are adding a foreign key, select the option This Table References Another; if you are adding a primary key, select the option This Table Referenced by Another.

4. Enter a name for the key and select the referencing or referenced table.

5. Select the column or columns that make up part of the key.

6. Press the Add button to add the key temporarily to the dialog box.

7. Press the Apply button to create the key in Sybase.

N O T E Because of the way the Sybase SQL Server Manager Table dialog box works, you can add multiple keys at once using the Add button, and then press the Apply button to have Sybase SQL Server Manager actually create them on the table. ▧

Using Create Table...Primary Key   The `Create Table` syntax has a place for adding a `Primary Key` or a `Foreign Key` in the `Constraint` section. A simplified syntax of the Create Table is shown as follows:

```
Create Table Table_Name
( Column_Name Data_Type Constraint ...,...)
```

In Listing 8.4, tables are created in various ways to show you how to use the `Create Table` syntax to add primary and foreign keys.

Listing 8.4   CHP08_04.SQL—Using Different Table Constraints to Enforce Referential Integrity

```
/* If creating a Table where the primary key name is not
   specified,  the database will assign it. */

Create Table Table_A
( COLUMN_A Smallint Primary Key)
Go

/* Now create a Primary Key specifying the name. */
Create Table Table_B
( COLUMN_B Smallint Constraint PK_COLUMN_B Primary Key)
Go

/* Now create a foreign key referencing Table_A. */
Create Table Table_C
( COLUMN_C Smallint References Table_A( COLUMN_A ) )
Go

/* Now Create a multi-column Primary Key;
   note that the constraint must follow the column list
   if it includes multiple columns itself. */
Create Table Table_D
( COLUMN_D1 Smallint,
  COLUMN_D2 Smallint,
  Constraint PK_D_Columns Primary Key( COLUMN_D1, COLUMN_D2 ) )
Go

/* Now create a foreign key referencing the multi-column
   Primary Key. */
Create Table Table_E
( COLUMN_E1 Smallint,
  COLUMN_E2 Smallint,
```

continues

Listing 8.4 Continued

```
    Constraint FK_E_Columns Foreign Key( COLUMN_E1, COLUMN_E2 )
            References Table_D( COLUMN_D1, COLUMN_D2 ) )
Go
```

Using Alter Table...Add Constraint   The Alter Table...Add Constraint syntax is very similar to the Create Table logic. In the examples in Listing 8.5, the same tables are created, but the Alter Table syntax is used to add the keys.

Listing 8.5 CHP08_05.SQL—Using the Alter Table Syntax of Transact-SQL to Add Constraints to a Table

```
/* Create the table. */
Create Table Table_A
( COLUMN_A Smallint )
Go

/* Add the basic Primary Key without specifying the name. */

Add Primary Key( COLUMN_A )
Go

/* Create the table. */
Create Table Table_B
( COLUMN_B Smallint )
Go

/* Add the Primary Key specifying the name. */
Alter Table Table_B
Add Constraint PK_COLUMN_B Primary Key( COLUMN_B )
Go

/* Create the table. */
Create Table Table_C
( COLUMN_C Smallint )
Go

/* Now create a Foreign Key referencing Table_A.*/
Alter Table Table_C
Add Foreign Key( COLUMN_C )
References Table_A( COLUMN_A )
Go

/* Create the table. */
Create Table Table_D
( COLUMN_D1 Smallint,
  COLUMN_D2 Smallint )
Go
```

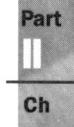

Part
II

Ch
8

```
/* Now Add the multi-column Primary Key. */
Alter Table Table_D
Add Constraint PK_D_COLUMNS Primary Key( COLUMN_D1, COLUMN_D2 )
Go

/* Create the table. */
Create Table Table_E
( COLUMN_E1 Smallint,
  COLUMN_E2 Smallint)
Go

/* Now Add the Foreign Key referencing the multi-column
   Primary Key. */
Alter Table Table_E
Add Constraint FK_E_COLUMNS Foreign Key( COLUMN_E1, COLUMN_E2 )
References Table_D( COLUMN_D1, COLUMN_D2 )
Go
```

Getting Information on Keys

Sybase has two ways to show information about keys. The graphical method is via Sybase SQL Server Manager's Table Manager. The Transact-SQL method is via the system-stored procedures sp_help and sp_helpconstraint, and the ODBC-stored procedures sp_pkeys and sp_fkeys.

Sybase SQL Server Manager's Table Manager has been discussed in detail in previous sections in this chapter. Please refer to the section, "Using Sybase SQL Server Manager To Add Primary And Foreign Keys" for information on how to view the constraints on a table.

Using sp_helpconstraint   Sybase's primary way of displaying information about keys is through the system-stored procedure sp_helpconstraint. Its syntax is as follows:

```
sp_helpconstraint Table_Name
```

In the above, Table_Name refers to the table about which you are trying to find whether there are any constraints.

Using sp_help   sp_help is a generic system-stored procedure that returns information about database tables. Part of the output from sp_help is information on keys on a table. The syntax for sp_help is

```
sp_help Table_Name
```

In the above, Table_Name refers to the table about which you are trying to find any descriptive information.

Using sp_pkeys and sp_fkeys   Sybase provides two system-stored procedures, sp_pkeys and sp_fkeys, that can be used to view key information stored in the database. sp_pkeys and sp_fkeys are procedures that have been created to help ODBC implementers access Sybase's system catalog tables easily.

The syntax for the two procedures is identical and is as follows:

```
sp_pkeys | sp_fkeys Table_Name
```

In the preceding, *Table_Name* is the table for which the keys need to be found.

Using Alter Table...Drop Constraint   To drop a foreign key using Transact-SQL, use the `Alter Table...Drop Constraint` statement. The syntax for this Transact-SQL statement is:

```
Alter Table Table_Name Drop Constraint Constraint_Name
```

The *Table_Name* is the name of the table that the constraint applies to. The *Constraint_Name* is the name of the constraint.

N O T E   You can't drop a primary key if other tables reference it as a foreign key. You must drop those foreign keys first. ■

Using Keys for Documentation

Sybase provides three system-stored procedures that can be used to document your database and make it easier for third-party applications to interact with the database to determine *key* data. These stored procedures are `sp_primarykey`, `sp_foreignkey`, and `sp_commonkey`; all they do is mark certain columns in the database in such a way that application programs can query the system catalog easily to determine indexed or keyed columns. The system-stored procedure `sp_dropkey` is provided to enable you to drop a key from a table.

You can use the system-stored procedures `sp_helpkey` and `sp_helpjoins` to help you query the database for information about keys defined on a table.

Using sp_primarykey   To identify columns in a table that are the primary key, you use the system-stored procedure `sp_primarykey`. The syntax for `sp_primarykey` is as follows:

```
sp_primarykey Table_Name, Column_Name1 [, Column_Name2, ...]
```

Table_Name is the table for which you are adding a primary key and `Column_Name1`... refers to the columns that are used to make up the key.

For example, to add a primary key on the *sales* table, you would execute:

```
sp_primarykey sales, stor_id, ord_num
Go
```

Using sp_foreignkey   To identify columns in a table that are being used as a foreign key to other tables, you use the system-stored procedure `sp_foreignkey`. The syntax for `sp_foreignkey` is as follows:

```
sp_foreignkey Table_Name, Primary_Table_Name, Column_Name1 [, Column_Name2, ...]
```

Table_Name is the table for which you are adding a foreign key, *Primary_Table_Name* is the table that you are referencing, and *Column_Name1*... refers to the columns that are used to make up the key.

For example, to add a foreign key on the *sales* table, you would execute:

```
sp_foreignkey sales, stores, stor_id
Go
```

CAUTION

Make sure that you have added a primary key to the table identified by *Primary_Table_Name* prior to executing `sp_foreignkey`, or Sybase will return an error informing you that no key exists on the primary table.

Using sp_commonkey   To identify columns in two tables that are often used for joining, you use the system-stored procedure `sp_commonkey`. The syntax for `sp_commonkey` is as follows:

```
sp_commonkey Table_Name1, Table_Name2, Column_Name1a, Column_Name2a
        [, Column_Name1b, Column_Name2b, ...]
```

In the above, `Table_Name1` is the first table and `Table_Name2` is the second table.

For example, to add a common key between the *roysched* and *titles* tables, you would execute:

```
sp_commonkey roysched, titles, title_id, title_id
Go
```

Using sp_dropkey   The system-stored procedure `sp_dropkey` is provided to remove keys that you no longer require. The syntax for `sp_dropkey` is as follows:

```
sp_dropkey {'primary' | 'foreign' | 'common' }, Table_Name [, Table_Name2]
```

In the above, `Table_Name` refers to the primary table, and `Table_Name2` refers to the dependent table if the key you are dropping is either a foreign or common key.

For example, to drop the common key created earlier, you would execute:

```
sp_dropkey 'common', roysched, titles
Go
```

Using sp_helpkey   The system-stored procedure `sp_helpkey` is provided to list keys that exist on a table. The syntax for `sp_helpkey` is as follows:

```
sp_helpkey Table_Name
```

In the above, `Table_Name` refers to the table that you want to inquire about.

For example, to find keys associated with the `sales` table, you would execute:

```
sp_helpkey sales
Go

For information on declarative integrity features: PRIMARY KEY, UNIQUE,
FOREIGN KEY, CHECK CONSTRAINT, REFERENTIAL CONSTRAINT, NULL/NOT NULL,
and DEFAULT, use sp_helpconstraint, a new system-stored procedure.

keytype    object    related_object  object_keys
related_keys
-----------------------------------------------------------------
foreign    sales     stores          stor_id, *, *, *, *, *, *, *
stor_id, *, *, *, *, *, *, *
primary    sales     -- none --      stor_id, ord_num, *, *, *, *, *, *
*, *, *, *, *, *, *, *
```

> **N O T E** sp_helpkey does not report information in the form of keys that were created as referential constraints through either `Create Table` or `Alter Table`. You will need to use sp_helpconstraint to find these objects on the table. ■

Using sp_helpjoins The system-stored procedure `sp_helpjoins` is provided to list suggested joins (defined with `sp_commonkey`) that exist between two tables. The syntax for `sp_helpjoins` is as follows:

```
sp_helpjoins Table_Name, Table_Name2
```

In the above, *Table_Name* and *Table_Name2* are the two tables that you want to join.

For example, to find suggested joins between the *roysched* table and the *titles* table, you would execute:

```
sp_helpjoins roysched, titles
Go

a1        a2        b1        b2        c1        c2
d1        d2        e1        e2        f1        f2
g1        g2        h1        h2
----------------------------------------------------------
title_id   title_id
```

From Here...

In this chapter you learned how to create, view, and manage indexes on your data tables. This information is very important in helping you create an optimized database that won't be bogged down by user queries that force table scans. Take a look at the following chapters for more information:

- Chapter 4, "Introducing Transact-SQL," shows some of the ways of writing `Select` statements that retrieve data based on the indexes you create.

- Chapter 23, "Using Sybase's Configuration Options," explains how to make changes to your global server, database, and query configurations to further optimize your queries.

Working with Views

Views provide a way of giving a user a look or *view* at table data that is returned from a `Select` statement. Views provide a *logical* table that is a representation of a query. The advantage of a view is that it can be the data from many tables joined, and it also can be exclusionary in that a `view` can be the result of a query that limits the rows returned by using a `Where` clause.

By now, you should be fairly comfortable with the basic table as a way of storing and organizing data in the database. Tables are made up of columns, and each table can have zero, one, or many rows in it. Also, by now, you should be happy with formulating basic SQL `Select` statements to retrieve data from a table or tables. If you have any problems or queries about how to do either of these steps, you should consult either Chapter 6, "Understanding Tables and Datatypes," or Chapter 4, "Introducing Transact-SQL," for more information.

Views are simply the combination of the `Create` statement that you learned in Chapter 6 to create a table and the `Select` statement that you learned about in Chapter 4. The result of the view is a *logical table* or `view` that can be manipulated just like a regular table. ■

Creating views

Using Transact-SQL, you learn how to create views on database tables. Views simplify database access for those users of your data that are not comfortable with writing joins between tables.

Managing views

Transact-SQL makes views seem very similar to tables. This chapter introduces management tools that are needed when working with views.

Using views for security

Views provide a convenient and easy way to manage security on the data in tables because with a view, you can limit via SQL the data that a user can see or have access to.

Why Use Views?

Views provide a number of advantages over tables that can be basically summarized as follows:

- **Partitioned data**—Through the use of a view, you can partition your data along either horizontal or vertical lines. What this means is that you can split up the data vertically by using one or more tables and only including specific columns that you want a user to have access to. Splitting up the data horizontally works by using a Where clause to eliminate and/or conditionally show records in the view to a user.

- **Enhanced security**—Views are objects in the database just like tables. This means that you can grant and revoke permissions on a view in the same way as a table. By granting and revoking permissions from a user or group of users, you can effectively control the data access that is achieved through the view. For example, in a highly secure environment, there may be no access at all to the underlying tables that make up a view. The only permitted access may be through the view itself. Different groups of users could have different views on the same data that further limits the data that they can access.

- **Simplified data access**—Many computer workgroups have novice or unsophisticated users who have no skills nor need to have the skills to access data using joins and complicated SQL. By creating views for users, it is possible to simplify the access to the table. Views become excellent report writing tools for users that just want to be able to execute simple queries, such as Select * From View_Name.

- **Data abstraction**—If the only access to data in a database is through views, then the Database Administrator can change the underlying tables that make up the view without concern for application programs that reference the data through the view (provided the DBA maintains the same view structure). This provides significant benefits when it is necessary to split up large tables on a historical basis. Say, for example, you have a one million row table that is historically based by month with about 100,000 rows per month. You could split up the table into 12 sub tables and then join the results together for those applications that still need to refer to the complete data set.

Creating and Managing Views

Creating a view is a straightforward process that can be achieved by using the Create View statement in Transact-SQL. Sybase SQL Server Manager also provides a convenient view creator, which can be used to manage the view creation process. I find that the syntax of the Create View statement is so simple (it's really just a Select with a Create in front of it) that this is my preferred way of working with the view. The user interface of Sybase SQL Server Manager is nice if you forget the syntax required to manage the view-creation process.

N O T E Because views are based on standard SQL statements, they can be based on other views. This is a very convenient way of sub-classing data to different levels of abstraction. If you define a view, View2, based on another view, View1, and you need to drop View1 to change its behavior, you can. Doing so will not cause an error for View2 unless a user tries to request data from it. If, however, you re-create View1 before View2 is accessed, then no errors are received and everything is OK.

Creating a View Using Sybase SQL Server Manager

To create a view using Sybase SQL Server Manager, follow these steps:

1. Launch Sybase SQL Server Manager from the Sybase for Windows NT or Sybase for Windows 95 groups.

2. Log on to the server that has the database you want to manage, and open the database in the left pane of the Sybase SQL Server Manager explorer view (see Fig. 9.1).

FIG. 9.1

The explorer view of SSM shows in the left pane a tree representing the highest level of the servers, and then at various detail levels, the objects in the server. In the right pane, the details of the currently selected object are displayed.

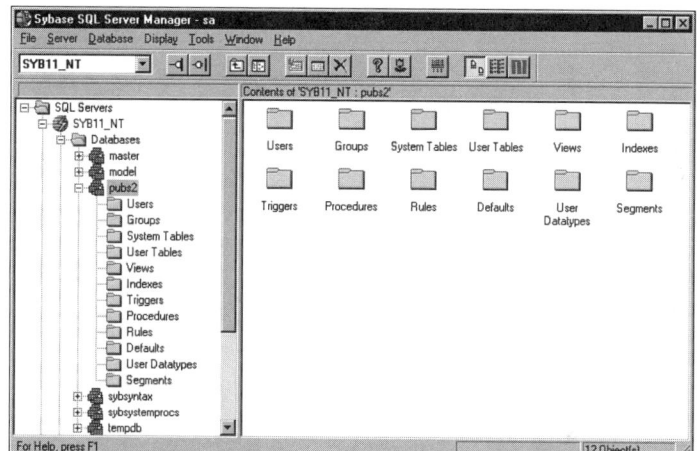

3. In the left pane of the explorer, click the Views folder, or double-click the Views folder in the right pane. This displays the list of views currently created on the database, as shown in Figure 9.2.

FIG. 9.2

In the right pane of the SSM, you can see the list of Views that are created in the *pubs2* database by default.

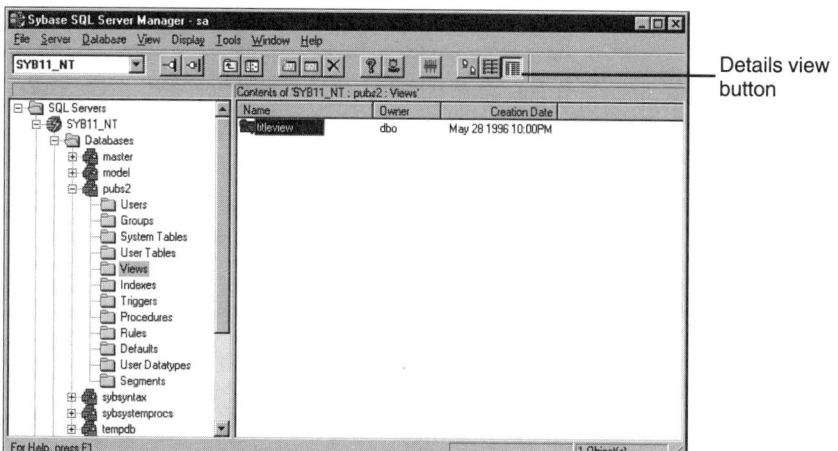

Details view button

4. Choose <u>D</u>atabase, Crea<u>t</u>e, and select <u>V</u>iew to display the Create View dialog box shown in Figure 9.3.

T I P In Sybase SQL Server Manager, it is possible to do things in several different ways. For example, to create a view, you also could have either right-clicked anywhere in the right pane of the explorer view and selected Create View from the context menu that was displayed, or right-clicked the Views folder in the left pane and also selected Create View.

Don't forget that there are plenty of ways to skin a cat, and the one that is most comfortable and easiest to remember will be the one that you end up using.

FIG. 9.3
The SSM Create View dialog box is like all of SSM's dialog boxes: it is modeless and enables you to minimize it independently from any other window or dialog box that you may have previously opened. Use the <u>W</u>indows button to get a list of other windows that are currently open.

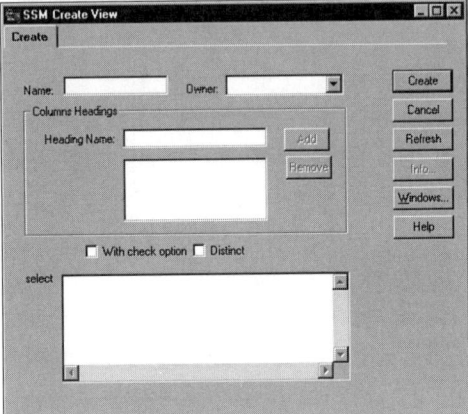

5. Enter the name of the view that you are creating in the Name field and optionally select the owner of the view. If you do not indicate an owner, it will be owned by the database owner (dbo).

6. Enter the column headings that you want to use for the data returned from the view. If you omit column headings, then the columns returned from the Select statement will be used instead.

N O T E   You also can use column aliasing in the body of the Select statement to change the title of the column returned when selecting from the view. ▪

▶ **See** "Renaming Column Titles in Results," **p. 81**

7. Select whether you want the view to be created With Check Option or Distinct. These options are described later in the section titled "Creating a View Using Transact-SQL."

8. Enter the Select statement that will be used for the view. Note that you must not include the keyword Select in the statement itself; Sybase SQL Server Manager automatically prepends the keyword Select to the statement you enter. In Figure 9.4, a basic view is created that returns two columns of data, which have the full name of the author and the author's identifier.

FIG. 9.4

The SSM Create View dialog box simplifies the creation of a view. In this case, a simple view is being created to help access the *authors* table in the *pubs2* database.

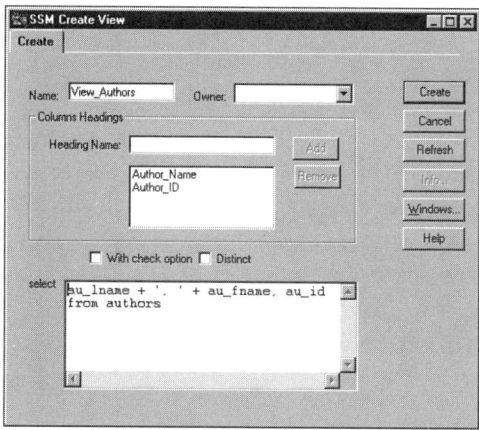

9. Click the Create button to create the view. Doing so changes the appearance of the dialog box so that it enables two additional tabs. These tabs enable you to review any of the underlying tables referred to by the view (Dependencies) and to alter user privileges of the view itself (Permissions), as shown in Figure 9.5.

FIG. 9.5

To change an existing view, alter the text in the SQL field, and click the Apply button that will be enabled after the modification.

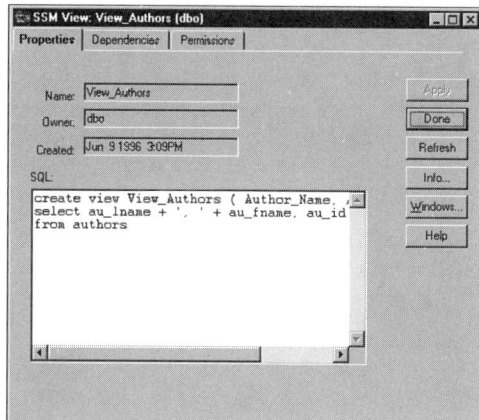

To test the view, you would execute a statement like this:

```
Select *
From   View_Authors
Go
```

The results of the Select would be:

```
Author_Name                                Author_ID
-----------------------------------------  ----------
White, Johnson                             172-32-1176
Green, Marjorie                            213-46-8915
```

```
Carson, Cheryl                          238-95-7766
O'Leary, Michael                        267-41-2394
...
Ringer, Albert                          998-72-3567
```

Creating a View Using Transact-SQL

The simplified syntax for the `Create View` statement is as follows:

```
Create View View_Name [(Column_Name [, Column_Name2...])]
As Select [Distinct] Select_Statement
[With Check Option]
```

The options for the Transact-SQL command `Create View` are as follows:

- `View_Name`—This is the name of the view. To create a view owned by another user, prefix the `View_Name` with the owner name.

- `Column_Name`—This is the title or column name alias that you want to give the columns as when referencing the view's columns.

- `Distinct`—The `Distinct` keyword works as it does in any regular `Select` statement by removing duplicate values from the returned dataset. Note that `Distinct` views cannot be updated.

- `Select_Statement`—This is any valid `Select` statement and has the following limitations: You cannot have a view with either an `Order By` or `Compute` clause; you cannot reference a temporary table in a view.

- `With Check Option`—This forces Sybase to validate that a record modification performed by either an `Insert` or an `Update` still leaves a record visible in the view. For example, say you have a view that only shows authors with home addresses in Florida. If you add a record with a home state of California and the `With Check Option` is enabled on the view, you will get an error due to the fact that the record wouldn't be visible when retrieving data from the view.

To create a view like the one shown in Figure 9.4, you would execute the following SQL:

```
Create View View_Authors ( Author_Name, Author_ID )
As      Select au_lname + ', ' + au_fname, au_id
From    authors
Go
```

TIP If you prefix all the views you create with the letters `View_` or `Vw_`, it will make it easier to identify and differentiate views from regular tables.

To create a view that might be used for aggregating the data in the *titles* table for reporting, you would execute something like the statement in Listing 9.1.

> **Listing 9.1 CHP09_01.SQL—Creating an Aggregate View to Demonstrate the Value of Views for Simplified Reporting**

```
/*
   This simple view demonstrates how to
   aggregate data in the Titles table of the
   pubs2 database for easier reporting
*/

Create View View_TitlesAgg
As
Select type, Count(*)
From    titles
Group By type
Go
```

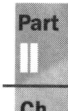

Part
II

Ch
9

If you selected from the view created in Listing 9.1, you would get the following:

```
Select *
From    View_TitlesAgg
Go

type
- - - - - - - - - - - - - - -
business       4
mod_cook       2
popular_comp      3
psychology     5
trad_cook      3
UNDECIDED      1
```

Getting Information on Views

There are a number of system-stored procedures that are valuable when trying to get information about views that are in the database. Sybase SQL Server Manager uses these views to consolidate the information for you when you browse the view.

Using Sybase SQL Server Manager to Inspect Views

To use Sybase SQL Server Manager to get information about a view, follow these steps:

1. Launch Sybase SQL Server Manager.

2. Connect to the Server and Database where the view is located.

3. Select the view you want to manage, and choose View, Properties. This displays the Sybase SQL Server Manager View dialog box for the view you had selected. The first tab of this dialog box is shown in Figure 9.5. On the first tab, you can review the SQL Select statement used to create the view, and also the owner and create date.

4. To view additional properties of the view, such as the tables from which data is retrieved to populate the view, select the Dependencies tab. Figure 9.6 shows the Dependencies tab for the View_Authors created earlier in this chapter.

5. To view and modify any permissions associated with the view, select the Permissions tab (see Fig. 9.7).

FIG. 9.6

The Dependencies tab of the SSM View dialog box shows you the tables and views that are referenced by the view and also the procedures, views, and triggers that reference the view itself.

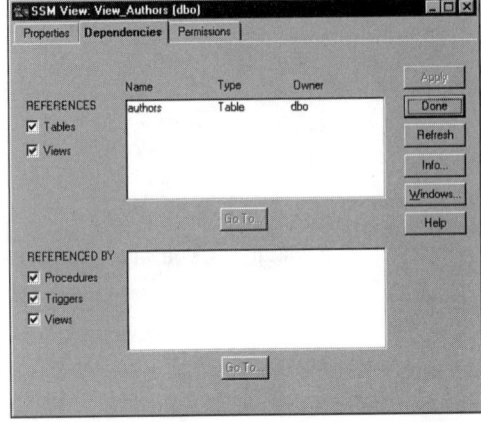

FIG. 9.7

The Permissions tab of the SSM View dialog box gives you the controls to modify any of the permissions associated with the view you currently are working on.

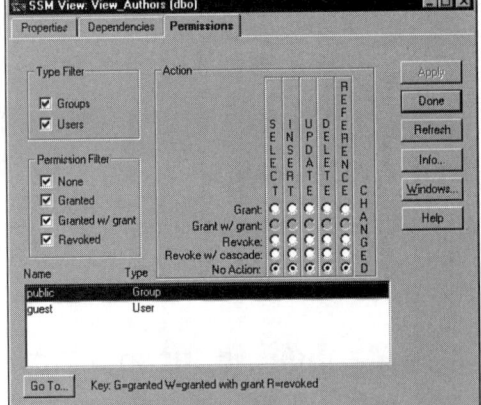

Using System-Stored Procedures to Inspect Views

There are three key system-stored procedures that will help you to find out information about views in the database. The system-stored procedures that you learn about here are as follows:

- sp_depends
- sp_help
- sp_helptext

In addition to these system-stored procedures, it is important to remember that a reference to all database objects is stored in the system catalog table *sysobjects*. In Listing 9.2, you can see a stored procedure that will list all objects from *sysobjects* that are of type 'V' (for views).

Listing 9.2 CHP09_02. SQL—Using sp_listviews to Return a List of Views in the Current Database

```
/*
    This system extension stored procedure is provided for you
    to easily get a list of views in a given database.

    It should be run in the sybsystemprocs database so that it
    is then available for execution in all other databases on the
    same server.
*/

Create Procedure sp_listviews
As
/* Declare a local storage variable */
Declare @sDbName Varchar(32)

/* Get our database name */
Select @sDbName = Db_Name( )

/* Return a string so that the user can identify from where this
   procedure was being run */
Print 'Views in the database: %1!', @sDbName

Select   name, crdate
From     sysobjects
Where    type = 'V'
Order By name
Go
```

If you run this procedure in the *pubs2* database, you would get the following returned:

```
Views in the database: pubs2
name                             crdate
------------------------------   --------------------------
titleview                        May 28 1996 10:00:30:930PM
View_Authors                     Jun  9 1996  3:09:29:710PM
View_TitlesAgg                   Jun  9 1996  4:47:17:173PM
```

Using sp_depends The system-stored procedure sp_depends returns any information that is stored in the system tables indicating dependencies to a supplied object. This procedure works on all database objects, not just views, and its syntax is as follows:

```
sp_depends Object_Name
```

To review information on the View_Authors view that was created earlier, you would execute:

```
sp_depends View_Authors
Go
```

```
Things the object references in the current database.
object                type             updated   selected
--------------------- ---------------- --------- ----------
dbo.authors           user table       no        no
```

Using sp_help   The system-stored procedure sp_help is a generic procedure that returns information about objects stored in the database. The syntax for sp_help is as follows:

```
sp_help [Object_Name]
```

If *Object_Name* is omitted, you will get a list of all the objects in the current database, sorted by object type. For example:

```
sp_help
Go

Name                      Owner  Object_type
----------------------    ----   ----------------
titleview                 dbo    view
au_pix                    dbo    user table
deltitle                  dbo    trigger
sysalternates             dbo    system table
byroyalty                 dbo    stored procedure
pub_idrule                dbo    rule
datedflt                  dbo    default
...
User_type  Storage_type    Length Nulls Default_name    Rule_name
---------  -------------   ------ ----- --------------- ----------
id         nvarchar           11      0
...
```

If you execute sp_help on a particular object, you will get more detailed information. For example, to view detailed information about the view View_Authors created earlier, you would execute:

```
sp_help View_Authors
Go

Name         Owner Type
------------ ----- -----
View_Authors dbo    view
Data_located_on_segment            When_created
---------------------------------  --------------------------
not applicable                     Jun  9 1996  3:09:29:710PM
Column_name Type    Length Prec Scale Nulls
 Default_name Rule_name Identity
-------------------------------------------------------------
Author_Name varchar 62                      0
                                   0
Author_ID   id      11                      0
                                   0
No defined keys for this object.
```

Using sp_helptext   The system-stored procedure `sp_helptext` is provided to enable you to retrieve the text stored on a view, trigger, or stored procedure. The text is stored in the system table *syscomments* and is put together by `sp_helptext` for easy reading. The syntax for `sp_helptext` is as follows:

```
sp_helptext Object_Name
```

For example, to review the text stored for the `View_Authors` view created earlier, you would execute:

```
sp_helptext View_Authors
Go

# Lines of Text
--------------
1

text
----------------------------------------------------------------------------
create view View_Authors ( Author_Name, Author_ID ) as
select au_lname + ', ' + au_fname, au_id from authors
```

Performing DML on Views

Views can be thought of essentially as tables. When you retrieve or reference a view, the view itself is *resolved* so that a full query can be executed on the database tables. This resolution phase is how Sybase determines what data you receive when you execute a query. The reason a resolution takes place is so that Sybase does not have to actually store any data in the database that is in the form of the view itself. If there were no resolution phase, Sybase would have to create a new "table" for each view that was created by a user. This would be extremely costly in terms of database size and performance.

Say you create a view on the *salesdetail*, *stores*, and *titles* tables in the *pubs2* database that looks like the one created in Listing 9.3.

Listing 9.3   CHP09_03.SQL—Using a View to Provide Consolidated Table Access

```
/*
   Simple view to demonstrate the use of
   joins and other DML on a view.
*/

Create View View_SalesInfo ( Store_Name, Book_Title, Quantity )
As
Select st.stor_name, t.title, Sum(qty)
From   salesdetail sd, stores st, titles t
```

continues

Part

II

Ch

9

Listing 9.3 Continued

```
Where  sd.stor_id = st.stor_id
And    sd.title_id = t.title_id
Group By st.stor_name, t.title
Go
```

If you executed a simple query that selected from the view and added an additional piece to get only the records where `Book_Title` was like `'E%'`, you would execute this:

```
Select *
From   View_SalesInfo
Where  Book_Title Like 'E%'
Go
```

Under the covers the resolution phase of Sybase would be executing the following query for you:

```
Select "Store_Name" = st.stor_name, "Book_Title" = t.title,
       "Quantity" = Sum(qty)
From   salesdetail sd, stores st, titles t
Where  sd.stor_id = st.stor_id
And    sd.title_id = t.title_id
And    t.title Like 'E%'
Group By st.stor_name, t.title
Go
```

Selecting Data from a View

As you can see in the previous few paragraphs, selecting data from a view is very straightforward. You can perform all normal operations that are permitted on a table including unions.

For example, using the view created in Listing 9.3, it is possible to generate some interesting results. In Listing 9.4, you can see that all basic SQL operations are supported on `Views`, even the use of a `Union`.

Listing 9.4 CHP09_04.SQL—Showing that Views are Similar to Tables

```
/*
   Performing a union with the results
   of a view
*/

Select 'Books that start with E', Count(*)
From   View_SalesInfo
Where  Book_Title Like 'E%'

Union

Select 'Books that start with G', Count(*)
From   View_SalesInfo
Where  Book_Title Like 'G%'
```

```
Union

Select 'Books that start with L', Count(*)
From   View_SalesInfo
Where  Book_Title Like 'L%'
Go
```

The results of the query are:

```
- - - - - - - - - - - - - - - - - - - - - - - - - - - - - - -
Books that start with G 0
Books that start with L 1
Books that start with E 5
```

A neat trick that views enable you to do is a double grouping. Remember that the view created in Listing 9.3 already is grouped by store name and title. In the following select, we *regroup* the data to show some meaningful cross bookstore sales information:

```
Select Book_Title, "Total Sold" = Sum(Quantity), "# of Sales" = Count(*)
From   View_SalesInfo
Group By Book_Title
Go


Book_Title                       Total Sold # of Sales
- - - - - - - - - - - - - - - - - - - - - - - - - - - -   - - - - - - - - - -  - - - - - - - - - -
But Is It User Friendly?         8780       5
Computer Phobic and Non-Phobic I 375        1
Cooking with Computers: Surrepti 3876       5
Emotional Security: A New Algori 3336       5
Fifty Years in Buckingham Palace 15096      7
Is Anger the Enemy?              2045       2
Life Without Fear                111        1
Onions, Leeks, and Garlic: Cooki 375        5
Prolonged Data Deprivation: Four 4072       4
...
```

Inserting Data Through a View

Inserting data through a view is the same as inserting data into a table. The same Insert syntax is used; the only difference is that you reference the columns described by the view and not those of the underlying table (unless the underlying table's column names are the same as the view's). The following are some restrictions that should be remembered when inserting into a view:

- If you do not have permission to Insert data into the underlying tables, your Insert will be rejected.

- If there are some Not Null columns in the underlying table and they are not available in the view, then your Insert will fail because of the null values. Similarly, any rules or constraint-bound columns that are not accessible from the view also will cause an error.

■ You can perform an Insert, Update, or Delete only on columns in a view that do not contain result data or the results of a function. For example, you would not be able to Insert a record into the view View_Authors because it uses a concatenation of strings in one of the logical columns of the view.

■ You cannot Insert a record into a view that has aggregate data normalized through the use of a Group By clause.

■ You cannot Insert into a multitable view that uses the With Check Option clause.

In Listing 9.5, a view is created that will be used for the demonstration of inserting into a view.

Listing 9.5 CHP09_05.SQL—All the Royalty Arrangements Assigning the Author Greater than 20%

```
/*
   View that will be used to demonstrate inserts,
   updates, and deletes
*/
Create View View_RoySched
As
Select *
From   roysched
Where  royalty > 20
Go
```

The data in this result is as follows:

title_id	lorange	hirange	royalty
BU2075	12001	14000	22
BU2075	14001	50000	24
MC3021	10001	12000	22
MC3021	12001	50000	24
TC3218	12001	14000	22
TC3218	14001	50000	24
BU1111	24001	28000	22
BU1111	28001	50000	24
TC4203	40001	50000	22
BU7832	30001	35000	22
BU7832	35001	50000	24

To add a record to the view View_RoySched and thereby a record to the underlying *royalty* table, you would execute something like this:

```
Insert View_RoySched( title_id, lorange, hirange, royalty )
Values ( 'BU2075', 50001, 75000, 27 )
Go
```

N O T E   In this Insert, a single table was involved in the view. If, however, you have multiple tables in the view, then you would only be able to perform an Insert if you only reference the columns from a single table at a time. ■

To review the effects of the With Check Option, the View_RoySched is re-created in Listing 9.6 to enable view data checking. The With Check Option helps eliminate bad DML from affecting the view's data.

Part

II

Ch

9

Listing 9.6   CHP09_06.SQL—Using the With Check Option Clause

```
/*
    View that will be used to demonstrate inserts,
    updates, and deletes

    Note that this view is checked, so that if you
    try to Insert a record with a royalty less than
    or equal to 20%;
    or Update a record to set the royalty to be less
    than or equal to 20% you will receive an error
*/
Create View View_RoySched_Checked
As
Select *
From    roysched
Where   royalty > 20
With Check Option
Go
```

If an Insert is performed on the data that causes the check to execute, an error occurs. For example:

```
Insert View_RoySched_Checked( title_id, lorange, hirange, royalty )
Values ( 'BU2075', 50001, 75000, 7 )
Go

- - - - - - - - - - - - - - - - - - - - - - - - - - - - - - - - - - - - - - - -
The attempted insert or update failed because the target view was
either created WITH CHECK OPTION or spans another view
created WITH CHECK OPTION.  At least one resultant row from
the command would not qualify under the CHECK OPTION constraint.

Command has been aborted.
```

Updating Data in a View

Updating a view is exactly the same as updating a table. The only exception is when a view contains more than one table. In this case, it is necessary to update values only from a single table at a time.

For example, the view titleview that comes in the *pubs2* database is as follows:

```
create view titleview
as
select title, au_ord, au_lname,
price, total_sales, pub_id
from authors, titles, titleauthor
```

```
where authors.au_id = titleauthor.au_id
and titles.title_id = titleauthor.title_id
Go
```

If you wanted to change both the author's last name and the title of the book, you might think you could execute something like this:

```
Update titleview
Set    au_lname = 'Yakomoto',
       title = 'Sashimi Anyone?'
Where  au_lname = 'Yokomoto'
Go
```

However, you actually get a slightly ambiguous error message:

```
View 'titleview' is not updatable because the FROM clause
names multiple tables.
```

However, you can perform these updates provided you do them individually, for example:

```
Update titleview
Set    title = 'Sashimi Anyone?'
Where  au_lname = 'Yokomoto'
Go
```

```
Update titleview
Set    au_lname = 'Yakomoto'
Where  au_lname = 'Yokomoto'
Go
```

N O T E   The With Check Option clause applies to an Update as well as an Insert, so if you tried to execute the following statement, you would get an error:

```
Update View_RoySched_Checked
Set    royalty = 15
Go
```

This guarantees that you don't accidentally Update a record and then "lose" it from the view—which would probably be quite confusing! ▪

Deleting Data from a View

Deleting data from a view is similar to deleting data from a table with one key consideration. You cannot delete a record from a multitable view.

For example, to delete the record that was previously added to the view created in Listing 9.5 (View_RoySched), you would execute the following:

```
Delete View_RoySched
Where  title_id = 'BU2075'
And    royalty = 27
Go
```

Using Views to Enforce Security

The following are three different ways that views can be used to enhance the security on a database:

- Views enable you to further segment or define addition objects in the database for which different permissions can be granted and revoked independently of the underlying tables.

- Views can limit the columns visible from underlying tables, thereby limiting the sorts of data columns that a user can inquire on.

- Views can limit the rows returned in a table or joined set of tables by applying `Where` clauses.

Part
II
Ch
9

Using Views with Permissions

Assigning permissions to views is a very convenient way of segmenting or redefining the security that applies to a given table or tables. Because you can create multiple views each with different column and row restrictions and then grant permissions on the view, you can give different users access to the same data in a table in different ways without compromising the security of the database.

Say, for example, that you are trying to impose some security restrictions on the authors table in the *pubs2* database. The first thing you should probably do is revoke all permissions from the table so that you know you have a baseline from which to continue working. Assuming that you have all users as members of the default group `public`, you would execute the following:

```
Revoke All On authors From public
Go
```

Having done that, you might create the different views that you want, as shown below in Listing 9.7.

Listing 9.7 CHP09_07.SQL—Several Different Types of Views at Work

```
/*
   This listing creates a few different views
   on the authors table so that you
   can see how to grant different permissions
   to different users of the same table
*/

/* This view has all power */
Create View View_Authors_All
As
Select *
From    authors
Go
```

continues

Listing 9.7 Continued

```
/* This view limits the columns
    that a user can see so that the
    user can't get the authors' addresses */
Create View View_Authors_Limited
As
Select au_lname, au_fname, au_id
From   authors
Go

/* This view limits the rows
    that a user can see so that the
    user can't get access to those
    authors that live in Utah */
Create View View_Authors_Limited2
As
Select *
From   authors
Where  state != 'UT'
Go
```

Now that you have several different views, it is a simple matter to grant permissions on each of them. Say you have three different users—Fred, Barney, and Wilma—and they are going to get access to the views in different ways. The following example shows the sort of SQL you would execute:

```
/* Fred gets full power! */
Grant all on View_Authors_All to Fred
Go

/* Wilma gets limited access to the authors
    that don't live in Utah */
Grant all on View_Authors_Limited2 to Wilma
Go

/* Barney only gets select power on the authors'
    names */
Grant select on View_Authors_Limited to Barney
Go
```

Hiding Columns with Views

In Listing 9.7, the view that was created called View_Authors_Limited demonstrated the power of a view to shield and/or hide sensitive data columns from the user.

For example, if you wanted to give an author access to the titleview view that's created as part of Sybase's *pubs2* database, there may be a concern that they should not be able to see the volume of books sold or the author so that they have no way of negotiating good royalties with the publisher. In this case, a new view might be created based on the titleview view:

```
Create View View_Titles_For_Authors
As
Select title, price, pub_id
From    titleview
Go
```

Then you could be confident that if you gave access to the new view `View_Titles_For_`
`Authors`, the most that an author could find out is that there are other books out there published.

Hiding Rows with Views

In Listing 9.7, the view that was created called `View_Authors_Limited2` demonstrated the
technique of partitioning the data or hiding data that was not suitable by row selection criteria.
Using the `Where` clause is a powerful security enhancement to the database and means that you
can limit which sets of data are visible to a given user or group of users.

For example, if you were concerned about letting other publishers have access to the database
and you didn't want them snooping about in the stores table (which is where you sell all your
books), you might add a view that made it seem as if there are stores only in Oregon:

```
Create View View_Stores
As
Select *
From    stores
Where   state = 'OR'
Go
```

This is a little bit of a nonsense example, but does demonstrate the flexibility of the view as a
method for enforcing security in your database.

Removing Views

Removing or dropping a view is very easy. To do so in Sybase SQL Server Manager, find the
view that you want to remove using the explorer, and choose <u>V</u>iew, <u>D</u>elete. To drop a view
using Transact-SQL, you need to use the `Drop View` command. The syntax for `Drop View` is as
follows:

```
Drop View View_Name
```

`View_Name` refers to the view that you want to drop. You must be the owner of a view in order to
drop it. In addition, a view cannot be in use (i.e., nobody can be performing SQL on it) when
you are dropping the view.

Renaming Views

The process of renaming a view is identical to that of renaming any other database object—you
use the system-stored procedure `sp_rename`. The syntax for `sp_rename` is as follows:

```
sp_rename Old_Object_Name, New_Object_Name
```

`sp_rename` has some limitations, as follows:

- You cannot rename any objects that are not in the current database. You must change to the database in which they reside before renaming them.

- You cannot change any other user's views unless you are the database owner (`dbo`) or the system administrator (`sa`).

- The new name given to the view must be a valid Sybase identifier.

For example, to change the name of the `View_Authors` view created earlier, you would execute:

```
sp_rename View_Authors, Vw_Authors
Go
```

```
---------------------------
Object name has been changed.
```

From Here...

In this chapter, you learned all about views and how they can be used to help you simplify and secure your database. Views are a cheap option for the database in that they don't incur much storage space (just enough to store the text of the view itself), and they don't need to store the underlying data. Views are an excellent object and should be exploited in your database design to help you create a more secure and simplistic database.

Views, however, are not a panacea for extremely complex queries that require more than 16 tables in the join. The same limits still apply to the query; the only benefit is that you don't have to see all the joins when performing a `Select` on the view, making it easier for a novice user to understand the data.

From here, you might want to look at the following chapters:

- Chapter 4, "Introducing Transact-SQL," shows some of the ways of writing `Select` statements that retrieve data from the views that you create.

- Chapter 6, "Understanding Tables and Datatypes," explains how to create tables that are used by the views that you create on top of them.

CHAPTER 10

Understanding Stored Procedures

As your systems become more complex, you'll need to spend more time carefully integrating SQL code with your server-based, stored procedure code. In this chapter, you will learn how to use the logic and flow control statements that are available in Transact-SQL—and how to put them together to make a sensible and usable stored procedure.

> **N O T E** It's important to keep in mind the client/server model when you're building your systems. Remember that data management belongs on the server, and data presentation and display manipulation for reports and inquiries should reside on the client in the ideal model. As you build systems, be on the lookout for those items that can be moved to the two different ends of the model to optimize the user's experience with your application. This is the idea of application partitioning, which is discussed more fully in Chapter 16, "Partitioning an Application." ■

Although SQL is defined in the standards and specifications of SQL89 and SQL92 as a non-procedural language, Sybase System XI permits the use of flow-control keywords to create a procedural program. These keywords enable you to create and store a procedure for subsequent execution. Instead of writing programs using conventional programming language, you can use these stored procedures such as C or Visual Basic, to perform operations with a Sybase database and its tables.

Which flow-control statements are available and how to use them

Programming languages were built around flow control, but databases were built around data. Flow-control statements were added to databases to facilitate the writing of stored procedures.

How to work with server-based Transact-SQL, returning information about the success or failure of your routine

Return codes or visual output to the user can increase the effectiveness of a stored procedure.

How to work with variables within your stored procedures

Variables must be assigned a datatype and a scope.

Some of the advantages that stored procedures offer over dynamic SQL Statements are

- Stored procedures are compiled the first time they are run and are stored in memory in the procedure cache. When compiled, they are optimized to select the best path to accessing information in the tables. This optimization takes into account the actual data patterns in the table, indexes that are available, table loading, and more. These compiled stored procedures can greatly enhance the performance of your system.

- Another benefit is that you can execute a stored procedure on either a local or remote SQL Server. This enables you to run processes on other machines and work with information across servers, not just *local* databases.

- An application program written in C or Visual Basic can also execute stored procedures, providing an optimum "working together" solution between the client side software and SQL Server. This is probably the greatest benefit because it means that you can get the full benefits of server computing performance and still retain the easy-to-use front end of Visual Basic or PowerBuilder.

- Stored procedures can also significantly reduce network traffic because the text for the procedure is stored in the database. When calling a stored procedure, you are only sending the name of the procedure across the network, not an entire set of commands as you would with a batch file. Using stored procedures in heavy transaction processing environments is key to reducing the amount of bandwidth required for many network users.

- You can use stored procedures to provide an additional layer of security on your database. You can grant the `Execute` permission to a use a stored procedure, while not granting any privileges to the tables accessed by the stored procedure. This means that the only way a table could be read or modified would be through a stored procedure. For more information on using stored procedures for security, see Chapter 21, "Managing and Monitoring Security."

- Stored procedures can also be used to help ensure data integrity. Because a stored procedure can be executed as a logical unit of work, if all of the table update processing is not successful, the entire transaction can be rolled back. ■

Creating Stored Procedures

There are two ways that you can create a stored procedure in Sybase: either by using the Transact-SQL command, `Create Procedure`, or by using the graphical Sybase SQL Server Manager. In reality, 99 percent of your stored procedures are going to be created using straight Transact-SQL and a database editor such as RapidSQL or even straight ISQL. However, using Sybase SQL Server Manager is not a bad thing for the ad hoc stored procedure that is created to address your organization's needs. Sybase SQL Server Manager is also a convenient database browser that you can use to get information on existing procedures in your database.

TIP You should always maintain your stored procedure scripts in ASCII files so that you can easily recreate or modify them. Once you have created a stored procedure, the only way to modify it is to drop it and recreate it.

Using Sybase SQL Server Manager to Create a Procedure

To use Sybase SQL Server Manager to create a stored procedure, follow these steps:

1. Launch Sybase SQL Server Manager and logon to the server you work with.

2. Select the database in which you want to create the stored procedure, and in the left pane of the explorer, click the Procedures folder to display a list of stored procedures that have been compiled onto the database (see Fig. 10.1).

FIG. 10.1

The Procedure detail display in SSM shows you the date the procedures were created and who created them.

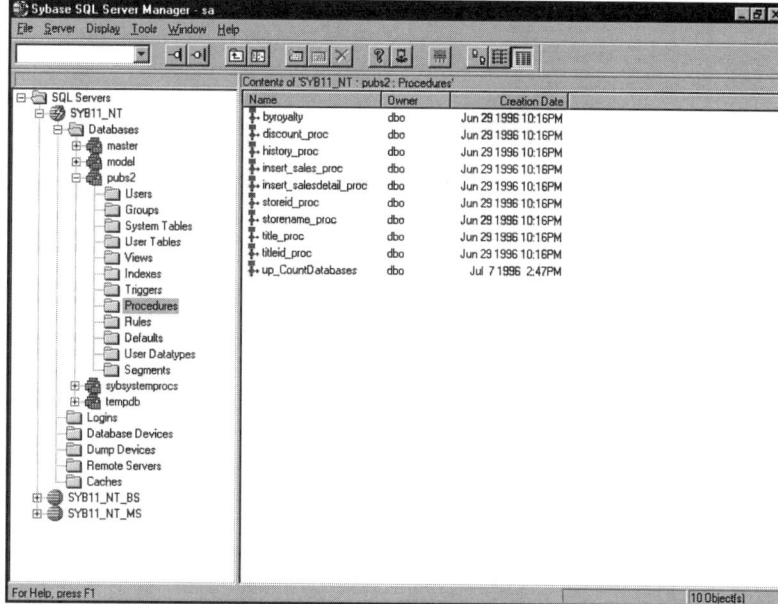

3. From the Database menu, select Create, Procedure to display the Sybase SQL Server Manager Create Procedure dialog box, as shown in Figure 10.2.

4. Enter a name for the stored procedure in the Name field, and optionally specify an owner for the procedure if you don't want to own it.

5. Check the Recompile check box if you want the server to recompile the procedure each and every time the procedure is run. Using the Recompile option is typically required for those procedures that have Transact-SQL; these would be greatly influenced by compilation due because their passed-in parameters might change each time the procedure is executed.

6. Enter a name and datatype information for each of the parameters that you want this procedure to have by clicking Add after each parameter.

7. Fill in the Default field if you want the parameter to have an automatically supplied value in case the user doesn't specify a parameter when the procedure is executed.

8. Check the Output check box if you want the parameter to be a receive argument—and so that the procedure can set the variable in the calling application. Another name for a receive or output variable is to *pass by reference*.

9. Enter the required Transact-SQL statements in the SQL field.

10. Click the Create button to add the procedure. If there are no errors in the procedure, the dialog box will change its fields around a little, so that you can have access to two new tabs (Dependencies and Permissions) and you have a bigger field with which to review the SQL used in the procedure (see Fig. 10.3).

FIG. 10.2

The SSM Create Procedure dialog box makes it easy for you to specify the name and parameters that will be used in the stored procedure, but you still have to write the Transact-SQL code yourself in the large SQL field!

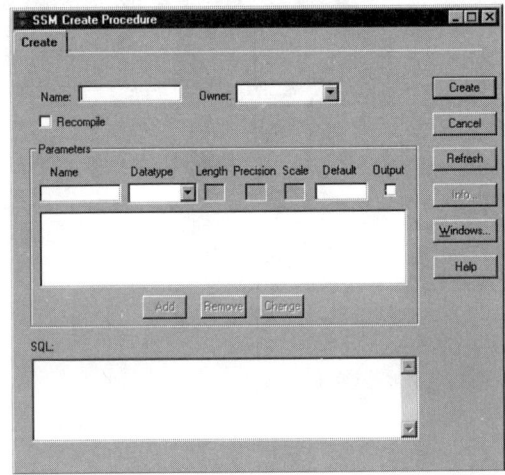

FIG. 10.3

The insert_sales _proc is a standard procedure that is installed in the *pubs2* database. The SSM Procedure dialog box enables you to review the SQL that it executes and then using the other tabs you can see if any other procedures rely on this one, and to whom permissions have been granted to execute the procedure.

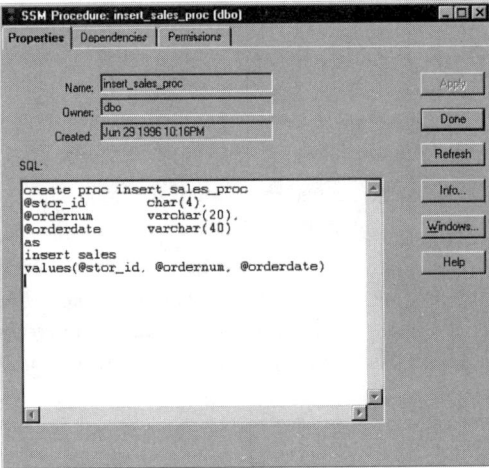

Using Transact-SQL to Create a Procedure

Using Transact-SQL to create a procedure, you execute the `Create Procedure` statement. Permission to execute the procedure that you create is set by default to the owner of the database. An owner of the database can change the permissions to enable other users to execute the procedure. The syntax that you use to define a new procedure is as follows:

```
Create Procedure [owner.]Procedure_Name; Procedure_Number
[@Parameter_Name datatype [=default] [Output]
...
[@Parameter_Name datatype [=default] [Output]
[With Recompile]
AS Sql_Statements
```

The options for the Transact-SQL command `Create Procedure` are as follows:

- *Procedure_Name*—This is the name of the procedure, which must conform to standard Sybase naming conventions.

- *Procedure_Number*—This is an integer used to differentiate two procedures with the same name. (See the following section, "Creating Multiple Procedures with the Same Name.")

- *Parameter_Name*—This is the name of a parameter that you want to apply to this procedure.

- =*default*—This is a default value that you want applied to the parameter if no value is supplied by the calling application.

- `Output`—Include the word `Output` after a parameter if you want the procedure to be able to set the value of this parameter in the calling procedure. This is equivalent to pass by reference in C.

- `With Recompile`—Each time the procedure is executed, this option forces Sybase to recompile, and therefore to reformulate the query plan to be used by the procedure.

Part
II

Ch
10

CAUTION

Be sure you reload your stored procedures each time that information has been saved in the database tables; those tables represent, both in volume and content, the information that your application can expect to see. Because stored procedures are compiled and optimized based on the tables, indexes, and data loading, your query can show significant improvement just by reloading it after "real" information has been placed in the system.

In the following example in Listing 10.1, a simple procedure is created that contains a `Select` statement to display all rows of a table. Once the procedure is created, its name is simply entered on a line to execute the procedure. If you precede the name of a stored procedure with other statements, you need to use the `Execute` procedure-name statement to execute the procedure.

Listing 10.1 CHP10_01.SQL—Creating the Procedure That Performs a Select

```
/*
   The first stored procedure is used to
   demonstrate the form of a simple procedure.
*/

Create Procedure up_All_Authors
as
Select *
From    authors
Go
```

N O T E Naming conventions for SQL objects are an important part of your implementation plan. In a production system, you will often have hundreds of stored procedures, many tables, and many more supporting objects. You should consider coming up with a naming convention for your stored procedures that will make it easy to identify and document them as procedures. In many installations, a common prefix for the user- stored procedures is up_. ■

You can only create a new procedure in the current database. If you're working in ISQL, you can execute a Use statement, followed by the name of the database in which the procedure should be created. Stored procedures are treated like all other objects in the database: they are subject to all of the same naming conventions and other limitations. The stored procedure is stored in the database currently in use, but may reference objects in other databases as long as those other objects exist when the stored procedure is created.

N O T E You can create an object within your stored procedure, and then reference that object. However, the types of references that you perform have two caveats:

- When you write a stored procedure, you cannot have code in that procedure that creates an object, drops that object, and creates a new object with the same name because SQL Server does not create the objects defined in a stored procedure until the stored procedure is actually executed.

- You also cannot create a table and then insert data into that table in your stored procedure because at the time that the insert statement is compiled, the table into which you want to insert the data does not yet exist. ■

CAUTION

If you use Select * in a stored procedure, and then later add additional columns to the table, the new columns will not be picked up by the stored procedure. You have to drop the procedure and recreate it to pick up the new columns. This rule applies even if you use the With Recompile statement when you execute your stored procedure.

Creating Multiple Procedures with the Same Name

The semicolon and integer after the name of a procedure enable you to create multiple versions of a procedure with the same name. In Listing 10.2, two procedures with the same name are created as version one and two. When the procedure is executed, the version number can be specified to control which version of the procedure is executed. If no version number is specified, the first version of the procedure is executed by default.

Listing 10.2   CHP10_02.SQL—Creating the Same Named Procedure More Than Once

```
/*
   Create two procedures with the same name, using the
   semicolon syntax to differentiate between the two
   instances of the procedure.
*/

Create Procedure up_MultipleInstance;1
As
Print 'Executing Version 1'
Return 0
Go

Create Procedure up_MultipleInstance;2
As
Print 'Executing Version 2'
Return 0
Go
```

The syntax for executing either procedure is to type the name of the procedure and then follow it with a semicolon and the version that you want to run. In the following sample, you can see the procedure run three ways to demonstrate each option's results:

```
Exec up_MultipleInstance;1
Go
Exec up_MultipleInstance;2
Go
Exec up_MultipleInstance
Go


- - - - - - - - - - - - - - - - -
Executing Version 1
Executing Version 2
Executing Version 1
```

T I P You can use the Set Noexec On command in Transact-SQL the first time that you execute a procedure to check it for errors, rather than executing the procedure when errors may cause it to fail.

Part

II

Ch

10

Working with and Understanding Stored Procedures

Stored procedures are made up of standard parts that are generally used in each and every procedure that you will write. In this section, you'll learn all about how to write and work with these basic elements of stored procedures. After reading this chapter, you should have enough of an understanding of each of these components that future stored procedure development should be a straightforward task. You'll likely find out that after you've written about ten or so different types of stored procedures, you'll have covered most of the common situations; each procedure after that will merely be a variation on a theme.

Using Parameters to Procedures

You can define one or more parameters in a procedure. You use parameters as named storage locations just as you would use the parameters as variables in conventional programming languages, such as C and Visual Basic. You precede the name of a parameter with an *at* symbol (@) to designate it as a parameter. Parameter names are local to the procedure in which they're defined.

You can use parameters to pass information into a procedure from the line that executes the parameter. Parameters are placed after the name of the procedure in the statement executed to create the procedure; commas separate the list of parameters if there are multiple parameters. You can use system datatypes to define the type of information to be expected as a parameter. For more information on system and custom datatypes, see Chapter 6, "Understanding Tables and Datatypes."

Before looking at the actual syntax for using parameters in stored procedures, there are a few general rules of which you should be aware when using parameters in procedures:

- You can define up to 255 parameters for a stored procedure.
- Parameter names can be up to 30 characters in length, including the @ symbol.
- You can include wild-card characters in the values you pass to a parameter if that parameter is used in a Like clause.
- Character strings must be enclosed in single or double quotes when passed to a parameter.
- You cannot pass an object name as a parameter.
- You can specify a default value for a parameter, provided that you specify the default value when the procedure is created.

Using Input Parameters   Input parameters are optional parts of a stored procedure that enables you to input value information from a calling program. Calling programs might include another procedure so that you can do conditional execution and logic in the current procedure. Parameters turn stored procedures into the same basic thing as a function in any other language, such as C or PowerBuilder.

Input parameters are passed by value. This means that their value is evaluated exactly inside the procedure. For example, say you have a procedure that gives you the details of an author, like this one in Listing 10.3.

Listing 10.3 CHP10_03.SQL—Using a Parameter to Retrieve a Particular Author

```
/*
   Create a simple procedure that will return
   the details of an author with one parameter to
   specify the author's ID.
*/

Create Procedure up_AuthorInfo
        @psAuthorID Char(11)
As

/* Select the author record that corresponds
   to the passed-in parameter value. */

Select *
From    authors
Where   au_id = @psAuthorID
Return 0
Go
```

To use this procedure you would execute the following:

```
up_AuthorInfo '724-80-9391'
Go

au_id       au_lname   au_fname phone        address
city        state country postalcode
----------------------------------------------------------------------
724-80-9391 MacFeather Stearns  415 354-7128 44 Upland Hts.
Oakland     CA    USA      94612
```

> **TIP** When a procedure is executed as the first statement in a series of statements (also known as a *command batch*), it does not have to be preceded by the keyword `Execute`. The name of the procedure to be executed is simply placed as the first keyword on the line.

Using Output Parameters The purpose of output parameters is to enable you to pass values to and from multiple stored procedures with ease. Because result sets are always sent back to a client process and not to another stored procedure, the only way to transfer information between procedures without creating a temporary table to store the results of actions is by using output parameters.

The best way to understand output parameters is to see them in action. In Listing 10.4, two stored procedures are created the second procedure up_DoMath is used to perform mathematical analysis on the data passed into the first parameter up_Multiply.

N O T E In Listing 10.4, note carefully that when up_DoMath is called from up_Multiply, the variable in up_Multiply used to store the results is called the @nMathResult. The @nMathResult is passed to the up_DoMath stored procedure with an Output declaration. This instructs Sybase that you want to pass the memory address of the variable to the called procedure so that the called procedure can set its value.

Note also that you won't get an error if you fail to use the Output declaration; Sybase will just assume that you really meant to pass the value of the variable instead. ■

Listing 10.4   CHP10_04.SQL—These Two Procedures Demonstrate Parameter Passing and Output Parameters

```
/*
    These two procedures demonstrate the use of
    output parameters to perform data transfer
    between two or more procedures.

    Note: These procedures are obviously limited to
          integer math, so be careful if you don't supply
          valid values to them!
*/

/* First Create a general math procedure
    that can operate on two numbers and
    return the results. */

Create Procedure up_DoMath
        @psOperator      Varchar(12),
        @pnFirstNumber   Int,
        @pnSecondNumber  Int,
        @rnResult        Int    Output /* This is the answer going here */
As

/* Print a statement to tell the user we're working.  */
Print 'Starting up_DoMath'

/* Conditional Math statements */
If @psOperator = 'Multiply'
Begin
    Select @rnResult = @pnFirstNumber * @pnSecondNumber
    Return 0
End
Else If @psOperator = 'Add'
```

```
Begin
      Select @rnResult = @pnFirstNumber + @pnSecondNumber
      Return 0
End
Else If @psOperator = 'Subtract'
Begin
      Select @rnResult = @pnFirstNumber - @pnSecondNumber
      Return 0
End
Else If @psOperator = 'Divide'
Begin
      Select @rnResult = @pnFirstNumber / @pnSecondNumber
      Return 0
End
Else
Begin
      /* Error condition! */
      Select @rnResult = 0
      Return -99
End

Return 0

Go

/* Now create a high-level function that's going to do some multiplication
   for the user. */
Create Procedure up_Multiply
          @pnFirstNumber  Int,
          @pnSecondNumber Int
As

Declare    @nRC           Int,       /* used to store return status */
           @nMathResult   Int

/* Print a statement to tell the user we're working. */
Print 'Starting up_Multiply'

/* Now execute the up_DoMath procedure.*/
Exec up_DoMath 'Multiply', @pnFirstNumber, @pnSecondNumber,
                           @nMathResult Output

/* Return the result to the front end. */
Select @nMathResult

Return 0
Go
```

Using Multiple Parameters   You can define multiple parameters for a stored procedure, and when you want to pass values to them, just separate them with a comma (,). For example, in Listing 10.5, a simple procedure with multiple parameters is created.

Listing 10.5   CHP10_05.SQL—A Procedure Using Multiple Parameters

```
/*
   A simple procedure with three parameters used
   to demonstrate call by name or call by position.
*/

Create Procedure up_MultipleParams
        @psParameter1 Char(5),
        @pnParameter2 Int,
        @pnParameter3 Int
As
Return 0
Go
```

Each of the parameters can then be specified by either position or by name. For example, to execute the procedure that was created in Listing 10.5 by position, you would execute:

```
Exec up_MultipleParams 'Hello', 25, 100
Go
```

You could also execute the same procedure by referencing each of the parameter's names as follows:

```
Exec up_MultipleParams @psParameter1 = 'Hello', @pnParameter2 = 25, @pnParameter3
= 100
Go
```

The significant advantage of using the call by name feature of stored procedures is that if you don't want or need to pass all of the parameters to a procedure because there are defaults in use or because the parameter isn't required, you can use the call by name to simplify your execution statement and to only use the parameters you need.

 TIP Despite the fact that it is easier to read a parameter being passed by name, it is better to pass parameters by position because doing so dramatically improves the execution time for the server. Passing parameters by position means that the server doesn't need to look up the parameter you are passing on the parameter list.

Defining Default Values for Parameters   If you want to ensure that a value is always passed to a procedure to make sure that there are no errors when it is executed, you can take advantage of the Default characteristic of a parameter. For example, if you wanted to ensure that the procedure up_Multiply created in Listing 10.4 always had a value in each of its parameters, you could alter it like this:

```
Create Procedure up_Multiply
        @pnFirstNumber  Int = 1,   /* Default is 1 */
        @pnSecondNumber Int = 1    /* Default is 1 */
As
```

```
Declare     @nRC            Int,        /* used to store return status */
            @nMathResult    Int

/* Print a statement to tell the user we're working. */
Print 'Starting up_Multiply'

/* Now execute the up_DoMath procedure. */
Exec up_DoMath 'Multiply', @pnFirstNumber, @pnSecondNumber,
                        @nMathResult Output

/* Return the result to the front end. */
Select @nMathResult

Return 0
Go
```

Executing Procedures

To execute a stored procedure, you need to use the execute command. The syntax is as follows:

```
Execute Procedure_Name
```

For example, to execute the procedure created above you would execute:

```
Execute up_Multiply
Go
```

N O T E   The Execute command must be included unless the statement is the first command in the calling program. Also, note that the keyword Exec may be substituted for the full-text equivalent of Execute.

Stored procedures can be executed from any calling program. Calling programs can be any of the following:

- A stored procedure
- A command batch
- A trigger
- A Client-Library or DB-Library program
- Any program written in a client/server development tool

If you execute a stored procedure that calls another procedure, the called procedure can access objects that were created by the calling procedure.

SQL Server uses a global variable called @@error to hold the error number most recently generated by the system. When your stored procedure successfully completes, the @@error value is set to zero.

Renaming Procedures

If you want to rename an existing procedure, you need to use the system stored procedure sp_rename. The syntax is:

```
sp_rename Old_Object_Name, New_Object_Name
```

Old_Object_Name is the old object that you are renaming and New_Object_Name is the name you want the old object to have.

If you wanted to rename the procedure up_DoMath to up_Mathematics, you would execute:

```
sp_rename up_DoMath, up_Mathematics
Go
```

> **CAUTION**
>
> If you rename a stored procedure that is referenced in another stored procedure, in a trigger, or even in a batch program, you will need to modify the calling stored procedure or trigger so that it references the new procedure name. Take great care when renaming any object in your database. Remember to use the system-stored procedure sp_depends to identify all database references to a particular stored procedure.

Understanding the "Life" of a Procedure

The benefit of using a stored procedure for the execution of a set of Transact-SQL statements is that it is compiled when it first runs. At the time of execution, if the procedure is not already in the procedure cache, the stored procedure's text is retrieved from the *syscomments* system catalog table and is brought into a common single piece of memory for compilation. During compilation, the Transact-SQL statements in the procedure are converted from their original character representation into an executable form. During compilation, any objects that are referenced in procedures are also converted to alternate representations. For example, table names are converted to their object IDs and column names to their column IDs.

An execution plan is also created just as it would be for the execution of even a single Transact-SQL statement. A specific list of the indexes to be used to retrieve rows from tables that are referenced by the procedure is one example of the contents of an execution plan. The execution plan is kept in a cache and is used to perform the queries of the procedure each time it's subsequently executed.

T I P You can define the size of the procedure cache so that it is large enough to contain most or all the available procedures for execution and save the time that it would take to regenerate the execution plan for procedures.

To configure the size of the procedure cache, use the system-stored procedure sp_configure. For more information on using sp_configure, see Chapter 23, "Using Sybase's Configuration Options."

Recompiling Stored Procedures

When a stored procedure is compiled, SQL Server creates a query plan that maps out the most effective way to execute the commands in the stored procedure. Each time the stored procedure is executed, the query plan is reused. This provides a significant performance improvement because the query plan doesn't have to be recreated. There are times, however, when you don't want to have SQL Server use the same query plan each time. Depending on how your stored procedure is written and the actions it takes, you may want to have a query plan generated every time the stored procedure is executed. The `With Recompile` option of the `Create Procedure` command accomplishes this when creating the stored procedure. The syntax looks like this:

```
Create Procedure Procedure_Name
...
With Recompile
```

Part

II

Ch

10

You can also force a stored procedure to be recompiled when it is executed by including the `With Recompile` clause in the `Exec` statement. For example:

```
Exec up_Multiply 100, 300 With Recompile
```

If you aren't sure why a query plan would need to be recreated each time a stored procedure is executed, take a look at the following example.

Assume that you need to create a lookup procedure that enables a user to enter the name of two companies and retrieve a list of all companies that fall between the entered names. This stored procedure might look like this:

```
Create Procedure up_Company_Search
  @psCompanyFirst Varchar(50),
  @psCompanyLast  Varchar(50)
With Recompile
As
Select Company_Name
From   Company
Where  Company_Name Between @psCompanyFirst And @psCompanyLast
```

Depending on the names selected, SQL Server will either use an index, assuming you have created one, or perform a table scan to retrieve the required data. For example, the following statement will be processed more quickly by SQL Server using an index of company names.

```
Exec up_Company_Search 'Centura', 'Century 21'
```

Whereas the following statement:

```
Exec up_Company_Search 'Apple Computer', 'Sybase Corporation'
```

will not benefit from the use of an index; instead, the query will need to read almost every page of the table.

N O T E It may be difficult to determine whether a procedure should be created with the `With` `Recompile` option. If in doubt, you'll probably be better served by not creating the procedure with the `With` `Recompile` option. Because—if you create a procedure with the `With` `Recompile` option—the procedure is recompiled each time the procedure is executed, you may waste valuable CPU time to perform these compiles . You can still add the `With` `Recompile` clause to force a recompilation when you execute the procedure. ▪

By having SQL Server recompile the stored procedure each time it is executed, you can force it to create a new query plan based on the information provided in the parameters passed.

> **CAUTION**
>
> Whenever certain changes are made to the database, like dropping and recreating indexes or tables, stored procedures are automatically recompiled. You should make sure that your database is large enough to handle a possible increase in the size of your stored procedures.

Using Nested Stored Procedures

Your stored procedures can call other stored procedures, which can call other stored procedures, and so on and so forth. This is known as procedure nesting. Each time your stored procedure calls another stored procedure, the nesting level is increased by one. When the called stored procedure completes execution, the nesting level is decreased by one.

Procedure nesting is limited to 16 levels of nesting of stored procedures. Once that limit is exceeded, the transaction fails. You can determine the current nesting level by looking at the global system variable `@@nestinglevel`.

Using a Command Batch

Sets of Transact-SQL statements that aren't preceded by a `Create` `Procedure` statement are referred to as a command batch, which includes stored procedures. The rules or syntax for the use of Transact-SQL statements in batch apply to the following list of objects:

- Procedures
- Rules
- Defaults
- Triggers
- Views

The syntax is primarily a set of restrictions that limits the types of statements that can be used in batch. Most of the restrictions are the statements that create objects or change the database or query environment; they don't take effect within the current batch.

For example, although rules and defaults can be defined and bound to a column or user-defined datatype within a batch, the defaults and rules are in effect until after the completion of the batch. You also can't drop an object and reference or re-create it in the same batch.

Some additional Set options that are defined with a batch don't apply to queries contained in the batch. For example, the Set option Set Nocount On will affect all queries that follow it with a stored procedure and suppress the count line for the execution of Select statements. The Set Showplan On option does not affect the queries used within a stored procedure, and a query plan isn't displayed for the queries in the procedure.

Dropping Procedures

You use the Drop Procedure statement to drop a stored procedure that you've created. Multiple procedures can be dropped with a single Drop Procedure statement by listing multiple procedures separated by commas after the keywords Drop Procedure in the syntax:

```
Drop Procedure Procedure_Name_1, ..., Procedure_Name_N
```

Multiple versions of a procedure can't be selectively dropped. All versions of a procedure with the same name must be dropped by using the Drop Procedure statement that specifies the procedure without a version number. All versions of a procedure with the same name must be dropped together.

If you wanted to drop the stored procedure up_DoMath and up_Multiply created earlier, you would execute the following:

```
Drop Procedure up_DoMath, up_Multiply
Go
```

TROUBLESHOOTING

I created a procedure in a previous session, but I was unable to find the procedure again in a subsequent session. Procedures are defined within a database. In your subsequent session, you probably found yourself in a different database than the database in which the procedure was originally defined. You can ask the database administrator to define to your default database the database in which your procedure was defined and you'll always be positioned to it each time you begin a session. You can also enter the Use command followed by the name of the database in which your procedure was defined to locate the procedure.

Understanding Remote Procedures (RPCs)

Remote procedures are simply stored procedures on another SQL Server. If your system is properly configured, you can execute a stored procedure on another server simply by prefixing the stored procedure name with the name of the remote server and database. To configure a server to execute remote procedures, all you need to do is add the remote server's name into the `master` system catalog table *sysservers*, by executing the system-stored procedure `sp_addserver`. The syntax for the use of `sp_addserver` is as follows:

```
sp_addserver Server_Name, Null, Physical_Net_Name
```

`Server_Name` is the logical name of the remote server that you want to add a reference to and `Physical_Net_Name` is the name of the server as identified in the interfaces file (SQL.INI) on the server.

> **N O T E** Sybase uses the `Physical_Net_Name` parameter so that it can do a remote connection to the server that you identify when you try to execute a procedure on the remote server. ■

Once you have added the server, you can execute a remote stored procedure using the syntax that looks like this:

```
EXEC [[[Server_Name].database_name.][owner].]Procedure_Name
```

For example, if your company or organization had another server called `server_2`, which contained a database called `enterprise`, and you wanted to run the stored procedure `up_department_report`, you would execute it like this:

```
Exec server_2.enterprise.dbo.department_report
```

Understanding Chained Transactions

When you create a stored procedure, SQL Server tags it with the transaction mode that you are in at the time of creation: chained or unchained mode. This means that a stored procedure created while in chained mode cannot be run while in unchained mode and vice versa. Attempting to run the stored procedure in a mode different from the one that created it will cause SQL Server to send an error message. You can use the system procedure `sp_procxmode` to find out what transaction mode the stored procedure was created in, and to change the transaction mode. You can only use `sp_procxmode` with the server explicitly in non-chained transaction mode (`set chained off`). The syntax for using `sp_procxmode` is as follows:

```
Exec sp_procxmode [Procedure_Name [, Transaction_Mode]]
```

Executing `sp_procxmode` and supplying just a Procedure_Name will report the current transaction mode that a procedure has been compiled with. To change the transaction mode of a procedure, supply the `Transaction_Mode` parameter with either `'Chained'`, `'Unchained'`, or `'Anymode'`. The value `'Anymode'` transaction mode enables the stored procedure to be executed in chained or unchained mode.

Using Flow-Control Statements

Transact-SQL contains several statements that are used to change the order of execution of statements within a set of statements such as a stored procedure. Flow-control statements permit you to organize statements in stored procedures to provide the capabilities of a conventional programming language, such as C or COBOL. You may find that some of the retrieval, update, deletion, addition, and manipulation of the rows of database tables can be performed more easily through the use of flow-control statements in objects, such as stored procedures.

Using If...Else

You can use the keywords If and Else to control conditional execution within a batch, including a stored procedure. The If and Else keywords permit you to test a condition and execute either the statements that are part of the If branch or the statements that are part of the Else branch. You define the condition for testing as an expression following the keyword If. The syntax of an If...Else statement is as follows:

```
If Expression
      Statement
[Else]
      [If Expression]
      Statement]
```

Part
II

Ch
10

N O T E   It's impossible to show examples of the use of conditional statements that can be formed with the keywords If and Else without using other keywords. The next examples use the keywords Print and Exists. In the subsequent examples, the keyword Print is used to display a string of characters.

The keyword Exists is usually followed by a statement within parentheses when used in an If statement. The Exists statement is evaluated to either True or False, depending upon whether the statement within the parentheses returns one or more rows, or no rows, respectively.

You needn't use an Else clause as part of an If statement. The simplest form of an If statement is constructed without an Else clause. In the following example, a Print statement is used to display a confirmation message that a row exists in a database table. If the row doesn't exist in the table, the message, "No author found," is displayed; unfortunately, the message is also displayed after the verification message because you're not using the Else option.

```
If Exists( Select *
           From    authors
           Where   au_id = '712-45-1867' )
      Print 'Author found'
Print 'No author found'
Go


----------------------
Author found
No author found
```

In the following example, the row isn't found in the table, so only the Print statement that follows the If statement is executed.

```
If Exists( Select *
           From    authors
           Where   au_id = '712-45-1868' )
```

```
      Print 'Author found'
Print 'No author found'
Go


- - - - - - - - - - - - - - - - - - - - - -
No author found
```

The previous two examples show the problem of using an `If` statement that doesn't contain an `Else` clause. In the examples, it's impossible to prevent the message, `'No author found'`, from appearing. You would add an `Else` clause to the `If` statement to print the message, `'No author found'`, if a row isn't found and the condition after the `If` isn't `True`.

In the following example, the first example is rewritten to use an `If` and `Else` clause. In this case, you no longer receive the additional 'No author found' message when the author is actually found correctly.

```
If Exists( Select *
           From    authors
           Where   au_id = '712-45-1867' )
      Print 'Author found'
Else
      Print 'No author found'
Go


- - - - - - - - - - - - - - - - - - - - - -
No author found
```

> **CAUTION**
>
> Unlike some programming languages you may have used, when used alone, the Transact-SQL `If` statement can have only one statement associated with it. As a result, there is no need for a keyword, such as `End-If`, to define the end of the `If` statement. See Using `Begin...End` in the next section for information on grouping statements and associating them with an `If...Else` condition.

Using Begin...End

You use the keywords `Begin` and `End` to designate a set of Transact-SQL statements to be executed as a unit. You use the keyword `Begin` to define the start of a block of Transact-SQL statements. You use the keyword `End` after the last Transact-SQL statement that is part of the same block of statements. `Begin...End` uses the following syntax:

```
Begin
      Statements
End
```

You often use `Begin` and `End` with a conditional statement such as an `If` statement. `Begin` and `End` are used in an `If` or `Else` clause to permit multiple Transact-SQL statements to be executed if the expression following the `If` or `Else` clause is `True`. As mentioned earlier, without a `Begin` and `End` block enclosing multiple statements, only a single Transact-SQL statement can be executed if the expression in the `If` or `Else` clause is `True`.

In the following example, Begin and End are used with an If statement to define the execution of multiple statements if the condition tested is True. The If statement contains only a If clause, no Else clause is part of the statement.

```
If Exists( Select *
          From    authors
          Where   au_id = '712-45-1867' )
Begin
     Print 'Author found'
     Select au_lname, au_fname
     From    authors
     Where   au_id = '712-45-1867'
End
Else
     Print 'No author found'
Go

Author found
au_lname                                          au_fname
----------------------------------------- --------------------
del Castillo                                      Innes
```

Using While

You use the keyword While to define a condition that executes one or more Transact-SQL statements when the condition tested evaluates to True. The statement that follows the expression of the While statement continues to execute as long as the condition tested is True. The syntax of the While statement is as follows:

```
While Boolean_Expression
     Sql_Statement
```

N O T E As with the If...Else statements, you can only execute a single SQL statement with the While clause. If you need to include more than one statement in the routine, you'll need to use the Begin...End construct as described earlier. ■

In the following example, a While statement is used to execute a SELECT statement that displays a numeric value until the value reaches a limit of five. Because a variable is a named storage location it is like a parameter, as shown in the following example. You define the datatype of a variable using a Declare statement to control the way information is represented in the variable. A variable is always referenced preceded by an *at* sign (@) like a parameter.

In the example, the value stored in the variable is initialized to one and subsequently increased. The statements associated with the While execute until the variable *x* reaches a value of five.

```
/* Declare a variable. */
Declare @nNumber Int

/* Initialize its value. */
Select @nNumber = 1

/* Perform while. */
```

```
While @nNumber < 5
Begin
     Print 'Number still less than 5'
     Select @nNumber = @nNumber +1
End
Go

.........................
1 row(s) affected
Number still less than 5
1 row(s) affected
Number still less than 5
1 row(s) affected
Number still less than 5
1 row(s) affected
Number still less than 5
1 row(s) affected
```

A more meaningful example of the use of a While statement can be shown after two additional Transact-SQL keywords are introduced and explained. An example using While along with the keywords Break and Continue will be given a little later in this section.

Using Break

You use the keyword Break within a block of Transact-SQL statements that is itself within a conditional While statement in order to end the execution of the statements. The execution of a Break results in the first statement following the end of block to begin executing. The syntax of a Break clause is as follows:

```
While Boolean_Expression
     Sql_Statement
Break
     Sql_Statement
```

In the following example, the Break within the While statement causes the statement within the While to terminate. The Print statement executes once because it is located before the Break. Once the Break is encountered, the statements in the While clause aren't executed again.

```
/* Declare a variable. */
Declare @nNumber Int

/* Initialize its value. */
Select @nNumber = 1

/* Perform while. */
While @nNumber < 5
Begin
     Print 'Number still less than 5'
     Select @nNumber = @nNumber +1
     Break
End
```

```
Go

- - - - - - - - - - - - - - - - - - - - - - - -
1 row(s) affected
Number still less than 5
1 row(s) affected
```

Using Continue

You use a `Continue` keyword to form a clause within a conditional statement, such as a `While` statement, to explicitly continue the set of statements that are contained within the conditional statement. The syntax of the `Continue` clause is as follows:

```
While Boolean_Expression
    Sql_Statement
Break
    Sql_Statement
Continue
```

In the following example, a `Continue` is used within a `While` statement to explicitly define that execution of the statements within the `While` statement should continue as long as the condition specified in the expression that follows `While` is `True`. The use of `Continue` in the following example skips the final `Print` statement:

```
/* Declare a variable. */
Declare @nNumber Int

/* Initialize its value. */
Select @nNumber = 1

/* Perform while. */
While @nNumber < 5
Begin
    Print 'Number still less than 5'
    Select @nNumber = @nNumber +1

    /* The continue statement causes the next iteration of the while to
       be executed, and no further lines of code will execute. */
    Continue
    Print 'This statement will be ignored'
End
Go

- - - - - - - - - - - - - - - - - - - - - - - -
1 row(s) affected
Number still less than 5
1 row(s) affected
Number still less than 5
1 row(s) affected
Number still less than 5
1 row(s) affected
Number still less than 5
1 row(s) affected
```

Part

II

Ch

10

Examples of Using While, Break, and Continue

Although the two previous examples use Break and Continue alone, you don't typically use either Continue or Break alone within a While statement. Both Break and Continue are often used following an If or Else that is defined within a While statement, so an additional condition can be used to break out of the While loop. If two or more loops are nested, Break exits to the next outermost loop.

In the following example, a Break is used with an If statement, both of which are contained within a While statement. The Break is used to terminate the statements associated with the While if the condition specified by the If statement is True. The If condition is True if the value of the local variable, @y, is True.

```
/* Declare variables. */
Declare @nNumber  Int,
        @nNumber2 Int

/* Initialize their values. */
Select @nNumber  = 1,
       @nNumber2 = 1

/* Perform while. */
While @nNumber < 5
Begin
     Print 'Number still less than 5'
     Select @nNumber = @nNumber +1,
            @nNumber2 = @nNumber2 + 1

     If @nNumber2 = 3
     Begin
          Print 'Number2 is 3 so break out of loop'
          Break
     End
End

Print 'Out of while loop'
Go

---------------------------------
1 row(s) affected
Number still less than 5
1 row(s) affected
Number still less than 5
1 row(s) affected
Number2 is 3 so break out of loop
Out of while loop
```

In the following example, a While statement is used to permit only the rows of a table that match the criteria defined within the expression of the While statement to have their values changed:

```
/* Begin a transaction so that we can undo it later on. */
Begin Transaction
While ( Select Avg( price )
        From Titles ) < 30
```

```
Begin
     Select title_id, price
     From   titles
     Where  price > 20

     Update titles
     Set    price = price * 2
End
Rollback Transaction
Go

title_id price
-------- -----
PC1035   22.95
PS1372   21.59
TC3218   20.95
18 row(s) affected
title_id                           price
--------  -------------------------------
BU1032                             39.98
BU1111                             23.90
BU7832                             39.98
MC2222                             39.98
PC1035                             45.90
PC8888                             40.00
PS1372                             43.18
PS2091                             21.90
PS3333                             39.98
TC3218                             41.90
TC4203                             23.90
TC7777                             29.98
18 row(s) affected
```

You must be careful in defining the While statement and its associated statements. As shown in the following example, if the condition specified with the While expression continues to be True, the While loop will execute indefinitely.

```
While 5 * 9 > 10
    Print '5 times 9 is really greater than 10!'
Go

5 times 9 is really greater than 10!
5 times 9 is really greater than 10!
5 times 9 is really greater than 10!
...
```

Defining and Using Variables

You may recall that earlier in this chapter in the section titled "Using Parameters to Procedures," variables were described as similar to parameters because they are named storage locations. Variables in Transact-SQL can be either local or global. You define local variables by using a Declare statement and assigning the variable a datatype. You assign an initial value to local variables with a Select statement.

You must declare, assign a value, and use a local variable within the same batch or stored procedure. The variable is only available for use within the same batch or procedure, hence the term local.

You can use local variables in batch or stored procedures for such things as counters and temporary holding locations for other variables. Recall that local variables are always referenced with an at symbol (@) preceding their names. You can define the datatype of a local variable as a user-defined datatype as well as a system datatype. One restriction that applies to local variables is that you can't define a local variable as a text or image datatype.

The syntax of a local variable is as follows:

```
Declare @Variable_Name datatype [, Variable_Name datatype...]
```

The Select statement is used to assign values to local variables, as shown in the following syntax:

```
Select @Variable_Name = expression |select statement
[,@Variable_Name = expression select statement]
[From list of tables] [Where expression]
[Group BY...
[Having ...]
[Order By...]
```

If the Select statement returns more than a single value, the variable is assigned to the last value returned. In the following example, two local variables are defined and used to return the number of rows in the table.

```
/* Declare a counter variable. */
Declare @nCount    Int

/* Count the number of publishers. */
Select @nCount = Count( * )
From    publishers

/* Print the results of the count.*/
Print 'There are %1! publishers in the pubs2 database.', @nCount
Go

1 row(s) affected
There are 3 publishers in the pubs2 database.
```

Each Select statement returns a count message in the previous example. If you want the count message suppressed, you must first execute the Set Nocount statement.

Using Global Variables

A global variable is a variable that is defined by Sybase. You can't define a global variable with your routines; you can only use the pre-declared and pre-defined global variables. You always reference a global variable by preceding with two *at* signs (@@). You reference a global variable to access server information or information about your operations. You can only declare local variables. You shouldn't define local variables that have the same name as system variables because you may receive unexpected results in your application.

Table 10.1 lists the names of all Sybase System XI global variables and a brief description of the information that's contained within them.

Table 10.1   Global Variables Available for Use in Sybase System XI

Global Variable	Description
@@Char_Convert	If equal to 0 then no character conversions are being performed, otherwise equal to 1
@@Client_CsName	The current character set name in use on the client
@@Client_CsID	The current character set ID in use on the client
@@Connections	The total logons or attempted logons
@@CPU_Busy	The cumulative CPU Server time in ticks
@@Error	The last system error number: 0 if successful
@@Identity	The last inserted identity value
@@Idle	Cumulative CPU Server idle time
@@IO_Busy	Cumulative Server I/O time
@@Isolation	Current isolation level
@@LangId	Current language ID
@@Language	Current language name
@@MaxCharLen	Maximum length in bytes of a character in the current character set. Use this value to determine if the client is using double byte character sets (DBCSs)
@@Max_Connections	Max simultaneous connections permitted on the server
@@NCharSize	Average length in bytes of a national language character
@@NestLevel	Current nested level of calling routines from 0 to 16
@@Pack_Received	Number of input packets read
@@Pack_Sent	Number of output packets written
@@Packet_Errors	Number of read and write packet errors
@@ProcId	Current stored procedure ID
@@RowCount	Number of rows affected by last query
@@ServerName	Name of local server
@@SPID	Current process server ID

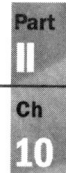

Part
II

Ch
10

continues

Table 10.1 Continued

Global Variable	Description
@@SQLStatus	Status of the last Fetch statement
@@TextColId	The ID of the column that is currently being referenced by the value @@TextPtr
@@TextDBId	The ID of the database that is currently being referenced by the column with the value @@TextPtr
@@TextObjId	The ID of the object that is currently being referenced by the column with the value @@TextPtr
@@TextPtr	A numeric pointer to the value of the last column of Image or Text type that was either inserted or updated
@@Textsize	Current of max text or image data with default of 4K
@@TextTTS	The Timestamp associated with the value in @@TextPtr. This value is a Varbinary(8).
@@Thresh_Hysteresis	The amount of free space that must be consumed before the threshold stored procedure will be fired to dump the logs
@@TimeTicks	Number of microseconds per tick-machine independent. Tick is 31.25 milliseconds/1/32 sec.
@@Total_Errors	Number of errors during reads or writes
@@Total_Read	Number of disk reads (not cache)
@@Total_Write	Number of disk writes
@@TranChained	The current chained status: 0 = unchained; 1 =chained
@@TranCount	Current user total active transactions
@@TranState	The state of the current transaction after it has been begun: 0=transaction in progress; 1=transaction completed, commits successful; 2=previous statement aborted with no effect on the transaction; 3=transaction aborted and rolled back
@@Version	Date and version of Sybase

In the following example, two global variables are printed:

```
/* Print The Server Version. */
Print @@Version
Go
/* Print the Language in use. */
```

```
Print @@Language
Go

SQL Server/11.0.1/P/PC Intel/Windows NT 3.5/1/OPT/Tue Mar 5 1996 13:22:45.60
us_english
```

Using Additional Procedure and Batch Keywords

Several additional keywords can be used within stored procedures or batches of Transact-SQL commands. These additional keywords don't fall into a single descriptive category of common or similar function. Some of these keywords are Goto, Return, Raiserror, and Waitfor.

Using Goto

You use a Goto to perform a transfer from a statement to another statement that contains a user-defined label. A Goto statement used alone is unconditional. The statement that contains the destination label name follows rules for identifiers and is followed by a colon (:).

You only use the label name without the colon on the Goto line. The syntax of the Goto statement is

```
label:

Goto label
```

The following example shows an instance of the Goto statement's being used to transfer control to a statement that displays the word *yes* until the value of a variable reaches a specified value. The Count was turned off prior to execution of the statements in the example.

```
/* Turn off row counting. */
Set Nocount On
Go

/* Declare a Variable. */
Declare @nCount smallint

/* Initialize its value. */
select @nCount = 1

/* Goto Label. */
Restart:

Print 'Yes'

Select @nCount = @nCount + 1
While @nCount <= 4
    Goto Restart

yes
yes
yes
yes
```

Part

II

Ch

10

TIP You can make your code far easier to read simply by indenting sections such as the Goto Restart under the While, and blocking statements under If or Begin in indented text.

Using Return

You use the Return statement to formally exit from a query or procedure and optionally provide a value to the calling routine. A Return is often used when one procedure is executed from within another. When used alone, the Return statement is unconditional, though you can use the Return within a conditional If or While statement. The syntax of the Return statement is:

```
Return [integer]
```

You can use a Return statement at any point in a batch or procedure. Any statements that follow the Return are not executed. A Return is similar to a Break with one difference: unlike Break, a Return can be used to return an integer value to the procedure that invoked the procedure that contains the Return. Execution of statements continues at the statement following the statement that executed the procedure originally.

To understand the use of the Return statement, you must first understand the action performed by Sybase when a procedure completes execution. Sybase always makes an integer value available when a procedure ends. A value of zero indicates that the procedure executed successfully. Negative values from –1 to –99 indicate reasons for the failure of statements within the procedure. These integer values are always returned at the termination of a procedure even if a Return statement isn't present in a procedure.

NOTE A procedure that is invoked within another procedure with an Execute statement is most often referred to as a *called procedure*. Call refers to an equivalent operation used in some programming languages. The keyword used in these languages to invoke the equivalent of a section of code from a program is Call. This is the same as running a subroutine or function in these other languages. ■

You can optionally use an integer value that follows the Return statement to replace the Sybase value with your own user-defined value. You should use non-zero integer values so that your return status values don't conflict with the Sybase status values. If no user-defined return value is provided, the Sybase value is used. If more than one error occurs, the status with the highest absolute value is returned. You can't return a NULL value with a Return statement. Table 10.2 shows several of the return status values that are reserved by Sybase.

Table 10.2 Selected Sybase System XI Status Values

Return Value	Meaning
0	Successful execution
–1	Missing object
–2	Datatype error

Return Value	Meaning
−3	Process was chosen as a deadlock victim
−4	Permission error
−5	Syntax error
−6	Miscellaneous user error
−7	Resource error, such as out of space
−8	Nonfatal internal problem
−9	System limit was reached
−10	Fatal internal inconsistency
−11	Fatal internal inconsistency
−12	Table or index is corrupt
−13	Database is corrupt
−14	Hardware error

Part
II
Ch
10

You must provide a local variable that receives the returned status in the EXECUTE statement that invokes the procedure that returns status. The syntax to specify a local variable for the returned status value is the following:

```
Exec[ute] @Return_Status = Procedure_Name
```

The following example shows a return value from a called procedure that executes successfully and returns zero (0). The example shows the definition of the called procedure proc1. This stored procedure is executed from a set of Transact-SQL statements entered interactively.

N O T E When a set of Transact-SQL statements execute together, whether the statements are part of a procedure or not, the rules for batch operations apply. This is true even if the set of statements are typed in interactively.

Although the called procedure doesn't contain a Return statement, Sybase returns an integer status value to the procedure that called proc1.

```
/* Create the procedure. */
Create Procedure up_Publishers
As
select *
From    publishers
Go

/* Declare a Return Code variable and execute. */
Declare @nRC int
Exec    @nRC = up_Publishers
Go
```

```
/* Return the status of the procedure. */
Select status = @nRC
Go

pub_id  pub_name                    city                    state
------  ----------------------      ------------------      -----
0736    New Age Books               Boston                  MA
0877    Binnet & Hardley            Washington              DC
1389    Algodata Infosystems        Berkeley                CA
        status
        -----------
                  0
```

In the following example, up_Publishers has been enhanced to return a user status of 5:

```
/* Create the procedure. */
Create Procedure up_Publishers
As
select *
From    publishers
Return 5
Go

/* Declare a Return Code variable and execute. */
Declare @nRC int
Exec    @nRC = up_Publishers
Go

/* Return the status of the procedure. */
Select status = @nRC
Go

pub_id  pub_name                    city                    state
------  ----------------------      ------------------      -----
0736    New Age Books               Boston                  MA
0877    Binnet & Hardley            Washington              DC
1389    Algodata Infosystems        Berkeley                CA
        status
        -----------
                  5
```

In the following example, the returned value is checked as part of a conditional statement and a message displayed if the procedure executed successfully. This third example of Transact-SQL return statements is more typical of the usage of return status in a production environment.

```
/* Declare a Return Code variable and execute. */
Declare @nRC int
Exec    @nRC = up_Publishers
If @nRC = 0
        Print 'No Errors occurred'
Else
        Print 'Error return occurred: %1!', @nRC
Go

pub_id  pub_name                    city          state
------  ----------------------      ----------    -----
```

```
0736    New Age Books        Boston    MA
0877    Binnet & Hardley     Washington DC
1389    Algodata Infosystems Berkeley  CA
No Errors occurred
```

 T I P You can nest procedures within other procedures up to 16 levels in Transact-SQL.

Using Raiserror

You use the `Raiserror` statement to return a user-specified message in the same form in which Sybase returns errors. The `Raiserror` also sets a system flag to record that an error has occurred. The simplified syntax of the `Raiserror` statement is:

```
RaiseError Integer_Expression [Message_Text] [,Message_Tokens]
```

Part

II

Ch

10

The *Integer_Expression* is a user-specified error or message number and must be greater than 50,000. The *Integer_Expression* is placed in the global variable, `@@Error`, which stores the last error number returned. An error message can be specified as a string literal or through a local variable in the parameter *Message_Text*. A local variable that contains an error message can be used in place of the text of the message. If the *Message_Text* is tokenized like a print statement (e.g., `'Hello %1!'`, where `%1!` will be replaced by a variable's value) you must supply an appropriate number of tokens as variables following the call to `Raiserror`.

Using sp_addmessage   You can also add your message text and an associated message number to the system table sysmessages. You use the system-stored procedure, sp_addmessage, to add a message with a message identification number within the range 50,001 and 2,147,483,647. The syntax of the `sp_addmessage` system procedure is as follows:

```
sp_addmessage Message_Id, Message_Text [, language]
```

User-defined error messages that are generated with a `RaiseError` statement (but without a number in the sysmessages table) return a message identification number of 50,000.

When specifying messages, you enter an error message within single quotes of up to 255 characters. The remaining parameters of the `sp_addmessage` procedure are optional. The language parameter specifies one of the languages installed with Sybase. U.S. English is the default language if the parameter is omitted.

The following example shows the use of the `sp_addmessage` system-stored procedure that adds a system message with an associated identification number and severity. A subsequent `Select` statement retrieves the message from the system table sysmessages. Finally, the `RaiseError` statement is used to return the user-defined system message.

```
/* First add the message. */
sp_addmessage 99999, "I'm not feeling well, Dave..."
go

/* Check that it's in the system catalog. */
Select *
From    sysusermessages
```

```
Where  Error = 99999
Go

/* Now test it by raising the error. */
Raiserror 99999
Go

The message has been inserted.
error    uid description                          langid
------------------------------------------------ ------
99999       1 I'm not feeling well, Dave...
I'm not feeling well, Dave...
```

Using sp_dropmessage   You can use the system stored procedure, sp_dropmessage, to remove a user-defined message from the system table sysmessages when it is no longer needed.
The syntax of the sp_dropmessage is as follows:

```
sp_dropmessage [Message_Id [, language | 'all']]
```

You're only required to enter the message number to drop the message. The two additional
optional parameters permit you to specify the language from which the message should be
dropped. You can use the keyword All to drop the user-defined message from all languages.

In the following example, a user-defined message in the default language of U.S. English is
removed from the system table, sysmessages.

```
sp_dropmessage 99999
Go

- - - - - - - - - - - - - - -
Message deleted.
```

Using Waitfor

You use a Waitfor statement to specify a time, a time interval, or an event for executing a statement, statement block, stored procedure, or transaction. The syntax of the Waitfor statement
is as follows:

```
Waitfor {Delay <'time'> | Time <'time'> | ErrorExit | ProcessExit |  MirrorExit}
```

The meaning of each of the keywords that follow the Waitfor keyword is shown in the following list:

- Delay—Specifies an interval or time to elapse

- Time—A specified time (no date portion) of up to 24 hours

- ErrorExit—Until a process terminates abnormally

- ProcessExit—Until a process terminates normally or abnormally

- MirrorExit—Until a mirrored device fails

In the following example of a Waitfor statement, a Delay is used to specify that a pause of forty seconds is taken before the subsequent Select statement is executed.

```
Waitfor Delay '00:00:40'
    Select *
    From    authors
```

In the second Waitfor example, a Time is used to wait until 3:10:51 PM of the current day until the subsequent Select statement is executed.

```
Waitfor time '15:10:51'
    Select *
    From    authors
```

From Here...

In this chapter, you've seen how you can use Transact-SQL to control the flow of your Sybase-based application. Remembering to use these techniques to manipulate information on the server can significantly improve performance for your application.

The following are some other areas of interest that relate to the materials you've been working with here:

- Chapter 6, "Understanding Tables and Datatypes," explains how to create and use user-defined datatypes.

- Chapter 7, "Using Rules, Defaults, and Triggers," teaches you how to create and use rules, defaults, and triggers to help maintain the integrity of your database.

- Chapter 11, "Understanding Transactions and Locking," provides more information on how to manage locks that are acquired by your transactions.

- Chapter 13, "Using Advanced Stored Procedures and Triggers," gives a detailed walkthrough of some complex stored procedures and triggers that you can learn from and use in your own applications.

- Chapter 22, "Managing and Monitoring Performance," teaches you ways to optimize the operation of Sybase System XI, including the correct sizing of the procedure cache.

Understanding Transactions and Locking

A good understanding of transactions and locking is essential for anybody who is going to write database applications for more than one user. Even single-user applications require some understanding of locking, though the impact of locking your own individual computer is not nearly as drastic as that of locking an enterprise network of hundreds of users.

Sybase System XI has a number of different styles of locking available to the programmer. This chapter provides you with the information required to make an accurate assessment of what is needed for your application for transaction control and locking.

You can never be too cautious in a multi-user application. As a programmer you should always concentrate on attempting to minimize the amount of locking that can occur so that there is less chance of users interfering with each other. ■

How to work with transactions

Sybase enables you to manipulate data in a transaction and to undo your changes if you want to.

How to lock records and tables

You learn how to force explicit locks on the data that you are working with.

Tips and tricks for managing locks on Sybase

Sybase has a number of features that enable you to manage the locks on your server.

N O T E Special thanks to Peter Thawley, Senior Manager, Advanced Technologies, Server, and Connectivity Group, Sybase, Inc., for providing background information for this chapter. Universally regarded as the "god" of Sybase databases, Peter Thawley gets to play with every little piece of hardware at Sybase and has the good fortune of being able to try out everyone else's theories on large applications and multi-user systems. ▪

Defining Transactions

A *transaction* is a logical unit of work that you want Sybase to perform for you. That unit of work may include one or many SQL statements, provided the unit of work is appropriately delineated to the server.

Single-statement transactions can be executed in ISQL just by entering their text and typing **Go**. In fact, a large part of this book has been using transactions and you probably never gave them a second thought. Single-statement transactions are ideal where the results required are simple and self-contained. In Listing 11.1, the SQL statement will return a list of tables from the database currently being used.

Listing 11.1   CHP11_01.SQL—Fetching Tables from Sysobjects

```
/*
   This simple select statement
   returns a list of user-created
   tables in the current database.
*/
Select name, id, uid, crdate
From    sysobjects
Where   type = 'U'  /* user defined tables */
Order By name
Go

name              id         uid   crdate
- - - - - - - - - - - - - - - - - - - - - - - - - - - - - - - - - - - - - - - - -
au_pix            304004114  1     May 27 1996 10:16:02:680AM
authors           16003088   1     May 27 1996 10:16:01:680AM
authors2          656005368  1     May 27 1996  2:28:21:476PM
blurbs            336004228  1     May 27 1996 10:16:02:680AM
discounts         272004000  1     May 27 1996 10:16:01:680AM
publishers        48003202   1     May 27 1996 10:16:01:680AM
roysched          80003316   1     May 27 1996 10:16:01:680AM
sales             112003430  1     May 27 1996 10:16:01:680AM
salesdetail       144003544  1     May 27 1996 10:16:01:680AM
salesdetail2      688005482  1     May 27 1996  2:44:59:456PM
stores            240003886  1     May 27 1996 10:16:02:680AM
titleauthor       176003658  1     May 27 1996 10:16:01:680AM
titles            208003772  1     May 27 1996 10:16:02:680AM
```

System XI treats every operation that is not *explicitly* started with `Begin Transaction` as a single-statement transaction that is independent of all other actions on the server.

But what do you do when you need to do more than one thing in a transaction and conditionally undo it if something goes wrong? That is where multi-statement transactions come into play. Multi-statement transactions enable you to put two or more SQL statements together and send them to the server for processing; then, on some basis that you decide, you may choose to undo the work submitted. In Listing 11.2, you can see an example of a multi-statement transaction.

Listing 11.2 CHP11_02.SQL—A Multi-Statement Transaction

```
/*
   A slightly more complex example:
   here you create two tables, Table_A and Table_B,
   then you do a little bit of data entry through some
   quick inserts, and then do a transaction.
*/

/* First create the work tables. */
Create Table Table_A(
      X        Smallint Null,
      Y        Smallint Null)
Go

Create Table Table_B(
      Z        Smallint Null)
Go

/* Now add some dummy data for Table_A. */
Insert Table_A
Values ( 1, 100 )
Go

Insert Table_A
Values ( 3, 100 )
Go

Insert Table_A
Values ( 5, 200 )
Go

/* Now add some dummy data for Table_B */
Insert Table_B
Values ( 1 )
Go

Insert Table_B
Values ( 2 )
Go

Insert Table_B
Values ( 3 )
Go

Insert Table_B
```

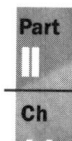

Part

II

Ch

11

continues

Listing 11.2   Continued

```
Values ( 4 )
Go

Insert Table_B
Values ( 5 )
Go

Insert Table_B
Values ( 6 )
Go

/* Now Begin the transaction and do some work! */
Begin Tran
      Print 'Start of the Transaction!'

      /* Update the first table.*/
      Update Table_A
      Set    X = X + 1
      Where  Y = 100

      /* Check for errors and for successful updating,
          if @@RowCount = 0 then you didn't hit anything;
          if @@Error != 0 then a SQL Error must have occurred */
      If @@RowCount = 0 or @@Error !=0
      Begin
             Rollback Tran
             Print 'Error Occurred, no rows were updated'
             Return
      End

      /* Update all the records in the second table. */
      Update Table_B
      Set    Z = Z + 1

      /* Check for errors and for successful updating.*/
      If @@RowCount = 0 or @@Error !=0
      Begin
             Rollback Tran
             Print 'Error Occurred, no rows were updated'
             Return
      End
Commit Tran
Go

Print 'End of the Transaction, therefore we must have committed!'
Go
```

TIP

To make your scripts and stored procedures easier to read, format them with indented sections inside transaction blocks.

By using transactions, you can guarantee that your access to the table data will be consistent and unaffected by other users for the duration of the transaction. This is key to building a system that has reliable data processing. Furthermore, transactions provide you with the capability to recover in the event of a media failure or other problem. If a transaction is left in an uncommitted state at the time of a disk crash, Sybase will faithfully undo all the work when the server is restored to life and you will have a database that has been left in a known state.

Types of Locking: Optimistic versus Pessimistic

When you write multi-user database applications, you can take one of two approaches to transaction control: optimistic or pessimistic locking. *Optimistic locking* assumes that you are going to do nothing in your application code to explicitly enforce locks on records while you work on them. Instead, you will rely on the database to manage this on its own while you concentrate on application logic. *Pessimistic locking* relies on the programmer to explicitly manage the locking process on the data or objects. The application is responsible for acquiring, sharing and releasing any locks on data that it is using.

To implement optimistic locking in your application without having it grind to a halt because of excessive locks on the server, you must take care to observe some simple rules, as follows:

- Minimize the amount of time that a transaction is held open by limiting the amount of SQL that occurs inside a `Begin Tran…Commit Tran` section.
- Rely on application code to guarantee that updates are hitting the right record rather than holding locks while a user browses data.
- Ensure that all application codes update and select from tables in the same order. This will stop any deadlocks from occurring.

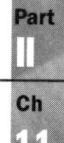

Most marketing literature has attempted to tell application developers that Sybase is going to manage locking and that there is nothing to worry about. This is a *very* optimistic locking approach. Unfortunately, it is not very pragmatic because it assumes that there is nothing a programmer or user can do to explicitly cause locking. In fact, there are many situations that will cause a large amount of locking to occur on a server, potentially disabling it for the enterprise that it is supporting.

How Locks Are Managed by Sybase

I think it will be useful as background to first discuss some of the basics of locking as they pertain to (and are implemented by) Sybase, so that some of the more detailed items discussed in the sections below are not without a base of understanding. Specifically, I want to focus on the following two key areas of locking:

- Page sizes and granularity of data
- Types of locks

Learning about Page Sizes and Granularity of Data   Up until System XI, Sybase's internal basic unit of work was a 2K data page. What this means is that any activity that is executed on the server must do work on at least 2K of data. To further explain, a table has a number of pages of data associated with it (depending on the number and size of rows that it contains); Sybase can only reference data in that table a page at a time. So, if an update hits a single record in a table and a lock is held for some period of time, it is more than likely that more than one row is in fact being locked.

 In System XI it is possible to define larger I/O pages in private named caches. This feature is typically used to improve performance when writing to the transaction logs. For more information on how to configure and work with named caches, see Chapter 22, "Managing and Monitoring Performance."

How does this affect a database application? One of the most important considerations when writing a multi-user application is that there must be a way for multiple users to work independently of one another. For example, two users must be able to update customer records at the same time while answering phone calls from customers. The greater the capability to manipulate data in the same table without affecting other users by locks, the greater the concurrency of an application and the greater the chance of its being able to support a lot of users.

A highly-accessed table, such as a table of unique values for the rest of the system, should be made as concurrent as possible. By forcing as few as possible rows of data onto the same data page, you thereby limit the number of coincidental rows locked as the result of a user action. Additionally, users' transactions should be kept to a minimum duration when hitting these tables.

Two other types of locks can occur that lock data more greatly than a single data page: table and extent. *Table* locks occur because a user issued a query to update a table without including a Where clause, thereby requesting an update of every row. When the number of data pages locked exceeds the Lock Escalation Threshold defined for the particular table or database, a *Table* lock is incurred, which locks all rows of the table.

Extent locks occur when Sybase needs to create a new database extent (eight pages of data) to respond to a user query. Unfortunately, there are no controls at your disposal to handle or deal with extent locks, so you simply should know that they occur and what they mean.

For more information on lock escalation, refer to the following section titled "Understanding Table Lock Promotion."

Understanding the Types of Locks Available in System XI   Sybase can place several types of locks on database pages and tables. The page locks that are possible are Shared, Exclusive, and Update. Shared locks and Exclusive locks are reasonably self-explanatory in that they either enable another process to acquire a lock on the same page or they don't.

Multiple processes may have Shared locks on the same data page; they are usually acquired when data is being read. It's important to note that no other process may take an Exclusive lock (to perform DML) until all Shared locks have been released.

Exclusive locks of table pages are given to a process that is updating a record on a page, inserting a new record at the end of a page, or deleting a record from a page. Exclusive locks disallow any other process from accessing the page.

The Update lock type is a middling lock. It sits in between Shared and Exclusive in that it will enable a process to acquire a Share on the page until an actual update has occurred on it. Update locks are acquired when a Cursor is being built in the server. Update locks are automatically promoted to Exclusive when an update occurs on one of the pages associated with the cursor.

At the table level, Sybase has Shared and Exclusive locks that work in the same fashion as the page level. Sybase also has Intent locks. Intent locks indicate that a table has a number of pages on it that Sybase is *intending* to lock at the page level in response to a user process.

▶ **See** "Using Sybase Cursors," **p. 315**

Understanding Isolation Levels

There are a number of ways in Sybase that you can cause locks to be held or released while querying the database. One of those ways is by setting a transaction's isolation level. As its name implies, an *isolation level* specifies to the database how "isolated" to keep the data that is currently being worked on by the other users and requesters of data on the server. The Sybase isolation levels are documented as follows:

- Isolation Level 0: dirty or uncommitted data
- Isolation Level 1: committed data
- Isolation Level 2: undefined and not used
- Isolation Level 3: repeatable read data

N O T E Transaction isolation levels are set for the entire time that a session is connected to the database. If you change isolation levels for a specific part of your application, do not forget to change back to the default so that other parts of the application are not adversely affected.

To achieve the same effects as isolation levels for a single Select statement, refer to the section below, "Holding a Lock Explicitly," for more information. ■

Sybase has several ways of referring to each of the isolation levels available to you. In this chapter, you see how to use both the set statement, which uses the Transaction Isolation Level keywords in Transact-SQL, and the at keyword appended to a Select statement, which uses the more English-like terms such as Read Committed, Read Uncommitted and Serializable. Note that by using the at keyword in a Select statement, you are affecting just that Select; the overall setting of the set isolation level will remain in effect for all the other queries and elements of the transaction.

T I P There's an easy way to find out what your current isolation level is by inspecting the global system variable @@isolation. For example:

```
Select @@isolation
Go
```

```
-----------------
0
```

Part

II

Ch

11

Transaction Isolation Level 0

Transaction Isolation Level 0 is the same as the Nolock keyword on an individual Select statement. No Shared locks are placed on any data that you pass over in the query; additionally, no locks held by other users are observed. For example, if another user has deleted a whole table that you are about to select from, but has yet to Commit a transaction, you will still be able to read the data from it and not receive any error conditions.

This isolation level when used in a Select statement is known as Read Uncommitted.

> **CAUTION**
>
> The Read Uncommitted transaction isolation level is not recommended for any applications that require data integrity because you cannot be guaranteed that the data you are working with is still as it was or, indeed, in the database at all. Use Read Uncommitted sparingly in your applications and possibly only for such procedures as reporting applications on tables that are statistically unaffected by the average transactions that post against your server.

To set your isolation level to Level 0, perform the following SQL transaction:

```
Set Transaction Isolation Level 0
Go
```

If you want to use this isolation level in a query, execute something like this:

```
Select *
From    sysobjects
At      Isolation Read Uncommitted
Go
```

Transaction Isolation Level 1

Transaction Isolation Level 1 (Read Committed) is the default method of operation for Sybase. It does not allow you to have data returned from the database that is *dirty* or *uncommitted*. Read Committed acquires Share locks on all the pages it passes over inside a transaction. You may receive some data pages that are not re-readable or that may contain values that only temporarily exist in the database because of another user's performing a delete or insert that is committed or rolled back during the life of your query.

If it is important that the query's results be completely unaffected by other users during the life of a particular transaction, then make sure that you use the Repeatable Read isolation level.

To set your isolation level to Level 1, perform the following SQL:

```
Set Transaction Isolation Level 1
Go
```

If you want to use this isolation level in a query, execute something like this:

```
Select *
From    sysobjects
At      Isolation Read Committed
Go
```

N O T E All Sybase system stored procedures execute in `Read Committed` isolation level to guarantee data consistency. You cannot alter their isolation level; they will override any session or environment isolation level that is currently in effect. ■

Transaction Isolation Level 3

`Transaction Isolation Level 3` (`Serializable`) is the most *exclusive* type of locking that you can force Sybase to maintain. In other DBMSs, `Serializable` is referred to as `Repeatable Read`, which guarantees that the data you are reading will be unaffected by other transactions issued from other users during the life of a given transaction you are working on. Because of `Repeatable Read`'s explicit locking of data from other users, it reduces the concurrency of the database. It also reduces the number of different users who can access data at the same time without affecting one another. Take care that you do not use `Repeatable Read` unwisely in your application; there are not that many places where it is actually required.

To set your isolation level to `Level 3`, perform the following SQL transaction:

```
Set Transaction Isolation Level 3
Go
```

If you want to use this isolation level in a query, execute something like this:

```
Select *
From    sysobjects
At      Isolation Serializable
Go
```

N O T E Applications and databases that claim to be SQL92 compliant are supposed to default their isolation level to `Repeatable Read` or `Serializable`. In this respect, Sybase is not SQL92 compliant because it defaults a connection to be `Level 1` (`Read Committed`). ■

Part

II

Ch

11

Working with Transactions

In the opening section of this chapter, you saw how to delineate a transaction using `Begin`, `Commit` and `rollback`. Sybase has several keywords or Transact-SQL statements that are required for transaction control. They are described below for clear definition going forward.

CAUTION

It is very important to remember that every `Begin Tran` must be followed at some point in the code by a matching `Commit Tran` or `Rollback Tran`. Transactions must begin and end in pairs; otherwise the server will continue holding locks until the client is disconnected. See the section below on "Using Named Transactions and SavePoints" for more information.

Beginning a Transaction with Begin Tran

When you issue a `Begin Tran` to the database, Sybase marks a point in the database's transaction logs and identifies a point to be returned to in the event of a `Rollback Tran`. `Begin Tran` explicitly tells Sybase that all the work following should be treated as one logical unit until a `Commit` or `Rollback` is encountered—despite the fact that the logical transaction may contain many operations.

It is possible to issue operations without a `Begin Tran` statement, and they will effect the database. The danger of not explicitly beginning a transaction is that you will not be able to conditionally undo the work that you sent to the server. If an operation is not preceded by a `Begin Tran`, Sybase will be unable to roll back in the event of an error or some other condition that is programmer controlled.

> **N O T E** Sybase's transaction logs monitor those transactions that are contained inside of `Begin` and `Commit` statements. In the event of a media failure on a database before data is physically changed on the database, Sybase will recover or ensure that those changes are applied by "rolling forward" those unapplied transactions to the database when the server is next brought back online. ▓

Finishing a Transaction with Commit Tran

Issuing a `Commit Tran` to the database signals Sybase that you are happy with the work done so far and no longer want to group any additional work inside the transaction. `Commit Tran` is not reversible.

Undoing a Transaction with Rollback Tran

`Rollback Tran` is Sybase's equivalent of the Edit, Undo menu option in your favorite word processor. Sending a `Rollback` to the database server will cause it to undo all the work to the most recent `Begin Tran` statement. Typically, a `Rollback Tran` would be issued during a long transaction if any particular part of it encountered a SQL error of some kind.

> **CAUTION**
>
> Sybase will enable you to call *remote* stored procedures inside a transaction; however, because of the nature of the *Remote Procedure Call* (RPC) interface with the other server on which the RPC executed, Sybase will not be able to `Rollback` any such calls. Take care when writing applications that require RPCs that there are additional RPCs to programmatically undo your previous work.

Transaction Limitations

Sybase manages transactions by writing data to the log file that it maintains internally. Due to the design and implementation of this log, there are some sorts of SQL statements that cannot be represented in the logs. Consequently, any statement that cannot be placed in the logs cannot be placed inside a transaction.

N O T E Sybase's replication methods are derived in part from replicating data that occurs, or is represented, in the transaction logs. For the same reason that DDL and permissions-type SQL cannot be placed in a transaction, it cannot be replicated to other servers. ■

DDL and Database Statements *DDL* (Data Definition Language) and database modification statements are not allowed inside a transaction because they are considered to be immediately in effect on a database. To add "rolling back" capabilities for some of these commands, you will have to programmatically reverse them with corresponding `Creates` or `Drops`. The following are the commands that are affected by this limitation:

ALTER DATABASE	CREATE DATABASE	CREATE INDEX
CREATE PROCEDURE	CREATE TABLE	CREATE VIEW
DISK INIT	DROP...	DUMP TRANSACTION
LOAD DATABASE	LOAD TRANSACTION	RECONFIGURE
SELECT INTO	TRUNCATE TABLE	UPDATE STATISTICS

TIP Sybase does not allow a table column to be dropped, but there is a way to work around it. Create a new table with the required schema (minus the column) and use the `Select Into` Transact-SQL command to copy the data.

Part
II

Ch
11

Permissions Sybase also limits your capability to modify user permissions inside a transaction through the `Grant` and `Revoke` statements. However, unlike most DDL statements, permissions are pretty easy to undo because they have matching pairs of `Grant` and `Revoke` permissions.

So rather than require that this syntax be supported inside a transaction, all you need to do is perform the opposite operation programmatically. In Listing 11.3, Sybase refuses to execute or compile the SQL because it tries to perform `Grants` inside a transaction.

Listing 11.3 CHP11_03.SQL—Using Invalid SQL in a Script Causes an Error

```
/*
   This example script demonstrates Sybase's stopping a transaction
   due to the existence of an invalid statement.
*/

/* First create a table.*/
Create Table Table_A(
     X      Smallint Null,
     Y      Smallint Null)
Go

/* Now add a security group. */
sp_addgroup Grp_Private
Go
```

continues

Listing 11.3 Continued

```
/* Now work on a transaction that will be disallowed. */
Begin Tran
      Grant Select On Table_A To Grp_Private
      If @@error != 0
      Begin
              Rollback Tran
              Print 'Failed to grant select to Grp_Private'
              Return
      End
Commit Tran
Go
```

In Listing 11.4, the script is modified slightly so that it no longer is a cause of error with Sybase.

Listing 11.4 CHP11_04.SQL—Moving the Offending SQL Outside of the Transaction

```
/*
   This example script will compile because
   the Grant statement is outside of a transaction
*/

Create Table Table_A(
      X       Smallint Null,
      Y       Smallint Null)
Go
sp_addgroup Grp_Private
go

Grant Select On Table_A To Grp_Private
If @@Error != 0
Begin
      Print 'Failed to grant select to grp_private'
      Return
End
```

N O T E This is kind of a spurious example because it is unlikely that Sybase would have actually performed the operation if a SQL error had occurred. However, it is reasonable to expect that there will be times in an application program when it will be necessary to revoke permissions conditionally, and this is possible—only not inside a transaction. ■

Using Named Transactions and SavePoints

One thing that becomes obvious during the writing of large stored procedures and applications with large bodies of SQL code is that no matter how it is looked at, the code is pretty unreadable. It is text-based and greatly relies on programmers who are all working with the same style of format and layout. When transactional programming is involved, it becomes even more important for people to use good indenting to clearly mark blocks of code.

However, even the most careful programmer will find that it becomes a bit of a nightmare to remember how many indents to Rollback out of in the event of an error condition or some programmatic constraint. Named Transactions and SavePoints are used for just this purpose: They provide a way of rolling back work to a given *named* or *saved* portion of the code that has been executing, even if that portion is at a higher nesting level.

Working with Named Transactions   Named transactions provide a convenient way of attaching an identifier to a whole body of work. Use named transactions to make it easier to undo large portions of code. To create a named transaction, add the name of the transaction to the Begin Tran statement, as in Listing 11.5.

Listing 11.5   CHP11_05.SQL—Using Named Transactions

```
/* Open outer transaction. */
      Update authors
      Set    phone = '415 986-7020'
      Where  au_id = '341-22-1782'

      /* Open inner transaction. */
      Begin Tran Update_TitleAuthor
            Update titleauthor
            Set    royaltyper = royaltyper + 25
            Where  au_id = '341-22-1782'

            /* Check for errors. */
            If @@Error != 0
Begin
                  Rollback Tran Update_TitleAuthor
                  Print 'Failed to update Royalties'
                  Return
            End
      Commit Tran Update_TitleAuthor
Commit Tran Update_Authors
Go
```

N O T E   If you omit the transaction's identifier or name when committing or rolling back a transaction, Sybase will simply undo the work to the most recent Begin Tran, regardless of its name. Take care when using named transactions that all work is coded in a consistent manner— either using names or not. Otherwise, programmers may end up stepping on each others' transactions inadvertently. For more information on naming conventions, have a look at Appendix A, "Suggestions for Naming Conventions." ∎

Working with SavePoints   SavePoints are really just another way of doing a named transaction. They provide a method of marking a place in the code to which a Rollback can be used to undo work. To create a SavePoint, issue the SQL command:

```
Save Transaction Tran_Name
```

Then just use the identifier, *Tran_Name*, when performing your Rollback. In Listing 11.6, you can see that SavePoints provide a very convenient way of undoing or rolling back SQL statements.

Listing 11.6   CHP11_06.SQL—Using Saved Transactions

```
Begin Tran
        Update authors
        Set     phone = '415 986-7020'
        Where   au_id = '341-22-1782'

        /* Save your work to this point. */
        Save Transaction AuthorDone

        Update titleauthor
        Set     royaltyper = royaltyper + 25
        Where   au_id = '341-22-1782'

        If @@Error != 0 Or @@RowCount > 1
Begin
            /* Rollback and exit. */
            Rollback Tran AuthorDone
            Print 'Error occurred when updating TitleAuthor'
            Return
        End
Commit Tran
Go

Print 'Transaction Committed'
Go
```

CAUTION

Despite the fact that the transaction above rolled back the Update on *authors*, Sybase will hold locks on the *authors* table until the entire transaction is completed by either Commit or Rollback. This is a side effect of using a SavePoint; it is also something that may cause unexpected locking in an application.

 TROUBLESHOOTING

I have an application that seems to continuously hold locks after the first transaction executes. I'm sure that I'm committing properly. What's going on? The most likely scenario is that you have issued more Begin Trans than you have corresponding Commit Trans or Rollback Trans. Remember that transactions *must* be enclosed in pairs of Begin and Commit/Rollback. If you fail to provide commands in pairs, Sybase will think that you want to keep the transaction open for a longer period.

To help identify your code problems, do a walkthrough of your application and monitor error conditions carefully. Chances are that an error condition is occurring and some code is returning control before closing an open transaction. Also, check the value of the system variable @@trancount to tell you how deeply nested in transactions you really are. Note that transactions can be nested 16 layers deep.

Serialized Columns Without Identity

Sybase System 10 introduced a new *serial* datatype, called the Identity, in which Sybase will automatically assign the next sequential value to a column in a table. Identitys are very valuable in applications that have high transaction volume in order to identify each record uniquely.

For some applications that must support multiple database back ends and for those applications that require Sybase 4.x compatibility, it is possible to implement the same kind of feature as an Identity column by performing the following steps:

1. In Listing 11.7, a table is created with columns in it to store a table name and the current value.

Listing 11.7   CHP11_07.SQL—Creating a Table for Identity Simulation

```
/*
   This DDL is designed to create a table
   that will be used for keeping track of IDs
   or record labels for the database.
*/
Create Table Record_IDs(
     Table_Name   Varchar(30),
     Current_ID   Int)
Go

/* Add a primary clustered index. */
Create Unique Clustered Index PK_Record_IDs
On Record_IDs( Table_Name )
With Max_Rows_Per_Page = 1
Go
```

Part

II

Ch

11

2. In Listing 11.8, records are inserted into the table that correspond to tables in the target database.

Listing 11.8   CHP11_08.SQL—Inserting System Identity Records

```
/*
   This simple insert adds a record
   to the Record_IDs table for each
   of the user-defined tables found
   in the current database.
*/
Insert Record_IDs
Select name, 1
From   sysobjects
Where  type = 'U'
Go
```

3. In Listing 11.9, a stored procedure is created that will have a consistent access interface to the table and will lock the table so that no other users can modify the data while a given process is accessing it.

Listing 11.9 CHP11_09.SQL—Using Serialized Procedures to Lock Data

```
/*
    This stored procedure is the "user interface"
    to the Record_IDs table, which enables you to
    fetch from the database a valid record
    identifier.
*/

/* First create the procedure. */
Create Procedure up_GetID              /* up = user procedure */
     @psTableName      Varchar(30),   /* p = parameter */
     @rnNewID          Int Output     /* r = receive or output parameter */
As
Declare
        @nSQLError      Int,
        @nRowCount      Int

Begin Tran
        /* First update the record to acquire the exclusive lock on the page. */
        Update Record_IDs
        Set    Current_ID = Current_ID + 1
        Where  Table_Name = @psTableName

        /* Check for errors. */
        Select     @nSQLError = @@error,
                   @nRowCount = @@rowcount
        If @nSQLError != 0 OR @nRowCount != 1
        Begin
             Rollback Tran
             Return -999 /* failed to update record correctly */
        End

        /* Select back the value from the table that you've already locked. */
        Select @rnNewID = Current_ID
        From   Record_IDs
        Where  Table_Name = @psTableName

        /* Check for errors */
        Select     @nSQLError = @@error,
                   @nRowCount = @@rowcount
        If @nSQLError != 0 OR @nRowCount != 1
        Begin
             Rollback Tran
             Return -998 /* failed to select record correctly */
        End
```

```
Commit Tran
Return 0
Go
```

4. In Listing 11.10, the procedure is tested and used to generated IDs for the table *authors*.

Listing 11.10 CHP11_10.SQL—Using the Serializing Stored Procedure to Create an ID for Later Use

```
/*
   This script demonstrates how you
   might use the stored procedure up_GetID
   to fetch data for a unique ID.
*/

/* First declare some local storage variables. */
Declare @nRecordID  Int,
        @nRC        Int

/* Fetch a record ID for use in inserting new record. */
Exec @nRC = up_GetID 'authors', @nRecordID Output

If @nRC != 0
     Print 'An error occurred fetching new Record ID'
Else
Begin
     Print 'New Record value is: %1!', @nRecordID
End
Go
```

Part

II

Ch

11

 TIP Always use the new `Identity` column to create identifying columns instead of the `Timestamp` datatype. The `Identity` column is far easier to reference and use in application code and consumes less database space.

Understanding Locks

In addition to the background information provided above in the section, "Types of Locks," it is important to know how to handle locking when it occurs in your database. In this section, you learn the techniques needed to analyze and understand the locking that is occurring on your database server. In addition, you learn how to *Kill* a user who is holding locks on the server and thereby affecting performance or functionality for other users.

 TIP Transaction control, locking, and optimization tips seem to be abundant on electronic forums. Check out the CompuServe and Microsoft Network forums for Sybase and Sybase to find some new "TechNotes."

Viewing Lock Information in the Server

There are two ways to review information about locks held in the database: by using the Sybase SQL Server Manager or through the execution of the system-stored procedure, sp_lock. Sybase SQL Server Manager, under the covers, is selecting records from the *master* table *sysprocesses* and presenting the data for you in the display. You should know how to use both methods, in case you are at a site that doesn't have access to Sybase SQL Server Manager.

Using Sybase SQL Server Manager to Review Locking Processes   To view information that is being locked using the Sybase SQL Server Manager, perform the following steps:

1. Run Sybase SQL Server Manager from the Sybase for Windows NT group in Program Manager and connect to the Server you want to administer.

TIP   Instead of having to specify and connect to the server each time you start Sybase, it is possible to specify command-line options with which you can specify the server name (-S), user id (-U), and password (-P) that you want to use to log on. Note that these same parameters apply to Sybase's other utilities, ISQL and WISQL32.

2. Choose Server, Processes to view the currently active processes on the server selected (see Fig. 11.1).

FIG. 11.1

The SSM Server Processes dialog box enables you to monitor all the active processes on the server and to kill one if you want to.

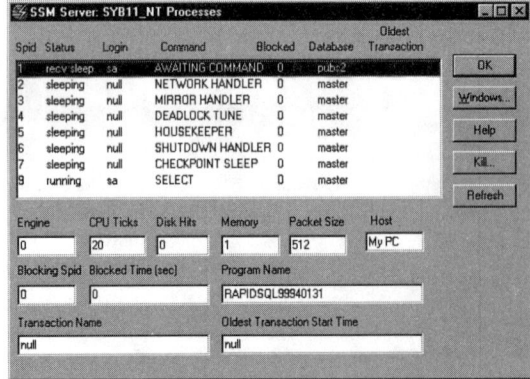

To refresh the display, press the Refresh button.

Using sp_lock   The sp_lock system-stored procedure will return a list of processes and the types of locks that they are holding on the system. To get the locks held by a particular process, add the process ID to the command (sp_lock *spid*). Listing 11.11 is some example code to show you the output of sp_lock:

Listing 11.11 CHP11_11.SQL—Using sp_lock to Query the Database for Active Table Changes

```
/*
   This sample script demonstrates
   the use of sp_lock and shows you
   the output.
*/

/* Begin a transaction. */
Begin Tran
      /* Update all the records in the authors table
         so that the sp_lock call will show a number
         of pages being locked. */
      Update authors
      set au_id = au_id
Go

/* Query the active locks from the system. */
sp_lock
Go

/* Undo the transaction. */
Rollback Tran
Go
```

The output of the sp_lock is shown below:

```
The class column will display the cursor name for locks associated
with a cursor for the current user and the cursor id for other users.
  spid locktype       table_id   page dbname   class
------ -------------- ---------- ---- -------- ----------------
     1 Sh_intent      432004570  0    master   Non Cursor Lock
     1 Ex_table       16003088   0    pubs2    Non Cursor Lock
```

 TIP   Many system procedures return an `Object_ID` column to identify a database object. To quickly get the name of that object, use the system function `Object_Name( )`. For example, select `Object_Name( 1232324 )`. Note that the spaces around the object name 1232324 are optional and can be omitted if you want, and are placed there for easier reading.

Specifically, to identify the two tables listed above you would execute:

```
Select Object_Name( 432004570 )
Go
Select Object_Name( 16003088 )
Go


---------------
deltitle
authors
```

continues

continued

These results are interesting, because it seems that Sybase is holding a lock on a trigger *deltitle*. This would seem to be impossible. However, if you notice the results from sp_lock, the database is different. The correct SQL to be executed is:

```
Use master
Go
Select Object_Name( 432004570 )
Go
Use pubs2
Go
Select Object_Name( 16003088 )
Go


- - - - - - - - - - - - - - -
spt_values
authors
```

These results are far more satisfactory and believable!

Killing a Locking Process

If a process or user is holding locks on a table or set of tables, it is sometimes necessary to kill them. Killing a process forces a Rollback of any transactions that the process may have open and thereby enables other processes and users to access the locked table or set of tables. Killing a process is generally an act of last resort that is necessary if an application program incorrectly holds locks and is unable to release them. It is important that before you attempt to kill a process that is holding locks on the database, you verify with the sp_who and sp_lock system procedures that the spid (server process id) that you are targeting to kill is in fact the user holding the locks.

When reviewing the output from sp_who, look at the blk spid column to identify a user that is blocked. Trace the tree of the blocks back to the parent spid, and kill that user. To kill a user process, you can either use Sybase SQL Server Manager or execute the Kill command.

Using Sybase SQL Server Manager to Kill a Process Using Sybase SQL Server Manager to kill a process involves first finding the process that is causing locking; the steps to accomplish this are outlined above in the section on sp_lock. Click the Kill button on the Sybase SQL Server Manager Processes dialog box to kill the blocking process (see Fig. 11.2). A warning dialog box appears so you can change your mind and undo your action (see Fig. 11.3).

Using KILL Having identified the user process (spid) that you want to kill, execute the following SQL to kill it:

```
Kill spid
```

This will kill most processes that are existing on the server. Under some circumstances, it is possible to have processes that can't be killed. Usually this occurs when it is in an Extent or Resource lock awaiting the underlying operating system to complete a task. Monitor the process with sp_who until it leaves this condition and then execute the KILL command.

FIG. 11.2
In the SSM Processes dialog box, you can see that `spid 8` is being blocked by the transaction on `spid 1`.

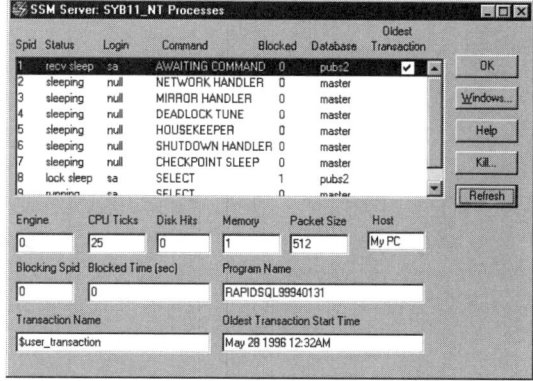

FIG. 11.3
This warning is the last chance you have to change your mind before dropping a user's connection to the database.

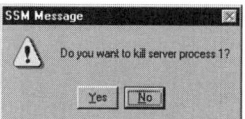

Holding Locks on Data Explicitly

If you have application code that really needs to explicitly hold locks on particular sets of data, Sybase provides you with extensions to the basic `Select` statement that perform this functionality. Sybase enables you to add *optimizer hints* or keywords to your `Select` statements, which tell it how to process the data that matches your results. There are several kinds of hints that you can place on a set of data affected by a `Select` statement: `Noholdlock`, `Holdlock`, and `Shared`.

Using Noholdlock `Noholdlock` is an option that enables the query to read from dirty data. *Dirty* data is data that may or may not have been affected by other user's updates and deletes. Selecting records from a table with the `Noholdlock` keyword ignores any other user's `Exclusive` locks by indicating that they had updated a record. It does not place any locks on the data itself.

`Noholdlock` is a very useful option for those people writing applications in which the data is statistically unaffected by a small sample of records having fluctuating values (for example, if you are more interested in trends of data than in the actual values themselves). Care should be taken, and it is important to clearly differentiate between data fetched with the `Noholdlock` keyword and data that is legitimately accurate according to the known condition of the database as a whole.

> **CAUTION**
>
> When selecting data with the Noholdlock keyword, it is possible that another user has affected your data in such a way as to make it invalid during the time you are reading from the data page in which it resides. For example, another user could have deleted a record that you are reading, and while you are reading it, their Commit is processed and the record is removed.
>
> If you are reading data and it is no longer available, you will receive error messages 605, 606, 624, or 625. It is recommended that you process these errors in the same way that you process a deadlock condition. That is, inform the users that an error has occurred and ask them to retry their operations. Advanced applications may want to auto retry the first time to avoid confusing the users unnecessarily.

Using Holdlock   Normal Selects on tables acquire a Shared lock on a page while the Select is passing through the data pages. A Shared lock does not prohibit another user from updating a record or attempting to gain an Exclusive lock on the data page that is currently being processed by the Select. In addition, the Shared lock expires on a data page as the next page is being read. If you want to maintain data integrity for the life of the Select because you may need to scroll backwards and forwards through the result set, use the Holdlock command to force Sybase to hold the Shared lock (for example, make it essentially exclusive in nature) until the transaction is complete.

Using Shared   Shared locks are provided for when you create a cursor and you want to force Sybase to use a Shared lock on the underlying data without a full table lock. For example, this Declare Cursor statement instructs Sybase to use a Shared lock when the cursor is opened:

```
Declare Cur_Authors Cursor
For     Select au_id, au_lname, au_fname
From    authors Shared
Where   au_lname Between 'A' and 'F'
Go
```

Creating Row Level Locking in Sybase

A common complaint among users of Sybase System XI and Sybase System 10 is that they do not support row-level locking. What this means is that Sybase's smallest granularity (lowest level) of locking is at the page level. Because Sybase's data pages are 2K in size, it is quite easy for the average table to have a number of data rows per page. The problem is that when you update any given row on that page, all the rows are in turn locked for the duration of the transaction, thereby unnecessarily locking rows that you were not actually updating, but that were casualties of your other actions.

A simple solution exists. Prior to System XI, you had to make sure that each record on the table was wide enough to force it to fit on one data page by itself. It is easy enough to calculate an approximate amount of space used by the columns on any given table by adding up its bytes of data. As an example, take the table below:

```
Create Table Employee2(
      LastName    Varchar(40)   Not Null,
      FirstName   Varchar(40)   Not Null,
      TIN         Char(11)      Not Null,
      BirthDate   SmallDatetime Not Null,
      EmployeeID  Smallint      Not Null )
Go
```

A single row of data on this table would take approximately 97 bytes (40 + 40 + 11 + 4 + 2), given full values in the column. Rounding to 100 bytes and taking off 10 percent of a data page as general overhead, you could expect up to 18 rows of data per page. This could be quite costly in terms of locking if you needed to have lots of users hitting this table. To fix the problem, append some "filler" columns on to the end of the table of type `Char(254)` `Not Null` until you have stretched the row wide enough to force only one row per page. At most on a table, you should need to add only four such columns because they alone will be adding a kilobyte of data to your records. For example, a revised table structure might be something like this:

```
Create Table Employee2(
      LastName    Varchar(40)   Not Null,
      FirstName   Varchar(40)   Not Null,
      TIN         Char(11)      Not Null,
      BirthDate   SmallDatetime Not Null,
      EmployeeID  Smallint      Not Null,
      Filler1     Char(254)     Not Null,
      Filler2     Char(254)     Not Null,
      Filler3     Char(254)     Not Null,
      Filler4     Char(254)     Not Null,
      Filler5     Char(254)     Not Null,
      Filler6     Char(254)     Not Null,
      Filler7     Char(254)     Not Null )
Go
```

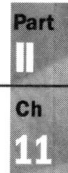

 TIP To simplify managing "filler" columns, bind defaults to the table columns, so that a value is inserted into them automatically without programmer intervention.

There is one other way in Sybase System 10 to force a table to have only one row per page by using a `FillFactor` on a clustered index. `FillFactors` specify to the database how much space to leave free on an index page before going on to a new page to add data. If you use a clustered index, Sybase physically places rows in the data pages in the order of the index; thus, if you only allow a limited number of rows in the index page, you similarly limit the number of rows per data page. The index and data pages for the clustered index are, in fact, the same.

 Both of these methods are somewhat messy and Sybase has addressed them by adding a new option to the `Create Table` statement in System XI. You now have the option of specifying the `Max_Rows_Per_Page`. For example, to create this table with a single row per page, this is all you would need to execute:

```
Create Table Employee2(
      LastName    Varchar(40)   Not Null,
      FirstName   Varchar(40)   Not Null,
      TIN         Char(11)      Not Null,
```

```
        BirthDate    SmallDatetime Not Null,
        EmployeeID   Smallint      Not Null )
With Max_Rows_Per_Page = 1
Go
```

▶ **See** "Choosing Datatypes for Your Data," **p. 149**

N O T E There is a definite downside to forcing a single row per data page because your tables will grow in size very rapidly. Take care that you don't run out of space in your database because you underestimated the amount of space consumed by your one row per page tables.

If you really need row-level locking on tables other than small tables that have relatively few records, you may be better off waiting for Sybase System XI.1 that is due by the end of 1996. ■

Understanding Table Lock Promotion

Sybase locks data on the page level. Any query that you execute on the server will hold locks on at least one full page. If you start updating or locking multiple pages on a table, Sybase starts consuming resources to manage your requests. At a certain point based on a percentage of pages locked per table, it becomes more efficient for the database to lock the entire table (a table lock) than to keep managing the individual pages being locked by a given transaction.

Fortunately, Sybase enables you to configure the way in which it chooses to *promote* locks from page level to table level. These are options that are set at the server level with the server-stored procedure, sp_configure.

Using sp_configure, it is possible to set three different types of lock promotion thresholds: lock promotion HWM (high water mark), lock promotion LWM (low water mark), and lock promotion percent.

The lock promotion HWM is used by the server to determine when to escalate a set of page locks to a table lock. The default for the server is 200 pages. To change this value, you can use the example script shown in Listing 11.12.

Listing 11.12   CHP11_12.SQL—Raising the Lock Promotion HWM

```
/*
    You can use this script to change the
    lock promotion HWM on your server.
    Adjust the numeric value to the required
    value for your server.
*/

/* Note that you use master because all configurations
    must be changed in the master database first */
Use master
Go
```

```
sp_configure 'lock promotion HWM', 400
Go

Reconfigure
Go
```

N O T E The lock promotion options of sp_configure are dynamically configurable and do not require that you shut down the server before they take effect. ▪

The lock promotion LWM is used in conjunction with the lock promotion percent to stop a table lock escalation occurring on a table with few rows. Suppose you set the lock promotion percent to 50 percent, meaning that if more than half the data pages were being locked, you wanted the whole table locked. This is not an unreasonable proposition until you have a small table with only a few pages. The lock promotion LWM that defaults to 20 pages stops the threshold percentage from escalating page locks to table locks unless its minimum number of pages has been locked.

The lock promotion percent is used to enable you to set a generic level at which you want to escalate a set of page locks to a single table lock; this level is relative to the number of rows in the table. The default value of this configuration option is zero (0), meaning that the lock promotion LWM should be used to determine escalation.

Part

II

Ch

11

N O T E As you saw above, despite the lock promotion thresholds, it is possible to force locking on pages and tables by using the Holdlock keyword when issuing a Select statement on the server. ▪

Understanding Deadlocks

Deadlocks are a special sort of lock that can occur in highly transactional databases that have a lot of concurrent users. The premise of a deadlock or a "deadly embrace," as it is sometimes called, goes like this: User 1 is holding locks on Table A, and is attempting to acquire locks on Table B; at the same time User 2 is holding locks on Table B and is attempting to acquire locks on Table A.

In this scenario, both users have arrived at the same conclusion: They cannot continue because each is waiting for the other's lock to expire. Rather than waiting forever and leaving the users permanently disabled, Sybase detects this condition and terminates the second user's (or the user that entered the embrace last) transaction and issues an error saying that the transaction was terminated due to a deadlock.

As a result of the termination, you would typically expect the client program of User 2 to automatically reissue the command in a few seconds on the assumption that User 1 will have completed his or her transaction by that time.

To minimize the likelihood of a deadlock, some suggestions follow:

- Minimize the length of time that any transaction is held open.
- Ensure that all table updates and modifications are done via the same access path. If you need to Update three different tables for any given transaction, make sure that you always do the Updates in the same order.

 If you are having undiagnosable deadlocks and you cannot figure out where the problem is occurring, you can use the newly configurable option print deadlock information with sp_configure to get Sybase to write information about the deadlock to the error log. You should be aware that this option may seriously effect and degrade the performance of the server; it should only be used in cases where you have no other diagnostic tools.

Note that this option was previously available in System 10 as a trace flag T1204.

From Here...

In this chapter you learned about the fundamentals of locking and transactions and how they will affect your application. In addition, you learned about the internals of Sybase and how it manages many users hitting the same table.

Take a look at the following chapters to further develop your Sybase and application programming knowledge:

- Read Chapter 6, "Understanding Tables and Datatypes," so that you can redefine some of your tables to enable better concurrency.
- Consult Chapter 8, "Understanding Indexes and Keys," so you can optimize table access through the creation of a clustered index with a sparse Fill Factor and Max_Rows_Per_Page.
- See Chapter 23, "Using Sybase's Configuration Options," to get an understanding of how the options you set up for the server affect database applications and transaction locks.

CHAPTER 12

Understanding and Using Cursors

In System 10, probably the biggest feature that Sybase added to the release was back-end, or server, cursor support. *Cursors* are a way of manipulating data in a set on a row-by-row basis, instead of the typical SQL commands that operate on all the rows in the set at one time. Specifically, Sybase added a full implementation of *back-end cursors*—cursors managed by the database and that have an easy access method from front-end application development tools, such as SQLWindows and PowerBuilder. In referring to *back end,* the distinction is made so that it's understood that Sybase always could have cursors, but these were provided by the DBLibrary and Client Library layer, not the server.

Cursors provide a way of doing result-set processing inside the server without the need for a client program to manage the datasets being worked on. For example, before System 10, it was difficult to write a fast-performing application that had to perform multiple actions on a set of data. This was because each row in the data would need to be sent back to the front end, and the client application would be responsible for initiating further activity on each row. Cursors provide a way for advanced Transact-SQL stored procedures to do all this processing without needing to return to the client.

Learn the difference between front-end cursors and the new back-end cursors

Sybase System 10 introduced back-end cursors that enable the processing of results without returning to the client application.

Creating and using cursors

Learn tips and tricks on how to use cursors in your application to take advantage of their performance gains.

Working with nested cursors

Cursors can create a heavy burden of locks on your server. This chapter helps you to eliminate unnecessary locks on the server.

Contrary to the beliefs published in some books on Sybase System XI, cursors represent the fastest way known to process data on the server. In fact, they are even likely to outperform Embedded SQL written in C on the server itself. You owe it to yourself to invest in the learning of the cursor syntax so that you can take advantage of it in your environment. ■

Distinguishing Between Front-End and Back-End Cursors

As just mentioned, with Sybase, two types of cursors are available for use in an application: front-end (client) cursors and back-end (server) cursors. They are two very distinct concepts, and it's important to be able to distinguish between them.

N O T E Sybase refers to back-end cursors, or cursors that are created and managed by the database, as *server cursors*. To avoid any confusion from this point on, unless the text specifically refers to cursors on the client or server, assume that any reference to the term *cursor* is describing a cursor that's created in the database server. ■

When writing an application, you often find that you need to perform a given operation on a set of data. This set-based operation can normally be performed by using an Update statement when it's necessary to change data values, or a Delete statement when it's necessary to remove data values. These set-based operations often provide great flexibility in an application—provided that the tasks that need to be performed can appropriately be defined by a Where clause. Suppose that you want to change the ZIP code for all those authors in the *Pubs* database who live in Menlo Park to 94024. A simple Update can be used, as Listing 12.1 shows.

Listing 12.1   CHP12_01.SQL—Using the Update Statement to Change the Value of a Record

```
Update authors
Set    zip = '94024'
Where  city = 'Menlo Park'
Go
```

▶ **See** "Modifying Data in a Table with Update," **p. 87**

But, what if you need to do different kinds of operations on a set of data? There are two possible solutions: You can perform multiple operations on exclusive sets, or you can get the whole set of data and, based on values in it, perform the required operations. This second solution is the concept of cursor-based processing.

Relying on the set-based updates and deletes can be inefficient because your updates may end up hitting the same row more than once. It's possible to create a "view" of data in the database called a *cursor*.

One of the best advantages of cursor processing is that you can perform conditional logic on a particular row of data in a set independently of the other rows that may be in a set. Effectively, you're issuing commands or SQL on single-row datasets. This granularity of processing is often required in complex applications, and has many benefits, as follows:

- **Performance**—Set-based operations tend to use more server resources, compared with cursor operations.

- **Better transaction control**—When you're processing sets of data, you can control what happens to any given row independent of the others.

- **Special syntax**—Cursors enable positioned `Updates` and `Deletes`, through the use of the `Where Current Of` clause, that apply to the row being fetched and directly hitting the table row without the need of an index.

- **Efficiency**—When you're performing a number of operations on a large dataset, such as calling multiple stored procedures, it's more efficient for the database to process the data doing all actions per row (because data is kept in memory caches) rather than perform each task serially on the entire data set.

Understanding Client Cursors

In prior versions of Sybase (version 4.9.2 and below), Microsoft and Sybase together realized that their customers needed to be able to process data and to scroll backward and forward through a result set. Customers needed scrolling to support complex applications that users needed for browsing data fetched from the database.

At the time, Sybase couldn't incorporate the server-based cursors that some of the other vendors supported. Sybase instead chose to mimic some of the cursor behavior in DBLibrary, its client API to the Sybase database.

N O T E DBLibrary is a client interface that was created by Sybase to interact with the Sybase database. DBLibrary is a set of commands and functions that can be executed in C to perform operations on the database. DBLibrary has been superseded from System 10 onwards with a newer (better?) API called Client Library. A full discussion of the use of Client Library can be found in Chapter 14, "Understanding the Sybase Client Model (Client Library.)"

To achieve this functionality, Sybase added cursors to the datasets on the client side: *client cursors*. These cursors work by having DBLibrary interact with the database as normal, fetching data from the *tabular data stream* (TDS) as quickly as the client requests. The TDS is the method of communication that DBLibrary uses to fetch data from the database. Typically, DBLibrary will discard any data that has been fetched from the database and then fetched to the client application—relying on the client to perform any additional work.

With cursors activated, DBLibrary will cache these records itself until the client cancels the cursor view on the data. This caching has a number of limitations:

Part
II

Ch
12

■ Sybase has no way of controlling or minimizing the locks held on the database, and so any locks held will be held for all data pages in the cursor, not just the affected data pages. This is because Sybase is basically unaware that anything other than a select activity is occurring on the data.

■ Client-side resources can be consumed very quickly if there are large sets of data.

■ The caching is inefficient when processing large amounts of data because all the data is being sent across the network unnecessarily.

Understanding Server Cursors

Clearly, Sybase's client cursors were just a stopgap measure until the real work of server cursors could be completed. Server cursors provide all the same benefits of client cursors without any of the overhead or limitations. Aside from backward-compatibility issues, there are few good reasons to use client cursors in a Sybase System 10 or higher application.

Server cursors are made up of essentially two components. The *result set* of the cursor is the list of rows that match the cursor's initially specified domain. In other words, these are the rows that the cursor was created to maintain. The *cursor position* is the current placement of the cursor. This is the row that the cursor is currently processing or working on.

N O T E Cursors behave very similarly to file pointers with one exception—they cannot process in reverse. By thinking about a *result set* as the list of records in a file, it is easier to understand the way that Sybase processes the *result set* data. Unfortunately, Sybase has yet to add the capability for you to fetch in reverse on a particular cursor. This feature (while not essential) is sorely missed and is often considered a shortcoming when you compare Sybase to other relational databases, such as its close siblings, Microsoft Sybase 6.5 and Centura's SQLBase. ■

Server cursors generally have five states when being used. These states or conditions are usually passed through when working with a cursor, and are shown in Table 12.1.

Table 12.1   The States of Existence of Sybase Cursors

State	Description
Declare	At this point, Sybase validates the query that's going to be used to populate the cursor. Sybase creates a structure in shared memory that has the definition of the cursor available for compilation at the Open phase.
Open	Sybase begins to answer the Declare statement by resolving the query and fetching row IDs into a temporary workspace for the use of the client, should it decide to fetch the rows that this cursor has identified.
Fetch	The data is now being returned from the cursor, and any activity that's required can be performed.

State	Description
Close	Sybase closes the previously opened cursor and releases any locks that it may have held as a result of opening it.
Deallocate	Sybase releases the shared memory used by the Declare statement, no longer permitting another process to perform an Open on it.

Using Sybase Cursors

Using a cursor in Sybase involves following the states described in Table 12.1. This section explains the steps required to use a cursor effectively in your applications.

The first thing you need to do when using a cursor is Declare it. Once a cursor has been declared, it can be opened and fetched from. During the fetch phase, or state, of a cursor, any number of operations can be performed on the currently active row in the cursor. When you have finished working with a cursor, you need to Close and Deallocate it so that Sybase does not waste resources managing it further.

Understanding Cursor Scopes

The scope of a cursor refers to the domain or level of containment within which it exists. For example, the scope of a table requires that it be uniquely named in the domain of a database. Because cursors can be used in a number of different areas of Transact-SQL, they have a different set of scopes within which they can exist. The following domains permit the creation of a cursor:

- **Session**—A *session* is defined as the time of a user connection. This is from the time that the user connects or logs on to a Sybase database to the time that the user disconnects. If a cursor is created in a session—that is, without explicitly beginning a transaction prior to the creation and thereby enclosing the cursor in transaction—then it must be uniquely named within that session. Cursors created in a session exist until either the user disconnects or they are explicitly removed. Cursors created in a session by a particular user are *not* accessible by other users, so for all intents and purposes do not even exist.

- **Stored procedure**—For the purposes of a cursor, a *stored procedure* provides a unique existence for the cursor. Each time a procedure is executed, it receives a new domain in which it can contain or host cursors. Stored procedures cannot access cursors that are created in other stored procedures except when the other stored procedure is executed as a parent of the child stored procedure. For example, if stored procedure 1 creates a cursor and then executes stored procedure 2, stored procedure 2 can reference the cursor created by stored procedure 1. In this case, the first stored procedure is acting as a *session* for the second stored procedure. By a similar extension, any cursors that are created in a session are accessible by any stored procedures that are subsequently executed in that same session.

■ **Trigger**—Cursors created inside a *trigger* work within the domain of the trigger. Trigger-created cursors are not accessible by any other processes unless the trigger in turn calls or executes a stored procedure (see the explanation provided above for the stored procedures).

N O T E   When a higher level domain declares a cursor for use by subsequently executed stored procedures, the name must still remain unique. If, for example, you create a like-named stored cursor inside your stored procedure, you will not get a domain uniqueness violation and will be permitted to create the cursor. All access from that point would refer to the cursor that was created by the procedure.

Note also that Sybase only detects domain uniqueness violation at runtime. It would be perfectly acceptable to write a stored procedure that creates two cursors of the same name. The reason that Sybase permits this is so that you can use a single cursor name in your code and have different Where clauses in use. For example:

```
/*
   Note that this is just a sample script
   and does not actually run!
*/
Declare @nTemp Int

Select @nTemp = 1

/*
   Here, based on the conditional logic, we
   create two different cursors that have the
   same name but different effects on the
   database.
*/

If @nTemp = 1
Begin
     Declare Cur_MySelect Cursor
     For     Select au_lname
             From   authors
             Where  au_lname Like 'D%'
             Order By au_lname
End
Else
Begin
     Declare Cur_MySelect Cursor
     For     Select au_lname
             From   authors
             Where  au_lname Like 'F%'
             Order by au_lname Desc
End
...
```

Declaring a Cursor

Declaring a cursor is very similar to requesting data using a standard `Select` statement. Note that the `Select` statement used to declare a cursor can't include any of the Transact-SQL extensions, such as `Compute`, `Compute By`, and `Select Into`. The syntax for declaring a cursor is as follows:

```
Declare Name_Of_Cursor Cursor
For Select_Statement
[For {Read Only | Update [Of Column_List]}]
```

N O T E Because cursors must fetch row values into variables inside the stored procedure or command batch, you can't use the asterisk (*) in your `Select` statement. You must use named columns in the data tables that correspond one-to-one with the variables used in the `Fetch` clause. (You also can use columns in a `Select` statement that are expressions if you want.) ▪

The options for the Transact-SQL command `Declare Cursor` are as follows:

- ▪ *Name_Of_Cursor*—The name of the cursor must comply with the standard object identifier rules of the database.

- ▪ *Select_Statement*—Any valid SQL statement that includes a column list that can be worked on.

- ▪ `Read Only`—As its name implies, this option stops the cursor's data from being modifiable. Internally, this makes a big difference in how Sybase chooses to retrieve the data and generally makes it more likely to hit a clustered index if one is available. Unless you need to modify data for which the cursor is declared, I recommend that you use the `Read Only` clause. This will provide substantial performance gains.

- ▪ `Update`—This is the default option on a single table cursor, such as those created when you issue a `Select` without any join conditions. A cursor declared in this fashion enables the `Where Current Of` syntax to be used when performing an `Update` statement. Specify any columns that you know you are updating in the `Column_List` section of the statement to give Sybase the maximum chance of optimizing the creation of the cursor.

Listing 12.2 shows a basic cursor that's being declared to fetch the data from a single table in the *pubs2* database *authors*.

Part

II

Ch

12

Listing 12.2   CHP12_02.SQL—Declaring a Simple Cursor to Retrieve All Records from the Authors Table

```
Declare Cur_Authors Cursor
For     Select au_id, au_lname,
                au_fname
        From    authors
        Order By au_id
Go
```

T I P As part of a set of tips on naming objects, I suggest that you name all your cursors with a prefix of `Cur`. That way, if you ever see an object in the database, you will be able to easily identify it.

When using the `Declare Cursor` syntax in a transaction batch, it must be the first command that you execute. You cannot open a cursor until it has been declared or you will get an error saying that no cursor by the name you opened exists.

N O T E If you `Declare` a cursor that is the result of joining more than one table in the `Select` statement, Sybase forces you to be in a `Read Only` mode. This is because the data that you are manipulating is not actually based on a particular underlying table. If you need to modify the data fetched on such a query, you must use a fully qualified `Update` that has all the columns that uniquely identify the record being worked on in the `Where` clause. ▪

Opening a Cursor

After a cursor is declared, Sybase reserves handles for its use. To use a cursor and fetch data from it, you must open the cursor using the following syntax:

`Open Cursor_Name`

To open the cursor created in Listing 12.2, you would execute the following:

`Open Cur_Authors`

When a cursor is opened, Sybase resolves any unknown variables with its current state. If a cursor was declared with a variable in the `Where` clause and then opened, for example, the value used to resolve the query would be the value that the variable held at the time the cursor was opened. For example, in Listing 12.3, you can see a variable, `@nLowAuID`, being used in the `Where` clause for the cursor `Cur_Authors_Where`.

> **Listing 12.3   CHP12_03.SQL—Resolving Variables at the Time the Cursor Is Opened**

```
/*
   Note that the id datatype used below is a
   user defined datatype created in the pubs2
   database
*/

Declare     @nHighAuID id,
            @nLowAuID  id

Declare Cur_Authors_Where Cursor
For   Select au_lname, au_fname
      From   authors
      Where  au_id Between @nLowAuID And @nHighAuID

/* note that if the cursor were to be opened now,
probably no data would be returned because the values
```

```
of @nLowAuID and @nHighAuID are NULL */

/* now we set the values of the variables */
Select @nLowAuID = '213-46-8915',
       @nHighAuID = '672-71-3249'

/* open the cursor now */
Open Cur_Empl_Where
...
```

This feature of being able to have the Where clause dynamically interpreted is what makes the use of cursors inside stored procedures so compelling. You can define a *functional* stored procedure that can do a whole bunch of SQL related processing and then simply pass parameters to it, which will be evaluated when the cursor is opened.

> **CAUTION**
>
> Sybase has to build a result set at the time you Open the cursor. If you perform ordering in the declaration of the cursor, Sybase *may* need to build a temporary table to store the results of the query prior to enabling you to fetch the data. To avoid building a temporary table, Sybase requires that a unique index be placed on a column that is being *ordered by* in the declaration of a cursor.
>
> If you perform ordering in your declaration of the cursors, make sure that the ordering of the cursor (by columns) corresponds to the underlying table's ordering; otherwise, you will incur a performance penalty while Sybase builds a temporary table.

Fetching a Cursor

After a cursor is in an opened state, you can fetch data from it. Sybase only supports serial or sequential fetching. By fetching a record, you are instructing Sybase to transfer the record to the client. If, however, you specify variables in the Into clause, you will read the values returned from the cursor and assign them to the variables. The syntax for the Fetch statement is as follows:

```
Fetch cursor_name
[Into @Variable_Name1, @Variable_Name2...]
```

For example, to fetch from the cursor created in Listing 12.3, you would execute the following:

```
Fetch Cur_Authors
Go

au_id       au_lname                 au_fname
---------   ----------------------   --------------------
172-32-1176 White                    Johnson
```

Subsequent executions of the Fetch statement cause Sybase to return the next rows from the result set. For example:

Part
II

Ch
12

```
Fetch Cur_Authors
Go
Fetch Cur_Authors
Go
```

au_id	au_lname	au_fname
213-46-8915	Green	Marjorie

au_id	au_lname	au_fname
238-95-7766	Carson	Flagstaff

N O T E If you attempt to fetch from a cursor that has not yet been opened, Sybase reports an error informing you that you need to open a cursor prior to fetching from it. ■

It is possible to fetch multiple rows to the client from a cursor by using a configurable option, `cursor rows`. This option controls the number of records that are affected by a `Fetch` statement. For example, to retrieve five records at a time from the `Cur_Authors` cursor, execute the following:

```
Set cursor rows 5 for Cur_Authors
Go
Fetch Cur_Authors
Go
```

au_id	au_lname	au_fname
213-46-8915	Green	Marjorie
238-95-7766	Carson	Flagstaff
267-41-2394	O'Leary	Michael
274-80-9391	Straight	Dick
341-22-1782	Smith	Meander

N O T E You can change the number of cursor rows at any time after the cursor has been declared. If you want to change it after fetching a row or rows, Sybase will start sending larger result sets back to the client after you execute the `set cursor rows` statement. ■

Closing a Cursor

Closing a cursor releases any resources and locks that Sybase may have acquired while the cursor was open. A closed cursor is available for fetching only after it's reopened. To close a cursor, use the following syntax:

```
Close Cursor_Name
```

To close the cursor `Cur_Authors`, execute the following:

```
Close Cur_Authors
Go
```

Deallocating a Cursor

Deallocating a cursor completely removes any data structures that Sybase was holding open for a given cursor. Unlike closing a cursor, after a cursor is deallocated, it no longer can be opened. To deallocate a cursor, use the following syntax:

```
Deallocate Cursor Cursor_Name
```

For example, to deallocate the Cur_Authors cursor created earlier, execute the following:

```
Deallocate Cursor Cur_Authors

Go
```

An Example of Using Cursors

In the previous sections, you saw all the separate elements that are used to work with cursors in Sybase. However, you haven't seen how all the elements are put together—we'll examine that in this section.

Listing 12.4 shows cursors in action. Refer to the comments in the script (placed between /* and */) to get a good understanding of what the cursors are doing.

Listing 12.4   CHP12_04.SQL—Creating an Advanced Stored Procedure that Uses a Cursor

```
/* In this example, I will be working with the stores table
of the pubs database.

To illustrate the cursors most easily, I will create a stored
procedure that when executed:

- declares,
- opens,
- fetches, and
- processes

the data returned from a cursor.  */

/* First drop the procedure if it exists. */

If Object_Id( 'proc_Stores') Is Not Null
 Drop Procedure proc_Stores
Go

/* Step 0: Declare the procedure. */
Create Procedure proc_Stores
As

/* Step 1: Declare some working variables. */
```

Part

II

Ch

12

continues

Listing 12.4 Continued

```
Declare     @nOrderCount      integer,
            @nSQLError        integer,
            @nStorCount       tinyint,
            @sState           char(2),
            @sStorId          char(4),
            @sStorName        varchar(40),
            @sCity            varchar(20)

/* Step 2: Turn off result counting.

Turns off unnecessary "0 rows affected messages" showing on the front-end */

Set NoCount On

/* Step 3: Declare the cursor that is going to find all the data.

This step causes Sybase to create the required
resource structures needed to manage the cursor. */

Declare Cur_Stores Cursor
For    Select    stor_id, stor_name,
                 city,     state
       From      stores
       Order By stor_id

/* Step 4: Open the cursor.

This step causes Sybase to create the initial result set
and prepare the data for returning to the "Fetching process. */

Open Cur_Stores

/* Step 5: Perform the first fetch.

Fetch data from the cursor into our variables for processing
and evaluation. */

Fetch Cur_Stores
Into   @sStorId, @sStorName,
       @sCity,   @sState

/* Step 6: Initialize counters. */

Select @nStorCount = 0

/* Step 7: Fetch and Process Loop.

Process the data while the system variable @@sqlstatus is = 0
(meaning that a row has been fetched from the cursor */

While @@sqlstatus = 0
Begin
     /* Step 8: Increment counter */
```

```
    Select @nStorCount = @nStorCount + 1

    /* Step 9: Do a quick operation to determine books on order */

    Select @nOrderCount = Sum(qty)
    From    salesdetail
    Where   stor_id = @sStorID

    /* Step 10: Return a result set to the front end so that it knows
    what is happening */

    Select "Store ID" = @sStorId,
           "Store Name" = @sStorName,
           "# Books on order" = @nOrderCount

    /* Step 11: Continue Fetching.

    If no rows are found, then @@sqlstatus will be set to a value other
    than zero, and the looping will end. */

    Fetch Cur_Stores
    Into   @sStorId, @sStorName,
           @sCity,   @sState
End

/* Step 12: Cleanup - Deallocate and close the cursors.

Note that for a stored procedure, this is really unnecessary because the
cursor will no longer exist once the procedure finishes execution.
However, it is good practice to leave the procedure cleaned up */

Close      Cur_Stores
Deallocate Cursor Cur_Stores

/* Step 13: Send a totaling result.

Send total count of employees to front end */

Select "Total # of Stores" = @nStorCount

/* Step 14: Turn on counting again */

Set NoCount On

/* Step 15: End Procedure */

Return 0
Go

/* Now we execute it to see the results. */

Execute proc_Stores
Go
```

Part

II

Ch

12

The output from running Listing 12.4 follows:

```
Store ID Store Name                               # Books on order
-------- ------------------------------------     ----------------
5023     Thoreau Reading Discount Chain           82674

Store ID Store Name                               # Books on order
-------- ------------------------------------     ----------------
6380     Eric the Read Books                      2430

Store ID Store Name                               # Books on order
-------- ------------------------------------     ----------------
7066     Barnum's                                 2430

Store ID Store Name                               # Books on order
-------- ------------------------------------     ----------------
7067     News & Brews                             2900

Store ID Store Name                               # Books on order
-------- ------------------------------------     ----------------
7131     Doc-U-Mat: Quality Laundry and Books     2097

Store ID Store Name                               # Books on order
-------- ------------------------------------     ----------------
7896     Fricative Bookshop                       1182

Store ID Store Name                               # Books on order
-------- ------------------------------------     ----------------
8042     Bookbeat                                 3733

Total # of Stores
-----------------
7
```

 TIP Sorting variables in large procedures alphabetically makes it much easier to find them. In addition, you can sort the variables by datatype, which makes them even easier to find. (This will happen automatically if you prefix variables with a datatype indicator, such as s for strings, n for numbers, and dt for date/times.)

Getting Information about Cursors

If you ever need to retrieve information about the status of a cursor for debugging or other purposes, Sybase provides a system-stored procedure, sp_cursorinfo, that will return all the known information about a cursor at the current time. For example, if you place an sp_cursorinfo statement immediately after the line that reads Select @nStorCount = @nStorCount + 1 in Listing 12.4, you would receive the following cursor information returned to you:

```
Cursor name 'Cur_Stores' is declared at nesting level '1'.
The cursor id is 65537.
```

```
The cursor has been successfully opened 1 times.
The cursor was compiled at isolation level 1.
The cursor is currently scanning at a nonzero isolation level.
The cursor is positioned on a row.
There have been 1 rows read, 0 rows updated and 0 rows deleted through this
cursor.
The cursor will remain open when a transaction is committed or rolled back.
The number of rows returned for each FETCH is 1.
The cursor is read only.
The cursor is read only because it contains an ORDER BY clause.
```

Using Nested Cursors

You can have multiple layers of cursors in a stored procedure that you can use to provide flexible result-set processing. An example of this might be when you're opening a cursor, as shown earlier in the Cur_Emp1 example in Listing 12.3. In addition to the cursor you've already reviewed, you can add nested cursors to impose some additional conditional logic and perhaps open a second cursor to perform additional work with the dataset.

In Listing 12.5, you can see a complex stored procedure that maintains all the authors in the *pubs2* database and, using outer and inner cursors, processes multiple layers of the data without ever needing to return to the client.

Listing 12.5 CHP12_05.SQL—Some of the Possibilities of Nested Cursors

```
/* First drop the procedure if it exists. */

If Object_Id( 'proc_Maint_Employees') Is Not Null
 Drop Procedure proc_Maint_Employees
Go

Create Procedure proc_Maint_Employees
As
/* First declare variables that are going to
be required in this procedure */

Declare     @dtPubDate    datetime,
            @nEmplCount   smallint,
            @sAuID        id,
            @nFirstHalf   smallint,
            @nRowCount    integer,
            @nSecondHalf  integer,
            @nSQLError    integer,
            @nTotalSales  integer,
            @sLName       varchar(30),
            @sLastType    char(12),
            @sType        char(12)

/* Now Declare the cursors to be used
Note that because variables are used in the
where clause on the second cursor, it is not
```

Part

II

Ch

12

continues

Listing 12.5   Continued

```
required that the second cursor be Declared inside the first.
Take advantage of this functionality so that unnecessary
declaring of cursors does not take place (this will
save resources on the server. */

Declare Cur_Authors Cursor
For     Select au_id, au_lname
        From    authors
        Order By au_id

Declare Cur_Titles Cursor
For     Select t.type, t.pubdate, t.total_sales
        From    titles t, titleauthor ti
        Where   ti.au_id = @sAuId
        And     t.title_id = ti.title_id
        Order By t.type


/* open the outer cursor and fetch the first row */

Open   Cur_Authors

Fetch Cur_Authors
Into   @sAuId, @sLName

/* Initialize counters */
Select @nEmplCount = 0

While @@sqlstatus = 0                /* only fetch while there are rows left */
Begin
        /* increment counter */
        Select @nEmplCount = @nEmplCount + 1

        /* Return a result set to the front end so that it knows
        what is happening */
        Select @sAuId,    @sLName

        If @sLName < 'D'   /* Skip all the Ds by using a GOTO */
            Goto Fetch_Next_Author

        /* Now open inner cursor and count the different types
        of books for this employee's publisher */

        Open Cur_Titles

        Fetch Cur_Titles
        Into   @sType, @dtPubDate, @nTotalSales

        /* Reset totals */
        Select @nFirstHalf = 0,
                @nSecondHalf = 0,
                @sLastType = NULL
```

```
     While @@sqlstatus = 0
     Begin
          If @sType != @sLastType AND @sLastType != NULL
          Begin
               /* send back a total record to the front end */
               Select @sLastType, @nFirstHalf, @nSecondHalf

               /* reset totals */
               Select @nFirstHalf = 0,
                      @nSecondHalf = 0
          End

          If @dtPubDate <= '6/30/95'
               Select @nFirstHalf = @nFirstHalf + @nTotalSales,
                      @sLastType = @sType
          Else
               Select @nSecondHalf = @nSecondHalf + @nTotalSales,
                      @sLastType = @sType

          Fetch Cur_Titles
          Into  @sType, @dtPubDate, @nTotalSales

     End

     /* Close the inner cursor so that the next time it is opened
        it gets re-created with new data based on the outer loop */
     Close  Cur_Titles

     Fetch_Next_Author:        /* label to skip inner loop */

     Fetch Cur_Authors
     Into  @sAuId,   @sLName

End

/* Deallocate and close the cursors. Note that for a stored
procedure, this is really unnecessary because the cursor
will no longer exist once the procedure finishes execution.
However, it is good practice to leave the procedure cleaned up */

Close Cur_Authors
Deallocate Cursor Cur_Authors
Deallocate Cursor Cur_Titles

/* Send total count of employees to front end */
Select @nEmplCount

/* End proc */
Return 0

/* Now execute it to see the results. */

Execute proc_Maint_Employees
Go
```

Part
II

Ch

12

The output from running Listing 12.5 follows:

```
.......... .............................
172-32-1176 White

.......... .............................
213-46-8915 Green

...
............. .... ..........
business    3876  0

.......... .............................
274-80-9391 Straight

...

.......... .............................
486-29-1786 Locksley

............. .... ..........
popular_comp 0     NULL

.......... .............................
527-72-3246 Greene

...
............. .... ..........
business    3876  0

...
.......... .............................
998-72-3567 Ringer

....
23
```

 TIP To make object names case-insensitive with Sybase, you must make sure that you install a sort order that offers case insensitivity. Insensitive sort orders are significantly quicker, and they enable you to reference objects without caring about the case of the object name.

This was a complex example of the things you can do with multiple nested cursors. However, it is important to remember that using cursors is really not that difficult provided that you follow the basic steps outlined in the previous examples and throughout this chapter. Note that you can nest a procedure up to 16 layers deep, and can check the current nesting level by inspecting the global system variable @@NestLevel.

Processing Cursors from Front-End Applications

A key consideration of using cursors in an application is how they're accessible from front-end programming tools, such as SQLWindows and PowerBuilder.

If the cursor returns a single set of data, which is the most common type, most front-end application languages won't be able to distinguish the data from that returned by a normal `Select` statement. Typically, the tool will have a function for executing `Select` statements. This function is designed to work with a single set of data and therefore probably will work fine with stored procedures or cursors that return a single result set. Most tools provide special functions for referencing data that comes from cursors if the cursor and its associated processing returns more than one result set. A common construction might be something like the following Centura Team Developer example snippet:

```
...
Call SqsExecuteProc( hSql, 'proc_Stores', gsResults )
While SqsGetNextResults( hSql, gsResults )
While SqlFetchNext( hSql, nReturn )
...
```

The execution of the stored procedure is followed by looping that forces the return of results to the front end and then the fetching of the data in each result. Most programming languages have similar functionality, and whatever programming language you choose for development should support anything that Sybase can return. For more information on using cursors with popular front-end client/server programming tools, see Chapter 15, "Using Client/Server Application Programming Tools."

From Here...

In this chapter, you learned about Sybase's server-based cursors and how they can be used to provide much more processing power to your applications without the need to return to the client for help.

After I spoke with the performance-tuning group at Sybase—whose understanding of Sybase's cursors is very intimate—it became clear that server cursors provide greater performance than all other results-set processing mechanisms, including Embedded SQL in a C application running on the server. The reason? No networking is involved. Unless the type of work you're doing can't be modeled in stored procedures, as may be the case with arrays, then just about all batch operations should be moved to cursor-based procedures running on the server.

Part
II

Ch
12

I suggest that you explore the following chapters to implement what you've learned:

- Chapter 10, "Understanding Stored Procedures," introduces the basics of stored procedures and Transact-SQL extensions to support control of flow programming in SQL.

- Chapter 13, "Using Advanced Stored Procedures and Triggers," provides an in-depth study of advanced procedure utilization.

- Chapter 15, "Using Client/Server Application Programming Tools," provides a full explanation of how your front-end tool of choice interacts with the database when using cursors.

Using Advanced Stored Procedures and Triggers

Somewhere in this book, I wanted to have the opportunity to share with you some of the more complex tricks and traps of Transact-SQL. In this chapter (the last of the "Using System XI" part of the book), I introduce you to some cool processing solutions, all written in Transact-SQL. Transact-SQL has so many different ways of being used that I can't possibly hope to examine every eccentricity of the Transact-SQL language in the space of a chapter or two. So what I've done here is to take some key principles that are demonstrated in some example procedures and then describe how they work. I hope that by reading this chapter you'll get a feel for some of the more advanced options that you have when using Transact-SQL (especially in a stored procedure) as your language of choice.

The other problem that I faced with coming up with subject matter for this chapter was to find some useful example procedures that I could show you and describe. Partly because I'm lazy, and mostly because I thought that the Sybase system procedures were actually quite good, I settled on using Sybase's system-stored procedures as the perfect examples. In this chapter, you see the internals of several key system-stored procedures that you probably use every day.

N O T E Each of these procedures was extracted from the database using the system-stored procedure sp_helptext. The system-stored procedure sp_helptext takes a single parameter: the name of a procedure that you want to get the text for. ■

One more thing: you may have noticed the title of this chapter is "Using Advanced Stored Procedures and Triggers," and yet if you've looked at the contents of this chapter, you'll probably notice a pretty obvious absence of any particular reference to triggers themselves. Why? Because everything you see here in this chapter applies as equally to code for a trigger as it does for a stored procedure. Transact-SQL's trigger implementation is really just a stored procedure that's fired automatically; thus, with basically no exceptions, everything that is valid for a procedure is valid for a trigger too. ■

Using Nested Procedure Calls

One of the simplest and yet most often overlooked features of Transact-SQL is the capability to nest or call one procedure from another. Typically, people tend to write procedures as self-contained functions or logical groups of code, and neglect the fact that they cannot only be called from the client or front-end application, but also by other procedures. This section is going to look at one of the more commonly used stored procedures that's also quite small: sp_helptext. Listing 13.1 shows the body text of sp_helptext used to create the procedure.

Listing 13.1 CHP13_01.SQL—System-Stored Procedure sp_helptext

```
/* Sccsid = "%Z% generic/sproc/%M% %I% %G%" */
/*     4.8     1.1     06/14/90     sproc/src/helptext */
/*
** Messages for "sp_helptext"            17nnn
**
** 17460, "Object must be in the current database."
** 17461, "Object does not exist in this database."
** 17679, "There is no text for object @objname."
*/
create procedure sp_helptext
@objname varchar(92)
as
declare @text_count int
declare @msg varchar(100)


if @@trancount = 0
begin
     set chained off
end

set transaction isolation level 1

/*
**   Make sure the @objname is local to the current database.
*/
```

```
if @objname like "%.%.%" and
    substring(@objname, 1, charindex(".", @objname) - 1) != db_name()
begin
    /* 17460, "Object must be in the current database." */
    exec sp_getmessage 17460, @msg out
    print @msg
    return (1)
end

/*
**  See if @objname exists.
*/
if (object_id(@objname) is NULL)
begin
    /* 17461, "Object does not exist in this database." */
    exec sp_getmessage 17461, @msg out
    print @msg
    return (1)
end

/*
**  Find out howmany lines of text are coming back.
**      and return if there are none.
*/
select @text_count = count(*)
    from syscomments
where id = object_id(@objname)

if @text_count = 0
begin
    /* 17679, "There is no text for object @objname." */
    exec sp_getmessage 17679, @msg out
    print @msg, @objname
    return (1)
end

/*
**  Return # how many lines of text that are about to come back.
**  This is required by the "old" report writer.
*/
select "# Lines of Text" = @text_count

/*
**  Now get the text.
*/
select text
    from syscomments
where id = object_id(@objname)
        order by number, colid2, colid

return (0)

go
```

Part

II

Ch

13

This system procedure, `sp_helptext` demonstrates one of the most frequently used system procedures, `sp_getmessage`, in action. When the procedure encounters an error condition, it calls `sp_getmessage` passing in a error ID that is looked up by `sp_getmessage` and the appropriate error message is returned. Sybase uses this model for handling errors so that they can import different language's errors into the *sysmessages* table of the *master* database and not affect the way the system procedures work. This is an elegant solution to a common problem that is faced by many application developers trying to manage multi-language error reporting in their systems.

Using nesting in procedures is an excellent way of solving the following problems:

■ **API layering**—If you have a set of complex stored procedures that normally take a default set of values or parameters to them and you want to simplify (reduce) the number of parameters required to execute the procedure, you can add a layer on top of the procedures that just calls the complex procedures with default parameters.

■ **Functional code**—Transact-SQL is a rich language; however, people have a tendency to make procedures big behemoths that are hard to manage and work with. By splitting up your long and complex procedures into small functions or *mini* procedures, you will gain both in terms of making your code more understandable and also easier to maintain. It is far easier to test a simple function's successful execution from end to end than it is to debug a lengthy tome of a procedure.

■ **Multiple programmer development**—By breaking up your code into smaller units or functions, you make it easier to have several programmers working on the code at the same time. It is completely impractical for more than one programmer to work on the same stored procedure at the same time. However, it is not unreasonable for two or more programmers to work on the same problem, provided that it is broken down into manageable chunks.

N O T E API Layering is a definitely recommended approach for those of you who tend to use the `= Default_Value` feature of a procedure's parameter where you get the parameter to take a default value if no value is supplied by the calling program. The reason you'd want to use API layering is that it speeds up the execution of the procedure because you are passing parameters to the procedure by position and not by name. Passing a parameter to a procedure by name incurs a performance penalty during execution because System XI has to evaluate the parameter's name and then read through the parameter list to the procedure and apply/pass it appropriately. ■

Using Temporary Tables

Quite often you come across a situation in which the data in a particular table or set of tables is in a form that makes joins difficult or makes it hard to return the data to the user/caller in a single result set. The advantage of a single result set for many client programs (especially many of the third-party report writers) is that this is all that they can handle. Despite the fact that it is possible to return multiple sets of results from a stored procedure, it is often a requirement for a system to not do this in order to simplify the client processing required to manage the returned data from the procedure.

A simple solution exists to the problem of multiple result sets (for most situations anyway): Use a temporary table. The purpose of the temporary table is to create a logical data storage area to contain the data that you are going to eventually return to the client. Into that temporary table, you will Insert data that you need to present to a user. After the table has all the required values in it that you need, all you need to do is perform a simple Select statement to return the information to the client or calling process.

N O T E You cannot use a Select statement to pass results from one procedure to another procedure. Any execution of a Select statement will send the results to the client application that invoked the procedure (or the parent procedure if the procedure was nested in execution). If you need to pass multiple records between different procedures, then your only option is to create a real table. For more information on creating real tables, see the next section, "Creating Real Tables for Data Transfer Between Procedures." ▮

Listing 13.2 shows the system stored procedure sp_databases at work using a temporary table, #databases. The temporary table in this example is designed to simplify the processing required on the *master* table, *sysusages*, which has multiple child records (for each of the database device fragments) for each database on the server.

Listing 13.2   CHP13_02.SQL—System-Stored Procedure sp_databases

```
/* Sccsid = "%Z% generic/sproc/%M% %I% %G%" */

create procedure sp_databases
as

    if @@trancount = 0
    begin
        set chained off
    end

    set transaction isolation level 1

    /* Use temporary table to sum up database size w/o using group by */
    create table #databases (
                    database_name varchar(32),
                    size int)

    /* Insert row for each database */
    insert into #databases
        select
            name,
            (select sum(size) from master.dbo.sysusages
                where dbid = d.dbid)
        from master.dbo.sysdatabases d
```

Part
II

Ch
13

continues

Listing 13.2   Continued

```
select
      database_name,
                  /* Convert from number of pages to K */
      database_size = size * (@@pagesize / 1024),
      remarks = convert(varchar(254),null)      /* Remarks are NULL */
from #databases

return(0)

go
```

Using temporary tables is also an option if you were considering using a Union in a Select and didn't want to compromise any flexibility in the ordering and formatting of the output data. You can create a temporary table for the columns that would have been in the Union and then use the Insert Into Table_Name Select * From Table_Name syntax to populate the table with the required data from the tables that you were going to Union. After you have performed all the inserts and data modifications required on the temporary table, all you need to do is issue a single Select statement to return the data in a single result set to the client.

TIP You can also use temporary tables to get around Sybase's 16-table join limit. Create a temporary table to insert the data from the first 16 tables and then perform a Select that joins from the temporary table to any of the other tables that you wanted to work with.

Creating Real Tables for Data Transfer Between Procedures

Sometimes it is necessary to create *pseudo temporary* tables that are used to share data between multiple stored procedures. A sample scenario might be a reporting *key* table. The table is created in a *temporary* fashion to store primary key information or *rollup* data that is going to be used for reporting later on. This scenario presupposes that passing the data once in large history tables (large means in the hundreds of thousand or million row size) is highly advantageous to the processing of the system.

For example, in your processing during a nightly update, you may already pass over this large table once, and during this pass, it may be possible to identify records that need to be reported on later during the night. You would use the reporting table to insert the key information (such as the customer number of the record) into a table that you could then join to when performing your report. The advantage is that you no longer have to perform large table scans and searches (which even on an index may be slow) and can instead join directly to this key data table.

The problem is that the data is *really* transient. It has no worth after the end of the day, and as such should not be placed in a real table permanently. However, you can't use a temporary table because these tables cease to exist at the exit of a session or the close of the execution of a stored procedure. So what's the best solution? Create a table in the *tempdb* database.

Why would you want to use *tempdb*? Because the *tempdb* database is a transient database like your transient table. The reason *tempdb* is described as a transient database is because it is completely rebuilt (i.e., it ceases to exist after the server is shutdown) each time the server is restarted. The advantage of the *tempdb* database being rebuilt is that you don't have to worry about maintaining the table after you are done with it. You can perform a simple existence check at the start of your overnight routine to determine if it currently has been created, and if you find it, you can `Truncate` the data from it. If you don't find the table, then all you need to do is create it again.

Using Cursors

Cursors, or specifically server-side cursors, are often used to write applications that process records of data on the server with multiple activities or actions on a row-by-row basis. The principle reason that you'd want to use a cursor is that you don't have to perform any networking when it is used. This alone can provide enormous performance advantages for an application. If you can perform all the processing on the server and eliminate any network traffic of the row-by-row data going back to the client, you drastically reduce the data transfer across the network.

Another reason that you might want to use server-side cursors is that they give you great flexibility in the processing of your data. No longer do you have to do multiple `Update` statements on different rows in a table; instead, you can process each row individually and differently as you see fit. This concept of row-by-row individual processing is key for many systems that have a strong sense of master detail in their database schema. A highly normalized database may have many *child* or *detail* tables that revolve or rely on a *parent* or *master* record. For example, you may have a database of houses; each of these houses may have several attributes stored in the primary table, but then there may be other *detail* tables for such items as the list of publications that are delivered to the house, the schedule of visits from utility companies, and so on.

Given a structure of a single central table and many dependent tables, you may have to write a batch routine that processes all the various aspects of the primary table's records. A traditional way of performing this function might be to fetch to the client a list of all the records in the central table (houses in the example) and then, based on each record that is returned, execute a number of functions on the record and its subsidiary records.

The negatives of this client driven approach are that you obviously incur networking overhead. An alternative might be to use mass `Update` statements that affect multiple records on the server without the need to send the records back to the client; however, this approach may not be effective due to the number of times that you are going to force the database to do a full table update. The best solution is to open a cursor on the data in the table and process it on the server.

▶ **See** "Opening a Cursor," **p. 318**

Part

II

Ch

13

In Listing 13.3, the system stored procedure `sp_helpcache` creates two temporary tables—
`#syscacheconfig` and `#sysdb`—that it uses to place data from the system catalog tables for easy
reference. After creating the temporary table, the procedure `sp_helpcache` opens cursors on
each of the tables and performs row-by-row processing to accomplish such tasks as estimating
the amount of memory used and free in each cache, and to check the status of each database
(whether it is `online` or `offline`).

You might wonder why temporary tables are used in this case. My theory is that a temporary
table is created for this data so that there are no locks left on the system catalog while the
cache and databases are being processed with their respective cursors. Reducing locking on
the system catalog is definitely a design goal of the Sybase system-stored procedures because
any locks on the system catalog may stop other processing on the database until the locks are
removed.

Listing 13.3   CHP13_03.SQL—System-Stored Procedure sp_helpcache

```
/* This stored procedure is for displaying cache overhead and bindings */
/* 17260, "Can't run %1! from within a transaction." */
/* 18174, "The database '%1!' is offline. To obtain cache-bindings for
objects in this database, please online the database and rerun sp_helpcache. */

create procedure sp_helpcache
@parm1          varchar(30) = NULL
as

declare @stat         int    /* cache status from sysconfigures */
declare @cstat        int    /* status return from config_admin */
declare @unit_loc     int    /* location of unit specifier in str */
declare @size         int    /* cache size from sysconfigures */
declare @row_count    int    /* # rows in #syscacheconfig */
declare @config_size  int    /* cache's configured size
                      ** (syscurconfigs
                      */
declare @run_size     int    /* cache's current run size from
                      ** syscurconfigs
                      */
declare @overhead     int    /* cache's memory overhead */
declare @total_config int    /* total configured cache memory */
declare @total_run    int    /* total running cache memory */
declare @total_overhead int   /* totalamount of overhead used */
declare @left_over_mem int    /* memory not explicitly configuured */
declare @status2      int    /* Sysdatabase[DAT_STATUS2] */
declare @first_char   char(1)    /* first char of parm1 */
declare @unit         varchar(5) /* unit of size for configuration */
declare @name         varchar(30)/* cache name from sysconfigures */
declare @config_sz_str  varchar(30)/* str value for run_size */
declare @run_sz_str   varchar(30)/* str value for config_size */
declare @overhead_sz_str varchar(30)/* str valuefor overhead size */
declare @print_str    varchar(255)/* general string to print info */
declare @curr_avail_cache_mem float    /* current amount of memory
                                   available
```

```
                        ** for named cache configuration.
                        */

/* Dont allow sp_helpcache to run with in a transaction. */
if @@trancount > 0
begin
     /*
     ** 17260, "Can't run %1! from within a transaction."
     */
     exec sp_getmessage 17260, @print_str output
     print @print_str, "sp_helpcache"
     return (1)
end
else
begin
     set transaction isolation level 1
     set chained off
end

select @first_char = substring(@parm1, 1, 1)

if (@parm1 = NULL or (patindex("%[a-z,A-Z]%", @first_char) != 0))
begin
     select name, value, value3, status
     into #syscacheconfig
     from master.dbo.sysconfigures
          where parent = 19 and name like "%"+ @parm1 + "%"
          and config = 19

     /*
     **  Find out the number of rows you want to look at.
     */
     select @row_count = count(*) from #syscacheconfig

     /*
     **  If no rows qualify then this cache doesn't exist.
     */
     if @row_count = 0
     begin
          exec sp_getmessage 18135, @print_str output
          print @print_str, @parm1
          return 1
     end

     declare sysc_cursor cursor
     for select name, value, status
          from #syscacheconfig

     open sysc_cursor

     print "Cache Name      Config Size    Run Size    Overhead"
     print "--------------  -------------  ---------   --------"

     select @total_config = 0
     select @total_run = 0
```

continues

Listing 13.3   Continued

```
select @total_overhead = 0

while (@row_count > 0)
begin
     fetch sysc_cursor into @name, @size, @stat

     if (@stat & 32 = 32)
     begin
          select @config_size = @size
          select @total_config = @total_config + @config_size
          /*
          **  The actual run size is in syscurconfigs
          */
          select @run_size = value, @overhead =  memory_used
          from master.dbo.syscurconfigs
               where config=19 and
               comment = @name
          select @total_run = @total_run + @run_size
     end
     if (@stat & 64 = 64)
     begin
          select @run_size = 0
          select @overhead = 0
          select @config_size = @size
          select @total_config = @total_config + @config_size
     end
     if (@stat & 128 = 128)
     begin
          /*
          **  The actual run size is in syscurconfigs
          */
          select @run_size = value, @overhead = memory_used
          from master.dbo.syscurconfigs
               where config=19 and
               comment = @name
          select @config_size = 0
          select @total_run = @total_run + @run_size
     end

     select @total_overhead = @total_overhead + @overhead
     /*
     **  Convert run_size ,config_size and overhead to megabyte
     **  values stored as strings
     */
     select @run_sz_str = rtrim(str(convert(float,@run_size)
               / 1024, 7, 2)) + " Mb"
     select @config_sz_str = rtrim(str(convert(float,@config_size)
               / 1024, 7, 2)) + " Mb"
     select @overhead_sz_str = rtrim(str(convert(float,@overhead)
               / 1024, 7, 2)) + " Mb"

     select @print_str =  convert(char(25), @name) + convert(char(15),
               @config_sz_str) + convert(char(15), @run_sz_str) +
               convert(char(15), @overhead_sz_str)
```

```
    print @print_str

    select @row_count = @row_count - 1
end

close sysc_cursor

/*
** If you're doing a helpcache on a specific cache, then don't print
** out info on global memory availability.
*/
if patindex("%[a-z]%", @first_char) = 0
begin
    select @curr_avail_cache_mem =
            config_admin(13, 0, 0, 0, NULL, NULL)
    /*
    ** Subtract all cache overhead from available cache
    ** memory.
    */
    select @curr_avail_cache_mem = @curr_avail_cache_mem -
            @total_overhead

    print " "
    print " "
    print "Memory Available For    Memory Configured"
    print "Named Caches            To Named Caches"
    print "-------------------     ----------------"
    select @print_str = convert(char(28),
            str(convert(float,@curr_avail_cache_mem)
            / 1024, 7, 2) + " Mb") + str(convert(float,@total_config)
            / 1024, 7, 2) + " Mb"
    print @print_str
    print " "
    select @left_over_mem = @curr_avail_cache_mem - @total_config
    if @left_over_mem > 0
    begin
        select @print_str = "There is " + str(convert(float,
            @left_over_mem) / 1024, 7, 2) + " Mb of memory left
            over that will be allocated to the default cache"
        print @print_str
    end
    print " "
end


print " "
print "------------- Cache Binding Information: ------------- "
print " "

/*
** Find out the number of rows you want to look at.
*/
select @row_count = count(*) from #syscacheconfig
```

Part

II

Ch

13

continues

Listing 13.3 Continued

```
declare bindings_cursor cursor
for select name from #syscacheconfig

open bindings_cursor

print "Cache Name    Entity Name       Type  Index Namd        Status"
print "----------    ----------        ----  ----------        ------"
while (@row_count > 0)
begin
    fetch bindings_cursor into @name

    select @cstat = config_admin(9, 2, 0, 0, NULL, @name)

    select @row_count = @row_count - 1
end

close bindings_cursor

/* Now print error message for offline databases. The built-in
** function config_admin() ignores offline databases, and you handle
** them here after all online databases have been handled.
*/
select name, status2
   into #sysdb
   from master.dbo.sysdatabases

/*
** Find out the number of rows you want to look at.
*/
select @row_count = count(*) from #sysdb

declare offlinedb_cursor cursor
for select name, status2 from #sysdb

open offlinedb_cursor

while (@row_count > 0)
begin
    fetch offlinedb_cursor into@name, @status2

    if (@status2 & 16 != 0)
    begin
        /* 18174, "The database '%1!' is offline. To obtain
        ** cache-bindings for objects in this database,
        ** please online the database and rerun sp_helpcache.
        */
        exec sp_getmessage 18174, @print_str output
        print @print_str, @name
    end
    select @row_count = @row_count - 1
end
```

```
        close offlinedb_cursor
        return 0
  end
  else
  begin

      /*
      **  If you get here, parm1 must be of the form %d[M P K G].
      */
      exec @stat = sp_aux_getsize @parm1, @size output
      if @stat = 0
      begin
          return 1
      end

      select @overhead = config_admin(12, 0, @size, 0, NULL, NULL)
      select @overhead_sz_str = str(convert(float,@overhead)
              / 1024, 7, 2) + "Mb"

      select @print_str = convert(varchar(15), @overhead_sz_str) +
              " of overhead memory will be needed to manage a cache of size "
              + @parm1

      print @print_str
  end

  return 0

  go
```

Using Roles to Ensure that the Right People Execute a Procedure

One of the concerns that you may have as a security officer at your company or organization is that only the appropriately authorized users can perform certain tasks. Typical methods for ensuring security are discussed in some detail in Chapter 21, "Managing and Monitoring Security." However, using roles is a somewhat nebulous subject and is explored in a little more detail in this section.

Normally, you would grant permission to run a procedure to a particular user or group of users just as you would grant permission to Select from a table. However, there are some procedures that you simply don't want anyone to run unless they have one of the special roles allocated and defined in System XI. The roles that a user can assume are as follows:

■ SSO Role—This is the *system security officer* role and is designed to be used as a person who can create and manage security for the database or server.

- ■ SA Role—This is the *system administrator* role. The system administrator has full access to the system/server and can perform all functions on the server. However, when using Sybase Secure Server, you can revoke user management functions from the SA—leaving them with the SSO.

- ■ Operator Role—This is a class of user that you would want to give permissions to perform such things as backups and restores or to manage tape volume changing during a backup or restore process.

- ■ Replication Role—This is a special class of user that has special permissions to read from the transaction log on one server and then to write to the tables, indiscriminately, on a target server.

For example, say that irrespective of the user or group that a user belongs to, the only class of user that can perform an operation is the system administrator (sa) class. You can manage this by evaluating in the procedure the role of the user that's currently running the procedure. In Listing 13.4, the system-stored procedure is allowed only to be run by a user of the sa role. To enforce this, the procedure uses the system function proc_role to determine whether the current user has the appropriate privileges:

```
...
if (proc_role("sa_role") = 0)
      return (1)
...
```

If security is a concern for you, you can add a similar style of logic to your application to ensure that only the appropriately authorized users execute certain procedures in the database.

Listing 13.4 CHP13_04.SQL—System-Stored Procedure sp_modifylogin

```
/* Sccsid = "%Z% generic/sproc/src/%M% %I% %G%" */
/*    5.0   1.0   10/22/91    sproc/src/modifylogin */


/*
** Messages for "sp_modifylogin"          17920
**
** 17260, "Can't run %1! from within a transaction."
** 17880, "No such account -- nothing changed."
** 17920, "The given security label value is syntactically wrong."
** 17921, "The given maxwrite value cannot dominate the minwrite value from
**         syslogins -- nothing changed."
** 17922, "The given minwrite value is not dominated by the maxwrite value from
**         syslogins -- nothing changed."
** 17923, "The given security label is not dominated by the clearance value from
**         syslogins -- nothing changed."
** 17924, "The given clearance value cannot dominate the %1! value from
syslogins
**          -- nothingchanged."
** 17925, "Column name invalid -- nothing changed."
** 17926, "Column changed."
** 17927, "Error in changing the value of the specified column."
*/
```

```
create procedure sp_modifylogin
@account varchar(30),          /* the name of the account  */
@column  varchar(30),          /* the column to be updated */
@value   varchar(255)          /* the new value of column  */
as
declare @suid int         /* suid of account to be modified   */
declare @msg varchar(250)      /* message text */
declare @retstat int           /* return status from other procedures */

/*
**  If you're in a transaction, disallow this since it might make recovery
**  impossible.
*/
if @@trancount > 0
begin
     /* 17260, "Can't run %1! from within a transaction." */
     exec sp_getmessage 17260, @msg output
     print @msg, "sp_modifylogin"
     return (1)
end
else
begin
     set chained off
end

set transaction isolation level 1

/*
** If user is trying to modify someone else's login then
** check if user has sa role. Proc_role will perform auditing
** and print error message if required.
*/

if (suser_id(@account) != suser_id())
begin
     if (proc_role("sa_role") = 0)
          return (1)
end

/*  Check if the account exists */
select @suid = suid
     from master.dbo.syslogins
     where name = @account
if @suid is NULL
begin
     /*
     ** 17880, "No such account -- nothing changed."
     */
     exec sp_getmessage 17880, @msg output
     print @msg
     return (1)
end
```

continues

Part

II

Ch

13

Listing 13.4 Continued

```
/*
**  Update takes place here: column can only be fullname for C2
*/
if @column = "fullname"
begin
        update master.dbo.syslogins set fullname  = @value where suid = @suid
end
else if @column = "defdb"
begin
      execute @retstat = sybsystemprocs.dbo.sp_defaultdb @account, @value
      return (@retstat)
end
else if @column = "deflanguage"
begin
      execute @retstat = sybsystemprocs.dbo.sp_defaultlanguage @account, @value
      return (@retstat)
end

else /* error */
begin
      /*
      ** 17925, "Column name invalid -- nothing changed."
      */
      exec sp_getmessage 17925, @msg output
      print @msg
         return (1)
end

/*
**  Check @@rowcount when it works
*/
if @@rowcount = 1
begin
      /*
      ** 17926, "Column changed."
      */
      exec sp_getmessage 17926, @msg output
      print @msg
      return (0)
end
else
begin
      /*
      ** 17927, "Error in changing the value of the specified column."
      */
      exec sp_getmessage 17927, @msg output
      print @msg
      return (1)
end

   go
```

Splitting Up a Qualified Object Name

If you are writing some general purpose stored procedures that need to be able to operate on a fully qualified object name, such as `MyServer.MyDatabase.MyUser.MyObject`, you may need a tool to split up the components of the object name into easily usable parts. Fortunately, Sybase provides a useful system-stored procedure, `sp_namecrack`, that does just this. The syntax for the use of `sp_namecrack` is as follows:

```
sp_namecrack Object_Name, Server_Name Output, Database_Name Output,
            Owner_Name Output, Object_Name Output
```

The values of the parameters to the procedure `sp_namecrack` are as follows:

- *Object_Name*—This is an object name, which may have qualifiers, such as server, database, or owner, and based on these qualifiers, will be split out into the output parameters that follow.

- *Server_Name*—This is an `Output` parameter to the procedure, and it will contain the name of the server (if any) specified in the object name.

- *Database_Name*—This is an `Output` parameter to the procedure, and it will contain the name of the database (if any) specified in the object name.

- *Owner_Name*—This is an `Output` parameter to the procedure, and it will contain the name of the owner (if any) specified in the object name.

- *Object_Name*—This is an `Output` parameter to the procedure, and it will contain the name of the object.

N O T E When calling a stored procedure with `Output` parameters, you *must* remember to use the `Output` keyword in your calling program. If you don't, Sybase will not be able to assign the values to the variables, and will just assume that you are passing in regular parameters to the procedure. ■

For example, if you wanted to run `sp_namecrack` on the object specified in the first example of this section, you would execute:

```
/* First declare some receive variables */
Declare  @sServerName   Varchar(30),
         @sDatabaseName Varchar(30),
         @sOwnerName    Varchar(30),
         @sObjectName   Varchar(30)

/* Now execute the proc */
Exec sp_namecrack "MyServer.MyDatabase.MyUser.MyObject",
            @sServerName    Output,
            @sDatabaseName  Output,
            @sOwnerName     Output,
            @sObjectName    Output

Print "Here comes the cracked name:"
```

Part

II

Ch

13
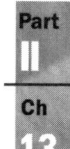

```
/* Now Return the results */
Select "Server Name"   = @sServerName,
       "Database Name" = @sDatabaseName,
       "Owner Name"    = @sOwnerName,
       "Object Name"   = @sObjectName
Go

Here comes the cracked name:
Server Name     Database Name   Owner Name    Object Name
--------------  --------------  ------------  ------------
MyServer        MyDatabase      MyUser        MyObject
```

From Here...

In this chapter, you were introduced to the guts of several key Sybase system-stored procedures. The purpose was to show you some well-coded examples of the best way to solve problems using Transact-SQL as the solution. A lot of these examples and coding styles can be used in your own applications and stored procedures, and I encourage you to adopt some of these tricks in your own programs.

I suggest that you look at the following chapters for more information on using Transact-SQL to enhance your applications:

- Chapter 15, "Using Client/Server Application Programming Tools," provides a comprehensive review of the four top ranked client/server tools on the market today: PowerBuilder, Centura Team Developer, Delphi, and Visual Basic. Using these client-side tools is a perfect way to integrate the stored procedures that you can now develop.

- Chapter 17, "Using Third-Party Products," reviews some of the more popular and powerful third-party application programs that will help you work with a database and develop a database schema with a modeling tool.

- Chapter 23, "Using Sybase's Configuration Options," shows you how to use query options to control the display of data through Set command options. These options help you optimize the performance of your application.

Application Programming

Understanding the Sybase Client Model (Client Library)

Since the early days of database management systems, high-order languages (HOLs) have been used to retrieve and manipulate data. In fact, the majority of functional requirements were satisfied in this manner. Entire systems were developed using both interactive and batch programs. Over time, database vendors and third-party software developers created interpreted programming languages specifically for database applications such as report writing languages.

In the early to mid-1980s, embedding data manipulation language commands within HOLs was a popular means of interfacing with databases that required pre-compiling and often led to inefficient code created by the pre-compiler. At around the same time, libraries of functions encapsulating database interfaces were developed. This adoption of database APIs (application programming interfaces) through functions was a natural progression for the C programming language. In an attempt to compete with host language interfaces, several report writing languages added advanced capabilities. Although widely used, even these improved tools had numerous shortcomings. In recent years, development of these products has been focused toward easy-to-use interfaces accompanied by development tools.

Today, there are numerous methods available for writing programs to retrieve and manipulate data stored in relational client/server databases. This chapter covers three methods: Sybase's DBLibrary, Client Library, and Structured Query Report Writer (SQR) Version 2.5.

Programming interfaces enable you to perform heavy processing of data, to create files, to execute data-oriented tasks, and to run programs on multiple operating systems. More advanced applications use the library functions to encapsulate communications with the database, hence creating a layered programming architecture.

Because the Open Client functions, DBLibrary, and Client Library, are most widely used within C programs, examples for these methods will be presented in C. However, remember that these executable functions can be used in other programming languages. A thorough understanding of how the library functions and Sybase work together will provide the necessary foundation for developing efficient, robust programs. ∎

Comparing Programming Interfaces to Sybase

A general comparison of the capabilities available from the three options covered in this chapter is shown in Table 14.1.

Table 14.1   Comparing the Capabilities of DBLibrary, Client Library, and SQR

Capability	DBLibrary	Client Library	SQR
Cursors	[1]	✔	[2]
Full Access to Operating System	✔	✔	
Control-of-flow Language	✔	✔	✔
Variables	✔	✔	✔
Execute all Transact-SQL Commands	✔	✔	[3]
Compiled	✔	✔	[4]
Calls to Remote Stored Procedures	✔	✔	
Transactions	✔	✔	✔
Executes on Client Machine	✔	✔	✔
Executes on Server	✔	✔	✔
Windows GUI Development	✔	✔	

1. *DBLibrary emulates cursors on the client side.*
2. *SQR will use cursors if they are available. However, no method of cursor control is provided.*
3. *SQR can specify only the* Use Database *command in the initial program setup.*
4. *SQR interprets report files. However, runtime files can be created that have already been scanned and compiled.*

Selecting one programming method over another will depend on several factors. You must think about a number of issues that may affect the development process, for example:

- What are the performance requirements?
- How complex is the task?
- Will it be executed online, in batch, or both?
- What skills do you have among staff?
- Will additional interfaces be required?
- How reliable must this capability be?

C/DBLibrary programs provide an excellent means of manipulating large volumes of data and creating large data files. SQR is very easy to learn and provides a quick method of formatting data into reports. It can also be used to output files that can embed formatting instructions for PCL, which is HP's LaserJet page definition language, as well as PostScript and raw/ASCII.

Another factor to consider is where on the network will the program be executed. Should you target PC-based or server-based processing? The fundamental basis of employing a client/server architecture is to maximize performance by dividing the processing between client and server. You might want to consider the following things:

- The amount of data traversing a network
- The relative capabilities of the client and server hardware
- The sort of user interface required (GUI, text, or none)

Programs that require heavy throughput of data should be executed on the database server machine. When large data throughput tasks execute on the server, the network does not need to get involved with data transfer between client and server, and this is a major performance advantage.

This chapter briefly covers programming using DBLibrary, Client Library, and SQR. A detailed explanation of these programming interfaces could fill several books and is beyond the scope of this chapter. Therefore, you will focus primarily on the essential aspects of each method. Though not exhaustive, you will be provided with information intended to enable you to begin programming.

Working with DBLibrary

What is DBLibrary? DBLibrary is a set of functions written in C, enabling application programs to communicate with a Sybase System XI server or any Sybase Open Server application. Programs written using the DBLibrary functions can be run on client machines, i.e., PCs connected to a UNIX database server on a LAN. They can also be run on the database server.

DBLibrary uses a structure called a LOGINREC to gain access to specific servers. Programs use one or more objects, called DBPROCESSES, to communicate with Sybase System XI. A DBPROCESS is a unique handle to the database and represents a set of environment variables that control

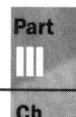

Part

III

Ch

14

the connection to the database. Each DBPROCESS operates independently and is responsible for the following activities:

- Commands sent to the server
- Results returned from the server
- Messages provided by the server

Any information that is stored in DBPROCESS buffers can be accessed by using functions or functions defined in the DBLibrary API. Result sets are returned from Sybase as a batch of one or many rows to an internal buffer in the DBPROCESS. The results that are stored in a buffer are then fetched by the client program one record at a time, using the dbnextrow API of DBLibrary.

If you have existing applications written to DBLibrary, don't be concerned that Sybase may drop the API altogether. Because of the multitude of programs currently written in DBLibrary, it will continue to be effectively supported by Sybase. However, after the System 10 release of DBLibrary, it is unlikely that Sybase will spend much time adding new features to the API; instead, the company will concentrate on improving and further developing Client Library.

The examples that are provided in this section will clarify how to use the LOGINREC and DBPROCESS structures in your applications. One word of caution: Pay special attention to specific rules for datatypes and proper use of the DBLibrary functions.

N O T E Although you are actually able to access information stored in the DBPROCESS structure directly, as a precaution, you should use only the DBLibrary/C functions provided. Manually working with DBPROCESS is not recommended because of the critical impact it has on your application. A DBPROCESS is your active connection to the database; direct manipulation could have unpredictable results. ■

Understanding the Basic DBLibrary Functions

There are over 250 functions available in the DBLibrary API. You will use several of them in every DBLibrary program you write. However, some functions will be used less frequently, depending on the requirements and design of a specific application. Many will be used infrequently. In order to write optimum programs and minimize complexity, you should be familiar with the entire DBLibrary API.

The most commonly used functions are described below. After a brief explanation of each function is a list of possible return values.

dbinit   Initializes DBLibrary. DBLibrary programs must always call this function first.

Returns: SUCCEED or FAIL

dblogin   Allocates a structure (defined by LOGINREC), which will be used for connecting all DBPROCESS to Sybase. The term "allocate" refers to retrieving a pointer to a large enough space in memory where the data will be stored.

Returns: Pointer to a LOGINREC structure or NULL when allocation of structure fails.

DBSETLUSER   This C macro sets the username of a LOGINREC.

Returns: SUCCEED or FAIL

DBSETLPWD   This C macro sets the user password of a LOGINREC.

Returns: SUCCEED or FAIL

DBSETLHOST   This C macro sets the host server name of a LOGINREC.

Returns: SUCCEED or FAIL

N O T E   DBSETLUSER, DBSETLPWD, and DBSETLHOST may be used to modify logon information for each DBPROCESS structure (e.g., to connect to different servers). ■

dbopen   Connects a DBPROCESS to Sybase. This function must be performed to create the DBPROCESS, which has already been defined earlier.

Returns: A pointer to a DBPROCESS structure or NULL, if logon to server or creation of structure failed.

dbloginfree   Destroys the specified LOGINREC structure and frees its allocated memory.

Returns: Nothing

dbuse   Directs a DBPROCESS to use a particular database on the server to which it is connected.

Returns: SUCCEED or FAIL

dbcmd   Appends text (e.g., Transact-SQL statements) to the command buffer of a specified DBPROCESS.

Returns: SUCCEED or FAIL

dbfcmd   Appends text with formatted input to the command buffer of the specified DBPROCESS. Program variables are formatted into the command text exactly as in the standard C function printf.

Returns: SUCCEED or FAIL

dbsqlexec   Sends the contents of the specified DBPROCESS command buffer to Sybase. It is worth mentioning that you can use two separate DBLibrary functions (dbsqlsend followed by dbsqlok) in place of dbsqlexec and achieve the same results. The DBLibrary function dbsqlsend sends the contents of the command buffer to the server. A return value of SUCCEED indicates that the contents of the command buffer were successfully sent to the server, but does not necessarily indicate correct execution. The dbsqlok function checks for correct execution of the commands sent to the server and waits until the results are ready to be retrieved.

Returns: SUCCEED or FAIL

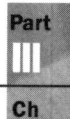

Part

III

Ch

14

dbresults Informs the program of the results of the command executed by dbsqlexec. You must issue a dbresults command for each result set returned from a command batch or a stored procedure; hence, it is typically issued within a while loop.

Returns: SUCCEED, FAIL, or NO_MORE_RESULTS

dbbind Binds (i.e., associates) a column that is returned as a member of a result set to a program variable.

Returns: SUCCEED or FAIL

dbnextrow Places the next row of the result set being read into the variables specified by dbbind function calls.

Returns: REG_ROW, *computeid*, NO_MORE_ROWS, BUF_FULL, or FAIL

dbcancel Halts execution of a command batch and cleans up the DBPROCESS buffers once the DBPROCESS buffers are cleared and ready to be used again. Typically used when errors occur or when results are pending, but when you are done with the data being retrieved.

Returns: SUCCEED or FAIL

dbclose Closes the connection for a specific DBPROCESS and de-allocates its memory.

Returns: Nothing

dbexit Closes all structures used by DBLibrary. Closes all DBPROCESS connections and de-allocates their memory.

Returns: Nothing

CAUTION

You may not use any DBLibrary functions after calling dbexit. However, you may continue to use variables declared with the DBLibrary datatypes provided that you don't try to fetch the next row or something like that.

Many of the functions you will use in DBLibrary are logically grouped. In other words, they should not be used randomly throughout a program. To simplify development of DBLibrary application programs, you should structure your programs using the following "nested" format:

```
Connect to Sybase System XI( dbinit, dblogin )
  Open DBPROCESS structures( dbopen, dbuse )
  Install Message/Error Handlers( dberrhandle, dbmsghandle )
    Send commands to Sybase( dbcmd, dbfcmd, dbsqlexec )
      Retrieve data( dbresults, dbbind, dbnextrow )
        Process the results on the client
      Clean up after using DBPROCESS (dbcancel, if required)
  Close all DBPROCESS structures( dbclose )
Close the connection( dbexit )
```

The range of DBLibrary functions available is quite extensive. Although you may have little need for many of them, take the time to look them over. It is advisable to at least be aware of what is available to you through the DBLibrary functions.

Declaring Variables for Use by DBLibrary Functions

Variables used by DBLibrary functions should be declared using the DBLibrary-defined datatypes. These datatypes are defined in the `<sybfront.h>` and `<sybdb.h>` header files, which you must include in all DBLibrary programs. In Table 14.2, you can see a cross-reference between DBLibrary program variable types and Sybase column types that will help you remember the appropriate datatypes to use when working with Sybase stored procedures and database objects.

Table 14.2   Cross-Reference of Sybase Datatypes and DBLibrary Program Variable Types

Sybase Datatype	DBLibrary Program Variable Type
Binary	DBBINARY
Bit	DBBIT
Char	DBCHAR
Datetime	DBDATETIME
Decimal	DBDECIMAL
Float	DBFLT8
Image	DBBINARY
Int	DBINT
Money	DBMONEY
Numeric	DBNUMERIC
Real	DBREAL
Smalldatetime	DBDATETIME4
Smallint	DBSMALLINT
Smallmoney	DBMONEY4
Text	DBCHAR
Tinyint	DBTINYINT
Varbinary	DBBINARY
Varchar	DBCHAR

Part

III

Ch

14

Here are a few examples of variables declared using the DBLibrary datatypes:

```
DEBTOR    *Company_Name;        /* Pointer To Character String */
DBCHAR    Company_Name[81];     /* Array Of Characters */
DBINT     Number_Of_Calls;      /* Integer */
DBFLT8    Cost_Per_Call;        /* Float */
```

N O T E   When using a numeric variable such as DBINT or DBFLT8 within a DBLibrary function, precede the name of the variable with an ampersand (&) as follows:

```
dbbind(dbproc, 1, INTBIND, (DBINT)0, (BYTE *) &Number_Of_Calls);
```

so that the C compiler knows that the value is a receive or output parameter of the function and that only the pointer to the memory location should be passed, not the value of the variable itself. ▪

The DBLibrary datatypes are actually typedefs and structures. What this means is that the datatypes aren't raw datatypes; they hold additional information accessible to the DBLibrary functions. Use of the DBLibrary datatypes improves the portability of programs because these datatypes are compiler and platform independent. In addition, the DBLibrary datatypes ensure that program data retrieved from and returned to the database will be compatible with Sybase datatypes.

CAUTION

Failure to use these datatypes could produce unexpected results and is definitely not recommended.

T I P   When using the following definition for an array of characters:

```
DBCHAR        Company_Name[81];
```

Always remember to define the variable one character greater than the length of the field defined in the database. This is especially important in C programs, because character strings are null-terminated ('\0'). Data returned from the database and bound to these variables could overwrite the memory allocated to adjoining variables. This will create unexpected results and could easily cause a General Protection Fault (GPF) or Application Exception (AE) in Windows.

In addition to your standard variables, you must define structures that will enable the program to log into and communicate with Sybase. You declare the logon and database processing structures within your program as follows:

```
DBPROCESS    *dbproc;
LOGINREC     *login;
```

N O T E   Because data within a relational database and data stored in structures (groups of one or more variables specified by the same name) are so similar, records retrieved from Sybase are typically moved into arrays of structures. Consequently, "child" data can be organized in substructures: arrays of structures declared as elements of other structures. This method improves program readability, simplifies future modifications, and keeps the relationships between database entities intact. ▪

Using DBLibrary to Create a Simple Program

Now let's look at an example of a C program using DBLibrary functions. In Listing 14.1, you can see a program that connects to Sybase System XI, creates a LOGINREC and a DBPROCESS, builds a query in the command buffer, sends the query to Sybase, executes the query, retrieves the results (one row at a time) from the row buffer, writes data to a file, closes the DBPROCESS, and disconnects from the server. I hope that the commands and concepts that have been presented so far will begin to come together when you read this code listing.

Listing 14.1 CHP14_01.C—First Sample Application Using DBLibrary with Sybase

```c
/***********************************************************/
/*  File Name: CHP14_01.C                                  */
/*  Description: Sample app. using C and DBLibrary         */
/*  ENVIRONMENT: SunOS 5.3                                 */
/*  Sybase 10.0                                            */
/***********************************************************/
#include        <sybfront.h>
#include        <sybdb.h>
#include        <syberror.h>
#include        <stdio.h>
#include        <stdlib.h>
#include        <string.h>


/***********************/
/* MAIN FUNCTION.      */
/***********************/
main()
{
    DBPROCESS       *dbproc1;
    LOGINREC        *login;
    FILE            *fp_out;
    FILE            *fp_error;

    DBCHAR          company[61]; /* Don't forget the extra character. */
    DBINT           count_calls;

    memset(company,'\0',sizeof(company));  /* Initialize memory to nulls. */

    fp_error = fopen("error_file","w");
    fp_out = fopen("out_file","w");

    if (dbinit() == FAIL)
    {
        exit(ERREXIT);
    }

    login = dblogin();
    DBSETLUSER(login, "my_username");       /* Set username for Dbproc. */
    DBSETLPWD(login, "my_password");        /* Set password for Dbproc. */
    DBSETLHOST(login, "Sybase_SERV");       /* Set server for Dbproc. */
```

continues

Part
III
Ch
14

Listing 14.1 Continued

```
    dbproc1 = dbopen(login, "Sybase_SERV");

    dbuse(dbproc1, "CALL_TRACKER");

    dbcmd(dbproc1, " select ");           /* Enter the SQL Statement   */
    dbcmd(dbproc1, " company_name, ");    /*  into the command buffer. */
    dbcmd(dbproc1, " number_of_calls ");
    dbcmd(dbproc1, " from COMPANY_CALLS ");

    dbsqlexec(dbproc1);

if (dbresults(dbproc1) == SUCCEED)       /* Test query for success. */
    {
        dbbind(dbproc1, 1, NTBSTRINGBIND, (DBINT)0, (BYTE *) company);
        dbbind(dbproc1, 2, INTBIND, (DBINT)0, (BYTE *) &count_calls);

        while (dbnextrow(dbproc1) != NO_MORE_ROWS)
        {
            fprintf(fp_out,"%s   %d\n",company,count_calls);
        }
    }
    else
    {
        fprintf(fp_error,"Sybase query for CALL RECORD unsuccessful !!!");
        dbcancel(dbproc1);
    }

    dbclose(dbproc1);

    printf("Program Completed.\n");

    dbexit();
    exit(0);
}
```

 You can output the information returned from the server directly to the screen by using dbprrow in place of dbnextrow. This method does not require binding columns to program variables with the dbbind command. For example, the previous example could print result rows to the screen by using the following code:

```
if (dbresults(dbproc1) == SUCCEED)
    {
    dbprrow(dbproc1);
    }
```

Compiling and Executing DBLibrary Programs

Compiling programs using DBLibrary functions is no different than compiling any other C program. However, you must make provisions for the DBLibrary functions, which will be linked to your programs. Therefore, when you compile your programs, you will use several compiler options to provide additional information. These options will depend on the specific compiler you are using.

A typical command to compile a C program using DBLibrary functions looks like this:

```
cc my_db_prog.c -I/sybase/include -L/sybase/lib -lsybdb -lm -lnsl -o my_db_prog
```

The options required to compile a C program using DBLibrary functions may vary depending on the operating system being used, the specific compiler, and which DBLibrary capabilities are being used. The command-line options used in the above compile statement are explained as follows:

- ▪ *-I*—Full path to the directory where the Sybase #include files are located
- ▪ *-L*—Full path to the directory containing Open Client Library functions
- ▪ *-l*—Instructs compiler to link with a specific object library (e.g., *libsybdb.a*)
- ▪ *-o*—Name of the executable program to be created

Handling Errors and Messages

DBLibrary automatically raises messages and errors returned from Sybase. These events will trigger the installed message- or error-handling function to execute. Host operating system errors will trigger execution of the error-handling function. Use the DBLibrary functions and dberrhandle after connecting to a server and opening your DBPROCESS. Once installed, the program will run the specified functions for the specific situation. For instance, the functions My_Error_Handler and My_Message_Handler could be set up to handle errors and messages after creating and opening DBPROCESS, as follows:

```
dberrhandle( My_Error_Handler );
dbmsghandle( My_Message_Handler );
```

Based on the specific errors that have occurred, the installed functions can determine whether to write an error message to the console/display and exit the program, or to write a message to a file, to repair any damage caused by the disruption, and to continue executing. You can either code your own functions or copy those provided in the Sybase example programs.

The following error handler in Listing 14.2 will be run when an error is returned from Sybase or the operating system. The file identified by the file pointer fp_error must be open for writing.

Listing 14.2   CHP14_02.C—A Simple Error Handler for Error Processing in Your Applications

```
/****************************************************************/
/*  File Name: CHP14_02.C                            */
/*  Description: Sample error handler for DBLibrary   */
/*  ENVIRONMENT: SunOS 5.3                           */
/*  Sybase 10.0                                      */
/****************************************************************/
```

continues

Listing 14.2 Continued

```
int   My_Error_Handler(DBPROCESS *proc, int severity, int dberr, int oserr,
   char * dberrstr, char * oserrstr)
{
char           sqlstatement[1201];

if (proc == NULL)     /* Check for Null DBPROCESS */
   { fprintf(fp_error, "DB process is null - %d\n", dberr);
     fflush(fp_error);     /* Flush output to file */
     return(INT_CANCEL);   /* Return with DBLibrary defined value. */
   }
else
   { if (DBDEAD(proc))    /* Check for Dead Process */
       { fprintf(fp_error, "DB process is dead - %d\n", dberr);
         fflush(fp_error);
         return(INT_CANCEL);
       }
     else
        { dbstrcpy(proc, 0, 1200, sqlstatement);
          fprintf(fp_error, "DBLibrary error: %d\n\t%s\n", dberr, dberrstr);
          fprintf(fp_error, "%s\n", sqlstatement); /* Print contents of the
                                         ** current command buffer.*/

          fflush(fp_error);

          if (oserr != DBNOERR)   /* Check for operating system error. */
             { fprintf(fp_error, "Operating-system error:\n\t%s\n", oserrstr);
               fflush(fp_error);
             }
          return(INT_CANCEL);
        }
   }
  return(0);
}
```

An installed error handler will be called when

- A syntax error occurs in a SQL command;
- A logon to the server fails;
- A DBLibrary function is used incorrectly;
- A server can no longer communicate with the client application;
- A server does not respond within the time-out period for a logon or an executed command;
- A fatal server error is raised.

The following message handler in Listing 14.3 will be run when Sybase returns a message to the program. The file identified by the file pointer fp_error must be open for writing.

Listing 14.3   CHP14_03.C—Trapping and Handling Messages Raised Through DBLibrary

```
/***********************************************************/
/*  File Name: CHP14_03.C                                  */
/*  Description: Sample message handler for DBLibrary      */
/*  ENVIRONMENT: SunOS 5.3                                 */
/*  Sybase 10.0                                            */
/***********************************************************/


int   My_Message_Handler(DBPROCESS *proc, DBINT msgno, int msgstate, int
   severity,
   char *msgtext, char *srvname, char *procname, DBUSMALLINT line)
{
char    sqlstatement[401];

fprintf (fp_error, "Message %ld, Level %d, State %d\n",
        msgno, severity, msgstate);   /* Print message info to file. */

dbstrcpy(proc, 0, 400, sqlstatement);
fprintf(fp_error, " SQL = %s\n", sqlstatement);

if (strlen(srvname) > 0)
       fprintf (fp_error, "Server '%s', ", srvname);
if (strlen(procname) > 0)
       fprintf (fp_error, "Procedure '%s', ", procname);
if (line > 0)
       fprintf (fp_error, "Line %d", line);

fprintf(fp_error, "\n\t%s\n", msgtext);   /* Print message to file. */
fflush(error);
return(0);
}
```

An installed message handler will be called when

- A syntax error occurs in a SQL command;
- A SQL error is raised;
- A DBPROCESS becomes deadlocked;
- A logon to the server fails;
- A Print command is executed on Sybase;
- A Use Database command is executed on Sybase;
- A fatal server error is raised.

 T I P It is recommended that errors and messages returned from Sybase be written to a file. Then use fflush to ensure that the information physically gets to the file.

Part

III

Ch

14

Executing Transact-SQL Commands with DBLibrary

DBLibrary enables programs to execute valid Transact-SQL commands on the server. Commands are placed in the command buffer, using dbcmd and dbfcmd; then they are executed on the server by using dbsqlexec followed by dbresults. Stored procedures can also be executed in this manner. Additionally, you can create objects in the database including permanent and temporary tables, indexes, and stored procedures. With very little effort, you could write a program to manage an interactive session to Sybase or Open Server.

Using DBLibrary Cursors

DBLibrary can emulate cursors. A cursor enables you to operate on database records one row at a time. In contrast to true Sybase cursors, DBLibrary tracks the rows in a result set on the client side. DBLibrary cursors enable your program to operate on data more freely than the browse mode capability, discussed in detail later. DBLibrary cursors can do things that Sybase cursors cannot, such as scrolling backwards through a result set. However, your program and Sybase will pay significant performance penalties for these additional capabilities. The primary restriction for using a cursor within your DBLibrary application is that you must have a unique key defined for the table or tables on which you are operating.

There are three types of cursors in DBLibrary: static, keyset-driven, and dynamic:

- **Static:** The result set returned by the cursor will not reflect any modifications made while the cursor is open.

- **Keyset-driven:** Changes made in the database are reflected in the result set. Specifically, uncommitted changes made by the cursor owner and committed changes by other users will be visible. Inserted and deleted rows do not affect the number of cursor rows returned. Therefore, the program may move the cursor either *relative* to the current row or to a specific (*absolute*) row number.

- **Dynamic:** Changes made to data will be reflected in the result set as it is being viewed. The cursor recognizes inserted and deleted rows; therefore, the program may move only the cursor relative to the current row.

 TIP It's easy to identify a function call being made that is working with a local cursor, because they all begin with the prefix dbcursor.

DBLibrary cursors enable the program to define concurrent use of the database when a cursor is opened, for example, when control locks are placed on database table pages. This is very important in a large-scale, multi-user database. Minimizing locks in the database must be considered a high priority when designing and coding your programs. The program should use the minimum level of locking required to run successfully.

The following DBLibrary functions are used for cursor manipulation:

dbcursoropen   Declares the cursor, sets several options (such as concurrency control), and opens the cursor for use.

Returns: Handle to the cursor or NULL (indicating that the open failed)

dbcursorinfo   Gets row (keyset) and column information for a cursor.

Returns: SUCCEED or FAIL

dbcursorcolinfo   Gets information for a specific column returned by a cursor.

Returns: SUCCEED or FAIL

dbcursorbind   Binds a cursor column to a program variable.

Returns: SUCCEED or FAIL

dbcursorfetch   Fetches the next cursor row, placing column data into program variables.

Returns: SUCCEED or FAIL

dbcursor   Manipulates data on the server through the fetch buffer.

Returns: SUCCEED or FAIL

dbcursorclose   Closes the DBLibrary cursor.

Returns: Nothing

Executing Remote Stored Procedures with DBLibrary

The capability to run remote stored procedures is referred to as an RPC. An RPC enables a DBPROCESS connected to one server to execute a stored procedure located on another server. Stored procedures located on the server that a DBPROCESS is connected to may also be run using an RPC. There are three functions that DBLibrary programs must use when executing remote stored procedures. Once a remote stored procedure has been successfully executed, you can use the standard DBLibrary functions to retrieve and process the information returned. RPC functions are similar to the functions used for regular communications with the server.

N O T E   The remote stored procedure functions all begin with the prefix dbrpc.

dbrpcinit   Initializes the RPC for a specific DPROCESS (i.e., define the stored procedure to be executed). This function is similar to dbcmd.

Returns: SUCCEED or FAIL

dbrpcparam   Adds parameters to be passed to the RPC. Analogous to using dbfcmd to insert variables into the where clause of a Transact-SQL command.

Returns: SUCCEED or FAIL

dbrpcsend   Sends the remote stored procedure call to the server to which the DBPROCESS is connected, and execute it on the remote server. This function is similar to dbsqlsend.

Returns: SUCCEED or FAIL

Part
III

Ch

14

Several standard DBLibrary commands are typically used to retrieve and process data from the server: `dbsqlok`, `dbresults`, and `dbnextrow`.

The following sample code demonstrates the use of the RPC functions:

```
if (dbrpcinit(dbproc, "SERVER_NAME.dbname.owner.stored_proc_name",
   (DBSMALLINT)0) == FAIL)
   {
    fprintf(fp_error,"dbrpcinit failed for stored_procedure.\n");
    return -1;
   }

if (dbrpcparam(dbproc, "@proc_parameter_name", (BYTE)0, SYBCHAR, -1, 1,
   company) == FAIL)
   {
    fprintf(fp_error,"dbrpcparam(1) failed for stored_procedure\n");
    return -1;
   }

if (dbrpcsend(dbproc) == FAIL)
   {
    fprintf(fp_error,"dbrpcsend failed for stored_procedure\n");
    return -1;
   }

if (dbsqlok(dbproc) == FAIL)
   {
    fprintf(fp_error,"dbsqlok failed for stored_procedure\n");
    return -1;
   }

while (dbresults(dbproc) == SUCCEED)
   {
    dbbind(dbproc, 1, NTBSTRINGBIND, (DBINT)0, (BYTE *) company);
    dbbind(dbproc, 2, INTBIND, (DBINT)0, (BYTE *) &count_num_calls);

    while (dbnextrow(dbproc) != NO_MORE_ROWS)
       {
         /* Process results one row at a time. */
       }
   }
```

Understanding Additional DBLibrary Functions

There are several groups of functions within DBLibrary that provide support to Sybase capabilities:

- **Bulk copy:** The bulk copy utility can be operated using DBLibrary functions. All DBLibrary bulk copy functions begin with the prefix `bcp_`. The DBLibrary bulk copy capability provides the speed and functionality of BCP with the control that complex database loads typically require.

- **Two-phase commit:** Two-phase commit functions enable DBLibrary to simultaneously update data located on different servers. The two-phase commit functions have no specific prefix.

- **Browse mode:** Browse mode enables DBLibrary programs to retrieve data one record at a time, to analyze the information, to modify the information, and to update that specific record. There are several restrictions involved with browse mode: It requires two DBPROCESS structures: one for reading, and another for updating.

Troubleshooting DBLibrary Programs

As with any code, programs do not always do what you want them to do; they nonetheless tend to execute exactly as you have coded them. You must carefully design your programs to handle situations introduced by the database interface and client/server communications. Rather than attempt to enumerate all possible error conditions that could be encountered, I recommend that you take a proactive approach and use all the information that is available for the DBLibrary functions. In particular, you may want to think about the following points:

- Install error and message handlers. You can use the examples that have been provided or write your own. Providing more information to the program reduces the guesswork involved in debugging and troubleshooting.

- Make sure that you understand exactly what a DBLibrary function does before using it.

- Ensure that the command buffer and result buffer have been cleared after you are done with a command batch, especially when an error has occurred. Attempting to use a DBPROCESS while results are pending will cause an error.

- Remember that the DBLibrary cannot perform any Sybase functions that you cannot perform through ISQL. All privileges and roles continue to be enforced.

TIP

Most DBLibrary functions return information to the DBPROCESS structure. This information typically indicates the results of the interaction with Sybase. For example, dbinit can return either SUCCEED or FAIL.

It is a good practice to always execute these functions within a conditional statement. For example:

```
if (dbinit() == FAIL)
{
    printf("Sybase Error: dbinit returned FAIL\n");
    exit(ERREXIT)
}
```

Taking advantage of the information that the DBLibrary functions return will make testing and debugging easier, as you will decrease the amount of time spent troubleshooting when the system is in the target production environment.

Part

III

Ch

14

Using Client Library

The Sybase's Client Library is quite similar to DBLibrary. Both consist of functions which are callable from within a program. In fact, they contain many functions that serve the same purpose. Client Library applications provide a generic means of accessing any server, including those requiring a gateway application to translate between non-compatible clients and servers.

Client Library was introduced with Sybase System 10 as the initial version of the new programming interface that is sometimes referred to as *CTLib*. The current version of Client Library is 10.0.3, with various EBFs depending on operating system platform. The added ability to directly use server-side (*native*) cursors with Sybase 10.0 is unique to Client Library applications. Cursors enable you to operate on database records one row at a time, typically referred to as the *current row*. As previously stated, Client Library cursors are different from DBLibrary cursors.

▶ **See** "Using Sybase Cursors," **p. 315**

If you are just now selecting a programming interface for your RDBMS, Client Library is an excellent choice. Client Library has been developed around the System 10 database capabilities, as opposed to DBLibrary, which is limited to buffering result sets. Client Library has simplified many of the capabilities that were added to DBLibrary over time. For example, SQL statements and remote procedure calls can be sent to Sybase using the same Client Library command, whereas in DBLibrary, you are expected to code them differently. The introduction of cursors in Sybase System 10 has greatly improved client/server coordination. Although DBLibrary can now emulate cursors, DBLibrary's functionality was originally developed to compensate for the lack of cursors and doesn't interact with the new cursors that are built into the server very well.

High-level design of client programs will be similar for both Client Library and DBLibrary. The basic nested approach described earlier should be implemented for both applications. Similar functions are available in both libraries for connecting to Sybase, creating structures to communicate with the database, issuing requests to the server, and retrieving information from the server. After that, however, the two APIs diverge as to specific interaction with the server and the methods of manipulating data.

Client Library also differs from DBLibrary in that you may write application programs to communicate with servers other than Sybase. Therefore, it is notable that Client Library will not enforce database rules specific to Sybase. You should design your program to accommodate all the servers that it might possibly encounter, but coding will typically favor the specific production server for which the program is being developed.

N O T E At runtime, your Client Library program will be able to access information about the specific server to which it is interfacing using the `ct_capability` function. ∎

Client Library programs can also make calls to Client/Server-Library functions. CS-Library functions provide utilities that are common to application programs for clients and servers. In particular, CS-Library is required by all Client Library programs to allocate and de-allocate a context structure. A context structure holds information required to connect to a server, and has some of the elements of DBLibrary's `DBPROCESS` structure. The main difference is that with a context structure, you can have multiple contexts on the server per connection to the database server that enables you to process and work with data without the need for multiple connections to the server. You can use the following statement to define a global context structure for a Client Library program:

```
CS_CONTEXT    *context;
```

Instead of using DBPROCESS, Client Library uses CS_COMMAND structures to send commands and retrieve result sets from Sybase. Also, Client Library programs use a connection structure (CS_CONNECTION) in place of the LOGINREC used by DBLibrary.

You can define structures for connecting to Sybase System XI and maintaining commands that will be sent to the server like this:

```
CS_CONNECTION    *connection;
CS_COMMAND       *command;
```

 TIP All Client/Server Library (CS Library) functions are prefixed with cs_, which makes them easy to spot in some application code!

Understanding the Basic Client Library Functions

As you have probably guessed, the Client Library functions are very similar to the DBLibrary functions covered in the previous section. Client Library functions are easy to identify in a program because they all begin with the prefix ct_.

To access the Client Library functions through the C prototype definitions, you must use the C header file <ctpublic.h> and include it in each of your applications.

Like the descriptions of functions in the previous section on DBLibrary, what follows is a list of the most commonly used Client Library functions.

cs_ctx_alloc (CS-Library) Allocates the CS_CONTEXT structure. *Allocation* refers to retrieving the required amount of space from the client's memory, where the structures of data will be stored. The context structure will hold information required for your program to connect to and communicate with a server. Although cs_ctx_alloc is not a Client Library function, it is required for Client Library programs.

Returns: CS_SUCCEED, CS_FAIL, or CS_MEM_ERROR

ct_init Initialize the Client Library interface, which is like DBLibrary's dbinit. You call ct_init after allocating a context structure, but it must be the first Client Library function called within a program, or you will get an error on subsequent Client Library calls.

Returns: CS_SUCCEED, CS_MEM_ERROR, or CS_FAIL

ct_callback Installs a user-created callback function to be executed for a specific type of callback (e.g., server message or client message). Additionally, this function can be used to retrieve the address of a callback function that has already been installed.

Returns: CS_SUCCEED, CS_FAIL, or CS_BUSY

ct_con_alloc Allocates a structure to store information about a specific connection (CS_CONNECTION).

Returns: CS_SUCCEED or CS_FAIL

Part
III

Ch
14

ct_con_props   Sets or retrieves properties stored in the CS_CONNECTION structure.

Returns: CS_SUCCEED, CS_FAIL, or CS_BUSY

ct_connect   Connects the executing program to a server using the information stored in the CS_CONNECTION structure.

Returns: CS_SUCCEED, CS_FAIL, CS_PENDING, or CS_BUSY

ct_cmd_alloc   Allocates a CS_COMMAND structure. The connection does not have to be opened to successfully allocate this structure, which the program will use to manage commands sent to the server.

Returns: CS_SUCCEED, CS_FAIL, or CS_BUSY

ct_command   Sets up (initiates) a command in preparation of its being sent to the server. The command may be one of several types. For example, a Transact-SQL statement is a *language command*, whereas the name of a stored procedure located on another server is defined as an *RPC command*.

Returns: CS_SUCCEED, CS_FAIL, or CS_BUSY

TIP   The ct_command API simplifies the database interfacing required to the server. If you use ct_command, you don't have to parse the statement that is about to be compiled in order to determine whether it's an RPC or a regular Transact-SQL statement—ct_command does this for you.

ct_send   Sends a command to a server once it has been initiated using the ct_command function.

Returns: CS_SUCCEED, CS_FAIL, CS_CANCELED, CS_PENDING, or CS_BUSY

ct_bind   Binds a column returned from Sybase to a program variable (defined using the Client Library typedefs).

Returns: CS_SUCCEED, CS_FAIL, or CS_BUSY

ct_results   Prepares result data for processing by the program. The result data consists of the information returned by the server. Multiple commands sent to the server in a batch can return several types of result data (e.g., regular rows of data or cursor rows).

Returns: CS_SUCCEED, CS_END_RESULTS, CS_FAIL, CS_CANCELED, CS_PENDING, or CS_BUSY

ct_cancel   Sends a message to server instructing it to cancel the command being executed. Three types of cancellation may be issued from the program:

CS_CANCEL_ALL causes the current command to be terminated and discards all result data.

CS_CANCEL_ATTN causes the current command to be terminated. Results cannot be read by the program even though they will not be discarded until another result set is returned from the server.

CS_CANCEL_CURRENT causes the results returned from the current command to be discarded.

Returns: CS_SUCCEED, CS_FAIL, CS_CANCELED, CS_PENDING, CS_BUSY, or CS_TRYING

N O T E Using the CS_CANCEL_ALL or CS_CANCEL_ATTN type of cancel could affect the connection's cursor(s), so take care that you don't issue it arbitrarily unless you are in an error-processing routine and you are trying to clean up the user's environment and database connection.

ct_fetch   Fetches the result set returned from a command executed by Sybase. Use ct_fetch within a while loop to ensure complete processing of results returned from the server.

Returns: CS_SUCCEED, CS_END_DATA, CS_ROW_FAIL, CS_FAIL, CS_CANCELED, CS_PENDING, or CS_BUSY

ct_cmd_drop   De-allocates a command structure (CS_COMMAND).

Returns: CS_SUCCEED, CS_FAIL, or CS_BUSY

ct_close   Closes a connection to a server.

Returns: CS_SUCCEED, CS_FAIL, CS_PENDING, or CS_BUSY

ct_con_drop   De-allocates a connection structure (CS_CONNECTION).

Returns: CS_SUCCEED, CS_FAIL, or CS_BUSY

ct_exit   Terminates Client Library.

Returns: CS_SUCCEED or CS_FAIL

cs_ctx_drop (CS-Library)   De-allocates a context structure (CS_CONTEXT).

Returns: CS_SUCCEED or CS_FAIL

N O T E Remember to explicitly complete all command processing and close any server connections; otherwise, cs_ctx_drop will fail.

As with DBLibrary, there is a logical grouping of commands. You should structure your programs using the following "nested" format:

```
Allocate a context structure( cs_ctx_alloc )
  Initialize Client Library( ct_init )
  Install error and message handlers( ct_callback )
    Connect to Sybase System XI( ct_con_alloc, ct_con_props, ct_connect )
      Allocate command structures( ct_cmd_alloc )
        Send commands to Sybase( ct_command, ct_send )
          Retrieve data( ct_results, ct_bind, ct_fetch )
            Process the results on the client
          Clean up after using CS_COMMAND( ct_cancel )
      De-allocate command structure( ct_cmd_drop )
    Close connection to Sybase( ct_close )
    De-allocate the connection structure( ct_con_drop )
  Terminate Client Library( ct_exit )
De-allocate context structure( cs_ctx_drop )
```

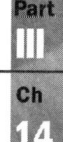

Part
III

Ch
14

Declaring Variables for Use by Client Library Functions

Variables used by Client Library functions should be declared using the Client Library-defined datatypes. These datatypes are defined in the <ctpublic.h> header file, which you must include in all Client Library programs. In Table 14.3, you can see a cross-reference between Client Library program variable types and Sybase column types that will help you use the correct Client Library variable datatype definitions in your programs.

Table 14.3 Cross-Reference of Sybase Datatypes and Client Library Program Variable Types

Sybase Datatype	Client Library Program Variable Type
Binary	CS_BINARY
Bit	CS_BIT
Char	CS_CHAR
Datetime	CS_DATETIME
Decimal	CS_DECIMAL
Float	CS_FLOAT
Image	CS_IMAGE
Int	CS_INT
Money	CS_MONEY
Numeric	CS_NUMERIC
Real	CS_REAL
Smalldatetime	CS_DATETIME4
Smallint	CS_SMALLINT
Smallmoney	CS_MONEY4
Text	CS_TEXT
Tinyint	CS_TINYINT
Varbinary	CS_BINARY
Varchar	CS_CHAR

An example of using the Client Library program variable datatypes would look like this:

```
CS_CHAR    Company_Name[61];
CS_INT     Count_Calls;
CS_FLOAT   Total_Hours;
```

Using Client Library to Create a Simple Program

In this section, you will see an example of a C program using Client Library functions. In Listing 14.4, the application connects to Sybase System XI server, creates the required structures (CS_CONTEXT, CS_CONNECTION, and CS_COMMAND), builds a query in the command buffer, sends the query to Sybase, executes the query, retrieves the results (one row at a time) from the row buffer, writes data to a file, closes the structures, and disconnects from Sybase.

Listing 14.4 CHP14_04.C—Using Client Library API Calls to Create a Simple Application

```
/***********************************************************/
/*  File Name: CHP14_04.C                                  */
/*  Description: Sample app. using C and Client Library    */
/*  ENVIRONMENT: SunOS 5.3                                 */
/*  Sybase 10.0                                            */
/***********************************************************/
#include      <stdio.h>
#include      <stdlib.h>
#include      <string.h>
#include      <ctpublic.h>


CS_CONTEXT    *ctxt;

/***********************/
/* MAIN FUNCTION.      */
/***********************/
main()
{
   CS_CONNECTION    *conn1;
   CS_COMMAND       *cmd;
   FILE             *fp_out;
   FILE             *fp_error;

   char              *sql_command;

   CS_DATAFMT        cols[100];

   CS_INT            f_datalength[100];
   CS_SMALLINT       f_indicator[100];
   CS_INT            f_count;
   CS_RETCODE        f_return;
   CS_CHAR           company[61];
   CS_INT            count_calls;

   CS_RETCODE        result_type;

   memset(company,'\0',sizeof(company));  /* Initialize memory to NULLs. */

   fp_error = fopen("error_file","w");
   fp_out = fopen("out_file","w");
```

continues

Part

III

Ch

14

Listing 14.4   Continued

```
cs_ctx_alloc(CS_VERSION_100, &ctxt);

if (ct_init(ctxt, CS_VERSION_100) != CS_SUCCEED)
{
    exit(-1);
}

ct_con_alloc(ctxt, &conn1);
ct_con_props(conn1, CS_SET, CS_USERNAME,
             "my_username", CS_NULLTERM, NULL);
ct_con_props(conn1, CS_SET, CS_PASSWORD,
             "my_password", CS_NULLTERM, NULL);
ct_con_props(conn1, CS_SET, CS_HOSTNAME,
             "Sybase_SERV", CS_NULLTERM, NULL);

ct_connect(conn1, "Sybase_SERV", CS_NULLTERM);

ct_cmd_alloc(conn1, &cmd);

strcpy(sql_command, " select company_name, number_of_calls from \
                     CALL_TRACKER.dbo.COMPANY_CALLS ");

ct_command(cmd, CS_LANG_CMD, sql_command, CS_NULLTERM, CS_UNUSED);

ct_send(cmd);

while (ct_results(cmd, &result_type) == SUCCEED)
{
    cols[0].datatype = CS_CHAR_TYPE;
    cols[0].format = CS_FMT_NULLTERM;
    cols[0].maxlength = 60;
    cols[0].count = 1;
    cols[0].locale = NULL;
    ct_bind(cmd, 1, &cols[0], company, &f_datalength[0],
            &f_indicator[0]);

    cols[1].datatype = CS_INT_TYPE;
    cols[1].format = CS_FMT_UNUSED;
    cols[1].maxlength = 0;
    cols[1].count = 1;
    cols[1].locale = NULL;
    ct_bind(cmd, 2, &cols[1], &count_calls, &f_datalength[1],
            &f_indicator[1]);

    if (result_type = CS_ROW_RESULT)
    {
        while (ct_fetch(cmd, CS_UNUSED, CS_UNUSED, CS_UNUSED, &f_count)
               == CS_SUCCEED)
        {
            fprintf(fp_out,"%s    %d\n",company,count_calls);
        }
    }
}
```

```
    ct_cmd_drop(cmd);
    ct_close(conn1, CS_UNUSED);
    ct_con_drop(conn1);
    ct_exit(ctxt, CS_UNUSED);
    cs_ctx_drop(ctxt);

    exit(0);
}
```

Compiling and Executing Client Library Programs

Compiling programs using Client Library functions is no different than compiling any other C program. As with DBLibrary, you must make provisions for the Client Library functions, which will be linked to your programs. Therefore, when you compile your programs, you will use several compiler options to provide additional information. These options will depend on the specific compiler you are using.

A typical command to compile a C program using Client Library functions looks like this:

```
cc my_ct_prog.c -I/sybase/include -L/sybase/lib -lct -lcs \
 -ltcl -lm -lnsl -o my_ct_prog
```

The options required to compile a C program using Client Library functions may vary depending on the operating system being used, on the specific compiler, and on what Client Library capabilities are being used. The command-line options used in the above compile statement are explained as follows:

- ▪ -I—Full path to the directory where the Sybase #include files are located
- ▪ -L—Full path to the directory containing object Client Library functions
- ▪ -l—Instructs compiler to link with a specific object library (e.g., *libsybdb.a*)
- ▪ -o—Name of the executable program to be created.

Handling Errors and Messages

Unlike the DBLibrary message and error handlers, Client Library recognizes callback events that are triggered either internally or by the server. Client Library automatically calls installed functions based on the type of callback event. There are several different types of callbacks and they can be triggered by the client, the server, and the operating system. You use the Client Library function ct_callback to install your own functions for a specific type of callback. Once installed, the program will run that function when Client Library recognizes the callback event. For instance, the function My_Callback_Handler could be set up to run when a server message callback event is received:

```
ct_callback(context, connection, CS_SET, CS_SERVERMSG_CB,
  (CS_VOID *)My_Callback_Handler);
```

Client Library programs may optionally use in-line message handling to check for errors and messages with the ct_diag function. A single connection to a server can use both callbacks and in-line message handling, but not at the same time.

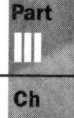

Part

III

Ch

14

Executing Transact-SQL Commands with Client Library

Client Library enables programs to execute any valid Transact-SQL command. Commands are placed in the command buffer by using `ct_command` function and then executed on the server using `ct_send` followed by `ct_results` to return result information. All information returned from Sybase is bound to program variables and then stored in the variables (using `ct_bind` and `ct_fetch`). The Client Library functions enable the program to send multiple commands to the server and process them based on the type of data returned: result set, result status, or cursor row.

Using Cursors in Client Library Applications

Server cursors were new with Sybase System 10. Simply put, a cursor is a server's "place-holder" for data being returned to a client. Row buffering, in which the client receives the data as a batch of one or more rows, is still utilized in Client Library; however, the client and the server maintain the concept of a *current row*. The *current row* can be manipulated (deleted or updated) by the client's issuing a command to the server. Because of this coordination between client and server, modification of the *current row* becomes quite easy.

There are two types of cursors that a Client Library application may use to retrieve data from a server: language-based cursors and Client Library-based cursors. Both are native Sybase cursors, as opposed to DBLibrary's emulated cursors.

Language-based cursors are declared within a `ct_command` statement. Language-based cursors are those that you manually declare with Transact-SQL statements, such as `Declare Cursor` and then open using `Open Cursor`. Because you are opening and managing these cursors yourself, you may define several cursors per command in this manner, and then use `ct_fetch` to return a regular result set. Therefore, this data is not received as cursor rows by the application program.

Client Library-based cursors are explicitly declared at the rate of one per command structure using the `ct_cursor` function. The advantage of Client Library-based cursors is that they enable the program to perform data manipulation as they navigate through a result set. Additionally, these cursors manage the locks placed on the data currently being read.

Both of these *server-side* cursors are limited to forward-only processing of the data returned due to the underlying limitations of Sybase's cursor implementation.

You can define Client Library-based cursors as either `For Update` or `Read Only`. Updatable cursors enable the program to modify columns in the database for the *current row* being read. For data integrity, specific columns can be set as not updatable.

Executing Remote Stored Procedures

Client Library programs can initiate remote stored procedure commands using the `ct_command` function. Two functions, `ct_remote_pwd` and `ct_param`, are required to set remote server passwords and pass parameters. There are very few differences between executing remote stored procedures and standard Transact-SQL commands from Client Library.

Using SQR

Structured Query Report writer is an application programming interface for creating reports and performing data manipulation. As with DBLibrary and Client Library, you can use SQR to create applications to interface with Sybase System XI. Even though SQR has undergone major improvements in the past few years, it is cumbersome for creating large applications, and is definitely *not* recommended for general purpose application development. However, SQR excels as a report-generating tool. In fact, it is easy to develop simple or complex reports with very little coding. The major benefits of SQR are as follows:

- SQR is very easy to learn.
- Reports are very simple to develop.
- Reports operate on multiple DBMSs, such as Oracle, Sybase, and Informix.
- Reports operate on multiple platforms, such as Windows 3.1, Windows NT, and UNIX.
- Reports operate over a client/server architecture.

SQR can execute all SQL commands and includes its own procedural language. The main difference between SQR and the previously discussed programming interfaces is that SQR programs are interpreted, not compiled. Actually, SQR is a program which runs commands from ASCII report files. You can write and edit your report files in any editor capable of outputting standard ASCII format. You then use SQR to execute the commands in your report files.

If you want to find out more information about SQR, then the best place to look is at MITI's home page on the World Wide Web at **http://www.miti.com**.

Understanding the Basics of SQR

SQR is an easy-to-learn report-writing and file-generating tool that can create simple or complex reports with very little code. SQR is one of the best report writers on the market for large volumes of data processing, given its internal speed and performance that is optimized for various operating systems, as well as the way in which it compiles dynamic stored procedures for some of the work directly on the Sybase server. Besides reports and data manipulation, you can use SQR to create interactive querying programs.

In addition to its stand-alone capabilities, SQR can be called from other programs, by execution from the command line. It uses database cursors (when available) to retrieve data; it can perform several SQL statements concurrently; and it can create SQL statements dynamically.

Understanding the Sections of an SQR Report

SQR executes commands from report files that you create. Report files are logically broken up into five sections:

- SETUP
- REPORT
- HEADING

Part
III

Ch
14

- ■ FOOTING

- ■ PROCEDURE

An entire SQR program could consist of only the REPORT section. Of course, for purposes of readability, reliability, and maintenance, you will typically declare procedures to perform specific tasks as your programs grow in size and complexity.

 Another way of thinking about a section within an SQR report is as analogous to one paragraph of a document. In fact, you will see paragraph, section, and even block used interchangeably when talking about an SQR report's sections.

Understanding the SETUP Section   The SETUP section of a report file describes report characteristics. You can prompt the user for information, define the size of the report, set printer specifications, and execute SQL paragraphs. A typical SETUP section would look like this:

```
! Report Setup section
begin-setup
page-size 60 80      ! 60 lines, 80 columns per line
use CALL_TRACKER     ! Important, only for Sybase System XI
ask eff_date 'Enter Effective Date of Report'
end-setup
```

This example of a SETUP section defines a page size of 60 lines and 80 columns per line, informs SQR of the database to use, and prompts the user to enter an effective date. The variable eff_date is referenced within the REPORT and PROCEDURE sections as {eff_date}.

 You can issue the Sybase Use Database command only within the SETUP section of your report file. In other words, you cannot issue this command inside a SQL paragraph. To reference an object in another database (located on the same server), you must use a fully qualified object name. For example: database2.dbo.clients.

Understanding the REPORT Section   The REPORT section of the report file is equivalent to the main( ) function in a C program. For simple reports, you could place all SQL paragraphs and print statements in the REPORT section, but it is a good practice to break tasks down to individual procedures because this makes the code more readable and reusable later on. Building on your previous example, your report file would begin to look something like this:

```
! Report Setup section
begin-setup
page-size 60 80
use CALL_TRACKER
ask eff_date 'Enter Effective Date of Report'
end-setup

! Main Reporting section
begin-report
do preliminary      ! Instructions to run procedures
do write_report     !    that you will write.
do clean-up
end-report
```

TIP Comments can be inserted into report files using an exclamation point (!) as the designator.

SQR programs will always run commands in the SETUP section first. Then, SQR will execute the REPORT section. In the example, the do command is used to run three procedures: preliminary, write_report, and clean-up. You will define these procedures in the PROCEDURE section.

Understanding the PROCEDURE Section The PROCEDURE section will typically hold most of your work. You may write as many procedures as you require. You could define the three procedures for your example as follows:

```
begin-procedure preliminary          ! PROCEDURE preliminary
show 'Example report file'           ! Write to screen
show 'effective date ' {eff_date}
end-procedure

begin-procedure write_report         ! PROCEDURE write_report
position (2,0)                       ! Set current position to line 2
begin-select                         ! Select from Sybase
 company_name (+1, 2, 60)
 phone_number (0, 0, 14) edit (999) 999-9999
from COMPANY
order by company_name
end-select
end-procedure

begin-procedure clean_up             ! PROCEDURE clean_up
show 'Done with example report file.'
end-procedure
```

Now the example actually does something! It writes a message to the user that it is running (in procedure preliminary); then it prints data to the report file (in procedure write_report); finally, it informs the user that it has completed (in procedure clean_up). The variable &phone_number will be formatted so as to look like a phone number, instead of just numbers. For instance, (555) 555-1111 will appear in the report instead of 5555551111.

N O T E In the procedure write_report, you probably noticed the numbers in parentheses following the columns selected from the COMPANY table. These are called *position qualifiers*. Position qualifiers instruct SQR to output data to your report starting at a specific position. The numbers inside the parentheses represent, respectively: line number, column number, and data length. By using position qualifiers, you do not have to create your report one line at a time from top to bottom. You can also use position qualifiers in the PRINT command, like this:

```
print $company_city (12, 7, 30)
```

The *current position* on the report is the line and the column of the position immediately following the last character printed on the report. For example, after executing the previous command, the current position would be line 12, column 37. A zero (0) position qualifier for the line or column instructs SQR to print beginning at the current line or current column. A zero used in the length field instructs SQR to print the actual length of the data in the specified SQR variable. You can also specify line and column position qualifiers relative to the current position. For example, the command:

Part
III

Ch
14

continues

continued

```
print $company_state (0, +2, 0)
```

would print the entire contents of the variable $company_state on the current line two columns after the current column. ■

Understanding the HEADING Section   For reports requiring a heading for each page, you use the HEADING section to define what and where SQR will place information. You define the number of heading lines in the begin-heading line. To add a simple three-line heading to a report, you would add the following to the SQR report file:

```
begin-heading 3                         ! HEADING will be 3 lines long
  string 'Company Names/Phone Numbers as of ' {eff_date} by ''
     into $rpt_title
  print $rpt_title (2) center           ! Print $rpt_title to primary report
end-heading
```

Using the string command, you have appended the variable {eff_date} to a literal string and placed it all into a text variable $rpt_title. The variable $rpt_title will be centered on line 2 of the heading.

Understanding the FOOTING Section   The FOOTING section is very similar to the HEADING section. To add a simple one-line footer to each page, you would add the following to the SQR script file:

```
begin-footing 1                         ! FOOTING will be 1 line
  page-number (60, 65, 0) 'Page '       ! Put page number in bottom right
end-footing
```

The report will now have the page number (printed as 'Page n') on the last line, beginning in column 65 of each page.

Using Variables in SQR

You can create global and local variables to store and manipulate your data. The datatype of a variable within your report file is identified by special characters:

- Text variables begin with $.
- Numeric variables (integer and decimal) begin with #.
- Marker location variables (used within BEGIN-DOCUMENT paragraphs) begin with @.
- Data retrieved from the database in a SELECT paragraph begins with &.

Unlike the programming library functions you have covered, variables are not explicitly declared in SQR. To create a new variable, you have to use it only in your report file. The following rules apply to all variables in SQR:

- Unless specifically made local, all variables are global.
- Variables are automatically initialized when they are first declared or used. (Numbers are set to 0; text variables are set to NULL.)
- Variable names can be of any length.

- Variable names are case-insensitive.
- The length of a character string stored in a text variable is device-dependent.
- All numbers are stored as double-precision floating point.

CAUTION

Variables in SQR are not declared. Therefore, if you copy a character string into a variable called $company_name, but then print a report with a variable called $compnay_name, your program will not work correctly, but will also not incur an error. Keep in mind that simply using a variable declares that variable if it does not already exist.

Using Global Variables   Variables that you create within report files are automatically available throughout the entire report. In other words, everything not specifically made a local variable is global.

There are several predefined variables that are global within all report files. SQR provides information as to the status of interactions with the database and statistics on the report being created. For example, #sql-count lets you know how many rows have been affected by a SQL paragraph in the database; #page-count lets you know on which page the program is currently writing data.

Using Local Variables   There are two methods of creating local variables within your PROCEDUREs. You may either declare a PROCEDURE as LOCAL, or pass information as arguments to your procedures. For example:

```
...
do write_error_msg
...
begin-procedure write_error_msg LOCAL
  string "An Error Has Occurred." into $err_msg
  show $err_msg
end-procedure

do local_calc(2, 5, #total)
...
begin-procedure local_calc(#num_1, #num_2, :#num_total)
  #num_total = #num_1 + #num_2
end-procedure
```

Procedure write_error_msg uses a text variable, $err_msg, which is not visible to the rest of the report file. Procedure local_calc will add the arguments passed as input, and return the output argument #num_total. Output arguments are preceded by a colon (:) in the BEGIN-PROCEDURE command.

To access a global variable from within a local procedure, place a "_" between the identifier (i.e., $, #, or &) and the variable name. For example, $_company_name would refer to the global variable $company_name within a local procedure.

Part

III

Ch

14

Using Arrays in SQR   You can create arrays of variables using the CREATE-ARRAY command as follows:

```
CREATE-ARRAY name=companies size=1000
     field=name:char
     field=id_number:number
```

The preceding declaration creates an array called companies with 1,000 instances or array elements. Each instance consists of a character field—name—and a number field—id_number.

An array in SQR is very similar to the structures available in many high-order languages. However, in SQR, you cannot directly access the data stored in an array. You must manipulate the array using the PUT and GET commands, like this:

```
PUT $company_name #id into companies(#i)
GET $company_name #id from companies(#i)
```

The PUT command inserts data ($company_name and #id) into the elements identified by #i of the companies array. The GET command reads data from the elements identified by #i of the companies array into $company_name and #id.

Creating Output from Report Files

Every SQR report file will create a primary report. You write information to the primary report using the PRINT command like this:

```
print 'SQR is easy to understand !' (+1, 20)
```

You can specify a file name for your primary report when SQR executes a report file by using the -F flag. For example, you could instruct SQR to create a report file with the name *sample.txt* as follows:

```
SQR report_2.sqr username/password -Fsample.txt
```

In addition to the primary report created when you execute SQR report files, you can create and read operating system files. Only 12 files may be opened at one time; however, you can CLOSE files when you are done with them and OPEN others as required. To OPEN an existing file called *calls.dat*, you would use the following command:

```
open 'calls.dat' as 1 for-reading record=100:vary status=#openstat
```

The preceding OPEN command makes the file *calls.dat* accessible within the report file for reading only. You have selected '1' as your identifier within the report file, and indicated that records read from the file are variable in length, and that they can be a maximum of 100 characters. Finally, the numeric variable #openstat will either be 0 (success) or –1 (fail) when SQR attempts to open *calls.dat*.

> **CAUTION**
>
> For variable length record files, SQR will ignore data beyond the length specified in the OPEN command for that file.

If you do not specify a variable to accept the status returned from the OPEN command, an open failure will cause the execution of your report file to halt. As long as you are returning the status of the OPEN command to a variable, you may continue processing and inform the user of a problem as follows:

```
if #openstat = -1
 show 'Could not open file for reading!'
 stop                 ! HALT execution of report file.
end-if
```

More complex report files will typically create several output files. To OPEN a new file called *calls.out*, you would use the following command:

```
open 'calls.out' as 2 for-writing record=80 status=#openstat
```

You have seen that the PRINT command inserts information into your primary report. To put information into the other files you are creating, you need to use the WRITE command. The syntax for writing information to *'calls.out'* would look something like this:

```
write 2 from $company_name:60
```

To close a system file, use the CLOSE command, like this:

```
close 2
```

The file, identified within the report file as ', will no longer be accessible after it is closed.

Issuing DML and DDL Commands in SQR

Data manipulation language commands can be executed from the REPORT section or from a procedure. Select statements are issued with the following syntax:

```
begin-select
company_name
from company
end-select
```

The data returned from Sybase will be stored in the column variable &company_name by default. To alter the bound variable, you can specify it in the Select statement. For example:

```
begin-select
company_name &company_name_text
from company
end-select
```

In this case, the data will be stored in the variable &company_name_text. You can perform operations on each row returned from a result set by placing commands between the last column selected and the FROM clause, like this:

```
begin-select
company_name &company_name_text
 print &company_name_text (10, 7, 0)
from company
end-select
```

Update and insert commands can be issued in a `begin-sql` paragraph. Inserting a new row of data into the company table would be done like this:

```
begin-sql
insert into company (name, id_number)
values(_$name, #id_number)
end-sql
```

More than one SQL command can be issued in the same paragraph, but they must be separated by a semicolon (;) and each command must begin on a new line. Therefore, if you wanted to commit after each insert, you could have programmed the command like this:

```
begin-sql
insert into company (name, id_number)
values(_$name, #id_number );
commit
end-sql
```

Issuing data definition language commands to the server is also accomplished using `begin-sql` paragraphs:

```
begin-sql
create table valid_company_names
(company_name char(60) not null)
end-sql
```

N O T E To reference a temporary table in SQR, you must place an additional pound sign (#) in front of the table name, as in this example:

```
begin-sql
create table ##temp_company_names
(company_name char(60) not null)
end-sql
```

Using SQR to Create a Simple Program

The following example program performs the same job as the previous DBLibrary and Client Library examples. You should, at the very least, appreciate the simplicity of using SQR for basic reports and simple data manipulation.

```
! SQR program
!
begin-setup
 use CALL_TRACKER
 page-size 60 80
end-setup
begin-report
do main
end-report
begin-procedure main ! PRINT THE DATA TO OUTPUT FILE
begin-select
company_name,
count_calls
    print &company_name (+1, 1, 60)
    print &count_calls (0, +4, 6)
```

```
from COMPANY
end-select
end-procedure
```

As with the two previous examples written in DBLibrary and Client Library, this SQR report file performs a select from your database, and prints out the results to a file. The PRINT commands will be executed for each row returned from the database. The first position qualifier (+1, 1, 60) instructs SQR to write &company_name on the line after the current position line, beginning at column 1, 60 characters in length. The second position qualifier (0, +4, 6) instructs SQR to write &count_calls on the same line as &company_name, beginning on line 65, 6 characters in length.

Executing SQR Files

To run a report file, you use the SQR command from your operating system prompt. For example, execution of a report file called my_report.sqr, could appear as follows:

```
SQR my_report_file my_username/my_password
```

The output report will be stored in the current directory with the name my_report.lis. You can specify the name of the output file using the -F flag option. For example, if you wanted to produce a report named new_report.txt, you would have executed the report file like this:

```
SQR my_report_file my_username/my_password -Fnew_report.txt
```

A list of available command-line options is listed below in Table 14.4.

Table 14.4 Command-Line Options Available in SQR

Flag	Description
-A	Appends output to existing file.
-C	Displays Cancel dialog box while report is running (Windows).
-D##	Displays up to ## lines of report output on computer screen.
-DEBUG*xxx..*	Compiles DEBUG directives and executes them. Optional levels of debugging are specified by letters following DEBUG flag.
-E*filename*	Specifies *filename* for error file.
-F*filename* or	Specifies *filename* or *directory* for output *directory* file.
-G*file_mode*	Instructs VMS to use specified file mode.
-G*attributes*	Specifies file attributes on VAX applications.
-I*directories*	Specifies path for #INCLUDE files.
-ID	Displays copyright banner.
-M*filename*	Specifies file for defining internal array sizes.
-O*filename*	Specifies *filename* for log messages.

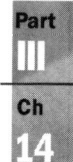

Part
III

Ch
14

continues

Table 14.4   Continued

Flag	Description
-P	Sends output to printer (VMS).
-RS	Creates runtime file with file type .*SQT*.
-RT	Directs SQR to use a runtime file (see -RT).
-S	Displays cursor status after report is run.
-T##	Tests report file for ## pages.
-V*server*	Specifies which server SQR is to use.
-XB	Suppresses extraneous SQR messages.
-XC	Suppresses commit.
-XL	Runs report file without logging into database.
-XP	Runs report file, but does not enable temporary stored procedures to be created.
-ZMF*filename*	Instructs SQR to use a specified SQR Error Message file.

As previously mentioned, you can provide command-line options and pass arguments to your report file. Optionally, you could specify a file containing all or some of the items following the SQR command. You may want to do this because some operating systems (especially DOS and Windows 3.x) have a limitation of 152 characters for a single command. For instance, you could create a file run_call_report as follows:

```
call_report.sqr
call_username/call_password
MEGA COMPANY, INC.
-Fnew_report.txt
```

and then execute your report like this:

```
SQR @run_call_report
```

Debugging SQR Programs   SQR enables you to perform commands based on whether or not the DEBUG flag (-DEBUG) has been included in the SQR execution statement on the command line. Consider the following statement:

```
#debug show 'I am still running.'
```

The previous line if placed in your report file will be compiled and run only when you execute the report file like this:

```
SQR reportdb username/password -DEBUG
```

SQR enables for 10 levels of debugging within a report file. For example, you could insert the following lines of code in your report file:

```
#debug show 'I am still running.'
#debuga show 'Company = ' $company_name
#debugb show 'id_number = ' #id
```

The three debug statements would all be executed when SQR ran your report file with the following command:

```
SQR reportdb username/password -DEBUGab
```

However, only the first two debug statements would be executed if you ran a report file with the following command:

```
SQR reportdb username/password -DEBUGa
```

Additionally, SQR provides us with five conditional debug compiler directives:

```
#IF
```

```
#ELSE
```

```
#END-IF
```

```
#IFDEF
```

```
#IFNDEF
```

These directives are used similarly to #DEBUG, and are detailed in the SQR Command Reference section of the SQR User's Guide.

Creating SQR RunTime Files   You can create runtime versions of your report files that do not require scanning and compilation, as typical SQR report files do. You can create a runtime file as follows:

```
SQR my_report my_username/my_password -RS
```

The -RS flag instructs SQR to create the runtime file my_report.sqt. You execute a runtime file using either of the following two commands:

```
SQR my_report my_username/my_password -RT
```

or

```
SQRT my_report my_username/my_password
```

The second example, which uses the SQRT command, requires that SQR-Execute be installed on the machine issuing the command. The advantage of using SQR-Execute is that it is deployable and significantly cheaper for the customer who is running your SQR reports.

From Here...

After reading this chapter, you should be pretty confident that you can write an application in C or C++ to do some basic Transact-SQL and to interact with the database sensibly. If you were already a C/C++ guru and just wanted to know how the database is accessed, then I hope you have acquired a competent understanding of the database interfaces available from DBLibrary and Client Library.

Of course, there's an alternative to writing applications in C/C++ and to even having to think about DBLibrary or Client Library. One of those alternatives (at a somewhat lower level) is SQR. Many other client/server development tools exist such as PowerBuilder, SQLWindows, Centura, Delphi, and so on. You can find out more about these other languages in later chapters in this book.

I suggest that you have a look at the following chapters to further your application development progress:

- Chapter 10, "Understanding Stored Procedures," teaches you how to define storage structures, such as parameters and local variables, by using system variables. Stored procedures are a fundamental part of any serious Sybase application and should be used all the time.

- Chapter 15, "Using Client/Server Application Programming Tools," offers a comprehensive review of the four top-ranked client/server tools on the market today: PowerBuilder, Centura Team Developer, Delphi, and Visual Basic.

- Chapter 16, "Partitioning an Application," gives tips and tricks to take advantage of popular three-tier partitioning schemes to make your application more robust and powerful.

- Chapter 17, "Using Third-Party Products," contains guides and reviews of some of the more popular and powerful third-party application programs that will help you work with a database and develop a database schema with a modeling tool.

- Chapter 23, "Using Sybase's Configuration Options," shows you how to use query options to control the display of data through Set command options. These options help optimize the performance of your application.

Using Client/Server Application Programming Tools

What good is a database if you can't give your users access to it? Client/Server application development tools are designed to help you write programs that will enable your users to interact with the database. This chapter is a review-like introduction to the top four tools on the market today: PowerBuilder 5, Centura, Delphi 2.0, and Visual Basic 4. What you will learn in this chapter is how these top-notch client/server tools perform and how you work with them to create database applications.

Writing client/server software for most people reading this book is a profession. The choice of development tool is critical to your success, and by using this chapter as a reference, you can compare and evaluate the most commonly used tools and judge whether a given tool is suitable for your project.

This chapter's focus is on developing applications under 32-bit Windows operating systems—either Windows 95 or Windows NT (version 3.51 or 4.0). The reason for this focus is that between Windows 95 and Windows NT, probably 80 percent of the entire business marketplace can be addressed. OS/2 and MacOS are both viable environments for application development, but are definitely on

Using and working with the top-rated client/server development tools on the market

In this chapter, you'll see the four best ranked and most popular application programming tools in action: Centura Team Builder, Delphi 2.0 Client/Server, PowerBuilder 5 Enterprise, and Visual Basic 4.0 Enterprise.

Configuring ODBC

Many third party tools and report writers take advantage of ODBC to control access to the database. Microsoft's Visual Basic also needs ODBC. This chapter helps you install and use ODBC effectively.

Tips and tricks for client/server development

Each of the tools that are discussed in this chapter has benefits and traps to their programming environments. You will learn tips and tricks for application development that will help you write better, faster, and cleaner applications.

the outer edge of the commonly chosen development environments and are certainly not where the major client/server development vendors are putting their energies. ■

N O T E With the intensity behind Java and the various development environments that support Java code generation, it may seem as though there is little time or incentive left for independent software language companies such as Centura and Borland to stay with their proprietary languages. I suspect that a number of these tools will end up being front ends for real Java development. ▨

 T I P One of the most important points to remember about working with any database front-end programming tool like PowerBuilder and Centura Team Developer is that they are only as strong as the connectivity that you implement for them to the database. What this means is that you should stay up with the latest EBFs (Emergency Build Fixes) and Rollup Releases available from Sybase.

Without the correct software in place, you could be experiencing bugs in the connectivity and think it is the front end. At the time of the writing of this book, the most current version of the connectivity to Sybase for Windows (3.1) is Open Client 10.0.3 EBF 6131. The current version of the Sybase for Windows NT (Windows 95 included) 32-bit is Open Client 10.0.3 EBF 6184.

Sybase's Open Client is probably the least robust of all the components of the Sybase toolkit; thus, the EBFs are pretty frequent from Sybase. Make sure that you have the current versions of all the required connectivity software to eliminate any bugs in the code on which you are working.

Working with ODBC

Most client/server development tools such as PowerBuilder and Centura come with native drivers that interface directly to the database vendor's programming interface, which in Sybase's case is Client Library for 32-bit applications and either DBLibrary or Client Library for 16-bit Windows applications. Direct interfaces to the drivers from Sybase provide optimum performance and access to all the native features of the Sybase drivers.

Open Database Connectivity (ODBC) was created by Microsoft in 1991 as a solution to the problem of standardization of interfaces by database vendors such as Sybase and Oracle. The goal of ODBC was to create a common API that all vendors would support. The advantages are obvious: From a client application, you code to one interface and instantly have a connection to all the databases on the market. ODBC is such a generic interface that vendors have written ODBC drivers for all the majors servers such as Sybase, Oracle, and Informix, and have also written drivers for systems like DB2, SQL/400 (the AS/400's database), Dbase, FoxPro, and even the humble Comma Separated Variable (CSV) file!

The downside of ODBC is that it is almost always slower than a direct API access to the database. Why? Because there's an additional layer of communication between APIs involved. Typically, the database vendor will write the ODBC driver for their database. This ODBC driver will simply be a layer over the top of their existing proprietary interface to the database. Sybase's case is typical: They licensed a third-party ODBC driver from Intersolv and use this as their standard public ODBC interface.

Part
III

Ch
15

> **N O T E** A number of different vendors now supply ODBC drivers for Sybase. Check out the CompuServe forum for a list of current suppliers of ODBC drivers. In fact, OpenLink Software's drivers are actually not an interface to Client Library at all, but go straight to Net Library for significant performance gains. OpenLink Software can be visited on the Web at: **http:// www.openlink.co.uk** in the United Kingdom, or on their U.S. mirror at: **http://www.openlinksw.com/ index.html**.

> If database independence is an important part of your application design, I highly recommend that you investigate the OpenLink drivers for ODBC. They are basically a slick piece of software that gets away from all the traditional concerns people have with ODBC and presents high-speed, generic connectivity to a variety of database engines such as Sybase, Microsoft SQL Server, Oracle, Informix, and Progress. ■

Installing and Configuring ODBC

ODBC is configured through a Control Panel Applet: ODBC (16-bit systems) or ODBC32. To configure ODBC for use with Sybase System XI, follow these steps:

1. Install the ODBC drivers that you received from Sybase.

2. From the Start menu in Windows 95 or Windows NT 4, select Settings, Control panel to display a list of applets that can be configured using Control Panel (see Fig.15.1).

FIG. 15.1

Windows NT Workstation's Control Panel is really just a window with several icons in it. Each icon is an applet—a small application that manages a particular part of the operating system's behavior.

3. Double-click the ODBC icon to display the Data Sources dialog box, as shown in Figure 15.2.

4. Click Add to bring up a list of installed drivers that you can use to install ODBC connectivity to the database (see Fig. 15.3).

FIG. 15.2

The Data Sources dialog box lists all the configured ODBC sources and the drivers that those ODBC sources are using to get to the database.

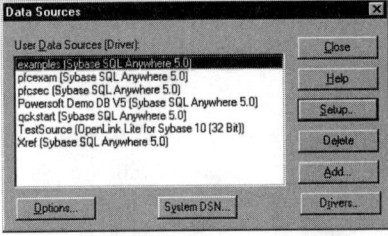

FIG. 15.3

The Add Data Source dialog box shows for which installed software you currently have active ODBC drivers.

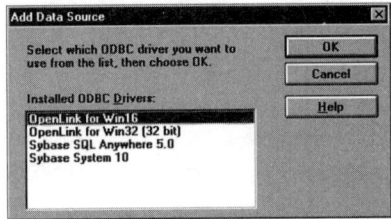

5. Select Sybase System 10 from the list and click OK. After clicking OK, a large dialog box, ODBC Sybase System 10 Driver Setup, will be displayed. A filled-in dialog box can be seen in Figure 15.4.

N O T E   Sybase has yet to release System XI-specific ODBC drivers, so you need to use the System 10 drivers that are currently the supported interface to the database via ODBC. ▄

FIG. 15.4

The Driver Setup dialog box has a lot of options; you can basically skip over most of them because they can be programmatically set by client front-end programs.

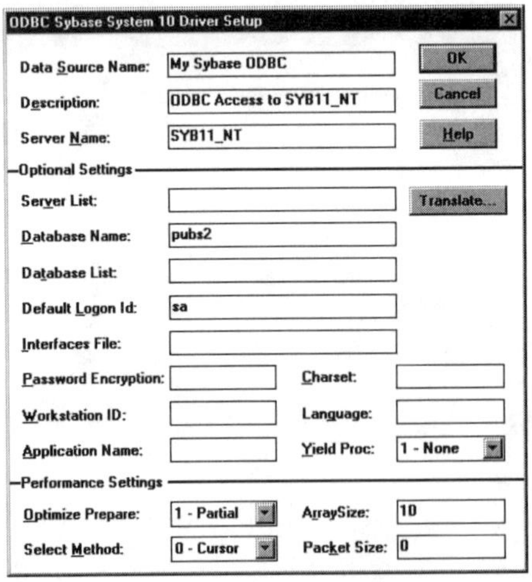

6. Enter a Data Source Name; this is any logical name that you want to use, such as "My Sybase ODBC" (see Fig. 15.4).

7. Enter a Description that will be displayed on client programs that are connecting to the data source.

8. Enter the Server Name, which should correspond to a server that you have configured using SQLEDIT. For more information on using SQLEDIT, please see Chapter 3, "Installing Sybase."

9. Enter a Database Name if you want this data source to be specifically associated with a particular database; otherwise, leave this blank and assume that the client program connecting to the data source will prompt the user for a database to be connected to.

10. Enter a Default Logon Id if you want this data source to be specifically associated with a particular user; otherwise, leave this blank and assume that the client program connecting to the data source will prompt the user for a user id and password.

11. If you don't want to use the default SQL.INI file that is found, based on the client workstation's SYBASE environment variable, enter a path to the required SQL.INI file in the Interfaces File field.

12. If you want passwords to be encrypted when sent across the physical network, put a 1 in the Password Encryption field. Entering a 0 (zero) or leaving this field blank will not encrypt the password as it travels across the network to the database.

13. Enter a character set to be used for character set conversion on the client in the Charset field. This field is optional and if left blank, the default character set's conversion will take place as defined in the configuration of the server.

14. If you want to identify this workstation with a unique name, enter it in the Workstation ID field.

15. If you want to override the default language of English, enter the required language in the Language field.

16. Enter a name by which you want this data source to be recognized in the Application Name field.

17. If you want to alter the way the database driver yields (returns control) to other applications on the desktop, change the setting in the Yield Proc combo box. I strongly urge you not to change this from the default of 1 (meaning no yielding) because you will incur a substantial performance penalty. The remainder of the performance options are described below in the section "Using the Performance Options of Sybase's ODBC Driver."

18. Click the OK button to add the driver. This will redisplay the Data Sources dialog box with the new driver *My Sybase ODBC* driver listed in the Data Sources list box (see Fig. 15.5).

FIG. 15.5
After a driver has been
added, you can click it
again and hit Setup if
you want to change any
of its characteristics
and configurations.

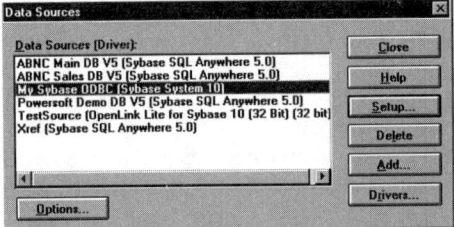

N O T E   You can use the Server List and Database List fields to enter a comma-separated list of
servers and databases that would be displayed to a user connecting to this data source.
Generally, I'd leave these fields blank and have a specific data source for each particular database and
server to which you are giving users access. ▪

Using the Performance Options of Sybase's ODBC Driver

There are a few options that you can use to help improve the performance of certain applications that connect to a Sybase database through ODBC. Like any performance configuration,
they will require benchmarking at your site in order to determine if any particular option is
going to actually provide any kind of benefit to your application.

Using Optimize Prepare   The Sybase ODBC connectivity driver typically maps all prepared
SQL statements (statements executed with the ODBC call SqlPrepare) through a stored procedure. This stored procedure is created so that you can use host variables and have the ability
to retrieve data through input and output parameters from the calling program. The advantage
is that your application code can be more flexible in the way it interacts with the database. The
downside of this approach is that its development will cost time and server resources for the
procedure to be made ready for execution.

N O T E   The System 10 driver is actually smart if you use the driver in its default setting of
1 -Partial because it will not create a stored procedure unless it detects that there are
parameters and/or host variables in use in the SQL statement that is being executed. In cases where
no parameters are detected, the driver will just cache the SQL statement in a local buffer and execute
it at the time SqlExecute is executed by the client program. ▪

If you anticipate that you will not use host variables, and you don't want to incur the performance cost of either having a stored procedure built or the actual detection of host variables
from occurring, you should set the Optimize Prepare field = *2 - Full*. If you want to force the
creation of stored procedures (which is *not* recommended), set the Optimize Prepare
field = *0 - None*.

Using Array Sizing   The array that is being referenced in this case is not actually a result set
space that you can touch or see, but is the internal cache that the ODBC driver uses when
interacting with the database. This controls the number of records that are transferred from
the server in a single-fetch request.

The advantage of this parameter is that it can help make dramatic differences in the database interaction times when working on different sorts of applications. For highly transactional programs that have small data sets being sent to and from the database server, you might want to try a lower value or even 1 (one) to force the database to send each transaction as soon as the buffer is full with the first result.

The default for ArraySize is 10 rows. For reporting systems that do a lot of data across the network, you may find better application and reporting speed by increasing this value to a greater number (20 or 30).

Using Select Methods   Another configurable option on the ODBC driver is the ability to set the way you want `Select` statements to be processed. In a similar fashion to the detection of parameters and/or variables causing stored procedures to be created, the ODBC driver can detect a `Select` statement and create a cursor on the server through which it can be used. The most significant advantage of this approach is that it enables you to have multiple contexts on the database server and to have multiple concurrently open SQL `Select` statements that do not interfere with one another and *don't* require additional connections to the database.

The default is *0 - Cursor,* which will create a cursor for each `Select` and does incur a performance penalty from the server because of the additional resources that are required to manage the cursor on the server's side. If you set the Select Method field = *1 - Direct,* you will not get a cursor created for your `Select` statements; this is a generally faster way of working with the database.

There's a negative aspect of disabling cursor support on the host side: If you need to perform multiple concurrent `Select` statements, you may need to connect an additional handle to the database, which would COST substantially more in terms of performance than using the ODBC driver's in-built cursor support. However, with some savvy programming, you can create your own cursors by executing a `Declare Cursor` statement through a single connection to the database and then programmatically control the cursor's results. It is highly recommended that you disable cursor creation through the ODBC driver and manually create cursors as needed in your application program (or connect a second handle if necessary).

▶ **See** "Using Sybase Cursors," **p. 315**

Using Packet Sizing   Being able to set the size of a logical database packet that forms the transport layer to the database is a standard feature of both the DBLibrary and Client Library interfaces to Sybase System 10 and higher servers. It is a natural assumption that the ODBC driver would also support this feature because it makes such a significant impact on the performance of the client.

The purpose of this option is to enable you to specify the underlying packet's size in numbers of bytes. Why does this make a difference? Well, it works in conjunction with the ArraySize option to determine how many physical network requests need to be made to send a piece of data to the client.

Take the default setting of 512 bytes for the Packet Size and 10 for the ArraySize. What this means is provided that each row in the 10 records required for the array is under 51 bytes in length, a single network operation (or in reality, a *logical* database network operation) can be performed to transfer the required data. What's the chance of a record being 51 bytes long? Pretty slim. So, what happens in the default scenario is that the database driver makes multiple requests to the server and the data is split up across each of those requests.

For normal send requests such as `Insert`, `Update`, and `Delete` statements, the 512 bytes of the default are normally sufficient; they were probably the reason for the default. You will, however, most likely see substantial performance gains if you set this value to a higher number for applications that are `Select` intensive, such as reporting systems.

When set to the default of zero, the ODBC driver will negotiate with the server for the default network packet size to use. You can configure the default on the server by using the system stored procedure `sp_configure` with the option `default network packet size`.

▶ **See** "Configuring and Managing Servers," **p. 635**

If you want the driver to take or allocate the maximum permitted packet size as defined on the server, set the Packet Size field to –1; the ODBC driver will negotiate with the server for the maximum size and then save it in the ODBC.INI file on the local computer for future use.

If you want to force the use of a particular size of network packets, set the Packet Size field to a value between 1 and 10. This value specifies the number of 512 byte increments in the packet size to request. For example, setting Packet Size to 4 would request a 4 * 512 = 2048 bytes network packet size from the server.

It is important to remember that setting the packet size on the client requires a corresponding amount of memory to be allocated on the server to buffer network operations. This means that if you have 100 users each utilizing a 4096 byte (4K) buffer for networking, you are going to consume 400K on the server just to manage network connections. Take care that you don't underestimate the magnitude of server-side resources that will be consumed by the use of a larger-than-default network packet size.

N O T E   Remember that the underlying network protocol such as TCP/IP or IPX can also have significant impact on the performance of the Packet Size option because the *logical* database packets still have to be *physically* transported across the underlying network protocol. If the protocol has a very small physical packet size, then this will result in multiple network trips *per* logical database packet, as defined by the packet size that you specify.

In contrast, a very large physical network packet size can also have an impact on an application that needs to send a short request to the server; the networking driver will not by default send the request until the packet has been completely filled with data for transmission. A work-around for this behavior is to start the server with special trace flag: T1610 (*TCP no delay*). With T1610 in use, the database server will send out network requests to clients even if the physical network packet is not full.

Testing a Connection Through ODBC to Sybase

You should have by now installed the necessary ODBC software. You want to check that you have successfully managed to get everything set up correctly. To do so, Microsoft supplies a simple application, CPPDemo, that can be used to test the connectivity. To use the CPPDemo application, follow these steps:

1. After installing the Sybase ODBC drivers from either OpenLink or Sybase, launch the CPPDemo application from the program group that was created (see Fig. 15.6).

FIG. 15.6
The main window of the CPPDemo application is pretty Spartan and is designed just as a straight results display area.

2. From the Environment menu, select Open Connection to display the SQL Data Sources dialog box (see Fig. 15.7).

3. Select the data source that you want to connect to, and click OK. You should now be prompted with a Logon dialog box as seen in Figure 15.8. Enter your password, and click OK. A successful connection will change the title of the main CPPDemo window to include a dash and then the name of the ODBC database to which you have connected.

FIG. 15.7
The SQL Data Sources dialog box lists all the data sources that you have currently configured through the standard ODBC setup.

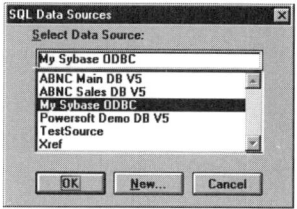

FIG. 15.8
The Logon to System 10 dialog box enables you to override the defaults for the ODBC connection if you need to and then to enter your password to connect to the required server and database.

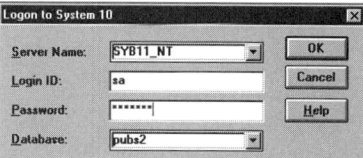

4. To test that the SQL execution is working correctly, from the SQL menu, select Execute SQL. This will display a dialog box stating that you can enter a SQL statement that will be executed on the server when you click OK (see Fig. 15.9).

FIG. 15.9

The SQL statement dialog box is very basic, and the editor, is rather poor. To enter the statement shown, you need to use CTRL+Enter instead of just a plain Enter statement. The Enter key is interpreted as pressing OK.

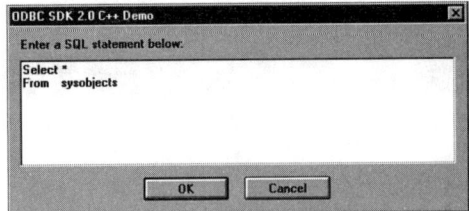

5. Enter the statement as shown in Figure 15.9 (Select * From sysobjects) and click OK to execute the statement. Executing the SQL statement will change the display to show the results of the query, as you can see in Figure 15.10.

FIG. 15.10

The CPPDemo application displays the results of queries in a standard tabular view that can be scrolled vertically and horizontally if there's too much data to display.

name	id	uid	type	userstat	sysstat	indexdel	schemacnt	
sysobjects	1	1	S	0	113	0	1	0
sysindexes	2	1	S	0	81	0	0	0
syscolumns	3	1	S	0	81	0	2	0
systypes	4	1	S	0	113	0	4	0
sysprocedures	5	1	S	0	81	0	0	0
syscomments	6	1	S	0	81	2	0	0
syssegments	7	1	S	0	1	0	0	0
syslogs	8	1	S	0	1	0	0	0
sysprotects	9	1	S	0	81	1	1	0
sysusers	10	1	S	0	113	0	0	0
sysalternates	11	1	S	0	81	0	0	0
sysdepends	12	1	S	0	81	0	0	0
syskeys	13	1	S	0	81	0	0	0
sysgams	14	1	S	0	1	0	0	0
sysusermessages	15	1	S	0	113	0	2	0
sysreferences	16	1	S	0	113	6	2	0
sysconstraints	17	1	S	0	113	0	0	0
systhresholds	18	1	S	0	81	0	0	0
sysroles	19	1	S	0	81	0	0	0
sysattributes	21	1	S	0	8305	0	0	0
syspartitions	22	1	S	0	81	0	0	51
authors	16003088	1	U	0	115	0	1	0
publishers	48003202	1	U	0	83	0	1	0

Using Delphi 2.0 Client/Server

Borland's Delphi 2 is at the cutting edge of client/server application development. It is a new object-oriented programming language based on Pascal. Delphi 2 is the new version of Delphi that was released in 1996 to much fanfare. Delphi 2 is a 32-bit development environment that has received many awards. Using Delphi is an interesting experience. The closest other language that is available, in terms of an experience, is Visual Basic.

The model of development in Delphi is very (if not too much) object-oriented and you are forced to work with a property customizer for each object and form, rather than being able to visualize the whole project in one clear view.

All the source code that follows for the Delphi 2 application can be found in DPHI20.PRJ and DPHIDEMO.* on the CD-ROM.

On the CD

Establishing a Connection

Delphi 2 has native drivers for Sybase System XI that are directly interfacing to Sybase's Client Library interface. The simplest way to prepare Delphi 2 for use with a database is to use the Database Explorer Applet that ships with Delphi 2.

To use the Database Explorer to prepare the ODBC interface, perform the following steps:

1. Install Delphi 2 from the CD-ROM.
2. From the program group in which Delphi 2 is installed (usually Borland Delphi 2.0), select the Borland Delphi folder and double-click the Database Explorer icon to launch the DB Explorer (see Fig. 15.11).

FIG. 15.11

Delphi 2's SQL Explorer has just been started. Note that after an install, unless you choose to install the Borland Database Engine or Interbase, you will not have any databases defined here for browsing.

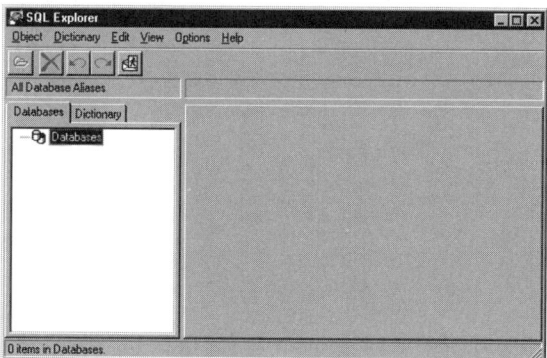

3. From the Object menu, choose New. Select SYBASE (for Sybase System XI or Sybase System 10) from the New Database Alias dialog box and click OK (see Fig. 15.12).

FIG. 15.12

The New Database Alias dialog box in SQL Explorer has SYBASE selected as the driver/database type that will be used for this database.

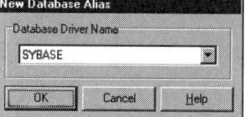

4. At this point, the word SYBASE1 will be highlighted in the left pane of the Database Explorer. Enter a name for the database's *alias* and press Enter.

Part
III

Ch
15

TIP Unless you plan to have multiple aliases for the same server, it's a good plan to set the alias name equal to the name of the server as defined in SQL.INI by the SQLEDIT program. By setting up the aliases with the same name as the SERVER you will have no doubt which server you are currently connecting to.

5. Click the editable portion of the DATABASE NAME property in the right pane and enter the name for the database to be referenced: *pubs2*.

6. Enter the name of the server in the SERVER NAME property in the right pane.

7. Enter the name of the user who will by default connect to this database in the USER NAME property in the right pane: *sa*.

8. Enter any additional configurations that you want to select for this database. The completed dialog box is shown in Figure 15.13.

FIG. 15.13

A completed database definition is ready to be applied (made usable) using the SQL Explorer from Delphi 2. Note that there is a highlighted arrow pointing to the database being worked on, indicating that it has not been activated yet.

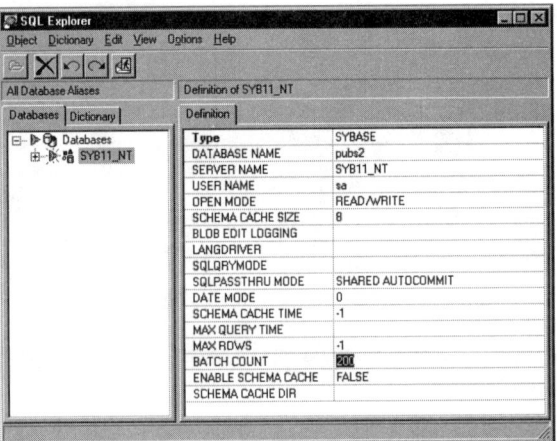

9. From the Object menu, select Apply to activate this database; you will notice that the arrow goes away.

NOTE If you want to change the alias name for this database at any time from either the default of SYBASEX (where X corresponds to the number of default databases installed so far), or from any other name, highlight the database in the left pane of the Explorer. From the Object menu, select Rename. Enter the new name for the database alias and press Enter. ■

10. To test that everything is configured correctly, click the plus sign to the left of the database alias name to expand the Explorer view. This will display a Database Login dialog box, as shown in Figure 15.14.

FIG. 15.14

This is the Database Login dialog box from the SQL Explorer. Enter your password (and change the logon being used if necessary) and click OK.

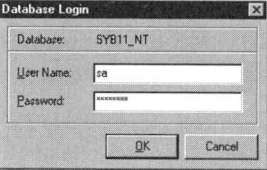

11. Enter the *sa* password and the Explorer tree will expand, indicating the various components of the Sybase that are available for manipulation via SQL Explorer (see Fig. 15.15).

FIG. 15.15

After connecting to the database, you can expand the items in the SQL explorer to get a view of any of the database objects that you want to manipulate. Also, note that the Sybase driver goes and returns the current version information in the Type field at the top of the right pane.

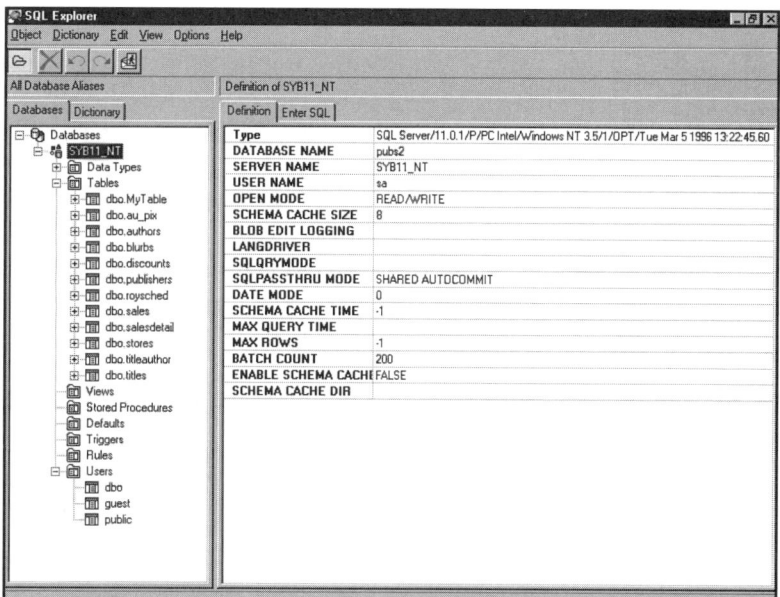

Understanding the Delphi 2 Database Model

In its most common use, Delphi 2 has a layered approach to interfacing with databases. This layering provides several levels of abstraction from the database itself, enabling a very generic application programming interface through common objects.

Delphi 2 has a number of classes that can be used to actually manipulate the data. These classes are responsible for executing the appropriate queries to perform any DML required. The classes that can be used vary from TTable, which is used for representing a table, to TQuery, which enables a custom query to be presented to the visual objects. These physical data interface classes are typically non-visual.

These physical data sources are then mapped to a class that is responsible for interfacing with user interface objects/controls, such as data fields and lists. This interface is performed through a non-visual class, `TDataSource`, which transfers data from the physical data class to the visual objects that you place on an edit form.

Manipulating the data in `TQuery` or `TTable` to fetch records, update them, and so on, can be performed by invoking the methods that they have or by adding a Navigation control to the edit form. `TDBNavigator` is a class that interacts with `TDataSource` and provides the standard Next, Previous, Insert, and Update buttons to manipulate the data on the form. By placing one of these controls on an edit form and then hooking—either at design time by setting its property or at runtime by adjusting its property to the required data source on the form, you will have all the necessary components to build an edit window to a data structure (defined as either a query or a database table).

Finally, in Delphi 2, it is necessary to add controls to view/edit the actual data. Delphi 2 provides all the standard edit controls (including list boxes and combo boxes) that have properties that enable them to be hooked to a particular `TDataSource`. Placing the control on the form and setting its `DataSource` and `DataField` properties is all that is required.

In Figure 15.16, you can see the sort of user interface that Delphi provides the developer. At the top of the window is a toolbar/palette that enables you to select any control that you want to place on a form. On the left side of the window is an Object Inspector that shows any of the properties that relate to the current object selected. On the right, you can see the code editor for Delphi 2 and underneath it is the working window that is currently being edited.

FIG. 15.16

The user interface of the Delphi 2 environment makes it easy to work with the code and the properties of any particular object that you are programming.

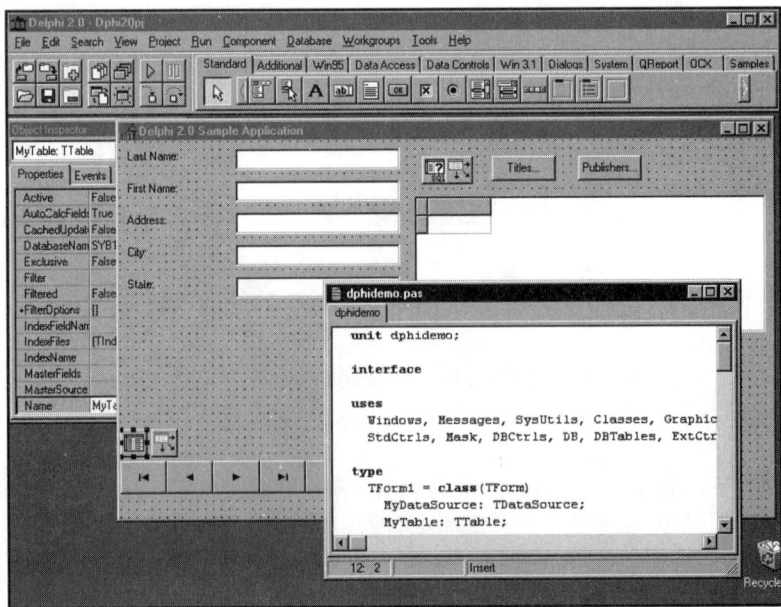

About the Sample Application DPHIDEMO

The sample application provided here demonstrates a simple edit form to the authors table in the *pubs2* database. This application took less than ten minutes to write and shows how easy it is to use Delphi 2.

TIP   This application is designed to use a database alias of SYB11_NT to interact with the database. To simplify things while working with this sample code, I recommend that you create an alias with the name SYB11_NT. If you are comfortable working with Delphi, you can change all the DatabaseName properties of the TTable and TQuery objects to any database alias that you have defined.

The application demonstrates the use of basic TTable.Table_Authors to read from the database table directly. On top of this class is TDataSource.MyDataSource that performs the data source manipulation. There are data fields on the form that enable editing of the basic name and address information in the table; they are all of class TDBEdit.

Finally, to control the interaction with the database, TDBNavigator.MyNavigator is hooked to TDataSource.MyDataSource. To "beef up" the application and to learn a tiny part of Delphi 2, some code executes whenever the form is resized so that the Navigator control stays "docked" to the bottom of the window. The code in Listing 15.1 is so simple that it's amazing to anyone who has ever had to write this in a language such as C.

Listing 15.1 DPHI20.PRJ—Dynamic Form Resizing with Objects that Paint Inside the Form's Boundaries

```
procedure TForm1.FormResize(Sender: TObject);
begin
    MyNavigator.Top := Form1.ClientHeight - MyNavigator.Height;
    MyNavigator.Width := Form1.ClientWidth;
    end;
end.
```

Perhaps the nicest feature of Delphi 2 is that the data access can be tested at design time. The TTable class has a property of Active, which, if enabled, will connect to the database and present data to the controls if they are hooked via a TDataSource. This enables you to at least see something of what the application is going to look like at runtime.

Preparing and Executing SQL Statements

Delphi 2 represents ad hoc queries through the class TQuery. TQuery is a non-visual class with has properties that enable it to be attached to a database. The SQL property is provided to enable the setting of the required SQL statement. TQuery then interacts with a TDataSource just like TTable.

In the sample application, the Active property is set to True when the Titles... button is clicked. This causes the SQL to be executed in TQuery.MyQuery and the Grid control to be populated with the results of the SELECT statement. The Grid control, TDBGrid.MyDBGrid, is hooked to the data source for presentation of the query results.

Clicking the Titles button executes the default SQL that was set in TQuery.MyQuery at design time. The Publishers button dynamically changes the SQL and executes it. Listing 15.2 shows what is required to do this SQL changing at runtime in Delphi 2.

Listing 15.2   DPHI20.PRJ—Setting a SQL Statement in a Delphi 2 Control and then Activating (Executing) It

```
procedure TForm1.Button2Click(Sender: TObject);
begin
    MyQuery.Active := False;
    MyQuery.SQL.Clear;
    MyQuery.SQL.Add( 'Select * from publishers');
    MyQuery.Active := True;
end;
```

Using Stored Procedures and Command Batches

Delphi 2's implementation, which consists of Stored Procedures and Command Batches, is identical to that of the general query execution principle. A StoredProcName property is provided to enable you to hook the object with a stored procedure in the server. The TStoredProc is then attached/hooked to a TDataSource and accessed as normal through other data controls.

More Information and Examples

The documentation (both printed and online) was excellent and very comprehensive. A neat feature of Delphi 2 is that class-specific help is invoked whenever F1 is pushed during design time and when an object is highlighted. This will make it easy for you to find information about the properties and methods of the Delphi 2 classes provided by Borland.

There's a lot of source code available on the Delphi 2 CD that shows you how to create all sorts of applications. In addition, Borland supplies the source code for the VCL (Borland's Visual Objects) so that you can learn how they are implemented internally, or how to customize their behavior through sub-classing if you want.

Another avenue for support and information is the Delphi forum on CompuServe, where you will get a lot of help from other Delphi users. This is a very active forum and is highly recommended for the new user of Borland's tool.

Using Centura Team Developer

Centura Software Corporation is a new name for a well-established player in the Client/Server development community: Gupta Corporation. Gupta's SQLWindows is a classic front-end tool that has been around since the late 1980s. Since that time, it has acquired various drivers written natively to provide communications to different DBMSs.

Centura Team Developer (hereafter referred to as Centura) is a full 32-bit rewrite of the SQLWindows product. Centura built on the base of a strongly written application development environment of SQLWindows; they reengineered the tool for scalable 32-bit application development. Centura is a new incarnation of the existing SQLWindows product: Porting an application from one environment to another is a straightforward process and is virtually automatic.

Support for Sybase is supported via a native driver written to the 32-bit Client Library interface from Sybase. Note that in SQLWindows, you could either use the Client Library router (Centura's term for a database driver) or an older (but more stable!) driver that used DBLibrary to communicate with the database.

The user interface in Centura is very different to that of SQLWindows and has added an explorer-like metaphor. In Figure 15.17, you can see the new UI used in Centura, which is very similar to products like Microsoft Visual C++'s Developer Studio and other explorers that are built into Windows 95 and Windows NT 4.

FIG. 15.17
The explorer in Centura makes it easy to navigate the source code on an object-by-object basis. For die-hard SQLWindows users, Centura also provides a full outline browser that is accessible at any time by selecting the Outline tab in the right pane.

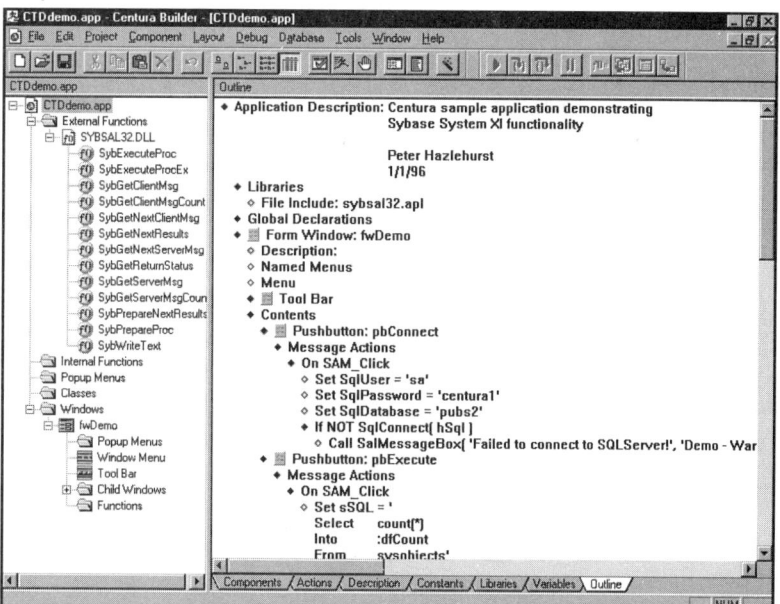

All the source code that follows for the SQLWindows application can be found in CTDDEMO.APP on the enclosed CD-ROM.

Establishing a Connection

Connecting Sybase and Centura Team Developer is a bit of a manual process that involves editing the file SQL.INI (this is the same name as Sybase's file!) that can be found in the installation directory of Centura. Centura does ship with a graphical utility name SQLEdit (again, the same name as Sybase), but it lacks the ability to correctly work with Sybase router information section.

TIP The fact that Sybase and Centura have chosen the same name for their INI files may seem like a cause for concern! But, in fact, it's not really that bad. Just make sure that Sybase's environment variable SYBASE is set correctly and that the path instruction to the Centura directory is after that of the Sybase installation directory.

If you want to be really adventurous, you can combine both INI files, but take care that you don't compromise either file by removing any required entries. A file COMBSQL.INI is supplied with this CD-ROM that indicates all the required sections from both INI files that need to be present. Once combined, you should place this INI file in the INI subdirectory under the directory pointed to by the SYBASE environment variable on the workstation.

Preparing Centura for Sybase System XI   In order to configure your workstation to support Centura, follow these steps:

1. Install Centura from the CD-ROM.

2. Using the Windows Explorer, find the file SQLEDIT.EXE in the installation directory of Centura and double-click it to launch Centura's SQL.INI file editor, as shown in Figure 15.18. (Don't ask me why no shortcut is created for this application—if you are going to work with Centura a lot, I recommend creating a shortcut for it in the Centura Folder.)

FIG. 15.18
The SQL.INI Editor provided by Centura permits you to edit both the server (for SQLBase) and client side of the SQL.INI file.

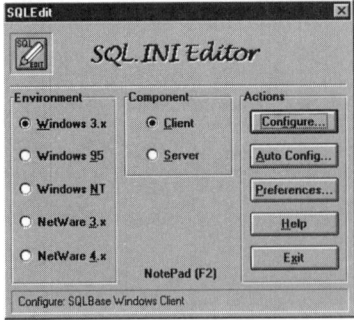

3. Select the Environment that you are working in (either Windows 95 or Windows NT), and click Configure.

4. SQLEdit will then ask you to confirm the INI file that you want to edit. If the file shown in the Open dialog box (see Fig. 15.19) is not the one you want to work with, navigate to it correctly and then click OK.

FIG. 15.19

The Open dialog box in SQLEdit is designed to help you find the SQL.INI file that you want to edit for use with Centura.

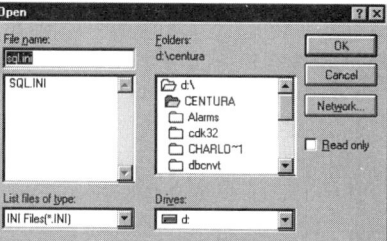

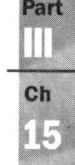

5. Select Sybase from the Interface Option(s) list and click the move right button (=>) to move it to the Selected Interfaces list (see Fig. 15.20)

FIG. 15.20

After saving the Win32 Client dialog box, SQLEdit will add the appropriate default settings to the SQL.INI file for you, including an entry to [Win32Client] and a complete default [sybgtwy] section.

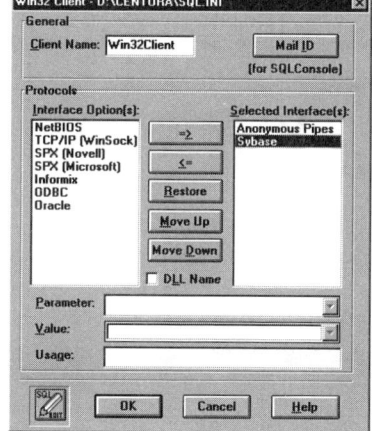

6. Click OK to make the changes to the SQL.INI file.

7. Click Exit to close the main window of SQLEdit.

8. Using the Windows Explorer, find the file SQL.INI in the installation directory of Centura and double-click it to edit the file.

9. In the SQL.INI file, go to the section titled [Win32Client] and confirm that the following entry has been added:

```
comdll=sqlsyb32
```

10. Now, go to the end of the file and you should see a section that looks like this:

```
[sybgtwy]
remotedbname=sys10,SERVERNAME,DBNAME
longbuffer=32650
locktimeout=0
sybautocommit=off
yieldonservercall=0
sybworkstationname=workstation_name
sybapplicationname=CENTURA Sybase App
checkexists=off
```

```
fetchrow=20
sybmaxmessages=0
enablemultipleconnections=off
closecursorateof=off
```

The important entry that you need to configure is the one that reads `remotedbname`. The `remotedbname` entry is used to define the remote database alias. The first value (in the default you can see `sys10`) refers to the alias that will be accessible from Centura. The second value is the server name as defined in Sybase's SQLEdit or Sybase's SQL.INI file. The third value corresponds to the database name on the server itself. So, to add a new remote database for the *pubs2* database, you would add:

```
remotedbname=pubs2,SYB11_NT,pubs2
```

N O T E The value of the database alias is that you can name a database and its reference from Centura's code differently than the name on the server. For example, say you wanted to have an alias called *PubsDB* for the *pubs2* database, you would add the following to the SQL.INI file:

```
remotedbname=PubsDB,SYB11_NT,pubs2
```

The only limitation is that the alias name may be only eight characters long. ▪

11. Save the INI file and launch Centura Team Developer.

12. From the Database menu, select Database Explorer to launch the database explorer that you will use to test connectivity to the Sybase server through Centura's tools (see Fig. 15.21).

FIG. 15.21

The Database Explorer after just being started shows on the right pane a list of the different database vendor brands that Centura can connect to.

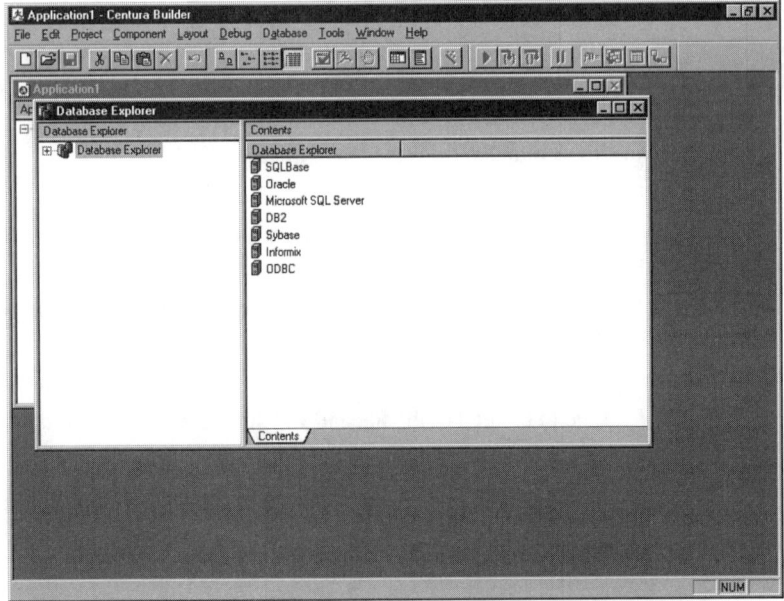

13. Double-click the entry in the right pane called sybase to bring up a list of remote databases (taken from the remotedbname entries in SQL.INI) that are available.

14. Select the database that you want to connect to and then enter the User Name and Password that you want to use to connect with in the right pane, which will have changed to a Logon window (see Fig. 15.22).

FIG. 15.22

The Database Explorer in Centura Team Developer doesn't use traditional dialog boxes as in Delphi's Database Explorer. Instead, Centura's Database Explorer paints dialog-like information in the right pane of the explorer's browser.

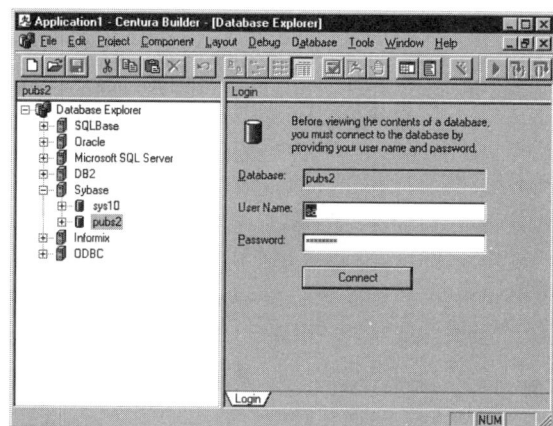

15. If you have successfully configured the connectivity, you should be able to click the Connect button, which will then connect to the database. The explorer will be activated with browsers for tables, views, and indexes (see Fig. 15.23).

FIG. 15.23

Once you have connected to the database, you will be able to edit the schema or work with the data in the tables of the database by using the Explorer's navigation and then double-clicking the object that you want to inspect.

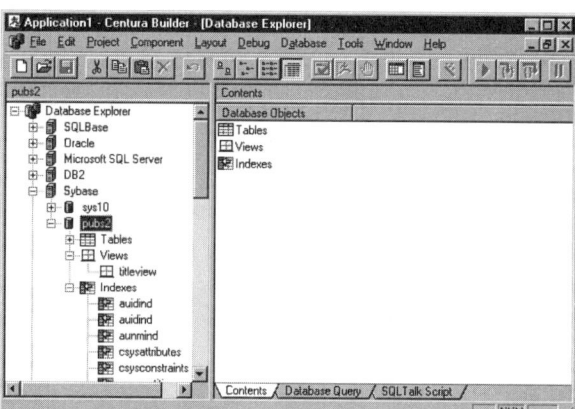

> **CAUTION**
>
> Centura Team Developer and Centura's other products, such as Quest and SQLWindows, require that you enter a password for the database that you are connecting to. If you do not enter a password, Centura will pass in the default password of SYSADM. You *must* have a password configured for the user that you want to access the database.
>
> Remember that the default installation of Sybase is to install SA with no password. This must be changed!

Connecting to Sybase System XI   Connecting to Sybase using Centura is relatively straightforward. Centura has three reserved words that are used to specify the user id, password, and database to which you are going to be connected. Listing 15.3 shows the setting of the variables with hard-coded values. In your application, you would probably have some kind of dialog box that you use to achieve the same result.

Listing 15.3   CTDDEMO.APP—Connecting to the Sybase System XI Remote Database Using Centura's SqlConnect( ) Function

```
Pushbutton: pbConnect
...
    Message Actions
        On SAM_Click
            Set SqlUser = 'sa'
            Set SqlPassword = 'centura1'
            Set SqlDatabase = 'pubs2'
            If NOT SqlConnect( hSql )
                Call SalMessageBox( 'Failed to connect to SQLServer!',
                                    'Demo - Warning', MB_IconAsterisk )
```

hSql is a local variable of type Sql Handle that is defined on the form. Centura uses Sql Handles to control the connectivity to the database. All activity is routed through the handle and this is the equivalent of a logon session to the database you specify.

Preparing and Executing SQL Statements

Centura provides a simple interface for executing statements. The same interface is used to prepare and execute queries on all database server types. Listing 15.4 shows the execution of a simple Select to count the number of objects and place the results in the data field on the screen dfCount.

Listing 15.4   CTDDEMO.APP—Executing a SQL Statement on Sybase Using Centura's SqlPrepareAndExecute( ) Function

```
On SAM_Click
    Set sSQL = '
            Select    count(*)
            Into      :dfCount
            From      sysobjects'
```

```
If NOT SqlPrepareAndExecute( hSql, sSQL )
    Call SalMessageBox( 'Failed to execute a select from the SQLServer!',
                        'Demo - Warning', MB_IconAsterisk )
If NOT SqlFetchNext( hSql, nReturn )
    Call SalMessageBox( 'Failed to fetch on the select from the
                        SQLServer!', 'Demo - Warning', MB_IconAsterisk )
```

Notice again the use of the Sql Handle, hSql, in all activity that involves the database. The SQL Handle is the logical entity through which all database interaction is performed.

Using Stored Procedures and Command Batches

In Centura, there are some extension functions for the use of executing stored procedures on the server. These functions are prefixed with the letters Syb. To add this functionality to an application, include the Centura-supplied include file: SYBSAL32.APL, which should be located in the root Sybase directory.

TIP If you are writing an application in SQLWindows and want to use these functions using the DBLibrary router, you need to change the prefix of Syb with Sqs and use the include file SQSSAL.APL.

A simple stored procedure is used to test stored procedure execution. Listing 15.5 shows the code for the stored procedure.

Listing 15.5 CHP15_01.SQL—A Simple Stored Procedure that Counts the Number of Databases on the Server

```
/*
    This is a really simple stored procedure
    that returns the number of databases that
    are installed and configured on the current
    server.

    This procedure is provided so that you can
    test connectivity with the Sybase System XI
    server and the ability to perform stored
    procedure executions.
*/

Create Procedure up_CountDatabases
As

Select Count(*)
From    master..sysdatabases

Return 0
```

Listing 15.6 shows results that are fetched and returned to the same dfCount data field.

Listing 15.6 CTDDEMO.APP—Executing a Stored Procedure on Sybase Using Centura's SybExecuteProc( ) Function

```
On SAM_Click
    Set sSQL = 'up_CountDatabases'
    If NOT SybExecuteProc( hSql, sSQL, ':dfCount' )
        Call SalMessageBox( 'Failed to execute a select from the SQLServer!',
                            'Demo - Warning', MB_IconAsterisk )
    If NOT SqlFetchNext( hSql, nReturn )
        Call SalMessageBox( 'Failed to fetch on the select from the
                            SQLServer!', 'Demo - Warning', MB_IconAsterisk )
```

More Information and Examples

Centura has provided a number of instructive sample applications—SQLSYB1.APP, SQLSYB2.APP, SQLSYB3.APP, SQLSYB4.APP, and SQLSYB5.APP—that can be found in the \SAMPLES directory below the Centura installation directory. These examples indicate in more detail how to connect to the database and perform various operations on them. I highly recommend that you run these applications at least once to get a feel for all the possibilities of the Sybase connectivity.

Centura's forum on CompuServe is very active and you're bound to get great help if you go there and ask questions—using CompuServe is an excellent support channel for a new user of Centura's products.

Using PowerBuilder 5

PowerBuilder 5 is the latest generation of Sybase's (Powersoft's) award-winning database programming language for client/server application development. A few years younger than SQLWindows, PowerBuilder is still a veteran in the Client/Server arena for applications development. The interesting thing about PowerBuilder is how completely different its approach is to database development, compared to all the other vendors. With PowerBuilder you either do it *their* way, or you just don't do it at all!

CAUTION

This is a big warning to you: If you are going to work with PowerBuilder on your server, *you must install the PowerBuilder Catalog Stored Procedures*. These stored procedures are found in the \server directory on the CD-ROM Distribution media. I have no idea why there's no directory created for them on installation of PowerBuilder, nor why they aren't run automatically, but that's the way it is.

These scripts provide PowerBuilder's data windows and all the object painters and other tools with Sybase System XI catalog information that are required to enable the visual representation of the database. Without these files being installed, you will not be able to work correctly with PowerBuilder, and you will not be able to program easily at all.

To run these files, you should execute the following at the command line (after either copying the files to your local machine, or changing directories to the CD- ROM drive):

```
isql -Usa -PPassword -SServer_Name -ipbsyc.sql
```

Where *Password* is the password, the System Administrator (sa) user and *Server_Name* are both the name of the Sybase server that you are going to be adding the procedures to.

For more information on these procedures, please consult the PowerBuilder book *Connecting to Your Database,* page 221.

The premise or style of PowerBuilder coding is built around a series of *Painters* of different types. Essentially, each of these painters is a freeform window that is almost completely independent of any other window. In PowerBuilder, just about everything you develop becomes available for reuse through a shared repository metaphor of existing objects. This is a nice way of organizing code and is an effective multi-developer sharing architecture. Source code is organized in PBL (PowerBuilder Library) files or *Pibbles* as they are known. The PBL files are sharable between multiple applications and are bound into the main code base or executable at compilation time.

All the source code that follows for the PowerBuilder application can be found in PB5DEMO.PBL on the enclosed CD-ROM.

On the CD

Creating a PowerBuilder Database Profile

After you have installed the PowerBuilder system stored procedures mentioned in the Caution above (and not before!), you can begin the process of connecting to a Sybase System XI database server. To create a database profile, follow these steps:

1. Launch PowerBuilder 5 from the Powersoft 5.0 program group into which it was installed. If this is the first time you have launched PowerBuilder after installation, you will see a window similar to that in Figure 15.24.

FIG. 15.24
The default installation of PowerBuilder shows a nice welcome page, but has a very empty work area behind it.

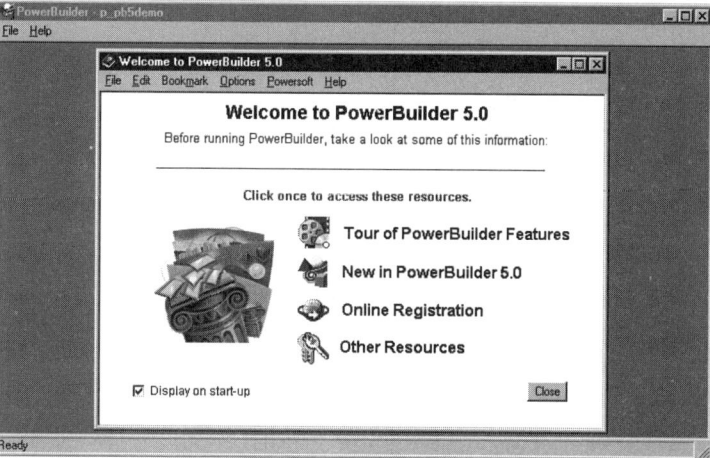

2. From the File menu, select PowerPanel (Ctrl+Shift+N) to display the PowerPanel dialog box (see Fig. 15.25).

3. Scroll down to the Database Profile panel (Shift+F7) and click OK after selecting it to display the Database Profiles dialog box (see Fig. 15.26).

4. Click the New button to display the Database Profile Setup dialog box (see Fig. 15.27).

FIG. 15.25

The PowerPanel dialog box lists all the installed Panels available for use in PowerBuilder. A Panel is just the PowerBuilder way of executing the internal utilities or sections of the development tool.

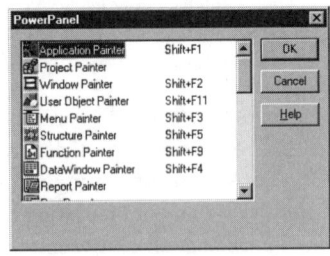

FIG. 15.26

The Database Profiles dialog box lists all the profiles that have been configured on this workstation. Profiles are similar to Delphi's aliases and Centura's `remotedbnames`.

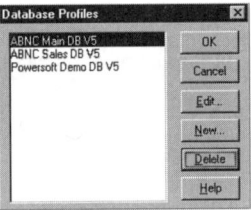

FIG. 15.27

The Database Profile Setup dialog box after having been completed with information for a profile to the *pubs2* database.

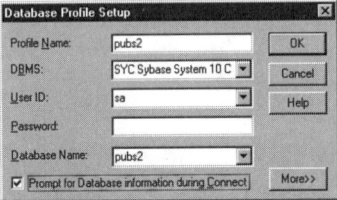

5. Enter a name for the profile in the Profile Name field. (I recommend that you use the same name for the profile that you have for the database that it is connecting to, for simplicity's sake.)

6. Choose SYC Sybase System 10 CTLIB as the DBMS to tell PowerBuilder to use the correct router or driver for the database.

7. Enter the default user that you want to connect to (usually the System Administrator—sa—when in development).

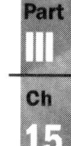

8. Do *not* enter a password. PowerBuilder places the password unencrypted in a file, PB.INI in the PowerBuilder install directory, and this is a significant security flaw.

9. Enter the database name in the <u>D</u>atabase Name field.

10. Turn on the option Prompt for Database Information on <u>C</u>onnect so that the database driver will ask you for the appropriate user information when connecting to the database.

11. Click OK to add the profile and PowerBuilder will prompt you to enter logon information (as you requested in step 10 above) with a standard logon dialog box (see Fig. 15.28).

FIG. 15.28

The Client Library Login dialog box enables you to specify all the attributes that are important to the connection to the server.

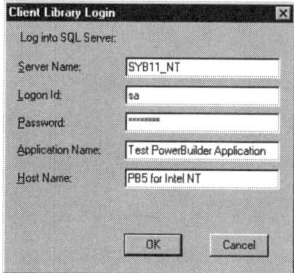

12. Click OK to close the Database Profiles dialog box, noting that the new *pubs2* profile has been added to the list.

Testing the Connectivity Profile to Sybase System XI

After creating the profile, it is necessary to make sure that you can actually talk to the database successfully. To do so, follow these steps:

1. From the <u>F</u>ile menu, select Po<u>w</u>erPanel (Ctrl+Shift+N) to display the PowerPanel dialog box (see Fig. 15.25).

2. Select the Database Painter and click OK, this will change the display to show you the Select Tables dialog box, which should be a list of the tables in the *pubs2* database (see Fig. 15.29).

3. Select the tables that you are going to work with and click OK at which point you should be shown a window that shows the properties of each of the tables you had selected.

After selecting basic table properties, you have shown that you have successful connectivity to the Sybase System XI server.

N O T E The database painter is actually a full-featured database administration tool that permits the management and manipulation of the schema of a System XI database. The database painter is a very powerful way of working with Sybase's system catalog efficiently and quickly to understand the nature of and structure of your databases. ▨

FIG. 15.29

The Select Tables dialog box is asking you for a list of tables that you are going to browse with the database painter. Click the tables that you want (for example, authors and roysched) and then click OK.

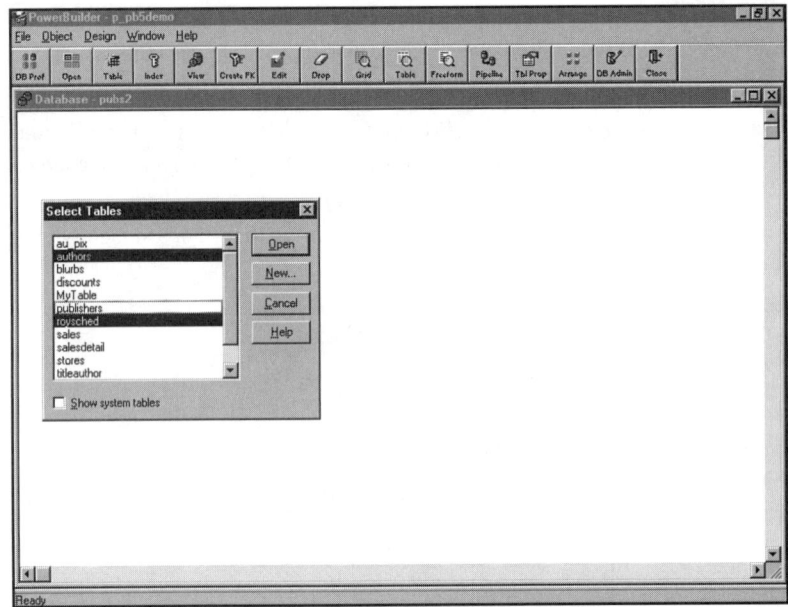

Working with DataWindows

A large part of PowerBuilder's unique development environment centers around the DataWindow. This is a truly amazing piece of software that is both a tabular and form-like browsing object in one. Understanding the DataWindow's full functionality is beyond the scope of this book, but I will point you to an excellent book also published under the Que banner, *Special Edition Using PowerBuilder 5* by Chuck Wood.

The neat thing about DataWindows is that you can write a whole application in them without really even needing to write much code at all. To create a simple DataWindow that browses the *authors* table in a similar fashion to that of the other sample applications you've worked on, follow these steps

1. Type Shift+F4 or select the DataWindow Painter from the PowerPanel dialog box (refer to Fig. 15.25)—if you haven't previously connected to a database, you may need to login and select a database to work with. This will display the Select DataWindow dialog box.

2. Click the New button to display the New DataWindow dialog box (see Fig. 15.30).

3. Select the Data Source that you want to use. The SQL Select is the most commonly used option; however, you can also use a stored procedure, a handwritten SQL query, or an external DLL. (For this example, you will see a SQL Select!)

4. Click the Presentation Style that you want to use from the available options and click OK.

FIG. 15.30

The New DataWindow dialog box shows you all the Data Sources that can be used for DataWindows and the particular styles for each of those data sources that are available.

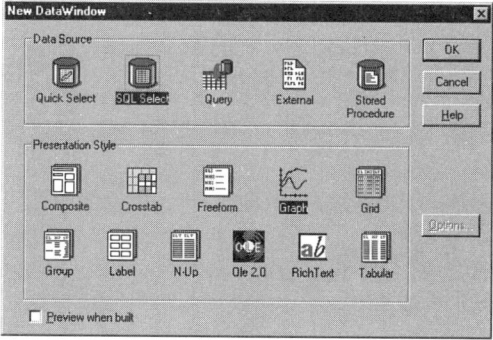

5. After choosing to do a SQL Select, you will be presented with a Select Tables dialog box that you can use to choose which tables you are going to be working with in the DataWindow. Choose the *authors* table. This will display a painter showing all the columns that are used for the Select (see Fig. 15.31).

FIG. 15.31

The graphical view of the tables involved in the SQL statement can be converted to a regular SQL statement by selecting Convert To Syntax from the Design menu.

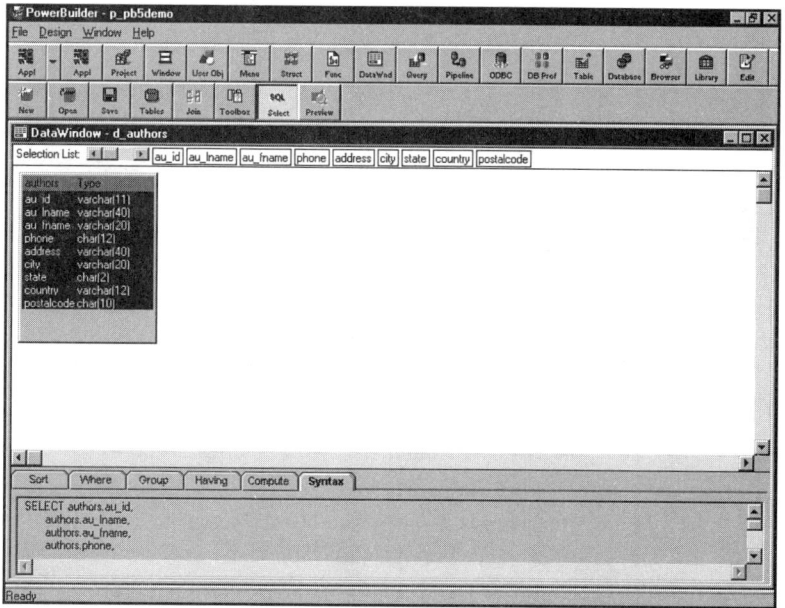

6. To view the layout area/display of the DataWindow, from the Design menu, select Data Source. This will display a field-like representation of the columns that are going into the SQL statement. You can double-click any of the items/objects and customize them by changing the fonts, colors, and so on of the objects (see Fig. 15.32).

FIG. 15.32

By customizing the data window, you can create pretty effective and advanced data entry screens for your users. To get a preview of the window, select Ctrl+Shift+P.

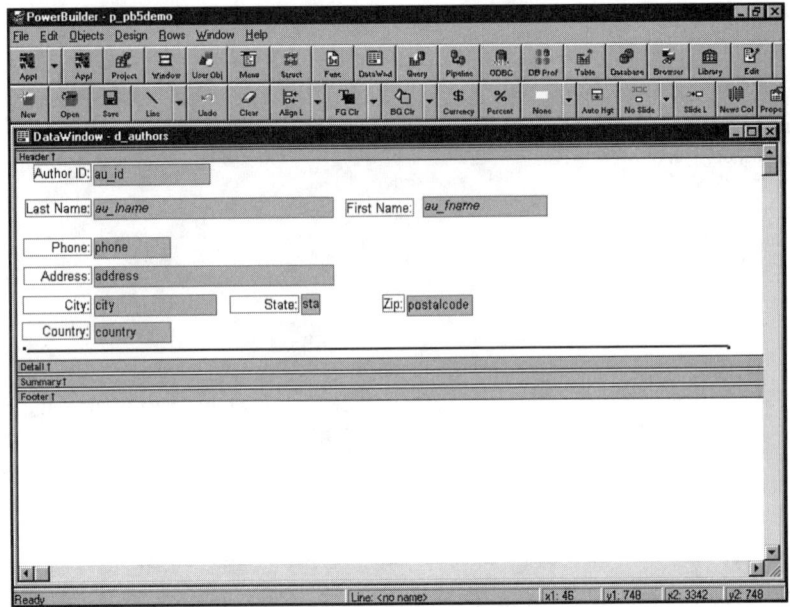

7. From the File menu, select Save (Ctrl+S) to save the DataWindow to the PBL file so that it can be used on a form/sheet later on.

Using a DataWindow

Once you have a DataWindow doing what you want it to be doing, it's time to start using it on a form or window that a user can access.

If you create a default project with which to do work, PowerBuilder provides a simple MDI framework that you can use to add your DataWindow to. To add the DataWindow created earlier to a window, follow these steps:

1. Open the Window Painter (Shift+F2) and select the window w_genapp_sheet from the Select Window dialog box (see Fig. 15.33).

2. From the Controls menu, select DataWindow and draw a frame on the form window that will enclose the required DataWindow.

3. Double-click the DataWindow frame to display the DataWindow properties dialog box (see Fig. 15.34).

4. Enter the DataWindow that was created earlier, or click Browse if you have forgotten its name and need a list to choose from.

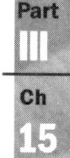

FIG. 15.33

The Select Window dialog box lists all the windows that you have created in the included PBL files.

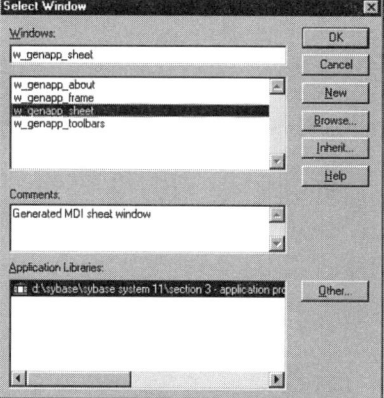

FIG. 15.34

The DataWindow properties dialog box enables you to customize how the DataWindow will be presented to the user, including titles, fonts, colors, shading, borders, and so on.

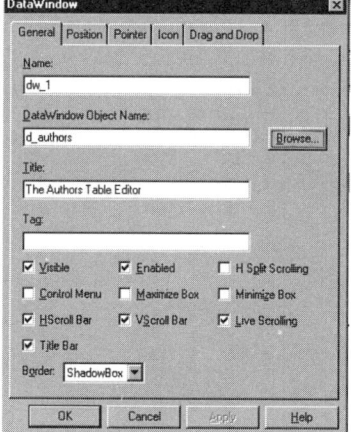

    5. Click OK to activate the DataWindow in the dropped region.

    6. Preview the operation of the DataWindow and the application by running the application (Ctrl+R).

This application doesn't actually seem to do very much because there's no code behind the DataWindow to connect to the database and perform the query. Adding code to the DataWindow is simple, and the logic of the code is also pretty straightforward. To add the required PowerScript code, follow these steps:

    1. Click the Form Window and from the Edit menu, select Script (Ctrl+K). This will display the PowerScript editor, as shown in Figure 15.35.

FIG. 15.35

The PowerScript editor built into PowerBuilder is a nice, multi-color, context-sensitive editor that makes it easy to work with the code associated with an object.

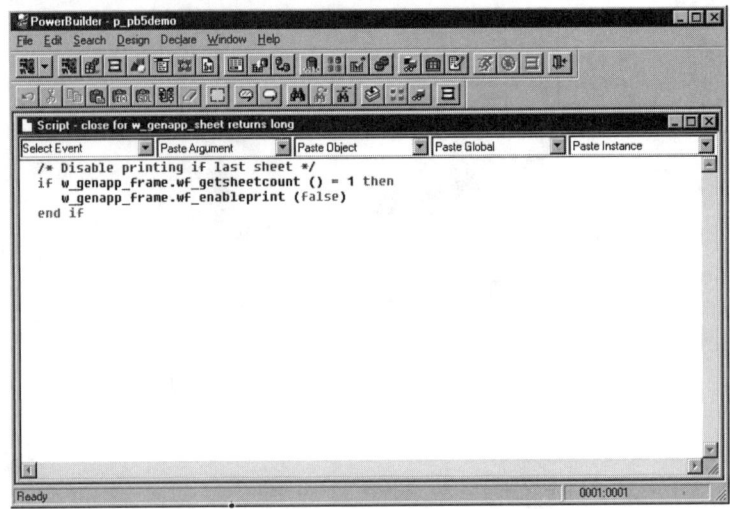

2. Select the Open event from the Select Event field, and add the following code to connect to the database using the default Sql Context handler SQLCA:

```
/* Set up the connection properties */
SQLCA.DBMS = "SYC Sybase System 10 CTLIB"
SQLCA.Database = "pubs2"
SQLCA.LogId = "sa"
SQLCA.LogPass = "centura1"
SQLCA.ServerName = "SYB11_NT"
SQLCA.UserId = "sa"
SQLCA.DBPass = "centura1"

/* now Connect to the database */
Connect Using SQLCA;
```

SQLCA is a logical object that has many properties (a few of which you can see here) and is designed to manage the connection to the database for you.

3. Then add the following logic to the same event to tell the DataWindow which handle to use (setTransObject( )) and to request the data from the server (Retrieve( )):

```
/* get some data */
dw_1.setTransObject(sqlca)
dw_1.Retrieve()
```

4. From the File menu, select Return (Ctrl+T) to return to the Window Painter.

5. From the File menu, select Save (Ctrl+S) to save the PBL file and make the changes permanent.

Making a Real Executable

Probably the best feature that Powersoft added to version 5 of PowerBuilder is the ability to create native executables. These executables are compiled with technology that Powersoft acquired when it bought Watcom (whose C/C++ compiler expertise is well-known). Making a true executable reduces the size of the code significantly and creates a high performance application that is self-contained and easily deployed.

To make an executable, follow these steps:

1. Activate the Project Painter from the PowerPanel, and click New to add a new project; this will display the Project Painter Window (see Fig. 15.36).

FIG. 15.36

The Project painter window is a simple screen that consolidates all the project-wide settings necessary to make an executable.

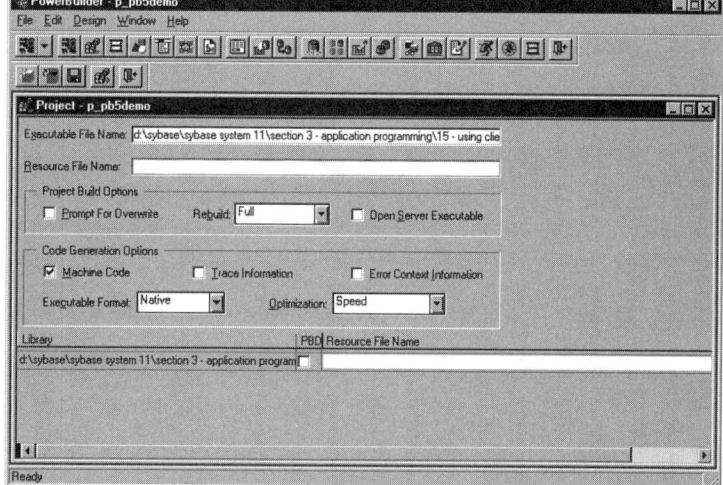

2. Enter the file path and name of the executable that you want.

3. Select the build options that you want to use and indicate whether you want Machine Code generated (required for native executables) or not.

4. Choose whether you want the application optimized for speed (which means the file is bigger) or size (smaller executable file).

5. From the Design menu, select Build Project and the compilation will begin.

The result of a machine code-generated native compile is a truly stand-alone executable that can be deployed with no other required DLLs (except any that you may have manually linked to in your application).

Using Microsoft Visual Basic 4

Visual Basic 4 is Microsoft's latest incarnation of the BASIC standard. As a general tool, it has great features and has a huge install base. Microsoft has always tried to latch on to client/server connectivity, and still has some work to do to support it as cleanly as Centura, PowerBuilder, or Delphi 2.

This was the first time I had ever tried to use Visual Basic for database connectivity, so to a certain extent, I have to accept a bit of the blame for not being a VB expert; however, I was consistently frustrated by a non-intuitive environment that clearly lacked the integration of a mature database development environment.

On the CD

All the source code that follows for the Visual Basic 4 application can be found in VB4DEMO.FRM and VB4.VBP on the CD-ROM.

Understanding the Visual Basic 4 Database Model

Visual Basic and Delphi 2 have a similar approach to data access. Data access is controlled by a Data object that resides on a form. Unlike Delphi 2, VB4 does not use truly non-visual object classes or container classes. Instead, it is possible to alter the visible property of the Data object to hide it if you want.

VB4's Data control is more of a combination of the TDataSource and TDBNavigator classes that are found in Delphi 2, and the visual nature of the arrow buttons explains the need to have it visible most of the time.

Once a Data control is correctly configured and bound to a particular table, it is possible to hook data fields to it as a declared data source on the form.

Connecting to Sybase

I had expected to find some kind of configuration utility in Visual Basic 4 for database connectivity; however, VB4 is so closely integrated to ODBC that ODBC is the only interface provided.

To set up a Data control, I tried to specify ODBC as the Connect property of the Data control that I was adding to the form; however, VB4 refused to correctly work with this. In the end, I gave up and used the Data Form Designer Wizard to create a data form and then copied the Connect string from there. This was truly an inelegant interface and is very surprising from Microsoft.

For future reference, the following is a Connect string for ODBC connectivity to Sybase:

```
ODBC;DSN=My Sybase ODBC;UID=sa;PWD=centura1;
APP=Data Form Designer;WSID=SYB_11;DATABASE=pubs2
```

The information in this string can be set at runtime by altering the Connect property of the Data control.

Preparing and Executing SQL Statements

VB4's Data control can be used to either represent tables or process queries directly. The RecordSource property can either be set to a table name or to a query. The following code snippet demonstrates a push button, changing the query used to populate the Data control. In turn, the Data control acts as a DataSource for a DBGrid control that is also on the form.

Performing the Refresh method of the Data control causes the query to execute and, in turn, causes the grid to be populated:

```
Private Sub Command3_Click()
    MyDataSource2.RecordSource = "select * from titles"
    MyDataSource2.Refresh
End Sub
```

This sort of flexibility is nice and is comparable to the functionality provided by Delphi 2.

About the Sample Application VB4DEMO

The sample application that is included on the CD-ROM demonstrates a basic form that enables browsing and editing of the *authors* table in the *pubs* database. The application has an Update button that interfaces with Data.MyDataSource and invokes its UpdateRecord method, as follows:

```
Private Sub Command1_Click()
    MyDataSource.UpdateRecord
End Sub
```

In a similar fashion, the Delete button removes a record from the table. However, for some obscure reason, there is no corresponding method in Data for DeleteRecord. Instead, you must resolve the reference manually by referring to the Data control's recordset, which is presumably the cache of data that the Data control is manipulating:

```
Private Sub Command2_Click()
    MyDataSource.Recordset.Delete
End Sub
```

Overall, the style of programming in Visual Basic is quite similar to Delphi 2. Here is the same logic to make the Data control appear docked to the base of the form window—this time as Visual Basic code:

```
Private Sub Form_Resize()
    MyDataSource.Top = Form1.ScaleHeight - MyDataSource.Height
    MyDataSource.Width = Form1.ScaleWidth
End Sub
```

From Here...

In this chapter, you learned about the basics of ODBC and how to configure it on a workstation. In addition, you were introduced to four of the best client/server development tools on the market: Centura Software Corporation's Centura Team Developer 1.0, Borland's Delphi 2.0 Client/Server, Powersoft's PowerBuilder 5 Enterprise, and Microsoft's Visual Basic 4. In addition, there are many fine tools that were not mentioned here.

Each of the products covered in this chapter is strong in certain areas and weak in others. Choosing one of these development tools should be done after carefully evaluating a project's needs. In addition, if you are embarking on a large project, you may want to get consultants from each of the companies to come and demonstrate and prototype the sort of application you will be developing to get an idea of how it might be achieved in the development tools that the company represents. Both Centura and Sybase (through its Powersoft group) have consultants that would be happy to come in and do a product evaluation and a walkthrough with you at your site. For Visual Basic and Delphi, unless you are a very large customer, your best bet is to use a local Microsoft or Borland Solution provider or Value-Added Reseller (VAR).

After reading this chapter, you're probably anxious to get into some heavy duty programming. I suggest that you have a look at the following chapters to further your application development progress:

- Chapter 10, "Understanding Stored Procedures," teaches you how to define storage structures, such as parameters and local variables, by using system variables. Stored procedures are a fundamental part of any serious Sybase application and should be used all the time.

- Chapter 16, "Partitioning an Application," gives tips and tricks on how to take advantage of popular three-tier partitioning schemes to make your application more robust and powerful.

- Chapter 17, "Using Third-Party Products," provides reviews of some of the more popular and powerful third-party application programs that will help you work with a database and develop a database schema with a modeling tool.

- Chapter 23, "Using Sybase's Configuration Options," shows you how to use query options to control the display of data through Set command options. These options help optimize the performance of your application.

Partitioning an Application

Everyone's talking about it... but is anybody doing it? No I'm not talking about high school and dating...I'm talking about application partitioning. No other topic is more often discussed among the most technically minded developers these days than application partitioning. The purpose of this chapter is to introduce you to some of the key concepts of application partitioning so that you can be aware of what it takes to split up a system to work on several different domains.

Typically, people think of partitioning an application as the straightforward process of moving client code onto the server or vice versa. People think that by partitioning an application, you will be able to reap the benefits of either the server or client for general benefits in performance. This *is* true. You can end up with a better performing system by splitting the application onto another platform; however, this isn't the only benefit of splitting up an application. ■

Understanding the types of partitioning

There are many different ways to partition an application to achieve better application software distribution and performance on large systems.

Knowing when and how to partition an application

With many options available to you to perform application partitioning, half the problem comes down to choosing a technology that will benefit your projects from a crowded marketplace. Use this chapter as an introduction to some of the better-known partitioning systems available today.

Working with Sybase Open Servers and Tuxedo

Sybase's Open Servers are a generic way of writing applications that act as application servers using the Open Server (a variation on Open Client) API. Tuxedo is a popular three-tier architecture in use in many corporations. This chapter will introduce you to how Tuxedo works.

Using Tempest

Tempest is a new partitioning technology developed by Tempest Software Corporation. This technology will serve as a demonstration of putting application partitioning into practice.

Performing Application Partitioning

There are a number of other reasons to perform application partitioning. These reasons include the following:

- **Code re-use**—By moving functions from either the server or client into another domain, you can use different protocols to interface with these functions that preserve the functional code irrespective of the client or server technology with which you end up developing your project.

- **Scalability**—By moving application code into another partition from either the server or the client, you can then introduce the concept of managed transaction processing to improve the performance of the system. By having the ability to move transactional logic onto different platforms, you instantly gain the ability to size your application using different hardware as required.

- **Platform neutrality**—Sometimes referred to as application database independence, a key benefit from a partitioned application is that it doesn't need to know how to interact with a database system. Instead, the partitioned logic can be responsible for interacting with the database and the transport of the partitioning software can make the required data available without knowledge of a database at all. This scheme is often employed for interfacing client/server applications with legacy databases through message-based gateways to the host. The client program uses standard calls to the messenger, and then the messenger is responsible for interacting with the mainframe host and then returning the data in a meaningful format to the client/server program.

- **Transaction Complexity**—If you have a complex transaction that must perform operations on several different systems, there's a lot to be gained by placing the responsibility for managing the integrity of that transaction on a separate server independent from the client. Say you are writing a Web-based banking system, and you are letting a customer perform a debit from their checking account that will be transferred to the customer's stock portfolio in the form of a trade, and to the customer's credit card as a payment on an outstanding bill. This sort of multi-part transaction may involve several different updates on different systems that would be difficult to manage reliably and efficiently on a large scale, on the client processor. By using an application partitioning scheme, this transaction could easily be managed and controlled by software like Novell's Tuxedo Transaction Processing Monitor. Tuxedo is more fully discussed below in the section titled, "Understanding Novell's Tuxedo."

These benefits are typically associated with the current buzzword in client/server circles these days—*three-tier applications*. It is important to remember that you don't have to consciously be trying to create a three-tier application to reap the benefits of one. You will be able to garner the benefits described above in your applications without having to go out and adopt a full three-tier development model at your site.

NOTE Three-tier applications separate the layers of an application into three (or more) distinct sets of operations: the user interface tier, the business logic tier, and the database tier.

Partitioning an application can be performed in several different ways that use very different styles of inter-process communication; in all of them, the goal is the same—to provide a mechanism that enables different components of an application to be placed on different execution systems. This means that you may, for example, move business logic to run on a different server from the database server, or move graphics processing and calculation from the smart workstation directly on to the server and simply use the terminal for graphical display. The typical separation of a system involves three tiers or layers of processing:

- The graphical user interface (the first tier)
- The business logic or application logic (the second tier)
- The database management system (the third tier)

These layers can easily be blurred and do not necessarily mean that separate computers have to be involved; this means that the technology is *logically* separated between these layers. The logical separation of these technologies enables you to scale an application in different ways according to the needs of the system without affecting the user's application physically. If, for example, the database is not performing adequately, a bigger server (perhaps of a different vendor) can be implemented and the only code that needs to change (if any) is the code in the business logic or application logic layer (tier two).

In a similar fashion, if the business logic is not up to scratch, or a different way of processing the data is desired, you can just plug in the new business layer without affecting the whole system.

Clearly, the most important nature of *all* application partitioning schemes is that they are based on sound communications protocols and strategies. The technology required for communicating between the layers or partitions of applications breaks down into several key groups, styles, or solutions, as follows:

- **Message-based**—Asynchronous or Synchronous messaging systems have been around for a long time in the computing world. Using messaging as a means of splitting up an application is a normal evolution of the computer systems from the legacy environment where message based processing has existed for decades. Message-based partitioning is the strongest and most portable of all the schemes because the only consideration between the different components of your application is that they can communicate with each other. After you have established effective and transparent communications, each component can be of any language, database, or operating system platform that makes sense for the job at hand.

- **Stored procedures**—This is the most common partitioning scheme employed in the client/server arena. The server vendor's procedural language is adopted on the server side of an application to improve performance of long-running procedural logic. The procedural language of Sybase is Transact-SQL, Oracle's is PL-SQL; both languages are essentially a derivative and combination of COBOL and BASIC.

Both languages support a wide variety of operations and enable quite complex business processes to be modeled on the server without the need for any external code written in another language such as C. Stored procedures have an obvious problem—they are (with very few exceptions) not portable to any other database vendor and thus tie you directly to a particular vendor's implementation of the stored procedure syntax.

- **Transaction processing monitors**—TP monitors are designed to manage large numbers of clients talking to a limited number of servers. TP monitors act as a gateway or traffic cop between the hundreds and thousands of users who are trying to access a database system. TP monitors typically operate over a discrete number of channels to the database. For example, a TP monitor may service 1,000 clients through 20 channels or connections to the database. In this way, you ensure that the database server does not become bogged down servicing the network when it should be working on the actual requests themselves.

  TP monitors, such as Novell's Tuxedo, usually have a proprietary programming language with which you write a service or *function* of the TP monitor that the remote clients can execute. This service is then responsible for performing the necessary operations on the server that it is connecting to. TP monitors are excellent choices for very large systems, and for those systems that must have guaranteed reliable communications with a database server.

- **Remote function/procedure calls**—Partitioning schemes in RPCs are a very effective and performance-enhanced way of separating the components of a system. RPCs work by having an *Interface Definition Language* (IDL) that specifies the interface of the remote procedure in terms of parameters expected to be sent and the data that is going to be returned.

  RPCs can communicate over publicly defined protocols, such as TCP/IP, or can be implemented in proprietary interfaces, such as Open Environment Corporation's Entera product. The advantage of the IDL is that it enables two independent applications to start communicating over the proprietary RPC protocol, provided each application can read and interpret the IDL.

- **Remote business objects**—RBOs are the natural extension and evolution of the RPC model into the object-oriented programming world of languages like Java and C++. RBOs work by letting you define in the client application an instance of a class that is created and defined on a different server or operating system. The underlying communication technology that makes any references to class methods execute transparently and can provide *in-process* or *out-of-process execution.*

  In-process execution means that the class is run in the same process as the client, which thereby eliminates the majority of the networking once the class has been transferred to the client. Out-of-process execution means that the class or object runs in a separate process, possibly on a separate server or servers and communications is used to transfer the data transparently to the client process. (Distributed or Network OLE [DCOM] is Microsoft's RBO solution.)

Understanding Two-Tier Applications

Two-tier applications are what 90 percent of modern client/server applications are today. A two-tier application naturally has two participants—the client and the server. In a two-tier application, there's a one-to-one ratio between clients and connections to the server. However, in some complex systems, the client may establish multiple independent connections to the server to perform particular operations such as nightly routines.

The typical two-tier application is written in traditional client/server development tools like PowerBuilder, SQLWindows, or Visual Basic. It communicates to any of a number of different back ends like Sybase System XI, Oracle, or SQLBase. The two-tier application generally houses a lot of logic on the client because procedural code must be executed in a programmatic form that is not employed on the server.

Two-tier applications are often described as the first generation of client/server programs because they adopted the model that was proposed in the late 1980s and early 1990s: that you should evenly split up applications so that all functional code would execute on the client and all the server would do is respond to SQL queries and return the data as quickly as possible.

Understanding Fat Client Applications

Fat Client applications are those applications that have all the application code residing on the client's computer. These applications are typically quite large in size and have a great deal of code that is executing on the client at one time to perform all manner of operations. *Fat Client* applications are generally written in such a way that all functional code executes on them with the only thing going across the network to the server being SQL queries, and the only thing coming back to the client being data.

Fat client applications are written in this manner for one of a couple of reasons that include the following:

- **Complete database independence**—With client code completely responsible for interacting with the database, you can be sure that your application is portable, provided the database supports a certain required level of ANSI SQL compatibility.

- **Support for Simple DBMSs**—Some database implementations (usually the older ones) still don't support the concept of server-based procedural code execution (stored procedures); you have no alternative to placing application logic in the client.

- **Simple systems**—Some applications simply don't require the use of server-based code because it offers no advantages. Many multimedia browsing types of applications that just perform simple queries and updates would get little benefit from a stored procedure.

There's a good market for the development of Fat Client applications because they are generally faster to write and easier to deploy because they have little code that is platform-specific. However, Fat Client applications have a significant problem with performance.

Fat Client applications rely on the client to perform all compute-intensive operations and as such cannot compete with server-driven or optimized applications. Take a typical operation that needs to be performed in a system every day, such as updating and performing some kind of operation on every record in a master file. For a fat client to process the data, each record must come across the network and then be operated on by the client. If the row by row processing is sufficiently complex, this data processing can be quite slow. For a server-based application, a single procedure can be executed on the server that will perform all of these tasks directly on the server with optimal performance.

Obviously a server-based solution is better suited for compute-intensive operations and for those systems that must process a lot of data. However, with the advent of three-tier application programming systems, it is sometimes unclear which server you should use.

Fat client applications typically have maintenance problems when the code at either the client or the database has to change. For example, upgrade and distribution is not very easy with a fat client application because any changes made to the client requires redistributing the client to all the users. This increases your maintenance and distribution costs. On the other hand, if the business or application logic resides on the server, any change made to it would automatically be reflected without having to redistribute the client application.

Understanding Fat Server Applications

Fat server applications are those applications that rely almost solely on the server to perform all the operations required: user interface, business logic, and database management. Sound like an improbable situation? Well, consider that a fat server application is mainframe-based and isn't a client/server system at all. On the mainframe, the only thing that was off-loaded to other systems was the display of the 3270 or 5450 (on an AS/400) text stream. Everything else, from keystroke management on the terminal to long batch processes, was managed and controlled on the mainframe, a single Fat Server.

You might ask, especially if you're new to the Information Technology business, why would anyone do this? Mainframes have been around for as long as the IT business itself, and the term legacy is almost universally applied to applications written on a mainframe because they are the legacy of the computing world. Mainframe systems have been developed over the last three or four decades and have a serious number of lines of code that will probably never be rewritten in the client/server arena. There are many technology companies from Attachment to IBM itself that make a lot of money interfacing to and selling mainframe systems that support the existing investments of large corporations, which can afford to maintain mainframe systems.

The other reason that people rely on mainframes is that it is proven technology that can support thousands and tens of thousands of users concurrently. It is ironic, but all the mid-range UNIX vendors from Sun, to DEC, to HP all refer to their high-end server solutions that are designed as the ultimate client/server solutions as *mainframe class,* implying that their UNIX boxes could replace a mainframe in your environment if you let it.

Mainframes are relied on for the most complex and largest systems in the world of IT today. Typical mainframe applications include flight-reservation systems, ATM networking switching systems, telephone network management, and large-scale commercial banking systems. Each of these systems is categorized by the small size of the transactions that are required to the host and the way that data is managed on the client. These systems are relatively non-interactive with the client and generally have a large volume of batch processing involved in them.

Mainframes excel at the management of huge datasets and the management of large numbers of clients. The load-balancing and transaction-processing capabilities are built right into the operating systems of a mainframe (such as the CICS on IBM hardware). As such, all applications that are written on these mainframes are inherently multi-user and designed to support large volumes of user traffic.

Part
III

Ch

16

These mainframe applications are the so-called *fat server applications* of today. They suffer in one key area—scalability. Ultimately, if all processing is being performed on a single server, be it a mainframe or a super high-end UNIX box, there's going to be a point at which you can no longer support the addition of extra users or more data to the system. At this point you are stuck: the only option you have is to purchase bigger and faster hardware. And ultimately, you run out of top-end hardware that you can throw at a problem. This problem of mainframes is what led to the advent of client/server computing and the notion of distributed processing.

The distributed processing model of client/server and/or tiered application environments seeks to find some kind of balance between the components of the application that are required for a user. For example, the first generation of client/server programming languages sought to off-load application or local validation from the host or mainframe to the client machines.

In this model, the client was responsible for validating that accurate data was going to be sent to the host (or database) and required no further validation. However, the problem that was soon discovered with client validation is that if a programmer failed to validate the data then erroneous data could make it into the system and cause harm to the integrity of the database. As a compromise, server-side triggers were added to most relational database products to allow for central management of the integrity of the data, independent of any client program.

Client/Server and Partitioned Application systems make better use of technology available today and try to make each computer involved in a transaction equally responsible for managing the effort or load of the transaction. The obvious advantage of this scheme is that you are much more able to scale the system with greater ease. Adding more clients has less of a burden on the server because the clients contribute to the processing.

Understanding Two-and-a-Half Tier Applications

Two-and-a-half-tier applications are the logical next step for two tier applications. As the database systems became more advanced, they began to introduce procedural extensions to the SQL standard that would enable the programmer to write procedural logic and have it execute on the server. These procedural language extensions in Sybase are in the Transact-SQL language and allow for robust application development completely on the server.

▶ **See** "Working with and Understanding Stored Procedures," **p. 256**

What these extensions enabled is that functional or procedural code that previously had to execute on the client could now be executed on the server. This typically lead to several advantages:

- **Reduced query processing overhead**—The benefits of stored procedures are due to the fact that the query plans for all operations are pre-compiled on the server, reducing the time the server requires to understand the request from the client.

- **Less network traffic**—If large SQL statements are sent over the network, and large datasets are returned, substantial network resources are required to manage the traffic. Using stored procedures eliminates the SQL's being transferred across the network. Instead, all that is sent is the stored procedure name and the required parameters. Furthermore, there is no need to send the data back across the network to process it. You can process the data right on the server inside the procedure using server-side cursors.

- **Generally faster servers**—Typically, your database server is going to have a faster CPU, more memory, and greater resources to process and perform operations. This will result in better performance of the application.

- **Shorter transaction time**—Because the event or the transaction involves less computing across the network and on the server itself, a stored procedure-based transaction executes faster and therefore more of them can be performed per second. For most applications, the more transactions per second that your application can perform, the better.

- **Transactional integrity**—Stored procedures can be treated as a single event from the client's point of view. Even if the stored procedure performs a number of operations, the client can roll back the transaction begun for the procedure if it chooses to. The advantage of this option is that you can have complex operations be performed on the server without the client's needing to understand the transaction's nature, and yet still give the client ultimate control of the transaction's completion or undoing.

Two-and-a-half-tier applications are almost universally the best performing applications that you can write. They combine the flexibility of client-based validation with the performance of stored procedure transactions. For most applications, with the exception of those that need to do multiple, disparate operations on different servers, writing two-and-a-half-tier applications is the best option you have. Any three or n tier partitioning scheme is going to impose an overhead that will cost you performance and add complexity to your application, an outcome you can generally do without.

There is a great big negative to writing applications based on the two-and-a-half-tier model— you are inextricably tied to a particular database vendor's stored procedure syntax. There's no denying that the benefit of server-side performance can come at the cost of portability. However, a general trend in the database server community these days is to see convergence in the functional toolsets available through each vendor's extensions to the SQL standard. The SQL standard itself is trying to define the standards for procedural languages, but each vendor is implementing extensions far more quickly than the standard can evolve.

I expect that you will see in the coming years each vendor effectively support everything each of the other vendors can do. Once that has been achieved, it's going to become a case of using a smart interpreter or parser to move procedures between different platforms such as Oracle and Sybase. Both Oracle and Sybase have rudimentary versions of these porting tools available for projects right now; however, both of them still require some hand tuning of the ported code.

Three- and n-Tier Applications

Once you have established that you can split some of your code off into a stored procedure to get the benefits of a two-and-a-half-tier application, it just becomes a matter of time before you want to split more and more of the code on to the server. However, some code doesn't make sense on the database server. Database servers inherently like to perform operations on textual data, and generally don't like to work with things like spatial data (for geographic systems) or complex mathematical data (for engineering systems). In these cases, you still want to split the business logic out of the client, but the database server is not necessarily the best place for the code to reside.

Welcome to the third tier. Three-tier applications split business logic or functional code onto any server platform that makes sense. Strictly conceiving of an application in three tiers is probably limiting; the business logic could be executing on any number of servers in your domain; thus, the generic term *n-tier computing* is used to define any computing performed on more than one device where each of the devices are peers of one another.

The concept of computing devices as peers of each other is an important one to grasp. In this model, all computers are participating with equal importance to the net or complex transaction. The downside of this model is that any particular break in the whole computing chain can affect the whole system, so inter-process communication and reliability is key to managing a well-designed n-tier system.

All *n*-tiered solutions rely on some form of communications to manage the inter-process (between tier) transactions. The key problem that most people have found when implementing *n*-tier solutions is that the configuration and management of these communications protocols are complex and difficult. In addition, the performance cost associated with transactions computing over multiple tiers of computers can adversely affect a system. Early adopters of products based on DCE (the Distributed Computing Environment) often complained of unreasonable performance costs associated with the DCE protocols, but acknowledged that the power of the process and computing distribution was worth the hit in performance.

There are many advantages to tiered application processing or distributed computing that mostly center around letting the right computer on the network perform the task that is being requested. By setting up a cluster of *application servers* that support remote procedure calls, or some other form of application partitioning, you can develop a smart network of computing devices accessible from any of the clients on the network. The goal of application development should be to make sure that all computing resources are accessible and sharable for the benefit of client computers on the network. This is the *component* application development model, where smart objects are developed that can be interfaced locally or remotely through the same computing technologies such as OLE or CORBA.

Another way of thinking about the *n*-tier partitioning model is not actually at the application level but at the data level. In this sense, the tiers correspond to data storage units. For example, one tier might be corporate data that's stored in a mainframe in a central location. Another tier might be departmental or divisional data that is stored in a regional or local database server on a UNIX-based machine. The third tier would be distributed data, such as data that's transferred to laptop computers for sales staff or other mobile officers of a corporation.

Understanding Sybase Open Servers

Sybase Open Servers are built with the Server Library API that looks very similar to the Client Library API documented in Chapter 14, "Understanding the Sybase Client Model (Client Library)." The major difference between the two APIs is that the Server Library API is designed around allocating server based resources and managing multiple threads or clients concurrently.

General processing of data is virtually the same in the Server Library API compared to the Client Library API. An Open Server exposes the same client interface as any Sybase Server, such as the Sybase System XI SQL Server or Data Server, the Monitor Server, or the Replication Server. The advantage of an Open Server is that any standard Sybase client can communicate to it through standard Sybase Open Client calls (Client Library or DBLibrary) to access its resources.

Using the Open Server technology is an excellent way of extending the Sybase environment for your corporation, because the clients do not need to purchase any additional middleware to communicate or interact with the Open Server. Open servers can perform any task permissible in C/C++ and therefore can be very powerful extensions to the standard environment. Microsoft has developed a full DOS interpreter, based on an Open Server. This means that you can execute DOS commands through a Sybase Client Library connection to the Open Server and effectively control any of the disk-based resources on the host server. Other things that you can do with Open Server include the following:

- **E-mail**—It would be easy to write an Open Server that, for example, accepted a text stream and a recipient list and then sent an e-mail through the MAPI application programming interface.
- **Complex mathematics**—Sybase's Transact-SQL provides some mathematical functionality, but the functions aren't all that advanced, and the Sybase math engine has never been speedy. Writing a mathematical processing engine like an Open Server would be a great resource for an engineering company.

■ **Data gateways**—Using Open Server technology makes it possible to write gateways to other data storage systems on other platforms and yet to be able to return the data to the client using standard Client Library protocols. In this manner, the Open Server acts as a data-conditioning agent, performing protocol exchanges with foreign systems such as mainframes and then presenting the data to the client in an understandable form.

Clients can connect directly to an Open Server, or can execute processes on the Open Server through the RPC mechanism provided in Transact-SQL. For example, say you were connected to an existing SQL Server and were performing normal transactions against the database. When you needed to perform some additional functions on the Open Server, you would prefix the procedure that you are executing on the Open Server with the server name (that must be defined to the SQL Server with `sp_addserver`) and execute it through a normal Transact-SQL command:

```
Exec Open_Server_Name...Procedure_Name [Parameters...]
```

N O T E   A key advantage of the Open Server design model is that the API is available on all 28 client platforms that the Sybase SQL Server supports, guaranteeing you the ability to integrate Open Server resources in just about any environment imaginable. ■

Writing a Simple Open Server

To write an Open Server, you will need access to a C Compiler capable of compiling Client Library and Server Library applications. Microsoft Visual C++ 4.x is a recommended compiler for Open Server applications.

Open server is an application that has two key components: network processing and data processing. The network processing components are designed to provide the threading and the client management technology needed to manage the users that connect to and execute procedures on the Open Server. The data processing logic is simply the code that you are going to write in C/C++ to perform the tasks that you want to be executed by the Open Server.

The application flow of an Open Server is very similar to that of an Open Client application:

```
Allocate a context structure( cs_ctx_alloc )
  Specify Server Properties( srv_props )
    Initialize Server Library( srv_init )
      Install error and message handlers( srv_callback )
        Start The Server( srv_run )
          Listen for clients and process their requests
        De-allocate any server acquired resources( srv_free )
De-allocate context structure( cs_ctx_drop )
```

N O T E   Full documentation for the Open Server API is provided in two Sybase manuals, *Open Server-Library/C Reference Manual* and *Open Client and Open Server Common Libraries Reference Manual*. Both of these resources are excellent tools that I have found to be most useful when writing Open Server applications. ■

Part
III

Ch
16

Understanding Open Server Events

When a client establishes a connection to the Open Server, they gain the ability to raise events on the Open Server. These events are the way in which you code procedures and application code into your Open Server. The default service handlers listen for common events like `ct_connect` from a client application and will respond with connection characteristics or an appropriate message such as `"No event handler <request_type> has been installed in the Server"` to the client program. In this way, if you forget to cater for a particular client request, your clients will at least be notified that the Open Server is up and running, but that it didn't know how to deal with the request.

Installing an event processor in Open Server code involves calling the Open Server API `srv_handle`. The `srv_handle` function installs an event handler in the server for the desired event type that you want to monitor and process. The types of events that you can process are as follows:

- **SRV_ATTENTION**—This is a synchronous event that occurs most often when a client cancels a request for data or cancels a long running task on the Open Server.
- **SRV_BULK**—A client is issuing a Bulk Copy (BCP) request.
- **SRV_CONNECT**—A client is requesting to connect to the Open Server using the Client Library call `ct_connect`. You might want to issue a particular event to the console of your Open Server when a client connects to it.
- **SRV_CURSOR**—A client is requesting a server-side cursor. Unless you are writing a pretty heavy-duty application, it is unlikely that you will ever process this event.
- **SRV_DISCONNECT**—A client is requesting to disconnect from the Open Server using the Client Library call `ct_exit`. You may also receive this event if one of your threads is killed for some reason by the underlying operating system.

N O T E   Any RPC based connections implicitly terminate at the end of the execution of the RPC. ■

- **SRV_DYNAMIC**—A client has transmitted a request to process Dynamic SQL. You could write a handler for `SRV_DYNAMIC` if you wanted to be able to process calls that include regular Transact-SQL to, say, pass them on to another SQL Server of System XI type or of another database vendor.
- **SRV_LANGUAGE**—A client has made a Transact-SQL statement request, using `ct_command` and `ct_send` to transmit it to the server. This is a typical event that you would want to handle to install your own parsing system.
- **SRV_MSG**—A client has sent a message to you. Typically, you can ignore this event.
- **SRV_OPTION**—A client has requested to change a server option. The typical use of this event is to enable the client to issue the equivalent of a Transact-SQL `set` statement through which they are trying to change the behavior of the server.

- ■ SRV_RPC—A client or Sybase System XI SQL Server has issued a Remote Procedure Call (RPC). This is a common event that you should process in order to install your own RPCs that other clients can execute.

- ■ SRV_START—This is the first event that is issued after the call to srv_run. You would normally place startup or initialization logic in a function designed to be executed on this message.

- ■ SRV_STOP—This is the complement of SRV_START and is sent immediately prior to the server's shutting down. You should use this message to clean up any resources that you have opened during the execution of the Open Server, and to notify any other services that you are shutting down (if necessary).

- ■ SRV_URGDISCONNECT—This message is sent to you when you execute a call to srv_event in your own code to tell the server to shut down. You would normally raise or execute this event if there was an urgent need to kill a server thread and to bypass the normal messages that have been queuing for that thread. Sending a SRV_URGDISCONNECT via srv_event will arrive immediately and will jump the normal message queue so that you can process it pseudo-synchronously.

Part
III

Ch
16

Understanding Novell's TUXEDO

Novell's TUXEDO is a similar style of programming system to the Open Server libraries provided by Sybase. The intent of TUXEDO is to provide a robust, three-tier, transaction-processing environment. Like Sybase's Open Server, TUXEDO has an API that you must code to in order to gain from its services. Coding a TUXEDO server is similar to coding an Open Server, and many of the same messaging models exist in both APIs. TUXEDO's communications protocol is either based on TCP/IP or the OSI Transaction Processing (TP) standard, which means that it's not quite as flexible as the Client Library protocols supported by Sybase.

Interfacing to a TUXEDO application server is done through proprietary client-side libraries on platforms such as Windows 3.1, Windows NT, and UNIX. These libraries perform the same sorts of functions that Client Library does for Sybase and act as a high-level transaction interface to the TUXEDO server.

One of the great advantages of TUXEDO is that it provides a simple way of managing the transactions that are being processed through the server. A single graphical workstation/console is provided, through which you manage the server transactions.

TUXEDO is also well known for its advanced security services. Like Sybase SQL Server, you can create users that have Access Control Lists (ACLs) or permissions to various services or objects on the application server. These ACLs can then be used in groups to manage multiple users concurrently. TUXEDO enables plug-in authentication code so that different vendors can implement their own authentication logic using security schemes like Kerberos.

An interesting feature of TUXEDO is that you can use it to send messages to clients, as well as receive and process application events. By this mechanism of messaging the client base, you can notify the clients of events that occur that require application handling or management. This is the concept of application service-based triggers. In the same fashion as writing a trigger on a database server, you can write a trigger on the application server that can either notify the originating process, that is, the user who executed a process on the application server, or any other process, such as a systems management queue, on the network of special events. This is a great way to log any suspicious activity on particular application services for later review.

TUXEDO is implemented through RPC calls. You execute abstractly named services (or RPCs), like *PerformSystemValidation* on the TUXEDO application server. That server will respond with the appropriate data stream. TUXEDO application servers can be set up in a domain scheme. If multiple servers exist on a network, and they each have been notified that the other exists, then if a request comes in that one server doesn't know how to handle, it will pass it on to another server to see if that server can handle it. RPC calls in the TUXEDO environment require uniquely named process names that enable the RPC to exist on any of the registered TUXEDO servers on the network.

TUXEDO's transaction processing is very capable and provides built-in load balancing capabilities, which help you to prioritize and schedule transactions on TUXEDO application servers according to rules and message queues that you define. You can also use TUXEDO as a marshall that interacts with database resources and helps you manage hundreds of users connected to a single database through a secure and guaranteed transaction-processing architecture.

N O T E You can learn more about Novell's TUXEDO product and other offerings from Novell Corporation at their Web site: **http://corp.novell.com/market/apr96/ mm000035.htm**. ▪

Using Tempest

Now that you have seen and read about several different partitioning systems available to you from leading vendors, I thought I would introduce you to a new piece of technology that is coming to market this year from a startup company, Tempest Software Corporation. Tempest is a messaging system based on the notion of mailboxes. A central mail server, the *Tempest Server*, is a messaging server that receives and dispatches messages to any mailboxes that are connected to the server on a TCP/IP based network.

Tempest has a very simple programming interface consisting of just nine functions. These functions are designed to implement and manage the messaging protocol for you in a simple fashion. With limited functions, it is quite obvious that the design goal for this product was simplicity.

In this section you'll see a sample application written using the Tempest messaging protocols to distribute the processing across multiple computing environments. The sample applications are written using Centura's Team Developer; however, the Tempest API is supported on any Win32 or UNIX-based application development language through either a DLL or through shared libraries on UNIX. The Tempest server is written in POSIX compliant C and is initially supported on Windows NT and Sun Solaris. In the future, the server will be ported to other server platforms such as HP-UX 10.10 and DEC Alpha.

The power of Tempest cannot be underestimated by its simplicity. Writing a Tempest application provides you with protocol transparent communications and a clean asynchronous way of sending transactions across the network to one or many recipients. In addition, the Tempest server is based on a store and forward model. What this means is that if you queue a message for a given mailbox, the Tempest server will hold the message in the server until the client has received it. Unlike many protocols used to perform Tempest-style messaging, the Tempest model is a push model. In this manner, messages are sent to clients: clients do not have to request messages from the server. They will instead be invoked on the client through a sent message.

N O T E You can find detailed information on the Tempest Server and Client products at Tempest Software's Web site: **http://www.tempestsoft.com**. There are some excellent Java based demonstration applications also available on their Web site that show how powerful the Tempest messaging architecture is, and how easy it is to create distributed applications. ▪

Starting the Tempest Server

N O T E All the sample code and screen shots are based on an early beta version of the Tempest product, which was (at least) feature complete. It is quite possible that some of this code will require some modification when the Tempest product ships; please feel free to e-mail me at **phazlehurst@phoenixint.com** if you have questions on how to get this sample code to work with the shipping version of the Tempest product. ▪

Starting the Tempest Server on Windows NT is very simple, and to do so, follow these steps:

1. Launch a command shell in Windows NT.

2. Use the cd command in the command shell to change directories to the directory in which you installed the Tempest Server.

3. Execute the Tempest server from the command line as follows:

```
Tempest
```

Launching the Tempest server will consume a 10M disk area for messaging queuing and will cause the console application to be started and the server to enter a message receiving loop (see Fig. 16.1).

FIG. 16.1

The Console Screen for the Tempest Server lists the number of messages that it has received and sent every second.

```
Command Prompt - tempest2.exe
D:\Centura\Tempest>tempest2.exe
960721/220843 <LOG_Info> TEMPEST(tm) Messenger (INTERNET edition) version 2
960721/220843 <LOG_Info> Copyright (C) 1996 by Heldenleben Corp.
960721/220843 <LOG_Info> Written by Francis Cianfrocca and Paula Hostetter
960721/220843 <LOG_Info>
960721/220844 <LOG_Info> mem-mgr ok (10485760 msg-space)
960721/220845 <LOG_Info> QList started (1000 queues)
960721/220845 <LOG_Info> Watchdogs started
960721/220845 <LOG_Info> local address determined to be: 127.0.0.1
960721/220845 <LOG_Info> started system queue
960721/220845 <LOG_Info> Initialization complete
960721/220845 <LOG_Info> Listening on port 11600 (100 cxns max)
960721/220845 <WRN-Assert> ignoring max-connections
P(0/0)(0/0), Messages:0
P(0/0)(0/0), Messages:0
P(0/0)(0/0), Messages:0
P(0/0)(0/0), Messages:0
P(0/0)(0/0), Messages:0
P(0/0)(0/0), Messages:0
P(0/0)(0/0), Messages:0
P(0/0)(0/0), Messages:0
P(0/0)(0/0), Messages:0
P(0/0)(0/0), Messages:0
P(0/0)(0/0), Messages:0
```

N O T E The shipping version of Tempest will be implemented as a Windows NT service that you can start and stop through the Services applet in Control Panel. ■

Configuring a Client to Communicate with a Tempest Server

Client configuration in the Tempest environment consists of setting a few entries in the System Registry. To configure the registry correctly, you can either run the supplied application or run the script file shown in Listing 16.1.

Listing 16.1   TEMPEST.REG—Registry Settings for a Tempest Client

```
REGEDIT4

[HKEY_CURRENT_USER\Software\Tempest Software, Inc.]

[HKEY_CURRENT_USER\Software\Tempest Software, Inc.\Tempest Messenger]

[HKEY_CURRENT_USER\Software\Tempest Software, Inc.\Tempest
Messenger\Client Settings]
"Server Address"="localhost"
"IP Port"="11600"
```

 T I P To import these registry settings, use the Windows Explorer to find the registry file TEMPEST.REG on the CD-ROM that ships with this book, and then double-click the file. The Windows Explorer should automatically run the Registry Editor and load the file for you. You will receive a notification of success: Information in TEMPEST.REG has been successfully entered in the registry.

These Registry settings configure the location in terms of IP addresses that the Tempest server can be found. You can use a host name such as "MyTempestServer" if you have declared the host on either a Domain Name Server, on a WINS Server, or in your local hosts file. Alternately, you can enter an IP address, such as 205.160.254.102, to connect to a Tempest server installed on a machine that has the IP address of 205.106.254.102 (which is unlikely because that's my machine at work!).

In addition, you specify the port on the server to which you want to connect. Tempest servers default to listening on the IP Port 11600. In the release version of the Tempest server, you will be able to specify the listener port when starting the Tempest server by using the command line switch -P and indicating the port that you want to listen on. For example, to change the port from the default of 11600 to 999, you would execute the following to start the Tempest server:

```
Tempest -P999
```

T I P   In Listing 16.1, the IP address of the server is defined as localhost. The localhost server is a special IP address that always is defined as the same machine that you are currently running on. In this configuration, it is assumed that the Tempest client and the Tempest Server are actually on the same Windows NT server.

Connecting to the Tempest Server

Once you have configured the client to know where the Tempest Server is located, and you have started the server in a listening mode, you need to connect to the server. The function call required to the server is TEMPEST_Connect. The syntax for using TEMPEST_Connect is as follows:

```
TEMPEST_Connect( hWndMessageRecipient )
```

Note that *hWndMessageRecipient* is the window handle to which you want the Tempest server to send messages. For example, in Centura, to register the currently active form window as the recipient of messages and to connect to the server you would execute:

```
On SAM_Create
    If NOT TEMPEST_Connect( hWndForm )          ! hWndForm is Centura's
                                                      current Form
            Call SalMessageBox( "Could not connect to Tempest Messenger!",
                              "Message",0 )
```

TEMPEST_Connect returns TRUE or FALSE (1 or 0) to notify you whether a connection was established or not.

Sending a Message Using TEMPEST_Send

The simplicity of the API of Tempest is shown by the fact that all communications are managed by essentially a single function call, TEMPEST_Send. The syntax for using TEMPEST_Send is as follows:

```
TEMPEST_Send( sRecipient, sMessage, nLength_Of_Message, bBroadCast )
```

The values of the TEMPEST_Send function are described as follows:

- *sRecipient*—This is the name of the server or recipient client to which you want to send the message. The Recipient must have connected to the Tempest server and must have created and opened a mailbox of the name specified in the string *sRecipient*.

- *sMessage*—A text stream that contains a message. This text stream can be a pointer containing any textual data, including numeric values and binary data that's converted to text. Typically, you would include in *sMessage* some form of tokenized data; this ensures that when a message is received, you can process it intelligently, knowing what the client is requesting.

- *nLength_Of_Message*—This is the length of the buffer in *sMessage*.

- *bBroadCast*—This is a Boolean parameter used to specify whether you want the message sent to the particular recipient or to all clients subscribing to the mailbox.

For example, to send a message like "Hello World" to a recipient called "Console" using Centura Team Developer, you would execute:

```
Set sMessage = "Hello World"          ! don't forget to declare the variable
Call TEMPEST_Send( "Console", sMessage, SalStrLength( sMessage ), FALSE )
```

Creating and Opening a Mailbox

To write a server application for Tempest, all you need to do is to write an application that connects to the Tempest server and then creates and opens a Mailbox through which messages will be delivered. Creating and opening a mailbox on the Tempest server instructs the Tempest server to deliver to the registered window handle (specified with TEMPEST_Connect) messages sent to the mailbox using TEMPEST_Send. To create a mailbox, you use the TEMPEST_CreateMailbox function. The syntax for TEMPEST_CreateMailbox is as follows:

```
TEMPEST_CreateMailbox( Mailbox_Name )
```

Mailbox_Name is the name of the mailbox that you want to receive messages for.

To open the mailbox and start receiving any messages that have been sent and are queued in the mailbox, you use the TEMPEST_OpenMailbox function. The syntax for TEMPEST_OpenMailbox is as follows:

```
TEMPEST_OpenMailbox( Mailbox_Name )
```

Mailbox_Name is the name of the mailbox that you want to open.

N O T E Note that the notion of client and server is strictly for convenience of understanding the example. In Tempest, all nodes on the Tempest network are really peers, and as such there is no real client or server, with the exception of the given state of a transaction. A client in Tempest can act as a server for another client or even for the server that it sent a message to. This kind of flexibility through a common server and client API makes it easy for you to choose how you want the application to work. ■

Receiving Messages from the Tempest Server

Now that you have successfully connected to and sent a message to a recipient, you need to actually process the message and do something with it. Messages are received by the window handle that you specified with the call to TEMPEST_Connect. The message is sent with a message number of 10,000. So, to trap the message in Centura, you would typically define a constant for the message like this:

```
Global Declarations
...
    Constants
        System Constants
        User Constants
            Number: TEMPEST_Message = 10000
            ...
```

Then to trap the message in your Centura code, you would add the following to the window that you had defined as the message recipient:

```
On TEMPEST_Message
    ! Process the message
    ...
```

Two key APIs are required to help you work with the data sent through a TEMPEST_Message: TEMPEST_ConvertMsgToHstring and TEMPEST_Reply.

Using TEMPEST_ConvertMsgToHstring

Data that is sent to a mailbox in Tempest arrives in the lParam of the TEMPEST_Message sent to the recipient window handle. In order to extract the text from the lParam, it is necessary to crack or break out the text. You use the function TEMPEST_ConvertMsgToHstring to extract the components of the message. The syntax for TEMPEST_ConvertMsgToHstring is as follows:

```
TEMPEST_ConvertMsgToHstring( lParam, sMessageBuffer )
```

lParam is the system variable for the long parameter sent with the message, and sMessageBuffer is defined as a string variable available to receive text.

 TIP Some application programming languages require that you preallocate buffer space in *sMessageBuffer* prior to calling TEMPEST_ConvertMsgToHstring. Use the required buffer allocation function in your language, if necessary, to avoid receiving a protection or exception fault due to writing to unallocated memory.

Using TEMPEST_Reply

The TEMPEST_Reply API is provided so that you can send a message back to the sender who placed the message in the mailbox you were listening on. The syntax of TEMPEST_Reply is as follows:

```
TEMPEST_Reply( lParam, sReplyMessage, nLength_Of_Message )
```

lParam is the message's long parameter, sReplyMessage is the text message that you want to send back to the sender, and nLength_Of_Message is the length of the string buffer in sReplyMessage.

Understanding the Tempest Sample Application

On the CD-ROM included with this book, you will find two applications written in Centura Team Developer that demonstrate the simplicity of Tempest in distributing processing on your network. These applications are designed to work as a telephone area code lookup service. To find out whether the area code exists, the server application connects to the area code database and does a query for any Tempest client that sends a message to the Area Code Server. If it does, it returns a notification to the Area Code Client.

A Web-enabled version of this application can be seen on the Tempest Software Web site. The Web version is written in Java on the client and connects using Tempest to a Centura-based application server on the other side of the Internet at the Tempest Software Corporation's office. You can see the demo (and it's really pretty cool) for yourself at **http:// www.tempestsoft.com**, then choose Demos and Area Code Locator (see Fig. 16.2).

FIG. 16.2

The Area Code Java Applet in Action at Tempest Software's Web site.

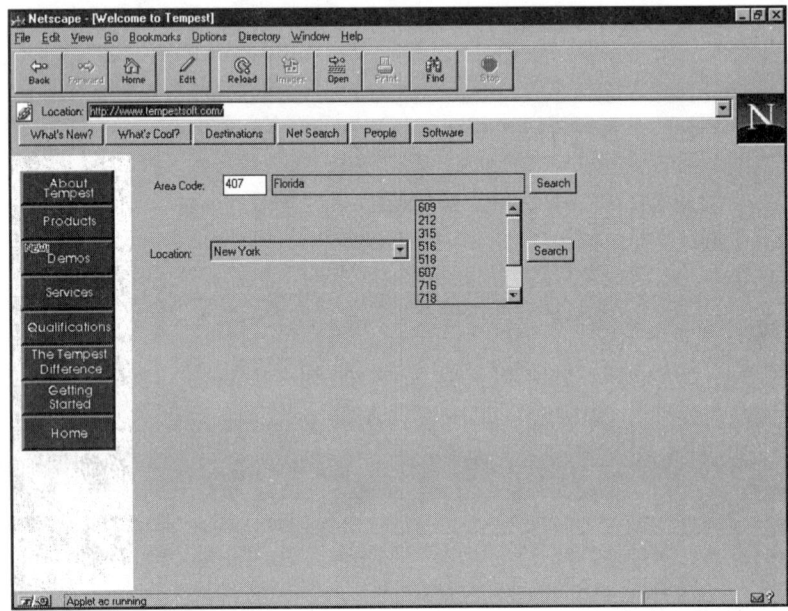

Installing the SQLBase Database   To use the application, you first need to install the sup-plied SQLBase 6.0.1 database on your SQLBase server. The simplest way to install the data-base is to follow these steps:

1. Create a new subdirectory under your SQLBase root directory called AC.

2. Copy the AC.DBS database file from the CD-ROM to the newly created AC subdirectory.

3. In the SQLBase server's SQL.INI file, add an entry to install the database on the server like this:

   ```
   dbname=AC,SQLAPIPE
   ```

4. Shut down and restart the SQLBase server.

Understanding the Area Code Server Application   After the SQLBase database is available, open the file ACSER.APP, which is the server application. This application is designed to listen on the AreaCode mailbox and, whenever it receives a TEMPEST_Message, process it and send back the appropriate data from the database to the sender of the message. In this way, the client application is shielded from the underlying database access and is just working with the text stream. The code in Listing 16.2 shows the processing of the TEMPEST_Message by the application:

Listing 16.2   ACSER.APP—Processing a TEMPEST_Message to Fetch Data and Return It

```
Call TEMPEST_ConvertMsgToHstring (lParam, sMessage)
Set nLastMsg = lParam
Set dfMsgNum=dfMsgNum+1
Set dfMessage = sMessage
Call SalStrTokenize( sMessage, "", ",", sMessageParts )
Set sCommand = sMessageParts[0]
Set sQueryObject = sMessageParts[1]
If sCommand = "SearchAreaCode"
    Set gsSQL= 'Select Description from AreaCode into :sLocation
              where AreaCode = :sQueryObject'
    Call SqlPrepareAndExecute( ghSQL, gsSQL )
    Call SqlGetResultSetCount( ghSQL, gnCount )
    If gnCount=0
       Set sLocation = 'Area Code Not Found'
    Else
       Call SqlFetchNext( ghSQL, gnCount )
    Set sReply = "LocationFound," || sLocation
    If nLastMsg
       Call TEMPEST_Reply( nLastMsg, sReply, SalStrLength( sReply ) )
...
```

 T I P   You can use the Centura SAL function SalStrTokenize to break up a text stream into array elements based on starting and ending delimiters that you specify.

The user interface of the Area Code Server is pretty simple, and just shows the messages being processed as they are received (see Fig. 16.3).

Understanding the Area Code Client Application   The Area Code client application is a very simple application that sends a message to the Tempest server mailbox AreaCode and then waits for a formatted reply that tells it to populate either the data field Location or the table window with data from the Tempest server. The client logic of the Area Code client is also placed under the TEMPEST_Message message handler in the Centura Team Developer code. In Listing 16.3, you can see the client application breaks up the message into message parts, using SalStrTokenize. Based on the first part (array element zero) Centura Team Developer decides what to do with the results. If the first part, sCommand is equal to "AreaCodeFound", then the field dfLocation is set to the second part of the message, sQueryResult.

FIG. 16.3

The Tempest based Area Code Server Locator window shows the number of messages sent and received through the Tempest server and the AreaCode mailbox.

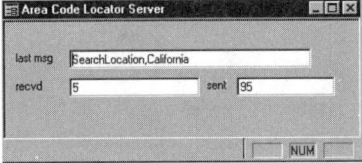

Listing 16.3   ACCLI.APP—The Client Application Processes the Reply

```
Call TEMPEST_ConvertMsgToHstring( lParam, sMessage )
Call SalStrTokenize( sMessage, "", ",", sMessageParts )
Set dfMsgNum=dfMsgNum+1
Set dfMessage = sMessage
Set sCommand = sMessageParts[0]
Set sQueryResult = sMessageParts[1]
If sCommand! = "AreaCodeFound"
    Call SalStatusSetText( hWndForm, 'Message:'||sMessage||'end' )
If sCommand = "LocationFound"
    Set dfLocation = sQueryResult
...
```

The user interface of the Area Code Locator shows the interaction with the Area Code server and demonstrates that data transferred across Tempest is usable in a client application (see Fig. 16.4).

FIG. 16.4

The Area Code Locator was used to look up an individual location and also to receive tabular data for a whole state (California).

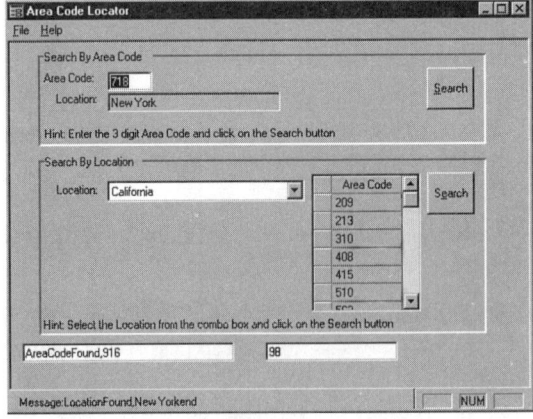

From Here...

This chapter introduced you to some of the benefits and curses of application partitioning. It also gave you a brief introduction to a couple of the more popular application partitioning and monitoring technologies available today. From Sybase's proprietary Open Servers, to Java Remote Method Interface applications, the choices for application partitioning are diverse and varied. The problem is no longer how to split up an application, but which API to use. Hopefully, after reading this chapter, you've seen a little bit more about the technologies available and know where to go for more information.

One thing that you shouldn't discount as you embark on an application partitioning process for your system is the cost in terms of overall transactional performance. Be careful that you have measurable performance numbers for your existing system before attempting to partition the application; that way you can be sure that you aren't adding substantial delays to the transaction times simply to improve the application architecture.

I suggest you look at the following chapters for additional information:

- Chapter 10, "Understanding Stored Procedures," gives information on how to work with Sybase's procedural extensions to the ANSI SQL standard: Transact-SQL.

- Chapter 15, "Using Client/Server Application Programming Tools," teaches you to examine how clients connect to the database and perhaps tune the ODBC interface on the client.

- Chapter 21, "Managing and Monitoring Security," attempts to make sure that you have appropriately addressed any security issues that may present themselves now that you have opened up your database to remote applications and partitioned systems.

- Chapter 22, "Managing and Monitoring Performance," enables you to measure and quantify the capability of your system to seriously evaluate whether you need to split up your application or not.

CHAPTER 17

Using Third-Party Products

The measure of a relational database (or *any* product, for that matter) is the acceptance in the community of that product, as represented by third-party development. Sybase's case is typical. A huge industry of third-party vendors has emerged around Sybase's core products: System XI, Replication Server, MPP, and IQ. These vendors have taken advantage of openings and areas in which Sybase has chosen not to provide technology.

Sybase's vendors provide a wide variety of tools and products that are useful to the application development company. In this chapter, you learn how to use the top applications in the market today. In addition, you will get a subjective review of each of the products in order to help you navigate the many products available in the market.

For a complete list of Sybase-certified partner solutions, you can visit Sybase's Web site and go to the following page: **http://www.sybase.com/Partners/ application.html**. ▪

Working with third-party products

Sybase has literally hundreds of different third-party products at your disposal to do development and to aid you. This chapter introduces you to some of the better-known products in the market today.

Querying the database

Are you a little tired of ISQL or WISQL32? I don't blame you. These products should actually be billed as a way of confirming connectivity, not as real database management tools. Real database querying tools exist, and in this chapter you get to sample a few of them.

Using tools for database design and modeling

Database Design and Modeling is an important part of working with Sybase. This chapter introduces you to the key modeling tools available for Sybase and will demonstrate what sorts of possibilities you have among the tools.

Administering Sybase System XI

Sybase SQL Server Manager is a great product, but there are other companies that have been doing graphical management of Sybase for quite some time. Use this chapter as a resourceful introduction to them.

Using Querying Tools

Without a doubt, the most important thing that you need when working day in and day out with the Sybase database is a good program to interact with and to execute SQL on the server.

Sybase's ISQL is basically a stop gap program to show you that it is actually possible to connect to the database and run queries. Nobody in his right mind would try to use it for normal day-to-day activity because it's pretty awful. What does this mean? It means that a bunch of different third-party software vendors have sprung at the opportunity to deliver software to meet this need.

These products are really pretty good and deserve your attention. Above all, pick a product to replace ISQL as soon as possible. Doing so can only help your going forward.

Using SQL-Programmer

Company:	Sylvain Faust, Inc. (SFI)
Current version:	1.85
Platforms:	Windows 3.x (Windows 95 and Windows NT in alpha right now)
Web page:	**http://www.sfi-software.com**
CD-ROM:	\demos\sqlprog\install.exe

SQL-Programmer from Sylvain Faust, Inc. is a venerable tool that has been used by thousands worldwide. It has established a quite sizable market share and is a well-rounded product.

There's only one thing that is a bit strange about this product: It has the weirdest toolbar you have ever seen (see Fig. 17.1). I think that the company designed the toolbar as a differentiator between this product and others; at least, it has tried to make the user interface very distinctive. SQL-Programmer is unique visually. The UI is quite unusual—even the default colors are quite "loud." However, these quirks are just a strange cover over some pretty powerful technology. Changing colors is very straightforward, as is removing the toolbar.

The scope of SQL-Programmer is quite large; it tries to do a number of things, including the following:

- **Batch Object**—This is an excellent editor for ad hoc SQL to be executed on the server.
- **Report Writer**—This is an innovative tool that reports on the system catalog in a database and enables you to print the output.
- **Stored Procedure Editor**—This is a clear and easy tool that simplifies the creation and management of stored procedures on your server.
- **Version Control Manager**—This is a simple but effective version control system that helps make sure that two programmers don't work on the same stored procedure at the same time by imposing a check-out, check-in policy system.
- **DDL Extractor**—This is the excellent script generation capability of SQL-Programmer that enables simple extraction of just about everything on the server.

FIG. 17.1

The Batch Object window is where you enter ad hoc queries in SQL- Programmer. Notice the quirky toolbar with the odd-sized buttons.

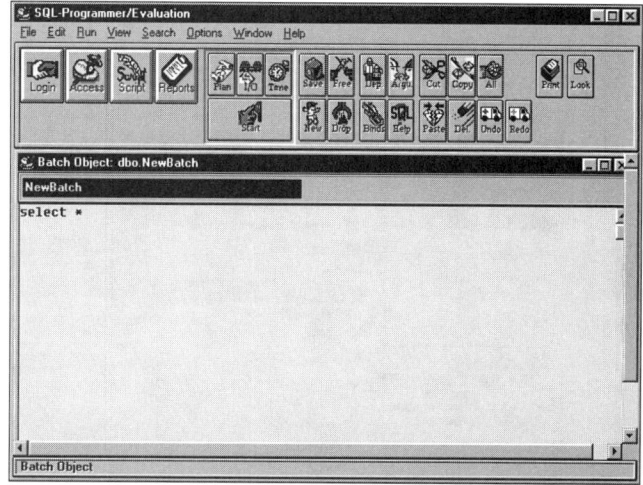

Using the Batch Object For the average database analyst or programmer, the Batch Object manager is going to be the place where you spend most of your time. SQL-Programmer's Batch Object manager is a very well-designed editor that supports files up to 16M, which is more than large enough. This capability enables execution of particular statements in a large file by simply selecting the text you want to execute and pressing Ctrl+E.

A rather limited feature of SQL-Programmer is the way it handles multiple errors in a script file. A typical problem that occurs when working with large scripts is that many errors exist during the initial phases. SQL-Programmer enables you to skip these errors and reports them in a separate window; however, there's no easy correlation between the error and the line of code causing the problem (see Fig. 17.2).

FIG. 17.2

The error management of the Batch Object lists any errors that occurred in the SQL most recently executed, but it doesn't give you access to the offending code in the script.

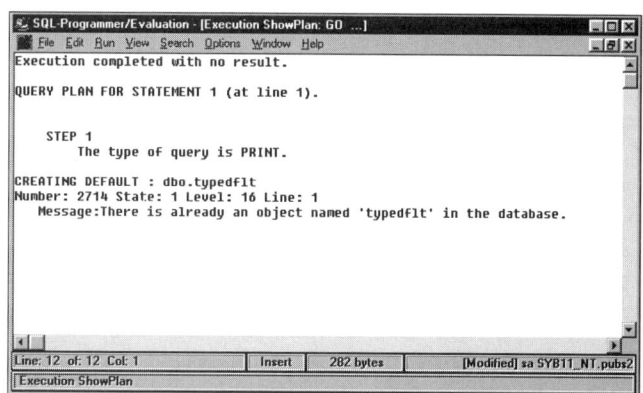

Have a look at RapidSQL below for a much better way of handling this sort of problem.

Using the Report Utility SQL-Programmer's reporting capabilities are an excellent way of creating documentation for the database on which you are working. To use the Report Writer (see Fig. 17.3) from the File menu, select Reports (Ctrl+R).

FIG. 17.3

The Report dialog box in SQL-Programmer permits you to specify the database and objects of various types for which you want to generate a report.

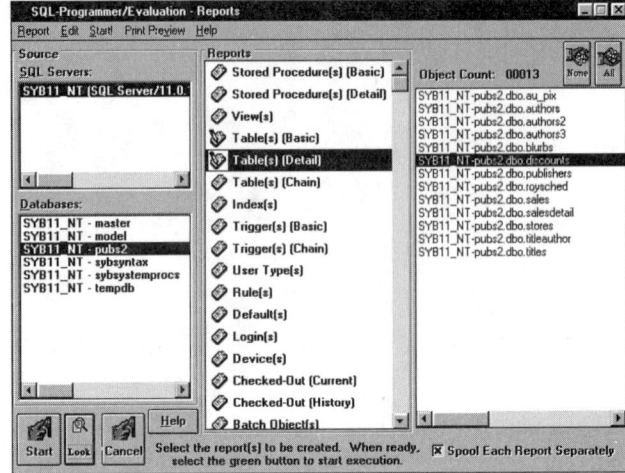

After selecting the options that you want for the report, click the Start button to begin the report and print it, or press the Look button. (Both buttons are found in the lower-left corner of the dialog box.) In Figure 17.4, you can see the sort of report that can be produced from SQL-Programmer.

FIG. 17.4

The Print Preview of the report enables you to confirm that the report you created is what you want to print. This is a sample report that shows the basic details of a table.

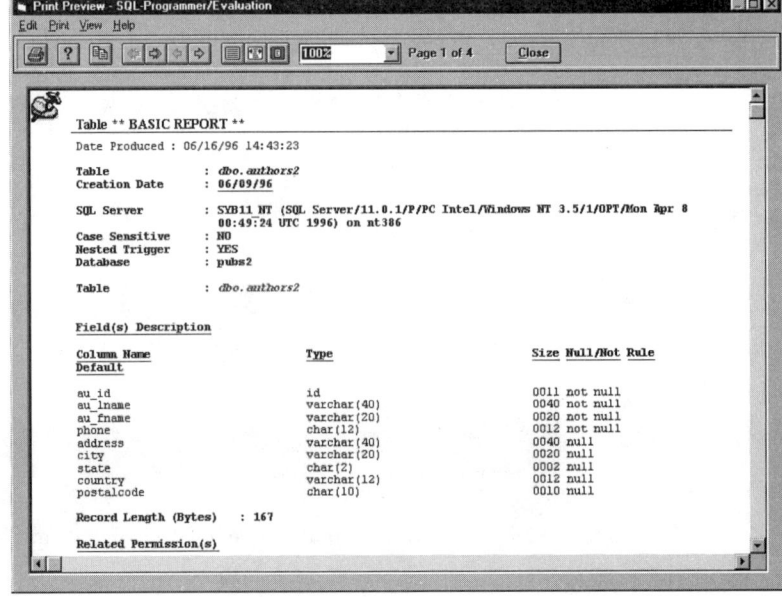

Using the Stored Procedure Editor The Stored Procedure Editor in SQL-Programmer is basically the same as the regular Batch Object Editor. The editor itself is identical, except for in the way that you open the editor and begin work. To create a stored procedure object in SQL-Programmer, follow these steps:

1. From the File menu, select New (Ctrl+N) to display the New object dialog box (see Fig. 17.5).

FIG. 17.5

The SQL-Programmer New dialog box enables you to create each of the basic objects and work areas that SQL-Programmer supports.

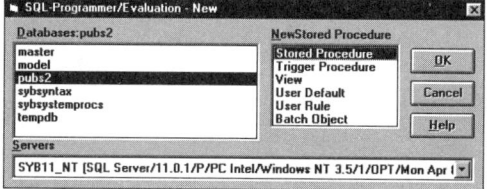

2. Click the database that you want to work with.

3. Select Stored Procedure from the New list and click OK.

After getting a new window for the stored procedure, you enter the Transact-SQL as normal for the stored procedure and execute just as though it were a Batch Object.

Using the Access Manager The Access Manager enables multiple programmers to share a database's stored procedures without the risk of two programmers' working on the same stored procedures. In Figure 17.6, you can see the main interface of the Access Manager, where you can choose the procedure on which you want to work. By using the Access Manager (on relatively simple projects) it would be possible to avoid needing to purchase an additional version control manager. The downside is that this model is tied to databases—if the Sybase server is down, you cannot work on your files!

FIG. 17.6

The Access Manager dialog box in SQL-Programmer is the central point from which you can check out a procedure to work on and execute it if you want.

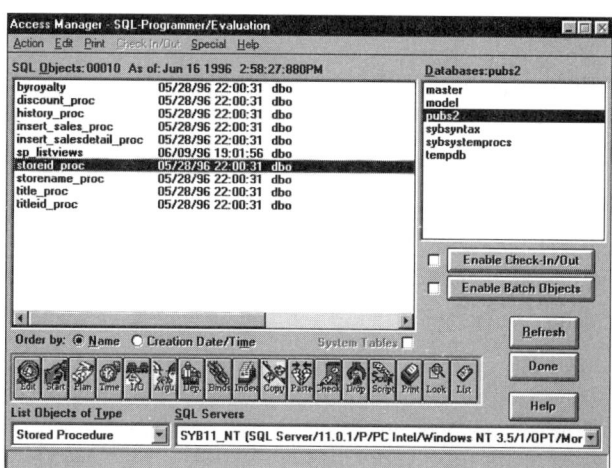

Part
III

Ch
17

Using the DDL Extractor   The user interface to the DDL Extractor is very similar to that of the Report Generation facilities (see Fig. 17.7). The advantage of this approach is that it enables you to generate a single script that has as many different objects in it as you require in a text file that can then be run at any time on the server.

FIG. 17.7

The DDL Extraction dialog box enables you to extract multiple objects and then generate a single script file to place them in.

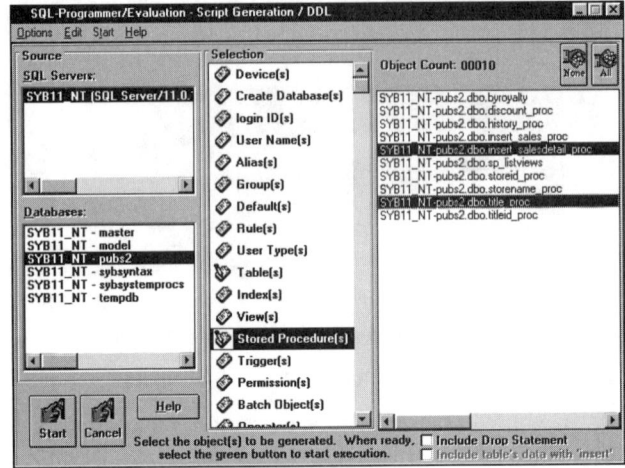

Final Word   SQL-Programmer is a neat product. It has all the elements that make up a good tool for the average database user. I find the quirkiness somewhat annoying, but then I'm a traditional Windows UI fan and think that Microsoft really knows how to do UI better.

SQL-Programmer's features are worthy and the ability to edit large files should not go unrecognized; however, my final word on this product would be to wait for their 32-bit version that's due in the third quarter of 1996.

Using RapidSQL

Company:	Embarcadero Technologies
Current version:	1.7
Platform:	Windows 3.x
Web page:	**http://www.embarcadero.com**
CD-ROM:	\demos\rapidsql\rapidsql.exe

RapidSQL was Embarcadero's fledgling product. Initially released in early 1994, Embarcadero has done little to enhance it in two years. But to be honest, they really haven't needed to.

RapidSQL is the perfect tool for the serious Sybase System XI database user. It is a bare bones tool that gives you all the basics for executing queries, and that's it. Look to Embarcadero's other product (that also seems to get a little more attention in the bug fix department). RapidSQL doesn't have the breadth of functionality that other products do in its class, but what it does, it does very well. The functionality of RapidSQL is focused around two key areas:

- **Database browsing**—The simple database browsing built into RapidSQL makes it easy to work with and get information about any of the objects in the database.

- **Script execution**—RapidSQL's editor interface is by far the best on the market. The ability to have multiple workspaces is truly an edge for the serious developer.

Browsing Database Objects with RapidSQL RapidSQL's database browser is an uncomplicated affair. To access its features, follow these steps:

1. Launch RapidSQL from the installed group and select the Connect! menu to bring up the database connection dialog box (see Fig. 17.8).

FIG. 17.8

RapidSQL's Connection dialog box is the only commercial product that goes the distance and actually attempts to find the valid SQL servers by either reading WIN.INI's [SQLServer] section or looking at your SQL.INI file.

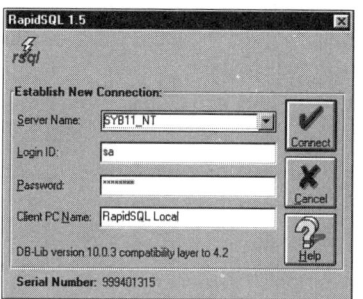

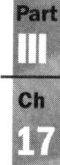

Part III

Ch

17

2. Select the Server Name that you want to connect to (or type it in if it's not listed), and enter the required user and password information.

3. Click the Connect button to log on to the database. In Figure 17.9, you can see RapidSQL after connecting to the *pubs2* database.

FIG. 17.9

The main interface of RapidSQL is centered around an editor. To browse any database object, click the appropriate button on the Toolbox supplied.

Toolbox ——

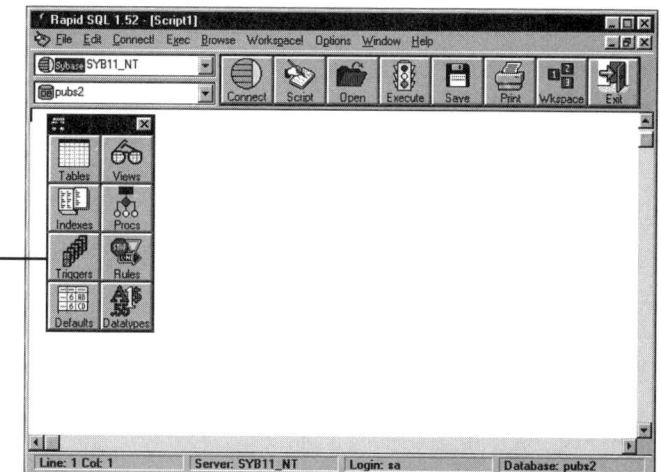

4. From the Browse menu select the object type that you want to review: Tables (F3), Views (Ctrl+F3), Indexes (Ctrl+F4), Stored Procedures (F4), Triggers (F6), Rules (F10), Defaults (Ctrl+F6), and Datatypes (Ctrl+F10).

5. To get an extraction of the DDL required to manage the object, click the object that you want to extract and then Choose Object, Extract DDL (see Fig. 17.10). RapidSQL will create a new window with that object's DDL in it (like the Table dbo.authors window shown).

FIG. 17.10

The DDL extraction can also be executed by right-clicking a database object and selecting Extract DDL from the context menu that pops up.

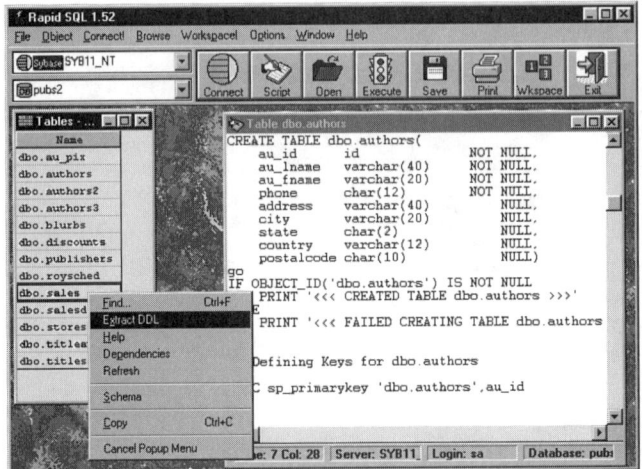

N O T E RapidSQL enables you to customize the elements that are extracted in the DDL, including generating Insert statements that will export the data from the database. ■

Working with RapidSQL's Editor RapidSQL's editor has several really nice features that make it a great way of working with a database:

- **Large files**—This supports unlimited file sizes with ease.
- **Advanced error support**—This shows you all the errors that occurred during execution of a script and then enables you to click any error and get to the place in the code causing an error.
- **Multiple workspaces**—This enables you to open three logical workspaces, each of which can have an unlimited number of files open.

The Advanced Error Support is probably the best feature of RapidSQL. In Figure 17.11, you can see the multiple errors generated in the lower portion of the window; click any of the errors and you will be taken to the part of the script that caused the failure.

Another great feature that has just been added to the latest version of RapidSQL is syntax highlighting. Although you can't easily change the colors of the syntax elements as you can in a proper editor, such as Brief, RapidSQL's new editor in Version 1.7 is really a great improvement.

FIG. 17.11
The multiple error support of RapidSQL lists all the errors that occurred in a script; by clicking each error, you can go to the offending code.

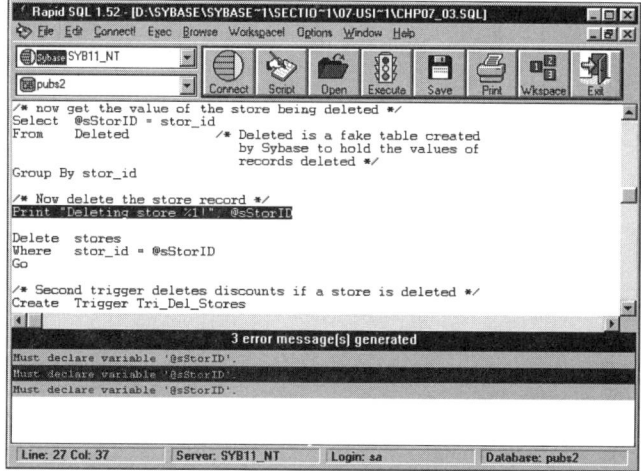

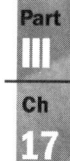

The biggest drawback of RapidSQL's editor is the frequency that it tends to cause a *general protection fault* (GPF) for no particularly good reason. Make sure that you save often because doing a lot of selecting of text, highlighting, and so on, is liable to cause a GPF. That being said, it's really quite reliable for general use, and only seems to be a problem under heavy use.

Final Word   Despite its apparent lack of features, RapidSQL is definitely something that you should look at seriously. It's one of the best products around for straight database procedure execution and management. If you *do* purchase it, I encourage you to give Embarcadero a push into getting the GPFs out of the Editor and to release a 32-bit version.

Using Aurora Utilities' Script Manager

Company: Northern Lights Software, Inc.

Current version: 1.2

Platform: Windows 3.x

Web page: **http://www.nlight.com**

Northern Lights Software is a relative newcomer to the tools business. Their products represent the new breed of tools. Script Manager is a very dedicated and specific product. It runs scripts that execute on a Sybase server. That's all. Why? Because Northern Lights also has a set of other products that perform the following tasks:

- **Performance Monitor**—This graphical system monitors Sybase and generates statistics.

- **SQL Scheduler**—Are you sick of ugly UNIX Cron jobs? Use SQL Scheduler to set up easy-to-manage scheduled tasks.

- **Object Manager**—This feature is designed to help you manage and work with Sybase's database objects.

- **The Bulk Copy Assistant**—This graphical utility acts as a convenient shell for BCP.

■ **Stress Tester**—Using this tool, you can organize and test a server's performance with a strategic and sensible approach.

■ **SSO Apprentice**—Are you worried about security? Use the SSO Apprentice to guide you through all aspects of security design and management.

This comprehensive suite of products works well together as a set of applets. However, their independence can be a little bit annoying; there's an argument to say that they might work better as a single executable with different options. Obviously, one benefit of having them separate is that you only need to buy the things that you are interested in or need.

Script Manager has little to distinguish it from the other utilities that you've seen so far in this chapter except for the fact that it is a really compliant Windows application. What this means is that there aren't any quirks that make it non-Windows standard. This is the most refreshing UI of all the applications. It is a true MDI application, with an easy and comfortable way of presenting results as a split window of the main query window (see Fig. 17.12).

FIG. 17.12

Aurora Script Manager's clean interface with a split window for the scripts provides an elegant solution to the problem of trying to determine which result set goes with which query.

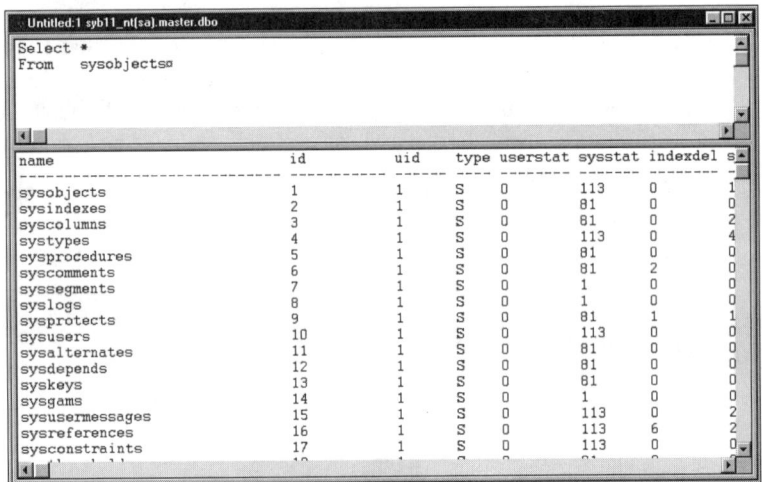

N O T E   Aurora Utilities was written in Visual Basic. This is an excellent example of the power of the new client/server development tools, and their ability to deliver true, commercially viable applications. No longer do you have to rely on C/C++ to develop applications that have real value to lots of users. ■

Working with Modeling Tools

Database design and modeling tools are an essential part of the DBA's toolkit. Using these tools, you can generate a model of the database's structure to determine how the database is going to work both logically and physically.

▶ **See** "Introducing Relational Theory," **p. 61**

For this section, I've chosen two products from the wide range of database modeling tools on the market to demonstrate for you:

- **S-Designor**—Well, it used to be a third-party! Sybase acquired SDP technologies in 1995 and introduced S-Designor as a Sybase product.

- **ErWin/ERX**—A mainstay of the CASE (Computer Assisted Software Engineering) industry, ErWin from LogicWorks is one of the top products on the market today.

N O T E Unfortunately, I wasn't able to get demo versions of either S-Designor (though you can download a copy from Sybase's Web Site) or ErWin/ERX. However, I have secured a demo version of a new product from Embarcadero Technologies called ER/1. You can install it from the CD-ROM, located in \demos\er1\er1.exe.

ER/1 is an interesting product, and is the first new data modeling tool to come on the market in quite some time. It's definitely a first release, however, and it lacks some of the features found in both ErWin/ERX and S-Designor. The second version of ER/1 is going to ship in the first quarter of 1997, and it looks like this will be the release that brings ER/1 into contention as a serious player in the data modeling market.

Part

III

Ch

17

Using S-Designor

Company:	Sybase
Current version:	5.0.1
Platforms:	Windows 3.x, Windows 95, Windows NT
Web page:	**http://www.powersoft.com/products/design/des_fam.html**

S-Designor is an excellent product that is designed to aid you in the development of databases and applications. Not only does it talk to and reverse engineer Sybase System XI databases, but it also has support for every other major database vendor on the market, including Oracle, Informix, Ingres, SQLBase, and DB2.

The implementation of S-Designor is broken down into two separate sections and applications: the Physical Data Model and the Conceptual Data Model. Each of these products works identically and is designed to make it easy to manage the database's structure.

Using the Conceptual Model   The Conceptual Model is provided so that you can define the database in terms of logical entities, prior to developing a database schema. In this step, you are removed from the physical layer of the database that would include the actual implementations of datatypes and tables. In Figure 17.13, you can see a sample model provided with S-Designor.

Each of the entities is defined in a separate box. By double-clicking any of the entities, you can get a view of its high-level properties, as shown in Figure 17.14. This is a useful way to define the basics about an entity and to include any information that you get from a systems designer in the Description and Annotations tab.

FIG. 17.13

The main display or workspace area of S-Designor enables you to lay out your database entities easily and colorfully to create easy-to-understand database models.

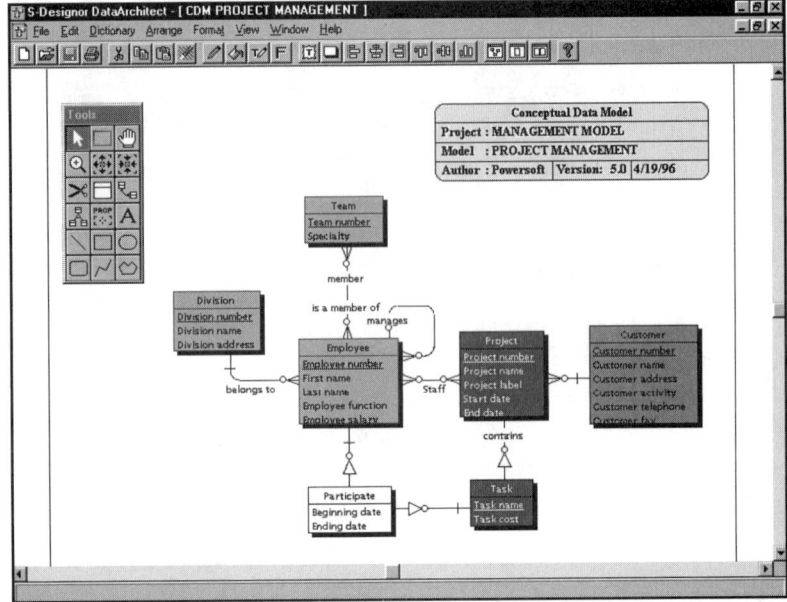

FIG. 17.14

The high-level Entity Properties dialog box enables you to specify the name of the entity and to document any important description or annotations for the model's readers.

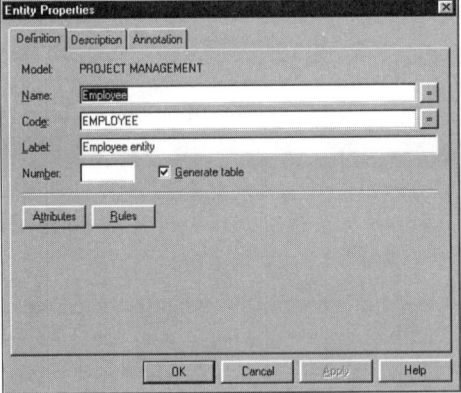

By clicking the Attributes button, you can get a detailed view of all the logical elements that make up this entity. In addition, you get to assign a logical datatype to each element at this stage of the design. These logical datatypes will be converted to physical datatypes and columns when the physical data model is created (see Fig. 17.15).

Using the Physical Model   Once you are satisfied with the development of your logical model using the Conceptual Modeling tool, you then need to generate a Physical Model. Before you do so, you should probably check that the model you created makes sense. To check a model for consistency and accuracy, from the Dictionary select Check Model (F4). Checking the model makes sure that you don't have any duplicate objects and that the data is sufficiently normalized. In Figure 17.16, the Messages dialog box shows the results of checking the sample model that was opened earlier.

FIG. 17.15

The attributes of the Entity dialog box enable you to work with the individual data properties or attributes that make up the entity.

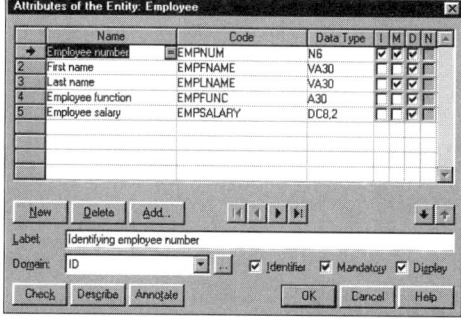

FIG. 17.16

The S-Designor Model checking takes some time; fortunately, there's a status window that informs you of any errors that are found as the model is processed.

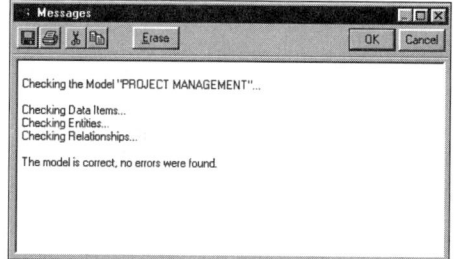

To generate the Physical Model follow these steps:

1. From the Dictionary menu, select Generate Physical Model (Ctrl+G)—this will display the Generating Physical Data Model dialog box (see Fig. 17.17).

FIG. 17.17

The Generating Physical Data Model dialog box is comprehensive and permits the configuration of the interpretation of the Conceptual Model that you have created. You can generate many models from the Conceptual Model, so experimentation here is often a good thing!

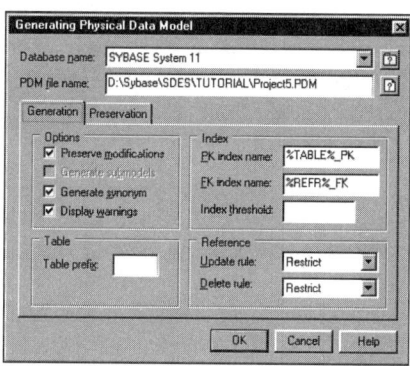

2. Select the Database Name from the list (SYBASE System 11) and enter a name for the output PDM (Physical Data Model) file.

3. Click OK to generate the model (see Fig. 17.18).

FIG. 17.18

The generated Physical Model for Sybase System XI shows all the tables that were created to interpret the Conceptual Model and how they were related to each other through primary and foreign keys.

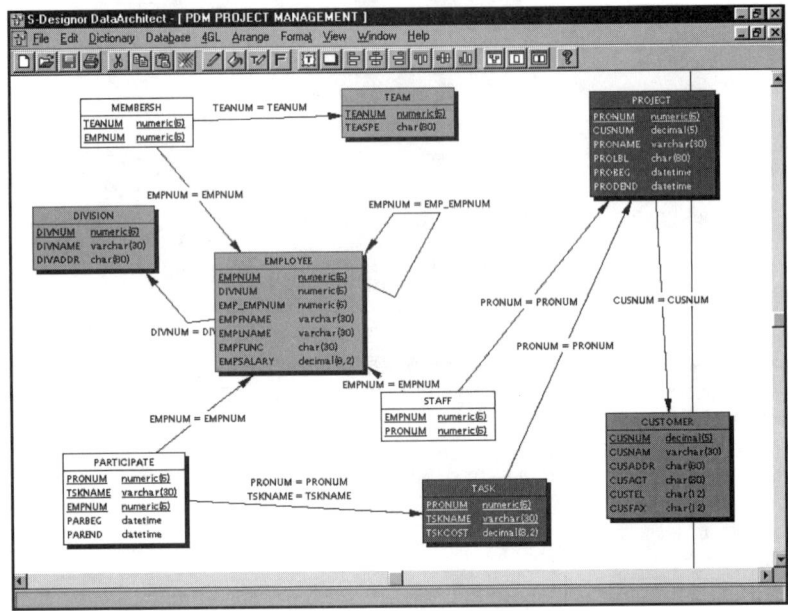

Working with the Physical Model is often easier for the DBA that's not such a great analyst. Double-clicking any table brings up a familiar list of columns and so on. In general, the user interface for S-Designor couldn't be better.

Final Word S-Designor is a great product: simple, elegant, and well-finished. With tight-hooks to many of the leading development tools like SQLWindows, PowerBuilder, and Visual Basic, it has all the capabilities of a real enterprise class product. S-Designor is also available as a full 32-bit product and as such is a much more reliable and quicker program than its 16-bit predecessor. I recommend that you look into purchasing or trying S-Designor in your company or organization.

The only negatives are that database reverse engineering and administration are performed through ODBC. This can mean that you are at the mercy of your ODBC vendor for a good interface to the database.

Using ErWin/ERX

Company:	LogicWorks
Current version:	2.5.01
Platforms:	Windows 3.x, Windows 95, Windows NT, Sun Solaris
Web page:	**http://www.logicworks.com**

LogicWorks' product ErWin is undoubtedly the market leader when it comes to market share and product life. ErWin is one of the oldest players in the data modelling business, and indeed that's all the company does—model data that is! ErWin's cross-platform capabilities are also incredibly beneficial to complex environments that have many different kinds of machines involved in database design. It is really good to know that you have support for both of Microsoft's different flavors of Windows and also for UNIX (Sun Solaris).

ErWin is a tool that shows its maturity by offering many convenient extra features over the S-Designor product from Sybase that make working with your models much more convenient. Fundamentally, all the modelling tools on the market are pretty similar; they all have ways of enabling you to specify the tables, columns, and attributes of the data that you are modelling and give you a nice graphical way of working with the data. ErWin has all the basics, and then adds a layer of additional functionality that really helps you in the day-to-day management of your data model.

Working with a Data Model   Using ErWin is a real pleasure: The flexibility with which you can customize the behavior of the user interface makes it an easy fit for however you want to work with the product. For example, when you double-click an entity, you would expect that some kind of property dialog box would be opened for you to work on. Well, this same behavior happens in ErWin. However, what differentiates ErWin from S-Designor is that the logical and physical models are available for editing in one place. Unlike S-Designor's requirement that you start another application to work with two separate executable programs—one for the logical model and one for the physical model—ErWin consolidates this functionality into one program.

To illustrate this neat feature, take a look at the simple model shown in Fig. 17.19. In this model, a few simple tables/entities are defined: CUSTOMER, MOVIE, MOVIE-COPY, and so on.

FIG. 17.19
This is ErWin's main display window for a sample model that ships with the ErWin product MOVIES.ER1.

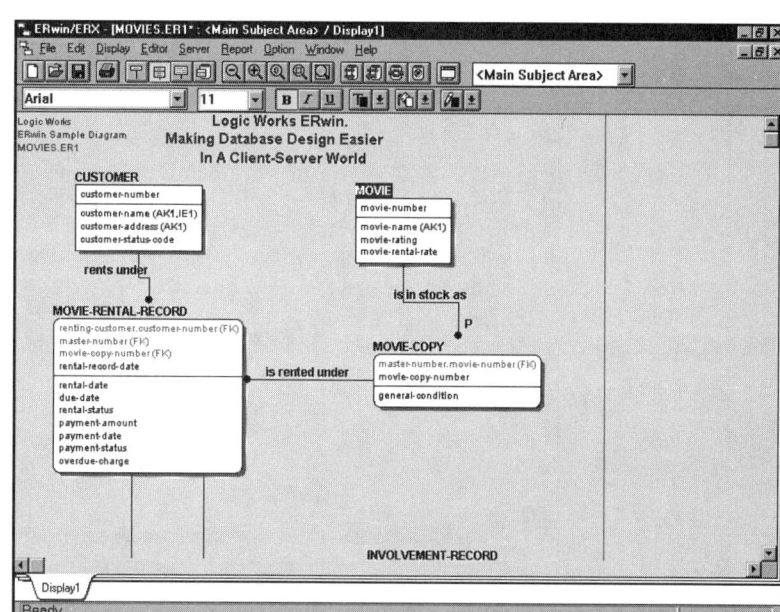

Part
III

Ch
17

From the Editor menu, you can select whichever browser or editor you want activated when you double-click an entity. The options are as follows:

- **Entity-Attribute**—This displays the attributes of the entity.
- **Database Schema**—This displays an editor for the columns and table definition.
- **Attribute Definition**—Choose this for a logical attribute definition editor.
- **Trigger, Index, and other Database Objects**—Choose this for a specific editor based on the type of object that you want to associate with the entity.
- **Entity Definition**—This gives the entity a logical definition and description.
- **Note, Query, and Sample**—This gives additional descriptive information, including some example data that should be associated with the entity.

In addition, by right-clicking an entity and then selecting from the context menu that is displayed, you can pick any of the above listed options and execute them right there.

Working with Displays   One very nice feature of ErWin is the ability to quickly and easily customize the information that is presented to you. There are two ways that you can change the visual appearance of your model. The first is to alter what you can see in terms of attributes associated with an entity. The Display menu has several options—including, Entity Level, Attribute Level, Primary Key Level, and Definition Level—that will help change what you can see when working with the model. If you look at the image in Figure 17.19, you will notice that there are some details of each entity visible. This is what is known as an Attribute Level display.

In Fig. 17.20, you can see the same figure; however, this time you can read the definition for each of the objects/entities—this is Definition Level view.

FIG. 17.20

This time, the Movies database model is displayed in Definition Level view.

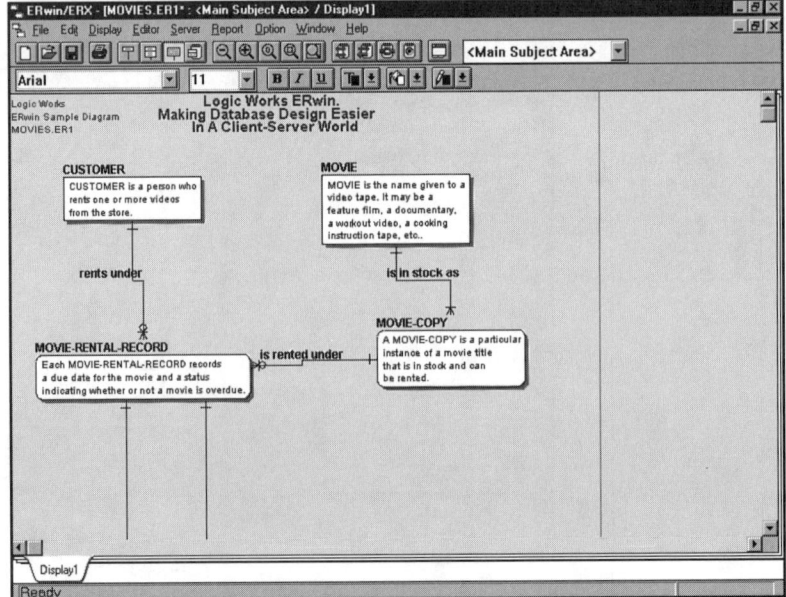

The second way to customize the display is to use *Subject Areas*. Subject Areas are a way of dividing a complex model into various sub-models, each of which contains a sub-set of entities from the main model. To configure a Subject Area, follow these steps:

1. Choose <u>W</u>indow, Subject <u>A</u>rea to display the Subject Area Editor dialog box shown in Figure 17.21.

FIG. 17.21

The Subject Area Editor dialog box is a simple screen that enables you to customize the entities that will be included in the particular named area that you are going to work with.

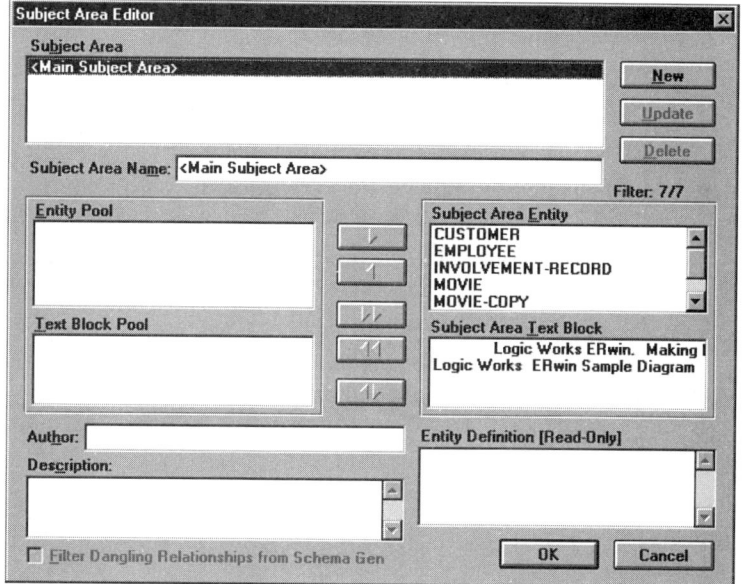

2. Enter the new name that you want to give the area in the Subject Area <u>N</u>ame field.
3. Click the <u>N</u>ew button to add the Area.
4. Select the entities and text blocks that you want included in the area.
5. Enter any additional descriptive information that is appropriate for the new area.
6. Click the OK button to create the logical area, which also takes you to either the area that you selected or the new area that you just created.

Final Word   ErWin is a great high-end relational modelling tool. It has all the same features as S-Designor and adds the flash and pizzazz that you would expect from the product that has been out for the longest time on the market. LogicWorks has clearly taken data modelling to a new level, and while the other vendors are playing catch up on the feature front, LogicWorks continues to make the user interface more straightforward and more complete.

LogicWorks has written more interfaces into ErWin than just about any program on the market today. So don't be afraid about connectivity and functionality with your system—chances are ErWin will have you covered.

Using Database Administration Tools

This section is devoted to tools that are designed to help you manage your database. Administering a database is quite a complex job, especially when you've got lots of servers in remote locations that need your assistance. The products that are discussed here are designed to help you with that problem.

There are many different sorts of things that beset a DBA, and by using some of the tools described here, your job should be easier:

- **Desktop DBA**—This is a classic product from PLATINUM Technology. It is both cross-platform (Windows, UNIX, NT, and so on) and cross-database (Sybase, Oracle, and DB2).

- **DBArtisan**—This product from Embarcadero Technologies is an excellent extension of RapidSQL to include all the essential elements of database administration.

- **SQL-Port**—This is a component of Desktop DBA that provides a cross-database (for example, Oracle to Sybase) export and import utility that is useful when trying to create fast database dumps.

- **Image Analyzer**—This is an excellent tool designed to help you work with database backups to determine whether they were successful or not.

Using Desktop DBA

Company:	PLATINUM Technology
Current version:	3.3.4
Platforms:	Windows 3.x, Windows 95, Windows NT, all major GUI UNIX environments
Web page:	**http://www.platinum.com**
CD-ROM:	\demos\platinum\desktop\setup.exe

Desktop DBA is a tool that is pretty all-encompassing. As a framework for the other components in the PLATINUM suite of products, Desktop DBA is a great way of putting everything under one roof.

CAUTION

Installing Desktop DBA was a little confusing, and required two tries. The main reason is that the default for installation of some key files is FALSE. What this means is that you get all the files installed from the basic install and then when you try to run the database setup program, you get a bunch of errors saying that various DLLs can't be found.

So as a general rule, install everything whether or not you are going to Oracle.

After installing Desktop DBA, a few stored procedures are needed to be added to your database. The only problem, however, is that the DBLibrary DLL that's shipped with Desktop DBA is an old one designed for SQLServer or Sybase System 4.9. The first thing you should do after installing Desktop DBA is track down the W3DBLIB.DLL that's in the installation directory and delete it.

N O T E The amazing thing about all of PLATINUM's products is that they are all cross-platform, meaning that they run on a bunch of different flavors of UNIX as well as the popular Microsoft OS's like NT, Windows 95, and Windows 3.x. This is a technological marvel and is not even close to being achieved by any of PLATINUM's competitors. ▨

There are so many features in Desktop DBA, I could write a book on describing them here; instead, I've picked a few key capabilities that I think might be interesting. Besides those described in the sections below, you can also look forward to the following:

■ **Search and Replace**—This is an excellent tool that permits you to search across all objects in the database and replace text in any of the object types of the server.

■ **Full DDL Extraction**—This makes it easy to extract scripts of the DDL for any object in the database.

■ **Server Saving**—This enables you to save the entire status of the server in a single script file, making it possible to rebuild the server in the event of a serious failure. This feature alone is worth its weight in gold!

Using the Explorer Desktop DBA's functionality is built around a central window that has an explorer-like view on the left pane and a detail view on the right pane (see Fig. 17.22).

FIG. 17.22

The main view of Desktop DBA gives you access to all the major components of the database server, and enables you to double-click any detail object for more information.

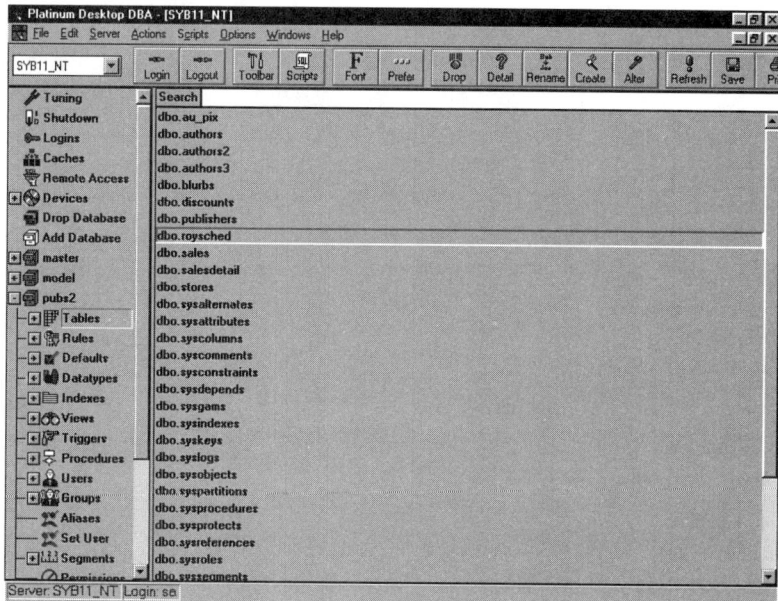

Part
III

Ch
17

This user interface is a simple solution to a difficult problem of trying to represent all the elements of the database to the user. Working with any of the database objects is a straightforward process of double-clicking the object and bringing up a self-describing dialog box that allows for the manipulation of any of the relevant attributes of the object. For example, in Figure 17.23, the Tables dialog box is shown and details all the elements that make up the *sales* table from the *pubs2* database.

Working with Scripts   Desktop DBA also provides an excellent script management utility. To access it, from the Options menu, select SQL Scripts. The editor is a simple and efficient database interface that supports the editing of large files and provides a neat facility in the toolbar that enables you to have access to the primary objects in the database. By selecting the type of object in the Type combo box and then choosing the object itself, all you need to do is click the Paste button to add the appropriate SQL to your current script.

In Figure 17.24, you can see the SQL Scripts window after pasting the SQL for a table, *au_pix*, and the SQL that would recreate the stored procedure *byroyalty*.

FIG. 17.23

Cross platform support is demonstrated in the dialog boxes provided in Desktop DBA. Some of the UI is not quite as slick as it would be in a native Windows 95 only application. Notice how additional buttons are used instead of tabs, probably because tabs aren't supported on UNIX GUIs.

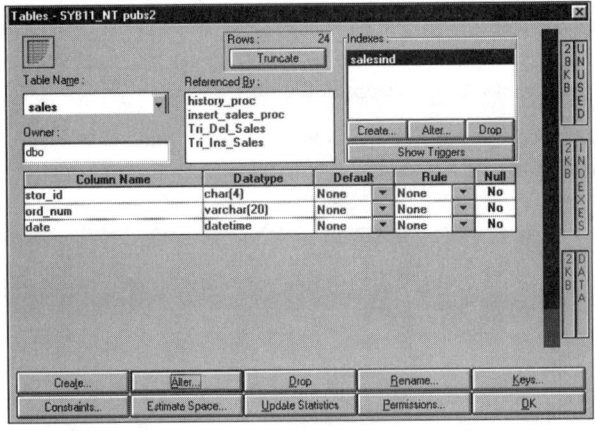

FIG. 17.24

The SQL Scripts window of Desktop DBA is an excellent way of working with and managing the database scripts that you use to create stored procedures and various objects in the server.

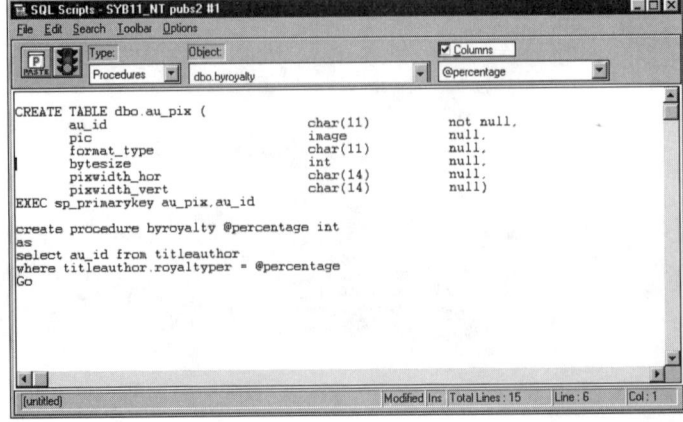

Another interesting feature of Desktop DBA that indicates its UNIX support is the ability to open and save remote files through FTP. This is a great feature if you have a lot of UNIX boxes in your shop and want a central tool that can be used to manage the scripts on the server (for example, Cron jobs) as well as those that are executed from the client for storage on the server (like stored procedures).

Using Database Comparisons   Desktop DBA has an excellent feature that enables you to compare two different databases to check for consistency related to the different objects and data in them. To access and use this feature, perform the following steps:

1. From the Options menu, select Compare Database to display the Database Compare dialog box (see Fig. 17.25).

FIG. 17.25

The Database Compare dialog box is a unique tool to Desktop DBA and helps you identify objects that are missing or new in different databases on different servers.

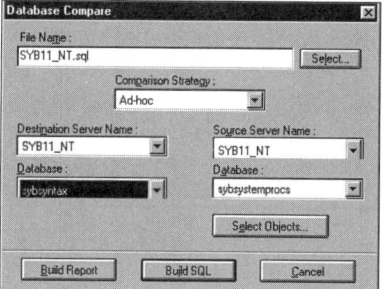

2. Enter a name for the output file in the File Name field.

3. Select the comparison methodology to be used: Ad-hoc compares the objects that you select; Intersection compares the objects in the destination database with respect to the source database; and Union compares all objects in the databases without repeating those objects in both databases.

4. Select the server and database for the Destination and Source, and then optionally, click the Select Objects button to customize the objects being compared (default is all objects).

5. Click either Build Report or Build SQL to generate the output that you require. Generating a SQL script is the normal approach. In Figure 17.26, you can see the result of doing the comparison between the *sybsystemprocs* and *sybsyntax* databases. While this is probably a little bit of crazy comparison, it does show you the power of this feature.

Final Word   Desktop DBA is a great tool. It solves just about every problem and caters to just about every database administrative need that I can think of and does so in a simple, elegant, and complete manner. On the negative side of things, it seemed to not quite understand all the new elements of the System XI catalog, especially when it comes to the tuning of sp_configure, so I'd wait for a later version than 3.3.4 to get complete integration with System XI.

I highly recommend that you evaluate Desktop DBA and introduce it as a product of choice at your company or organization.

FIG. 17.26

The result of a comparison as a script is a convenient summary that lists all the objects that differ between the source and the destination databases. (Note that this was an Ad-hoc comparision.)

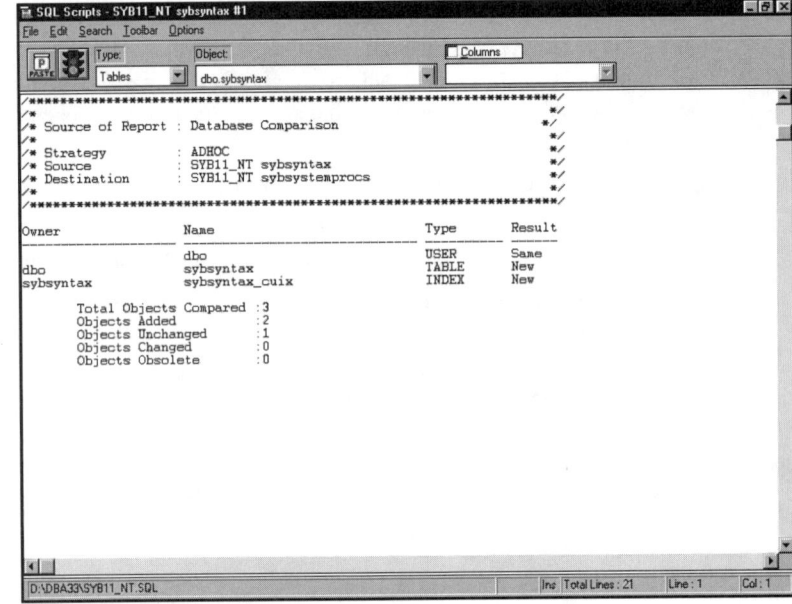

Using DBArtisan

Company:	Embarcadero Technologies
Current version:	2.5.5
Platform:	Windows 3.x
Web page:	**http://www.embarcadero.com**
CD-ROM:	\demos\artisan\artisan.exe

DBArtisan is Embarcadero's flagship product, which has pretty much the same feature set as Desktop DBA and features an Explorer-like browser that you can use to manipulate and work with the databases on your server. In Figure 17.27, you can see the browser at work.

Using System XI Extensions   Perhaps the best reason to use DBArtisan is that it has been specifically extended to add support for all the new features found in System XI. For example, the named cache and memory pool manager shown in Figure 17.28 makes light work of the sometimes complex syntax and logic required to create named caches and to allocate I/O buffer pools in those caches.

Another very useful dialog box in DBArtisan is the Server Configuration dialog box shown in Figure 17.29. The great thing about this dialog box is that it logically and graphically groups all the configuration options available in System XI into different tabs. By clicking a tab, you activate the particular group of options for configuration.

▶ **See** "Configuring and Managing Servers," **p. 635**

FIG. 17.27

The browser in Embarcadero's DBArtisan is called the Navigator. In this view, you can see the tables are being browsed on the *pubs2* database.

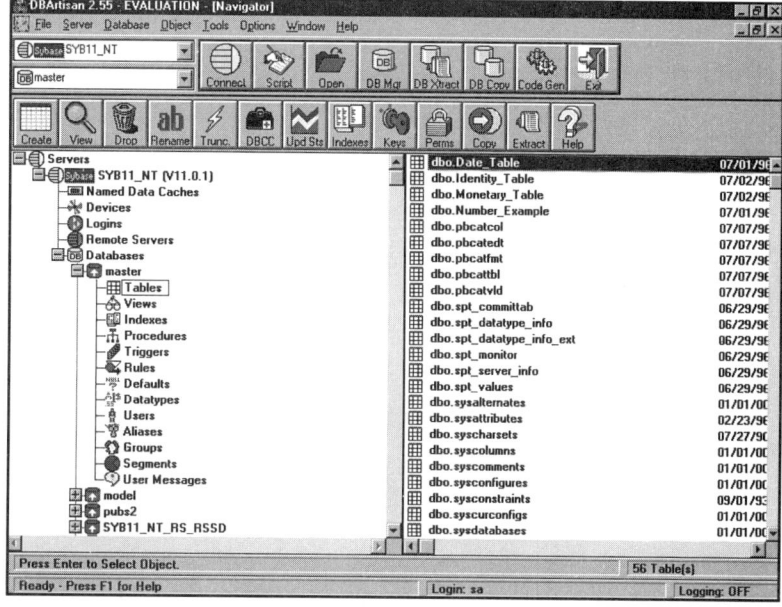

FIG. 17.28

Using DBArtisan's Named Cache manager is definitely a good idea. Buffer pool management is a big headache, and DBArtisan makes this somewhat tedious DBA task a trivial one.

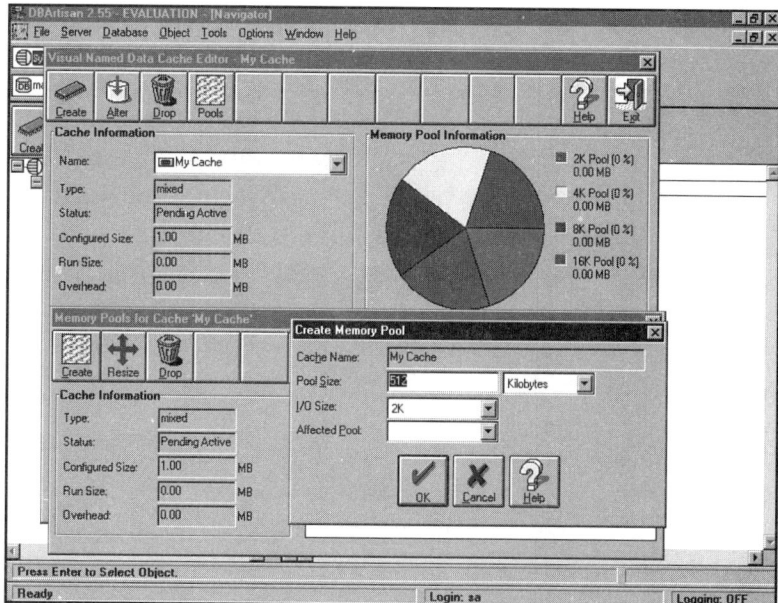

FIG. 17.29

The Server Configuration dialog box makes it easy to manage all the many configurable options available in System XI.

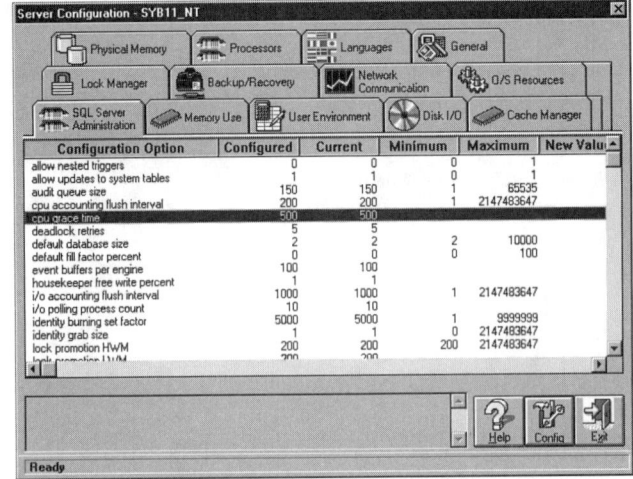

DBArtisan is full of neat utilities that you will find useful in your work with databases. One final utility that I have used quite extensively since first installing DBArtisan is the excellent Database Search facility. To use Database Search, follow these steps:

1. Launch DBArtisan and connect to the server that you want to search.

2. Choose Tools, Database Search to display the Database Search dialog box (see Fig. 17.30).

FIG. 17.30

The Database Search Dialog box enables you to search all the objects in the database for any particular piece of text that you specify. In this example, the text error was searched for and found in quite a few objects.

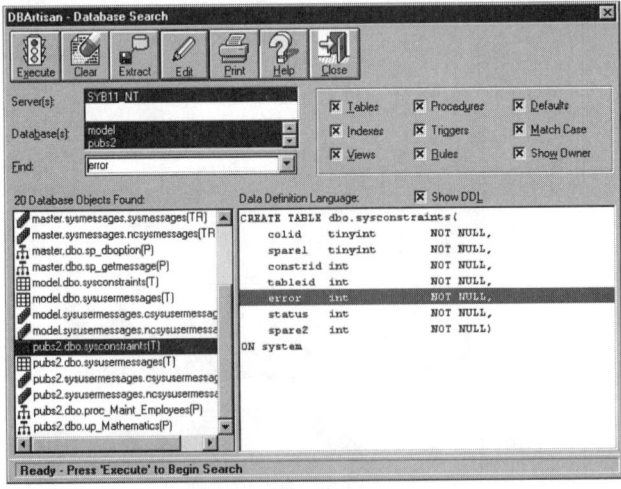

3. Select the databases in the Database(s) combo box that you want to search.

4. Enter the text that you want to search for in the Find field.

5. Select the object types that you want to search through or in (Tables, Indexes, Procedures, and so on).

6. Click the Execute button to start searching for the text.

7. Click each of the objects in the left-hand list to display the object's data or text in the Data Definition Language Window for browsing.

Final Word   DBArtisan is a good product with excellent support for all the new features of System XI. It is, however, a 16-bit program and, as such, is limited in the handling of large scripts and the way these scripts are executed on the server. DBArtisan is a DBLibrary program. Until DBArtisan is upgraded to Client-Library and supports 32-bit execution, DBArtisan will always be a step behind the tools from PLATINUM.

Using SQL-Port

Company:	PLATINUM Technology
Current version:	2.2
Platforms:	Windows 3.x, Windows 95, Windows NT, all major GUI UNIX environments
Web page:	**http://www.platinum.com**

SQL-Port is an add-on to the Desktop DBA product; actually, you can't use one without the other, so make sure that you get Desktop DBA installed before trying to get SQL-Port to work. Using SQL-Port, you can extract data from and insert data into the database with Sybase's BCP (Bulk Copy Program) to maximize performance. The interesting thing about SQL-Port is that the format of the output is readable and then usable with Microsoft SQL Server and Oracle databases. The cross-platform capabilities of SQL-Port and all of Desktop DBA is quite an advantage in a heterogeneous environment.

Configuring SQL Port   After installing SQL-Port, some additional options are made available under the Options menu. To configure SQL-Port, follow these steps:

1. From the Options menu select SQL-Port, Preferences, which will display the SQL-Port Preferences dialog box (see Fig. 17.31).

2. Choose the format of the output that you want to create/import: either Native, Character, or Customized. If you choose Customized, the two fields Field Delimiter and Row Delimiter will be enabled so that you can specify what sort of separation characters to use between the fields and rows in the import or output file.

N O T E   Note that for better compatibility with Oracle databases, you should probably not use the native file format. The other file formats are straight ASCII text files, which are more portable and easier to work with when inserting back into an Oracle database. ■

Part III

Ch 17

FIG. 17.31

The SQL-Port Prefer-
ences dialog box has a
great option that can
be used when exporting
large tables: Use the
First Row To Copy and
Last Row To Copy fields
to break up the table
into multiple files that
are a little more
manageable.

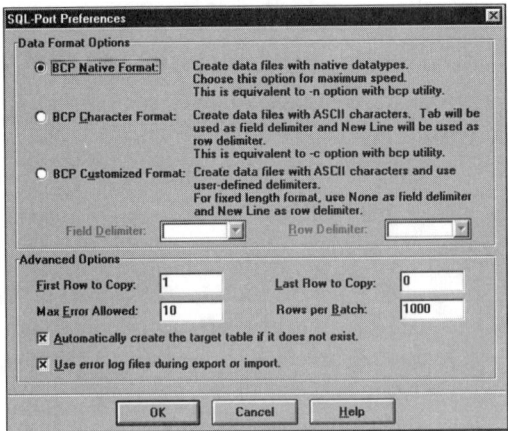

3. In the Advanced Options group, specify any additional characteristics of the export or
   import process, such as how many errors you want to permit before aborting (Max
   Error Allowed) and how many rows you want to do in a group before writing to disk
   (Rows per Batch).

4. Click OK.

 If you are having problems in your export process, turn on the option Use error log files during export
and import. SQL-Port will then generate a log file that you can use to help diagnose any problems that
occur.

Exporting a Database with SQL-Port   To use SQL-Port to dump a database is very easy.
For example, to export the entire *pubs2* database, follow these steps:

1. From the Options menu select SQL-Port, Export Data, which will display the Export
   Database dialog box (see Fig. 17.32).

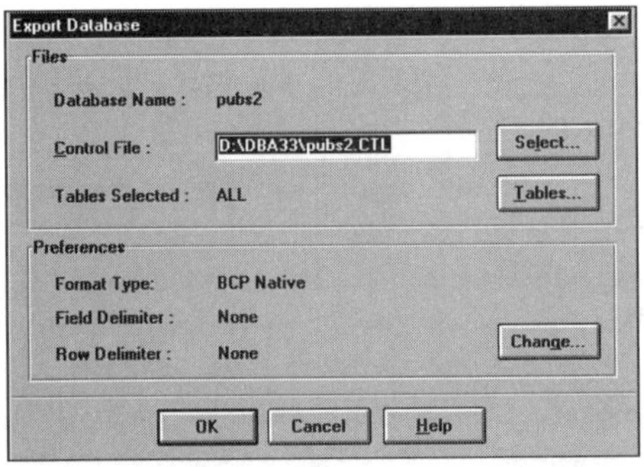

FIG. 17.32

The Preferences Group
of the Export Database
dialog box in SQL-Port
shows you the
selections that you
made on the Prefer-
ences dialog box. To
modify any of the
selections now, click the
Change button.

2. Choose a location for the Control File. The Control File is used by SQL-Port and BCP to manage the import process later on, so you will need to keep it along with the data. SQL-Port also places all the actual data export files in the same directory into which the Control File is placed, so make sure that the Control File is going where you want it to go.

TIP Create a separate directory for each database prior to opening the Export Database dialog box; then place the Control File in it. By using a separate directory for all the files in the database, you won't get confused as to which files belong to what database.

3. Click the Tables button if you want to change the list of tables being exported (the default is ALL).
4. Click OK to begin the export.

SQL-Port creates three files for each of the tables that is exported. The first file has an *f* in the file name extension and describes the options that would be needed to import the data using BCP. For example, here's the output from exporting the *publishers* table:

```
10.0
4
1    SYBCHAR    0    512    "\t"      1    pub_id
2    SYBCHAR    0    512    "\t"      2    pub_name
3    SYBCHAR    0    512    "\t"      3    city
4    SYBCHAR    0    512    "\r\n"    4    state
```

The second file created has an *s* in the file name extension and describes the table's characteristics, in the event that a new table needs to be created on the target database. Again, here's the output from exporting the *publishers* table:

```
(pub_id       char(4)         NOT NULL,
pub_name      varchar(40)     NULL,
city          varchar(20)     NULL,
state         char(2)         NULL)
```

Finally, a data file is created with all the rows from the table. The import file has a *t* in the file name extension and the output for the *publishers* table looks like this:

```
0736    New Age Books          Boston      MA
0877    Binnet & Hardley       Washington  DC
1389    Algodata Infosystems   Berkeley    CA
```

Importing a Database with SQL-Port   Importing a database with SQL-Port is the exact same process as exporting; the dialog box even looks the same (see Fig. 17.32), with exception that you don't have the option of excluding tables during the import phase—SQL-Port will import anything that's specified in the control file.

TIP To skip the importing of a particular table or tables, modify the control file generated by the export process to remove the files mentioned. The file format is very simple: You can just remove a line from the control file to avoid loading the table later on.

Final Word SQL-Port is really an essential part of Desktop DBA. They go hand in hand. Fortunately, if you've already written your own BCP scripts on the UNIX box, you may not need this functionality, which is why PLATINUM probably marketed it as a separate product. If you chose Desktop DBA as your tool of choice to manage your server, I recommend your picking up a copy of SQL-Port to add to the toolkit available to the DBA.

Using Image Analyzer

Company: PLATINUM Technology

Current version: 1.0.5

Platforms: Windows 3.x, Windows 95, Windows NT, all major GUI UNIX environments

Web page: **http://www.platinum.com**

CD-ROM: \demos\platinum\log\setup.exe

Image Analyzer is a separate product from PLATINUM Technology designed to help you work with and analyze the backups that you create using Sybase's Backup Server. PLATINUM must have worked with Sybase to get the file format for a backup image so that they would know how to interpret the files after they were created by Backup Server.

The premise of Image Analyzer is that you can use it to verify and work with the backup file in an offline mode, saving you time that you would normally spend doing a DBCC. Image Analyzer will guarantee that the backup file is restorable, and therefore good, meaning that you would not require a DBCC (which can save many hours of time in large databases).

▶ **See** "Performing Backups," **p. 492**

N O T E Image Analyzer failed to initially read my System XI database files due to a bug in the software provided. I had the pleasure of calling Technical Support and getting a response within 20 minutes from a callback center. We worked through the problems quickly and were able to get my backups loaded. Image Analyzer turned out to have quite a few problems, and I ended up calling technical support several times. This type of support was excellent and indicates the quality and nature of PLATINUM Technology. ▪

Viewing a Backup File with Image Analyzer Image Analyzer is a very easy product to use. On startup, you are presented with a dialog box that asks you to confirm the type of backup file that you are working with and whether it came from Sybase or Microsoft SQL Server (see Fig. 17.33).

After making your selections and indicating where the backup file can be found, click the OK button to process the file.

Final Word I can't really see the point in using this product in its current incarnation, there just doesn't seem any reason to do this offline verification with a user attended tool. The more realistic approach for a large company is to do an automated backup and then run the Image Analyzer to verify the contents of the backup; if an error is found, then staff can notify a DBA quickly.

FIG. 17.33

The first dialog box of Platinum Image Analyzer enables you to verify the backup file from all the current versions of both Sybase and Microsoft SQL Server.

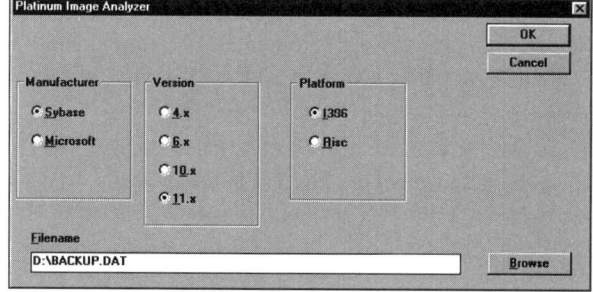

I spoke with PLATINUM and was surprised to find that the next version, which I just received an alpha for, has support for just that. A command-line interface has been added to the product so that you can include the execution of Image Analyzer in your backup strategy. Take a look at Image Analyzer when the new version comes out (fourth quarter 1996), and see if it saves you the time you normally would have allocated to the DBCC process.

Part
III

Ch
17

Keeping Up on the Latest Technology

An important part of doing application development is making sure that you know the latest information that's circulating in the industry. You owe it to your company to know what's new so that you can take advantage of the technology to further advance your company. However, Sybase's technology is not the only thing you should be concerned with. It's up to you to be abreast of all the advances in the information technology industry so that you can make sensible choices on the strategic direction of the company or organization that you work for.

In this section, you see a couple of tools that I have found invaluable in making sure that I knew what was what in the technology business:

- **MSDN**—The Microsoft Developer Network is probably the best consolidated piece of knowledge available to the developer. If you're not a subscriber now, you should be!

- **Sybase's InfoBase**—Sybase's InfoBase product is similar to MSDN in that it is published on a regular schedule and covers all the different products in the Sybase line. I recommend keeping up to date with InfoBase (you get a current copy with most Sybase products) as it will be invaluable to you as you continue to work with Sybase's technologies.

Subscribing to Microsoft Developer Network (MSDN)

MSDN is probably the best thing that you can get to stay current on all the important technologies that are available in the industry at any point in time. MSDN is based on a subscription; each quarter you are shipped a number of CD-ROMs that have different technology resources available on them. There are four different levels of subscription available for MSDN:

■ **Library**—A library subscription is the basic level, which provides you with a complete set of resources that describe all the existing APIs and toolkits available from Microsoft. Also included is Microsoft's Knowledge Base of common questions and problems related to programming and working with Microsoft products.

■ **Professional**—The next level of subscription available is the Professional Subscription. It provides the same benefits as Library, but adds access to the full SDKs that are available from Microsoft. In addition, you get access to all the "public" beta programs, such as Windows 95 and Windows NT 4.0, plus a copy of every operating system that Microsoft ships (in every language).

■ **Enterprise**—The Enterprise Subscription level builds on the Professional Subscription by adding a full development license to all of Microsoft's BackOffice products, including SQLServer 6.5, Exchange Server, Internet Information Server, and SNA Server.

■ **Universal**—This is the ultimate subscription. With it you get everything that Microsoft publishes—well, just about everything. In addition to all of the Enterprise benefits, you also get Microsoft Office products and Microsoft's Visual development tools—Visual C++, Visual Basic Enterprise Edition (including Visual SourceSafe), Visual FoxPro, and the Access Developer's kit.

As a common component of MSDN, you will get access to the MSDN Development Library (see Fig. 17.34). This unique tool has an explorer-like interface that makes it easy to find any piece of information that's stored in the very comprehensive repository.

FIG. 17.34
Even though MSDN is devoted to Microsoft tools and products, it still has a little bit of information that's useful for the Sybase developer.

For more information on MSDN, see the Web site devoted to it at **http:// www.microsoft.com/msdn.**

From Here...

Now that you've seen a bunch of third-party applications that are available for Sybase, it's up to you to go and pick up a couple of them. You can try them from the CD-ROM included with this book and start working with them in your company or organization. The trick with choosing a third-party application is that you must be comfortable that you can get the support that you need to keep working.

Unlike buying Sybase, where it is expected that you will outlay 10 to 15 percent of the purchase price per year for support, many people overlook the purchasing of support for third-party software. Without support, you will be in a bad position when you find bugs or want upgrades.

After reading this chapter, I recommend that you look at the following chapters for additional information and inspiration:

- Chapter 4, "Introducing Transact-SQL," demonstrates some of the ways of writing SQL that you will use with the scripting utilities that you may have chosen.

- Chapter 15, "Using Client/Server Application Programming Tools," introduces some of the third-party development tools that are also available to write software that works with Sybase.

- Chapter 23, "Using Sybase's Configuration Options," explains all the different configurable options available in System XI that you can manage with such tools as DBArtisan.

Part
III

Ch
17

Introducing the Internet

The Internet is probably the most influential technology to hit mainstream popularity in the last 20 years. Not since the evolution of television and radio has a single technology seen such diverse and rapid adoption across all facets of life. The impact of the Internet is hard to underestimate. Thousands of new users are logging on and plugging in to the Net every day. The popularity of the Net is sparking millions of users to contribute content of various different levels of quality and quantity in every possible type of field.

The beauty of the Internet is that it's made up of a number of different and flexible technologies that can be used in different ways to provide an excellent knowledge and data transfer medium. The sorts of things that you can do with the Internet are basically limitless. The only bounds for the Internet are your imagination. It is possible to represent virtual worlds, distribute news information, and publish various forms of data in just about any method you desire.

The momentum behind the Internet right now is probably the most interesting thing about it. There's such a wide industry support for the technology base that progress in Internet technologies is going incredibly fast. As an example, Microsoft recently adopted the Internet as its strategic focus and has poured its huge resources into developing an instant set of tools and technology that benefits all users of the Net.

This chapter is simply designed to whet your appetite for more information on the Internet. There are dozens of books on the Internet and especially on the World Wide Web. The following are three excellent books from Que that you might want to have a look at:

- *Student's Guide to the Internet,* 2nd Edition
- *Special Edition Using HTML,* 2nd Edition
- *Special Edition Using Java*

The Origins of the Internet

The Internet began as a project under the auspices of the US Department of Defense ARPA (Advanced Research Projects Agency), which various government agencies and research centers would use to send secure data transmissions and enable the sharing of ideas on a more expedient basis than just using faxes or other public network infrastructures. The research centers quickly demanded the inclusion of many of the major universities in the US and around the world. Soon the Internet had grown to link most of the universities and some select private organizations, mostly in the defense arena.

The problem for the Internet in its early stage was that it was inherently a hidden world. The common interface to the Internet was a Telnet terminal or an FTP program. This didn't lead to easily being able to distribute information, but served scientists fairly well because they knew where the information was and what they wanted to do with it.

It was not until CERN (a French acronym for European Laboratory for Particle Physics) in Geneva, Switzerland, created the world's first World Wide Web server and browser that the Internet started to gain real market volatility. It's hard to believe, but the prototype of the first Web server was only developed in 1991 and rolled out into major production in early 1993. In this short span of time, the Web and the Internet have acquired some hundreds of millions of pages of data and has proliferated at an astonishing rate.

The fundamental basis of the Internet is the protocol used for communications: the Internet Protocol or IP. Known more commonly as TCP/IP for *Transmission Control Protocol/Internet Protocol,* this universal data transmission and management protocol was used to route packets of information between the various different servers that made up the early Net. Indeed, today TCP/IP is the cornerstone of the Net and is responsible for almost all of the traffic sent across the public networks that the Internet now encompasses.

Users of the Internet and the World Wide Web owe thanks to Tim Berners-Lee, the inventor of the Web, URL (Uniform Resource Locator), HTTP (HyperText Transport Protocol), and HTML (HyperText Markup Language) while working at CERN. Tim's work was designed to make the Internet accessible to those who were uncomfortable with the text based terminals of Telnet, and also to take advantage of possibly the most advanced workstation of the time: the NeXT computer (the Pizza Box and the NeXT Cube) developed by Apple Computer cofounder

Steve Jobs. Without the availability of highly graphical computers, such as the NeXT Cube, Tim Berners-Lee would not have been able to design and create the Web.

Understanding Basic Internet Technologies

The Internet has a number of different technologies that make up its various offerings. The most well-known is, of course, the World Wide Web. But there are several other systems and communications media available on the Internet to just about any user that offer a different way of thinking about the resources of the Net. This section briefly introduces you to those technologies so that you can at least understand all the different components of the Internet.

Each of the technologies described below is managed on a central site by a server. The Internet is fundamentally a client/server-based network architecture.

Understanding URLs

URL or *Uniform Resource Locator* is a way of describing the location of a file or object/resource on the Internet. The principle of a URL is that it describes the server type on the left-hand side of a pair of slashes (//), and the right-hand side is the specifics of the object/resource.

You may have noticed that throughout this book there are references to various Web pages that are like this: **http://www.sybase.com**. Well, the *http:* is referring to a server of type HTTP (HyperText Transfer Protocol) or a standard Web Server. And the *www.sybase.com* is referring to the server's address.

In a similar way, there are other types of documents and services described by a URL, as follows:

- **ftp://**—An FTP site for file transfer
- **news://**—An Internet news server
- **wais://**—An Internet search engine on a Web Server
- **telnet://**—A Telnet server
- **gopher://**—A Gopher server or file retrieval agent server
- **file://**—Used to describe a local file on the local machine

Using Telnet

Telnet is a remote terminal emulation technology that is designed to enable you to emulate a UNIX console on any computer connected to an IP based network. The principal reason that Telnet was developed was so that you could remotely administer a server without needing to go to the physical location of the server itself. The primary advantage of Telnet is its extremely low bandwidth requirements. Telnet is the most modest of all the Internet technologies currently available.

Part
III

Ch
18

The interface of Telnet is strictly functional and low-tech. The basic Telnet application is supplied free in both Windows 95 and Windows NT. To use it, just type **telnet** at the command prompt. Then use the Connect menu to enter the name of the Telnet site that you want to access.

In Figure 18.1, you can see a Telnet session that has been opened to a custom Telnet site that is used by the Canadian Government as a basic way for people to get information.

FIG. 18.1

The CHAT port of the Government of Canada is available as an example of a Telnet site. This is a useful public domain site that is of great public interest.

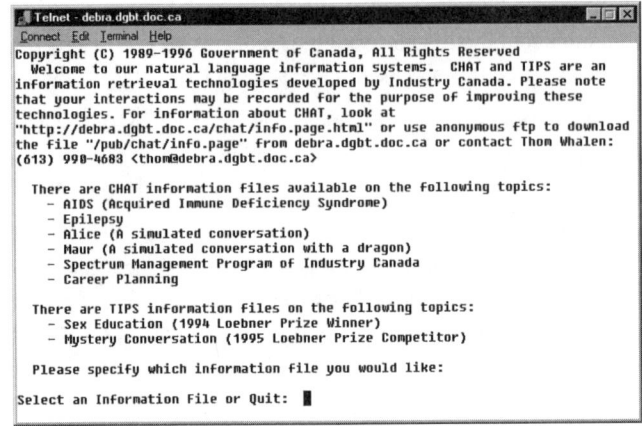

Using FTP

The Internet has a standard way of managing files and sending file-based data across the network to remote clients. FTP or the *File Transfer Protocol* was developed as a public standard for defining the way that files should be sent. There are many FTP programs currently available for Windows 95 and Windows NT that make it easy to send and receive files from FTP servers. The primary command set for FTP is text based and is a series of commands, such as get and put, that are used to request and send files to and from servers on the Internet.

It is highly recommended that you download one of the more popular FTP programs to simplify your access to FTP servers. I highly recommend the program WS_FTP that can be downloaded from **http://www.shareware.com**. Most major software companies have an FTP site that you can use to download beta or production copies of software from. It is often easy to identify or guess the name of a server by simply adding ftp to the front of a company's name, for example, **ftp.microsoft.com**, **ftp.netscape.com**, and **ftp.ibm.com.** Access to some FTP sites requires a password and valid user account, but most public companies offer free access to users who log on with the user name anonymous and pass a password as the e-mail address of the user logging on anonymously. For example, if I were to log on to Microsoft's FTP site I would enter:

```
User Name: anonymous
Password: phazlehurst@phoenixint.com
```

In Figure 18.2, you can see an example of being connected to Microsoft's FTP site at the top-most directory using WS_FTP.

FIG. 18.2

WS_FTP makes it easy to navigate an FTP server because it makes the FTP server look similar to the standard Windows 95 and Windows NT4 Explorer.

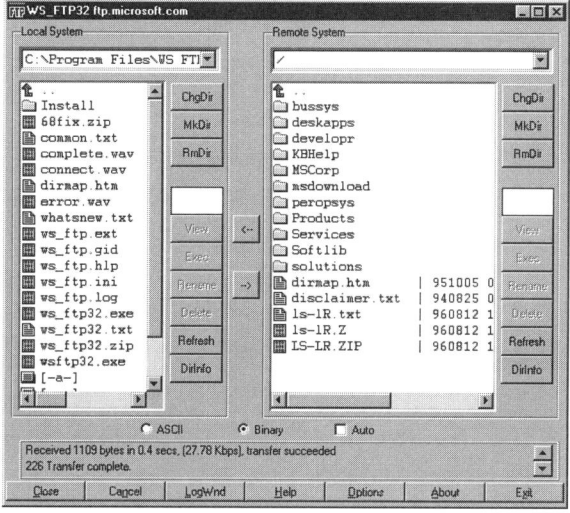

Using Internet Relay Chat (IRC)

The Internet also serves as an excellent mechanism for pseudo real-time conversations. *Internet Relay Chat* is an Internet protocol that can be used to transfer data between multiple real-time users of the Internet. IRC is typically implemented in a text fashion through a Telnet terminal. Recently, Microsoft released some neat technology called Microsoft Comic Chat. With Comic Chat, you are interacting with other users on the IRC, but are displaying a *comic* through a Web Browser. This may seem a bit odd at first, but it's really quite a nice way to have a "conversation" with someone on the Net and be able to show some kind of expression as you "talk" (see Fig. 18.3).

More information about Microsoft Comic Chat can be found at **http://www.microsoft.com/ ie/comichat**.

Using E-Mail

Internet mail is probably the most used feature of the Internet after surfing on the Internet. The ubiquity of the Internet's mail backbone is what makes it so appealing. You can literally send e-mail anywhere around the world and it only takes a few seconds to get there. The core parts involved in working with Internet mail are to have a mail account (usually managed either by your corporation or by an Internet service provider) and a mail reader.

There are scores of different mail readers on the market, and a good one is available from Microsoft called simply Internet Mail. The interface is very intuitive, and it makes negotiating with the different server-based mail protocols (SMTP, MIME, and UUENCODE) quite simple by managing all these steps for you (see Fig. 18.4).

Part

III

Ch

18

FIG. 18.3
While not the most practical way of communicating, you can even be an alien when talking to someone on the Net!

FIG. 18.4
The Internet Mail program from Microsoft succeeds the integrated Internet Mail browsing capabilities of the Microsoft Windows Messaging/Exchange reader.

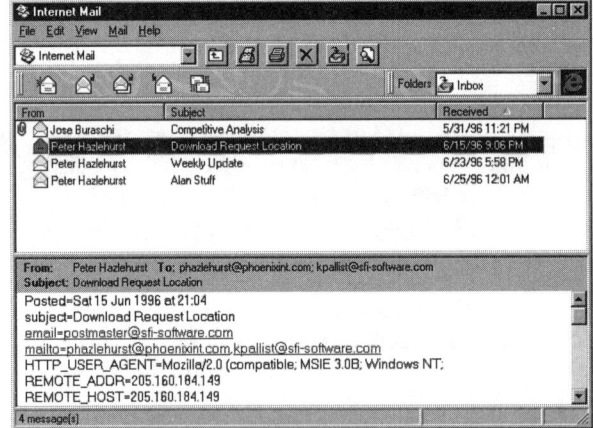

Using the Web (HTML and HTTP)

By now, you have heard much about the different Web pages mentioned throughout this book and probably can't avoid seeing references to the World Wide Web everywhere you look. IBM's recent presentation of the Olympic Games on the Internet was probably the most ambitious project yet undertaken on the Web, and it demonstrates the tremendous flexibility that the Web provides a content provider, such as IBM, to deliver information in a timely and effective way.

The Web is made up of three key technologies:

- **An HTTP server**—The server is responsible for delivering to a client the data that makes up the HTML page that you browse. The HTTP server is really just a special kind of file server that serves up files to the multiple clients that it is servicing. An important point about an HTTP server is that it is stateless. A session to the server lasts as long as it takes to send the file in its entirety. After that, you cease to exist from the point of view of the server.

- **One or many HTML documents**—An HTML document is a text file that uses special tags to mark up a work of text for presentation by browser software. The HTML tags are defined in various standards that are theoretically adhered to by the major vendors of HTML browsers.

- **An HTML-compatible browser**—The browser is the technology that interacts with the HTTP server to receive a text file that it then interprets for display and browsing. The two most important browsers on the market are Netscape's Navigator and Microsoft's Internet Explorer. Both products are neck and neck with functionality and are easily extensible with *plug-in* software components. These *plug-ins* or *ActiveX* controls are designed to add capabilities to the core browser for advanced functionality, such as streamed audio and video.

These three technologies interact with each other to deliver real-time multimedia to surfers on the Web.

Part
III

Ch
18

Understanding the Java Language

Java is a new language brought to you by one of the leaders in the enterprise and networking computing markets: Sun Corporation. The Java language is fully object-oriented and is a very elegant language that is very general purpose and suited to solving many different sorts of problems. The beauty of Java is that it's an interpreted language. Why is this good? Because Sun has developed what it calls the *Java Virtual Machine.* The JVM is a runtime environment for Java applets and applications that enables the Java code to run. Sun has developed JVMs for almost all of the major client operating systems, including Windows 95, Windows NT, Sun Solaris, HP-UX, the Macintosh (Mac OS), and IBM's OS/2. In addition, many software vendors, such as Novell, Microsoft, and IBM, are licensing the Java language so that they can embed it into the operating systems themselves rather than require a JVM to exist.

For the programmer who wants to target many different platforms, Java is an amazingly flexible language that allows for the development on one platform, such as Windows 95, and deployment on another, such as HP-UX, with no code changes. Java's only complaint is that it's slower in execution because it is interpreted; however, many of the compiler companies, such as Borland, Symantec, and Microsoft, have developed what is known as a *Just In Time* compiler or JIT. The JIT is used to compile the Java code at runtime on the client for optimized performance. JITs have been shown to improve some Java-based applications by factors of up to 80.

To stay in touch with the latest developments in the world of Java, go to Sun's Web site at: **http://java.sun.com**.

From Here...

This chapter is a very brief introduction to the technologies and components of the Internet. In this chapter, you learned a little about the creation of the Net and how the Web was developed. Also, you learned about FTP, HTML, IRC, and various other Internet standards.

There's one key source that goes with this book that is worth reading for more information on using the Internet to work with Sybase to publish your data effectively. In the manner of being easily accessible and updated, this reference has actually been published on the Internet at Que's Web site. The address is: **http://www.mcp.com/que...** This reference is an excellent eye opener for you if you are planning to develop Internet-hosted database applications and need some tips on how to publish your data, and it explores Sybase's new product, Web.SQL.

In addition, you should surf the Internet's World Wide Web looking at the many, many documents on the Internet's origins and capabilities—most such documents change frequently to address emerging technologies.

Advanced Features

Managing Data Availability

As a database administrator, you have a responsibility to your users to maintain and manage the access to the data on the servers that you manage. Also as a DBA, it is usually in your job description to help ensure that any data stored in the database server is adequately protected in the event of some kind of unforeseen disaster.

What this means is that *you* are required to make sure that you can keep giving users access to the database with minimal interruptions because of conditions that would down the server. For example, you are required to plan for horrible events, such as a database corruption, and be prepared to be able to restore from a backup copy of the database so that your users aren't left stranded without data.

In this chapter, you learn all about backups and restores (or *dumps* and *loads* in Sybase terminology), and you'll discover the importance of a clearly defined backup strategy that will save your company or organization time and money in the event of a disaster. ■

Performing backups and restores

Backups and restores (dumps and loads in Sybase's Transact-SQL) are extremely important tools that you will need to use every day to ensure the integrity and safety of your data.

Using thresholds

Sybase has a unique automatic option that can be used to dump the logs in the event that they exceed a user-specified limit. You will find that using a threshold is a convenient way to manage dumping of the transaction log.

Working with checkpoints

System XI performs a periodic activity called a Checkpoint, which is designed to flush transaction pages from the log to the disk area on the database. In this chapter, you learn how the checkpointing of the database affects the server's performance.

Using Bulk Copy Program (BCP) for data exporting

Sometimes it is necessary to copy a database at the logical level with just the data. Using BCP is Sybase's most efficient way of exporting data from the server into a format that can be loaded on another server independently of the underlying database's Operating System.

Performing Backups

The first time you really think about a backup is usually too late. There's not a lot of good in finding out that you haven't got a way to restore a critical environment and database when you really have a problem. However, if you haven't thought much about backups, you're really not all that alone. Many customers with whom I have spoken and advised have never even considered what the backup would provide them.

In this section, you'll learn how to work with and define a clear backup strategy that will help you to save the day in the event of a disaster. It is very important that you don't undervalue the time and resources required to manage and maintain a backup strategy in your company or organization. Take care that you inform management as to the importance of this task and insist that they make it a priority.

N O T E   This section is designed to instruct you on how to maintain and manage the server from the backup's point of view. There are a number of other steps that you can take to ensure the database server's functionality independently of the backup strategy that you choose. For more information on some general tips for keeping the server up and running, see the final section in this chapter, "Some Tips to Keep a Server Running." ▥

Designing a Backup Strategy

How often or frequently should you perform a backup? What's the point in a daily backup? Can I live with my data if it's a week old? These are all questions that you need to ask yourself prior to beginning to develop a backup strategy. Essentially, all these questions are trying to ascertain: *What's the value of the data, and what happens if it doesn't stay current?*

If you can answer this question, then you are a step closer to solving and defining your needs. My main field of experience is in mission-critical banking systems. For the financial sector, the data is of paramount importance. I do full backups twice a day—prior to the nightly processing run, and then after the run—to guarantee that we are able to restore the system to any known point in time.

In banking, transactions can happen at any point in time during the day, but they are really a temporary or memo transaction. The nightly processing is the key part of the system around which all the backups are centered. In addition, my customers are relatively unsophisticated Sybase users; many of them don't even have a member of staff dedicated to doing the database maintenance or DBA tasks. The idea of having to mess around with transaction log restoring and so on is not particularly appealing because it is a complex task.

Many other organizations have less data-critical schedules for backing up their systems: They can be more flexible in their backup plans. A very common model adopted in many data-processing environments is to back up the transaction logs on a once- or twice-a-day basis, with full backups once a week. The key advantage to this strategy is that it reduces the amount of time required to perform the backup phase of the system and effectively reduces the amount of time that the system is in a semi-down state. The disadvantage of a transaction log-based backup is that it is more difficult to restore the server in the event of a failure.

N O T E In each of these examples, it is assumed that the whole database fits on a single data tape. Digital Audio Tape (DAT) technology can typically hold a maximum of 8 Gbytes on a single tape in a compressed form (compression is usually pretty good on a database because of the sparse storage of the data on the data pages of the database itself). The newer tape medium of Digital Linear Tape (DLT) can hold nearly five times that much data on a single tape (up to 40 Gbytes).

If you have a large database and you need better performance during the backup and restore phase of your system's life cycle, I highly recommend considering purchasing a DLT backup unit for the server.

If your database requires multiple tapes per backup/restore, then you need to multiply all of the tape calculation requirements by the number of tapes that you need per backup. ■

Working with a Mission-Critical Backup Strategy   This strategy is designed around the principle that any loss of data would be catastrophic to the customer. This strategy requires a slightly high grade of tapes and assumes fairly normal activity windows on the server, where, during the evening, the load on the server is lower and there's a real opportunity to perform backups.

Performing Daily Backups   The daily backups of a mission-critical system involve the following steps:

■ **Routine backups of the transaction logs**—Depending on the volume of transactions and the size of the transaction log device that you have configured, these routine backups could take place at intervals of every few hours, or at least once per day.

■ **Full database backups**—These are usually performed twice per day.

The transaction log backups are designed to enable quick recovery during the day in the event of a media failure. The process would involve restoring the last known full backup and then rolling forward through each of the Transaction log backups that you had made throughout the day. The more frequently you perform the transaction log backups, the less incremental daily data will be lost.

The full database backups are typically performed twice per day. Usually a backup occurs at the end of the day after the daily activity by the majority of your users has been completed, and then a second time following any nightly activity.

This part of the backup scheme requires a minimum of 63 tapes when there are two tapes reserved per day of the month, and an additional tape is used for the incremental backups during the day. The same tapes can be used on a rotating schedule, month to month. As tapes become more than a week old, I recommend that you place the tape off-site so that if a fire or other disaster occurs at the primary site, you can recover from an earlier backup.

Part
IV

Ch
19

Performing a frequent backup (defined as once per day) of the *master* database, especially after you add any devices or make any changes that affect the *master* database's system catalog tables, is highly recommended. If you don't have a backup of the *master* database and you have a media failure on the device that holds the *master* database, too, you will need to manually re-create all the entries in the tables, such as *sysdatabases* (a list of all the created databases on the server), *sysdevices* (a list of devices on the server), and *syslogins* (all the valid logins to the server).

Performing Monthly Backups   Monthly backups are also full backups that are kept for a twelve-month period. Therefore, you are going to need 12 tapes that are used in a rotating schedule.

N O T E   Some institutions choose to keep monthly backups forever. This provides a level of control required for reporting to federal or governmental agencies at any point in time, and is something you may want to consider. ▨

Performing Yearly Backups   On large systems, the annual backup is a critical backup that is normally kept indefinitely; several copies are made to help protect the company/organization in the future. In addition, the year-end backup is often used for long-term analysis. You will need a tape per year (plus copies) that should be kept permanently and a copy of which should be placed off-site.

Working with a Standard Backup Strategy   A standard backup strategy would apply for those companies and organizations that are less concerned about the daily full backups.

The strategy involves a weekly full backup of the database, followed by daily backups of the transaction logs. In this scenario, I recommend that you keep the weekly backups for a month (so you'll need four tapes) and the daily backups can be rotated each week.

Therefore, you'll need seven tapes for daily backups of the transaction logs, and four tapes for each week for a total of 11 tapes.

Using a Double Backup Strategy   Independently of how frequently you back up your server's database, it is often useful to have an additional tape that can be used in the event of a media failure on the tape itself. There are two ways of achieving this requirement:

- **Backups to disk**—By using this option, you are doing a dump or backup to disk, and then using the operating system's backup to tape functionality to move the data onto a tape. The advantage of this method is that it reduces and eliminates a double backup from the database, which has the benefit of reducing the load on the server. The disadvantage is that it requires double the space in terms of disk on the server if you back up to the disks of the server where the database is located.

- **Backup/restore/backup**—In this scenario, you back up the primary database to tape, then restore the same tape to another database (of the same size, and so on), and then (finally) perform another backup of the second database to a second tape. The great advantage of this method is that not only do you get two tapes or copies of the database, but you also get to validate that the primary tape is a good backup that can be restored from.

Understanding How Backups Work

With the release of Sybase System 10, dumps and loads are performed by an open server program known as the Backup Server. Backup Server runs on the same machine as SQL Server. If you are running SQL Server on VAX clusters, Backup Server can run on any machine in the cluster that has access to every database device that will be dumped or loaded. Backups can also be performed over a network with a Backup Server installed on a remote computer, and another on the SQL Server machine.

Backup Server communicates with SQL Server through remote procedure calls (RPCs). Remote procedure calls are simply commands and messages passed between Backup Server and SQL Server. When a dump command is issued by a user, SQL Server interprets the command and sends a message to Backup Server with information about the operation to be performed. The message sent includes information about which database pages to dump, and what dump devices should be used. As the dump proceeds, Backup Server communicates with SQL Server, providing information about the progress of the dump. Some considerations are important when using Backup Server:

- A Backup Server must be running on the same machine as the SQL Server, or on the same cluster if you are using OpenVMS.

- You cannot use the dump and load commands unless SQL Server can communicate with its Backup Server.

- The Backup Server must be listed in the system catalog table: *master..sysservers*.

- SQL Server must be configured for remote access. The default setting for remote access when SQL Server is installed is enabled.

- The user who starts the Backup Server must have write permission for the dump devices used by the Backup Server.

Starting the Backup server is not very complex, and is usually something you would automate. If the backup server is not running, there are two ways to start it: using the Graphical Utility provided with the Windows NT version of Sybase, or by running a command from the UNIX command line.

Using Sybase's Services Manager to Start the Backup Server   To start the Backup Server using the Services Manager, follow these steps:

1. Start the Services Manager by double-clicking the icon in the Sybase for Windows NT program group.

2. In the Services combo box, select Backup Server, and you should see the Server change to something with a _BS extension (see Fig. 19.1).

3. Double-click the Start/Continue text to start the Backup Server. This should make the traffic light go green, indicating that it started successfully.

Part
IV

Ch
19

FIG. 19.1

The Sybase Services Manager enables you to start any Sybase server for which you have configured a port/ connection for Using SQLEdit.

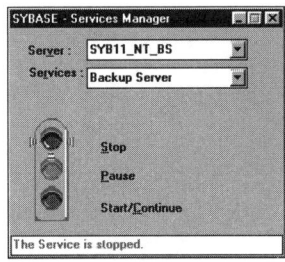

Using UNIX or the Sybase Scripts to Start the Backup Server   The other way of starting Sybase's Backup Server involves connecting to the UNIX server with a Telnet session. To do so, follow these steps:

1. Start a Telnet session to the host and log on as a user with Sybase privileges.

2. Type **cd $SYBASE** at the command prompt to change directories to the Sybase root directory on the UNIX box. Note that if you are doing this on Windows NT, you should enter, **cd %SYBASE%.**

3. Type **cd install** at the command prompt to change to the installation subdirectory off the Sybase root directory.

4. Type **ls** in UNIX or **DIR *.bat** on NT to identify the script files that are used to run a Sybase server. Each script should be something like RUN_<SERVER_NAME>. (Note that the backup server should have _BS as the last part of the name of the script or batch file.)

5. After you identify the correct file to run, type the name of it at the command prompt, e.g., **RUN_SYB11_NT_BS.**

TIP To run a task in the background on UNIX, use the ampersand (&) in the command line (e.g., RUN_SYB11_NT &). This will enable you to close the current Telnet session to the host without shutting down the Backup Server task that you just started.

On Windows NT, you can use the Start command to run a task in another Window/shell, but you cannot run anything in the background using the command line.

Performing a Local Backup

There are two ways to perform a backup in Sybase System XI: You can either use the graphical tool Sybase SQL Server Manager to aid you in the execution, or you can do it manually with the Transact-SQL command Dump. The graphical method is far easier for the average user and is recommended as a way of performing the backup in an online fashion. However, if you have to do an unattended backup (i.e., script driven), it is important that you understand the syntax for the Dump command.

  NOTE In order to perform a backup, you must have first installed a dump device that can be used to write the output to. If you have yet to create or install a dump device, or you have questions about how it is configured and managed, refer to Chapter 5, "Understanding Databases, Devices, and Transaction Logs." ■

Using Sybase SQL Server Manager to Perform a Backup   To use Sybase SQL Server Manager to perform a backup of a database, follow these steps:

1. Launch Sybase SQL Server Manager and log on to the server that has the database you are going to back up.

2. Select the database that you want to back up in the left pane of the explorer.

3. From the Database menu, select Backup to display the Sybase SQL Server Manager Backup dialog box (see Fig. 19.2).

FIG. 19.2

The SSM Database Backup dialog box makes it easy for you to perform backups. The best feature is that you can select from the dump devices created on the server, and SSM Database Backup will build the correct SQL for you to do the dump.

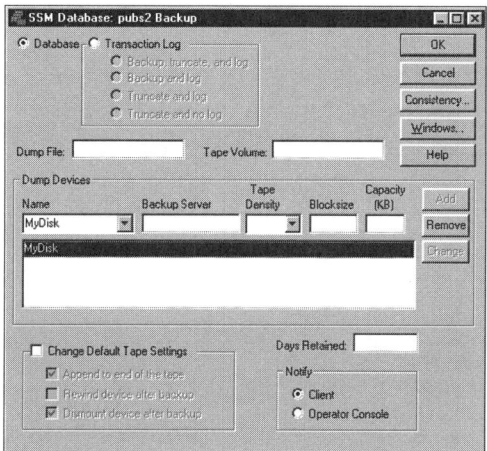

4. In the Dump Devices group box, select the dump device that you want to use. In Figure 19.2, you can see that a Disk device called *MyDisk* is being used. You may also override the existing dump devices by entering the full details in the available fields (described below in the section on Transact-SQL's Dump command).

5. Optionally, alter the default tape settings, which are to append the current backup to the end of the tape, and then to eject the tape.

 TIP If you are backing up several databases, make sure that you disable the option Dismount device after backup, or else you will have to keep putting the tape back in the drive.

6. You can add multiple dump devices if you want to do a dump to multiple devices in parallel, even if the devices are not identical.

7. Click OK to perform the backup: Doing so starts the backup. As the backup is progressing, a Sybase SQL Server Manager Output window is displayed to show the progress. Figure 19.3 shows the output from backing up the *pubs2* database to a disk volume.

N O T E Notice in the output listed in Figure 19.3 that there are multiple dump phases indicated. What this refers to is the fact that Sybase takes a snapshot when you start or initiate the Dump of what it thinks are pages that need to be written to the dump device. During the dump itself, however, users can be performing transactions that would have been missed because they didn't get entered in the first pass of the database's dumping process.

The second and third dump phases are Sybase's Backup Server going back into the transaction log to look for any activity that wasn't captured by the first pass of the backup. ▪

Part
IV

Ch

19

FIG. 19.3

The SSM Output window shows you all the messages that were generated from the Backup Server during the dumping of the *pubs2* database. If you get any errors, they will be shown here.

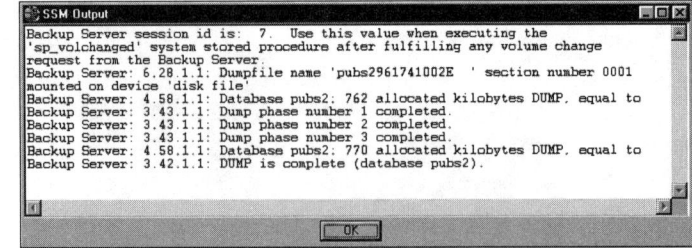

Using the Dump Command to Backup a Database   If you need to use Transact-SQL to perform a backup for whatever reason, you will need to know how to use the Dump command. The syntax for the Dump command is as follows:

```
Dump Database Database_Name
to Stripe_Device [ at Backup_Server_Name ]
    [Density = Density_Value,
     Blocksize = Number_Bytes,
     Capacity = Number_Kilobytes,
     Dumpvolume = Volume_Name,
     File = File_Name]
[stripe on Stripe_Device [ at Backup_Server_Name ]
    [Density = Density_Value,
     Blocksize = Number_Bytes,
     Capacity = Number_Kilobytes,
     Dumpvolume = Volume_Name,
     File = File_Name] ...]
[with {
    [Density = Density_Value,
     Blocksize = Number_Bytes,
     Capacity = Number_Kilobytes,
     Dumpvolume = Volume_Name,
     File = File_Name
[Dismount | Nodismount],
[Nounload | Unload],
 Retaindays = Number_Days,
[Noinit | Init],
 Notify = {client | Operator_Console}}]]
```

The options for the Transact-SQL command Dump are as follows:

- *Stripe_Device*—SQL Server enables you to dump a database to multiple dump devices simultaneously. The Backup Server will divide the database into approximately equal segments and dump each segment to the specified device. These devices are known as stripe devices. You can specify up to 32 stripe devices. Since the dumps are made simultaneously, the amount of time required to backup a database can be reduced significantly.

- at *Backup_Server_Name*—If you are doing a remote backup to a backup server on another machine, you must specify that machine's Backup Server Name here. If you are dumping to the current machine, you can leave this option alone without supplying a value at all.

■ *Density*—This option is only used when reinitializing a volume on OpenVMS systems. The density option enables you to override the default density for a tape device.

■ *Blocksize*—You can use this option to override the default Blocksize for a dump device. The Blocksize must be at least one database page (usually 2048 bytes) and must be an exact multiple of the database page size. If you are using OpenVMS, the Blocksize cannot exceed 15,384 bytes. It is recommended that you use the default Blocksize, since it is the most optimal Blocksize for your system.

■ *Capacity*—Capacity represents the maximum amount of data that can be written to a single tape volume. Capacity must be at least equal to five database pages, and should be smaller than the recommended capacity for the device. Note that if your version of UNIX cannot detect the end of a tape indicator when dumping, *you must* specify the *Capacity* of the tape; otherwise, an error will occur during the Dump.

 T I P   When calculating a valid *Capacity* for a device that is not implicitly recognized by the Backup Server, you should allocate about 70 percent of the manufacturer's specified limit for the device. The rest of the space will be consumed by System things on the tape, such as headers, spacing between records, and so on.

■ *Dumpvolume*—Dumpvolume represents the name that is assigned to the volume. The Backup Server will write the *Volume_Name* in the ANSI tape label when dumping the database. The load database command checks the label and will generate an error message if the wrong volume is loaded.

■ *File*—The file option holds the name of the dump file. There is a 17-character limit to the file name and it must conform to your operating system's naming conventions. If no name is specified, Backup Server will create a default.

■ *Dismount | Nodismount*—This option determines whether a tape is dismounted after the dump is complete. The default is to dismount the tape. Use *Nodismount* to keep the tape available for another dump or for a load. This option applies only to platforms that support logical dismounts.

■ *Nounload | Unload*—This option determines whether to rewind the tape after the dump completes. The default is to not rewind the tape. This enables you to make additional dumps to the same tape. When performing multiple dumps to the same volume, specify unload for the last dump so that the tape rewinds and is unloaded when the dump is complete.

■ *Retaindays*—This option applies only to UNIX systems. Use *Retaindays* to specify the number of days Backup Server should protect a tape from being overwritten by another dump. If an attempt is made to overwrite a dump before *Retaindays* expires, Backup Server will prompt for confirmation before overwriting the volume on tape. The *Retaindays* value is specified as a positive integer. If you want to be able to overwrite immediately, use 0. If *Retaindays* is not specified, Backup Server uses the "tape retention" value set using the sp_configure system procedure.

Part
IV

Ch
19

■ *Noinit | Init*—This option enables you to specify whether the dump should be appended to existing dump files or if the tape volume should be reinitialized. The default is to be appended to the tape following the last end-of-tape mark.

■ *Notify*—This option enables you to specify where messages are routed. If your operating system offers an operator terminal feature, volume change messages are sent to the operator terminal on the machine that is running Backup Server. You can use the notify = client option to route all other messages to the terminal session that initiated the dump database command. If your operating system does not offer an operator terminal feature, messages are sent to the client that initiated the dump database command. If you use *Notify = Operator_Console*, you can route messages to the terminal on the machine that is running Backup Server.

For example, to perform a backup of the *pubs2* to the tape device on the UNIX box that you want to keep for 30 days, you would execute:

```
Dump Database pubs2
    To   "/dev/nrmt0"
    With Unload,
        Retaindays = 30
Go
```

TROUBLESHOOTING

I've followed the steps for creating the backup, but when I run the backup, it fails. What should I be looking for to solve this problem? The first thing you'll need to examine is the free space on the dump device you've created. Make sure you have enough free space for the device to grow to accommodate the information you're saving. Remember, too, that if you are not dismounting the tapes, the information you save will be added to the prior information each time you run a backup. This will eventually lead to some very sizable dump devices. By using the rotating tapes as described in the earlier section "Designing a Backup Strategy," you can safely back up to separate dump devices each time you back up because you'll have the prior backup's information stored safely away.

Performing Remote Backups

Remote backups are similar to local backups except that the output from the Backup Server is redirected across the network to another Backup Server on another machine. There are several reasons why you might want to perform remote backups:

■ **Backup clusters**—If you have a number of servers available, each with tape drives, you can cluster them together through the Backup Server to improve the time of the backup because of the parallel writing of the output. (Note that the overhead of networking *can* have a negative impact on the performance of the Backup.)

■ **Redundancy**—If you have a remote location that you want to have backed up to the central office; or vice versa, you have a central office server that you want backed up to an off-site location, you can use the remote backup capabilities to enable you to achieve this goal.

- **Hardware failure**—If the tape device has failed on a server and you need to do a backup, you can use the remote backup solution to work around the temporary problem.

- **No hardware or other media required**—If the local server has no tape media, or a format that is no longer of any use, you can use the remote backup functionality to dump to the remote server.

Remote backups are fairly straightforward to set up, but do require some installation/configuration settings:

- The local interfaces file must have valid references for all the remote backup servers that are going to be used. Remote Backup Server is performed via DB-Library; as such, it needs to make a connection across the network.

- The network identification names for the two backup servers must be unique. To check that they are, you can execute the system-stored procedure sp_helpserver through ISQL on each server. For example, to see the name of the backup server in use you would execute:

```
sp_helpserver SYB_BACKUP
Go

name           network_name   status                                          id
----------------------------------------------------------------------------
SYB_BACKUP     SYB11_NT_BS    no timeouts, no net password encryption    1
```

In addition to these server level considerations, you should also think about the following issues:

- **Character sets**—In order to avoid any data conversion problems, it is highly recommended that the character sets installed and operating on both servers be the same. Unpredictable results could occur if you don't maintain the same data character sets.

- **Server memory on UNIX**—For each remote device that you stripe to, Sybase allocates an additional shared segment of memory of 54K. On most flavors of UNIX (Digital UNIX, Sun Solaris, and NCR), the default number of shared segments is six. If you are striping to more than this many devices remotely, you must increase the Operating System level parameter: SHMSEG.

- **Same server platforms**—You cannot use the Remote Backup Server as a way of performing a cross-platform backup, except in the case of a server running on SunOS and a server running on Solaris. Performing cross-platform backups is not supported by Sybase and will cause errors.

Part
IV

Ch
19

Dumping the Transaction Log

Dumping the transaction log is required because the log fills up with transactions during the day that are either no longer required or that need to be written to tape for disaster recovery purposes. In this section, you'll see a couple of different ways to dump the logs and you'll understand what it means to truncate the logs without concern for backing up the data.

Performing Normal Dumps

The user interface in Sybase SQL Server Manager for dumping the transaction log is very similar to that of a dump database. In Figure 19.2, you can see the additional configurations available for dumping the transaction log are grayed out. The meanings of those options are as follows:

- **Backup, truncate, and log**—This is the normal Dump option that should be taken. The log is backed up to tape, the inactive portions of the log are removed (truncated), and an entry is added to the log indicating that the Dump has taken place.

- **Backup and log**—This option performs a backup and records the backup in the log as well; however, the inactive information is not removed.

- **Truncate and log**—This option *does not* perform a backup and simply removes all the inactive transactions from the log. Using Truncate and Log also adds a record to the log indicating that the truncation has taken place.

- **Truncate and no log**—Used as a last resort Dump, this option is provided in the case that the log is completely full and needs to be dumped without adding an additional record to itself that indicates that the dump has taken place.

The Dump command in Transact-SQL has corresponding extensions that match up with the features on the Sybase SQL Server Manager Backup database dialog box.

The syntax for the Backup, Truncate, and Log option is as follows (which is the same syntax as the Dump Database command, except that Database has been replaced with Tran[saction]):

```
Dump Tran[saction] Database_Name
to Stripe_Device [ at Backup_Server_Name ]
    [Density = Density_Value,
     Blocksize = Number_Bytes,
     Capacity = Number_Kilobytes,
     Dumpvolume = Volume_Name,
     File = File_Name]
[stripe on Stripe_Device [ at Backup_Server_Name ]
    [Density = Density_Value,
     Blocksize = Number_Bytes,
     Capacity = Number_Kilobytes,
     Dumpvolume = Volume_Name,
     File = File_Name] ...]
[with {
    [Density = Density_Value,
     Blocksize = Number_Bytes,
     Capacity = Number_Kilobytes,
     Dumpvolume = Volume_Name,
     File = File_Name
[Dismount | Nodismount],
[Nounload | Unload],
 Retaindays = Number_Days,
[Noinit | Init],
 Notify = {client | Operator_Console}}]]
```

To avoid truncating the log after dumping it, you add the following keyword to the Dump command:

```
With No_Truncate
```

To perform a Dump of the transaction log that is not backed up, the syntax is as follows:

```
Dump Transaction Database_Name
With Truncate_Only
```

If you have run out of log space and you need to dump the logs without recording that you are performing the dump, you would use the following syntax:

```
Dump Transaction Database_Name
With No_Log
```

> **CAUTION**
>
> Performing a Dump Transaction Database_Name With No_Log is an operation that is not logged in any way and leaves the database in an unrecoverable state. Use this option only as a last resort after a With Truncate_Only Dump has failed.
>
> You should attempt to Dump the database as soon as possible after the No_Log has happened in order to make the database recoverable.

TROUBLESHOOTING

When I try to back up the Transaction Log, I get a message that indicates that I can't dump the transaction log while Truncate Log on Checkpoint is set. What do I do? The section later in this chapter titled "Understanding Checkpoints" explains that one way of helping to manage transaction log size is to turn on the Truncate Log on Checkpoint option. Another way to manage the size of the log is to dump the transaction log to a backup device. SQL Server will, by default, also truncate the log at that point after a successful backup. Because both operations take control over truncating the log, they are mutually exclusive. You'll need to turn off the option to truncate the logon checkpoint before you can successfully back up the transaction log.

Using Thresholds to Automatically Dump the Log

Monitoring the transaction log on a highly active database can be a very time-consuming and arduous task. Fortunately, Sybase provides a way of monitoring the freespace in the transaction log through a threshold mechanism. These thresholds are in effect for the life of the transaction log and are designed to look for a percentage of space free on the server, and then to execute a stored procedure specified by you to dump the logs or to perform an action.

This threshold can often be thought of as a *Last Chance Threshold* because it enables you to have some processing that will occur at the last chance before the logs fill up and the database is rendered unusable. Note that if the logs get full, all transactions and users are suspended until the logs are freed up.

N O T E To re-enable a user that has been suspended because the logs filled up, you need to execute the following SQL:

```
Select lct_admin("unsuspend", db_id)
Go
```

db_id is the *spid* (server process id) of the user account that has been suspended. Take care that you are ready to Kill the process if you suspect that it will fill the logs up again after it is unsuspended. ■

Sybase enables this functionality by executing the special system-stored procedure sp_thresholdaction in the event that the freespace threshold is crossed. In this section, you'll learn how to create a threshold and work with thresholds that are created on the server.

Displaying Information on Thresholds   Thresholds are not represented in Sybase SQL Server Manager, so you must use Transact-SQL to work with them. To see if any thresholds exist on the current database, you execute the system-stored procedure sp_helpthreshold. The syntax for sp_helpthreshold is as follows:

```
sp_helpthreshold [Segment_Name]
```

Segment_Name is the particular segment on the current database. If you execute sp_helpthreshold with no parameters, all the thresholds for all the segments in the current database will be returned. For example, to see all the thresholds on the *pubs2* database, you would execute:

```
Use pubs2
Go
sp_helpthreshold
Go
```

In the default Sybase System XI install of *pubs2*, there are no thresholds installed, and, therefore, no information is returned.

T I P   If you need to find information about the *Default* data segment on a database, you must enclose the word *Default* in quotation marks because it is a reserved word. For example:

```
sp_helpthreshold "Default"
Go
```

Adding a Threshold with sp_addthreshold   To add a threshold to a database, you need to use the system-stored procedure sp_addthreshold. The syntax for sp_addthreshold is as follows:

```
sp_addthreshold  Database_Name, Segment_Name, Free_Space, Procedure_Name
```

The options for the Transact-SQL system procedure sp_addthreshold are as follows:

- *Database_Name*—the name of the database for which you are adding the threshold.
- *Segment_Name*—the segment that you are wanting to monitor. To get a list of segments in a database, use either the sp_helpsegment or sp_helpdb system-stored procedures.

- *Free_Space*—the number of 2K pages that must remain free to keep the threshold procedure from being executed. If the number of free pages available on the segment falls below this number, then the Sybase SQL Server will execute the specified procedure.

- *Procedure_Name*—the name of the stored procedure that you want Sybase to execute when the *Free_Space* threshold has been exceeded. Sybase does not validate that the stored procedure exists at the time you execute `sp_addthreshold`, it just adds a record to the system catalog table *systhresholds*.

For example, to add a threshold to the *pubs2* database that will fire when the number of free pages falls below 60, you would execute:

```
sp_addthreshold pubs2, "default", 60, up_thresholdaction
Go

Adding threshold for segment 'default' at '60' pages.
DBCC execution completed. If DBCC printed error messages,
contact a user with System Administrator (SA) role.
```

You can confirm that the threshold was created by executing the system-stored procedure `sp_helpthreshold` as described in the preceding section:

```
sp_helpthreshold
Go
segment name    free pages last chance? threshold procedure
-------------------------------------------------------------
default                 60              0 up_thresholdaction
```

Defining a Stored Procedure to Execute on the Threshold   There are a number of special characteristics that must be considered when creating a threshold procedure. Because of the state the database will be in, you need to be careful about the actions that you take and guard the information that you return to the user.

N O T E   Sybase does *not* provide any threshold procedures (such as `sp_thresholdaction`) to you. You must create the procedure yourself and implement it as appropriate for the database/segment that you are managing.

When the procedure is executed, it will be passed four parameters that you must cater for in the procedure that you define:

- *@psDatabaseName Varchar(30)*—The database that caused the threshold to fire
- *@psSegmentName Varchar(30)*—The segment on the database that is so full that the threshold is firing
- *@pnFreeSpace* Int—The number of pages left free on the segment
- *@pnStatus* Int—The status of the threshold firing: 1 for last chance thresholds and 0 for all others

Typically, the stored procedure will, on the start of execution, write something to the errorlog so that you can determine that the event occurred at this point in time. Threshold procedures write all `Print` statements to the errorlog, so by some carefully thought out `Prints`, you can get some quite effective diagnostics. For example, you could print the size of the space free and the database getting dumped like this:

```
Print 'Database %1! being dumped due to threshold being exceeded.',
        @psDatabaseName
Print 'Space free: %1!', @pnSpaceLeft
```

There are generally two approaches that can be taken when writing a threshold procedure. The first is to dump the logs and keep going. This dump would just truncate the logs and have no consideration for the storage of the log data. In Listing 19.1, you can see a simple threshold procedure that you could use as the model for your own. It is designed to just dump the logs without caring about the fact that data may be lost.

Listing 19.1   CHP20_01.SQL—Simple Threshold to Dump the Logs and Keep Going

```
/*
  This is a threshold procedure that will
  be used to dump the logs without saving
  any of the data in the event that the logs
  fill up.

  Take care: this log dump is not recoverable!
             If you need to maintain the integrity
             of your log data, then you should not
             use this procedure.
*/

Create Procedure sp_thresholdaction
    @psDatabaseName Varchar(30),
    @psSegmentName  Varchar(30),
    @pnFreeSpace    Int,
    @pnStatus       Int

As

/* Dump the logs! */
Dump Transaction @psDatabaseName
With Truncate_Only

/* Write a record in the errorlog */
Print "Threshold Log Dump: '%1!' for '%2!' dumped",
      @psSegmentName, @psDatabaseName
Go
```

The second alternative when dumping the logs might be to write the output to a shared directory on the server for later transfer to a tape backup using the operating system's backup capabilities. In Listing 19.2, there's an example of how to write a threshold that will dump to the disk on the local server. This example is designed for UNIX but could easily be replaced with the correct disk structure required for Windows NT or other operating systems.

Listing 19.2   CHP20_02.SQL—An Advanced Procedure for Dumping During Thresholds that Will Back Up to Disk

```
/*
  This is a more advanced threshold procedure
  it takes into consideration whether or not this
  procedure is being fired because the logs are full
  and if not it reports that the data segment is out
  of space.

  In addition, it performs a backup to the
  root's /backup/<time> directory so that you
  can save the data off to a tape later on.

  Finally it adds timer entries into the log so that
  you can benchmark the performance of the dumps.

*/

Create Procedure sp_thresholdaction
    @psDatabaseName Varchar(30),
    @psSegmentName  Varchar(30),
    @pnFreeSpace    Int,
    @pnStatus       Int

As

/* Declare storage variables */
Declare    @dtCurrent        DateTime,
           @sBackupDirectory Varchar(60)

/* check if this is the log segment (always 2!) and if
   not print an error in the errorlog */
If @psSegmentName != (Select name
                      From    syssegments
                      Where   segment = 2)
Begin
    Print "The data segment '%1!' in database '%2!' is nearly full!",
          @psSegmentName, @psDatabaseName
    Return 0
End

/* Record Start Date */
Select @dtCurrent = GetDate( )
Print 'Dump beginning at: %1!', @dtCurrent

/* Build Backup Directory */
Select @sBackupDirectory = '/Backup/' + @psDatabaseName +
```

Part

IV

Ch

19

continues

Listing 19.2   Continued

```
        Str( DatePart( Year, @dtCurrent ) )+ Str( DatePart( Month, @dtCurrent ) ) +
        Str( DatePart( Day, @dtCurrent ) ) +  '_' +
        Str( DatePart( Hour, @dtCurrent ) ) + Str( DatePart( Minute, @dtCurrent ) )

/* Dump the logs! */
Dump Transaction @psDatabaseName
To    @sBackupDirectory

/* Record End Date */
Select @dtCurrent = GetDate( )
Print 'Dump ending at: %1!', @dtCurrent

/* Write a record in the errorlog */
Print "Threshold Log Dump: '%1!' for '%2!' dumped",
      @psSegmentName, @psDatabaseName
Go
```

Performing Restores

Restoring a database is a simple process using either Sybase SQL Server Manager or the Transact-SQL command Load. Using Sybase SQL Server Manager to perform restores is usually the easiest approach because a restore rarely happens in a script. However, if you need to perform automated database restores, you will need to know how to use the Load command.

Using Sybase SQL Server Manager to Restore a Database

Sybase SQL Server Manager's restore functionality is very easily accessed and is extremely similar to the backup functions. To perform a restore using Sybase SQL Server Manager, follow these steps:

1. Launch Sybase SQL Server Manager and log on to the server that has the database you are going to back up.

2. Select the database that you want to restore in the left pane of the explorer.

3. From the Database menu, select Restore to display the Sybase SQL Server Manager Restore dialog box (see Fig. 19.4).

4. Complete the options in the dialog box in the same way as you performed a backup, and click OK to begin the database-loading process.

FIG. 19.4

The SSM Database Restore dialog box is just about the same as the Backup dialog box, and it works in the same way.

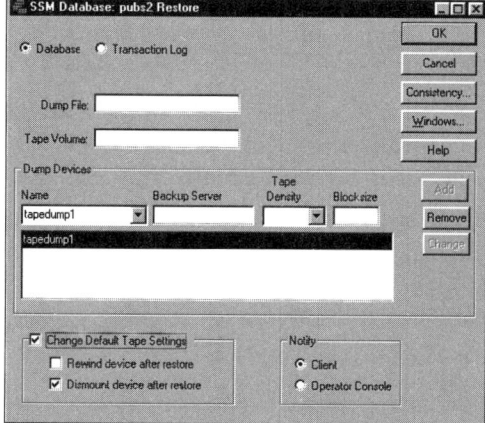

Using the Transact-SQL Command Load to Restore a Database

The Load command can be used to perform a database restore using Transact-SQL. The syntax for the Load command is the same as that of the backup command:

```
Load Database | Tran[saction] Database_Name
to Stripe_Device [ at Backup_Server_Name ]
    [Density = Density_Value,
     Blocksize = Number_Bytes,
     Capacity = Number_Kilobytes,
     Dumpvolume = Volume_Name,
     File = File_Name]
[stripe on Stripe_Device [ at Backup_Server_Name ]
    [Density = Density_Value,
     Blocksize = Number_Bytes,
     Capacity = Number_Kilobytes,
     Dumpvolume = Volume_Name,
     File = File_Name] ...]
[with {
    [Density = Density_Value,
     Blocksize = Number_Bytes,
     Capacity = Number_Kilobytes,
     Dumpvolume = Volume_Name,
     File = File_Name
[Dismount | Nodismount],
[Nounload | Unload],
 Listonly [= full],
 Headeronly,
[Noinit | Init],
 Notify = {client | Operator_Console}}]]
```

Part
IV

Ch

19

There are two additional options that can be used when doing a Load: Listonly and Headeronly. These two options are designed to help you determine what information is stored on a tape. Neither of these options causes the data on the tape to be loaded; they are informational only.

The Listonly option provides the details of the backups that are on a given piece of media (tape); using the full option provides extended information based on the ANSI tape label that was marked to the tape during the Dump.

The Headeronly option provides information about the first database that is backed up on the tape.

For example, to Load the *pubs2* database from the primary UNIX backup tape, you would execute:

```
Load Database pubs2
From "/dev/nrmt0"
Go
```

To get a list of databases that are backed up on a tape, you would execute:

```
Load Database pubs2
From "/dev/nrmt0"
With Listonly
Go
```

Bringing a Database Online

After you have restored the database from a backup, it is left in a state that makes it inaccessible to users— it is *offline*. This enables you to perform (as the System Administrator) any tasks that you need to after the dump is loaded and prior to the first user's gaining access to the database. In prior releases of Sybase, you would need to put the database in either Single User or dbo use only mode to achieve the same effect.

To bring a database online, you need to use the new Transact-SQL command online database. The syntax for online database is as follows:

Online Database *Database_Name*

For example, to bring a recently restored *pubs2* database online, you would execute:

```
Online Database pubs2
Go
```

After executing this command, Sybase makes the database accessible to any valid user of the database.

Handling Backups and Restores that Span Multiple Tapes

If you are backing up or restoring a very large database that requires the use of multiple tapes and you are not using multiple tape drives in parallel, you have some issues that are important to consider during the process. The primary point is that you need some way of telling the Backup Server that you are finished with one tape and that a second tape should be used. Sybase System XI enables you to interact with an active Backup Server through the system procedure `sp_volchanged`.

If you look at the output listed in Sybase's SQL Server Manager Output window (see Fig. 19.3), you will notice the following:

```
Backup Server session id is:  7.  Use this value when executing the
'sp_volchanged' system stored procedure after fulfilling any volume change
request from the Backup Server.
```

The Backup Server is actually warning you that you need to write down the value *7* in the event that you need to interact with the Backup Server. This session id corresponds to the channel of RPCs that is being used between the Sybase SQL Server (Data Server) and the Sybase Backup Server in order to transfer data.

If the tape gets full or the amount of data written to the tape exceeds the amount you specified in the `Dump` command, with the `Capacity` keyword, you will see a message like this in either the Output Window (under NT) or on the Sybase UNIX console itself:

```
Mount the next volume to write.
```

At this point, you need to go to another terminal or open another session to the database through ISQL to execute the `sp_volchanged` system procedure. The syntax for `sp_volchanged` is as follows:

```
sp_volchanged Session_Identifier, Device_Name, Action
[ ,File_Name [, Volume_Name] ]
```

The options for the Transact-SQL system-stored procedure `sp_volchanged` are as follows:

- *Session_Identifier*—This is the session identifier that the Backup Server reported in the first line of output from the `Dump` process.
- *Device_Name*—This can be either the physical address of the device in UNIX, such as `/dev/rmt/tape0/`, or it can be the logical name that is defined for it in the *sysdevices* system catalog table such as *tape_backup1*.
- *Action*—This is the action that you want performed, which has valid values of either: *Abort* to stop a dump/load; *Proceed* to tell the backup server to either continue loading or continue dumping (used after you have mounted the next tape); or *Retry* to retry using the same piece of media (in the case of media failures).

Part

IV

Ch

19

For example, if the *pubs2* database grew to 2 Gbytes and was being backed up to a medium that only supported 1 Gbyte per tape, you would need to execute the following statement after the first tape had been ejected by the Backup Server:

```
sp_volchanged 7, 'MyTapeDumpDevice', Proceed
Go
```

Understanding Checkpoints

Checkpoints are a function incorporated by Sybase to commit changes to a database or configuration option at a known, optimum point in time. As you work to configure the server or make modifications to the server that require a restart of that server, you may want to initiate the checkpoint process manually.

When a checkpoint is issued, whether by a manual intervention process or by naturally occurring server-based processes, all dirty pages are saved to disk. A *dirty page* is one containing updates that have not yet been applied to the disk image of the database. What this means is that when you are performing SQL transactions on the server, Sybase writes these transactions to the database's log temporarily. If you Commit the transaction, Sybase marks the pages on which those transactions reside as *dirty*. When a checkpoint occurs, Sybase writes all those transactions from the log to the database itself.

Checkpoints normally occur approximately every 60 seconds, when they occur without intervention on your part. The actual time frame in which they are called will depend on server loading, recovery options you've set, and general performance tuning that Sybase will be looking after—but should be very close to 60 seconds.

You may have noticed that if your Sybase goes down unexpectedly, it can take longer to start up the next time. This is because Sybase will roll back and roll forward transactions to the last checkpoint. When Sybase does this, it is restoring the database to the last known good state, which is defined as the one recorded when the last checkpoint was issued and successfully carried out.

 TIP You can manually shut down the server by issuing the Transact-SQL command, Shutdown. By issuing Checkpoint followed by a Shutdown, you can ensure that all transaction information is first saved appropriately.

The best trick is to write a script that would do a checkpoint on each database prior to performing a shutdown. For example:

```
/*
   This script uses each database on the server; performs a checkpoint
   and then performs a shutdown of the server
 */
/* First the pubs2 database */
Use pubs2
Go
Checkpoint
Go
```

```
/* other databases in here! */

/* Now, finally, the master database */
Use master
Go
Checkpoint
Go

/* Shutdown the server */
Shutdown
Go
```

If you know that you're shutting down the server, you can avoid the longer startup times by manually issuing the Checkpoint command. This will accomplish the same thing as allowing the server to issue the command automatically. All information will be saved to disk, and the system will be able to simply start up and "turn on" the databases for access by your client's applications. This is helpful if you're shutting down a server quickly, perhaps in a case where you've had power failure and the UPS that is sustaining the server is nearing the end of its life cycle.

> **N O T E** The Checkpoint command is issued at a database level and is applied against the current database. If you have more than one database in your system, you need to issue the command against each database. In order to issue the Checkpoint command, you must be the database owner. ▪

Understanding the Recovery Interval

After a system failure, Sybase will need some time to recover all of the databases. Depending upon the size of the database, and the size of the transaction log, it usually takes anywhere from a few seconds to a few minutes for Sybase to recover a database. Sybase provides a recovery interval configuration option to specify the maximum acceptable amount of recovery time. This recovery interval is measured in minutes. Based on the recovery interval specified, Sybase will perform an automatic checkpoint as often as is required so that the database can be recovered within that time period.

To set the recovery interval, you use the system-stored procedure sp_configure system procedure. The syntax for the use of sp_configure is as follows:

```
sp_configure 'Recovery Interval in Minutes', Required_Interval
```

Required_Interval is the number of minutes that you want to wait or deem acceptable on startup. The default recovery interval is five minutes. If you wanted to change the recovery interval to be 15 minutes, you would execute:

```
sp_configure 'Recovery Interval in Minutes', 15
Go
```

Part
IV

Ch
19

N O T E   Substantial performance benefits can be found in some applications that do a lot of
transactions in a *batch* mode (for example, a nightly processing activity) by setting the
recovery interval to a high number like 30 or 60 minutes. If you are confident that your database server
is unlikely to come down disgracefully (due to some unanticipated circumstance such as power failure)
and you don't want the server to checkpoint at a random time, you can set this option to a high
value. ▨

To examine the currently configured setting for recovery interval, you would execute:

```
sp_configure 'Recovery'
Go
```

```
Configuration option is not unique.
```

```
Parameter Name              Default Memory Used  Config Value Run Value
--------------------------- ------- -----------  ------------ -----------
Backup/Recovery                   0           0             0           0
print recovery information        0           0             0           0
recovery interval in minutes      5           0            10          10
Return status = 1
```

N O T E   The system-stored procedure `sp_configure` will return all matching configurable options
based on the text that you supply in quotation marks. If you had executed the following,
you would only have received the information on the recovery interval option:

```
sp_configure 'Recovery Interval'
Go ▨
```

To change the recovery interval on a server, you would execute the system-stored procedure
`sp_configure`, and then you would execute `Reconfigure` to tell the Sybase server to apply the
changes. For example:

```
sp_configure 'Recovery Interval', 10
Go
Reconfigure
Go
```

```
Parameter Name              Default Memory Used Config Value Run Value
--------------------------- ------- ----------- ------------ --------
recovery interval in minutes 5           0           10           10
Configuration option changed. The SQL Server need not be rebooted since
the option is dynamic.
```

T I P   When you change some of the system configuration options, you will need to restart the server. Watch
carefully the returned information from the database to determine whether the server needs to be
restarted.

▶ **See** "Configuring and Managing Servers," **p. 635**

Truncating the Log on Checkpoint

Another option that will prove quite helpful is the Truncate Log on Checkpoint option. This option will automatically truncate the transaction log whenever a checkpoint is reached. To set this option, follow these steps:

1. Start Sybase SQL Server Manager and connect to the server that you want to manage.
2. Select the database that is being configured in the right pane (or from the tree in the left pane).
3. From the Database menu, select Options (see Fig. 19.5).

FIG. 19.5
The SSM Options dialog box enables you to enable or disable any of the database-wide configuration options.

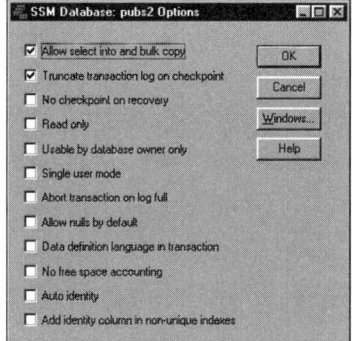

4. Check the option Truncate Transaction Log on Checkpoint.
5. Press OK.

N O T E If you elect to truncate the log when a checkpoint occurs, you won't be able to back up the transaction log during the course of standard backups. This may not present a problem in your installation, as you can still do database backups, but you should consider your overall backup plan prior to setting this option. ■

If you have enabled the truncation of the log for a database, the transaction log will be truncated up to the point of the last successfully committed transaction, provided replication is not in use. If replication is in use, the log is truncated up to the last successfully replicated transaction and successfully committed transaction. Because replication is transaction-log based, this prevents the log from being truncated in cases where replication has not been propagated to the subscribers for a given publication. More information on replication can be found in Chapter 24, "Managing Data Replication."

Working with BCP to Export Data at High Speed

The Bulk Copy Program (BCP) that is supplied with Sybase is designed to help you rapidly export and import data from the database in a table-by-table fashion. The great thing about

Part
IV

Ch

19

BCP is that it's also an API (Application Programming Interface) that can be accessed from either Client Library or DB-Library applications. For more information using the BCP API, refer to Chapter 14, "Understanding the Sybase Client Model (Client Library)." See Chapter 17, "Using Third-Party Products," for more information on some excellent programs, such as Embarcadero's DBArtisan and Platinum's SQL-Port, that encapsulate the BCP API in a clean Windows application (which makes it even easier to extract the data from the database).

Understanding the Syntax of BCP

Using BCP is really not that difficult; however, it does have quite a few options that you should learn and understand to use it effectively. BCP is a command-line application and so each of the options described below is used as an extension to the command line that you pass it. If you don't pass any commands to BCP, the program will return all the options that you can use:

```
D:\sybase\system11\bin>bcp
usage: bcp [[database_name.]owner.]table_name {in | out} datafile
        [-m maxerrors] [-f formatfile] [-e errfile]
        [-F firstrow] [-L lastrow] [-b batchsize]
        [-n] [-c] [-t field_terminator] [-r row_terminator]
        [-U username] [-P password] [-I interfaces_file] [-S server]
        [-a display_charset] [-q datafile_charset] [-z language] [-v]
        [-A packet size] [-J client character set]
        [-T text or image size] [-E] [-N] [-X]  [-y sybase_dir]
        [-Mlabelname labelvalue] [-labeled]
```

These parameters to BCP are defined as follows (note that the case of each of these options is important and must be matched):

- *table_name*—This is a fully qualified reference to a table in the database. You may omit the owner of the table if it is the same as the user that you are using to perform the BCP or if it is a unique name and the user doing the BCP has permission to read/Select from the table.

- *in | out*—Specify *in* to indicate that you want to import or load into the database table; specify *out* to indicate that you are going to export or dump from the database table.

- *datafile*—This is the name of the input or output file that you want to use. It can be fully qualified and will need to be correctly represented, based on operating system requirements. If you are loading from a file and the file name supplied is not accurate, you will get an error. Similarly, if you are exporting to a file that is invalidly named or if you don't have permissions to read/write from the directory, you will also get an error. The maximum file length is 255 characters.

- *-m maxerrors*—This is the maximum number of errors that you want BCP to ignore before aborting. For example, this enables you to ignore a specified number of duplicate key records during the Insert of a database table. The default for this value, if not specified, is 10.

- *-f formatfile*—This is the name of the format file that you want to use during the BCP process. BCP uses a format file to determine the characteristics of the file being imported or exported. If you don't specify a file format when performing BCP, Sybase will prompt you for the characteristics of each of the data elements being worked on. At the end of this prompting, you will be given the opportunity to save these values in a format file.

- *-e errfile*—This is the output file that you want BCP to use to send the output from the errors that occur to. If no errors occur, you will not get an error file created.

- *-F firstrow*—This is the first row in the output that you want BCP to copy to the output file. The default is the first row in the table. You can use this option to stagger the data extraction of a big database table into multiple BCP files.

- *-L lastrow*—This is the last row in the output that you want BCP to copy to the output file. The default is the last row in the table. You can use this option to stagger the data extraction of a big database table into multiple BCP files.

- *-b batchsize*—This is the number of inserts per transaction that you want to perform. By default, Sybase will perform all the inserts from a BCP operation in a single transaction. Specify a value with this option and Sybase will insert only that many records per committed transaction.

- *-n native*—This is the native file format for import/export. This is a pseudo-binary format that is not human readable but is quicker to import and export. This file format is specific to a particular operating system and is not portable between different operating systems, such as Windows NT and Sun Solaris.

- *-c character*—This is the character file format that writes a text file that is usable and readable by a person. The separator between fields is the <TAB> character. You must use this option if you want to create a file that can be used with other Sybase servers on different operating systems.

- *-t field_terminator*—This is the character that you want to use to separate each of the fields/columns in the output file.

- *-r row_terminator*—This is the character that you want to use to separate each of the rows in the output file.

- *-U username*—This is the user or logon that you want to perform the BCP as. This user must have sufficient privileges to perform the Select or Insert statements necessary to execute the BCP process.

- *-P password*—This is the password of the user that is running BCP. If you don't specify the password, BCP will prompt you for it.

- *-I interfaces_file*—This is the location of the sql.ini file that you want to use. If you don't specify a value for the *interfaces_file*, Sybase will look in the INI subdirectory under the directory specified in the host variable $SYBASE (%SYBASE% on Windows NT).

- *-S server*—This is the name of the server where the database and table reside.

- *-a display_charset*—This option is provided so that you can display the output to the terminal in a different character set from either the database or from the resulting output file itself. The value of this field is that in some circumstances (with different character sets) certain characters may not be visible on a terminal. To effectively perform character set translation, you normally need to specify a translation file using the *-J* parameter defined below.

■ *-q datafile_charset*—Like the *-a* option, this parameter is provided so that you can do character set conversion (but in this case to the output/input file). To effectively perform character set translation, you normally need to specify a translation file using the *-J* parameter defined below.

■ *-z language*—This option is provided so that you can have BCP itself present information in a different language from the default (based on the installed language on the server). You can add languages by using the setup/installation program.

■ *-v versioninfo*—This option displays the current version of BCP. The output for this version information is like the following:

```
bcp/10.0.3/P/PC Intel/Windows NT 3.5/2/1/OPT/Nov 13 1995 00:23:10

Confidential property of Sybase, Inc.
(c) Copyright Sybase Inc. 1987,1995
All rights reserved.

Use, duplication, or disclosure by the United States Government
is subject to restrictions as set forth in FAR subparagraphs
52.227-19 (a)- for civilian agency contracts and DFARS 252.227-7013
(1)(ii) for Department of Defense contracts. Sybase reserves all
unpublished rights under the copyright laws of the United States.
Sybase, Inc. 6475 Christie Avenue, Emeryville, CA 94608 USA.
```

■ *-A packet size*—This is the network packet size that you want to use for the BCP execution. For example to perform a BCP operation with a 4K packet size, you would execute:

```
bcp -A 4096
```

You will get substantial throughput benefits on large BCP operations by increasing this packet size, provided that the value you specify is less than the max network packet size configured with sp_configure.

▶ **See** "Configuring and Managing Servers," **p. 635**

■ *-J client character set*—This option specifies the character set to filter the client side output by. The BCP execution will do translation between the SQL Server's character set and the *client character set* that you specify with this parameter. Using the *-J* option without a character set (or by specifying NULL) will force no character set translation to occur.

■ *-T text or image size*—This option specifies the maximum size of Text or Image data that can be sent from the Sybase server. If the value that is sent from the server exceeds the value you specify or the default (32K), the extra information will be truncated.

■ *-E identity value*—By using this option during an import, BCP will take the value in the data file and explicitly use it for the Identity column on the table. This option has no effect when performing a BCP out.

- *-N skip identity*—If you created a file without exporting the `Identity` column, use this value to skip that column when performing the import. Sybase will then automatically assign appropriate values to the `Identity` column.

- *-X password encryption*—If you are performing an operation during BCP and the BCP operation crashes, the core dump file will include a human readable password. Use this option to encrypt the password going across the network and in the core dump file.

- *-y sybase_dir*—If you have to or want to move the default Sybase directory as specified in the `$SYBASE` (or `%SYBASE%` on Windows NT) host variable, use the *-y* option.

- *-Mlabelname labelvalue*—Undocumented.

- *-labeled*—Undocumented.

Performing an Export with BCP

Performing an export with BCP is quite easy; however, you should make sure that you have sufficient disk space for the data to be stored wherever you output. The following example would export the *authors* table from the *pubs2* database permitting up to 100 errors, and using the character mode output file format:

```
bcp pubs2..authors out d:\pubs2_authors.out -m100 -eerror.log
  -Usa -Pcentura1 -SSYB11_NT -c

Starting copy...

23 rows copied.
Clock Time (ms.): total = 1      Avg = 0      (23000.00 rows per sec.)
```

Note that the export speed is a little skewed because the *authors* table is so small. If you wanted to export a slightly larger table like *sysmessages* in the *master* database and you wanted to work in the native file format, you would execute:

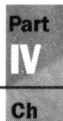

Part
IV

Ch
19

```
bcp master..sysmessages out d:\pubs2_authors.out -m100 -eerror.log
  -Usa -Pcentura1 -SSYB11_NT -n

Starting copy...
1000 rows successfully bulk-copied to host-file.
1000 rows successfully bulk-copied to host-file.
1000 rows successfully bulk-copied to host-file.

3403 rows copied.
Clock Time (ms.): total = -4      Avg = 0      (-850750.00 rows per sec.)
```

As you can see, the timings are again inaccurate. In general, don't rely on the timings; they tend to be quite misleading.

Performing an Import with BCP

If you wanted to import the file that was created previously with the Export from the *authors* table, you would execute a very similar command:

```
bcp master..sysmessages in d:\pubs2_authors.out -m100 -eerror.log
  -Usa -Pcentura1 -SSYB11_NT -c -b25
```

```
Starting copy...
Msg 2601, Level 14, State 3:
Attempt to insert duplicate key row in object 'authors' with unique
index 'auidind'

bcp copy in failed
```

As you can see in this example where an error of index duplicity occurs, BCP is just like any other application that you run; it is bound by the same rules.

TIP

Use the batch option -b to get less log contention on large table loads. By batching the work, Sybase will not hold open a massive transaction of every insert into the table, which could potentially fill your transaction logs.

TROUBLESHOOTING

I tried to do a BCP to load some data and kept getting the following message:

```
Msg 4806, Level 16, State 1:
You cannot run the non-logged version of bulk copy in this database.
Please check with the DBO.
```

The problem is that the database has not been configured/enabled to perform non-logged operations such as BCP. You need to use the system-stored procedure sp_dboption to change the state of the database. For example, to enable BCP operations on the *pubs2* database, you would execute:

```
Use master
Go
sp_dboption pubs2, 'select into', TRUE
Go
Use pubs2
Go
Checkpoint
Go
```

Some Tips to Keep a Server Running

There are many different things to consider when it comes to maximizing the up time on the server. I've tried to lump a bunch of them together here; if you know of others that you have tried successfully, write them down on this page so that you have a single resource in the future.

- **Use a UPS**—No, I'm not talking about the parcel service here! It is remarkable how many people don't place an uninterruptible power supply (UPS) on the database server to ensure it against power failures. This should be nearly the most important item on your list of purchases after you get a server. The minimum amount of time that you will require from the UPS is the time it takes to perform a full shutdown of the server, including powering down all external devices. Depending on the server, this usually can range anywhere from 10 to 30 minutes.

- **Use mirroring**—This is *the* most effective and highest performing option that you can take when it comes to media failure preparation. Straight mirroring speeds reads from the database and has a negligible effect on the server (provided that the mirroring is performed at the hardware or OS level) in terms of writes.

- **Use RAID**—If data integrity is of paramount importance to you and you want *more* redundancy than a single physical copy of the server on the mirrored device, you can use a RAID (Redundant Array of Inexpensive Disks) storage array to further complement your existing hardware. There are many different approaches to RAID, each with different performance costs and benefits. You can find out about the most commonly used levels of RAID in Appendix E, "Redundant Array of Inexpensive Disks (RAID)."

- **Prepare a hot-site**—Hot-sites are usually an expensive option for the smaller Sybase user. What is involved is a having a physically mirrored server in another location that can be switched in remotely via standard networking telecommunications. Typically what happens is that the primary server will basically explode and be completely down, then using the most recent backups, you will travel to the hot-site and restore the tapes and bring the system online with remote telecommunications, making it appear to the users as though the server is still in its primary location.

  Although this option is a costly one and involves setting up an additional server and good communications, it is required for many systems that are mission-critical. Evaluate the needs of your organization to decide whether the costs of maintaining this level of redundancy make sense.

- **Work with a service bureau**—If the cost of setting up a hot-site is prohibitive for your organization, it may be possible to set up a correspondence relationship with a local Service Bureau. Local Service Bureaus of major companies such as CompuServe, EDS, and IBM can provide servers to which you can switch over in the event of an emergency: They will provide all the communications infrastructure required to make the network bridging seem completely transparent.

- **Use replication**—If you have multiple servers that you *can* switch over to in the event of a failure, you should consider using Sybase's Replication Server to manage the data distribution, rather than relying on backup tapes. Replication Server will ensure that the other server is maintained at the transaction level, not just the whole database level. For more information on using Sybase's Replication Server, see Chapter 24, "Managing Data Replication."

From Here...

In this chapter, you've learned all about managing and maintaining the availability of the data on your Sybase System XI server. By now, you should be pretty familiar with all the steps required to perform backups and restores. In addition, (I hope) you should have prepared and implemented a strategy to help guide you through the rigors of a systematic backup.

I think it is really important that you recognize that a catastrophe of some kind will affect you— *soon*. If you haven't prepared and planned for this event, your users will be left stranded without data and the business of your company or organization may be left high and dry with no way of doing their day-to-day work.

In the following chapters, you will find extra information that will help you work with the server to provide an optimal environment for your users:

- Chapter 22, "Managing and Monitoring Performance," discusses ways of monitoring your server's performance to be able to determine when a good time is available to perform backups and restores.

- Chapter 23, "Using Sybase's Configuration Options," helps you fine-tune the server with the many different configuration options available to you.

- Chapter 24, "Managing Data Replication," offers instructions on how to configure and work with Sybase's Replication Server, which can be used to manage a live hot-site's data through a replication and data distribution model.

CHAPTER 20

Understanding the Joys, Secrets, and Mysteries of DBCC

The Database Consistency Checker or DBCC tool that Sybase provides has long been the most misunderstood component in the arsenal of tools that Sybase gives you to manage a server. DBCC was always known to provide somewhat useful information about the database tables (and indexes on those tables) and was pretty reliable at discovering problems on the database. The problem with DBCC is that it rarely can fix anything that it finds. Most of the time, you need to make sure that you have a clean backup and that you can restore from it.

Relying on DBCC to save you from a broken or defective database is a poor strategy for disaster recovery. In general, there are more things that DBCC can identify than it can fix. The only good way to protect yourself in the event of a database corruption is to have a clean backup.

Accessing DBCC from Sybase's SQL Server Manager

Sybase's SQL Server Manager is an excellent graphical tool that makes it easy to work all aspects of the database and to manage your server. Using Sybase's SQL Server Manager makes it particularly easy to perform basic DBCC operations on elements of the server such as databases, tables, and indexes.

Performing common DBCC commands using Transact-SQL

The normal way of interacting with DBCC is through Transact-SQL. In this chapter, you learn the most commonly used DBCC commands and how to put them in sensible scripts that can be used to automate the maintenance of your server's databases.

Working with the DBCC utilities

Sybase provides a number of additional utilities that are accessible by using the DBCC Transact-SQL command. It wasn't until System XI that Sybase really started to document a lot of these options, and so some of them fall into the "use at your own risk" category.

▶ **See** "Performing Backups," **p. 492**

A reasonable question that you may be asking yourself is why there is a DBCC command in the first place. It may seem odd that such an expensive database contains a known possibility of errors occurring for which the company provides a tool. You might be wondering how the database gets broken. Are there bugs that I have to worry about? The answer is simple—yes and no. Any piece of software that is as large and complex as Sybase is going to have bugs—there's no escaping that inevitability. However, the chances of self-corruption due to a Sybase bug are pretty slim and not something that you should really worry all that much about. I have heard of its happening; in five years, I have never actually seen it.

The more common reason for database corruption is because of hardware. Any number of hardware problems can cause a corruption: from crashing heads on the disk to spikes in power. The reason that problems occur usually is because the database sent a write to the disk controller that responded successfully, but the physical write actually incurred an error of some kind. In addition, in some very highly accessed systems with lots of users and activity, the database can queue multiple writes to the device asynchronously and then a hardware error on the device can occur. A hardware error or corruption on the device itself may not always be detected by the device until you take time to allow for a scheduled maintenance window on the device.

DBCC is designed to go through all the data on the database devices and to compare the data stored with the data expected to be stored.

The other thing about DBCC that's often not recognized is that it contains a lot more features than simple database checking and fixing. DBCC was Sybase's way of adding any utilities that technical support needed to help diagnose problems at customer sites. The use of many of these functions is at best scarcely documented, and in this chapter I attempt to remedy that problem. If you have more information about any of these options that you want to share with other users, please send me the details and I'll be sure to include them in the second edition of this book. ■

CAUTION

A lot of the undocumented or *slightly* documented information presented in this chapter can lead to dangerous consequences for the database, including (among other things) corruption and data loss. If you have any doubts about using any of these options, then don't use them.

The information supplied here is in a somewhat useful form that you can digest at your leisure, but that should not encourage you to be casual about testing it on your own database. You *must* understand that by using some of these DBCC commands, you are putting your database at risk. When in doubt—*perform a backup!*

I can't stress strongly enough that in some cases by using these DBCC tricks you will be rendering yourself without a legitimate channel for support. Sybase Technical Support will justifiably want to know what you did to crash the database, and, as soon as you tell them you used an undocumented DBCC call, they'll ask you how good your backup is.

In general, this chapter is not a good place for beginners. *You have been warned!*

Using DBCC with Sybase SQL Server Manager

Sybase SQL Server Manager is a great tool for the casual DBCC user who wants to check on the status of a particular object in the database. The best thing about using Sybase SQL Server Manager is that, as you traverse the database explorer and have an object selected, you can right-click it and perform a database consistency check right there. In Figure 20.1, you can see the context menu displayed for the database *pubs2*, which has the option of performing a database-wide DBCC.

FIG. 20.1

The DBCC option available from the context menu (right-click) for an object is Consistency. This option is available for Databases, Tables, and Indexes.

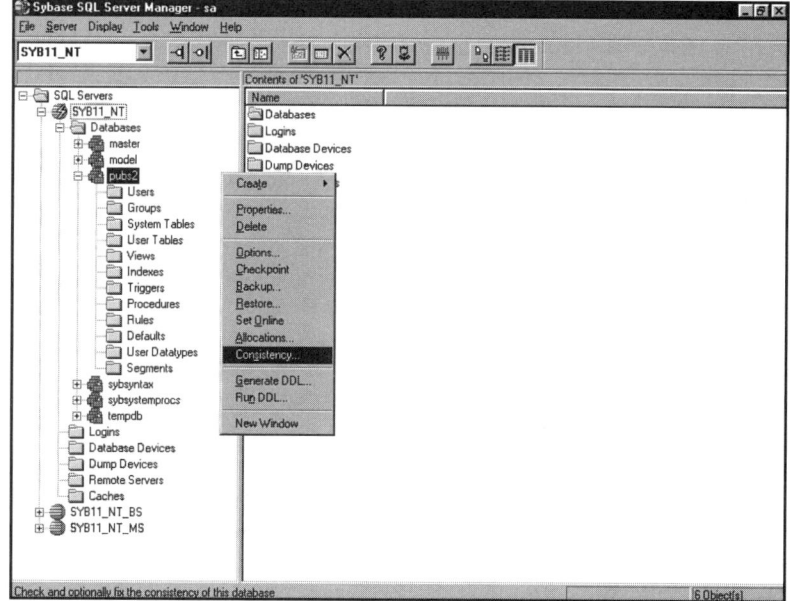

Performing DBCC on a Database

Database level DBCCs are designed to perform high-level analysis of all the objects in the database, and to verify that there are no major problems with those objects. To perform a database level DBCC, follow these steps:

1. Launch Sybase SQL Server Manager and log on to the server that has the database that you want to check.

2. Select the databases folder in the left pane of the explorer, and in the right pane, click the database that you want to DBCC.

3. Choose Database, Consistency to display the Database Consistency Check dialog box (see Fig. 20.2).

Part
IV

Ch
20

FIG. 20.2

The DBCC dialog box in SSM has four high-level options of operations that you can perform on the database. You can do only one test at a time, so if you want to do all of them, you will need to redisplay this dialog box several times.

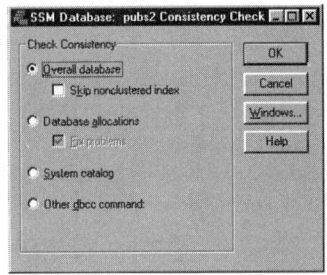

4. Choose the type of DBCC that you want to perform. The different DBCC options are as follows:

- **Overall database**—This option scans each table in the database and verifies that any index and data pages are correctly linked; it also verifies that indexes are sorted correctly, based on the installed sort page, and that any pointers to the data are consistent and accurate; and finally that the internally defined allocation page accurately describes the position of the rest of the rows of data pages and meaningfully points to good data.

 TIP Use the Skip nonclustered index to improve performance by ignoring the checking on indexes that can easily be rebuilt without any effect on the underlying data.

- **Database allocations**—This option specifically verifies that each and every database page is correctly allocated, that pages that have been allocated are in use, and that no page of data exists that hasn't been allocated by the database. The Fix problems check box controls whether or not you want Sybase to attempt to correct any allocation errors that it finds during the checking phase.

- **System catalog**—This option checks that the tables, indexes, and other objects that exist in the database have corresponding entries in the system catalog. The System catalog check also verifies the reverse: that no system catalog entry exists without a real object for it.

- **Other dbcc command**—This option is provided if you want to execute a particular DBCC command on the database that you may have been asked to execute by technical support.

5. Click OK to perform the DBCC.

N O T E DBCC execution is likely to take quite a lot of time, especially operations on the whole database or on tables with lots of data. Plan to have time to execute the DBCC and then go do something else. ▪

The output from a full database DBCC with the Overall Database is quite lengthy, even for a simple database like *pubs*. In Listing 20.1, you can see that the output goes through each table, telling you what the number of pages of data is on the table and how many rows of data there are.

Listing 20.1   Results from a Full DBCC on the pubs2 Database

```
Checking pubs2
Checking 1
The total number of data pages in this table is 3.
Table has 68 data rows.
Checking 2
The total number of data pages in this table is 5.
Table has 53 data rows.
Checking 3
The total number of data pages in this table is 8.
Table has 356 data rows.
Checking 4
The total number of data pages in this table is 1.
Table has 30 data rows.
Checking 5
The total number of data pages in this table is 79.
Table has 538 data rows.
Checking 6
The total number of data pages in this table is 8.
Table has 57 data rows.
Checking 7
The total number of data pages in this table is 1.
Table has 3 data rows.
Checking 8
The total number of data pages in this table is 2.
*** NOTICE:  Notification of log space used/free cannot be reported because the
log segment is not on its own device.
Table has 32 data rows.
Checking 9
The total number of data pages in this table is 1.
Table has 82 data rows.
Checking 10
The total number of data pages in this table is 1.
Table has 9 data rows.
Checking 11
The total number of data pages in this table is 1.
Checking 12
The total number of data pages in this table is 1.
Table has 39 data rows.
Checking 13
The total number of data pages in this table is 1.
Table has 53 data rows.
Checking 15
The total number of data pages in this table is 1.
Checking 16
The total number of data pages in this table is 1.
Checking 17
```

Part

IV

Ch

20

continues

Listing 20.1 Continued

```
The total number of data pages in this table is 1.
Checking 18
The total number of data pages in this table is 1.
Table has 1 data rows.
Checking 19
The total number of data pages in this table is 1.
Table has 6 data rows.
Checking 21
The total number of data pages in this table is 1.
Table has 16 data rows.
Checking 22
The total number of data pages in this table is 1.
Checking 16003088
The total number of data pages in this table is 1.
Table has 23 data rows.
Checking 48003202
The total number of data pages in this table is 1.
Table has 3 data rows.
Checking 80003316
The total number of data pages in this table is 2.
Table has 87 data rows.
Checking 112003430
The total number of data pages in this table is 1.
Table has 24 data rows.
Checking 144003544
The total number of data pages in this table is 3.
Table has 116 data rows.
Checking 176003658
The total number of data pages in this table is 1.
Table has 25 data rows.
Checking 208003772
The total number of data pages in this table is 3.
Table has 18 data rows.
Checking 240003886
The total number of data pages in this table is 1.
Table has 6 data rows.
Checking 272004000
The total number of data pages in this table is 1.
Table has 3 data rows.
Checking 304004114
The total number of data pages in this table is 1.
Checking 336004228
The total number of data pages in this table is 1.
The total number of TEXT/IMAGE pages in this table is 6.
Table has 6 data rows.
Checking 784005824
The total number of data pages in this table is 1.
Checking 816005938
The total number of data pages in this table is 1.
Table has 23 data rows.
DBCC execution completed. If DBCC printed error messages, contact a user with
System Administrator (SA) role.
```

TIP

The number listed after the word `Checking` (for example `Checking 784005824`) is the object id in the database of the object currently being worked on. To discover the name of the object, execute the following SQL on the database that was being checked:

```
Select Object_Name( 784005824 )
Go
----------------
authors2
```

The other DBCC options produce different kinds of information. For example, the output from the System Catalog DBCC trace is useful because it shows you the segments being utilized by the catalog tables and the database:

```
Checking pubs2
The following segments have been defined for database 5 (database name pubs2).
virtual start addr      size      segments
-------------------     ------    --------------------------
4612                    1024
                                       0
                                       1
                                       2
DBCC execution completed. If DBCC printed error messages, contact a user with
System Administrator (SA) role.
```

TROUBLESHOOTING

I tried to perform a DBCC on the database, but each time I did so I got the following error messages:

```
Database option 'single user' turned ON for database 'pubs2'.
Run the CHECKPOINT command in the database that was changed.
Attempt to set 'pubs2' database to single user mode failed because the usage
count is 2. Make sure that no other users are currently using this database and
rerun CHECKPOINT.
Checking pubs2
DBCC execution completed. If DBCC printed error messages, contact a user with
System Administrator (SA) role.
Server Message Number:  2595
Database 'pubs2' must be set to single user mode before executing this command.
```

The problem is that you cannot run a DBCC command with any users in the database. To fix the problem, you must get all the users to exit the database before attempting the DBCC. To get a list of users that are in the database, you can execute the system-stored procedure sp_who. For example:

```
sp_who
Go
```

Part

IV

Ch

20

continues

continued

spid	status	loginame	hostname	blk	dbname	cmd
1	running	sa	RapidSQL L	0	pubs2	SELECT
2	sleeping			0	master	NETWORK HANDLER
3	sleeping			0	master	MIRROR HANDLER
4	sleeping			0	master	DEADLOCK TUNE
5	sleeping			0	master	HOUSEKEEPER
6	sleeping			0	master	SHUTDOWN HANDLER
7	sleeping			0	master	CHECKPOINT SLEEP
8	recv sleep	sa		0	pubs2	AWAITING COMMAND

Performing DBCC on a Table

Performing a DBCC on a table is a very similar task to that of performing a DBCC on a database. Using Sybase SQL Server Manager, follow these steps:

1. Launch Sybase SQL Server Manager, and log on to the server that has the database on which you are going to be working.

2. Select the database in the left pane of the explorer and click the User Tables folder.

3. Select the table in the right pane of the explorer and from the Table menu. Select Consistency to display the Sybase SQL Server Manager Table Consistency Check dialog box, as shown below in Figure 20.3.

FIG. 20.3

The Table Consistency Check dialog box simplifies your use of DBCC and also gives you the option of fixing any problems found on the table.

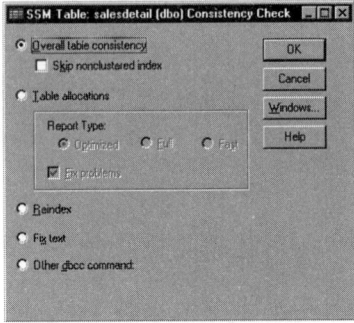

4. Choose the type of DBCC that you want to perform. The different DBCCs are as follows:

- **Overall table consistency**—This option works the same as the Overall Database option for the database-level DBCC, except that it only applies for a single table.

- **Table allocations**—This option specifically verifies that each and every database page is correctly allocated, that pages that have been allocated are in use, and that no page of data exists that hasn't been allocated by the database. The Fix Problems check box controls whether or not you want Sybase to attempt to correct any allocation errors that it finds during the checking phase.

• **Reindex**—This option is new to System XI and enables you to rebuild all the indexes on a table after a sort order change.

• **Fix text**—This option is used to fix the text columns associated with a database table after a multiple-byte character set has been installed on the server.

5. Click OK to perform the DBCC.

The output from the Table allocations DBCC is quite useful in determining if you have any problems on a particular table. The output shown in Listing 20.2 is the result of checking allocations for the table *salesdetail* in the *pubs2* database. In the output, you can see that the DBCC verified that all the data pages were correctly allocated and that the indexes were pointing to valid allocation pages.

Listing 20.2   DBCC Output from a Full Table Allocation Test on the pubs2 Table salesdetail

```
Database option 'single user' turned ON for database 'pubs2'.
Run the CHECKPOINT command in the database that was changed.
*************************************************************
TABLE: dbo.salesdetail         OBJID = 144003544
INDID=0      FIRST=433      ROOT=435      SORT=0
    Data level: 0.  3 Data pages allocated and 1 Extents allocated.
INDID=2      FIRST=402      ROOT=401      SORT=1
    Indid       : 2.  3 Index pages allocated and 1 Extents allocated.
INDID=3      FIRST=626      ROOT=625      SORT=1
    Indid       : 3.  3 Index pages allocated and 1 Extents allocated.
TOTAL # of extents = 3
Alloc page 256 (# of extent=2 used pages=8 ref pages=8)
Alloc page 512 (# of extent=1 used pages=4 ref pages=4)
Total (# of extent=3 used pages=12 ref pages=12) in this database
DBCC execution completed. If DBCC printed error messages, contact a user with
System Administrator (SA) role.
Database option 'single user' turned OFF for database 'pubs2'.
Run the CHECKPOINT command in the database that was changed.
```

 TROUBLESHOOTING

I was executing a query on a table and the server reported a strange error saying that the database table's indexes were invalid and that they needed to be rebuilt. The most likely problem that you are encountering is that the sort order for the server has been changed. Because indexes are built based specifically on the sort order currently installed on the server, changing the sort order will invalidate all of the indexes. In releases of Sybase prior to System XI, you would have had to manually drop all the indexes and then rebuild/recreate them by hand. In System XI, you have the option of using the Transact-SQL command DBCC Reindex(Table_Name). This will rebuild all the indexes on the table for you, but be warned that, if you have a very large table, this operation could take considerable time to execute.

Part

IV

Ch

20

Performing DBCC on an Index

DBCCing an index using Sybase SQL Server Manager is a very simple task and involves selecting the index that you want to check in the explorer. Having selected your index, you have two options to perform a consistency check: either right-clicking the index in the right pane of the explorer and selecting Consistency, or selecting Consistency from the index menu. After electing to perform a consistency check, you will be presented with the Index Consistency Check dialog box seen in Figure 20.4. Click the type of allocation check that you want to do and press OK.

The output from an index allocation check shows that Sybase goes through each data page of index data and checks that the data is meaningful and corresponds to real pages of data in the main data table (see Listing 20.3).

FIG. 20.4

The Index Consistency Check dialog box in SSM makes light work of the DBCC syntax and also enables you to run any of the undocumented DBCC options by selecting the Other dbcc command radio button.

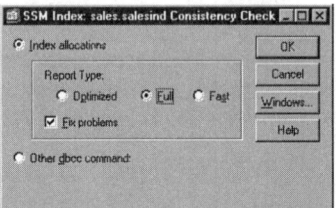

Listing 20.3   The DBCC Output from a Full Checking of the Allocations of an Index

```
Database option 'single user' turned ON for database 'pubs2'.
Run the CHECKPOINT command in the database that was changed.
******************************************************************
TABLE: sysprotects          OBJID = 9
INDID=1      FIRST=152      ROOT=320      SORT=1
     Data level: 1.  1 Data pages allocated and 2 Extents allocated.
     Indid      : 1.  2 Index pages allocated and 2 Extents allocated.
TOTAL # of extents = 4
Alloc page 0 (# of extent=2 used pages=2 ref pages=2)
Alloc page 256 (# of extent=2 used pages=4 ref pages=4)
Total (# of extent=4 used pages=6 ref pages=6) in this database
DBCC execution completed. If DBCC printed error messages, contact a user with
System Administrator (SA) role.
Database option 'single user' turned OFF for database 'pubs2'.
Run the CHECKPOINT command in the database that was changed.

Database option 'single user' turned ON for database 'sybsystemprocs'.
Run the CHECKPOINT command in the database that was changed.
******************************************************************
TABLE: sysprocedures          OBJID = 5
INDID=1      FIRST=88      ROOT=96      SORT=0
```

```
        Data level: 1.  5635 Data pages allocated and 708 Extents allocated.
        Indid     : 1.   80 Index pages allocated and 11 Extents allocated.
TOTAL # of extents = 719
Alloc page 0 (# of extent=1 used pages=8 ref pages=8)
Alloc page 0 (# of extent=1 used pages=8 ref pages=8)
Alloc page 256 (# of extent=9 used pages=72 ref pages=72)
Alloc page 512 (# of extent=30 used pages=240 ref pages=240)
Alloc page 768 (# of extent=1 used pages=8 ref pages=8)
Alloc page 768 (# of extent=28 used pages=224 ref pages=224)
Alloc page 1024 (# of extent=28 used pages=224 ref pages=224)
Alloc page 1280 (# of extent=28 used pages=224 ref pages=224)
Alloc page 1536 (# of extent=1 used pages=8 ref pages=8)
Alloc page 1536 (# of extent=28 used pages=224 ref pages=224)
Alloc page 1792 (# of extent=29 used pages=232 ref pages=232)
Alloc page 2048 (# of extent=1 used pages=8 ref pages=8)
Alloc page 2048 (# of extent=28 used pages=224 ref pages=224)
Alloc page 2304 (# of extent=29 used pages=232 ref pages=232)
Alloc page 2560 (# of extent=1 used pages=8 ref pages=8)
Alloc page 2560 (# of extent=28 used pages=224 ref pages=224)
Alloc page 2816 (# of extent=29 used pages=232 ref pages=232)
Alloc page 3072 (# of extent=1 used pages=8 ref pages=8)
Alloc page 3072 (# of extent=28 used pages=224 ref pages=224)
Alloc page 3328 (# of extent=29 used pages=232 ref pages=232)
Alloc page 3584 (# of extent=29 used pages=232 ref pages=232)
Alloc page 3840 (# of extent=1 used pages=8 ref pages=8)
Alloc page 3840 (# of extent=26 used pages=208 ref pages=208)
Alloc page 4096 (# of extent=28 used pages=224 ref pages=224)
Alloc page 4352 (# of extent=1 used pages=8 ref pages=8)
Alloc page 4352 (# of extent=27 used pages=216 ref pages=216)
Alloc page 4608 (# of extent=28 used pages=224 ref pages=224)
Alloc page 4864 (# of extent=31 used pages=248 ref pages=248)
Alloc page 5120 (# of extent=1 used pages=8 ref pages=8)
Alloc page 5120 (# of extent=26 used pages=208 ref pages=208)
Alloc page 5376 (# of extent=28 used pages=224 ref pages=224)
Alloc page 5632 (# of extent=29 used pages=232 ref pages=232)
Alloc page 5888 (# of extent=1 used pages=8 ref pages=8)
Alloc page 5888 (# of extent=25 used pages=200 ref pages=200)
Alloc page 6144 (# of extent=29 used pages=232 ref pages=232)
Alloc page 6400 (# of extent=29 used pages=232 ref pages=232)
Alloc page 6656 (# of extent=1 used pages=1 ref pages=1)
Alloc page 6656 (# of extent=21 used pages=162 ref pages=162)
Total (# of extent=719 used pages=5739 ref pages=5739) in this database
DBCC execution completed. If DBCC printed error messages, contact a user with
System Administrator (SA) role.
Database option 'single user' turned OFF for database 'sybsystemprocs'.
Run the CHECKPOINT command in the database that was changed.
```

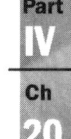

Using DBCC with Transact-SQL

DBCC can obviously be executed from Transact-SQL, and this is all that the Sybase SQL
Server Manager is doing when you click OK in any of the Consistency Check dialog boxes
shown in the section above. In this section, you will see the syntax to all of the major DBCC

commands so that you can use them in scripts or in other applications that you write to embed the database maintenance for your users.

Performing Database Checks

Using the dialog boxes in Sybase SQL Server Manager is actually a good way to get a feel for the syntax of the DBCC commands available at the Database, Table, and Index levels. The syntax for DBCC's main operations can be described in Transact-SQL as follows:

```
DBCC { CheckTable( { Table_Name | Table_Id } [, Skip_NCIndex])|
       CheckDB [ ( Database_Name [, Skip_NCIndex ] ) ] |
       CheckAlloc [ ( Database_Name [, fix | nofix ] ) ] |
       TableAlloc ( { Table_Name | Table_Id }
                   [, { full | optimized | fast | null }
                   [, fix | nofix ] ] ) |
       IndexAlloc ( { Table_Name | Table_Id }, Index_Id
                   [, { full | optimized | fast | null }
                   [, fix | nofix ] ] ) |
       CheckCatalog [ ( Database_Name ) ] |
       DBRepair ( Database_Name, DropDB ) |
       ReIndex ( { Table_Name | Table_Id } ) |
       Fix_Text ( { Table_Name | Table_Id } ) }
```

Each of the options *CheckTable, CheckDB, CheckAlloc, TableAlloc, IndexAlloc, CheckCatalog, DBRepair, ReIndex,* and *Fix_Text* correspond to each of the options that were used earlier through the graphical Sybase SQL Server Manager. For example, to perform a full allocation check on the *discounts* table you would execute:

```
DBCC TableAlloc( discounts, full, fix )
Go


****************************************************************
TABLE: discounts          OBJID = 272004000
INDID=0      FIRST=489      ROOT=489      SORT=0
    Data level: 0.  1 Data pages allocated and 1 Extents allocated.
TOTAL # of extents = 1
Alloc page 256 (# of extent=1 used pages=2 ref pages=2)
Total (# of extent=1 used pages=2 ref pages=2) in this database
DBCC execution completed. If DBCC printed error messages, contact a user with
➥System Administrator (SA) role.
```

Fixing Database Problems

DBCC permits you to perform a fix option when executing the allocation testing on a table or index. As you've seen in previous examples, this option is enabled with the third parameter that has values of fix or nofix. Sybase defaults to fixing all tables created by users, and defaults to nofix on system catalog tables.

In addition to the fixing of allocation problems, such as the ReIndex and Fix_Text options that were discussed earlier, DBCC has an extra command that can be used to drop a database when it is left in a damaged state. The reason that a DBCC command exists is that in some circumstances a database can be left in a state that makes it undroppable. The syntax for the DBRepair command is as follows:

```
DBCC DBRepair( Database_Name, DropDB )
```

This command will drop any database, so be careful that you don't accidentally drop a database that is not having any problems. You cannot drop a database that has active users in it, so you'll need to either Kill them or have them log off before you can drop the database.

Understanding the Sybase Technical Support Role

A number of operations performed with DBCC require that you have additional power and authority to perform them. For this sort of DBCC operation, you not only have to be the System Administrator (sa), but you need to have the authority known as the Sybase Technical Support Role. This role was specially created (and left undocumented) for the express purpose of having Sybase's Technical Support group walk you through fixing a database or repairing some part of the database with an undocumented call to DBCC.

> **CAUTION**
>
> Again, I'm going to warn you: using and/or granting the Sybase Technical Support Role to your sa logon and then using DBCC commands can leave your database in a corrupted state. If you have any doubts about using or performing any of these activities—*stop now!*

Another role that is useful to be assigned to the System Administrator is the System Security Officer (SSO) role. This role has no additional powers over the System Administrator but is needed to support some DBCC commands.

Enabling the support for the Sybase TS and SSO roles is a straightforward operation that requires you to use a combination of the system-stored procedure sp_role and a Set statement. To grant the required authorities to the System Administrator (sa), you would execute the following SQL:

```
sp_role "Grant", "Sybase_TS_Role", sa
Go
Set Role "Sybase_TS_Role" On
Go
sp_role "Grant", "SSO_Role", sa
Go
Set Role "SSO_Role" On
Go


--------------------
Authorization updated.
Authorization updated.
```

You can verify that the roles have been enabled by using the sp_displaylogin system-stored procedure like this:

```
sp_displaylogin sa
Go
```

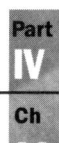

Part

IV

Ch

20

```
Suid: 1
Loginame: sa
Fullname:
Configured Authorization: sa_role sso_role oper_role sybase_ts_role
                          replication_role
Locked: NO
Date of Last Password Change: Jun 29 1996  9:14PM
```

▶ **See** "Managing Logins and Users," **p. 564**

To verify what roles are currently active for your user, you can use the system function
Show_Role( ). For example, to see the currently active roles for your user, you would execute:

```
Select Show_Role( )
Go
```

```
------------------------------------------------------------
sa_role sso_role oper_role sybase_ts_role replication_role
```

▶ **See** "Understanding Sybase System Functions," **p. 90**

Performing Traces with DBCC

DBCC TraceOn is an important command that you will need to learn in order to use a lot of the
other DBCC commands. The purpose of this command is to redirect the output from DBCC to
either the errorlog or to the user's console or display. The syntax for DBCC TraceOn is as follows where *TraceFlag* is a valid numeric value:

```
DBCC TraceOn( TraceFlag[, TraceFlag,...)
```

The valid trace flags that are available to you to use are the following:

- **200**—Produces the "before" image of a query tree
- **201**—Produces the "after" image of a query tree
- **302**—Reasons for index selection by the query optimizer
- **310**—Join selection criteria made by the query optimizer
- **317**—Full documentation on which index and why the query joined in a particular way
  to different tables
- **1204**—Trace information that displays what happened and/or what the users were
  doing when a deadlock occurs
- **3604**—Redirect the trace information to the display or console
- **3605**—Redirect the trace information to the errorlog

These trace flags are of variable value. The most valuable of them are 302, 3604, and 3605.
Why? Because with these commands you can clearly and concisely identify why index selection
was made and why a query performed the way it did.

For example, if you want to enable tracing and you want the information generated by the trace
to be sent to your workstation, you would execute the following:

```
DBCC traceon( 3604 )
Go
```

If you have trouble browsing the information returned from the database and it is not showing up correctly on your console/display, use DBCC TraceOn(3605) and this will write the trace information to the errorlog. You can review the errorlog at any time with a simple text editor. The errorlog is found in the Install subdirectory of the Sybase root installation directory.

At this point, all DBCC trace activity and information will be sent to you. Now, say that you have a problem query that you can't understand why it's choosing a particular index. To enable tracing of queries, you would execute the following:

```
DBCC TraceOn( 302 )
Go
```

Now that the server is prepared to trace or diagnose a query, you can execute one on the server, and you should get some very illuminating results. In the following SQL statement, you can see a simple join between the *authors* and the *publishers* table with an additional sub-Select to try to confuse the optimizer a little.

```
Select au_lname, au_fname, title
From   authors a, titles t, titleauthor ta
Where  a.au_id = ta.au_id
And       ta.title_id = t.title_id
Go


********************************
Entering q_score_index() for table 'authors' (objectid 16003088, varno = 0).
The table has 23 rows and 1 pages.
Scoring the JOIN CLAUSE:
    au_id EQ au_id
Base cost: indid: 0 rows: 23 pages: 1 prefetch: N
    I/O size: 2 cacheid: 0 replace: LRU
Relop bits are: 4
Estimate: indid 1, selectivity 0.041657, rows 1 pages 2 index height 1
Unique clustered index found--return rows 1 pages 2
Cheapest index is index 1, costing 2 pages and
    generating 1 rows per scan, using no data prefetch (size 2)
    on dcacheid 0 with LRU replacement
Join selectivity is 23.000000.
********************************
********************************
Entering q_score_index() for table 'titles' (objectid 208003772, varno = 1).
The table has 18 rows and 3 pages.
Scoring the JOIN CLAUSE:
    title_id EQ title_id
Base cost: indid: 0 rows: 18 pages: 3 prefetch: N
    I/O size: 2 cacheid: 0 replace: LRU
Relop bits are: 4
Estimate: indid 1, selectivity 0.055556, rows 1 pages 2 index height 1
Unique clustered index found--return rows 1 pages 2
Cheapest index is index 1, costing 2 pages and
```

Part
IV

Ch

20

```
          generating 1 rows per scan, using no data prefetch (size 2)
          on dcacheid 0 with LRU replacement
Join selectivity is 18.000000.
*******************************
*******************************
Entering q_score_index() for table 'titleauthor' (objectid 176003658, varno = 2).
The table has 25 rows and 1 pages.
Scoring the JOIN CLAUSE:
     au_id EQ au_id
Base cost: indid: 0 rows: 25 pages: 1 prefetch: N
     I/O size: 2 cacheid: 0 replace: LRU
Relop bits are: 4
Estimate: indid 1, selectivity 0.043478, rows 1 pages 2 index height 1
Relop bits are: 4
Estimate: indid 2, selectivity 0.043478, rows 1 pages 2 index height 1
Cheapest index is index 1, costing 2 pages and
     generating 1 rows per scan, using no data prefetch (size 2)
     on dcacheid 0 with LRU replacement
Join selectivity is 23.000000.
*******************************
*******************************
Entering q_score_index() for table 'titleauthor' (objectid 176003658, varno = 2).
The table has 25 rows and 1 pages.
Scoring the JOIN CLAUSE:
     title_id EQ title_id
Base cost: indid: 0 rows: 25 pages: 1 prefetch: N
     I/O size: 2 cacheid: 0 replace: LRU
Relop bits are: 4
Estimate: indid 3, selectivity 0.055556, rows 1 pages 2 index height 1
Cheapest index is index 3, costing 2 pages and
     generating 1 rows per scan, using no data prefetch (size 2)
     on dcacheid 0 with LRU replacement
Join selectivity is 18.000000.
*******************************
```

The output from the DBCC tracing is quite useful in that it shows you the reasons why Sybase chose to work in a particular way to resolve the query and send you back the answer. In the results from the trace, it is clear that the database is going for an index with the highest selectivity and the least number of physical I/Os required to perform the join operation.

N O T E   To disable tracing, you use the Transact-SQL command DBCC TraceOff(*TraceFlag*). This will disable any tracing that you have enabled for a particular connection to the database. Also, note that tracing is enabled only for a given session or connection to the database, so if you disconnect from the database, the tracing will be disabled implicitly. ▪

TROUBLESHOOTING

No matter what combination of TraceOn commands I try, I can't get the output to come to the console. It's very weird, but I think that the problem you are experiencing is due to the case of the Transact-SQL statement you send to the Sybase SQL Server. The following two SQL statements *do not* produce the same results:

```
/* This one doesn't work */
DBCC TraceOn( 3604 )
Go

/* This one does! */
DBCC traceon( 3604 )
Go
```

It seems that the `TraceOn` command specifically for the redirection to the console *must* be in lowercase. I don't know why, but it does make a difference, so try this out before giving up hope! Note that all the other commands *do not* require you to be case-particular.

Understanding DBCC's Undocumented Options

In this section, you see and learn about some of the undocumented options that you can execute with DBCC. I've done my best to find out and attempt to describe what some of them do, but there's very little information that's available on some of the DBCC commands. I've organized each of these DBCC commands in the order to get the most benefit from them—most valuable commands first. In addition, the DBCC commands that I just couldn't figure out are located at the end of this section.

N O T E   Many of these DBCC commands return trace information that you will not be able to see unless you have enabled the redirection of the trace information either to the console or to the errorlog. If you don't enable the redirection, it may seem like the DBCC didn't do anything and this could result in very misleading interpretation of the results of your actions. For more information on using tracing, see the section earlier titled "Performing Traces with DBCC." ■

Using DBCC Help

DBCC's `Help` command is probably the most valuable tool available to you to remind you how to use a particular DBCC command. The syntax for DBCC `Help` is as follows:

```
DBCC Help( DBCC_Command )
```

DBCC_Command is any other DBCC command available in the current release of Sybase. For example, to display the command syntax for the `Delete_Row` command you would execute the following:

```
DBCC Help( Delete_Row )
Go
```

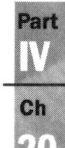

Part

IV

Ch

20

```
----------------------------------------------------------------
delete_row( dbid|dbname, pageid, delete_by_row = { 1 | 0 }, rownum )
```

Using DBCC Memusage

The DBCC `Memusage` command is what Sybase's SQLMonitor uses to determine the activity on the server in terms of open objects and stored procedures that are in the cache. There are no parameters to DBCC `Memusage`, so its use is fairly simple. The output from DBCC `Memusage` is really informative and useful to the DBA trying to analyze memory utilization on the server. In Listing 20.4, you can see the output is broken up into three main sections:

- The first section lists the breakdown of memory allocated by the server to the different core parts of the server's operation.

- The second section of the DBCC Memusage output describes each of the objects in the memory or data caches that you have created on the server. The objects are identified by their IDs, so you'll have to use the system function Object_Name to figure out what the actual object is.

- The third and final section of the DBCC Memusage output shows the details about the top five (most recently accessed) stored procedures that are in the stored procedure cache. This is an excellent way of diagnosing if your key stored procedures are being kept in memory or whether they're being recompiled each time they are used, thus incurring a substantial performance penalty.

Listing 20.4   The Output from DBCC Memusage

```
DBCC Memusage
Go


----------------------------------------------------------------

Memory Usage:
                     Meg. 2K Blks      Bytes
Configured Memory: 14.6484    7500   15360000

        Code size:  1.0000     512    1048576
Kernel Structures:  2.5040    1283    2625607
Server Structures:  3.7821    1937    3965838
     Cache Memory:  5.7715    2955    6051840
     Proc Buffers:  0.0536      28      56164
     Proc Headers:  1.5352     786    1609728

Buffer Cache Memory, Top 5:

Cache Buf Pool   DB Id  Object Id   Index Id        Meg.
default data c     1        8          0         0.0059
       2K          1        8          0         0.0059
default data c     5        8          0         0.0039
       2K          5        8          0         0.0039
default data c     2        8          0         0.0020
       2K          2        8          0         0.0020
default data c     3        8          0         0.0020
       2K          3        8          0         0.0020
default data c     4        8          0         0.0020
       2K          4        8          0         0.0020

Procedure Cache, Top 5:

Database Id: 1
Object Id: 656005368
Object Name: sp_dboption
Version: 1
```

```
Uid: 1
Type: stored procedure
Number of trees: 0
Size of trees: 0.000000 Mb, 0.000000 bytes, 0 pages
Bytes lost for alignment 0 (Percentage of total: 0.000000)
Number of plans: 1
Size of plans: 0.099387 Mb, 104215.000000 bytes, 52 pages
Bytes lost for alignment 1253 (Percentage of total: 1.202322)

----
Database Id: 4
Object Id: 2016010213
Object Name: sp_role
Version: 1
Uid: 1
Type: stored procedure
Number of trees: 0
Size of trees: 0.000000 Mb, 0.000000 bytes, 0 pages
Bytes lost for alignment 0 (Percentage of total: 0.000000)
Number of plans: 1
Size of plans: 0.066313 Mb, 69534.000000 bytes, 35 pages
Bytes lost for alignment 218 (Percentage of total: 0.313516)

----
Database Id: 4
Object Id: 272004000
Object Name: sp_displaylogin
Version: 1
Uid: 1
Type: stored procedure
Number of trees: 0
Size of trees: 0.000000 Mb, 0.000000 bytes, 0 pages
Bytes lost for alignment 0 (Percentage of total: 0.000000)
Number of plans: 1
Size of plans: 0.033715 Mb, 35353.000000 bytes, 18 pages
Bytes lost for alignment 124 (Percentage of total: 0.350748)

----
Database Id: 1
Object Id: 624005254
Object Name: sp_getmessage
Version: 1
Uid: 1
Type: stored procedure
Number of trees: 0
Size of trees: 0.000000 Mb, 0.000000 bytes, 0 pages
Bytes lost for alignment 0 (Percentage of total: 0.000000)
Number of plans: 1
Size of plans: 0.027628 Mb, 28970.000000 bytes, 15 pages
Bytes lost for alignment 90 (Percentage of total: 0.310666)

----
Database Id: 4
Object Id: 128003487
```

Part

IV

Ch

20

continues

Listing 20.4 Continued

```
Object Name: sp_getmessage
Version: 1
Uid: 1
Type: stored procedure
Number of trees: 0
Size of trees: 0.000000 Mb, 0.000000 bytes, 0 pages
Bytes lost for alignment 0 (Percentage of total: 0.000000)
Number of plans: 1
Size of plans: 0.027628 Mb, 28970.000000 bytes, 15 pages
Bytes lost for alignment 90 (Percentage of total: 0.310666)

----

DBCC execution completed. If DBCC printed error messages, contact a user
with System Administrator (SA) role.
```

Using DBCC NetMemusage

The DBCC NetMemusage command is a useful tool if you want to diagnose the way memory is being utilized for networking and active connections on the database server. Like DBCC Memusage, DBCC NetMemusage has no parameters. Listing 20.5 contains the output from DBCC NetMemusage, which shows how the server allocates 512 bytes minimum in anticipation of user connections based on the maximum packet size buffers required to send data between client and server. On a large system, the output from DBCC NetMemusage would be quite lengthy, so you may want to write a program or script that will get the important information out of the file for later review.

Listing 20.5 DBCC NetMemusage's Output When Run on a Small Server

```
DBCC NetMemusage
Go


-----------------------------------------------------------------
INUSE: 512: 1
INUSE: 512: 1
INUSE: 512: 1
INUSE: 512: 2
INUSE: 512: 2
INUSE: 512: 3
INUSE: 512: 3
INUSE: 512: 4
INUSE: 512: 4
INUSE: 512: 5
INUSE: 512: 5
INUSE: 512: 6
INUSE: 512: 6
INUSE: 512: 7
INUSE: 512: 7
RESERVED: 512
```

```
RESERVED: 512
...
RESERVED: 512
RESERVED: 512
RESERVED: 512
FREE: 1744

***************** TOTALS *****************
TOTAL MEMORY INUSE      =        7680 bytes
TOTAL MEMORY RESERVED   =      131584 bytes
TOTAL MEMORY FREE       =        1744 bytes
TOTAL MEMORY OVERHEAD   =        4396 bytes
                                 ================
TOTAL MEMORY ALLOCATED  =      145408 bytes

TOTAL NUMBER OF CONNECTIONS = 60 AND DEFAULT PACKET SIZE = 512
NUMBER OF CURRENT CONNECTIONS = 7

DBCC execution completed. If DBCC printed error messages, contact a user
with System Administrator (SA) role.
```

Using DBCC NetMemShow

If you want to customize the data that is returned from DBCC NetMemusage, you can use the lower-level DBCC command NetMemShow. The syntax for DBCC NetMemShow is as follows:

DBCC NetMemShow(*Option*)

The values for *Option* are the different sorts of output that you want to review. I believe that DBCC NetMemusage is using the same data, but just reporting it in a different way. The only different values that can be returned from DBCC NetMemShow occur when you use option 1:

```
DBCC NetMemShow( 1 )
Go


==================================================
=         NETWORK MEMORY ALLOCATIONS         =
==================================================
**** FREE MEMORY FRAGMENTS ****
NUMBER OF CONNECTIONS = 60 AND DEFAULT PACKET SIZE = 512
FREE memory found at address 0x205819fc of size 1744

   ***************** TOTALS *****************
TOTAL MEMORY USED       =      139268 bytes
TOTAL MEMORY FREE       =        1744 bytes
TOTAL MEMORY OVERHEAD   =        4396 bytes
                                 ================
TOTAL MEMORY ALLOCATED  =      145408 bytes

DBCC execution completed. If DBCC printed error messages, contact a user
with System Administrator (SA) role.
```

Part
IV

Ch
20

The other options return the same information as the DBCC NetMemusage, so there's no point in describing them again here.

Using DBCC PktMemShow

Another option that is useful when determining how your users are interacting with the net-working subsystem in Sybase System XI is the DBCC PktMemShow command. This command will show the buffer areas allocated by server process for handling read and write requests. The syntax for DBCC PktMemShow is as follows:

```
DBCC PktMemShow( spid )
```

If *spid* is omitted, DBCC will return information about all the processes on the server, as you can see in Listing 20.6.

Listing 20.6 The Output from DBCC PktMemShow

```
DBCC PktMemShow
Go


- - - - - - - - - - - - - - - - - - - - - - - - - - - - - - - - - - - - - - - - -
===============================================
=        NETWORK BUFFERS FOR ACTIVE PROCESSES =
===============================================
** NETWORK BUFFERS FOR SPID 1 **
READ BUFFER:       address=0x2055e8fc      size=512
WRITE BUFFER:      address=0x2055eb0c      size=512
OVERFLOW BUFFER:   address=0x2056e28c      size=512
** NETWORK BUFFERS FOR SPID 2 **
READ BUFFER:       address=0x2055ed1c      size=512
WRITE BUFFER:      address=0x2055ef2c      size=512
** NETWORK BUFFERS FOR SPID 3 **
READ BUFFER:       address=0x2055f13c      size=512
WRITE BUFFER:      address=0x2055f34c      size=512
** NETWORK BUFFERS FOR SPID 4 **
READ BUFFER:       address=0x2055f55c      size=512
WRITE BUFFER:      address=0x2055f76c      size=512
** NETWORK BUFFERS FOR SPID 5 **
READ BUFFER:       address=0x2055f97c      size=512
WRITE BUFFER:      address=0x2055fb8c      size=512
** NETWORK BUFFERS FOR SPID 6 **
READ BUFFER:       address=0x2055fd9c      size=512
WRITE BUFFER:      address=0x2055ffac      size=512
** NETWORK BUFFERS FOR SPID 7 **
READ BUFFER:       address=0x205601bc      size=512
WRITE BUFFER:      address=0x205603cc      size=512

DBCC execution completed. If DBCC printed error messages, contact a user
with System Administrator (SA) role.
```

Using DBCC Lock

DBCC Lock reports any locks on the server. It has no parameters and simply returns any page information in a formatted result list that shows any data locks that are currently in effect. In Listing 20.7, a few basic updates were done to leave some locks on the database and then the locks were reviewed using the DBCC command.

Listing 20.7 DBCC Lock's Output

```
/* Perform a few locking transactions first */
Begin Tran
Update publishers
Set    pub_id = pub_id
Go
Update authors
Set    au_id = au_id
Where. state = 'Ca'
Go

DBCC Lock
Go
- - - - - - - - - - - - - - - - - - - - - - - - - - - - - - - - - - - - - - - - - - - - - -
LOCKS:
TABLE LOCKS
2060fc80 Objid 48003202, dbid 5, (bucket 28)
2060fc60    swstatus=(), swskipped=0, swsemaphore=0x2060fc80
2060fc40        lrspid=8, lrtype=ex_tab, lrsemawait=0x2060fc60,
lrstatus=(granted ), lrsuffclass=0
2060fd40 Objid 16003088, dbid 5, (bucket 47)
2060fd20    swstatus=(), swskipped=0, swsemaphore=0x2060fd40
2060fd00        lrspid=8, lrtype=ex_tab, lrsemawait=0x2060fd20,
lrstatus=(granted ), lrsuffclass=0
PAGE LOCKS
ADDRESS LOCKS
SEMAPHORES

DBCC execution completed. If DBCC printed error messages, contact a user
with System Administrator (SA) role.
```

Using DBCC DBInfo

This DBCC command DBInfo is definitely not going to produce much information that could be deemed of use, unless that is, you can figure out what each of the variables it is reporting actually means. In any case, the syntax for DBCC DBInfo is as follows:

```
DBCC DBInfo( Database_Name )
```

The output from this command is rather odd, but does have some useful values in it (see Listing 20.8).

Part
IV

Ch
20

Listing 20.8 The Output from DBCC DBInfo

```
DBCC DBInfo
Go


- - - - - - - - - - - - - - - - - - - - - - - - - - - - - - - - - - - -
DBINFO STRUCTURE:

dbi_lastlr: (136,0)
dbi_dpbegxact: (441,7)
```

continues

Listing 20.8 Continued

```
dbi_oldseqnum: Jan  1 1900 12:00:00:000AM
dbi_curseqnum: Jun 29 1996 10:15:52:246PM
dbi_nextseqnum: Jan  1 1900 12:00:00:000AM
dbi_ltmtrunc_time_set: Jan  1 1900 12:00:00:000AM
dbi_deallocpgs: 1
dbi_nextcheckpt: (empty)
dbi_dbid: 5
dbi_suid: 1
dbi_version: 3
dbi_status: 0x0
dbi_checkpt: (870,13)
dbi_nextid: 640005311
dbi_complete: 0
dbi_crdate: Jun 29 1996 10:15:53:126PM
dbi_dbname: pubs2
dbi_status2: -32768
dbi_ldstate: 28
dbi_logvers: 2
dbi_rambots: 0x0000 0x00000000
dbi_dmplastckpt: (empty)
dbi_dmplastlr: (empty)
dbi_paretruncpg: 0
dbi_posttruncpg: 0
dbi_ltmtruncpg: 0
dbi_rep_stat: 0
dbi_rep_gen_id: 0
dbi_upgdvers: 1

DBCC execution completed. If DBCC printed error messages, contact a user
with System Administrator (SA) role.
```

Using DBCC Resource

DBCC Resource is a similar command to the DBInfo command, in that it reports internal statistics about the database, mostly related to the way the data server is currently configured and what internal resources are being utilized. Obviously, this DBCC command is intended for a Technical Support person, but it is quite illuminating if you get your hex calculator out and decode some of the locations and then use a heap walker to investigate the memory locations directly. In Listing 20.9, you can see the sorts of statistics that are returned to the user after executing the DBCC Resource command. Note the section titled DS_CONFIG, which corresponds to the configuration settings exposed through sp_configure.

Listing 20.9 The Output from DBCC Resource

```
DBCC Resource
Go

-----------------------------------------------------------------
RESOURCE:
```

```
rcaches=0x2059b790
rdbtab=0x2050f580
rdbtabfree=0x20515600 rfreelocklist=(0x20612a40,360) rpagelockhash=0x206145a8
➥rtablelockhash=0x206140e0
raddrlockhash=0x20617608 rlocksleeptaskq=0x20006960 rdlc_inprogress=536897888
rdlc_iteration_count=1 rdlc_dlsnotdone_count=0 rdlc_lockwait_seqno=1
rdlc_sleepownerlist=0x2059b920 rdlc_scanarray=0x2059c0d0 rdeadlock_id=0
rprotstamp=11 rckptalarmid=3 rdsinitkpid=196611
rsaspid=0
rfirstlock=0x0 rbufhmask=0x0 rinterfpath=D:\SYBASE\System11\ini
rbinaryversion=1101 rerrfile=D:\SYBASE\System11\install\errorlog rdiagstream=0x0
rdiagbuffer=0x207d9800 rnetworks=0x2000ff64 rnnetworks=1 rmaxuconn=2040
rfreedes=0x2047f7a0 rndeshash=0x204ee5cc rideshash=0x204eddcc rdeskept=0x0
rdeshmask=511
rdesunkept=0x2047b1dc rdesscavenge=0x2047f3f4 rmasterdes=0x204764c0
rprocfree=0x204661fc rmasterdbt=0x204f7380 rtempdbt=0x20503480
rslgroup_head=0x2061c880 rslicespin_cb=0x20621990
SPIN LOCKS:
    rlockfreelist_spin=0x2000b000 rlocksleeptask_spin=0x2000b040
    rlocksema_spin=0x2000b080
    rdesmgr_spin=0x2000cd00 rdesupd_spin=0x2000cd40 rdesidt_spin=0x2000cd80
    rprocmgr_spin=0x2000cdc0 raccmeth_spin=0x2000cf00
    rdumpdb_spin=0x2000cf40 rdbt_spin=0x2000ce00 rdbts_spin=0x2000ce40
    rdbt_ext_spin=0x2000cec0 rdbtnextid_spin=0x2000ce80
    rsysind_spin=0x2000cf80 rpssmgr_spin=0x2000cfc0 rsysgam_spin=0x2000d000
    rexerlog_spin=0x2000d040 rsysind_xspin=0x2000d100 rpage_xspin=0x2000d140
    rdes_xspin=0x2000d180 rdbt_xspin=0x2000d1c0 rrm_spin=0x2000d080
    rchatrm_spin=0x2000d0c0
    rslgroup_spin=0x2000b180
rdiagdes_lop=0x2047b1dc rdiagdes_hip=0x204eddcc
rdiagpss_lop=0x20395640 rdiagpss_hip=0x204661a0
rdiaglock_lop=0x2059c0e0 rdiaglock_hip=0x206140e0 rdiagstrmbuf_lop=0x0
rdiagstrmbuf_hip=0x0 rdiagbuf_lop=0x207da800 rdiagbuf_hip=0x20d9e580
rdiagproc_lop=0x204661b0 rdiagproc_hip=0x20473d14 rdiagdbt_lop=0x204f7380
rdiagdbt_hip=0x2053f980 rdiagphdr_lop=0x20665800 rdiagphdr_hip=0x207d6800
rprobestat=0x20552c90 rpstatfree=0x20552a90 risync_pageno=0
rexer_ptr=0x2065aca0
rlkunittrace=0 rlkunitscript=0x0 rlkunittime=0
rlkunitsemas=0x0 rmirror_mbox=2 rdskfreebufs=0 rmirrorexit=0
rpagesize=2048 rcmmtbuf=0 rcmmtind=0
rcaches_configured=1
hk_info.hk_max_few_percent=1

DS_CONFIG:
cconfsz=2048   cmajor=2   cminor=0   crevision=19
cbootsource=2  crecinterval=5  ccatalogupdates=0
cusrconnections=25  cmemsize=7500  cdbnum=12  clocknum=5000
cdesnum=500  cpcacheprcnt=20  cfillfactor=0
cavetimeslice=100  ccrdatabasesize=2  ctapreten=0  crecoveryflags=0
cwritestatus=0
cfgpss=60  cfgdbnum=12  cfgwqueuenum=32
cfgxdes=16  cfgsdes=16  cfgbuf=2955  cfgdes=500
cfgprocedure=738  cfglocks=5000  cfgcprot=15  cnproc=61
cstacksz=40960  cfgstacksz=36864  cguardsz=4096
cnmemmap=1  cnmbox=30  cnmsg=64
```

continues

Listing 20.9   Continued

```
cnmsgmax=64      cnvdisks=10      cnblkio=256
cnmaxaio_engine=2147483647      cnmaxaio_server=2147483647
cnsocket=52
cmasttype=0      cnalarm=40
cclkrate=100000      ctimeslice=1      ctimemax=500
clocdebug0      cfgmastmirror_stat=0
cfgupddate=34561      cfgupdtime=0
cfgrembuf=20      cfgsitebuf=10      cfglogconn=20      cfgdatabuf=3
cfgupgradeversion=1101      cmaxonline=1      cminonline=1
cfgcpuacctflush=200      cfgioacctflush=1000
cbufwashsize=256      cindextrips=0
cindextrips=0      coamtrips=0      cpreallocext=2
caddnetmem=0      cdfltpktsz=512      cmaxpktsz=512
cfgpasswordexp=0      clargextent=0      cchecksum=0
cfg_burn_factor=5000
csortbufsize=0 csortpgcount=0
cschedspins=2000      cmaxscheds=10
cfgcaches=1      calignment=2048  cchashsize=8192

cfgslspin=10      cfgslgroup=1024
cfg_hk_free_write_percent=1
idt_grab_size=1
```

```
DBCC execution completed. If DBCC printed error messages, contact a user
with System Administrator (SA) role.
```

Using DBCC DBTable

The DBTable option returns configuration information stored on the system pages of the database that apply to all the database's tables. The syntax for DBCC DBTable is as follows:

```
DBCC DBTable( dbid )
```

dbid is the number associated with the database and can be found by using the system function DB_Id. Note that you cannot pass a function to a DBCC command. The following Transact-SQL is invalid:

```
DBCC DBTable( DB_Id( pubs2 ) )
Go
```

Instead, you must manually execute the DB_Id command first to find out the identifier used for the *pubs2* database and then execute the DBCC command separately. In Listing 20.10, you can see the sorts of table statistics that the data server maintains for the *pubs2* database.

Listing 20.10   The Output from the DBCC DBTable Command

```
DBCC DBTable( 5 )
Go

------------------------------------------------------------------------
DBTABLES:
```

```
dbt_dbid=5    dbt_stat=0x0    dbt_state=0x2,    dbt_keep=1    dbt_lock=0
dbt_dbaid=1    dbt_crtime=24045938    dbt_dbname=pubs2
dbt_logrows=0    dbt_extstat=0x0
dbt_logvers=2
dbt_nextid=640005311dbt_dflinfo=0x0    dbt_dflstat=0x0
dbt_dbts=0x0001 0x000010b2    dbt_xdesqueue    next=0x2050f5c0
        prev=0x2050f5c0
dbt_xdesqueue_spin=0x2000ac00    dbt_lastckptts=0x0001 0x000010b2
dbt_sysindsrch=0    dbt_sysindstat=0x0
dbt_sysindstarve=0    dbt_sysindmod=0    dbt_sysindmodifywaiters=0
dbt_des=0x2047d694    dbt_udes=0x2050fe8c
dbt_stat2=0x80000000,0x40000000,0x20000000,0x10000000,0x8000000,
0x4000000,0x2000000,0x1000000,0x800000,0x400000,0x200000,0x100000,
0x80000,0x40000,0x20000,0x10000,0x8000,
dbt_upgdvers=1

dm_segmap:0x4,0x2,0x1,
dm_lstart=0    dm_vstart=4612    dm_size=1024

dbt_hklogflush=192

dbt_lkprom.lwm=200    dbt_lkprom.hwm=200    dbt_lkprom.pct=100
dbt_lkprom.status=1    dbt_lkprom.seqno=1

DBCC execution completed. If DBCC printed error messages, contact a user
with System Administrator (SA) role.
```

Using DBCC Buffer

DBCC Buffer is used to analyze exactly the memory allocation in the database server's buffer pools that are created to manage I/O. The syntax for DBCC Buffer is as follows:

```
DBCC Buffer( [ dbid ][, Object_Id][, Number_Of_Buffers][, Print_Detail][,
➥Buffer_Type]
[, Cache_Name] )
```

The values for each of the options to the Transact-SQL command DBCC Buffer are as follows:

- dbid—This is the database identifier that you are inspecting.
- Object_Id—This is the particular database object (table, index, and so on) for which you are checking buffer allocation.
- Number_Of_Buffers—This is the number of buffers about which you want to inquire.
- Print_Detail—This is the level of detail that you want to return to the client, ranging from 0 to 2.
- Buffer_Type—This is the type of buffer on which you want to inquire: *kept*, *hashed*, *nothashed*, and *ioerr*.
- Cache_Name—This is the particular data cache that you want to work on.

TIP By not supplying any parameters to DBCC `Buffer` and no parentheses, you will get a full dump of all the buffers on the whole server.

In Listing 20.11, you can see the very detailed information that can be pulled from the buffers in memory, including a full dump of a 2K memory block enabling complete access to the active memory areas for review and technical support reasons.

Listing 20.11 Performing a DBCC Buffer on the sysobjects Table

```
DBCC Buffer( 1, 1, 2, 2 )
Go

--------------------------------------------------------------------
BUFFERS (in MRU to LRU order):
starting with KEPT BUFFERS (not on LRU chain):
BUFFERS IN CACHE default data cache(ID 0):
BUFFERS IN POOL 0 (MASS SIZE = 2K):
BUFFER:
Buffer header for buffer 0x20d9c840
    page=0x20d36000 bdnew=0x20d9c840 bdold=0x20d9c840 bhash=0x0
    bmass_next=0x20d9c8a0
    bmass_prev=0x20d9d860 bvirtpg=8 bdbid=1 bkeep=0
     bmass_stat=0x4001010 bbuf_stat=0x0001 bpageno=4
     bxls_pin = 0x00000000 bxls_next = 0x00000000b
     bxls_flushseq 0 bxls_pinseq 0
PAGE HEADER:
Page header for page 0x20d36000
pageno=4 nextpg=0 prevpg=5 objid=1 timestamp=0001 08afcc69
nextrno=16 level=0 indid=0  freeoff=1427 minlen=64
page status bits: 0x100,0x1,
DATA:
20d36020:  02000100 31000000 00005100 00000000   ....1.....Q.....
20d36030:  00000000 00000000 a3850000 980c8701   ................
20d36040:  a3850000 980c8701 00000000 00000000   ................
20d36050:  00000000 00000000 00000000 53200000   ............S ..
20d36060:  57007379 736c6f67 696e726f 6c657300   W.sysloginroles.
20d36070:  00000003 534f4201 01010032 00000000   ....SOB....2....
20d36080:  00010400 00000000 00000000 00000000   ................
20d36090:  00000000 00000000 00000000 00000000   ................
20d360a0:  00000000 00000000 00000000 00000000   ................
20d360b0:  00000053 20000050 00737973 6c6f6773   ...S ..P.syslogs
20d360c0:  686f6c64 024d4202 020100da ddbf1900   hold.MB.........
20d360d0:  00530000 00000000 00000000 000000ab   .S..............
20d360e0:  8900004e f85701ab 8900004e f8570100   ...N.W.....N.W..
20d360f0:  00000000 00000000 00000000 00000000   ................
20d36100:  00000055 20000054 00737074 5f76616c   ...U ..T.spt_val
20d36110:  75657300 00000003 504c4202 0301004c   ues.....PLB....L
20d36120:  26a81b00 00430000 00000000 02000000   &....C..........
20d36130:  000000ab 890000e2 095801ab 890000e2   .........X......
20d36140:  09580100 00000000 00000000 00000000   .X..............
20d36150:  00000000 00000055 20000055 00737074   .......U ..U.spt
20d36160:  5f6d6f6e 69746f72 00000000 03514d42   _monitor.....QMB
20d36170:  02040100 f792841e 00004300 00000000   ..........C.....
20d36180:  00000000 00000000 ab890000 233a5801   ...........#:X.
```

```
20d36190:  ab890000 233a5801 00000000 00000000   ....#:X.........
20d361a0:  00000000 00000000 00000000 55200000   ...........U ..
20d361b0:  5f007370 745f6461 74617479 70655f69   _.spt_datatype_i
20d361c0:  6e666f5f 65787400 00000003 5b574202   nfo_ext.....[WB.
20d361d0:  05010069 db6c2000 00430000 00000000   ...i.l ..C......
20d361e0:  00000000 000000ab 8900004f 3b5801ab   ...........O;X..
20d361f0:  8900004f 3b580100 00000000 00000000   ...O;X.........
20d36200:  00000000 00000000 00000055 2000005b   ...........U ..[
20d36210:  00737074 5f646174 61747970 655f696e   .spt_datatype_in
20d36220:  666f0000 00000357 53420206 0100db23   fo.....WSB.....#
20d36230:  55220000 43000000 00000000 00000000   U"..C..........
20d36240:  0000ab89 00004f3b 5801ab89 00004f3b   ......O;X.....O;
20d36250:  58010000 00000000 00000000 00000000   X...............
20d36260:  00000000 00005520 00005900 7370745f   ......U .Y.spt_
20d36270:  73657276 65725f69 6e666f00 00000003   server_info.....
20d36280:  55514202 07010014 48492300 00040000   UQB.....HI#.....
20d36290:  000000a0 00000000 000000ab 8900007b   ...............{
20d362a0:  3c5801ab 8900007b 3c580100 00000000   <X.....{<X......
20d362b0:  00000000 00000000 00000000 00000050   ...............P
20d362c0:  20000056 0073705f 70726f63 786d6f64   ..V.sp_procxmod
20d362d0:  65000000 0003524e 42020801 004d6c3d   e.....RNB....Ml=
20d362e0:  24000004 00000000 00a00000 00000000   $...............
20d362f0:  00ab8900 00a73d58 01ab8900 00a73d58   ......=X......=X
20d36300:  01000000 00000000 00000000 00000000   ................
20d36310:  00000000 00502000 00560073 705f7661   .....P ..V.sp_va
20d36320:  6c69646c 616e6700 00000003 524e4202   lidlang.....RNB.
20d36330:  09010086 90312500 00040000 000000a0   .....1%.........
20d36340:  00000000 000000ab 890000d3 3e5801ab   ............>X..
20d36350:  890000d3 3e580100 00000000 00000000   ....>X.........
20d36360:  00000000 00000000 00000050 20000057   ...........P ..W
20d36370:  0073705f 6765746d 65737361 67650000   .sp_getmessage..
20d36380:  00000353 4f42020a 0100bfb4 25260000   ...SOB......%&..
20d36390:  04000000 0000a000 00000000 000000ab   ................
20d363a0:  0000ff3f 5801ab89 0000ff3f 58010000   ...?X......?X...
20d363b0:  00000000 00000000 00000000 00000000   ................
20d363c0:  00005020 00005600 73705f63 6f6e6669   ..P ..V.sp_confi
20d363d0:  67757265 00000000 03524e42 020b0100   gure.....RNB....
20d363e0:  f8d81927 00000400 00000000 a0000000   ...'............
20d363f0:  00000000 ab890000 57425801 ab890000   ........WBX.....
20d36400:  57425801 00000000 00000000 00000000   WBX.............
20d36410:  00000000 00000000 50200000 55007370   ........P ..U.sp
20d36420:  5f64626f 7074696f 6e000000 0003514d   _dboption.....QM
20d36430:  42020c01 0031fd0d 28000004 00000000   B....1..(.......
20d36440:  00800000 00000000 00ab8900 00834358   ..............CX
20d36450:  01ab8900 00834358 01000000 00000000   ......CX........
20d36460:  00000000 00000000 00000000 00502000   .............P .
20d36470:  005a0073 705f7072 74737962 7379736d   .Z.sp_prtsybsysm
20d36480:  73677300 00000003 56524202 0d0100a3   sgs.....VRB.....
20d36490:  45f62900 00530000 00000000 00000000   E.)..S..........
20d364a0:  000000ab 89000074 255901ab 89000074   .......t%Y.....t
20d364b0:  25590100 00000000 00000000 00000000   %Y..............
20d364c0:  00000000 00000055 20000057 00737074   .......U ..W.spt
20d364d0:  5f636f6d 6d697474 61620000 00000353   _committab.....S
20d364e0:  4f42020e 0100dc69 ea2a0000 04000000   OB.....i.*......
20d364f0:  00008000 00000000 0000ab89 0000242a   ..............$*
```

continues

Listing 20.11   Continued

```
20d36500:  5901ab89 0000242a 59010000 00000000  Y.....$*Y.......
20d36510:  00000000 00000000 00000000 00005020  .............P
20d36520:  00005800 6d6f6e5f 7270635f 61747461  ..X.mon_rpc_atta
20d36530:  63680000 00000354 5042020f 0100158e  ch.....TPB......
20d36540:  de2b0000 04000000 00008000 00000000  .+..............
20d36550:  0000ab89 0000242a 5901ab89 0000242a  ......$*Y.....$*
20d36560:  59010000 00000000 00000000 00000000  Y...............
20d36570:  00000000 00005020 00005900 6d6f6e5f  ......P ..Y.mon_
20d36580:  7270635f 636f6e6e 65637400 00000003  rpc_connect.....
20d36590:  555142                               UQB.
OFFSET TABLE:
Row - Offset
15 (0xf) - 1338 (0x53a),   14 (0xe) - 1250 (0x4e2),
13 (0xd) - 1163 (0x48b),   12 (0xc) - 1073 (0x431),
11 (0xb) - 988 (0x3dc),    10 (0xa) - 902 (0x386),
9 (0x9) - 815 (0x32f),     8 (0x8) - 729 (0x2d9),
7 (0x7) - 643 (0x283),     6 (0x6) - 554 (0x22a),
5 (0x5) - 463 (0x1cf),     4 (0x4) - 368 (0x170),
3 (0x3) - 283 (0x11b),     2 (0x2) - 199 (0xc7),
1 (0x1) - 119 (0x77),      0 (0x0) - 32 (0x20),
```

DBCC execution completed. If DBCC printed error messages, contact a user
with System Administrator (SA) role.

Using DBCC Ind

DBCC Ind is used to report all the information, including the actual data pages themselves on
any given table or object. The syntax for DBCC Ind is as follows:

```
DBCC Ind( dbid, Object_Id, Print_Detail )
```

dbid and *Object_Id*, refer to the database and object that you want to inquire on, and
Print_Detail is the level of information that you want returned from the DBCC execution. In
Listing 20.12, you can see that the individual data pages from the index are useful in determin-
ing how Sybase built the index.

Listing 20.12   DBCC Ind Output

```
DBCC Ind( 5, 1 )
Go


------------------------------------------------------------------
TAB:
Checking 1
The total number of data pages in this table is 3.
Table has 49 data rows.
DATABASE:5   OBJECT:1   INDEX:1   PAGE:8 (0x8)
Page header for page 0x20d35000
pageno=8 nextpg=0 prevpg=0 objid=1 timestamp=0001 00000e55
nextrno=50 level=0 indid=1  freeoff=59 minlen=9
```

```
page status bits: 0x80,
20d35020:  00010000 00010000 00006609 ad060300  .........f.....
20d35030:  0000004d 6c3d2404 000000            ...Ml=$.....
DATABASE:5  OBJECT:1  INDEX:2  PAGE:16 (0x10)
Page header for page 0x20d34800
pageno=16 nextpg=0 prevpg=0 objid=1 timestamp=0001 00000e7a
nextrno=1207 level=0 indid=2  freeoff=1229 minlen=9
page status bits: 0x1000,0x2,
20d34820:  01010003 00000006 00140061 755f7069  ..........au_pi
20d34830:  7802110b 01010001 00000015 00150061  x..............a
20d34840:  7574686f 72730212 0b010100 03000000  uthors..........
20d34850:  07001400 626c7572 62730211 0b010100  ....blurbs......
20d34860:  03000000 10001700 6279726f 79616c74  ........byroyalt
20d34870:  7902140b 01010003 00000009 00160064  y..............d
20d34880:  61746564 666c7402 130b0101 00030000  atedflt.........
20d34890:  000d0016 0064656c 7469746c 6502130b  .....deltitle...
20d348a0:  01010003 00000012 001b0064 6973636f  ..........disco
20d348b0:  756e745f 70726f63 02180b01 01000300  unt_proc........
20d348c0:  00000500 17006469 73636f75 6e747302  ......discounts.
20d348d0:  140b0101 00030000 0011001a 00686973  .............his
20d348e0:  746f7279 5f70726f 6302170b 01010003  tory_proc.......
20d348f0:  00000015 001f0069 6e736572 745f7361  .......insert_sa
20d34900:  6c65735f 70726f63 021c0b01 01000300  les_proc........
20d34910:  00001600 2500696e 73657274 5f73616c  ....%.insert_sal
20d34920:  65736465 7461696c 5f70726f 6302220b  esdetail_proc.".
20d34930:  01010003 0000000a 00170070 686f6e65  ..........phone
20d34940:  64666c74 02140b01 01000300 00000b00  dflt...........
20d34950:  18007075 625f6964 72756c65 02150b01  ..pub_idrule....
20d34960:  01000100 00001600 18007075 626c6973  ..........publis
20d34970:  68657273 02150b01 01000100 00001700  hers............
20d34980:  1600726f 79736368 65640213 0b010100  ..roysched......
20d34990:  03000000 00001300 73616c65 7302100b  ........sales...
20d349a0:  01010003 00000019 0073616c 6c6573  ..........sales
20d349b0:  64657461 696c0216 0b010100 03000000  detail..........
20d349c0:  14001a00 73746f72 6569645f 70726f63  ....storeid_proc
20d349d0:  02170b01 01000300 00001300 1c007374  ..............st
20d349e0:  6f72656e 616d655f 70726f63 02190b01  orename_proc....
20d349f0:  01000300 00000400 14007374 6f726573  .........stores
20d34a00:  02110b01 01000100 00000a00 1b007379  ..............sy
20d34a10:  73616c74 65726e61 74657302 180b0101  salternates.....
20d34a20:  00010000 0013001b 00737973 61747472  .........sysattr
20d34a30:  69627574 65730218 0b010100 01000000  ibutes..........
20d34a40:  02001800 73797363 6f6c756d 6e730215  ....syscolumns..
20d34a50:  0b010100 01000000 05001900 73797363  ............sysc
20d34a60:  6f6d6d65 6e747302 160b0101 00010000  omments.........
20d34a70:  0010001c 00737973 636f6e73 74726169  .....sysconstrai
20d34a80:  6e747302 190b0101 00010000 000b0018  nts.............
20d34a90:  00737973 64657065 6e647302 150b0101  .sysdepends.....
20d34aa0:  00010000 000d0015 00737973 67616d73  .........sysgams
20d34ab0:  02120b01 01000100 00000100 18007379  ..............sy
20d34ac0:  73696e64 65786573 02150b01 01000100  sindexes........
20d34ad0:  00000c00 15007379 736b6579 7302120b  ......syskeys...
20d34ae0:  01010001 00000007 00150073 79736c6f  ...........syslo
20d34af0:  67730212 0b010100 01000000 00001800  gs..............
20d34b00:  7379736f 626a6563 74730215 0b010100  sysobjects......
20d34b10:  01000000 14001b00 73797370 61727469  ........sysparti
```

continues

Listing 20.12   Continued

```
20d34b20:   74696f6e 7302180b 01010001 00000004   tions...........
20d34b30:   001b0073 79737072 6f636564 75726573   ...sysprocedures
20d34b40:   02180b01 01000100 00000800 19007379   ..............sy
20d34b50:   7370726f 74656374 7302160b 01010001   sprotects.......
20d34b60:   0000000f 001b0073 79737265 66657265   .......sysrefere
20d34b70:   6e636573 02180b01 01000100 00001200   nces...........
20d34b80:   16007379 73726f6c 65730213 0b010100   ..sysroles......
20d34b90:   01000000 06001900 73797373 65676d65   ........syssegme
20d34ba0:   6e747302 160b0101 00010000 0011001b   nts.............
20d34bb0:   00737973 74687265 73686f6c 64730218   .systhresholds..
20d34bc0:   0b010100 01000000 03001600 73797374   ...........syst
20d34bd0:   79706573 02130b01 01000100 00000e00   ypes...........
20d34be0:   1d007379 73757365 726d6573 73616765   ..sysusermessage
20d34bf0:   73021a0b 01010001 00000009 00160073   s..............s
20d34c00:   79737573 65727302 130b0101 00030000   ysusers.........
20d34c10:   000c001a 00746974 6c655f69 6472756c   .....title_idrul
20d34c20:   6502170b 01010004 00000000 00180074   e..............t
20d34c30:   69746c65 5f70726f 6302150b 01010003   itle_proc.......
20d34c40:   00000002 00190074 69746c65 61757468   .......titleauth
20d34c50:   6f720216 0b010100 04000000 01001a00   or..............
20d34c60:   7469746c 6569645f 70726f63 02170b01   titleid_proc....
20d34c70:   01000300 00000300 14007469 746c6573   ..........titles
20d34c80:   02110b01 01000300 00000f00 17007469   ..............ti
20d34c90:   746c6576 69657702 140b0101 00030000   tleview.........
20d34ca0:   000e001d 00746f74 616c7361 6c65735f   .....totalsales_
20d34cb0:   74726967 021a0b01 01000300 00000800   trig............
20d34cc0:   16007479 70656466 6c740213 0b         ..typedflt....
```

DBCC execution completed. If DBCC printed error messages, contact a user
with System Administrator (SA) role.

Using DBCC Log, DBCC Page, and DBCC Tab

DBCC Log and DBCC Page work identically to DBCC Ind in that they report page information either from the transaction log or from a database page (logical or from disk). The syntax for each of these commands is as follows:

```
DBCC Log( [ dbid ][, Object_Id ][, Page ][, Row ][, Number_Of_Records ][,
          Type = { -1...36 } ], Print_Detail )

DBCC Page( dbid | Database_Name, Page [, Print_Detail ][, Cache = {0|1} ][,
          Logical = {1|0} ][, Cache_Name | -1 ]   )
```

The output lists detail from the log and or data pages and can be useful in determining the effects of a SQL statement on the log itself.

DBCC Tab is similar to the DBCC Page command except that it will dump the entire data from the database table to either the errorlog or the console, depending on where you are redirecting the output. The format of the output is similar to DBCC Ind and is a hex with ASCII equivalents listing of all the data in the table. The syntax for DBCC Tab is as follows:

```
DBCC Tab( dbid, Object_Id, Print_Detail )
```

Using DBCC Des

The DBCC command Des is used to describe objects in the database. The output is relatively meaningless, unless you can get to a Sybase engineer to have the information explained to you. The syntax for DBCC Des is as follows:

```
DBCC Des( [ dbid ][,Object_Id ] )
```

If you omit any parameters, DBCC Des will describe all the objects in all the databases, which will take up quite a lot of space in returning results. In Listing 20.13, you can see the output given by DBCC Des when used to describe the *sysobjects* table in *master*. Note that the first object in the first database is always the sysobjects table in the master database on any server.

Listing 20.13 DBCC Des Output

```
DBCC Des( 1, 1 )
Go

-----------------------------------------------------------------
DESs:
dirty_chain=0x20475b60    dnew=0x20475b60    dold=0x20475b60
ddbid=1
objone=1  objrno=0  objuid=1
dobjstat.objid=1    dobjstat.objuserstat=0x0
dobjstat.objsysstat=0x40,0x20,0x10,0x1,
dobjstat.objindexdel=0    dobjstat.objschema=1
objdeltrig=0  objinstrig=0  objupdtrig=0
objseltrig=0  objckfirst=0 objtype [83],[32]
objcache=0  objlen=79  objname=sysobjects
dindc.ind_first=0  dindc.ind_root=0
dindc.ind_maxlen=104    dindc.ind_minlen=64
dindwork=0x0    dnextdes=0x204f7c8c
dihash=0x0    dnhash=0x0    ddbtable=0x204f7380    dkeepcnt=0
dstate=0x1
dslinfo.sd_numslices=1
dslinfo.sd_slice1.slicenum=0  sc_first=1  sc_ctrlpg=0
dlkprom.lwm = 0  dlkprom.hwm = 0  dlkprom.pct = 0
dlkprom.status = 0  dlkprom.seqno = 0
approx data pages = 0
lock promotion level = 200
Object mapped to cache -1.
Index 1 mapped to cache -1.
Index 2 mapped to cache -1.

DBCC execution completed. If DBCC printed error messages, contact a user
with System Administrator (SA) role.
```

Part
IV

Ch

20

Using DBCC Pss

DBCC Pss is provided for third-party applications that want to monitor the memory and activities performed by processes on the server. The output is basically meaningless, but does have a use if you can get it documented by Sybase. The syntax for the use of DBCC Pss is as follows:

```
DBCC Pss( Server_User_Id, Server_Process_Id, Print_Detail)
```

Server_User_Id and *Server_Process_Id* correspond to the user for whom you want to find out what is happening. The output shown in Listing 20.14 demonstrates all the counters and process monitors that Sybase maintains for all user processes on the server.

Listing 20.14   DBCC Pss Output for the System Administrator (sa)

```
DBCC Pss( 1, 1, 1 )
Go


-------------------------------------------------------------------
PSS:
PSS:
pstat=0x10000,   pcurdb=1   psuid=1   puid=1
puname=   ploginflags=15   prowcnt=0   pstatlist=0x0
pnumplan=0
plasterror=0  ppreverror=0  ptranstate=1
prowcount=0   plastprocid=0   pprocnest=0
pgid=0   phid=0   pspid=1   pkspid=720907
poptions=7 8 13 40 41 42   poffsets=0   pcurcmd=230
pcputot=24   pcpucur=0   pmemusage=2   pbufread=0
pbufwrite=0   pcmderrs=0   pntext=19   ptext=0x0
donestat=0x0   doneinfo=0   donecount=0
pxactcnt=0   ptimeslice=1   pcurcolid=0
pcompct=0   phdr=0x2066a000   pplan=0x2066a000
phosttype=0   phsocket=0   phindex=0   pline=1
ptrigdate=0x0   pwaitsema=0x0
precvbuf=0x2038c4b0   psendbuf=0x2038c4c8   pdbtable=0x204f7380   ppars=0x0
pcurstep=543597524   pnetid=0
pdbindex=-1   pdb_stat=1   pbackground=0
ploginrec=0x2038d010   ptdsversion=4.6.0.0
pstackbound=0x20074030   pguardbound=0x20075030
pmasterxact=0x0   pinternalxact=0x0
pplc=0x2063c030
IDENTITY_VAL info
      objid=0 dbid=0  idtnum=0
IDENTITY_INSERT settings
      objid=0 dbid=0  state=0
PHDR:PROC_HDR: (at 0x2066a000)
address=0x2066a000   p_hdrstep=0x2066a37c   p_hdrseq=0x20669cbc
p_hdrcrt=0x0
p_hdrpbuf=0x0   p_hdrtmps=0x0
p_hdrcaller=0x0   p_hdrelease=0  p_hdrtabid=0 p_hdrsub=0x0
p_hdrstatus=1024 (0x400 (SACREATED), )
p_lastpg=0  p_lastoff=0   p_procnum=0  p_lostcnt=1
Memory Allocation Map:
 0 mempgptr=0x2066a000   byte_count=1596   byte_save=892
DES:
TREE:
SEQ (!:0x20669cbc) (L: 0x20669cac R: 0x0)   (seqline:1 seqaction:1
seqstmttype:0 (GENERIC_TOKEN) seqgoto:0x0   seqprot:0x20669ed4
seqstmt:0x2066a37c  seqsetop:0x0
seqoffset:0   seqstat: 0x800 (POST_10), ) seqcursread: 0x0 0x0)
seqisolation: 0 (NOT_SPECIFIED))
```

```
CMD (L:0x20669cac) (L: 0x20669b7c R: 0x0)
ROOT (L:0x20669b7c) (L: 0x2066a458 R: 0x0)   (querytype:DBCC_CMD
rootname (0x20669ea8):pss  resvar:-1  workvar:-1  varct:0  workct:0
  subqct:0  workrg:0x20669c3c  rootstat:0x1 (USER),   root2stat:0x0
  root3stat:0x0  joindata:0x0  procnum:0  forupdlst: 0x0 )
SUBQUERY LIST: (at 0x20669c6c) (subqct=0) is empty.
  RESDOM (L:0x2066a458)  (resname:  colstat: 0x0 (0x0)  coltype:0x0
(GENERIC_TOKEN)  colen:0  resstat2: 0x0  resstat3: 0x0  resvarno:0
resnamelist: 0x0 )
     RESDOM (L:0x2066a4e4)  (resname:  colstat: 0x0 (0x0)  coltype:0x0
(GENERIC_TOKEN)  colen:0  resstat2: 0x0  resstat3: 0x0  resvarno:0
resnamelist: 0x0 )
       RESDOM (L:0x2066a570)  (resname:  colstat: 0x0 (0x0)  coltype:0x0
(GENERIC_TOKEN)  colen:0  resstat2: 0x0  resstat3: 0x0  resvarno:0
resnamelist: 0x0 )
         INT4 (R:0x2066a5d0)  (L: 0x2066a5d8 ) (prec:0 scale:0 len:4
  maxlen:4 constat: 0x0  value (2066a5f8): 1)
         INT4 (R:0x2066a544)  (L: 0x2066a54c ) (prec:0 scale:0 len:4
  maxlen:4 constat: 0x0  value (2066a56c): 1)
       INT4 (R:0x2066a4b8)  (L: 0x2066a4c0 ) (prec:0 scale:0 len:4
  maxlen:4 constat: 0x0  value (2066a4e0): 1)

DBCC execution completed. If DBCC printed error messages, contact a user
with System Administrator (SA) role.
```

Additional Undocumented DBCC Commands

Finally, for the undocumented DBCC commands, I leave you with a list of values that I couldn't figure out. Therefore, they seem dangerous to play with.

■ DBCC AllocDump(*dbid* | *Database_Name*, *Page*)—I believe that this allocates a dump page for a database table that would be used in the event that an inconsistency in the database allocations were found.

■ DBCC BHash(*Cache_Name* [, { Print_Bufs | No_Print }, Bucket_Limit])—This reports the utilized buckets in the database for your review. This has very little value except in Technical Support situations.

■ DBCC Bytes(Start_Address, Length)—This command I thought would return the memory at a particular location from the server; however, I couldn't figure out the correct format for the Start_Address parameter.

> **CAUTION**
>
> Executing DBCC Bytes without specifying any parameters crashes the server. Don't use the DBCC Bytes command unless you are instructed to do so by Technical Support.

■ DBCC Delete_Row(*dbid* | *Database_Name*, *Page*, Delete_By_Row, *Row_Number*)— This option is used to manually delete a record from a data page without using Transact-SQL. This option would be useful when a database page is corrupted due to invalid data and you can't delete the record with Transact-SQL statements.

Part
IV

Ch
20

■ DBCC `ExtentCheck( dbid, Object_Id, Index_Id, Sorted )`—This DBCC command checks for extents on the specified database, object, and index. The output can be sorted by placing a 1 in the final parameter (a zero indicates unsorted output).

■ DBCC `ExtentDump( dbid, Page )`—This displays information about the database extent on the database and page specified by you. This command is of little value except under the direction of Technical Support.

■ DBCC `ExtentZap( dbid, Object_Id, Index_Id, Sorted )`—This option drops an extent, but I have not tried it.

■ DBCC `FindNotFullExtents( dbid, Object_Id, Index_Id, Sorted )`—This option returns any extents on the given database, object, and index that are not completely filled with data. A high number of records returned here might indicate scattered data on a table and might warrant further inspection.

■ DBCC `LocateIndexPgs( dbid, Object_Id, Page, Index_Id, Level )`—This option searches for the index pages corresponding to data pages on an object, but I have not tried it.

■ DBCC `PgLinkage( dbid, Starting_Page, Number_Of_Pages, Print_Detail, Target_Page, Ordered_Results )`—This option is used by Technical Support to verify that pages in a database table are correctly linked together and are not suffering from page inconsistencies, but I have not tried it.

■ DBCC `ProcBuf( dbid, Object_Id, Number_Of_Buffers, Print_Detail )`—This command provides more detailed information about stored procedures in memory. The same information can be grabbed via DBCC `Memusage` and so this option is of little value unless you have a particular procedure that you want to find out about that isn't in the top five list.

■ DBCC `PrtIPage( dbid, Object_Id, Index_Id, Index_Page)`—This command can be used to dump information about index pages, but I couldn't get it to work.

■ DBCC `RebuildExtents( dbid, Object_Id, Index_Id)`—This command rebuilds the extents used by an index or database object. Unless you are in dire straits, I wouldn't use this option without guidance from Technical Support.

■ DBCC `Show_Bucket( dbid, Object_Id, Lookup_Type)`—This command displays information about hash buckets that are currently allocated on the server, but I haven't tried it.

■ DBCC `Undo( dbid, Page, Row_Number)`—This command is provided to undo a deleted row using DBCC `Delete_Row`; however, I don't know for sure and wouldn't advise that you use this command unless instructed to by Sybase Technical Support.

From Here...

This chapter was devoted to one of the less commonly used—and often misunderstood—components of the Sybase toolset: DBCC. You learned how to use DBCC effectively with the Sybase SQL Server Manager and you also learned the Transact-SQL equivalents of the Sybase

SQL Server Manager screens. Finally, you learned as much as anyone will know about the undocumented features of DBCC and how they can be used on your server to help diagnose problems.

From here, I'd suggest that you look into creating your own scripts that can run in automated fashion to perform regular DBCCs that check for errors on the database and either report them, or try to fix the errors. In addition, you may want to review the following chapters for some extra ideas relating to database management and configuration:

- Chapter 22, "Managing and Monitoring Performance," helps you find out ways to monitor your server to determine good times for performing backups and restores.
- Chapter 23, "Using Sybase's Configuration Options," helps you tune the server with the many different configuration options available to you.

CHAPTER 21

Managing and Monitoring Security

Have you ever wondered how easy it is to gain access to the database? Have you ever woken up in a cold sweat realizing that your sensitive data is open for abuse by internal and external agents to your company or organization? Just about everyone is concerned with the security of data. If you're not, then you may not have considered how easy it is to gain access to sensitive data on your server.

Managing security issues in System XI is a task that shouldn't be taken lightly, and is definitely something that you should carefully plan and organize to be effective. Perhaps more important than establishing security policies on your data at a physical database level is the establishment of policies at a corporate or institutional level. These policies should be mandated by senior management, and your role as a DBA should be simply that of an enforcer from the database server's point of view. If you impose security on a system without the public endorsement from your management team, the chances are that you are going to get a lot of flack and have little ground to stand on.

Learn the difference between logins and users

Sybase System XI manages server access through logins and database access through users. This chapter shows you the difference between logins and users and how to work with both.

Protect your data from unscrupulous browsing and the "casual" data criminal

This chapter introduces you to views and stored procedures as a way of hiding data from users. In addition, you learn how to assign permissions to database objects (such as tables and views) so that you can segment which users can see what information in the database.

Secure your environment

Get suggestions on how to secure not only SQL Server, but also your physical hardware, LAN, WAN, and Internet access.

Use AuditServer to track all access

Ultimately, it's impossible to guard against all database intrusion. However, AuditServer will create the ability to track everything that can happen to the database, and this way you'll be able to see what someone does—even if you can't actually stop it from occurring!

One thing to remember, however, is that sometimes too much security can get in the way of productivity. Make sure that you achieve a balance between your need to manage access to data and monitor users, and the users' needs to *use* the data.

A final introductory caution to you: No document can categorically define every possible security option; however, this chapter's purpose is to illustrate the features that System XI offers and to offer suggestions on what you can do to secure your environment from unauthorized access. ■

Understanding the Principles of Security

Securing your data from internal and external attacks is an important job for you as a database administrator. It is important that you can control who can access your data and how data is accessed on your server. Security in System XI will help you manage the access that you give to your users.

Securing your data from internal attacks is probably your primary concern for most corporate environments. This security will involve the monitoring and management of corporate databases at the direction of the managers of your company. Security is often designed to limit the sorts of data that your employees can see and when they can see it.

Securing your data from external attacks (such as over the Internet) is much more complicated, and is generally applicable only to those companies who are beginning to have an Internet presence with their System XI databases.

This chapter focuses more on internal security. This security will act in a layered approach, starting with logins and user permissions that secure the basic access to the server. The second layer adds views and stored procedures that limit data access. Finally, the third layer is an external security through things like physical LAN access, firewalls, and so on.

When thinking about security, it's probably instructive to get an overview of the principles or types of security that can be enforced in a system. The basic tenets of security that are discussed in this section of the chapter involve four key areas:

- **Discretionary Access Controls**—DAC is designed to enable you to specify who and how a user or group of users may access certain database objects and systems.

- **Authentication**—How do you know that the user making the request for data is who they really say they are? Authentication is the process of guaranteeing that only authorized and valid users can log in and have access to a system.

- **Role Separation**—A key element of security is that you have the ability to separate the powers of security among separate users of the system. This process ensures that even authorized users and system administrators are subject to validation and authorization.

- **Auditing**—Not so much a control mechanism as a means of recording all the events that actually occur, auditing is your system of watching all events, even by so-called trusted users.

Understanding Discretionary Access Controls

To enforce security, you need the ability to define it. DAC is designed to enable you to allocate permissions to the objects that you own. In Transact-SQL language, the method of giving these permissions is done through the Grant and Revoke commands. In System XI, it is possible to Grant or Revoke permissions to any object that you own, or to any object that you have been granted permission on yourself.

If you have the permission to perform a Transact-SQL command, such as Select, from a table, and you have been granted permission to pass on that Select permission, the database server will enable you to do so. That is, you will be allowed to grant a Select permission to another user or group of users, but that is the only control you can pass on to another user or group.

Some options and objects within the database can be accessed only by certain classes of users, and the permissions to these objects cannot be assigned or granted to any other users of the system.

Understanding Authentication

Sybase supports the separation of access to the server and the ability to use a particular data-base. Every user on a server is granted or created a login to the server with a unique system-assigned user ID. This ID is stored in the *suid* column of the system catalog table *syslogins* that is in the *master* database. This user or login account has the ability to connect to the server, but nothing else. Associated with that user or login is a password that is encrypted in a one-way encryption scheme that compares encrypted passwords on the server. There is no way to decrypt a server-stored password unlike some databases, such as Centura's SQLBase product, that permits a system administrator to decrypt the user's password with the @Decrypt system function.

Not only can the password be stored in an encrypted fashion, but you also can encrypt the password as it is sent across the network. This is highly recommended on environments and networks that are exposed on public networks, such as the Internet or over CompuServe's public backbone. If a password is not encrypted when sent across a network, it is a relatively straightforward task for a hacker to trap the data stream going across the network and then be able to access your system using the password that is extracted from the text stream.

Understanding the Separation of Roles

Most high-end security systems and users of secure data require that no single user has the power to completely and independently operate on the system regardless of the level of *trust* or *authority* that the user is supposed to have. Role separation is designed to permit the creation of an environment where everyone, irrespective of their system level, is subject to a review by a peer.

Role separation is well established in the banking community and an example can be found in the way DES encryption keys are stored and managed at a bank. DES encryption keys are

Part

IV

Ch

21

required to access ATM switch networks and are stored at a bank in the event that a computer system goes down and the switch connection needs to be renegotiated between the ATM switch and the bank. The DES key is actually made up of two components or pieces that are either stored electronically or on paper. Both parts of the key are required for successful negotiation with the network, and one part on its own is of little value.

The bank or switch network is required to store each part of the key in separate safes that are easily accessible but only operable by two different people within the bank or switch that have separate and independent combinations and are required to work in conjunction with each other to put together both pieces of the key. No person in the institution is permitted to know both combinations to the safes.

In a similar fashion, you will be able to separate those users who can perform system security critical operations within your site by adopting the use of roles that Sybase System XI provides.

Understanding Auditing

The purpose of auditing is to monitor all operations on specified resources on the server. Auditing is not designed as a preventive measure, but is designed to recognize that a security is ultimately only as secure as a single password. If that password is compromised, auditing is designed to at least track the effects of the unauthorized access.

Auditing also works in some institutions and organizations that require a full system-generated audit trail of all trusted users. By using the auditing capabilities of Sybase's AuditServer, you will be able to track everything that occurs on your server right down to the individual Transact-SQL statements that were executed on the server itself.

 You can use the results of the audit trail as a good way to get a feel for the way the system is being used. You will be able to see the amount and type of transactions that are being performed on the databases that are being audited. Using this information is a good empirical way of determining the performance of your system.

Managing Logins and Users

System XI separates or distinguishes between Logins and Users of a server and database. The distinction is made so that you can have different databases on a single server that are independently accessible to different groups of users and yet still maintain a single point of control when it comes to managing the physical connection to the server itself. This practice of separation of database access from the physical connection to the server is a pretty common way of managing security for server-based operating systems, such as Novell NetWare or Microsoft Windows NT Advanced Server. The corresponding relationship is that you have a login to the network (a Login to a Sybase server) and then are granted access to particular resources or directories on the network server (like a User being granted access to a particular database on the System XI server).

On UNIX-based implementations of Sybase, the login to the Sybase server typically does not have authority to connect to the UNIX server because they don't require access to the UNIX operating system on the server. Thus, on UNIX, there's no concept of an operating system user; the connection to the database server is completely independent of the underlying OS. This is why in most UNIX-based environments, the minimum number of concurrent user connections version of the OS is purchased, because the user of the Sybase database is not actually a connection to the OS, but just a TCP/IP access thread to the Sybase server's IP manager.

On Windows NT, Sybase was required to introduce a new or different level of integration with the operating system, due to Windows NT's design goal of providing a single login to all of the resources on the server. Under Windows NT's security model, the operating system is required to authenticate a user and then that user no longer is required to enter a password to access any resources that he or she has been granted access to by an appropriately empowered user or administrator of the Windows NT server itself. The advantage of this is obvious—one password to be remembered by the user, and consolidated login management facilities similar to those offered on many mainframe managed security systems, such as Computer Associates' TopSecret. This security model is known as a *Trusted Secure* environment, where each application (such as Sybase System XI) on the server trusts that the operating system will correctly authenticate the resources that a user may have access to, and once that trust has been established, will allow access to the application without the need for additional verification.

On Windows NT, the additional security or login management functionality option is described as `Integrated Security`. However, if you want to have Sybase still manage the user's authentication process, you can use the `Standard Security` that is installed by default when you install the server.

Configuring Sybase on Windows NT to Support Integrated Security

If you want the Windows NT-based Sybase System XI server to support Sybase's Integrated Security that means logins are managed by Windows NT, you should follow these steps:

1. Launch the Server Config utility that was installed in the Sybase for Windows NT folder on your desktop (see Fig. 21.1).

FIG. 21.1
The Configure Sybase Server dialog box makes it easy for you to access key server-based configuration options for any of the Servers (such as Data Servers, Backup Servers, and Monitor Servers) that you have installed on this particular Windows NT machine.

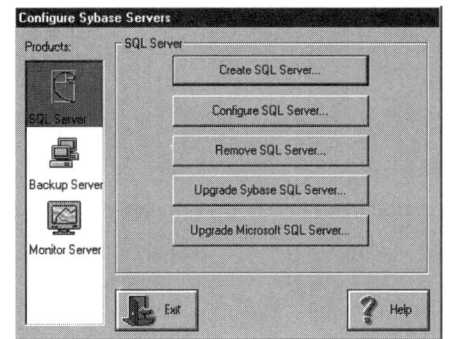

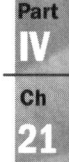

Part
IV

Ch
21

2. Click the Configure SQL Server button and select the server you want to manage from the provided list shown in the Existing Servers dialog box (see Fig. 21.2).

FIG. 21.2

The Existing Servers dialog box lists all the servers that you have defined in the interfaces file (SQL.INI).

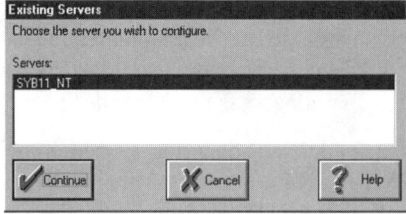

3. Enter the System Administrator's (sa) password and continue to display the Configure SQL Server dialog box, as shown below in Figure 21.3.

FIG. 21.3

Using the Configure SQL Server dialog box, you can (among other things) change sort orders, character sets, and auditing capabilities of the server being managed.

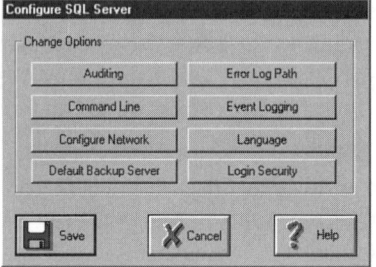

4. Click the Login Security button to display the Login Security Options dialog box (see Fig. 21.4).

FIG. 21.4

The Login Security Options dialog box shows the currently configured security scheme and enables you to change the scheme for the server.

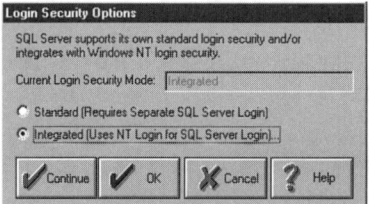

5. Click the Integrated (Uses NT Login for the SQL Server login) option and click OK. This returns you to the main Configure SQL Server dialog box shown in Figure 21.1.

6. Click the Save button to Save the changes and restart the SQL Server, if necessary.

Note, by installing the Integrated Security option, you are allowing the Windows NT machine to permit trusted connections to the Sybase database. This option is, however, available only for connections that are established with the Named Pipes communication protocol. To get more information on the particulars of the connection characteristics, click the Continue button that is available on the Login Security Options dialog box shown in Figure 21.4. By clicking the Continue button, you will be presented with the Integrated Login Options dialog box shown in Figure 21.5.

FIG. 21.5

The Integrated Login Options dialog box enables you to configure a mixed security mode where a Trusted Login is used for Named Pipe connections and non-Trusted Logins are used for any other communications protocols (such as TCP/IP).

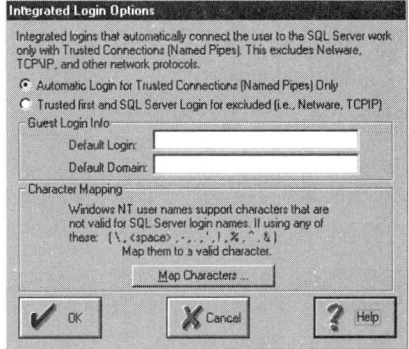

Use the Integrated Login Options dialog box to specify how connections should be managed, and if you want to supply the login to use in the event that a Sybase login hasn't been created for a user that is accessing the Sybase server (a Guest login), you can do that here, too.

Sybase's requirements for user or login names are a little more stringent than those of Microsoft's Windows NT. In Windows NT, you can use the following characters in a user's login name that are invalid in System XI: \, -, ., ', !, %, ^, &. Sybase's Integrated Login management provides you a way of mapping those characters to defaults when connecting to the server. Click the Map Characters button on the Integrated Login Options dialog box (see Fig. 21.5). Using the Character Mapping dialog box shown in Figure 21.6, you can define the way characters should be mapped between the operating system's login name and Sybase's trusted login name.

FIG. 21.6

The Character Mapping dialog box enables you to specify up to four characters that should be mapped from a Windows NT's login name to valid characters for a Sybase System XI login.

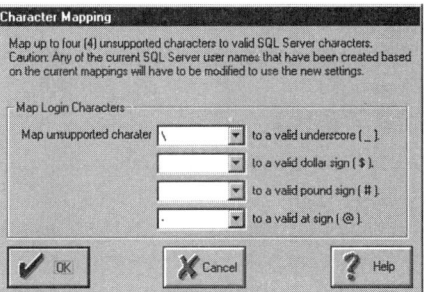

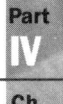

Part
IV

Ch
21

Using Integrated Security When System XI is run on Windows NT, Sybase can take advantage of, and integrate into, Windows NT's excellent security system. When operating in integrated security mode, Windows NT is responsible for managing user connections through its

Access Control List (ACL). The advantages of integrated security include single-password access to all resources on a Windows NT domain and password aging and encryption across the network.

When a user establishes a trusted connection to the System XI, the user is either

- Mapped to an existing System XI login if a name match is found;
- Connected as the default login (usually *guest*);
- Connected as SA if the user is the administrator on the Windows NT system.

All other database-based permissions, such as permissions on tables, views, and other objects, are managed by System XI in the same way as a server running in standard security mode. These security permissions are discussed in the section titled "Working with User Privileges."

Using Standard Security In Standard Security mode, System XI is wholly responsible for managing and maintaining accounts on the server. In this case, System XI is responsible for authenticating a user and for enforcing password/login restrictions. This is the most common way of configuring System XI because it behaves identically to Sybase on any hardware platform. The majority of the rest of this chapter covers the features of standard security. For more information on Windows NT's integrated security system, refer to Que's *Special Edition Using Windows NT Server*.

N O T E Standard security should be used when there are no Windows NT servers being used for file server duties. In this case, Windows NT's integrated security mechanisms provide no benefit to the System XI. Also, standard security should be used when you expect that various different protocols will be used to attach to the server. ■

Using Mixed Security Mixed security, as its name implies, is a combination of both standard and integrated security and means that users can login to the server in either way. When a user connects to a System XI in mixed security mode, the server validates the login by first checking whether the login name has already established a trusted connection to the NT server. If no connection is found, System XI then performs its own validation of the login name and password supplied. If the requested login is not a known System XI login, access is denied.

Understanding Logins and Users

System XI has two levels of a user that are important to understand. The first level of a user is a *login*. A login is the ability to attach to the Sybase server itself. System XI manages logins on a server-wide basis. All logins are stored in the *syslogins* table of the *master* database. The second level of a user is a *user*. Users are System XI's way of managing who has permissions to interact with resources (such as tables and stored procedures) in a given database. A user can be in one or many databases. All users are stored in the *sysusers* table of each database for which they have permission to access.

System XI uses these distinctions to enable a single user to have different levels of access based on the database that they are connecting to, and yet retain the same password. To support this, a user has a login or connection permission to the server. This login is what System XI associates a password to. Without a valid login to the server, a user will not have access to any of the server's databases with the possible exception of remote systems using remote stored procedures.

Once a login is created, it is then necessary to create a user of a database on that server. This process is very similar to creating a System XI system login and is described in the following sections.

You can create a login using either Sybase SQL Server Manager or the Transact-SQL Command sp_addlogin. Using Sybase SQL Server Manager is often convenient, because it simplifies connecting to many different servers and enables you to specify additional features of the user's login (such as roles that the user will be granted) in one place without you needing to perform additional manual steps.

Using Sybase SQL Server Manager to Add a Login   To use Sybase SQL Server Manager to add a login to a server, follow these steps:

1. Launch Sybase SQL Server Manager and login as the System Administrator (sa) to the server that you want to work with.

2. Choose Server, Create, and select Login to display the Sybase SQL Server Manager Create Login dialog box (see Fig. 21.7).

FIG. 21.7
The SSM Create Login dialog box simplifies login creation because it enables you to easily assign roles to the login being created.

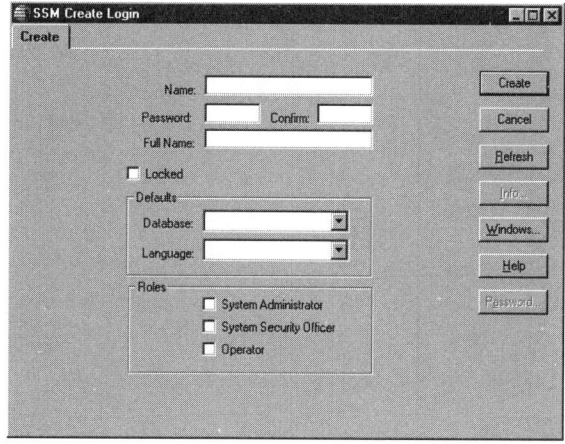

3. Enter the name of the user login (up to 30 characters).

4. Enter a password for the user and confirm what you typed in the Confirm field.

CAUTION
Check only the Locked option if you want to lock (restrict access) to the login until a later time. If you lock an account, the user will not be able to connect to the database until you unlock the account with the system-stored procedure sp_locklogin.

Part
IV

Ch
21

5. Enter an optional Full Name for the login.

6. Specify the Default Database and Language to use for the login.

7. Check any of the roles that you want the user to be granted.

8. Click the Create button to create the user. This will create the user and display output indicating the success or failure of the creation, as shown in Figure 21.8.

FIG. 21.8

The SSM Output window shows that the user's login was successfully created and that the authorization was updated three times (because the user was granted the three available security roles).

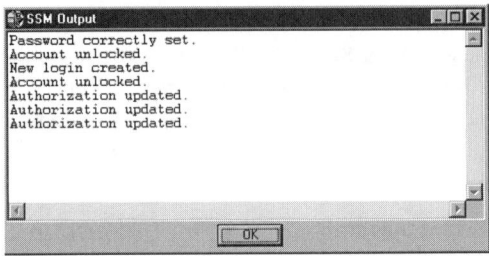

After you have created a login using Sybase SQL Server Manager, the main login dialog box will change and add two tabs that you can use to view additional properties about the login including the databases that the login owns and the databases that the login has access to (see Fig. 21.9).

FIG. 21.9

This is the SSM Login dialog box after adding the login Raistlin to the system.

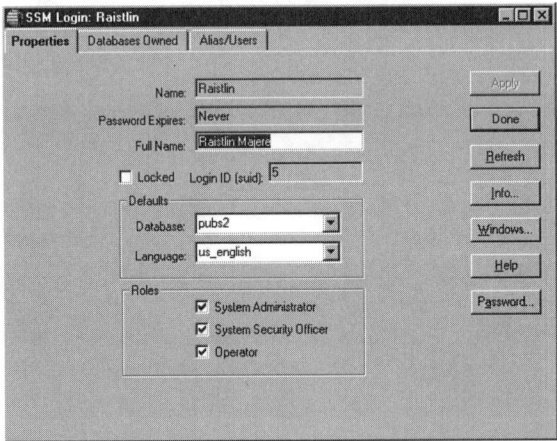

Using Sybase SQL Server Manager to Add a User to a Database To use Sybase SQL Server Manager to add a user to a database, follow these steps:

1. Launch Sybase SQL Server Manager and login as the System Administrator (sa) to the server that you want to work with.

2. Open the database that you want to manage in the left pane of the explorer and click the Users folder.

3. Choose <u>D</u>atabase, Crea<u>t</u>e, and select <u>U</u>ser to display the Sybase SQL Server Manager Create User dialog box (see Fig. 21.10).

FIG. 21.10
The SSM Create User dialog box is ready to add the user Raistlin to the *pubs2* database.

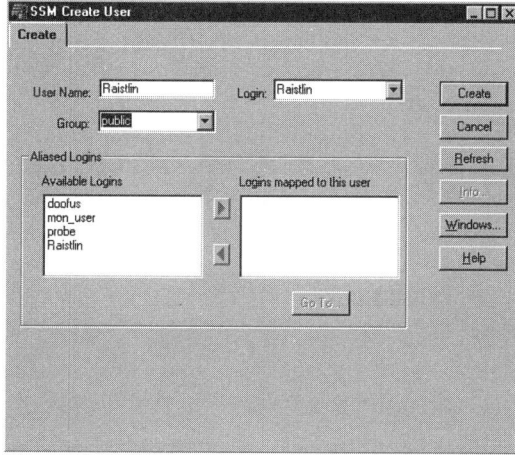

4. Enter the name of the user that you want the login to be known by (usually the same as the login name).

5. Choose the login from the login list that you are adding to the database.

6. Optionally specify the security group in which you want this user to be placed.

7. Use the aliasing features of this window if you want this login to be connected to this database through an existing alias on the server.

8. Click the Create button to create the user; this will alter the display of the dialog box and will add three tabs (Object Permissions, Objects Owned, and Command Permissions) that display additional information about the user in the database (see Fig. 21.11).

FIG. 21.11
The SSM User dialog box gives you comprehensive access to all the objects and permissions that a user (such as Raistlin) has created or been granted.

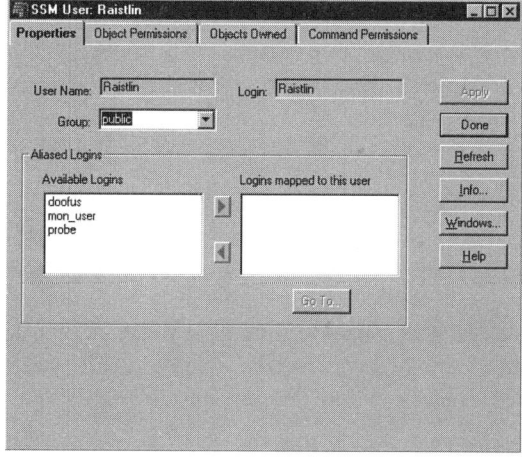

Part
IV

Ch
21

Using Sybase SQL Server Manager to Drop a Login or User Dropping a login or user with Sybase SQL Server Manager is a straightforward task that involves navigating through the explorer to the login on the server or user on a particular database (following the same steps outlined in the preceding two sections) and then clicking the login or user. From either the Login or User menu, select Delete to drop the login or user; you will be given a prompt message to confirm that you really want to drop the login or user, to which you should respond Yes and the login or user will be dropped.

> **N O T E** Note that you can't drop a login that owns any objects in a database or that has been created as a user in a database. You must first drop the user from the database before you drop the login from the server.

Using sp_addlogin to Add Logins to a Server The system-stored procedure sp_addlogin is provided in Transact-SQL to add a login to the server. The syntax for sp_addlogin is as follows:

```
sp_addlogin Login_Id, Password [, DefaultDB [, DefaultLanguage [,FullName ] ] ] ]
```

The options for the system-stored procedure sp_addlogin are as follows:

- *Login_Id*—This is the name of the login being added. A login follows standard System XI naming conventions.
- *Password*—This is the password to be assigned the login. Passwords must be supplied and must be at least six characters long. If you supply a password that's less than six characters, Sybase will return an error.
- *DefaultDB*—This is the default database that the Sybase should place the login in after connecting to the database. If left Null, Sybase leaves the login in the master database.
- *DefaultLanguage*—This is the default language that should be assigned to the login. If left Null, System XI assigns the default language for the server.
- *FullName*—This an optional full name of the user that will be displayed when you inquire on the user's information by selecting from *syslogins*.

 T I P The user can change his or her password at any time using the sp_password stored procedure. For example, sp_password 'Agent99', 'MaxwellSmart' changes the currently connected user's password from Agent99 to MaxwellSmart.

The following is an example of creating a login to the server with the default database of *pubs* and a password of Allen.

```
sp_addlogin 'Ronald', 'Allen', pubs2
Go
```

Using sp_adduser to Add a New User to a Database The system-stored procedure sp_adduser is similar in style to the sp_addlogin procedure. It takes an existing login and adds it to the currently active database. Note that you must issue a use database *Database_Name* and be in the required database to add a user to before running the `sp_adduser` stored procedure.

```
sp_adduser Login_Id [, UserName [, GrpName]]
```

The options for the system-stored procedure `sp_adduser` are as follows:

- `Login_Id`—This is the name of the login being added as a user to the database. Invalid logins will not be added to the database.

- `UserName`—This is provided to allow logins to be *aliased* in a database. This allows the same login to connect to different databases on the same server and have different names in each database.

- `GrpName`—This allows the specification of a user group to which the user will belong. Using groups simplifies security because instead of granting permissions to individual users, the permissions can be granted to the group and then all members of the group receive them.

Below is an example of adding a user to the currently active database. Because no username is supplied, the `Login_Id` is assumed for the username.

```
sp_adduser 'Ronald'
Go
```

Using sp_droplogin and sp_dropuser to Remove Logins and Users   To remove a login or user from the server or database, execute the system procedures `sp_droplogin` or `sp_dropuser`. Their syntax is very similar, especially when the username chosen for a given login to a database is the same as the `Login_Id`.

```
sp_droplogin Login_Id
```

and

```
sp_dropuser UserName
```

Understanding User Groups

System XI provides the ability to create groups of users so that security permissions granted to all members are the same. This provides far greater simplicity and is a more practical approach to security than granting individual users specific permissions on any particular set of tables. Most installations of Sybase use security groups to help manage the complex security allocated to particular objects in the database.

A group is really just a name of a set of security permissions; creating a group can be done either with Sybase SQL Server Manager or with the system-stored procedure `sp_addgroup`.

Using Sybase SQL Server Manager to Work with Groups   To create a group with Sybase SQL Server Manager, follow these steps:

1. Launch Sybase SQL Server Manager and login to the server that you need to work on.

2. Using the database explorer, navigate to the correct database, and click the Groups folder in the left pane.

Part

IV

Ch

21

3. Choose Database, Create, and select Group to display the Sybase SQL Server Manager Create Group dialog box (see Fig. 21.12).

FIG. 21.12
The SSM Create Group dialog box enables you to specify a name for the group, and optionally join available users in the database to the group.

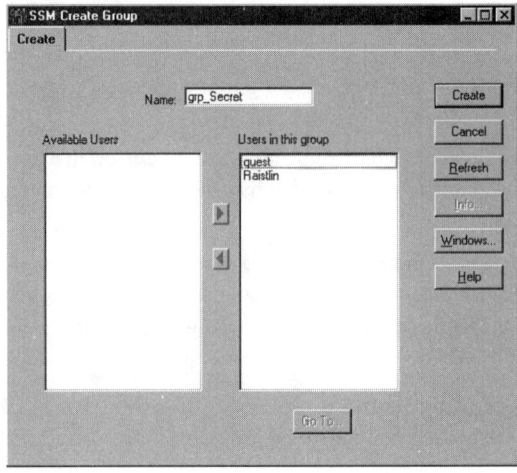

4. Enter a name for the group and move any users that you want to be a member of the group from the list of Available Users to the list of Users in This Group.

5. Click the Create button to create the group.

 TIP   A good naming convention to use for a group prefix is `grp_`. You can see a list of suggested naming prefixes in Appendix A, "Suggestions for Naming Conventions."

To drop a group with Sybase SQL Server Manager, navigate to the group that you want to remove with the explorer. Click the group, and from the Group menu, select Delete. Removing a group will not remove any users associated with those groups. Any permissions granted to users because they were members of the groups will be revoked.

Using Transact-SQL to Work with Groups   To create a group with Transact-SQL, you use the system-stored procedure `sp_addgroup`. The syntax for the use of `sp_addgroup` is as follows:

```
sp_addgroup Group_Name
```

`Group_Name` is the name of the group that you want to add. For example, if you wanted to add a group called `Grp_Secret`, you would execute:

```
sp_addgroup Grp_Secret
Go
- - - - - - - - - - - - - - - - - - - - - - - - -
New group added.
```

To drop a group, you use the system-stored procedure `sp_dropgroup`. The syntax for `sp_dropgroup` is the same as `sp_addgroup`. For example, to drop the group `Grp_Secret`, you would execute:

```
sp_dropgroup Grp_Secret
Go
------------------------
Group dropped.
```

Working with User Privileges

Permissions are the rights to access an object (such as a table) in the database. Permissions are granted to a user or group to allow that user or group to perform functions, such as select data, add new rows (insert), and update data. Several permissions exist on objects in the database and descriptions follow.

Permissions are implicitly granted to the owner or creator of an object. The owner can then decide to grant permissions to other users or groups as that user sees fit. Special permissions exist for owners of a database and users with the System Administrator role:

- The *Database Owner (dbo)* has full permissions on all objects in the database that he owns.
- The *System Administrator (sa)* has full permissions on all objects in all databases on the server.

System XI provides the `Grant` and `Revoke` commands to give or take away permission from a user. Sybase SQL Server Manager also provides an easy way to add and remove permissions.

Working with Object Permissions

Object permissions are the permissions to act on tables and other objects (such as stored procedures and views) in the database.

The following is a list of permissions available on tables and their descriptions:

- `Select` enables a user to select or read data from a table or view. Note that a `Select` permission can be granted to individual columns within a table or view, not just the entire table.
- `Insert` enables a user to add data to a table or view.
- `Update` enables a user to change data in a table or view. Note that an `Update` permission can be granted to individual columns within a table or view, not just the entire table.
- `Delete` enables a user to remove data from a table or view.
- `Execute` enables a user to execute a stored procedure.
- `DRI/References` enables a user to add foreign key constraints on a table.
- `DDL/Data Definition Language` enables a user to create, alter, or drop objects in the database. Examples are `Create Table`, `Drop Database`, `Alter Table`.
- `All` enables the user full permissions on the object. Note that only the SA can use `All` when DDL statements are being used.

Part
IV

Ch
21

Using Sybase SQL Server Manager to Grant and Revoke Permissions   Sybase SQL Server Manager makes it really easy to manage and work with permissions that belong to a user or group. To grant or revoke permissions from a particular user or group, follow these steps:

1. Launch Sybase SQL Server Manager and login to the server.

2. Connect to the database that has the user that you want to manage.

3. Open the Users or Groups folder depending on whether you are working on an indi-vidual user or a group.

4. Right-click the user or group that you want to work on and select Properties from the context menu that is displayed.

5. On the Sybase SQL Server Manager User dialog box that is displayed (see Fig. 21.11), click the Object Permissions tab to display the tab that will enable you to change the permissions for a given object or objects in the database (see Fig. 21.13).

FIG. 21.13

The Object Permissions tab has object and permission filters in the top left that make it easy to exclude certain objects and granted options.

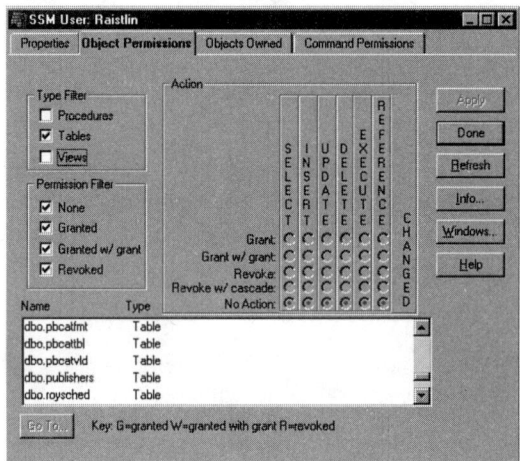

6. Highlight the object that you want to grant or revoke permissions from and make your selection from the Action group's list of available options.

7. Grant or revoke the required permissions from any other objects that you want to change, and then press the Apply button to have Sybase SQL Server Manager apply the changes to the database.

Using Transact-SQL's Grant and Revoke Commands   System XI's Transact-SQL interface to permissions is through the Grant and Revoke statements.

The Grant Transact-SQL command is used to give a permission or permissions to a user or group in System XI. Granting a permission allows the user or group to perform the granted permission.

The syntax for using the `Grant` command is as follows:

```
Grant Permission_List
On    Object_Name
To    Name_List
[With Grant Option]
```

Use the `Revoke` command to revoke permissions from a user. It's the opposite of `Grant` and is designed to undo or remove any permissions granted from a user or group.

The syntax for the Transact-SQL command `Revoke` is essentially the same as the `Grant` command and is as follows:

```
Revoke Permission_List
On    Object_Name
From  Name_List
```

The options for the Transact-SQL commands `Grant` and `Revoke` are as follows:

- *Permission_List*—The values for *Permission_List* is a list of permissions being granted or revoked. Multiple permissions should be comma-separated. If `All` is specified, then all permissions that the grantor has will be granted to the grantee.

- *Object_Name*—This is a table, view, or stored procedure for which permissions are being granted or revoked.

- *Name_List*—This is a list of user names or groups for which permissions are being granted or revoked. Multiple names should be separated by commas. Specifying *Public* will include all users.

- `With Grant Option`—If `With Grant Option` is appended to a grant statement, it will enable the grantee to also grant his rights to other users. This is a nice option, but it should be used very sparingly—if not only by the system administrator, for security reasons.

The following example grants `Select` and `Update` permissions on the `authors` table:

```
Grant  Select, Update
On     authors
To     public
Go
```

The following example revokes `Delete` permissions on the `sales` table:

```
Revoke  Delete
On      sales
From    public
Go
```

Using Views and Stored Procedures as Security Methods

Views provide a great way to enhance security because they limit the data that is available to a user. For example, you can have a group of users in Grp_Junior_Emp that are not allowed to view any of the authors that receive more than 50 percent royalties because these are to be available only to the senior managers or other employees within the company. Once you have created an exclusive view, you can then grant particular rights to that view that can eliminate the ability to Insert or Update statements to the underlying data (see Listing 21.1).

Listing 21.1   CHP22_01.SQL—Using Views and Groups to Help Secure the Authors Table

```
/*
   This script demonstrates the way
   views can be used to limit security and
   how groups can be used to manage the security
   permissions that are granted
*/
/* First add the group */
sp_addgroup Grp_Junior_Emp
Go

/* now revoke select on the base tables from the public group */
Revoke Select
On     titleauthor
From   public
Go

Revoke Select
On     authors
From   public
Go

/* now create the view that limits access */
Create View Vie_Authors
As
Select *
From   authors
Where  au_id in (Select au_id
                 From   titleauthor
                 Where  royaltyper <= 50)
Go

/* grant select on the view to the members of the group */
Grant Select
On     Vie_Authors
To     Grp_Junior_Emp
Go
```

Stored procedures can be used in a very similar fashion to views to provide a level of security on the data that completely conceals the data available to a user and/or the business processes involved in manipulating the data.

In Listing 21.2, you can see the same data concealment as demonstrated in using the view in Listing 21.1 except that it is achieved through the use of a stored procedure.

Listing 21.2 CHP22_02.SQL—Stored Procedures Can Be Used to Hide the Underlying Data

```
/*
   This script demonstrates the way
   stored procedures can be used to limit security and
   how groups can be used to manage the security
   permissions that are granted
*/
/* First add the group */
sp_addgroup Grp_Junior_Emp
Go

/* now revoke select on the base tables from the public group */
Revoke Select
On     titleauthor
From   public
Go

Revoke Select
On     authors
From   public
Go

/* now create the stored procedure that limits access */
Create Procedure up_SelectAuthors
As
Select *
From   authors
Where  au_id in (Select au_id
                 From    titleauthor
                 Where   royaltyper <= 50)
Go

/* grant execute on the view to the members of the group */
Grant Execute
On     up_SelectAuthors
To     Grp_Junior_Emp
go
```

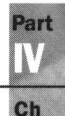

Part

IV

Ch

21

In Listing 21.3, the junior employees are allowed to update the contract flag on the AUTHORS table without having permission to update anything else on the table. This is the sort of procedure that enables you to hide data manipulation from the users while still giving them limited power to work on the data available to them in the server.

> **Listing 21.3 CHP22_03.SQL—Using a Stored Procedure to Limit Updates of the Authors Table**

```
/*
   This script demonstrates the way
   stored procedures can be used to limit security and
   yet still provide the ability to manipulate the data
   in the tables.
*/

/* First add the group */
sp_addgroup Grp_Junior_Emp
Go

/* now revoke privileges on the base table from the public group */


Revoke Update, Delete, Insert
On      authors
From    public
Go

/* now create the stored procedure that limits access */
Create Procedure up_SetStateForAuthor
        @pnAu_Id  char(11),
        @psState  char(2)
As
Update authors
Set     state = @psState
Where   au_id = @pnAu_Id

Print "Author's state modified."
Go

/* grant execute on the view to the members of the group */
Grant Execute
On      up_SetStateForAuthor
To      Grp_Junior_Emp
Go
```

Understanding and Using AuditServer

AuditServer is a component of the Sybase toolset that originally shipped as a feature of System 10. AuditServer is a unique tool that enables a full audit trail to be generated and captured for all activity on the server. The purpose of AuditServer is to act as a monitor. Eventually, you are going to come to the conclusion that all security is subject to the effectiveness of password management. If you have lax password security or you have unscrupulous employees at your corporation or organization, then you are open to fraud and other kinds of data abuse.

This limitation of the security system is addressed by an audit trail. Ultimately, you can't stop an operation from taking place; however, you can at least monitor it and then take actions following the event to trace the person who performed the operation.

AuditServer works by installing a new database on your server *sybsecurity*. This database is used as a storage area for the audit trail and is managed by a new process that is installed and made current on your server called the `Audit Process`. You can see the audit process in action by performing the system-stored procedure `sp_who` on the server. For example:

```
sp_who
Go
spid status    loginame hostname   blk   dbname    cmd
---- --------  -------- ---------- ----  --------- ----------------
   2 sleeping                       0     master    NETWORK HANDLER
   3 sleeping                       0     master    DEADLOCK TUNE
   4 sleeping                       0     master    MIRROR HANDLER
   5 sleeping                       0     master    HOUSEKEEPER
   6 sleeping                       0     master    SHUTDOWN HANDLER
   7 sleeping                       0     master    AUDIT PROCESS
   8 sleeping                       0     master    CHECKPOINT SLEEP
   9 running   sa       RapidSQL    0     master    SELECT
```

The purpose of the Audit Process is to monitor all transactions that you specify and then write an entry to the audit trail table *sysaudits* in the *sybsecurity* database. Any transaction that requires auditing is first written to an in-memory queue before being written to the disk for performance. This provides a substantial benefit because all auditable transactions can be written in a batch to the *sysaudits* table with larger IOs. However, the danger of using the in-memory queue is that these transactions will be lost if the server is brought down before the queue is written to disk. You must evaluate the performance requirements for your system and compare these needs to the need to have a full and comprehensive audit queue. The size of the audit queue can be managed with the system-stored procedure `sp_configure` and the parameter `audit queue size`.

▶ **See** "Configuring and Managing Servers," **p. 635**

Configuring Sybase to Use AuditServer

The first step to get AuditServer operational is to install the database *sybsecurity* and make it available. On UNIX, you will need to use the *SybInit* program, the documentation for which can be found in the Installation Guide for your particular operating system platform. You can also install AuditServer using the tools supplied for Windows NT on the Windows NT version of Sybase System XI. To enable auditing using AuditServer, follow these steps:

1. Launch the Server Config utility from the Sybase for Windows NT folder on the Start Menu (see Fig. 21.1).

2. Click the Configure Server button and log into the server as the System Administrator (sa).

3. Click the Auditing button to display the Activate Auditing dialog box (see Fig. 21.14).

FIG. 21.14

The Activate Auditing dialog box enables you to specify the size of the *sybsecurity* database that will be installed. Sizing the database is going to take some practice and will depend on the types of activity that you are going to monitor on the server.

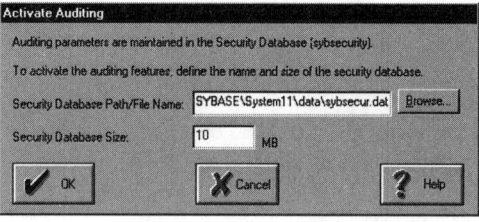

4. Enter the name of the data file that you want to use (the default will be *sybsecur.dat*) and the directory that you want to store it in.

If you are expecting heavy amounts of activity on the *sybsecurity* database due to auditing, you may want to consider placing the database on another physical device (i.e., a separate drive) to isolate the I/Os from the main devices that are serving data requests for the users.

5. Enter the size of the database in megabytes.
6. Click OK to close the Activate Auditing dialog box.
7. Click the Save button on the Configure SQL Server dialog box (see Fig. 21.1) to get the Server Config utility to add the *sybsecurity* database. (This task may take some time.)

CAUTION

The Sybase Server Config utility will redefine your interfaces file (SQL.INI) after the database is added, and will shut down the server and bring it back up for you. This can cause problems if you are relying on the SQL.INI file for anything other than Windows NT (Win32) type connections. You will need to use SQLEdit to re-add the supporting INI file entries required for things like 16-bit Windows or OS/2 support. For more information on using SQLEdit, see Chapter 3, "Installing Sybase."

Activating the Audit Trail

After you have installed the *sybsecurity* system database, you need to activate the audit trail. This is done by using the system-stored procedure `sp_auditoption` with the `Enable Auditing` parameter. To enable the audit trail, you would execute:

```
sp_auditoption "Enable Auditing", "On"
Go
```

Using the Auditing Stored Procedures

There are a number of system-stored procedures that are provided for you to manage the Audit trail in the database. These procedures should be used carefully and with consideration on the huge performance impact that can be felt on the database server if they are activated.

Using sp_auditoption   The system-stored procedure `sp_auditoption` is provided to manage the global controls for AuditServer, and its syntax is a bit like that of DBCC. Depending on the command being performed, it has different options. The overall syntax of `sp_auditoption` can be summarized like this:

```
sp_auditoption [Parameter, Switch_Setting]
```

`Parameter` can take a number of possible values, and `Switch_Setting` can be either `"On"`, `"Off"`, `"OK"`, `"Fail"`, `"Both"`, `"Fatal"`, or `"NonFatal,"` depending on the `Parameter` you are changing. All parameters require that you place them in quotation marks to work. If you supply no parameters to `sp_auditoption`, it will return the current global settings:

```
sp_auditoption
Go

name                          sval
----------------------------  ------
enable auditing               on
logins                        off
logouts                       off
server boots                  off
rpc connections               off
roles                         off
sa commands                   off
sso commands                  off
oper commands                 off
navigator commands            off
errors                        off
adhoc records                 off
replication commands          off
```

For example, to enable the audit of the booting of the server, you would execute:

```
sp_auditoption "Server Boots", "On"
Go
```

If you wanted to trap the failed logins, you would execute:

```
sp_auditoption "logins", "fail"
Go
```

If you were concerned about the super users having unmonitored access to the system, you would execute something like this:

```
sp_auditoption "sa commands", "Both"
Go
```

```
sp_auditoption "SSO commands", "Both"
Go
sp_auditoption "Oper commands", "Both"
Go
```

Using sp_auditlogin The system-stored procedure `sp_auditlogin` is provided to help you configure the auditing that will occur for an individual login to the server. The syntax for `sp_auditlogin` is as follows:

```
sp_auditlogin [Login_Name] [, "Table" | "View" | "CmdText" ]
              [, "Ok" | "Fail" | "Both" | "On" | "Off"]
```

The `Table` and `View` options are provided so that you can monitor successful and unsuccessful attempts to access data on either tables or views. The `CmdText` option enables you to monitor the individual SQL that is being used for every command being sent to the server.

For example, to monitor the user Raistlin's unsuccessful table accesses, you would execute:

```
sp_auditlogin Raistlin, "Table", "Fail"
Go
```

To track every SQL Statement made by the System Administrator, you would execute:

```
sp_auditlogin sa, "CmdText", "On"
Go
```

> **CAUTION**
>
> Monitoring SQL statements using the AuditServer consumes large amounts of disk space. Unless you have a particular reason to enable this feature, you are cautioned not to. It is quite likely you will run out of disk space more quickly than you expect with `CmdText` auditing enabled.

Using sp_auditdatabase The purpose of the system-stored procedure `sp_auditdatabase` is to provide you with a mechanism for tracking database-wide activities that occur that are normally non-logged operations (events that wouldn't normally be written to the transaction log).

The syntax for the use of `sp_auditdatabase` is as follows:

```
sp_auditdatabase [dbname [, "Ok" | "Fail" | "Both" | "Off"
[, {"d u g r t o"}]]]
```

dbname is the name of the database that you want to modify the auditing on, the single character values are as follows:

- d—Audit the execution of `Drop` statements, such as `Drop Table`
- u—Audit the `Use` command
- g—Audit the `Grant` command
- r—Audit the `Revoke` command
- t—Audit the use of the `Truncate Table` command
- o—Audit remote database object referencing that occurs when you perform a request from inside one database to fetch data from a table in another database

For example, to monitor all the successful and unsuccessful grants and revokes that occur in the *pubs2* database, you would execute:

```
sp_auditdatabase pubs2, "Both", "gr"
Go
```

Using sp_auditobject   To enable object-level audit trails of specific events, you use the system-stored procedure `sp_auditobject`. By using `sp_auditobject`, you can specify which events on a particular object are monitored and tracked. The syntax for `sp_auditobject` is as follows:

```
sp_auditobject objname, dbname
[, {"Ok" | "Fail" | "Both" | "Off"}
    [, "{d i s u}"]]
```

objname and *dbname* are the object and database that you are monitoring. If the object that you are auditing is not owned by the database owner (`dbo`), you will need to enclose the *objname* parameter in quotation marks and include the owner's name (e.g., `"Raistlin.Wizardry_Table"`). The values `d`, `i`, `s`, and `u` correspond to `Delete`, `Insert`, `Select`, and `Update`.

For example, to monitor all the failed deletes that occur on the *authors* table, you would execute:

```
sp_auditobject authors, pubs2, "Fail", "d"
Go
```

N O T E   The *objname* can be a special value of `"Default Table"` or `"Default View"` to track all tables created after the execution of `sp_auditobject` with the same criteria. For example, to audit all the tables' failed `Select` operations, you would execute:

```
sp_auditobject "Default Table", pubs2, "Fail", "s"
Go ▪
```

Using sp_auditsproc   The system-stored procedure `sp_auditsproc` works in the same way as `sp_auditobject` and allows you to either enable or disable the auditing of the execution of a particular procedure. The syntax for `sp_auditsproc` is as follows:

```
sp_auditsproc {ProcedureName | "All" | "Default"}, dbname[,
        {"Ok" | "Fail" | "Both" | "Off"}]
```

ProcedureName is the name of the procedure that you want to monitor. If you use `"All"`, then AuditServer will track all existing stored procedures in the server. If you use `"Default"`, then AuditServer will track all stored procedures that are created on the server going forward.

For example, to track all the procedures being executed in the *master* database, you would execute:

```
sp_auditsproc "All", master, "Ok"
Go
```

Using sp_addauditrecord   If you want to add your own custom entries to the audit trail, you can use the system-stored procedure `sp_addauditrecord`, provided the System Security Of-

Part
IV

Ch
21

ficer has granted you execute permissions to run it. The syntax for using `sp_addauditrecord` is as follows:

```
sp_addauditrecord [Text] [, Db_Name] [, Obj_Name]
[, Owner_Name] [, dbid] [, objid]
```

Each of these parameters is optional and they correspond to the columns that are available in the *sysaudits* table as described later in the section titled "Understanding the Output from AuditServer."

The most common way of using the `sp_addauditrecord` system-stored procedure is to add your own message to the audit trail like this:

```
sp_addauditrecord "My audit trail message will be going into sysaudits!"
Go
```

Moving Data Out of sysaudits

The *sysaudits* table is going to have a finite size, and it is your responsibility as the DBA to make sure that it doesn't overfill and cause errors. To move data from the *sysaudits* table, you should consider creating a set of tables that will serve as an archive. You should move data to those archive tables with a `Select Into` statement for optimal performance. For example, to move all the most recent auditable events from the *sysaudits* table to a dated archive table, you would execute:

```
Select *
Into    MyArchive_19960711
From    sybsecurity..sysaudits
Go
```

It is highly recommended that you then truncate the *sysaudits* table. This is the quickest way to remove the data from the audit trail tables and will minimize the number of lost audit records. To guarantee that you don't lose any audit records, you will need to make sure that your server's *sybsecurity* database is sufficiently large to hold a day's worth of transactions. Then, in a nightly process, you would need to bring all the databases on the server down and move the audit trail data to the archive.

What to Do if sysaudits Becomes Full

If the *sysaudits* table is full and you have a lot of auditing activated on the server, many users' events will be aborted or terminated by the server. For example, if you were logging the login process and the *sysaudits* table was full, then no users would be able to login to the server. This is a particularly serious problem, so you should be aware of how to deal with the problem quickly.

If the *sysaudits* table fills up, then all users with the System Security Officer role have the ability to perform events that are no longer audited. The SSOs can log into the server and truncate the *sysaudits* table (after making an archive of the data) and the operation of the server can continue.

N O T E While auditing is disabled for the SSO, all events that normally would have been written to the *sysaudits* table are actually written to the server's `errorlog` as warning events. So, it is still possible to track the actions of the SSO in this case. ■

Understanding the Output from AuditServer

The output from the AuditServer is written to the *sysaudits* table in the *sybsecurity* database. The data can be viewed by only a System Security Officer and is just a straight table. To read the logged transactions for sa, you would enter a select statement like this (after having first done a `Use sybsecurity`):

```
Select event, dbid, dbname, objname, extrainfo
From    sysaudits
Where   loginname = "sa"
Go
  event   dbid dbname          objname         extrainfo
      9      4 sybsystemprocs  sp_auditoption  EXEC sp_auditoption
      9      6 sybsecurity                     AUDIT OPTION
    105      1 master          sysmessages     SELECT
    105      6 sybsecurity     sysaudits       SELECT
    105      1 master          syslogins       SELECT
    107      6 sybsecurity                     USE sybsecurity
    107      6 sybsecurity                     select * from sysaudits
    107      6 sybsecurity                     Select event, dbid, dbname,
                                               objname, extrainfo From
                                               sysaudits Where  loginname
                                               = "sa"
    107      6 sybsecurity                     print 'hello'
```

The columns in the *sysaudits* table have the following values:

- ■ *event*—This is the type of event that occurred. See Table 21.1 for details on event types.

- ■ *eventmod*—This is indication of whether the audited event was successful. For example, if a login was successful, you would see it recorded here with an eventmod of 1. Valid values are 0 = no value for *eventmod* is required; 1 = successful event execution; 2 = event was not successful.

- ■ *spid*—This is the process ID on the server that initiated the event.

- ■ *eventtime*—This is the date and time that the event was created.

- ■ *sequence*—This is the internal sequence of an event if it spans more than one part. Typically, 107 events (command text lists) will span more than one event because the command text will be greater in length than the space available in *extrainfo*.

- ■ *suid*—This is the user ID of the process that initiated the event.

- ■ *dbid*—This is the database that was affected by the event.

- ■ *objid*—This is the ID of the object that was affected by the event, except in the case of a stored procedure or trigger, in which case it is the procedure or trigger's ID.

- ■ *xactid*—This is the physical transaction log's transaction ID. You can use this value to scan through the transaction log to see the effects of the transaction on the server.

Part

IV

Ch

21

■ *loginname*—This is the login name of the user that initiated the event.

■ *dbname*—This is the full name of the *dbid*.

■ *objname*—This is the full name of the *objid*.

■ *objowner*—This is the name of the owner login that owned the object affected by the event.

■ *extrainfo*—This is the extra information relating to the audit trail. The information in this column varies according to the event that is being logged (see Table 21.1).

Table 21.1   Event Types and the Sorts of Extra Information that You Can Expect

Event Type	Description	Extra Information (*extrainfo*)
1	Enable Auditing	Null
2	Disable Auditing	Null
3	Login	Host name
4	Logout	Host name
5	Server boot	Names of the server program, master device, interfaces file path, server, and error log file
6	RPC connection	Remote server name, host name
7	Use of set command to turn roles on and off	Role, new setting
8	Command requiring sa_role role	Command type
9	Command requiring sso_role role	Command type
10	Command requiring oper_role role	Command type
12	Command requiring navigator role	Command type
13	Error	Error number, severity, and state
14	Ad hoc audit record	User-supplied comment text
15	Command requiring replication_role	Command type
100	Database reference	Command type
101	Table reference	Command type
102	View reference	Command type
103	Stored procedure execution	Parameter list

Event Type	Description	Extra Information (*extrainfo*)
104	Trigger execution	Null
105	User's attempts to access a table	Command type
106	User's attempts to access a view	Command type
107	User's command text auditing	Command batch text

Removing the AuditServer

Removing the AuditServer is a task that is sometimes required when you are reconfiguring a server to work in a different way, or if you have changed the security requirements of the system. To remove the AuditServer, you need to first disable it. Disabling AuditServer is achieved by executing the system-stored procedure `sp_auditoption` as follows:

```
sp_auditoption "Enable Auditing", "Off"
Go
```

```
------------------------------------------------------------
Audit option has been changed and has taken effect immediately.
```

After the auditing is disabled, you can drop the *sybsecurity* database like this:

```
Drop Database sybsecurity
Go
```

N O T E   You must be a System Security Officer to drop the *sybsecurity* database.

Enforcing Security Beyond System XI

There are a number of steps that can be taken to provide a more secured environment in which System XI will operate. Some of the sections below may seem obvious, but are worth thinking about. I recommend that you designate a person to be responsible for system security at your workplace. This person will live, breathe, and eat security and should be clearly empowered to implement any of the steps outlined later. System Security Officers (SSO) are becoming more and more common within organizations due to the highly accessible nature of public access networks, such as the Internet. Their roles are that of company custodians.

Working with Physical Security

Often overlooked when designing the security of a system is the *physical security* of the server itself. Granted, it is unlikely that the average hacker will spend all day sitting on the system console hacking into a server trying various passwords without being noticed. However, if the server can physically be removed from its location, many unscrupulous users will be prepared to spend more time in the comfort of their homes. This would also include its mass data storage devices, such as tapes and hard drives.

Part

IV

Ch

21

Ensure that physical access to the server is limited. Provide locked doors, preferably with electronic locks, that secure the server, and optionally bolt the server to the structure on which it resides. Remember, in these days of smaller and smaller hardware, the server can be a laptop or similarly small device that's easy to steal.

Because UNIX and Windows NT provides excellent remote administration capabilities, you can remove monitors and keyboards from servers that must be placed in high access areas. This will stop the idle person from walking by and examining the server. As an alternative, there are plenty of hardware manufacturers that provide secure casings for server boxes that can be used to provide better security for your server.

It is assumed that the same level of physical security applied to the System XI will also be applied to the following:

- The network file servers
- The network hubs and routers
- Any other shared network device, such as bridges and remote WAN linkup devices

Securing Local Area Network (LAN) Access

A common mistake on LANs is to have unmonitored network nodes that allow access. Ensure that all nodes on the network that do not have computers actually attached to them have been disconnected from the hub so that no one can bring in a laptop and access the LAN at a physical level.

For highly secure environments, provide all users with SecureID cards or similar devices. These devices generate passwords that are authenticated by the Network file server and change constantly. This will stop users without valid identification cards from accessing the LAN, even if they have physical access to a node.

At a LAN software level, ensure that all the features of the LAN's software are being utilized. Most network operating systems provide at least government-approved C2 level of security, but only if you turn it on. Unlike the B2 standard of security, C2 provides the features but does not enforce their use. Windows NT, NetWare 4.1, and some versions of UNIX support C2 security. Make sure that you are doing all the basics of good user management on your local area network, as follows:

- Enforce password aging with a maximum life of 30 days.
- Require unique passwords.
- Require long (eight-character) passwords that are validated against a list of invalids. (Third-party applications exist that ensure good passwords are being used by a client.)
- Enforce security blockouts on logins that fail due to invalid passwords.

 TIP   An excellent resource for information on security can be found on the Internet at the Computer Security Resource Clearing House: **http://csrc.ncsl.nist.gov/**.

Securing Remote or Wide Area Network Access

It's much harder to control WAN or remote access to a network than the local access provided through the LAN. However, some of the steps that you can take are as follows:

- Assign IP addresses to all external users, and do not allow them to connect with their own addresses. This will enable you to monitor closely all remote connections to your LAN.

- Implement a software- and/or hardware-based firewall that physically limits external packet traffic on the server's network.

- Enforce routine password changing per the file server guidelines outlined above.

- Audit all remote transactions/IP traffic, and scan it for invalid requests.

- Implement secure WAN protocol transport by using hardware-based compression on each end of WAN bridges.

Using Application Security

There are a number of steps that you can take to make your applications secure independently of the security applied at the System XI level. Some things that you might want to consider are as follows:

- Permission trees that allow users access to windows within your application program. You may want to break down access into three levels: view, new, and edit.

- Application-based audit trails that track the changes of fields and the amount of time spent on any given window in the system.

- Application-based limits on the amount of money that can be posted (for financial systems).

Remember, if the security of your database is important to you, you should always ensure that the database itself is secure with or without application programs. You must do this because sophisticated users on your network and on the Internet (if you are connected) will always be able to use a different application to work with your data if they want. This would bypass any application-only security that was being enforced.

Understanding the Sybase Secure Server Product

If, after reading everything in this chapter, you still have the need for a more stringent security system that is server-enforced, then I suggest that you look to Sybase's Secure Server. Secure Server was created with the U.S. government and military in mind and has an upgraded security classification of B1. The U.S. government publishes several documents on security that contain standards and minimum features that describe how security should be implemented. These security standards come from the National Computer Security Center's (NCSC) Trusted Database Interpretation of the Trusted Computer Security Evaluation Criteria (TCSEC), otherwise known in the industry as the *Orange Book*.

Part

IV

Ch

21

The *Orange Book* defines several clear categories of security schemes that can be followed to reach certain classification levels. The basic level of compliance that most vendors of both network operating systems (such as Windows NT and NetWare) and databases (such as DB2, Informix, and Sybase) try to achieve is C2. The primary difference between those systems that implement C2 security at the database or network operating system is that C2 provides the mechanisms for the security to be enforced and B1 makes these restrictions and security schemes a mandatory requirement at the operating system or database level that cannot be bypassed by any user of the system.

N O T E Sybase Secure Server was also designed to meet the standards requirements for the following bodies:

- F-B1/E3 level of the European Information Technology Security Evaluation Criteria (ITSEC)

- International Standards Organization (ISO)/American National Standards Institute (ANSI) SQL89 level 2 and entry level SQL92

- Federal Information Processing Standard (FIPS) PUB127-1, including the Integrity Enhancement Feature and entry level 127-2. ▨

Sybase Secure Server implements B1 in a unique manner by enhancing the core security built into the base System XI product with additional functionality required to fully support B1 certification. Because these security enhancements are built around the core product, traditional Sybase users have a clear upgrade path to the more secure environments. Other competing products from other vendors typically introduce secure domains by mandating separate systems for classified data. Sybase's Secure Server implements all the domains in a single dataset, thereby reducing purchasing costs because you don't need multiple servers and improving system performance because multiple database systems are no longer required and no data replication is needed to move data between the secure and non-secure systems.

Secure Server's extensions to the core Sybase product include (among other things):

- **Mandatory access control**—MAC means you must impose and explicitly declare (through Grant and Revoke) security permissions on database, tables, and views.

- **Single and multi-level users**—The importance of a Multi-Level Secure (MLS) system is that you can have the same set of database tables with the data in them that is assigned a security level that a user's login must be granted permission to access. In this sense, a single table can contain multiple levels of secure data that can be browsed by different users without the user being aware that any other data exists in the table itself.

- **Trusted procedures and triggers**—Secure Server adds the ability to specify or denote that a procedure is trusted and that it can be executed by a user of a given security level. Trusted Procedures provide the DBA and System Security Officer a way of authenticating and managing transactions between users and the underlying data of the tables. Trusted Procedures can be executed against data in different security levels by users without the authority to normally access data at a higher level.

■ **Row-level polyinstantiation**—With row-level polyinstantiation, you can have two users create the same record in the database (i.e., they have the same primary key) with the same unique identifier, such as the same Social Security number, and the two users will not receive an indication that either insert is invalid. RLP is designed to prevent users from determining valid data in a system by performing any number of `Insert` statements that, if they fail due to primary key clashes, would indicate that a record exists. If, however, the same user attempts to add the same record twice, then that user will be notified of the error. Sybase implements RLP by adding the user's server-assigned login ID as a part of the primary key of every table in the database.

Sybase Secure Server has only one down side that you should be aware of: It is supported only on Sun hardware at this time.

From Here...

Having discovered the many facets of System XI security, it is most likely that you will spend the next few months trying to fill the holes that you now know exist. If you are lucky enough to be reading this book before you implement System XI in your environment, take advantage of what you have learned and apply as many security features as necessary to provide the appropriate control needed. Of course, the best secret of all is to make sure that your security policies and procedures are constantly under review so that you can close any loopholes that are exposed.

Take a look at the following chapters for more information that may be useful in creating a secure environment:

■ See Chapter 9, "Working with Views," to learn to hide underlying data tables with views that limit datasets available to users.

■ See Chapter 10, "Understanding Stored Procedures," to learn to create stored procedures to provide users with access to data without giving them access to the actual tables.

Part
IV

Ch
21

CHAPTER 22

Managing and Monitoring Performance

Performance tuning in the client/server world is somewhat of a magical art. A combination of so many factors can make an application perform well, and knowing where to focus your time is what's most important.

The most critical part of optimizing performance is to have good documentation. Document statistically how the system works or performs before even starting any performance tuning. As the performance tuning cycle begins, monitor and document the effects of all the changes so that it's easy to determine the changes that were positive and those that were negative. Never assume that all the changes made for one application automatically apply to another application. Remember you're ultimately tuning a product that a user is using, not just a database that's being accessed by some unknown client. ■

How to approximately size a database and how to estimate the amount of disk space required

Sizing a SQL Server database can make a difference with how you choose to buy hardware for your server. Make sure that you have enough disk to cope with the expected size of your system.

How to size the procedure cache for optimal performance

An optimally sized procedure cache will substantially improve performance because frequently accessed procedures will not need to be recompiled.

Using SQL Monitor

Sybase's SQL Monitor is an excellent tool that will help you accurately diagnose the performance of the server. You should become familiar with the way it works and how it will help you to understand your server's operation.

Sizing a Database

Estimating the size of a SQL Server database is relatively straightforward and can be done with a good level of accuracy. The principle of space calculation is that all the bytes of data per table should be added together along with the associated overhead per row and page of data and that this should be then used as a divisor to the page size (2K) to determine how many rows of data will fit in a page.

The actual available space of a page is 2,016 bytes because 32 bytes are reserved for fixed overhead to manage the rows on the page. In general terms these calculations are affected by the placement of and use of Fill Factor on indexes, the use of the new System XI keyword max_rows_per_page and if a clustered index is on the table.

Understanding the Size of a Datatype

Each SQL Server datatype consumes a certain amount of bytes based on the storage of the data. The following table defines the amount of storage that each datatype uses:

Datatype	Size
Char/Binary	The size indicated in the definition
Varchar/Varbinary	The actual data size (use an average estimate)
Int	4 bytes
Smallint	2 bytes
TinyInt	1 byte
Float	8 bytes
Float(b)	4 bytes (numbers with precision of 1–7 digits)
Float(b)	8 bytes (numbers with precision of 8–15 digits)
Double Precision	8 bytes
Real	4 bytes
Money	8 bytes
SmallMoney	4 bytes
DateTime	8 bytes
SmallDatetime	4 bytes
Bit	1 byte
Decimal/Numeric	2–17 bytes depending on the precision
Text/Image	16 bytes per table row plus at least one 2K page per NOT NULL column
Timestamp	8 bytes

SQL Server internally defines any nullable column as a var datatype. So a Char(12) Null column is actually a Varchar(12) column. Therefore, for any columns that permit Null values the average expected column size should be used.

Decimal and numeric precision affects the amount of storage required for these datatypes. The following table indicates the amount of bytes required for each range of precision:

Numeric Precision	Size
0–2	2 bytes
3–4	3 bytes
5–7	4 bytes
8–9	5 bytes
10–12	6 bytes
13–14	7 bytes
15–16	8 bytes
17–19	9 bytes
20–21	10 bytes
22–24	11 bytes
25–26	12 bytes
27–28	13 bytes
29–31	14 bytes
32–33	15 bytes
34–36	16 bytes
37–38	17 bytes

Calculating Space Requirements for Tables

The method of calculating a table's space requirements differs based on whether the table has a clustered index or not. Both calculation methods are shown here, and examples are drawn from the *pubs2* database to illustrate their use.

Some issues to be aware of when calculating table and index sizes are the following:

- Performing Update Statistics on an index adds an extra page for that index to store the distribution statistics of the data that it contains. Performing Update Statistics on the table will add one data distribution page per index on the table.

- For tables with variable-length columns, you should try to average the length of the row by estimating the anticipated average size of the columns on the table.

- SQL Server won't store more than 256 rows per page, even if the row is very short. So if your row is 7 bytes or less in size, the number of data pages required for N rows of data is calculated by N/256 = number of data pages required.

- Text and Image data will take up a minimum of 2K (one page) unless when a row is inserted the value for the column is specified as Null.

Sizing Tables with Clustered Indexes   The *publishers* table has a clustered index. This example estimates the space required for 5,000,000 rows, and assumes that the average length of the varchar columns is 60 percent of the defined length:

1. Calculate the row length. If the row contains only fixed-length, NOT NULL columns, the formula is

```
2 + (Sum of column sizes in bytes) = Row Size
```

If the row contains mixed variable-length fields and/or NULL columns, the formula is

```
2 + (Sum of fixed-length column sizes in bytes) + (Sum of average
➥ of variable-length columns) = Subtotal
Subtotal * (( Subtotal / 256) _+ 1) + (Number of variable-length
➥ columns +_ 1) + 2 = Row Size
```

For the *publishers* table, the second formula is required:

```
2 + 4 + (60% of 92) = 55.2
55.2 * ((55.2/256) + 1) + 5 + 2 = 75
```

2. Calculate the number of rows that will fit on a page. The formula is

```
2016 / (Row Size) = Number of rows per page
```

In this case,

```
2016 / 75 = 27
```

 T I P   For more accurate calculations, round *down* any calculations for number of rows per page.

3. Number Of Rows Required/Number of rows per page = number of 2K data pages:

```
5,000,000 / 27 = 18519
```

 T I P   For more accurate calculations, round up any calculations for number of pages required.

4. Next calculate the space required for the clustered index. The size of the clustered index depends on whether the key columns are variable- or fixed-length. For fixed-length keys, use this formula:

```
5 + (Sum of column sizes in bytes) = Clustered index size
```

For variable-length keys, use this formula:

```
5 + (Sum of fixed-length column sizes in bytes) + (Sum of average
➥ of variable-length columns) = Subtotal
Subtotal * (( Subtotal / 256) _+ 1) + (Number of variable-length
➥ columns +_ 1) + 2 = Clustered index size
```

For *publishers*, the key is a single fixed-length column, therefore

```
5 + 4 = 9
```

5. Now calculate the number of clustered index rows that will fit on a page. The formula is

```
(2016 / (Clustered index size)) - 2 = Number of rows per page
```

In this case:

```
(2016 / 9) - 2 = 222
```

6. Next calculate the number of index pages by using the following formula:

```
(Number of data pages) / (Number of clustered index rows per page) = Number
➡of index pages at index level N
```

For this example,

```
18519 / 222 = 84
```

Index pages are at multiple levels. To compute all the levels of the index, continue to divide the resulting number of index pages by the number of clustered rows per page until the result is 1 or less. In this case:

```
84 / 222 = 1,
```

which means that one index page is at the top of the index and all the other pages are actual pointers to data pages.

7. Compute the total number of 2K pages required for the database table:

Data Pages: 18,519

Index Pages (level 1): 1

Index Pages (level 0): 83

Total number of 2K pages: 19,403 (or about 38M)

Sizing Tables with Nonclustered Indexes   Tables with Nonclustered indexes are calculated in size the same way as a clustered index table except for the sizing of the index itself. In this example, assume that a nonclustered index has been added to the *Roysched* table on the `title_id` column, and that 7,000,000 rows are in the table. The following steps will help you size a nonclustered index:

1. The first step is to calculate the length of the leaf row in the index. A *leaf row* is the bottom row of an index tree and points to the data page. The leaf row's size is the size of the index's columns summed together and is affected by variable or fixed-length columns. Use this formula if you have only fixed-length columns in the index:

```
7 + (Sum of fixed-length keys) = Size of index row
```

Use this formula if you have fixed and variable-length columns in the index:

```
9 + (Sum of length of fixed-length keys) + (Sum of length of
➡ variable-length keys) + (Number of variable-length keys)
➡ + 1 = Subtotal
(Subtotal) + ((Subtotal / 256) + 1) = (Size of leaf index row)
```

In the *Roysched* table, the primary key is fixed-length and isn't null, therefore:

```
7 + 6 = 13
```

2. Next calculate the number of leaf pages that will be required by using the following formula:

```
2016 / (Size of leaf index row) = Number of leaf rows per page
```

In this case: `2016 / 13 = ` **155**

```
(Number of rows in table) / (Number of leaf rows per page) =
➥ Number of leaf pages
```

In this case: 7,000,000 / 155 = **45,162**

3. Next calculate the size of the non-leaf row, and calculate the number of non-leaf pages. The size of non-leaf row is calculated according to this formula:

```
(Size of leaf index row) + 4 = Size of nonleaf row
```

that is, 13+4=**17**

```
(2016 / Size of nonleaf row) - 2 = Number of nonleaf index rows
➥ per page
```

In this example, (2016/17)-2=**116**

```
(Number of leaf pages / Number of nonleaf index rows per page)
➥ = Number of index pages at Level N
```

or 45,162/117=**386** pages at level 1

Like the clustered index, the levels of the index are determined by result division until the result is 1 or less:

386 / 117 = **4** pages at level 2.

4 / 117 = **1** page at level 3.

4. Finally, compute the size of the Index by summing the number of pages at the various levels of the index:

Leaf Pages: 45,162

Level 1 Pages: 386

Level 2 Pages: 4

Level 3 Pages: 1

Total number of 2K pages: 45,553 (or about 89M)

Understanding the Effects of Fill Factor

Fill Factor alters the number of rows that SQL Server will place on a page. The most likely configuration of Fill Factor is to assume that the table will never change its dataset and therefore you set Fill Factor to 100 percent to maximize the use of data pages. This affects the calculations by increasing the number of rows that can fit on a page by 2.

If you're sizing an index with a Fill Factor of 100 percent, don't subtract 2 from the result of the number of rows per page because SQL Server won't preallocate these rows for page growth but will instead put user data there.

Any other value of Fill Factor alters the size of the page itself. For example, a Fill Factor of 70 percent reduces the amount of available space on the page to 1412 bytes.

Understanding the Effects of max_rows_per_page

The max_rows_per_page keyword is really just a more scientific way of using the Fill Factor keyword. By utilizing max_rows_per_page in the Create Table or Create Index statement that you use, you will be limiting the number of rows that a single data page can hold. If for example, you set the limit to 2 rows per page, then (provided that the individual row size isn't actually greater than 986 bytes) you won't need to calculate individual row sizes when performing the sizing steps outlined above. Instead you can use the fixed amount that was specified in max_rows_per_page.

Sizing the Procedure Cache

Sizing the Procedure Cache in Sybase System XI is basically a case of trial and error. Sybase documents an approximation based on the following formula:

```
Procedure Cache = (Maximum Concurrent Users) * (Size of Largest Plan) * 1.25
```

To determine the size of a plan in memory, the DBCC Memusage command should be used. The following SQL illustrates the output from DBCC Memusage:

```
dbcc Memusage
Go


------------------------------------------------------------------
Memory Usage:
                     Meg. 2K Blks      Bytes
Configured Memory: 14.6484     7500   15360000

        Code size:  1.0000      512    1048576
Kernel Structures:  2.5040     1283    2625607
Server Structures:  3.7821     1937    3965838
     Cache Memory:  5.7715     2955    6051840
     Proc Buffers:  0.0536       28      56164
     Proc Headers:  1.5352      786    1609728

Buffer Cache Memory, Top 5:

Cache Buf Pool   DB Id  Object Id   Index Id      Meg.
default data c     1        8          0        0.0059
        2K         1        8          0        0.0059
default data c     5        8          0        0.0039
        2K         5        8          0        0.0039
default data c     2        8          0        0.0020
        2K         2        8          0        0.0020
default data c     3        8          0        0.0020
        2K         3        8          0        0.0020
default data c     4        8          0        0.0020
        2K         4        8          0        0.0020

Procedure Cache, Top 5:

Database Id: 1
Object Id: 656005368
Object Name: sp_dboption
Version: 1
Uid: 1
Type: stored procedure
```

```
Number of trees: 0
Size of trees: 0.000000 Mb, 0.000000 bytes, 0 pages
Bytes lost for alignment 0 (Percentage of total: 0.000000)
Number of plans: 1
Size of plans: 0.099387 Mb, 104215.000000 bytes, 52 pages
Bytes lost for alignment 1253 (Percentage of total: 1.202322)
...
```

Assuming that sp_dboption was the largest procedure to be run on a server and that there were to be 150 concurrent users, then

```
150 * 52 * 2 * 1.25 = 19,500K
```

N O T E Memory in the procedure cache is managed as a set of 2K pages; therefore, the number of pages reported by DBCC Memusage is multiplied by 2K to derive the amount of memory that the plan actually consumes. ▦

Now that you know how much memory is required or needed for the procedures you can then determine how big to size the procedure cache. Say you have 64M of RAM in the server. If you know that 19.5M of that needs to be reserved for procedures, then it's a pretty simple calculation to determine the procedure cache percentage:

```
19.5 / 64 = 30%
```

An alternative sizing can be estimated based on the need to stop SQL Server from recompiling procedures that fall out of the cache frequently. The procedure cache like the data cache works on a Least Recently Used (LRU) algorithm, and procedures that are used infrequently are pushed out of the cache if there's no more room to compile a procedure that's requested by a user process.

Therefore, work out a list of the number of critical procedures or procedures that are most frequently accessed and execute each one, analyzing the memory used as reported by DBCC Memusage. Based on the total memory calculated, the size of the procedure cache can be determined.

Ultimately, the only true judge of an accurate size of procedure cache is to test, test, test an application, and monitor the effects of altering the amount of cache available.

It's possible to run out of procedure cache if the number of active procedures in use (and their combined plan sizes) is greater than the cache available. In this case, you'll receive error 701, and the calling process that was trying to execute a procedure will be rolled back. If you receive this message you should resize the procedure cache to a higher percentage of available memory.

Using Sybase SQL Monitor

Sybase's SQL Monitor is a comprehensive tool designed to extract performance information from the System XI server and present it to you in a readable and meaningful format. SQL Monitor has two key components:

■ An open-server-based Monitor that connects directly to the System XI server and extracts performance statistics in real time

■ An Open Client (Client Library) based graphical front-end tool that interfaces to the Monitor Server to display the statistics that are being gathered

This tiering architecture of SQL Monitor helps reduce the performance hits on the server due to the monitoring of the data. However, there is always going to be a cost associated with running the Monitor Server on a system, and you should not run it on a production system. If you have no other way of gauging a performance problem in production, then it is sometimes necessary to run SQL Monitor just for a short period of time to try to isolate the problem.

The Monitor Server establishes a server based connection to the Sybase System XI server and then caches statistical information in its own resources awaiting clients. The SQL Monitor Client for Windows NT/95 is a native 32-bit application that connects over standard Client Library network connections (i.e., through TCP/IP) to the Monitor Server and displays a graph-based output from the Monitor Server.

Installing and Configuring SQL Monitor

Of all of the elements of the Sybase toolkit, Sybase's SQL Monitor is by far the most finicky to install. Quite frankly, after installation on probably 10 different servers, I have never actually found the right steps to get it up and running the first time. Incidentally, there are many more quirks in the SQL Monitor for Sybase System 10 than in the Sybase System XI version, so if you've already been frustrated by the System 10 version, you will be (somewhat) pleasantly surprised by the installation for Sybase System XI.

Getting SQL Monitor to work requires a couple of things to be achieved. First, the Monitor Server needs to be installed. You can install the SQL Monitor server component using the standard installation that Sybase provides on Windows NT, or on UNIX you can use the `sybload` program.

▶ **See** "Installing the Server," **p. 34**

After installing the Monitor Server, you should have some additional entries in your interfaces file for a server with an extension _MS—this is the Monitor Server's interface. For example, if your server's name was SYB11_NT, then the name of the monitor server would by SYB11_NT_MS.

Starting Monitor Server should be a straightforward task. Under Windows NT, you should be able to run the Monitor Server by picking Monitor Server from the Sybase Services Manager and double-clicking the Start/Continue green light (see Fig. 22.1).

But this just never worked. No matter what I tried, there was no luck. So the result is that under Windows NT, you have to start the Monitor Server in the same way that you would under UNIX:

1. Launch a command prompt or terminal session to the operating system on the host that the server has been installed onto.

2. Change directories to the `%Sybase%\Install` directory.

3. Run the script file that was created by the installation program to launch the Monitor Server. The name of the script or batch file to run should be the server name prefixed with RUN_. For example, a server named SYB11_NT would use the following command to start the monitor server:

RUN_SYB11_NT_MS

FIG. 22.1

The Services Manager makes it easy to start and stop any database servers that you have defined.

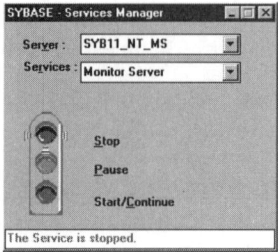

Starting the server in this fashion on a Windows NT PC forces the application to require a console window (see Fig. 22.2) to remain open as long as you want to run the Monitor Server. On most flavors of UNIX, you can launch a task like the Monitor Server in the background by using the ampersand (&) on the command line. For example, on HP-UX you would execute the following to run the Monitor Server and place it in the background:

RUN_SYB11_NT_MS &

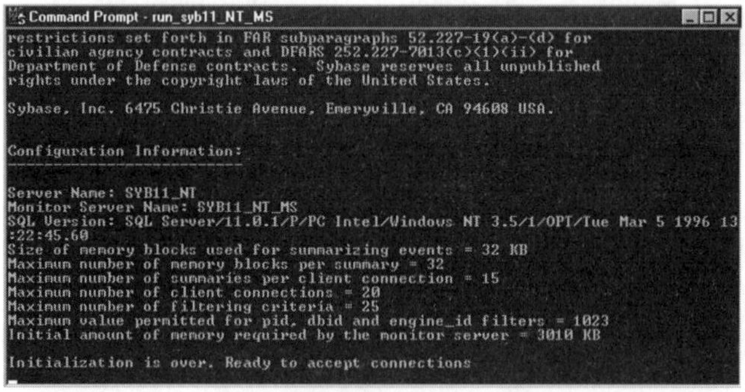

FIG. 22.2

After the Monitor Server starts in Windows NT, it tells you that initialization has completed successfully and that the server is ready to receive client requests (connections).

After SQL Monitor has been configured correctly and is in a listening mode you can get the client side running and talking to the server. To get the client connected to the server, follow these steps:

1. Launch the Sybase SQL Monitor Client from either the Sybase for Windows or Sybase for Windows NT folders (see Fig. 22.3).

FIG. 22.3

The main view of the Sybase Monitor Client has a simple toolbar with a network connection button, which is about to be clicked in this figure.

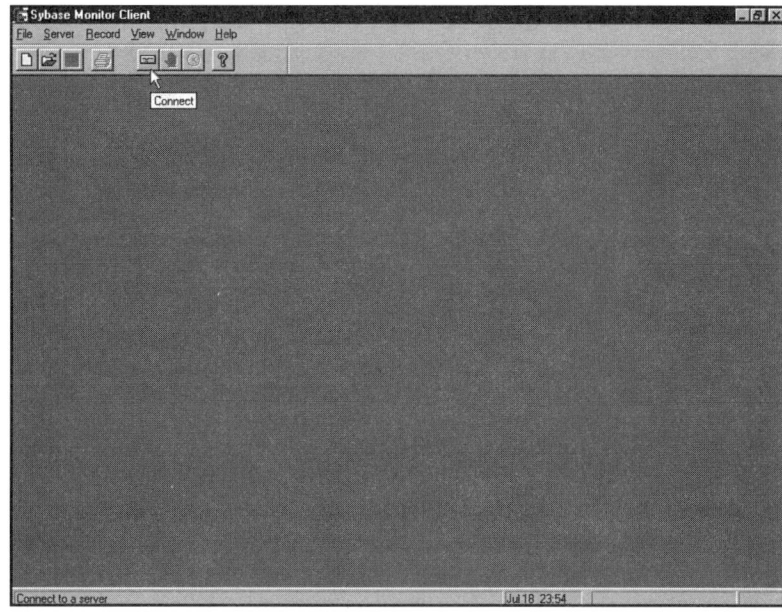

2. Choose Server, Connect to open the Server Connection dialog box (see Fig. 22.4).

FIG. 22.4

The Server Connection dialog box is used to establish a connection between this Client Monitor program and the Monitor Server.

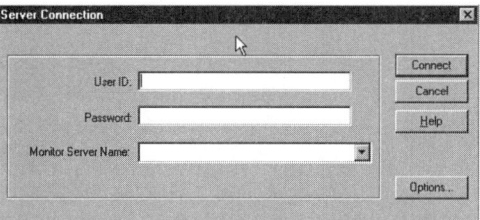

3. Enter the User ID (usually sa) and Password for the server that you are connecting to.

4. Select the Monitor Server from the Monitor Server Name combo box.

5. Click the Connect button to establish a connection. After connecting to the server, the name of the server currently connected to will be reflected in the title bar of the Monitor Client application.

Note that the Server Connection dialog box has an additional button, Options, that is useful if you want to alter the basic characteristics of the connection between the client and the server, perhaps, for performance reasons. By clicking the Options button, you will be presented with the Advanced Connect Properties dialog box shown below in Figure 22.5. This dialog box consolidates all the options that you have in terms of configuring the way that the connection is managed between the Monitor Server and the Monitor Client.

FIG. 22.5

Using the Advanced Connect Properties dialog box enables you to change the Interfaces file (SQL.INI) that is used to identify the server and alter such items as the packet size of the connection.

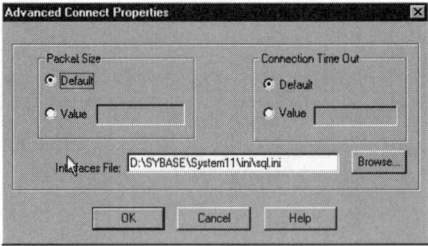

Using SQL Monitor

Fortunately, using SQL Monitor is a lot easier that getting a connection and is actually quite informative. SQL Monitor's interface is essentially a collection of different graphs that are designed to monitor the server's *heartbeats* and report them to you in a readable fashion. To display a graph, follow these steps:

1. From the Window menu, select New Window to display the Monitor Client Windows dialog box (see Fig. 22.6).

FIG. 22.6

The Monitor Client Windows dialog box gives you a list of available graphs that you can display. Take advantage of the Description group at the bottom to give you a simple description of the functions that this graph is showing.

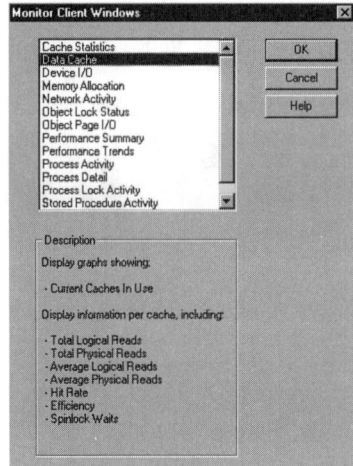

2. Select the graph to be displayed.
3. Click OK to create the graph.

After creating the graph that you want to display, Sybase Monitor Client opens it within the MDI Frame of the application (see Fig. 22.7).

FIG. 22.7

Monitoring Networking I/O using SQL Monitor is a very effective way of observing if the server is becoming bogged down in network activity.

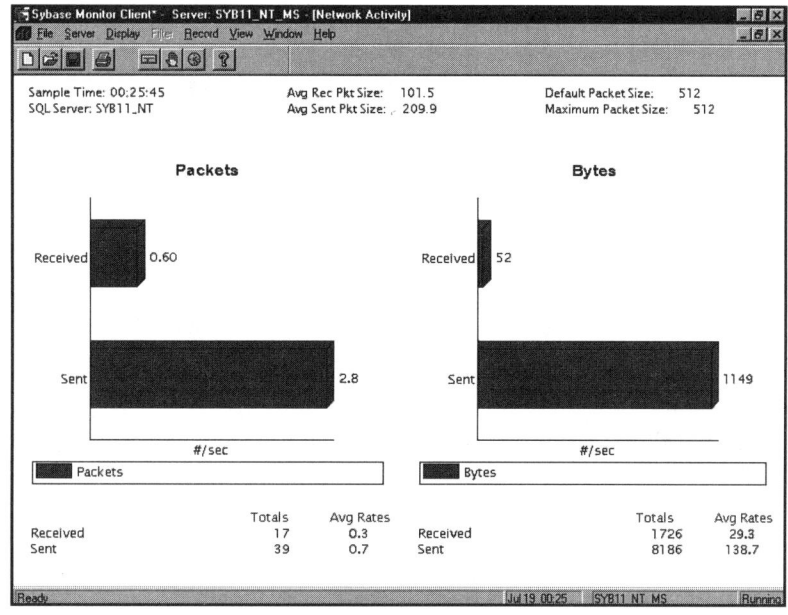

T I P After adding a few windows and getting them laid out in the way you like, you can take advantage of Sybase Monitor Client's workspace feature to save the status of the windows. The next time you successfully connect to the server, you will be able to open your saved workspace and Sybase Monitor Client will restore the layout for you. To save a workspace, Choose File, Save Workspace (Shift+F12).

You can customize the display characteristics (including color and display style of the graph) by working with the display options available under the Display menu. The most important option that this menu provides is the Update Interval option that enables you to configure how frequently you want the Monitor Client to poll the Monitor Server for up-to-date information on the status of the server. To configure this option, just choose Display, Update Interval to open the Update Interval dialog box (see Fig. 22.8).

FIG. 22.8

The default sample frequency is 5 seconds; use the Update Interval dialog box to change this by selecting the interval (an integer) and choosing the units (seconds, minutes, or hours).

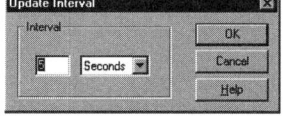

> **CAUTION**
>
> It is not recommended that you set the Update Interval to be less than 5 seconds because the frequency of polling for more information will skew the results due to the increased burden placed on the Data Server by the additional requests from the Monitor Server.

Analyzing SQL Monitor Information

SQL Monitor can report a wide variety of statistics to you, and it is important that you know how to interpret each of the available pieces of information accurately. In this section, you will see a sample graph from each of the statistics available for monitoring along with a brief discussion of why you would use the particular monitor graph.

Monitoring Cache Statistics   The Cache Statistics monitor should be used often in your environment to determine how effectively you are using memory to answer user requests instead of requiring reads from the disk. What you are hoping for on this graph is that your *L Reads* will be high indicating that you are performing a lot of reads from memory caches. In addition you are hoping that your *Proc Reads* are low because then you aren't having to read the procedure from the *syscomments* table and compile it before it is actually executed by the client.

If your *L Reads* (Logical Reads) are low, then you probably don't have enough memory configured or available to the Server. If your *Proc Reads* are high, then you haven't configured a large enough `Procedure Cache` (see Fig. 22.9).

FIG. 22.9
This Cache Statistics graph shows a slightly unusual, but excellently performing server that is reading 100 percent from logical pages (cache pages) and is executing 100 percent of precompiled procedures.

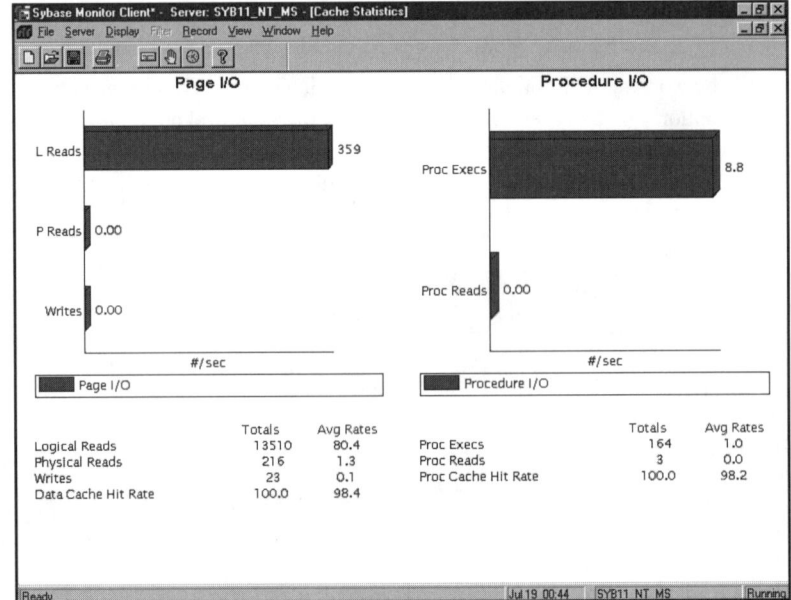

Monitoring the Data Cache   The purpose of the Data Cache monitor is to watch the Logical and Physical reads on the `default data cache` and any of the named caches that you have created. What you are looking for and hoping for is a large amount of L Reads to P Reads (Physical Reads) meaning that you are taking good advantage of the cache.

If *P Reads* are high, you should consider allocating more memory to the cache (see Fig. 22.10).

FIG. 22.10

This server only has a single data cache (the default data cache), and clearly, the data cache is working very efficiently and improving the performance of the system.

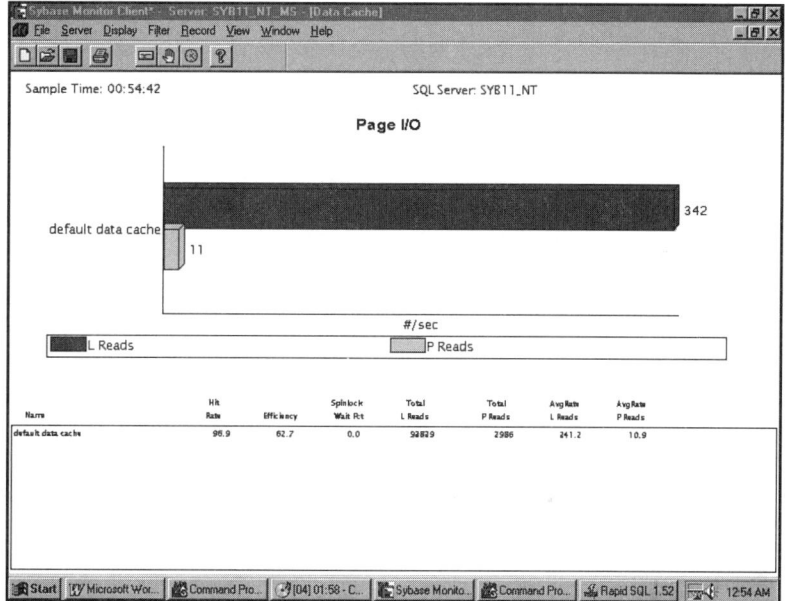

Monitoring Device I/O   The Device I/O monitor is an essential tool that you use to look for contention on a particular Sybase device due to it being I/O bound. If you are having throughput problems on your system and you suspect that a particular device is being hit heavily or not, you really need to run this monitor for quite some time to get empirical data that you will be able to compare the current performance of the system with (see Fig. 22.11).

Monitoring Memory Allocation   The Memory Allocation graph is just a graphical representation of the DBCC `Memusage` command, and as such, is a useful way of seeing quickly how memory has been allocated to the various components on the Sybase System XI Server (see Fig. 22.12).

Monitoring Network Activity   The Network Activity graph helps you monitor how your network is being responded to by the server. The data presented will have to be compared with what you learn over time. Obviously the higher these numbers go, the more operations that are being required across the network per second.

FIG. 22.11

In this monitor, the master device is being hit at the rate of about 3 I/Os per second, while the sybsecurity device is being hit at more than double that rate.

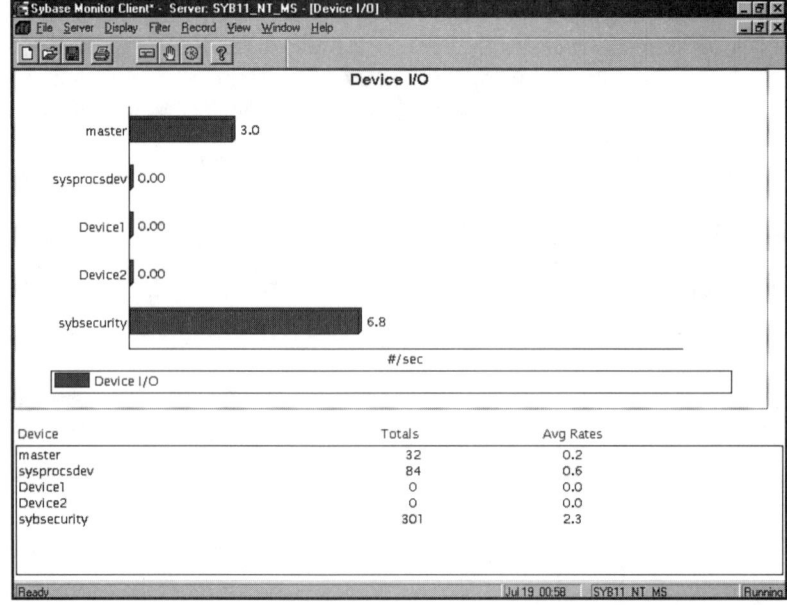

FIG. 22.12

The Memory Allocation graph helps you see the breakdown of memory use on the server. In this example, you can see that the fixed memory requirements for Sybase on Windows NT is about 7.3M for Code, Kernel Struct, and Server Struct.

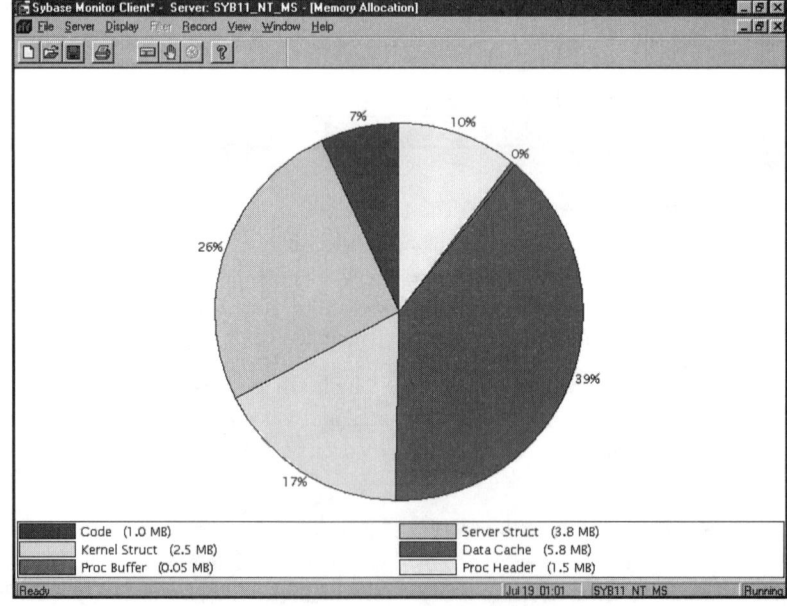

An interesting statistic available here is the `Avg Rec Pkt Size` and `Avg Sent Pkt Size` data points. By using these values you can determine how much wasted logical packet space there is on the net. If, however, you notice really high values in these statistics, you may want to consider increasing the `Network Packet Size` (see Fig. 22.13), so that your default packet size is closer to the average.

FIG. 22.13

This is an optimally performing server with an average number of transactions being performed on the network (per second) of 25.

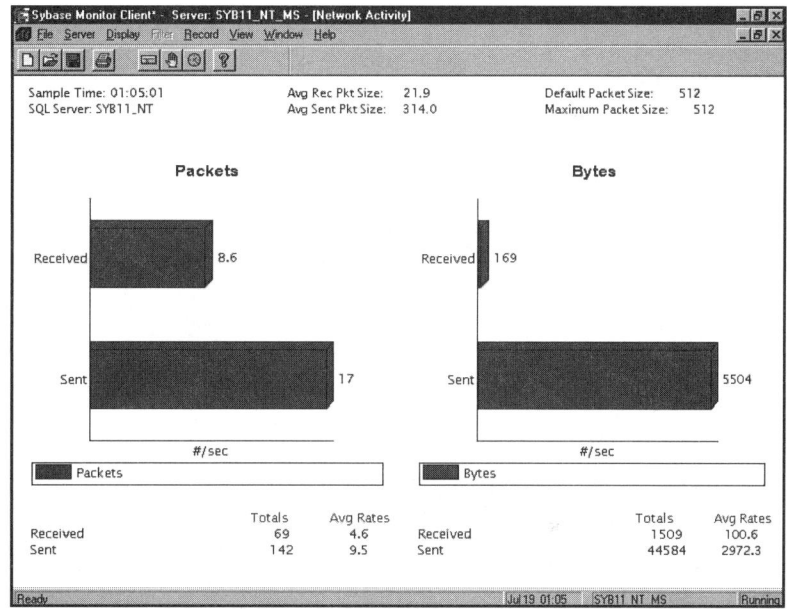

Monitoring Object Lock Status   The Object Lock Status graph is really not that much value to the normal Sybase user, but may have some worth in those environments that are keen to be proactive in the way that they manage user locks on objects on the Server. The output is just a tabular representation of all the objects on the server that are currently being locked.

 T I P   To customize this report and only monitor certain users, choose Filter menu, Process and then select the required processes (users) from the list of values in the Set Process Filter dialog box.

Monitoring Object Page I/O   You can use the Object Page I/O monitor if you are concerned that particular tables are being hit more frequently than others and you want to split the I/O to those tables by breaking up the table into several smaller tables. This report will show the live hits per sample frequency of the Monitor Server on every object in the system. By using this report it will be easy for you to figure out which tables are being highly accessed.

The report shows Logical Reads and Physical Reads on each object, and through the database object filter (choose Filter, Database Object), it is easy to customize which particular objects are either included or excluded from the report (see Fig. 22.14).

FIG. 22.14

The Set Database Object Filter gives you a list of all the database objects available on the server that you can select from. After making a selection, you can choose to either include or exclude these objects from the report.

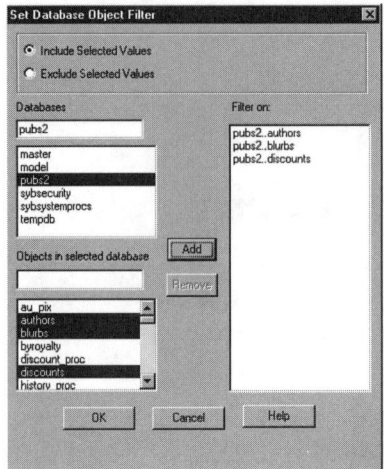

Monitoring the Performance Summary The Performance Summary monitor is a grouping of all of the most commonly used performance metrics in a single monitor window. You can use this window to have a good overall picture of the way a server is being used (see Fig. 22.15).

FIG. 22.15

You can use the artificial value Transactions Per Second at the top of this graph as your general benchmark from which to base the value of a particular configuration change when doing performance analysis.

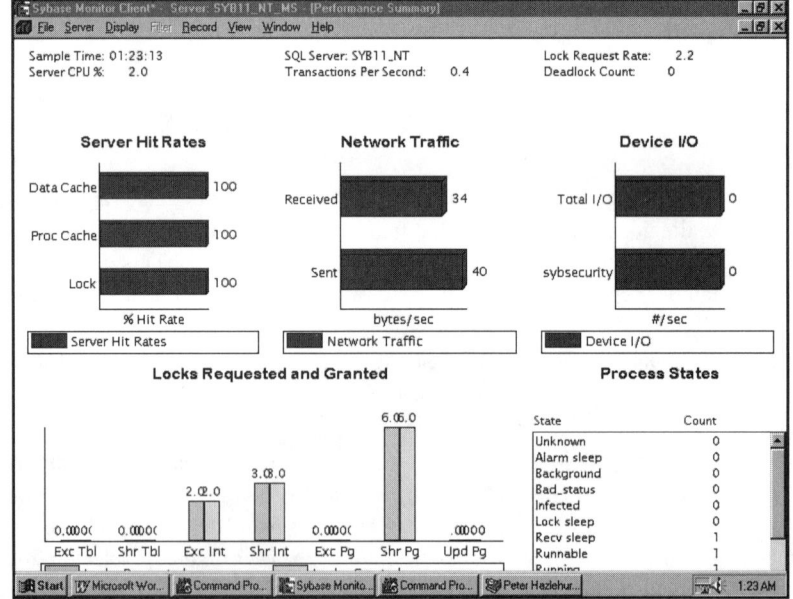

Monitoring Performance Trends   The Performance Trends monitor is a historical browsing meter that enables you to choose the sorts of statistics that you want to monitor over time. The advantage of this monitor is that it's a convenient way of easily seeing how the server is performing over time. To monitor a particular performance heuristic, choose Display, Options to open the Display Options dialog box (see Fig. 22.16).

FIG. 22.16

Use the Display Options dialog box to pick any of the options you want to monitor; however, be aware that by monitoring all of them, the graph will become very difficult to read.

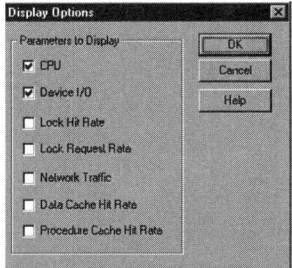

After you have selected a few options to monitor, let the trend analysis go on for some time. Then come back to SQL Monitor and look at the results to try and analyze overall bottlenecks (see Fig. 22.17).

FIG. 22.17

The most typically monitored options with the Performance Trends monitor is the percentage of CPU utilization, Device I/O, and Network Traffic.

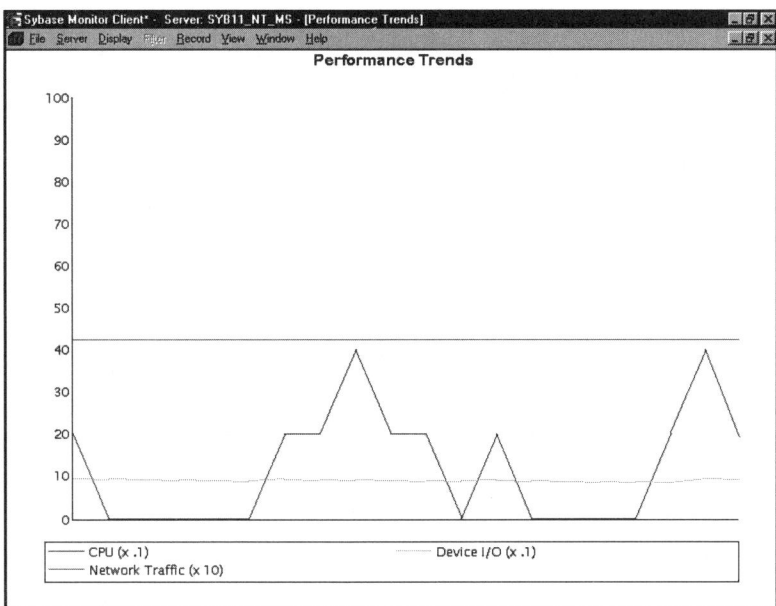

Monitoring Process Activity   The purpose of the Process Activity monitor is to enable you to monitor the behavior of individual users on the network (see Fig. 22.18). There's little to be gleaned from this graph unless your point in using it is to send messages to a user—who's overly taxing your server—to get off the system.

FIG. 22.18

A common theme in each of the monitors is to watch the number of physical and logical reads, compared to writes. In this particular graph, each individual user is scrutinized by the server.

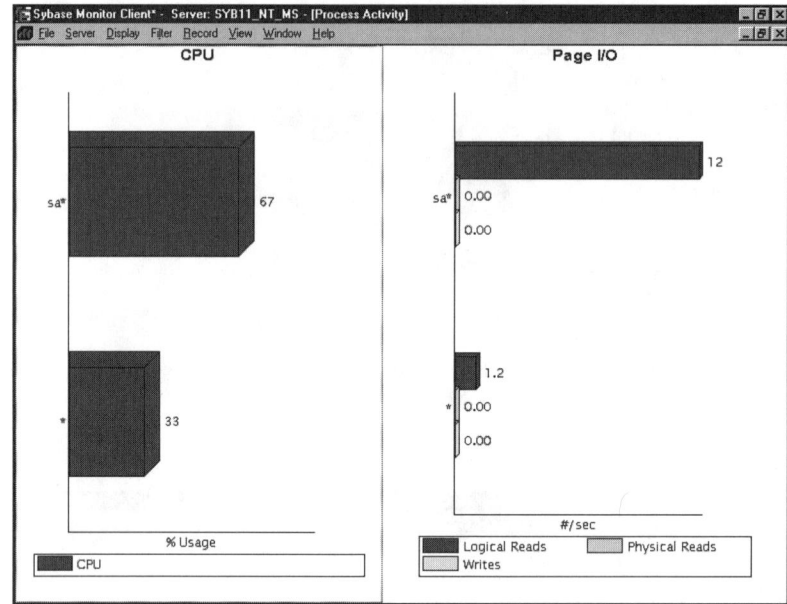

Monitoring Process Details   The Process Detail monitor takes the Process Activity monitor a little further and more finely describes all the events occurring on a single process. I have found little value in this report/graph, and I doubt that you will find much to gain by using it. The data is just a forms based representation of the *sysprocesses* table in the *master* database.

Monitoring Process Lock Activity   The Process Lock Activity monitor is useful if you suspect that a particular process or user is consuming or acquiring too many locks on the system. The output of this report is a simple bar chart graph showing the lock requests per second by process (see Fig. 22.19). Ideally, no particular process would consume a huge number of locks at any point in time.

Monitoring Stored Procedure Activity   The value of the Stored Procedure Activity report is that it shows you the frequency with which a particular stored procedure is being executed (see Fig. 22.20). You can use this frequency of execution information to determine if a particular procedure is being accessed too frequently and maybe requires an additional procedure to be created to split the load.

FIG.22.19

In this example, the System Administrator (sa) is clearly requesting far more locks than all the other users on the system combined.

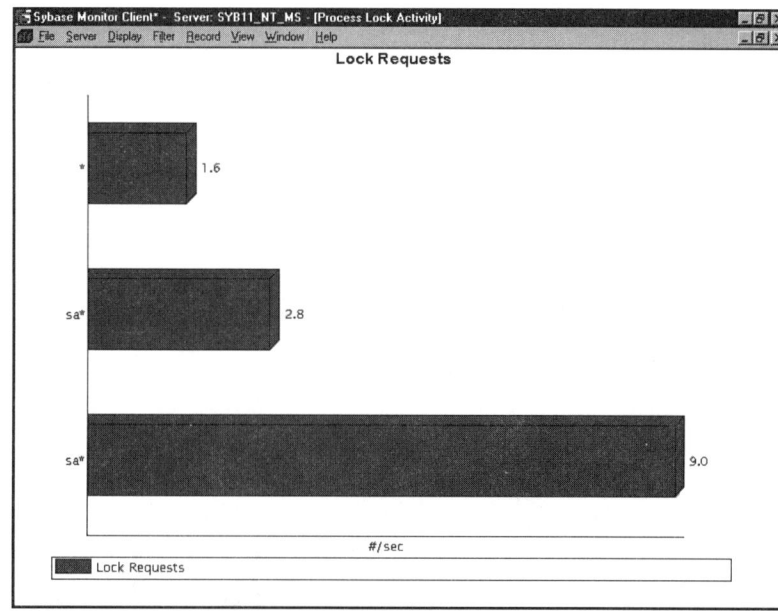

FIG. 22.20

The procedures used as sub-elements of sp_help are shown here being executed quite a few times due to a loop that executed sp_help on the authors table indefinitely.

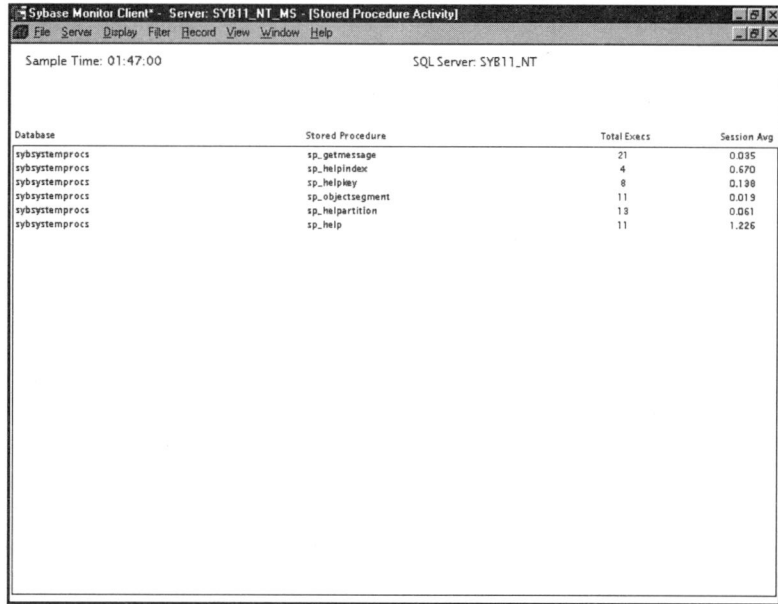

Monitoring Transaction Activity   Without exception, the Transaction Activity monitor is the most important tool that you have to monitor the performance of a system (see Fig. 22.21). The simple goal of this window is to monitor the peaks of the throughput as measured in operations per second (e.g., `Deletes` per second, `Transactions` per second, and so on) and then to tune different characteristics of the server to try and raise these values higher and higher.

You can use the averages column to help quantify whether any configuration changes that you make to your application have any effect on the net throughput of the server.

FIG. 22.21

Use the Totals column to keep track of how many operations were done in a particular benchmark. If the numbers are very different on the next benchmark, evaluate the methodology of the benchmark to make sure that you haven't materially changed what you were trying to measure.

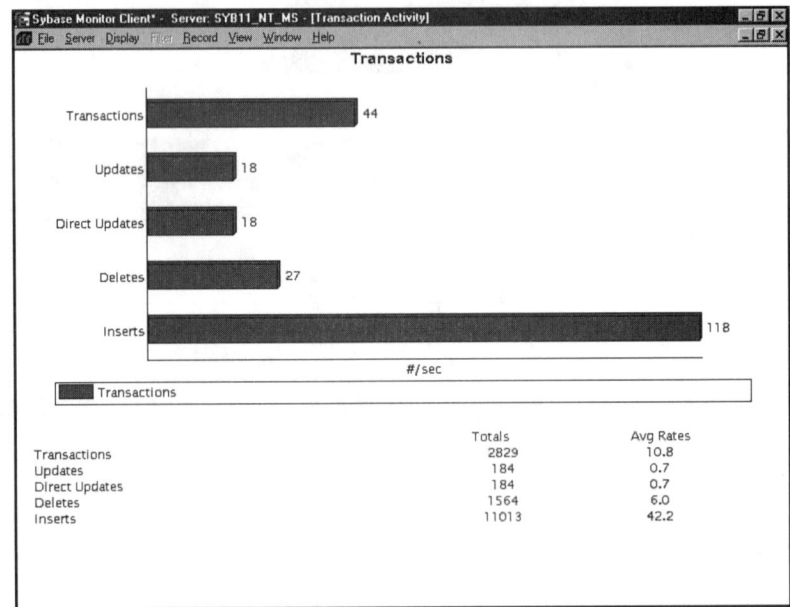

System-Stored Procedures that Reveal Performance Information

There are two key system stored procedures that you can use to monitor performance with on a server without the need for SQL Monitor: `sp_monitor` and `sp_sysmon`. Both of these stored procedures are designed to provide you with information that can help you judge the performance of the server and make valuable judgments about how it is working. However, unless you are prepared to write a statistical application that will execute these procedures on a frequent basis and capture the results and present it to the user in some graphical form, these procedures do not offer the dynamic performance monitoring capabilities of SQL Monitor.

Using sp_monitor

The system stored procedure sp_monitor has been around for quite some time in the Sybase system catalog and serves as a very basic analysis tool that you can use to look at some basic statistics on the server's current performance. There are no parameters to sp_monitor, so its operation is pretty simple; what you need to remember to do is to run it at least twice to get a measurable and sensible benchmark time. For example, you could execute something like this:

```
/* Execute first time to reset variables */
sp_monitor
Go

/* Wait for 1 minute */
Waitfor Delay "00:01:00"
Go

/* Now get the differential results */
Print "Use the results below!"
Print "==================================="
sp_monitor
Go
```

```
last_run                   current_run                seconds
------------------------   ------------------------   --------
Jul 17 1996 10:41:48:430PM Jul 17 1996 10:46:11:566PM    263
cpu_busy                   io_busy                    idle
------------------------   ------------------------   ---------------
11(0)-0%                   10(0)-0%                   13779(261)-99%
packets_received           packets_sent               packet_errors
------------------------   ------------------------   ---------------
100(3)                     224(4)                       0(0)
total_read        total_write       total_errors   connections
------------------   ------------------   --------------   -----------
665(5)               434(29)              0(0)             0(0)

Use the results below!
===================================
last_run                   current_run                seconds
------------------------   ------------------------   -----------
Jul 17 1996 10:46:11:566PM  Jul 17 1996 10:47:11:433PM       59
cpu_busy                   io_busy                    idle
------------------------   ------------------------   ---------------
15(3)-6%                   12(1)-2%                   13833(54)-92%
packets_received           packets_sent               packet_errors
------------------------   ------------------------   ---------------
106(6)                     258(34)                      0(0)
total_read        total_write       total_errors   connections
------------------   ------------------   --------------   -----------
771(106)             512(78)              0(0)             0(0)
```

As you can see from the output above, there's not a whole lot of information that can be gathered from these statistics, especially when formatted in this way. However, if you were to write an application in something like SQLWindows/Centura, it would be possible to graph these results over time to provide meaningful information.

> **N O T E** The information displayed in sp_monitor comes from the *spt_monitor* table in the
> *master* database. The *spt_monitor* table is updated at the end of the execution of
> sp_monitor with the current values in the system statistical, global variables: @@Cpu_Busy,
> @@IO_Busy, @@Idle, @@Pack_Received, @@Pack_Sent, @@Connections, @@Packet_Errors,
> @@Total_Read, @@Total_Write, and @@Total_Errors. So if you were writing an application, you
> could actually just poll these global variables and not rely on executing sp_monitor at all. ▪

Using sp_sysmon

The system stored procedure sp_sysmon is new to System XI and provides an incredibly
detailed report of all the activity on the server for the period of time that you specify. This extra
information is gathered by several sub-stored procedures that are designed to return information on particular areas of the server: sp_sysmon_dcache, sp_sysmon_diskio,
sp_sysmon_index, sp_sysmon_kernel, sp_sysmon_locks, sp_sysmon_memory, sp_sysmon_netio,
sp_sysmon_pcache, sp_sysmon_recovery, sp_sysmon_taskmgmt, sp_sysmon_xactmgmt, and
sp_sysmon_xactsum.

The consolidated information from each of these procedures is a lengthy report that needs to
be reviewed carefully to understand its components. The typical use of this report is to monitor
the difference of a standard benchmark after changing a particular configuration parameter.
Say you have a long running nightly process that utilizes a large amount of different stored
procedures. You might want to run the overnight process with a sp_sysmon executed two or
three times during the run to get an idea of how the currently running process is performing.
Then you could try something like increasing the procedure cache by 10 percent, performing
the same overnight, and running sp_sysmon at the same times during the run. Using both
runs' information you should be able to clearly get an understanding of how your system was
affected by the changes that you made to the procedure cache.

The syntax for the execution of the system stored procedure sp_sysmon is as follows:

```
sp_sysmon Sample_Period
```

Sample_Period is the number of minutes expressed as an integer that you want to sample the
server for performance information from one to 10 minutes. Here's a look at the results from
running sp_sysmon for a minute on a fairly lightly operated server:

```
===============================================================================
              Sybase SQL Server System Performance Report
===============================================================================
Run Date                   Jul 17, 1996
Statistics Cleared at         23:07:55
Statistics Sampled at         23:08:55
Sample Interval                1  min.
===============================================================================
Kernel Utilization
-----------------
```

```
Engine Busy Utilization:
   Engine 0                     71.0 %

CPU Yields by Engine            per sec      per xact       count   % of total
------------------------        ------------ ------------   -------- ----------
   Engine 0                      26.7          11.5          1597    100.0 %

Network Checks                    0.0           0.0             0     n/a
Disk I/O Checks
   Total Disk I/O Checks       3162.8        1363.4        189512     n/a
   Checks Returning I/O           9.4           4.1           565     0.3 %
   Avg Disk I/Os Returned         n/a           n/a       0.54513     n/a
===============================================================================
Task Management                 per sec      per xact       count   % of total
------------------------        ------------ ------------   -------- ----------
   Connections Opened             0.0           0.0             1     n/a

Task Context Switches by Engine
   Engine 0                   20201.7        8708.5       1210485    100.0 %

Task Context Switches Due To:
   Voluntary Yields           20193.9        8705.2       1210019    100.0 %
   Cache Search Misses            0.7           0.3            44      0.0 %
   System Disk Writes             0.2           0.1            10      0.0 %
   I/O Pacing                     2.3           1.0           138      0.0 %
   Logical Lock Contention        0.0           0.0             0      0.0 %
   Address Lock Contention        0.0           0.0             0      0.0 %
   Log Semaphore Contention       0.0           0.0             0      0.0 %
   Group Commit Sleeps            0.0           0.0             2      0.0 %
   Last Log Page Writes           0.7           0.3            44      0.0 %
   Modify Conflicts               0.1           0.0             5      0.0 %
   I/O Device Contention          0.0           0.0             0      0.0 %
   Network Packet Received        0.1           0.0             4      0.0 %
   Network Packet Sent            0.6           0.3            38      0.0 %
   SYSINDEXES Lookup              0.0           0.0             0      0.0 %
   Other Causes                   3.0           1.3           181      0.0 %
===============================================================================
Transaction Profile
-------------------
   Transaction Summary          per sec      per xact       count   % of total
------------------------        ------------ ------------   -------- ----------
   Committed Xacts                2.3           n/a           139     n/a

   Transaction Detail           per sec      per xact       count   % of total
------------------------        ------------ ------------   -------- ----------
   Inserts
      Heap Table                 12.4           5.4           745     84.2 %
      Clustered Table             2.3           1.0           140     15.8 %
------------------------        ------------ ------------   -------- ----------
   Total Rows Inserted          14.8           6.4           885     91.5 %
```

```
   Updates
      Deferred                  0.1            0.0              6      33.3 %
      Direct In-place           0.0            0.0              0       0.0 %
      Direct Cheap              0.2            0.1             12      66.7 %
      Direct Expensive          0.0            0.0              0       0.0 %
   ------------------------   ------------   ------------   ----------
   Total Rows Updated           0.3            0.1             18       1.9 %

   Deletes
      Deferred                  0.9            0.4             56      87.5 %
      Direct                    0.1            0.1              8      12.5 %
   ------------------------   ------------   ------------   ----------
   Total Rows Deleted           1.1            0.5             64       6.6 %
===============================================================================
Transaction Management
----------------------
   ULC Flushes to Xact Log    per sec        per xact          count  % of total
   ------------------------   ------------   ------------   ----------  ----------
      by Full ULC               0.0            0.0              0       0.0 %
      by End Transaction        0.8            0.3             45       6.4 %
      by Change of Database     0.0            0.0              2       0.3 %
      by System Log Record      9.4            4.0            562      79.7 %
      by Other                  1.6            0.7             96      13.6 %
   ------------------------   ------------   ------------   ----------
   Total ULC Flushes           11.8            5.1            705

   ULC Log Records             10.8            4.7            650        n/a
   Max ULC Size                 n/a            n/a            168        n/a

   ULC Semaphore Requests
      Granted                  21.8            9.4           1304     100.0 %
      Waited                    0.0            0.0              0       0.0 %
   ------------------------   ------------   ------------   ----------
   Total ULC Semaphore Req     21.8            9.4           1304

   Log Semaphore Requests
      Granted                  10.2            4.4            612     100.0 %
      Waited                    0.0            0.0              0       0.0 %
   ------------------------   ------------   ------------   ----------
   Total Log Semaphore Req     10.2            4.4            612

   Transaction Log Writes       1.2            0.5             71        n/a
   Transaction Log Alloc        0.4            0.2             24        n/a
   Avg # Writes per Log Page    n/a            n/a        2.95833        n/a
===============================================================================
Index Management
----------------
   Nonclustered Maintenance   per sec        per xact          count  % of total
   ------------------------   ------------   ------------   ----------  ----------
      Ins/Upd Requiring Maint   0.2            0.1             10        n/a
      # of NC Ndx Maint         0.2            0.1             10        n/a
      Avg NC Ndx Maint / Op     n/a            n/a        1.00000        n/a

      Deletes Requiring Maint   0.2            0.1             10        n/a
      # of NC Ndx Maint         0.2            0.1             10        n/a
      Avg NC Ndx Maint / Op     n/a            n/a        1.00000        n/a
```

```
        RID Upd from Clust Split       0.0            0.0             0        n/a
            # of NC Ndx Maint          0.0            0.0             0        n/a

      Page Splits                      0.0            0.0             0        n/a
      Page Shrinks                     0.0            0.0             0        n/a
===============================================================================
Lock Management
---------------
      Lock Summary                   per sec       per xact       count    % of total
      ------------------------       ------------  ------------   -------   ----------
      Total Lock Requests             102.7          44.3          6153       n/a
      Avg Lock Contention             0.0            0.0             0        0.0 %
      Deadlock Percentage             0.0            0.0             0        0.0 %

      Lock Detail                    per sec       per xact       count    % of total
      ------------------------       ------------  ------------   -------   ----------
      Exclusive Table
         Granted                      2.3            1.0           135       100.0 %
         Waited                       0.0            0.0             0        0.0 %
      -------------------------       ------------  ------------   -------
      Total EX-Table Requests         2.3            1.0           135        2.2 %

      Shared Table
         Granted                      0.2            0.1            11       100.0 %
         Waited                       0.0            0.0             0        0.0 %
      -------------------------       ------------  ------------   -------
      Total SH-Table Requests         0.2            0.1            11        0.2 %

      Exclusive Intent
         Granted                      2.0            0.8           118       100.0 %
         Waited                       0.0            0.0             0        0.0 %
      -------------------------       ------------  ------------   -------
      Total EX-Intent Requests        2.0            0.8           118        1.9 %

      Shared Intent
         Granted                      5.7            2.5           344       100.0 %
         Waited                       0.0            0.0             0        0.0 %
      -------------------------       ------------  ------------   -------
      Total SH-Intent Requests        5.7            2.5           344        5.6 %

      Exclusive Page
         Granted                      2.0            0.8           117       100.0 %
         Waited                       0.0            0.0             0        0.0 %
      -------------------------       ------------  ------------   -------
      Total EX-Page Requests          2.0            0.8           117        1.9 %

      Update Page
         Granted                      1.3            0.6            79       100.0 %
         Waited                       0.0            0.0             0        0.0 %
      -------------------------       ------------  ------------   -------
      Total UP-Page Requests          1.3            0.6            79        1.3 %

      Shared Page
         Granted                      43.5          18.8          2607       100.0 %
         Waited                       0.0            0.0             0        0.0 %
      -------------------------       ------------  ------------   -------
      Total SH-Page Requests          43.5          18.8          2607       42.4 %
```

```
Exclusive Address
  Granted                      23.6          10.2        1417      100.0 %
  Waited                        0.0           0.0           0        0.0 %
 -------------------------   -----------   -----------   ----------
  Total EX-Address Requests    23.6          10.2        1417       23.0 %

Shared Address
  Granted                      22.1           9.5        1325      100.0 %
  Waited                        0.0           0.0           0        0.0 %
 -------------------------   -----------   -----------   ----------
  Total SH-Address Requests    22.1           9.5        1325       21.5 %

Last Page Locks on Heaps
  Granted                      12.4           5.4         745      100.0 %
  Waited                        0.0           0.0           0        0.0 %
 -------------------------   -----------   -----------   ----------
  Total Last Pg Locks          12.4           5.4         745       12.1 %

Deadlocks by Lock Type       per sec       per xact        count   % of total
 -------------------------   -----------   -----------   ----------  ----------
  Deadlock Detection            0.0           0.0           0         n/a
  Deadlock Searches             0.0           0.0           0         n/a

  Lock Promotions               0.0           0.0           0         n/a
===============================================================================
Data Cache Management
---------------------
  Cache Statistics Summary (All Caches)
  -------------------------------------
  Cache Search Summary
    Total Cache Hits          118.6          51.1        7107       97.7 %
    Total Cache Misses          2.7           1.2         164        2.3 %
   -------------------------   -----------   -----------   ----------
    Total Cache Searches      121.3          52.3        7271

  Cache Turnover
    Buffers Grabbed             0.7           0.3          44         n/a
    Buffers Grabbed Dirty       0.0           0.0           0        0.0 %

  Cache Strategy Summary
    Cached (LRU) Buffers      152.4          65.7        9134      100.0 %
    Discarded (MRU) Buffers     0.0           0.0           0        0.0 %

  Large I/O Usage
    Large I/Os Performed        0.0           0.0           0        0.0 %
    Large I/Os Denied           0.0           0.0           1      100.0 %
   -------------------------   -----------   -----------   ----------
    Total Large I/O Requests    0.0           0.0           1

  Large I/O Effectiveness
    Pages by Lrg I/O Cached     0.0           0.0           0         n/a

  Dirty Read Behavior
    Page Requests               0.0           0.0           0         n/a
 ---------------------------------------------------------------------------
```

default data cache	per sec	per xact	count	% of total
	0.0	0.0	0	n/a
Utilization	n/a	n/a	n/a	100.0 %
Cache Searches				
Cache Hits	118.6	51.1	7107	97.7 %
Found in Wash	2.0	0.9	119	1.7 %
Cache Misses	2.7	1.2	164	2.3 %
Total Cache Searches	121.3	52.3	7271	
Pool Turnover				
2 Kb Pool				
LRU Buffer Grab	0.7	0.3	44	100.0 %
Grabbed Dirty	0.0	0.0	0	0.0 %
Total Cache Turnover	0.7	0.3	44	

Buffer Wash Behavior
 Statistics Not Available - No Buffers Entered Wash Section Yet

Cache Strategy				
Cached (LRU) Buffers	152.4	65.7	9134	100.0 %
Discarded (MRU) Buffers	0.0	0.0	0	0.0 %
Large I/O Usage				
Large I/Os Performed	0.0	0.0	0	0.0 %
Large I/Os Denied	0.0	0.0	1	100.0 %
Total Large I/O Requests	0.0	0.0	1	

Large I/O Detail
 No Large Pool(s) In This Cache

Dirty Read Behavior				
Page Requests	0.0	0.0	0	n/a

Procedure Cache Management	per sec	per xact	count	% of total
Procedure Requests	0.0	0.0	0	n/a

Memory Management	per sec	per xact	count	% of total
Pages Allocated	0.0	0.0	2	n/a
Pages Released	0.0	0.0	2	n/a

Recovery Management

Checkpoints	per sec	per xact	count	% of total
# of Normal Checkpoints	0.0	0.0	2	100.0 %
# of Free Checkpoints	0.0	0.0	0	0.0 %
Total Checkpoints	0.0	0.0	2	n/a

```
   Avg Time per Normal Chkpt     0.00000 seconds
================================================================================
Disk I/O Management
-------------------
  Max Outstanding I/Os          per sec     per xact       count   % of total
  ------------------------      --------    --------    --------   ---------
    Server                         n/a         n/a            8         n/a
    Engine 0                       n/a         n/a            8         n/a

  I/Os Delayed by
    Disk I/O Structures            n/a         n/a            0         n/a
    Server Config Limit            n/a         n/a            0         n/a
    Engine Config Limit            n/a         n/a            0         n/a
    Operating System Limit         n/a         n/a            0         n/a

  Total Requested Disk I/Os       5.1         2.2          307         n/a

  Completed Disk I/O's
    Engine 0                      5.1         2.2          308       100.0 %
  ------------------------      --------    --------    --------   ---------
  Total Completed I/Os            5.1         2.2          308

  Device Activity Detail
  ----------------------
  d:\sybase\system11\data\device1.dat
  Device1                       per sec     per xact       count   % of total
  ------------------------      --------    --------    --------   ---------
                                  0.0         0.0            0         n/a
  ------------------------      --------    --------    --------   ---------
  Total I/Os                      0.0         0.0            0         0.0 %


  ----------------------------------------------------------------
  d:\sybase\system11\data\device2.dat
  Device2                       per sec     per xact       count   % of total
  ------------------------      --------    --------    --------   ---------
                                  0.0         0.0            0         n/a
  ------------------------      --------    --------    --------   ---------
  Total I/Os                      0.0         0.0            0         0.0 %


  ----------------------------------------------------------------
  D:\SYBASE\System11\DATA\SYBPROCS.DAT
  sysprocsdev                   per sec     per xact       count   % of total
  ------------------------      --------    --------    --------   ---------
                                  0.0         0.0            0         n/a
  ----------------------------------------------------------------
  Total I/Os                      0.0         0.0            0         0.0 %


  ----------------------------------------------------------------
  D:\SYBASE\System11\data\sybsecur.dat
  sybsecurity                   per sec     per xact       count   % of total
  ------------------------      --------    --------    --------   ---------
    Reads                         0.0         0.0            0         0.0 %
    Writes                        2.5         1.1          151       100.0 %
  ------------------------      --------    --------    --------   ---------
  Total I/Os                      2.5         1.1          151        49.2 %
```

```
Device Semaphore Granted          2.5          1.1          151      100.0 %
Device Semaphore Waited           0.0          0.0            0        0.0 %


 ----------------------------------------------------------------------
master.dat
master                         per sec      per xact      count   % of total
 --------------------------    ----------   ----------    -------  ----------
    Reads                         0.7          0.3           44       28.2 %
    Writes                        1.9          0.8          112       71.8 %
 --------------------------    ----------   ----------    -------  ----------
Total I/Os                        2.6          1.1          156       50.8 %

Device Semaphore Granted          2.6          1.1          156      100.0 %
Device Semaphore Waited           0.0          0.0            0        0.0 %
 ----------------------------------------------------------------------
==============================================================================
Network I/O Management
 ----------------------
    Total Network I/O Requests    1.5          0.6           90        n/a
    Network I/Os Delayed          0.0          0.0            0        0.0 %

Total TDS Packets Received     per sec      per xact      count   % of total
 -----------------------       ----------   ----------    -------  ----------
                                  0.0          0.0            0        n/a
 -----------------------       ----------   ----------    -------  ----------
Total TDS Packets Rec'd           0.0          0.0            0

Total Bytes Received           per sec      per xact      count   % of total
 -----------------------       ----------   ----------    -------  ----------
                                  0.0          0.0            0        n/a
 -----------------------       ----------   ----------    -------  ----------
Total Bytes Rec'd                 0.0          0.0            0


 ----------------------------------------------------------------------
Total TDS Packets Sent         per sec      per xact      count   % of total
 -----------------------       ----------   ----------    -------  ----------
                                  0.0          0.0            0        n/a
 -----------------------       ----------   ----------    -------  ----------
Total TDS Packets Sent            0.0          0.0            0

Total Bytes Sent               per sec      per xact      count   % of total
 -----------------------       ----------   ----------    -------  ----------
                                  0.0          0.0            0        n/a
 -----------------------       ----------   ----------    -------  ----------
Total Bytes Sent                  0.0          0.0            0
============================= End of Report ================================
```

Rather than reinventing the wheel and completely redocumenting sp_sysmon, I'm going to point you to an excellent chapter in the Sybase documentation that you *must* read to get a full understanding of the information presented by sp_sysmon: Chapter 19, "Monitoring SQL Server Performance with sp_sysmon," of the *Performance and Tuning Guide.*

From Here...

In this chapter you learned how to identify and manage statistics that will help you determine the performance characteristics of your server. You also learned how to size a database and how to size the procedure cache. This chapter was designed to provide you with the educational tools required to figure out performance issues in the future. Performance tuning always boils down to sensible and measurable benchmark analysis. I hope that after reading this chapter, you have an idea of *how* to measure the performance of your systems.

Consider looking at the following chapters to further develop your Sybase System XI knowledge:

- Chapter 6, "Understanding Tables and Datatypes," provides clues on how to improve the performance of your tables by choosing the right datatypes.

- Chapter 8, "Understanding Indexes and Keys," provides comprehensive information on how to organize the indexing of your data to improve data access time.

- Chapter 15, "Using Client/Server Application Programming Tools," teaches you to examine how clients connect to the database, and perhaps tune the ODBC interface on the client.

- Chapter 23, "Using Sybase's Configuration Options," teaches you to further tune the server after analyzing the information provided by the SQL Performance Monitor.

Using Sybase's Configuration Options

How to configure your server, database, and query with the available options

Sybase System XI is the most configurable version of Sybase yet. Sybase has added dozens of new options that you can use to optimize the performance and change the operation of your system. This chapter shows you how to configure many of the options in Sybase System XI.

The purpose of each server, database, and query option

Sybase System XI has numerous options that can be configured. This chapter helps you understand them and give you some examples on their use.

Using Sybase's Windows-based utilities for server management

Sybase's graphical utilities Sybase SQL Server Manager and Sybase Server Configuration Utility are excellent tools that help you manage the multitude of options that are available for configuration.

After the release of Sybase System 10 in late 1993/early 1994, Sybase realized that there were significant performance obstacles that needed to be overcome before the release of System XI. One of the key concerns of many major Sybase accounts was that the DBA wasn't given enough flexibility to tune the database in any way they wanted to. Part of the problem was that Sybase's earlier releases had been targeted to solving the problems of many different types of customers, and Sybase thought that a "one size fits all" approach to managing the problems of configuration was better.

System XI completely reverses that design goal. Much of the previously unconfigurable, or difficult to configure options, have now been exposed for you to manage effectively and easily. What this means is that you can still take the defaults that Sybase provides—or if you think you know how better to tune your environment, Sybase now gives you that option.

Sybase System XI has a number of ways of being configured. Those ways are roughly broken down into the three following areas:

- **Server options**—These are global options that affect all operations on the currently active server. These options apply to all logons on the server and to all databases and other objects that the server owns. Server options are generally used for performance tuning and capacity or object handling management.

- **Database options**—These are global options that affect all operations on the currently active or *used* database. Database options are generally used to limit access to the database and to enable high-speed BCP operations.

- **Query options**—These are local options that affect only the currently executing query or a stored procedure or trigger that is being executed on the server. Query options enable the tuning and monitoring of the activities of individual queries, and they enable the displaying of additional statistical information about the query's execution.

Using the Configure Sybase Servers Utility

Sybase's Configure Sybase Servers utility is a convenient tool that Sybase provides to give you easy access to a number of the configuration options that are either in the configuration file (usually `Server_Name.CFG` in your root Sybase directory) or are built into the database server's core configuration tables in the *master* database.

This section documents the use of some of the options of the Configure Sybase Servers utility and gives you some pointers about the important server-wide characteristics that you need to be aware of when installing Sybase.

Configuring the Sybase System XI Server

After installing the Sybase System XI server on Windows NT, it can be necessary to reconfigure some of the default options that were picked during the installation process. For some reason on Windows NT, Sybase has taken the approach that you should be given defaults that are chosen by some Sybase engineer, and then if you want to change those options, you will need to manually return to the Configure Sybase Servers utility program to alter those options. On UNIX however, Sybase's installation program clearly prompts you for language, character set, and other options that are available here in this configuration program.

Understanding Languages   Language selection for the Sybase server has little bearing on anything other than the warning and error messages that are returned to you as a user of the database. In Sybase, all error messages in stored procedures are simply indicated by a number in the source code of the system-stored procedure. When the error condition is raised, another system-stored procedure, sp_getmessage, is responsible for going to the *sysmessages* database table and retrieving an appropriate message. The *sysmessages* table is localized on installation of the Sybase database server to the language or languages that you pick. When the error condition is raised, the sp_getmessage procedure then looks at the currently set @@langid system variable to determine which language (if there's more than one currently installed on the server) should be returned to the client program.

This localization of languages enables Sybase to deliver a core, unaltered product for all national languages and then be able to drop in or plug in country- and language-specific messages required for each region that Sybase is sold in.

To configure Sybase's selection and availability of languages using the Configure Sybase Servers utility, follow these steps:

1. Launch the Configure Sybase Server Utility from the Sybase for Windows NT program group/folder (see Fig. 23.1).

FIG. 23.1

The Configure Sybase Servers utility centralizes the maintenance of the core server components and helps you work with the configuration files that are the underlying way of modifying the behavior of your server.

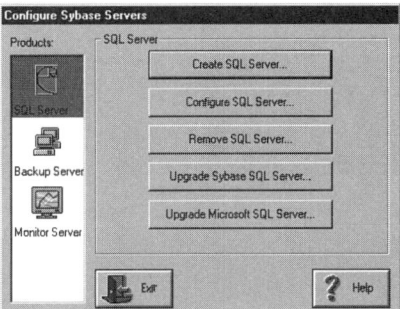

2. Select the SQL Server icon in the Products list on the left-hand side of the dialog box, and click the Configure SQL Server button to display the Existing Servers dialog box (see Fig. 23.2).

FIG. 23.2

The Existing Servers dialog box lists any servers that are available for management (i.e., listed in the interfaces file SQL.INI) from this workstation.

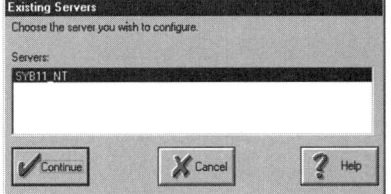

3. Select the server (if you have more than one) from the list of Servers that you want to manage, and click Continue to display a System Administrator Password dialog box (see Fig. 23.3).

FIG. 23.3

The Enter the System Administrator Password dialog box is required because all the configuration options that you are performing require System Administrator (sa) privileges on the server.

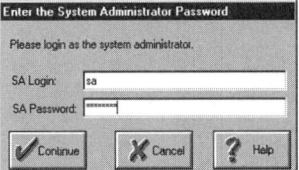

4. Enter the System Administrator (sa) password and click Continue to log on to the server and display the Configure SQL Server dialog box (see Fig. 23.4).

FIG. 23.4

The Configure SQL Server dialog box has all the server-wide options that are available for configuration through the Configure Sybase Servers utility. After working with each of the sub-dialog boxes (accessed by clicking a button), you click the Save button to perform the server change.

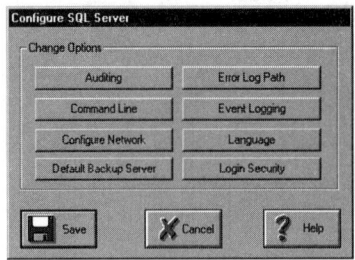

5. Click the Language button to display the Language Options dialog box (see Fig. 23.5).

FIG. 23.5

The Language Options dialog box shows the currently selected Language, Sort Order, and Character Set installed on the server. To change any of the selections, use the Add/Remove and the Set Default buttons.

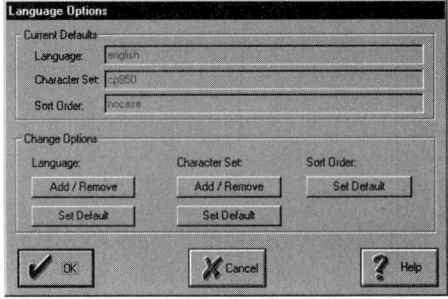

6. Click the Add/Remove button under the Language prompt. Select the languages that you want to be active on the server, and the click OK in the Install Languages dialog box that is shown in Figure 23.6.

FIG. 23.6

The Install Languages dialog box lists any languages on the left that were selected for installation at the time the server was installed and have yet to be made active.

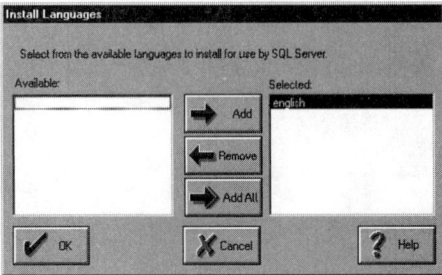

7. Click OK in the Language Options dialog box to return to the Configure SQL Server dialog box (see Fig. 23.4).

8. Click the Save button in the Configure SQL Server dialog box to have the Configure Sybase Servers utility alter the configuration of the server.

Understanding Character Sets   Character set selection is a key part of installing your server. The character set of the server controls the sorts of data that you can store in the database, and how special language characters will be presented and returned to the client program. Choosing a character set for the server in turn chooses the available set of characters that can be physically represented in the database. On Sybase, as in most application programs, data is stored in hexadecimal and binary equivalents of the text that is sent to it. So the choice of the character set determines how those numerical representations of values and characters will be presented when requested by a Select statement.

Character set selection can be confusing at times because even though you have chosen a character set that doesn't correctly store the data that you need (such as Roman 8 not being able to store such Spanish characters as the ñ) it will appear correctly in your own applications because the Windows client is translating the text stream on the fly. You really start to notice an incorrect character set selection when you start running application programs on other platforms, such as UNIX.

> **T I P**
>
> A good way to test whether your character set selection is accurately storing the data the way you expect is to run ISQL natively from the Windows NT command line or on the UNIX box through Telnet. Perform a Select on the data to guarantee that what you Insert is what you can retrieve.

On most Sybase installations, the most commonly selected character set is Code Page 850 (cp850). If you have a specific reason for modifying the default character set, follow these steps:

1. Launch the Configure Sybase Server Utility from the Sybase for Windows NT program group and navigate to the Configure SQL Server dialog box, following the steps shown in the earlier section "Understanding Languages."

2. Click the Add/Remove button under the Character Set prompt to display the Install Character Sets dialog box (see Fig. 23.7).

FIG. 23.7

The Install Character Sets dialog box lists the available character sets that have yet to be installed on the server.

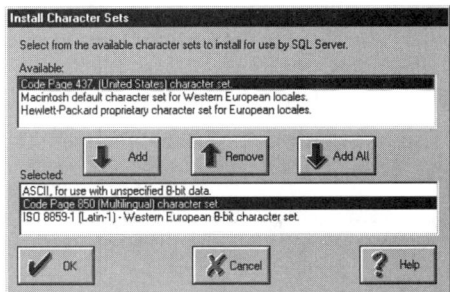

3. Select the Character Sets that you want to add and then press OK.

4. Click the OK button in the Language Options dialog box to return to the Configure SQL Server dialog box.

5. Click OK in the Language Options dialog box to return to the Configure SQL Server dialog box (see Fig. 23.4).

6. Click the Save button in the Configure SQL Server dialog box to have the Configure Sybase Servers utility go and alter the configuration of the server.

Understanding Sort Orders   Sort orders control the way Sybase orders the data that is returned in the results of a `Select` statement that uses an `Order By` clause. There are several different types of sort orders that are available for selection when you install the Sybase server. Each of the sort order options have different characteristics that make them valuable in different circumstances. However, you should be aware that your sort order selection can drastically affect the performance of the server in query intensive applications.

If you are requiring complex, accurate sorts that also take into consideration the special characters of a localized character set, you need to know that this will cost you server time, because it requires more work for the results to be placed in the desired order.

N O T E   Note that all languages that you install will have a sort order available of *Binary Order* sorting. However, only some of the other options, such as *Dictionary Order*, will be available, depending upon the language. ▪

The sort order options are described as follows:

- **Binary sort order**—This sorting places all values in the binary order of equivalence as the data is stored. This is the most efficient sorting algorithm. Uppercase values are sorted before lowercase values.

- **Dictionary order, case insensitive**—This option sorts the data in the order of a dictionary and ignores the case of a value when choosing the order of the data. This is the most recommended installation option because it means that you don't have to consider accurately setting the case of object names when referring to them.

- **Dictionary order, case sensitive**—This sorts in dictionary order, except that case is considered a critical component of the sort. Uppercase values are sorted before lowercase values.

- **Dictionary order, case sensitive, accent sensitive**—An extension of the Dictionary order, case sensitive option, this sort also considers whether or not a character is accented. Accented values are sorted after the corresponding unaccented value.

- **Dictionary order, case insensitive, accent insensitive**—This sort order treats all forms of a character in the same way.

To alter the currently configured sort order, follow these steps:

1. Launch the Configure Sybase Server Utility from the Sybase for Windows NT program group and navigate to the Configure SQL Server dialog box, following the steps shown above in "Understanding Languages."

2. Click the Set Default button under the Sort Order prompt to display the Select Default Sort Order dialog box (see Fig. 23.8).

FIG. 23.8

The Select Default Sort Order dialog box enables you to pick the sort order that you want to use for the server. The previously selected option will default in this dialog box prior to your changing it.

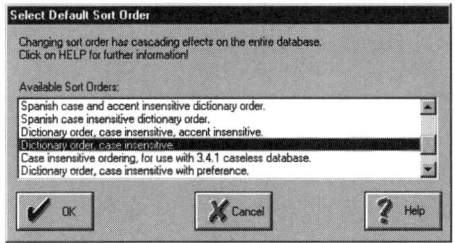

Part

IV

Ch

23

3. Select the Sort Order that you want to use and then press OK.

4. Click the OK button in the Language Options dialog box to return to the Configure SQL Server dialog box.

5. Click OK in the Language Options dialog box to return to the Configure SQL Server dialog box (refer to Fig. 23.4).

6. Click the Save button in the Configure SQL Server dialog box to have the Configure Sybase Servers utility go and alter the configuration of the server.

CAUTION

Changing the sort order on a server that already has installed databases is a bad thing to do because it invalidates all the indexes and can drastically affect the storage of the data. I highly recommend that you perform a logical unload of your data using BCP or some other third-party program, and then rebuild the database after choosing the required sort order for your database server.

To fix a broken index, you can use the DBCC command DBCC Reindex(*Table_Name*). For more information on the different ways to use DBCC, see Chapter 20, "Understanding the Joys, Secrets, and Mysteries of DBCC."

Configuring the Backup Server

There are some options that you may want to configure in the Backup Server that relate to the way it will be interacting with the SQL Server you already have installed. To manage the options in the Backup Server, follow these steps:

1. Launch the Configure Sybase Server Utility from the Sybase for Windows NT program group/folder.

2. Select the Backup Server icon in the Products list on the left-hand side of the dialog box, and click the Configure Backup Server button to display the Existing Servers dialog box (see Fig. 23.2).

3. Select the server (if you have more than one) from the list of Servers that you want to manage, and click Continue to display the Configure Backup Server dialog box (see Fig. 23.9).

FIG. 23.9

The Configure Backup Server dialog box lists all the global options that control the behavior of the Backup Server. Note that you can click the Command Line Parameters and Network Addresses buttons to further customize the Backup Server's operation.

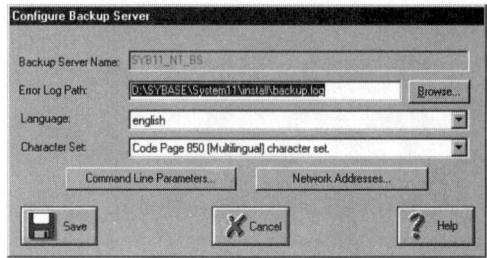

4. Modify the Error log field if you want to move the error log from its default of the %Sybase%\install directory.

5. Select the language that you want to use for the backup. Note: the only available languages for selection will be those that you have currently installed on the server.

6. Select the character set that you want to use for the Backup Server's output.

7. Click the Save button in the Configure Backup Server dialog box to have the Configure Sybase Servers utility alter the configuration of the Backup Server.

Configuring the Monitor Server

The Monitor Server has few options that can be configured through the Configure Sybase Servers utility. To access these configurable options, follow these steps:

1. Launch the Configure Sybase Server Utility from the Sybase for Windows NT program group/folder.

2. Select the Monitor Server icon in the Products list on the left-hand side of the dialog box, and click the Configure Monitor Server button to display the Existing Servers dialog box (refer to Fig. 23.2).

3. Select the server (if you have more than one) from the list of Servers that you want to manage, and click Continue to display the Configure Monitor Server dialog box (see Fig. 23.10).

4. Modify the Error log field if you want to move the error log from its default of the %Sybase%\install directory.

5. Click the Save button in the Configure Backup Server dialog box to have the Configure Sybase Servers utility alter the configuration of the Backup Server.

FIG. 23.10
Configure Monitor
Server is a simple
dialog box that enables
you to change the
output of the error log
and the name of the
server that is being
monitored.

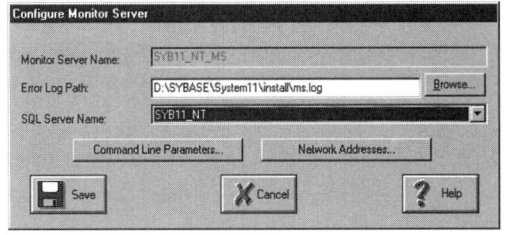

Configuring and Managing Servers

Sybase System XI provides a number of configuration options to enable varied and different installations of the server. These options are used to customize the way Sybase System XI's resources are managed. The sorts of resources that are available for management are the following:

- Memory
- User and logon handling
- Sizes of objects
- Network and physical I/O handling
- Memory, disk, procedure, and read-ahead cache
- Symmetric Multi-Processing (SMP) management

N O T E *Symmetric Multi-Processing* (SMP) computers are computers that conform to a published standard for incorporating more than one CPU in the system unit. SMP computers typically offer substantial performance improvements over single CPU boxes because they can distribute the processing workload to as many CPUs as are available. Windows NT and UNIX based SMP systems have been shown to provide near-linear performance improvements on computers with as many as eight CPUs on Windows NT 4 and up to 14 CPUs on UNIX. ▪

CAUTION
Changing server configurations can sometimes make a server unable to be restarted after the change (such as over-committed memory). To restart a server in this situation, it may be necessary to start the server in *minimal configuration mode,* which enables you to bring up the server without it attempting to apply the configurations that you set.

Displaying and Setting Server Options

Sybase System XI provides two ways to display and set configuration options for the server. The graphical method is via Sybase SQL Server Manager. The Transact-SQL method is by using the system-stored procedure, `sp_configure`.

Using Sybase SQL Server Manager to Configure Server Options Sybase SQL Server Manager is a very convenient tool for the DBA to use when changing server options. The user interface makes it unnecessary to remember the syntax required for sp_configure or to know all the different options.

To use the Sybase SQL Server Manager to display and set server options, perform the following steps:

1. Run Sybase SQL Server Manager from the Sybase for Windows NT program group and select the Server that you want to manage (see Fig. 23.11).

FIG. 23.11

The SSM displays the available servers for configuration in the left pane of the explorer view, and in the right pane is a list of appropriate options that are configurable.

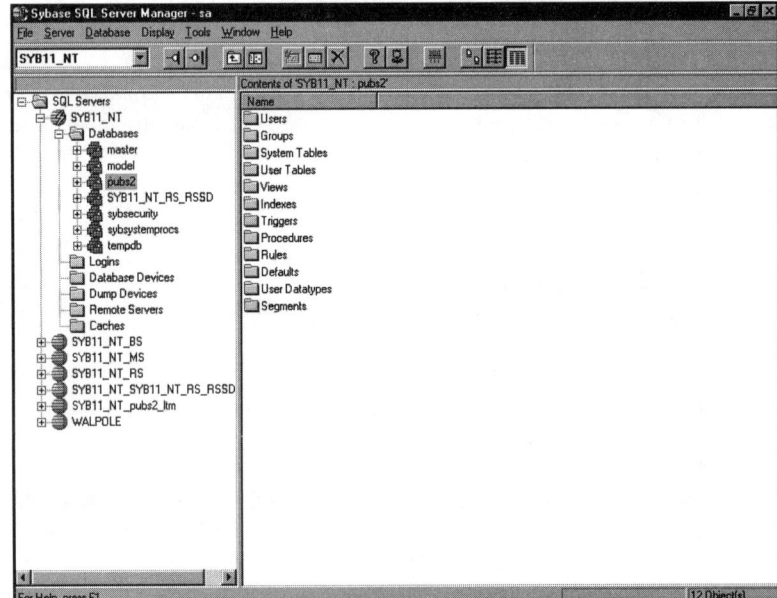

2. From the Server menu select Configuration. When the Server Configuration Parameters dialog box is displayed, click the required level of detail set of radio buttons to display different options for configuration in the table at the bottom of the dialog box (see Fig. 23.12).

3. To change any of the settings for the server, click the option, and then enter the required value in the New field.

4. Click the Change button that activates after you modify a value to save the change into the table, and place it in a list of changes to be applied.

5. Click the OK button to perform any configuration changes and save the newly configured values into the *syscurconfigs* table in the master database.

6. Click the Cancel button to ignore any configuration changes that you have made.

FIG. 23.12

The SSM Configuration Parameters dialog box has a set of radio buttons that control the level of detail or complexity of the options that are available for configuration: Standard, Advanced, and Complete.

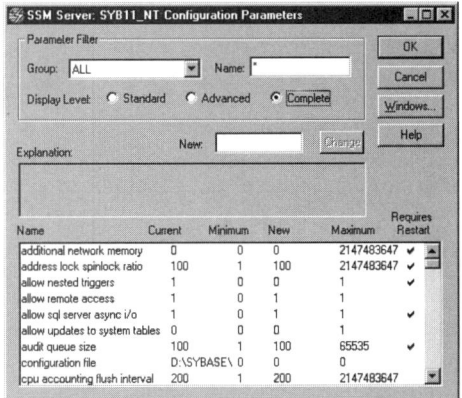

 T I P Use the explanation field on the dialog box to give you tips on the meaning of the value that you are currently configuring.

Using the System-Stored Procedure sp_configure The system-stored procedure, sp_configure is provided to enable the changing of settings on the server. You can use sp_configure for writing automated scripts that update the server without user intervention.

The syntax for the use of the system-stored procedure sp_configure is as follows:

```
sp_configure [configuration option, [configuration value]]
```

The configuration option is the value that is needed to change in the server. Sybase System XI uses a Like operator on the text that is supplied so that any unique set of characters is recognized without requiring the full text value. Sybase System XI requires that any text with spaces or other formatting in the configuration option parameter be enclosed in quotation marks. Listing 23.1 shows that all of the sp_configure statements perform the same function.

Listing 23.1 sp_configure—Requires Only That the Option Being Changed Is Uniquely Identified

```
sp_configure "nested Triggers", 0
Go
sp_configure "nested", 1
Go
sp_configure "triggers", 0
Go
sp_configure "trig", 0
Go
```

Part

IV

Ch

23

N O T E You can get a list of configurable options at a high level by executing `sp_configure` and passing in an invalid value:

```
sp_configure '1'
Go

----------------------------------------------------------------
No matching configuration options.  Here is a listing of groups:
Backup/Recovery
Cache Manager
Configuration Options
Disk I/O
General Information
Languages
Lock Manager
Memory Use
Network Communication
O/S Resources
Physical Memory
Physical Resources
Processors
SQL Server Administration
User Environment
```

To then get a list of specific options you just execute `sp_configure` for the given group. For example, to get a list of the current User Environment configurations and their current values you would execute:

```
    sp_configure 'User Environment'
Go
```

Group: User Environment

Parameter Name	Default	Memory Used	Config Value	Run Value
default network packet size	512	#136	512	512
number of pre-allocated extent	2	0	2	2
number of user connections	25	1870	25	25
permission cache entries	15	#29	15	15
stack guard size	4096	#244	4096	4096
stack size	36864	#2197	36864	36864
systemwide password expiration	0	0	0	0
user log cache size	2048	0	2048	2048
user log cache spinlock ratio	20	0	20	20

TROUBLESHOOTING

I'm trying to change a configuration option, and sp_configure keeps returning:

Permission denied. Only users with role 'sa_role' can change this configuration option.

You're not logged in to the database as SA. Only SA can change a server configuration. Log off from ISQL/W or the database tool that you are using, and reconnect to the database as the SA user.

Understanding the Reconfigure Command   The `Reconfigure` command was used in previous releases of Sybase to tell the server to implement a change made with `sp_configure`. In Sybase System XI, it is no longer required and actually doesn't do anything.

The `Reconfigure` command will probably not be supported in later releases of Sybase, and so you should remove the command from any scripts or application code that you have as soon as possible.

Server Options Explained

The following is a comprehensive list of all the most important server options. The options are organized alphabetically and the configuration group that the option belongs to is listed in parentheses after the option.

In each item below, there are indications of the minimum, maximum, and default values. These values indicate the range of values that the item can have and the default value to which Sybase System XI is configured when first installed.

additional network memory (Physical Memory)

Minimum: 0

Maximum: 2,147,483,647

Default: 0

This server option allocates memory on the server for any connections that are made to the server by clients requesting bigger network packet sizes than the default network packet size. If no memory is allocated with this option, the users will not be able to connect with larger than default network packet sizes.

address lock spinlock ratio (Lock Manager)

Minimum: 0

Maximum: 2,147,483,647

Default: 100

This option controls the way memory is managed inside Sybase. Normally, Sybase allocates a spinlock mechanism by which all requests for a common piece of memory are managed through a central program schedule. By allocating more spinlock managers for the available memory, you effectively make the memory manager parallel, which improves performance because the spinlock managers need to do less work while managing a smaller area of memory. This can improve performance on multi-CPU systems because each CPU can physically manage a spinlock manager. A single CPU system will not be affected by this configuration setting.

allow nested triggers (SQL Server Administration)

Minimum: 0 (Off)

Maximum: 1 (On)

Default: 1

If set to True, the default, Sybase will permit a trigger to call another trigger or to cause an additional trigger to execute, if an action is performed on another table.

▶ **See** "Using Nested Triggers," **p. 193**

TROUBLESHOOTING

I'm concerned that too many triggers are firing, and it seems as if triggers are causing other triggers to fire. I don't know how to monitor this effectively. You can use the Nested Triggers configuration to stop Sybase System XI from allowing a trigger to cause another trigger to execute a procedure. Turning off this option will enable you to more closely examine the behavior of triggers in your application.

allow remote access (Network Communication)

Minimum: 0 (Off)

Maximum: 1 (On)

Default: 1 (On)

This configuration option controls whether remote Sybase System XI installations are allowed logon access to the server. If set to 0 (zero), Sybase System XI will deny access to remote Sybase System XI servers.

allow sql server async i/o (Disk I/O)

Minimum: 0 (Off)

Maximum: 1 (On)

Default: 0 (Off)

This option controls whether asynchronous write events are permitted to the drive controllers. With asynchronous I/O turned on, you can send multiple events to the drives without awaiting acknowledgment for the returns from the operating system. This option should be enabled wherever possible because it yields dramatic performance improvements.

allow updates to system tables (SQL Server Administration)

Minimum: 0 (Off)

Maximum: 1 (On)

Default: 0 (Off)

The `allow updates to system tables` configuration option allows the system catalog to be updated. If the value is set to 1 (one) then the system catalog is updateable. Stored procedures created while the system catalog is updateable will be able to update the system catalog even when this value is returned to 0 (zero).

Part

IV

Ch

23

> **CAUTION**
>
> Allowing updates on the system catalog is an extremely dangerous decision. It should only be done under very controlled situations and should probably be done with the server in single-user mode to prevent other users from accidentally damaging the system catalog.
>
> To start the server in single-user mode, execute `sqlservr -m` from the Win32 command prompt.
>
> ```
> sp_configure "allow updates", 1
> go
> ```

audit queue size (SQL Server Administration)

Minimum: 1

Maximum: 65,535

Default: 100

This server option controls the number of transactions that are held in the server's queue before the audited transactions are written to the *sybsecurity* database for auditing purposes. This option can make a big difference to the performance of your server. The higher this number is set, the less frequently writes will physically occur to the *sybsecurity* database, yielding less of an impact on the server's overall performance. However, if the server crashes and there are items in this buffer, they will not be written to the audit trail and this could potentially compromise the integrity of your auditing of a system.

cpu accounting flush interval (SQL Server Administration)

Minimum: 1

Maximum: 2,147,483,647

Default: 200

This server configuration option is used to control the amount of time (measured in machine clock ticks) that the server waits before dumping statistical information from the *sysprocesses* table to the *syslogins* table. If you are writing a system that charges a user for the amount of server time they consume, you would want to have a relatively low value in this field, so that you can accurately charge a customer and also get a periodically changing value for display. Note, like the audit queue size option, if the server goes down with uncommitted (transferred) values sitting in the buffer, you will lose those statistics and they will not be written to the individual login's records.

cpu grace time (SQL Server Administration)

Minimum: 0

Maximum: 2,147,483,647

Default: 500

This option is provided to help you tune the performance of long running, CPU-intensive operations. If a task is consuming the whole CPU and you want the server to kill the task or to skip processing it and move on to the next task, you need to make sure that you configure this option appropriately. This configuration setting is measured in milliseconds.

deadlock checking period (Lock Manager)

Minimum: 0

Maximum: 2,147,483,647

Default: 500

This is the amount of time in milliseconds that Sybase waits when a lock is detected before attempting to determine whether the lock is actually deadlocked. Setting this value to a higher number can improve performance on highly transactional systems because the time it takes to evaluate a deadlock condition is quite large. If there's a higher waiting period, the other locking user might have finished their transaction by rolling back and then there would be no deadlock.

deadlock retries (Lock Manager)

Minimum: 0

Maximum: 2,147,483,647

Default: 500

This option controls the number of times a locking operation will attempt to acquire a lock before giving up and assuming that the lock is being deadlocked.

default character set id (Languages)

Minimum: 0

Maximum: 255

Default: 1

This option controls the default character set that will be used by the Sybase Server.

default database size (SQL Server Administration)

Minimum: 2

Maximum: 10,000

Default: 2

This option controls the default number of megabytes to reserve for a new database being created. If the majority of the databases that are being created on a given server are greater than 2M, it would be advisable to change this value. If the *model* database grows to be greater than 2M, it will be required to adjust this value.

default fill factor percent (SQL Server Administration)

Minimum: 0

Maximum: 100

Default: 0

This configuration option controls the default `fill factor` to use when creating indexes. The `fill factor` refers to how much space Sybase System XI will reserve in an index page for the potential growth of key values on the index. This option is overridden if a `fill factor` is specified when the `Create Index` command is executed.

A `fill factor` of 100 will force Sybase System XI to fill the index pages completely and should *only* be used for extremely static tables whose key values never change, grow, or are inserted into. Smaller `fill factor` values will allow or force Sybase System XI to reserve space on the index page for new values that may be added to the table/index after the initial table load.

▶ **See** "Creating an Index with Create Index," **p. 209**

default language id (Languages)

Minimum: 0

Maximum: 32,767

Default: 0

This option controls the default language ID to be used for the server. US English is the default and is always 0 (zero). If other languages are added to the server, they will be assigned different language IDs.

default network packet size (Network Communication)

Minimum: 512

Maximum: 52,428

Default: 512

This option controls the amount of memory that will be allocated to a connection for network transmission of data between client and server. Note that setting this value to a higher amount will cause the memory requirements of the server to jump dramatically because each user connection will require more RAM. This option is measured in bytes.

default sortorder id (Languages)

Minimum: 0

Maximum: 255

Default: 50

This option controls the sort order that the server will be using. The sort order controls the way Sybase System XI sorts data and returns it to the client. The default is binary sort order.

CAUTION

Do not use sp_configure to change the sortorder. Use the Sybase System XI setup program if you want to change this value. Changing the sortorder will require that you unload and reload the database because the data will need to be stored in a different format.

---

event buffers per engine (SQL Server Administration)

Minimum: 1

Maximum: 2,147,483,647

Default: 100

This option controls the number of buffers that are allocated by Sybase for the interaction with SQL Monitor. SQL Monitor uses these buffers to retrieve timely information on the performance of the server.

freelock transfer block size (Lock Manager)

Minimum: 1

Maximum: 2,147,483,647

Default: 30

You can use the freelock transfer block size option to tune how many locks Sybase will move from the global lock list to a specific engine to be managed locally on the CPU.

housekeeper free write percent (SQL Server Administration)

Minimum: 0

Maximum: 100

Default: 1

This option controls the way the housekeeper task works in writing modified cache pages to disk. The housekeeper works in the background by detecting when I/O is at a low level and then engages itself to move the data. The percentage refers to how much overhead is permissible for the housekeeper to increase the overall load of the server. For example, in its default mode, the housekeeper will only be activated if the load it places on the server is *at most* an additional one percent.

i/o accounting flush interval (SQL Server Administration)

Minimum: 1

Maximum: 2,147,483,647

Default: 1,000

Part

IV

Ch

23

This option controls the number of machine clock ticks that Sybase waits before writing I/O statistical information from the dynamic table sysprocesses to the static user/login table syslogins.

i/o polling process count (SQL Server Administration)

Minimum: 1

Maximum: 2,147,483,647

Default: 10

This option controls the amount of processes that Sybase will run in succession before checking that there's a free I/O resource. This option can greatly improve performance on systems because it enables you to tune how frequently you want Sybase to stop doing real work and go and look for free I/O resources.

Generally, if you increase the value of i/o polling process count you should see better throughput on the writes to the drives because there's less time spent actually checking for success and free resources, instead Sybase will try and fill the drive up more often. If you decrease the value of i/o polling process count you should expect to see better performance or response time from the application, because the server will be balancing operations more evenly, and will have more opportunity to listen to various different user requests in sequence.

identity burning set factor (SQL Server Administration)

Minimum: 1

Maximum: 9,999,999

Default: 5,000

Sybase manages all of the Identity columns that are on tables in the database by having a pool of available Identity values that can be assigned to the next records that are inserted into a table. For performance reasons, Sybase pre-allocates these numbers into a memory area so that instead of reviewing the last number allocated on the table each time,
Sybase can just read from memory. The advantage is the lack of Physical I/O that needs to be

performed to determine the required number. After all the identities have been allocated from the memory pool, Sybase then goes and re-evaluates the allocation and creates a new pool.

This option controls how many records Sybase places in the pool for allocation to inserted records. If you set this value very high and the server is shut down disgracefully (shutdown with nowait), you will lose the allocated (pooled) values for use with the table, and may end up with large gaps in the identity values that are used in your system.

identity grab size (SQL Server Administration)

Minimum: 1

Maximum: 2,147,483,647

Default: 1

This option controls the number of Identity values that are grabbed for a particular table during a set of inserts. If you want to have sequential Identity values assigned to each record inserted into a table in a batch, you will want to set this value to a higher number than the default of 1. You should probably set the identity grab size option to be equal to the largest number of contiguous inserts that you expect to perform in a normal day of operation.

lock promotion LWM (SQL Server Administration)

Minimum: 2

Maximum: 500,000

Default: 20

This configuration option controls the minimum number of page locks that Sybase System XI will require a single query to acquire before escalating a set of page locks on a table to a full table lock. This configuration option is provided so that the lock promotion threshold percentage will not hit on tables with small numbers of pages of data. Note: LWM stands for *low water mark.*

lock promotion HWM (SQL Server Administration)

Minimum: 2

Maximum: 500,000

Default: 200

This configuration option controls the maximum number of page locks that Sybase System XI will permit a single query before escalating a set of page locks on a table to a full table lock. If the number of pages is exceeded, Sybase System XI will force a table lock—irrespective of the lock promotion threshold percentage configured for the table. Lock escalation is performed to improve performance on the server because of unnecessary memory being allocated to manage the individual page locks. Note: HWM stands for *high water mark.*

lock promotion PCT (SQL Server Administration)

Minimum: 1

Maximum: 100

Default: 0

This configuration option controls the percentage of page locks to pages of data in the table that need to be acquired on a table before Sybase System XI will escalate the lock to a full table lock. A value of 0 (zero), the default, will not allow Sybase System XI to perform lock escalation unless the lock escalation threshold maximum is reached.

lock shared memory (Physical Memory)

Minimum: 0 (Off)

Maximum: 1 (On)

Default: 0 (Off)

This option will stop the SQL Server from allowing the operating system to page Sybase memory pages from physical memory to disk. Some operating systems do not support the ability to physically lock down memory, and so this may fail on your operating system. The reason to lock the shared memory in the first place is straight performance— if you can avoid ever needing to go to disk for memory-related activities you will receive great magnitudes of performance improvement.

max async i/os per engine (Operating System Resources)

Minimum: 1

Maximum: 2,147,483,647

Default: 2,147,483,647

This configuration option controls the maximum number of asynchronous I/O requests that the Sybase System XI can make to the hardware devices from a given online engine in an instance of Sybase.

Generally speaking, this value should be set to the maximum number of asynchronous I/O operations permitted by your underlying operating system. Letting Sybase attempt an unsuccessful asynchronous I/O operation is an expensive (in terms of CPU time) operation and should be avoided.

max async i/os per server (Operating System Resources)

Minimum: 1

Maximum: 2,147,483,647

Default: 2,147,483,647

This configuration option controls the maximum number of asynchronous I/O requests that the Sybase System XI can make to the hardware devices from a given server, regardless of how many online engines you have running.

Generally speaking, this value should be set to the maximum number of asynchronous I/O operations permitted by your underlying operating system. Letting Sybase attempt an unsuccessful asynchronous I/O operation is an expensive (in terms of CPU time) operation and should be avoided.

max engine freelocks (Lock Manager)

Minimum: 1

Maximum: 50

Default: 10

This option controls the percentage of the global locks that can be moved to a particular engine on a multi-CPU machine. On a single CPU machine, all locks are migrated from the global lock area to the primary CPU for management. If you have a multi-CPU, multi-engine machine, Sybase balances the load of the lock management process by migrating a lock from the global lock area to a free engine that has yet to exceed its max engine freelocks configuration setting.

For example, say you have 20,000 locks and 10 CPUs, each with its own engine. Setting max engine freelocks (which acts as a percentage) to 25 will mean that 25 percent of 20,000 or 5,000 locks are to be managed by each engine independent of the global lock area. Because there are 10 engines running, each engine will be allocated 500 locks in the freelock area for managing locks that need to be distributed from the global lock area.

max network packet size (Network Communication)

Minimum: 512

Maximum: 32,767

Default: 4,096

This configuration option controls the server-wide maximum network packet size that is requested by a client. If the client requests a size less than the value specified in the current value, Sybase System XI will accept it; however, greater values than the current value will be negotiated to the maximum value specified here.

This option can improve performance on networks whose base topology supports wider or larger packets than TCP/IP's default of 4,096 bytes. This is especially useful if you are running over a satellite service and want to batch large packets of data to send through the satellite packet service.

This option should be adjusted to a higher value for reporting-only databases that are not acquiring any locks on the datasets because it will allow larger batches of data to be sent to the client at one time, improving network throughput.

CAUTION

Setting the packet size too high can cause locking problems on high-transaction databases. This is because Sybase System XI will hold locks for an unnecessarily long time in order to fill up a network packet to send to the client. Take care when adjusting this value, and perform statistical analysis to prove that the values you have chosen are beneficial to you.

max number network listeners (Network Communications)

Minimum: 0

Maximum: 2,147,483,647

Default: 15

This option enables you to set the maximum number of listener services that you configure on the Sybase server. Typically, you have a single listener for each network type and protocol that you are expecting to receive a connection from (e.g., you might have a listener for TCP/IP and also for Named Pipes).

max online engines (Processors)

Minimum: 1

Maximum: 32

Default: 1

This option configures the maximum number of online engines that you want Sybase to have running. Typically this should be set to the number of physical CPUs in the box minus one. So if you have a 10 CPU machine, you'd set this value to 9.

N O T E Note that recovery and initialization of the server is a single engine task and will be performed only by the first engine that starts up the server. The last thing that is done during the startup of the server is that the other engines are brought online and tasks are migrated to run on the other engines. ■

min online engines (Processors)

Minimum: 1

Maximum: 32

Default: 1

This option configures the number of online engines that you want Sybase to have running. Typically, this should be set to the number of physical CPUs in the box minus one. So if you have a 10-CPU machine, then set this value to 9. This option is effectively the same as max online engines described above.

number of alarms (SQL Server Administration)

Minimum: 0

Maximum: 2,147,483,647

Default: 40

Alarms are used by Sybase as timers to manage users that execute the `Waitfor` command. If you have a large number of concurrent requests for *timed* activities, you should increase the `number of alarms` option.

number of devices (SQL Server Administration)

Minimum: 1

Maximum: 256

Default: 10

This option controls the number of devices that you can have open at any one time by the Sybase server. If you restart the server with a low number of devices and then find that you can't get access to some of your databases, it's probably because the number of devices has been exceeded. Make sure that you correctly size the `number of devices` option so that you aren't overly generous (it wastes memory) and yet still allow all database devices to be accessed.

number of extent i/o buffers (SQL Server Administration)

Minimum: 0

Maximum: 2,147,483,647

Default: 0

This option controls the number of extents (eight 2K page buffers) that Sybase pre-allocates for the creation of indexes. By setting this value high, you can drastically improve the performance of index creation on a server because the I/O is less frequent and for greater chunks of contiguous disk. Note that this allocation of extent buffers is actually in memory prior to writing to disk, so if you run this in production with a lot of users, you could quickly run out of physical memory available to the server.

number of index trips (Cache Manager)

Minimum: 0

Maximum: 65,535

Default: 0

This value controls the number of times an index page can be traversed by the memory manager looking for pages to drop from the Least Recently Used/Most Recently Used page list, before it gets dropped. This configuration can help you force certain pages to stay in memory if you know that those pages will provide benefits to the users in the long run. However, be aware that if you set this value too high, your index page cache could be filled up with pages from indexes that aren't in use and this could keep required pages from being placed in the cache—causing a server error and a task to be suspended.

number of languages in cache (Languages)

Minimum: 3

Maximum: 100

Default: 3

This configuration option controls the number of languages that Sybase System XI can store in the language cache simultaneously.

number of locks (Lock Manager)

Minimum: 5,000

Maximum: 2,147,483,647

Default: 5,000

This configuration option controls the number of locks that the Sybase System XI can maintain at any time. Each lock consumes 32 bytes of RAM, and so increasing this value to a large number will most likely require more RAM to be made available to the server. For example, setting this value to 20,000 will result in $20,000 \times 32$ bytes = 640,000 bytes or 625K of RAM consumed just by the lock manager.

number of mailboxes (SQL Server Administration)

Minimum: 0

Maximum: 2,147,483,647

Default: 30

This option is used internally by Sybase to manage the sending and receiving of events and messages between the different processes running on the server. You should not modify this value unless instructed to do so by Sybase Technical Support.

number of messages (SQL Server Administration)

Minimum: 0

Maximum: 2,147,483,647

Default: 64

This option is used internally by Sybase to manage the sending and receiving of events and messages between the different processes running on the server. You should not modify this value unless instructed to do so by Sybase Technical Support.

number of oam trips (Cache Manager)

Minimum: 0

Maximum: 65,535

Default: 0

This option is like the `number of index trips` option of the `Cache Manager`, except that it applies to OAM pages. OAM (Object Allocation Map) pages store information and pointers on the pages in the physical tables pointed to by the particular `object_id` that is being processed by the Cache Manager. The value you are configuring controls the number of times that an OAM page can be traversed (and ignored because the required data was not found on it) before it is dumped from the cache and its space reclaimed by another OAM page with pointers to other database pages.

number of open databases (SQL Server Administration)

Minimum: 5

Maximum: 32,767

Default: 20

This configuration option controls the maximum number of databases that Sybase System XI can maintain in an open condition at any one time. It should not be arbitrarily set to a high value because each open database does consume some server memory.

TROUBLESHOOTING

The DBA has created a new database, but nobody can connect to it. Check to see that you haven't exceeded the number of open databases on the server. If you have, use `sp_configure` to increase the number of open databases available on the server, and try to connect again.

number of open objects (SQL Server Administration)

Minimum: 100

Maximum: 2,147,483,647

Default: 500

This configuration option controls the maximum number of objects that Sybase System XI can hold in memory at one time. An object can be a table page, stored procedure that is executing, or any other object in the database. Increase this value if the server ever reports that the maximum number of objects has been exceeded.

Take care when assigning values to this option because it may be necessary to allocate more memory to the server due to the consumption of memory resources by the open objects configuration option.

number of pre-allocated extents (SQL Server Administration)

Minimum: 0

Maximum: 31

Default: 2

This option helps highly transactional systems by pre-allocating physical extents for writing data to during times of high load. If you specify a value for this option, Sybase will maintain that number of extents ($8 \times 2K$ data pages) in the physical disk area associated with the database for use as needed. Currently, BCP is the only Sybase utility that can take advantage of this configuration option.

number of remote connections (Network Communications)

Minimum: 0

Maximum: 32,767

Default: 20

This option controls the number of remote, logical connections that can be active between two Sybase System XI SQL Servers. These are logical connections at the server level, and don't imply a user transaction is necessarily required to initiate or create the connection.

number of remote logins (Network Communications)

Minimum: 0

Maximum: 32,767

Default: 20

This option controls the number of open user connections that can be alive between a primary server and a remote server.

number of remote sites (Network Communications)

Minimum: 0

Maximum: 32,767

Default: 10

This option controls the number of remote sites that can have a connection to a given SQL Server. You may want to limit your server to only be hit by three or four other servers—set this value appropriately to limit the number of remote site connections.

number of sort buffers (SQL Server Administration)

Minimum: 0

Maximum: 32,767

Default: 0

This option controls the number of buffer areas that Sybase allocates for the data read from a table prior to placing it in the cache. If you are also tuning your server to take advantage of the number of extent i/o buffers feature, then you would want this value to be set to eight times the value selected in number of extent i/o buffers.

number of user connections (User Environment)

Minimum: 5

Maximum: 32,767

Default: 20

This configuration option controls the maximum number of user processes that can connect to the server at one time. The logical limit is 32,767; however, it is very likely that practical limits of server hardware will be exceeded before this limit is ever achieved.

There is a minimum fixed overhead for each user connection of about 40K. If this value is set to a large value it may be necessary to allocate more memory to the Sybase System XI.

TROUBLESHOOTING

Periodically—usually at times of heavy load on the server—users are reporting that they can't connect. It's possible that you are running out of available user connections on the server. Use sp_configure to increase the number of user connections to a higher value so that more concurrent users are permitted.

page lock spinlock ratio (Lock Manager)

Minimum: 1

Maximum: 2,147,483,647

Default: 100

This option is like all the other spinlock ratios that are configurable in Sybase—it enables you to configure the ratio between page lock resources and the simple spinlock managers that manage the multiple, concurrent requests for the same resource. Each spinlock consumes 256 bytes, so if you attempt to tune this feature to reduce the concurrency on a particular page lock, you should be careful to consider the amount of memory being utilized.

page utilization percent (Disk I/O)

Minimum: 1

Maximum: 100

Default: 95

This option controls whether, during an Insert, you get Sybase to traverse the table's OAM (Object Allocation Map) to look for free areas on pages already allocated to the table, or simply allocate another extent's worth of data pages for inserting into. This is a percentage-based option, and it says that if the space free in the current table is less than the specified `page utilization percent`, the Sybase server will go ahead and look for free space on the OAM. If the percentage utilized in a given table is greater than the specified value, Sybase will allocate another extent for the data to be placed in. By setting this value to 100, you will force Sybase to *always* attempt to look for free space that will accept the row being `Inserted`.

partition groups (SQL Server Administration)

Minimum: 1

Maximum: 2,147,483,647

Default: 1,024

This configuration option is used to tell the Sybase server how many partition groups to allocate per database. A group is designed to manage information up to about 16 partitions, and can be assigned to only a single table. So if you have less than 16 partitions on a single table, the remaining partition storage holders in the group will be wasted. Likewise, if you have more than 16 partitions for a given table, you will need to cross over into a second group. The default for this option would allow 1,024 tables of 16 partitions to exist in a given database. It is unlikely that you will ever approach this limit, but if you do, Sybase System XI will enable you to configure and change it.

▶ **See** "Partitioning Tables," **p. 171**

partition spinlock ratio (SQL Server Administration)

Minimum: 1

Maximum: 2,147,483,647

Default: 10

This option controls the number of spinlocks that will be allocated per partition to manage the process of sharing resources to the partitioned table data. The default configuration of this parameter is probably going to be okay for almost all situations.

permission cache entries (SQL Server Administration)

Minimum: 1

Maximum: 2,147,483,647

Default: 15

This configuration option controls the amount of or number of permission items (granted or revoked authorities) that can be cached on a per task basis by the server. Reading from the cache is dramatically quicker than requiring a read from the system catalog table *sysprotects*, so you should try to configure this value high if you have a complex authorization system.

▶ **See** "Working with User Privileges," **p. 575**

print deadlock information (SQL Server Administration)

Minimum: 0 (Off)

Maximum: 1 (On)

Default: 0 (Off)

This option controls whether, during a deadlock scenario, you want the server to drop any information that was known about the deadlock to the error log file. This option has severe impacts on the performance of a server and should only be turned on for diagnostic purposes.

print recovery information (Backup and Recovery)

Minimum: 0 (Off)

Maximum: 1 (On)

Default: 0 (Off)

This configuration option controls the information that is displayed during the Sybase System XI startup process. If set to 0 (zero), the default, then Sybase System XI will only report that the database is being recovered/restored by name. If set to 1 (one), then Sybase System XI will report in detail the status of every transaction that was pending at the time the server was shutdown, and what activity Sybase System XI took to resolve it.

TIP To view the information captured in the error log, select Error Log from the Server menu in Sybase SQL Server Manager.

procedure cache percent

Minimum: 1

Maximum: 99

Default: 30

This configuration option controls the proportion of memory that Sybase System XI grabs and allocates to store the stored procedures that have most recently been executed. For systems that have large amounts of stored procedures, it may be necessary to set this value higher than 30 percent, if the total amount of memory available to Sybase System XI is relatively low.

It is recommended that this value be reduced to 10 percent or less on systems with more than 512M of RAM. It is extremely unlikely that the amount of stored procedures in memory cache will exceed 50M.

N O T E The reason Sybase System XI has a stored procedure cache is because it does not store the desired query plan/execution plan of the procedure in the database until it is first executed. This explains why the first time a procedure is executed it takes more time to run. Sybase System XI is pulling the tokenized procedure text out of private tables and is evaluating the text and determining the correct execution path. This execution path is what is stored in the procedure cache.

recovery interval in minutes (Backup and Recovery)

Minimum: 1

Maximum: 32,767

Default: 5

This configuration option controls the number of minutes that Sybase System XI will require to recover a database in the event that there is a system failure of some kind. This option combined with the amount of activity that is occurring on the server controls the amount of time between database Checkpoints.

A database Checkpoint forces the writing of all the changes to dirty data pages from the transaction log information to disk instead of residing in the transaction log buffers. A Checkpoint can take considerable time if there has been a lot of activity on the server, but frequent checkpointing will reduce the amount of time required to restart the server because it will not have to Rollforward as much work from the transaction log.

remote server pre-read packets (Network Communication)

Minimum: 0

Maximum: 32,767

Default: 3

This option manages how much information a particular site handler will be buffering ahead of anticipated requests for transmittal to a remote server. Setting this value to a higher number can improve performance on some systems because the primary server that is responding to remote user connections and requests can anticipate the sort of data required for transmittal to the other server.

size of auto identity column (SQL Server Administration)

Minimum: 1

Maximum: 38

Default: 10

This configuration option controls the number of digits that will be allocated to the identity column that is automatically appended to any tables designed and created when the database option auto identity is in effect.

stack guard size (SQL Server Administration)

Minimum: 0

Maximum: 2,147,483,647

Default: 4,096

Sybase manages a given user's operations in a stack of pending events. If the number of events that the user is requesting to perform exceeds the amount of space allocated in this stack, the user will receive an error, and the task will be aborted. It is very unlikely you will run into this error condition, (you will be able to see the error recorded in the error log) but if you do, you should increase the `stack guard size` in a 2K increment (2,048 bytes), and then retry your operation that caused the stack to overflow.

systemwide password expiration (User Environment)

Minimum: 0

Maximum: 32,767

Default: 0

This option controls the frequency at which the Sybase server will expire a password and require that the password be changed by the user before being able to log in to the server again. Make sure that your application programs written for Sybase can successfully negotiate an expired password error condition prior to activating this feature or you may find that your users cannot connect to the database at all!

table lock spinlock ratio (Lock Manager)

Minimum: 1

Maximum: 2,147,483,647

Default: 20

This option is like all the other spinlock ratios that are configurable in Sybase—it enables you to configure the ratio between table lock resources and the simple spinlock managers that manage the multiple, concurrent requests for the same resource. Each spinlock consumes 256 bytes, so if you attempt to tune this feature to reduce the concurrency on a particular table lock, you should be careful to consider the amount of memory being utilized.

tape retention in days (Backup and Recovery)

Minimum: 0

Maximum: 365

Default: 0

This configuration option controls the number of days that a given backup is expected to be retained before it can be reused. If this value is other than 0 (zero), Sybase System XI will warn the user that they are performing a backup over an existing backup that has not expired its number of retention days.

This is a useful configuration for Sybase System XI servers that are in remote areas where a full-time administrator is not available to manage the environment and where it is likely that the user may incorrectly reuse backup tapes that should be kept for a prescribed period.

TROUBLESHOOTING

My users keep overwriting their historical backup tapes with the latest backups of the database. I'm happy they're doing backups at all, but how can I stop them from using the same tape twice? It is impossible to stop a user from using the same tape twice. However, by using the media retention configuration option, you can stop them from using the tape too quickly after a backup is made. A good setting is 7, which will stop the tape from being used more than once a week.

tcp no delay (Network Communication)

Minimum: 0 (Off)

Maximum: 1 (On)

Default: 0 (Off)

This option enables you to change the way Sybase sends data physically across the network at the TCP/IP level. Typically, Sybase will wait until a TCP/IP data packet is completely full before sending it out on the network. This waiting could negatively impact a system that has a small transaction volume and a small transaction size because Sybase wouldn't attempt to put the data packet out on the net until it was full.

If you enable this option, you will greatly increase the amount of network traffic because Sybase will simply start sending any data it receives immediately after it is received—it will not wait for the packet to be full prior to sending the data onto the network.

total memory (Physical Memory)

Minimum: 3,850

Maximum: 2,147,483,647

Default: Depends on the hardware platform

This configuration option controls the maximum number of 2K pages of memory that Sybase System XI will consume upon startup. To fully optimize your server for use as a database server, you should allocate all available memory to the server after subtracting the minimums required by Windows NT.

> **CAUTION**
> If you overcommit the amount of available memory, Sybase System XI may not start.

user log cache size (User Environment)

Minimum: 2,048

Maximum: 2,147,483,647

Default: 2,048

Sybase uses `user log caches` to manage more efficiently the writing of events to the master transaction log. As a user event occurs, it is first written to the user's cache. If the cache becomes full, or the transaction is committed, Sybase then sweeps the transactions from the user's cache to the main transaction log in a batch process. By taking advantage of private log cache areas, Sybase greatly reduces the contention on the end of the log because it can choose when to sweep from the local caches to the log.

sysconfigures and syscurconfigs: System Catalog Tables

sysconfigures and *syscurconfigs* are system catalog tables that Sybase System XI uses to store information about configuration options that are in use on the server. They are stored in the master database.

sysconfigures has information about the available options and their defaults that the server has created. Note that the `sp_configure` option that you see comes from the `spt_values` table in the master database. Rather than relying on the formatted results returned from sp_configure, it's sometimes necessary to be able to select back (and process in a result set) the configurations available and configured on the server. In Listing 23.2, the query shows you the defaults for all the configurable options in the server.

Listing 23.2   CHP24_01.SQL—Querying the sysconfigures Table to Review the System Defaults

```
/* Simple query to return all of the options
    that are configurable in Sybase System XI
*/
Select V.NAME,   COMMENT = substring( C.COMMENT, 1, 60 ),
       "DEFAULT" = c.value
From   MASTER.DBO.SPT_VALUES V,
       MASTER.DBO.SYSCONFIGURES C
Where  V.NUMBER = C.CONFIG
And    V.NAME is not null
Order by V.NAME
```

The results from the query in Listing 23.2 are as follows:

NAME	COMMENT	DEFAULT
abort tran on log full	Configuration Options	0
add	Configuration Options	0
additional netmem	additional netmem	0
all	General Information	0
allow updates	Allow updates to system tables	0
alter	Backup/Recovery	0
and	Cache Manager	0
any	Disk I/O	0
arith_overflow	Languages	0
arithabort	Network Communication	0
arithignore	Languages	0

```
as                            Memory Use                      0
asc                           Network Communication           0
...
floatn                        Disk I/O                        0
foreign                       General Information             0
i/o flush                     I/O Accounting Flush Interval   1000
identity burning set factor   Identity Burning Set Factor     5000
identity grab size            identity grab size              1
int                           Languages                       0
int high bit                  General Information             0
...
view                          number of alarms                40
waitfor                       number of pre-allocated extents 2
where                         event buffers per engine        100
while                         sql server clock tick length    100000
with                          runnable process search count   2000
work                          i/o polling process count       10
writetext                     deadlock retries                5
yes                           Configuration Options           0
```

TIP In the above query, the reserved Sybase System XI keyword DEFAULT was used as a column title. To use any reserved words as text in a column title, enclose it within quotation marks.

The system table *syscurconfigs* stores the currently configured values that are being used by the server. In Listing 23.3, the query shows how to get the current values for each of the configurable options in the server. Using SYSCONFIGURES and SYSCURCONFIGS together will enable you to write your own programs to dynamically set options and report options on the server.

Listing 23.3 CHP24_02.SQL—Querying the syscurconfigs Table to Review the Current Server Configurations

```
Select V.NAME,   COMMENT = substring( C.COMMENT, 1, 60 ),
       "CURRENT VALUE" = c.value
From   MASTER.DBO.SPT_VALUES V,
       MASTER.DBO.SYSCURCONFIGS C
Where  V.NUMBER = C.CONFIG
And    V.NAME is not null
Order by V.NAME
```

The results from the query in Listing 23.3 are as follows:

```
NAME                     COMMENT    CURRENT VALUE
------------------------ ---------- -------------------------
abort tran on log full   0          0
add                      0          0
additional netmem        0          0
all                      0          0
allow updates            0          0
```

```
alter                          0         0
and                            0         0
any                            0         0
arith_overflow                 0         0
arithabort                     0         0
arithignore                    0         0
as                             0         0
asc
...                            0         0
floatn                         0         0
foreign                        0         0
i/o flush                      0      1000
identity burning set factor    0      5000
identity grab size             0         1
identity in nonunique index    0         0
ignore duplicate keys          0         0
ignore duplicate rows          0         0
int                            0         0
int high bit                   0         0
...
view                           1        40
waitfor                        0         2
where                        #10       100
while                          0    100000
with                           0      2000
work                           0        10
writetext                      0         5
yes                            0         0
```

N O T E   Both queries above are joined to the Sybase System XI system table spt_values. This is
a special table that Sybase System XI uses for displaying value and configuration data. ■

Configuring and Managing Databases

Sybase System XI has several options available at a per-database level that enable the database
administrator (DBA) to configure how different databases perform/act on a given server.

Displaying and Setting Database Options

Sybase System XI provides two ways to display and set configuration options for the database.
The graphical method is via Sybase SQL Server Manager. The Transact-SQL method is by
using the system stored procedure, sp_dboption.

Using Sybase SQL Server Manager to Configure a Database   To configure a database using
Sybase SQL Server Manager, follow these steps:

1. Run Sybase SQL Server Manager from the Sybase for Windows NT program group/
   folder.

2. Select the Server and Database that you want to work on.

3. Choose <u>D</u>atabase, <u>O</u>ptions to display the Sybase SQL Server Manager Database Options dialog box (see Fig. 23.13).

FIG. 23.13
The SSM Database Options dialog box makes it a simple job of clicking the required options and then pressing the OK button to configure the database.

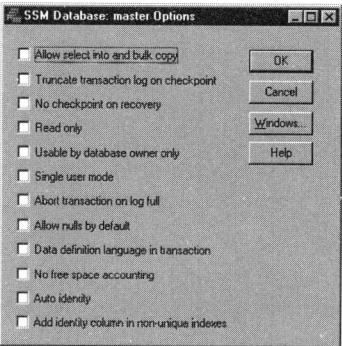

4. To change any of the settings for the database, click the required options and then press OK to apply the changes and return to the main Sybase SQL Server Manager window.

Using sp_dboption to Configure a Database The system stored procedure sp_dboption can be used instead of the Sybase SQL Server Manager to set options for the database. The syntax for sp_dboption is as follows:

```
sp_dboption [Database_Name, Database_Option, Database_Value]
```

The values of the options for the sp_dboption stored procedure are as follows:

- ■ *Database_Name*—This is the name of the database that is being viewed or changed.

- ■ *Database_Option*—This is the name of the option being viewed/changed. Place quotation marks around the option being set if it contains any embedded spaces.

- ■ *Database_Value*—This is the new value for the option.

If no parameters are supplied to sp_dboption, it will return the available parameters that can be set for any current database, for example:

```
sp_dboption
Go

Settable database options.
database_options
--------------------------
abort tran on log full
allow nulls by default
auto identity
dbo use only
ddl in tran
identity in nonunique index
no chkpt on recovery
no free space acctg
```

```
read only
select into/bulkcopy
single user
trunc log on chkpt
```

The system-stored procedure `sp_dboption` is similar to `sp_configure` because of the option being set, it performs a wildcard-style search on the passed in option parameter (so that `dbo`, `dbo use`, and `dbo use only` are all the same parameter).

Database Options Explained

The following is a list of all the database options that are available for configuration in user databases. In parentheses following the option name is the equivalent name that Sybase SQL Server Manager uses for the option.

Abort tran on log full (Abort transaction on log full)   This database option controls what happens if the transaction log gets full while a long running transaction is in progress. If the log fills, and this value is set to `True`, Sybase will abort and roll back the transaction, thereby freeing up log space. The default behavior would leave the database in a locked status until the logs were dumped by another user of System Administrator privileges.

Allow Nulls by Default   This database option controls the way the `Create Table` statement is parsed by the SQL interpreter when defining columns. By default, if the `Null` keyword is omitted in Sybase System XI, the SQL interpreter assumes that the column is supposed to be `Not Null`. However, the ANSI standard specifies the reverse, that if not specified, a column is `Null`.

If the database scripts being used to create a table or set of tables have been created for an ANSI compatible database, it will be necessary to have this option turned on so that the tables generated/created behave the same way as they would on another ANSI-compatible database.

Auto identity   This database option instructs the System XI server to automatically add a system column `SYB_IDENTITY_COL` to each table that is created by a user. This identity column is a 10-digit number and can be used to uniquely identify each record in the database table.

DBO use only (Usable by database owner only)   This database option controls the user access to the database. If set to `True`, then the only user that may access the database is the database owner (dbo). If this option is turned on while existing users have connected, they will not be killed. They will be allowed to stay on the database until they disconnect voluntarily.

DDL in tran (Data definition language in transaction)   This database option controls whether or not a user is permitted to place statements like `Create Table`, `Create Index` or any other DDL-based command inside an explicitly begun transaction. If not set to `True` the user/client program will receive an error when a `Create` statement is executed inside the transaction.

▶ **See** "Understanding Data Definition Language (DDL)," **p. 66**

Identity in nonunique index (Add identity column in non-unique indexes)   This database option will automatically add an identity column as part of the key to a non-unique index so that the index becomes a unique index. This can have drastic impact on the size of your indexes and should not be used unless you have a specific reason for maintaining unique values in the index.

▶ **See** "Creating Indexes," **p. 206**

No chkpt on recovery (No checkpoint on recovery)   This database option controls the behavior on recovery of a database. The default is False, meaning that after a recovery of database or transaction log, a Checkpoint operation will occur.

If multiple databases are being used in a primary and secondary fashion and transaction logs are being rolled forward from one database to another, this option should be turned on. It will stop the database from rejecting further transaction logs being applied.

No free space acctg (No free space accounting)   This database option controls the way the database manages the amount of free space available in the database segment on which the database and the transaction log reside. If you set this option to True the System XI server will not attempt to calculate when space is running out, and will not execute any user-defined threshold actions that might have been written to dump the logs.

Read only (Read Only)   This database option, if enabled, places a database in read-only mode, making it impossible for any Inserts, Updates, or Deletes. This is a useful option to turn on for reporting databases. For example, if you are writing an application that simply does a lot of reports for your users, the read only flag will guarantee that the data does not change.

Select into/bulkcopy (Select Into/Bulk Copy)   This database option controls whether non-logged database operations are permitted in the current database. A non-logged operation, such as the Select Into... command, is highly optimized and does not write any entries to the database transaction log, making it unrecoverable.

This option must be enabled if bulkcopy (BCP) operations are to be executed against a database table without indexes. However, if a table has indexes, Sybase System XI will always use the slow load algorithm so that it has a chance to update the indexes.

Single user (Single User)   This database option limits database access to a single user. If enabled and a user connects, then that user may stay connected; however, any other user will be denied access. If single user mode is turned on, then trunc. log on chkpt. will be disabled because it requires an additional user connection to the database to act as a monitor.

Trunc. log on chkpt. (Truncate Log on Checkpoint)   This database option controls whether or not the database logs will be truncated when a checkpoint activity occurs. By default this option is off and it should always be off in production when it may be necessary to use the transaction logs for replication, backup, or recovery.

Configuring and Managing Queries

Sybase System XI has a number of individual options that can be set while querying the database. These options control the behavior of queries when they are executed. They are also useful statistical and informational gatherers that can be helpful in diagnosing query problems, such as queries that run really slow for no apparent reason.

Displaying and Setting Query Options

Sybase System XI provides the Set Transact-SQL command that you can use to display and set configuration options for a query. If used in a stored procedure, the Set statement is in effect for the life of the procedure and overrides any previous settings. The syntax for the Set statement is as follows:

```
Set Option On | Off
```

where Option is any valid Sybase System XI query option.

Query Options Explained

The following is a list of the most important query options that are configurable, and what they do. Use this information to help determine whether you should enable an option for any given situation.

Arithabort (Abort on Arithmetic Error)   This option controls what Sybase System XI will do when an arithmetic error occurs. If set to On, Sybase System XI will abort any query that causes a divide by zero or numeric overflow (a value is greater than the defined datatype that it is declared for) condition to occur. There is no opportunity to capture this error at runtime, so if this option is not set, the resulting output could be Null.

In Listing 23.4, Arithabort is used to stop a command batch from continuing with invalid data.

Listing 23.4   CHP24_03.SQL—Using the Arithabort Option

```
/* Declare working variables */
Declare @nDecimal Decimal( 8, 2 ),
        @nInteger Integer

/* ensure that the error does not cause an abort */
Set Arithabort off
/* do a division that is going to cause an erro
   note that the print statement doesn'
   get executed because this is a special erro
   condition that Sybase System XI doesn't "publish
   for handling *

Select @nDecimal = 8 /
If @@error !=
      Print 'Error

/* abort processing if the error occurs again *
Set Arithabort o

/* This time the division will cause an error and
   the SQL command batch will be terminated, not
   that the termination stops any further activit
   and the print statement again is ignored */
```

```
Select @nDecimal = 8 / 0
If @@error != 0
     Print 'Error'
```

The following is the output of Listing 23.4:

```
Divide by zero occurred.
Command has been aborted.
Error
Divide by zero occurred.
```

Arithignore (Ignore Arithmetic Error)   Arithignore is the opposite of Arithabort in that it will stop the Sybase System XI from reporting an error condition if an arithmetic error occurs. In Listing 23.5, Arithignore is demonstrated and shows Sybase System XI not reporting any error conditions.

Listing 23.5   CHP24_04.SQL—Using Arithignore to Ignore Arithmetic Overflows

```
/* Declare working variables */
Declare @nDecimal Decimal( 8, 2 ),
        @nInteger Integer

/* ensure that the error does not cause an abort */
Set Arithignore on
/* do a division that is going to cause an erro
   note that the print statement doesn'
   get executed because this is a special erro
   condition that Sybase System XI doesn't "publish
   for handling *

Select @nDecimal = 8 /
If @@error !=
     Print 'Error

/* do a print so that you know you are through th
   first part of the query *

Print 'Second Query

/* abort processing if the error occurs again *
Set ArithIgnore of

/* This time the division will cause an error an
   the SQL command batch will be terminated, not
   that the termination stops any further activit
   and the print statement again is ignored *

Select @nDecimal = 8 /

If @@error != 0
     Print 'Error'
```

The following is the output of Listing 23.5:

```
Second Query
Divide by zero occurred.
```

Chained (Chained Transactions)   If set on, the `Chained` command option instructs Sybase to implicitly perform a `Begin Tran` statement prior to each statement that executes outside of a transaction, thereby implicitly placing the statement in a transaction that can be rolled back.

Nocount (No Count Display)   This option disables the display of the number of rows processed by any SQL statement. The `@@Rowcount` global variable is still maintained, even though this option is turned off.

Noexec (No Execute)   This option controls whether Sybase System XI will actually execute a SQL statement. If you turn this option on, Sybase System XI will not execute the query, but will perform only the work to determine how the query would have been answered. This option is most commonly used when viewing the `Showplan` that a query generates without fetching the data.

> **N O T E**   Sybase System XI processes queries in two phases: *compilation* and *execution*. In the compilation phase, Sybase System XI validates that the query is OK, checks that all the objects exist and are readable, and generates the query plan or best path to the actual data. In the execution phase, Sybase System XI starts performing the query, which could be updating the records, fetching the data, and so on. ▪

Parseonly (Parse Query Only)   This option is like `Noexec` except that Sybase System XI does not even compile the query (generate the access path to the data); all it does is check that the query is syntactically accurate.

Showplan (Show Query Plan)   This option shows the query plan that Sybase System XI generated to answer a query.

For a complete and detailed discussion on interpreting the SHOWPLAN output, refer to Chapter 8, "Understanding Query Plans," in Sybase's *Sybase System XI Performance and Tuning Guide.*

Statistics Time (Show Stats Time)   This option shows the amount of time the server spent in different areas of parsing, compilation and execution, and answering a query. This information can be very useful in helping to tune queries; however, the data can be skewed because of server caching.

Statistics Io (Show Stats I/O)   This option shows the number of logical and physical reads that the server did to answer a query. Logical reads are reads that come from cache pages; physical reads cause the database to go to disk. The number returned is the number of 2K pages read.

From Here...

In this chapter, you learned how to configure your server, database, and queries to get optimal performance and to maximize your use of the server. Take a look at the following chapters for more information:

- See Chapter 4, "Introducing Transact-SQL," which shows you how to take advantage of some of the configuration options discussed in this chapter and improve the performance of your Selects.

- See Chapter 10, "Understanding Stored Procedures," which shows you how to take advantage of the new options to stop your stored procedures from getting error conditions and aborting.

- See Chapter 21, "Managing and Monitoring Security," which provides tips on how to configure the server environment to be more secure.

Part
IV

Ch
23

CHAPTER 24

Managing Data Replication

Installing and configuring Replication Server

Sybase's Replication Server is an open server that is used to move data between two or more Sybase System XI data servers. This chapter shows you how to install and configure the Replication Server correctly.

Understanding how replication works

Knowing the ins and outs of the way Sybase's Replication works (at least conceptually) will help you to understand what you can and can't replicate.

Writing your own replication

The way that Replication Server moves transaction logs between servers may not be appropriate in your corporation or organization. This chapter gives you some practical tips and ideas on how to write your own replication.

Replication is one of *the* hot topics in the computer industry for the 90s. With the ever-changing model of data processing moving from centralized, mainframe-based data servers to distributed, PC-based remote and mobile data centers, the importance and need for replication has greatly increased.

There are many different ways of solving the replication challenges created for a database vendor, such as Sybase. Sybase's solution is mostly designed for high-speed, transaction-based replication. This model of replication-by-transaction monitors the database's transaction log, and as soon as a transaction has been marked, is committed to the database (i.e., pending transactions are ignored, in case they are rolled back by the client that initiated them). The transactions are then marked as pending replication to another server—that is, they are put in a queue of transactions to be sent to other servers on the network.

Sybase's replication model minimizes the impact, or load, on the primary data server, and the responsibility for moving appropriate data to one or more remote servers is placed on the Replication Server. The Replication Server applies any pending transactions to one or more other remote servers (these are the subscribers of the replicated data) and the transaction is marked as removable from the log.

The key problem with Sybase's replication model is that it's a big chore to get it installed and up and running correctly. This chapter helps guide you through the installation procedures and get the Replication Server going properly. In addition, you'll be introduced to some of the more basic functions of the very rich Replication Server API. There are over 100 different commands in the Replication Server ranging from system functions in the Replication Server itself to definition commands like `Create Replication Definition` to the special system stored procedures (prefixed with `rs_`)that are installed in publishing and subscribing databases. It's impossible to cover all of these commands in a single chapter; however, you'll get an appreciation for the flexibility of the Replication Server API here, and you can follow up this information with the detailed (if somewhat dull) manuals supplied by Sybase:

- *Replication Server Administration Guide*—Leads you through all the key tasks of administration and management of the Replication Server API and all the key components of the server itself. This is definitely a recommended read and something that you should become intimately familiar with.

- *Replication Server Commands Reference*—A comprehensive guide that lists all of the functions and documents in detail the syntax and use for all the API commands, functions, and stored procedures that Replication Server provides.

- *Replication Server Design Guide*—This is a user-style document that helps you think about replication issues and how they might be solved using Replication Server. It steps you through the thought processes necessary to generate and implement a replication system in your environment. This is the most practically oriented document in the Sybase set of Replication Server documentation.

- *Replication Server Troubleshooting Guide*—As one of the most complex components of the Sybase toolkit as a whole, the Replication Server Troubleshooting Guide is going to be essential reading for all DBAs placed or empowered with the responsibility for managing a replication system. ■

Installing Replication Server

Installing and preparing Replication Server for use is really quite simple; there are just a lot of steps that have to be taken to complete the installation successfully. In this section, you see how to install Replication Server for use with Windows NT. Much of the information on how to install Replication Server on Windows NT is very similar to that on UNIX. For specific information on installing Replication Server on your particular UNIX platform, please consult the excellent documentation provided by Sybase.

Planning for Replication

Before installation of the Replication Server, you should be aware of some of the following important considerations:

■ **Memory**—Make sure that you have sufficient RAM free (after the installation of the Database Server to manage the Replication Server). If you don't have enough RAM, then Replication Server either will not start at all, or will be forced to use virtual memory (reading and writing from disk) and will suffer substantial performance hits. A minimum requirement is 32M of free RAM.

■ **Disk**—You need to have at least 35M of free disk space to install the Replication Server. 15M will be used by the server software and support files, and then a 20M partition will be created for each Replication Server disk that you are using.

N O T E Disk consumption can be very great if you have lengthy downtime when no communications are supported between the two servers that are being replicated. Make sure that you plan to have enough available disk to manage the longest period of time that you expect or anticipate being without communications between the two servers. ■

■ **Number of Replication Servers**—In order to plan for the installation of Replication, you need to know how many Replication Servers you are going to use; where those Replication Servers are going to be located; and how the servers are going to physically communicate with each other either on a LAN or WAN.

■ **Location of the master Replication Server**—The master or central Replication Server in a group of Replication Servers is known as the ID Server. It supplies or assigns IDs to the other databases and servers and manages versions across the replication system.

■ **Logical design of the replication system**—In order to successfully implement replication, you need to first identify the data that you want to replicate and where it needs to be sent. Once you have determined the nature of the replication, it is often useful to draw a diagram to document how you want data to move throughout the system. The diagram will serve you well later on as a checklist to make sure that you have got everything moving data correctly around the network. The diagram can also be seen as the foundation of any documentation that you produce on replication at your corporation.

Installing the Replication Server Software

After you have prepared your site and have thought a bit about the sort of replication that you want to construct for your network, you need to actually get the software installed in order to get the replication working.

 T I P I highly recommend that you close or shut down all other applications prior to the installation of the Replication Server software. This ensures that the installation program has the full opportunity to get access to any of the resources on the server. In the case of the System XI data server, you *must* shut it down prior to installation or you will see the warning shown in Figure 24.1.

FIG. 24.1

The Replication Server software cannot be installed if Sybase is actually up and running.

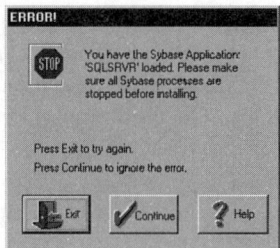

To perform the software installation, follow these steps:

1. Insert the Replication Server CD-ROM in the server's CD-ROM player, and using the Windows 95/NT 4 Explorer, double-click the Setup Program (SETUP.EXE). (Note: The installation program takes a while to start, so be patient.)

2. Enter your Customer Authorization String (CAS) in the Welcome dialog box that is displayed after the Setup Program has been loaded (see Fig. 24.2).

FIG. 24.2

Your CAS can be found on either the product invoice from Sybase, or the distribution media's packaging.

3. Choose the installation directory for the Replication Server software by entering it in the Sybase Release Directory dialog box, and click the Continue button (see Fig. 24.3).

FIG. 24.3

The defaulted release directory will be set to the system variable $SYBASE on UNIX or %SYBASE% on Windows NT.

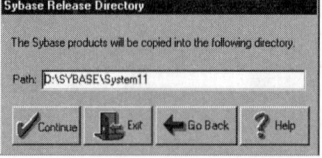

4. Choose to install 16- or 32-bit application software on the Product Set Selection dialog box, and click the Continue button. Note: the Replication Server CD-ROM does not have any 16-bit software on it, so you can uncheck the Windows Products (16-bit versions) option (see Fig. 24.4).

FIG. 24.4

The install program for the Replication Server CD-ROM is identical to that of the main System XI product, which is why the 16-bit software option is shown. There's no point in checking this option because there's nothing that you can install on the CD.

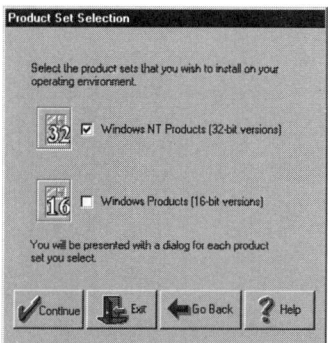

5. Click Continue on the Windows NT Product Selection Screen—Replication Server will already be checked, and this is your only option (see Fig. 24.5). After clicking to continue, the software will be decompressed from the CD-ROM and copied to your server.

FIG. 24.5

The Windows NT Product Selection Screen has a Custom button associated with Replication Server. By clicking it, you can optionally choose to not install the Log Transfer Manager for this server.

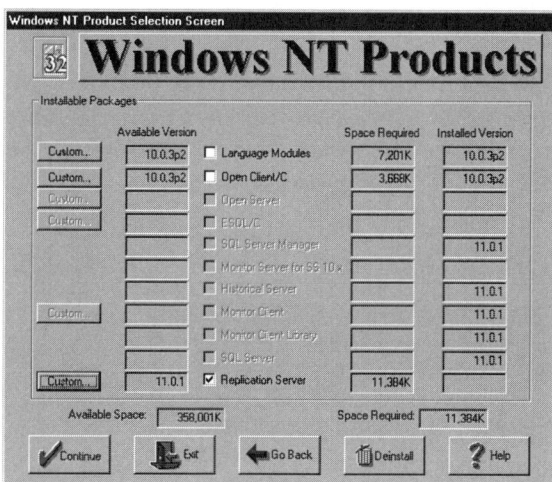

6. Click the Resume button after all the files are copied to end the Setup program (see Fig. 24.6).

Part

IV

Ch

24

FIG. 24.6

The Information dialog box at the end of the install is reminding you to run the Configuration (RS_INIT) program before attempting to use Replication Server.

Setting Up and Configuring the Primary or Publishing Server

After the Replication Server software has been installed, you need to configure it to make it work correctly in your environment. To do so, you'll need to run the Replication Server Configuration program that was just installed. The Replication Server Configuration program can be launched by double-clicking its icon in the Sybase for Windows NT program group on your server (see Fig. 24.7).

FIG. 24.7

The Sybase for Windows NT program group or folder is where all the shortcuts or icons to all the Sybase applications installed on the server are found.

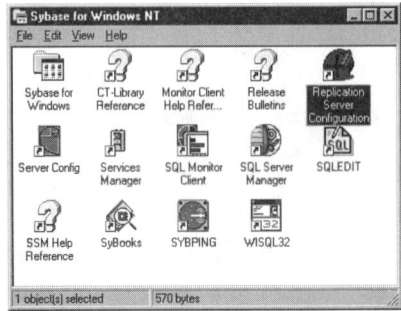

The Replication Server Configuration program under Windows NT has a similar counterpart on UNIX and when they are run, both programs actually call themselves the same thing: RS_INIT. Configuring the Replication Server is a process that involves many steps and should be documented as you go so that you have a written copy of all the passwords and user names that you define.

To configure the Replication Server, follow these steps:

1. Run the Replication Server Configuration program to display the primary RS_INIT dialog box (see Fig. 24.8).

FIG. 24.8
The RS_INIT dialog box enables you to configure either the Interfaces file or the actual Replication Server that you are currently working on.

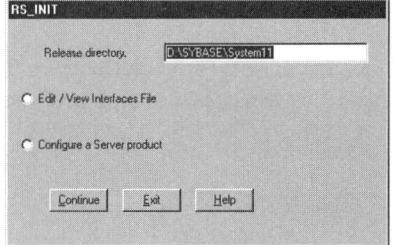

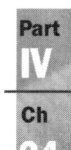

Part

IV

Ch

24

2. If you need to modify the SQL.INI (the Sybase interfaces file) click the Edit/View Interfaces File radio button and click Continue. Note that you are probably better off using SQLEdit because it is a far better and easier-to-use program.

▶ **See** "Using SQLEDIT," **p. 46**

3. To configure the Replication Server, click the Configure a Server Product radio button and click Continue. This will display the CONFIGURE SERVER PRODUCTS dialog box shown in Figure 24.9.

FIG. 24.9
The CONFIGURE SERVER PRODUCTS dialog box offers only one choice: Replication Server.

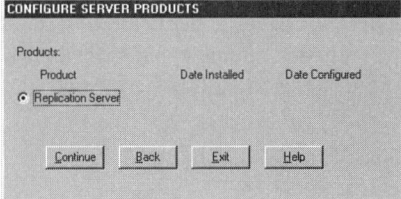

4. Click the Replication Server radio button, and click Continue. You will now be presented with the CONFIGURE REPLICATION SYSTEM dialog box (see Fig. 24.10).

FIG. 24.10

The CONFIGURE REPLICATION SYSTEM dialog box enables you to manage all the different areas of the Replication Server installation from one place.

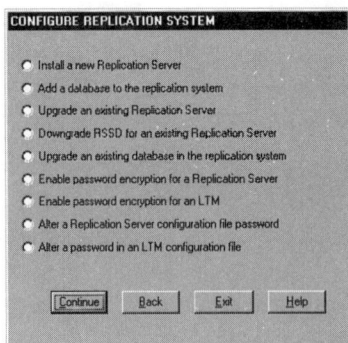

5. Click Install a new Replication Server and then click Continue. This will display the NEW REPLICATION SERVER dialog box, which is designed as a sort of a worksheet or guided installation (see Fig. 24.11).

FIG. 24.11

Each of the installation steps will be marked Incomplete until you have successfully worked through them in the install process.

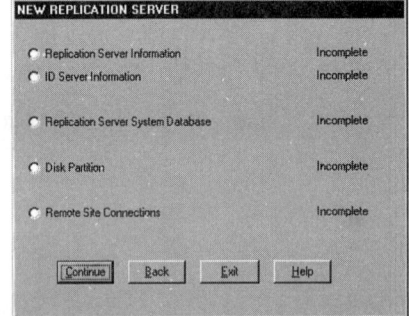

6. Click Replication Server Information and then click Continue.

7. Enter the name of the Replication Server in the REPLICATION SERVER NAME dialog box shown in Figure 24.12, and click Continue to display the REPLICATION SERVER INFORMATION dialog box (see Fig. 24.13).

FIG. 24.12

The name of the Replication Server must be unique on the network. I recommend that you use the Sybase System XI Data Server's name and append _RS.

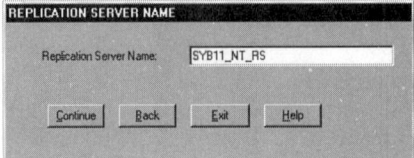

FIG. 24.13

The REPLICATION
SERVER INFORMATION
dialog box is where you
customize the settings
for this particular
Replication Server. In
this example, the server
is being set up as a
primary or publishing
server and is the ID
server on the network.

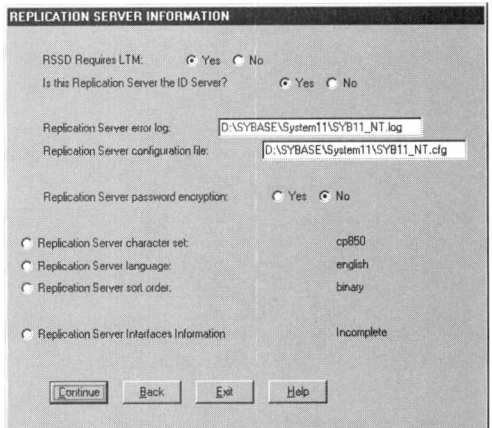

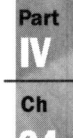

8. Select whether you want the Replication Server to use the Log Transfer Manager (LTM) or not. The LTM is required on all the originating or source databases because this is the way that the Replication Server transfers transactions from the database's transaction log to the Replication Server for distribution to the subscribing databases.

9. If this is the primary Replication Server on the network, select the Yes option for Is this Replication Server the ID Server? (An ID Server is a Replication Server that monitors and manages multiple *other* Replication Servers and manages the interchange of addresses between them.)

10. Modify the names and locations of the Error log and Configuration files if necessary. By default, they tend to be files that would be used by a regular data server, so it is recommended that you add _RS to their names to help distinguish them correctly.

11. Select whether you want the passwords to be encrypted in the Replication Server database. This option should always be checked to yes; otherwise, any user will be able to look at the rs_users table in the RSSD (Replication Server System Database) and see the passwords!

12. If you have modified the installation of the Sybase Data Server from the default character set of cp850, then you must modify the option on this INFORMATION dialog box so that they are the same as the Sybase Data Server. If you don't use the same character set, data will be lost and rendered unusable as it is replicated across the network to other servers/databases. To change the character set, select the Replication Server character set radio button and click Continue. This will display a list of valid character sets from which you can pick and then click Continue (see Fig. 24.14).

13. Modify the language and sort order if necessary to be as desired for the Replication Server. You can use any language or sort order provided it is compatible with the character set that you installed.

FIG. 24.14

The REPLICATION
SERVER CHARACTER
SET dialog box shown
here is going to change
from the default of
cp850 to HP's normal
default installation of
ROMAN8.

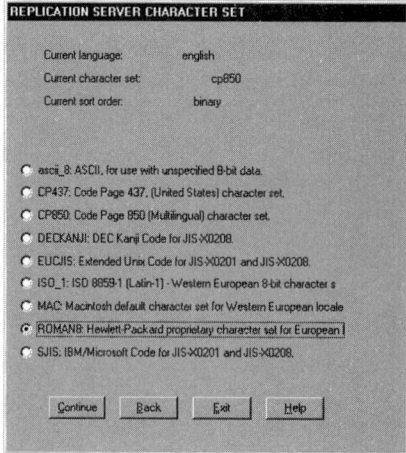

14. If you haven't yet added a listener service for the Replication Server, the Replication
Server Interfaces Information will be incomplete. Select the option, and use the SQLEdit
program to add a listener for the Replication Server (see Fig. 24.15).

FIG. 24.15

The SQLEdit program
supplied with Replica-
tion Server is a little bit
different (and a lot less
intuitive) from the
SQLEDIT program that
comes with Sybase
System XI.

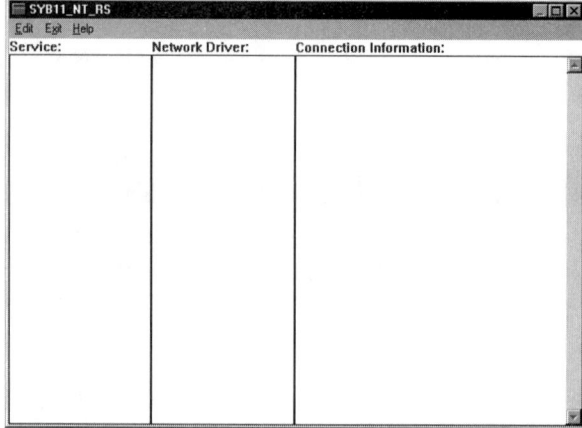

15. From the Edit menu, select Add Service to display the Add Service dialog box shown in
Figure 24.16.

16. Enter the details for the service you are adding and click OK.

17. Repeat steps 14 and 15 to add a `query` service for Windows NT application software, and
a `win3_query` service if you have any 16-bit applications that need access to the Replication Server. After adding the services, you will see them listed in the details views of the
main window (see Fig. 24.17).

FIG. 24.16

The Add Service dialog box lets you pick the type of service (master is a listener service) and network protocol and then specific information for the listener that you are adding.

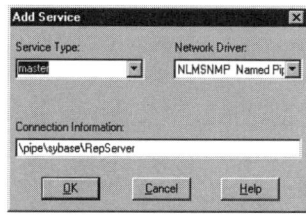

FIG. 24.17

This Replication Server is designed for communication using Windows NT's preferred communications protocol Named Pipes. A listener has been added for the server (a master listener), 16-bit clients (a win3_query listener), and for 32-bit clients (a query listener).

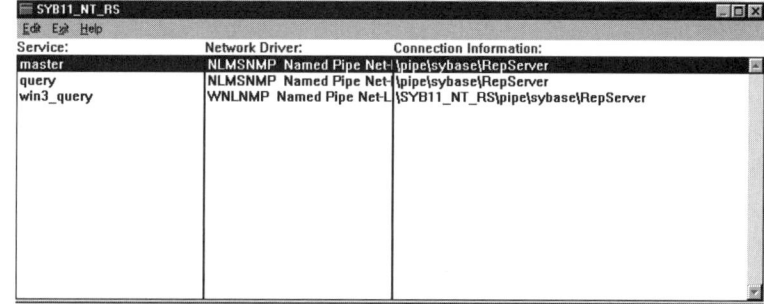

18. From the Exit menu select Exit Edit Services to return to the main installation program.

19. Click Continue on the REPLICATION SERVER INFORMATION dialog box (Fig. 24.13) to return to the NEW REPLICATION SERVER dialog box (Fig. 24.11).

20. Click the ID Server Information option and then click Continue to activate the ID SERVER INFORMATION dialog box (see Fig. 24.18).

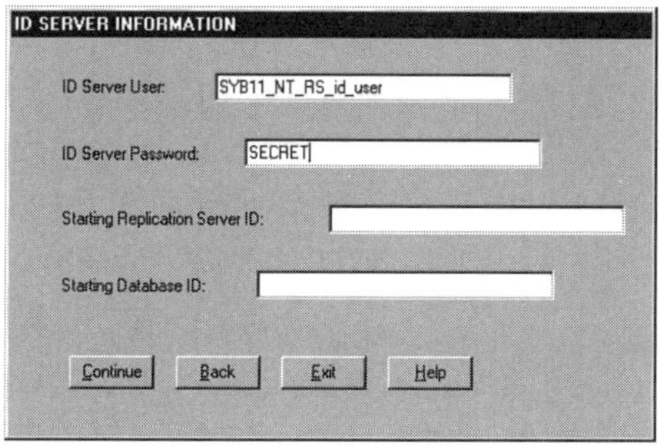

FIG. 24.18

The ID SERVER INFORMATION dialog box enables you to define the user and password information required for other servers and users to log in to the ID SERVER, and it also gives you the option of changing the defaults for IDs being assigned to servers and databases.

21. Enter the name of the user that will be the administrative/server level login to the ID Server (usually use the name of the Replication Server with _id_user appended on the end).

22. Enter a password for the ID Server user. (In the example, SECRET is entered as the password.)

23. If you plan to have multiple ID Servers involved in Replication Server, then you will need to provide values for the range of Replication Server IDs and Database IDs so that the ID Servers don't think that they are replicating the same databases to each other. On a typical installation, you can leave these fields blank for the defaults to be assigned to them.

24. Click Continue to return to the NEW REPLICATION SERVER dialog box.

25. Click the Replication Server System Database option to configure the System Database used for replication and to optionally create it. Click Continue to display the REPLICA-TION SERVER SYSTEM DATABASE dialog box (see Fig. 24.19).

FIG. 24.19

The REPLICATION SERVER SYSTEM DATABASE dialog box helps you configure user and login information related to the database that is going to be installed on the SQL Server to manage data that needs to be distributed to other servers and databases on the network.

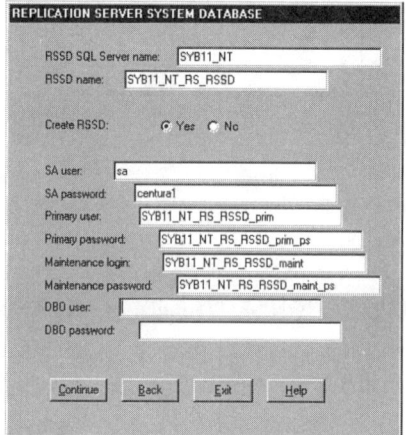

26. Enter the name of the Sybase System XI server that is going to store the RSSD, and enter the System Administrator (sa) password required to login to the server.

27. Select Yes to have RS_INIT create the RSSD database for you now.

28. Modify any of the default user names and passwords to your desired requirements. The Primary User/Login is used as a login between multiple Replication Servers to replicate System Catalog table updates across the network. The Maintenance User/Login is used as a login between Replication Servers for System Catalog updates that are not being replicated.

29. Enter the DBO's (Database Owner's) user name and password for the database that is going to be replicated. If you don't enter a name and password, Replication Server will use the System Administrator (sa) login to read the transaction log.

30. Click Continue to return to the NEW REPLICATION SERVER dialog box.

31. Click the RSSD Device Information option and then click <u>C</u>ontinue to configure the database devices that will be used by the RSSD database (see Fig. 24.20).

FIG. 24.20

The RSSD DEVICE INFORMATION dialog box takes your input to determine the physical disk devices that will be used by the Replication Server to hold the RSSD database.

RSSD DEVICE INFORMATION

Size of the RSSD database:	10
RSSD device name:	RSSD_data
Create the RSSD device:	⦿ Yes ○ No
RSSD device physical name:	d:\sybase\system11\data\RSSD_data.dat
RSSD device size:	10
Size of the RSSD log:	10
RSSD log device name:	RSSD_log
Create the RSSD log device:	⦿ Yes ○ No
RSSD log device physical name:	d:\sybase\system11\data\RSSD_log.dat
RSSD log size:	10

[Continue] [Back] [Exit] [Help]

32. Enter the required information for the data and log devices that will be used by the RSSD and click <u>C</u>ontinue to return to the NEW REPLICATION SERVER dialog box.

T I P   RS_INIT cannot create devices on a remote SQL Server correctly because the file system does not permit the remote association of the disk names. You should create the disk devices using Sybase's Sybase SQL Server Manager on the remote SQL Server prior to installing the Replication Server, and then use those created devices for the RSSD.

33. Click the Disk Partition option and then click <u>C</u>ontinue to configure the special file that will be used on Windows NT to store events that need to be replicated outside of the Sybase System XI database server. These files are designed to be outside of the scope of the System XI Server so that in the event of a failure in the database server, replication data is not lost (see Fig. 24.21).

FIG. 24.21

The DISK PARTITION INFORMATION dialog box enables you to specify the physical file that will be used to manage replicated events.

DISK PARTITION INFORMATION

Disk Partition path:	base\system11\data\SYB11_NT_RS.PAR
Logical Identifier for Disk Partition:	SYB11_NT_RS_PAR
Size of Disk Partition:	20
Vstart value for partition:	0

[Continue] [Back] [Exit] [Help]

34. Enter the file name and path to the disk partition file.

T I P For greater redundancy, this file should normally be placed on a separate physical disk to the main System XI database server.

35. Enter a logical name for the disk partition file. This logical name will be used when you need to write transactions to the partition and when you need to work with the partition manually.

36. Modify the size, if necessary, of the partition and then click Continue to return to the NEW REPLICATION SERVER dialog box. (There's no need to modify the Vstart value under Windows NT.)

37. If you want to modify the user and password required to login remotely to the Replication Server, click the Remote Site Connections option and then click Continue. This will display a simple dialog box that you can use to modify the password and user name for the login to the Replication Server (see Fig. 24.22). Click Continue.

FIG. 24.22
The REMOTE SITE CONNECTIONS dialog box enables you to specify the user name and password required to log on to the Replication Server for other Replication Servers that are performing the replication across the network.

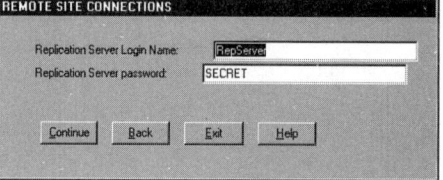

38. Click the Database Log Transfer Manager option and click Continue to configure the LTM. This will display the LTM NAME dialog box, which you can use to modify the default name of the LTM (see Fig. 24.23).

FIG. 24.23
The LTM Name defaults to the name of the SQL Server plus the name of the RSSD database and appends _ltm to the end.

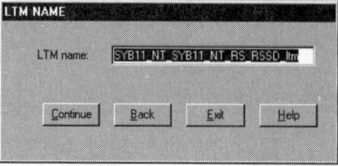

 T I P If you have installed Windows NT on the FAT file system and are limited to 8.3 naming conventions, you will need to change the LTM NAME to something that is less than or equal to eight characters long. Sybase Replication Server uses the LTM NAME to control the creation of certain system files that will fail if they use an invalid (because of length) file name. Installations of Replication Server either on UNIX or on the NTFS file system do not have this restriction.

39. Revise the name of the LTM, if necessary, and then click Continue to display the
    DATABASE LOG TRANSFER MANAGER dialog box (see Fig. 24.24).

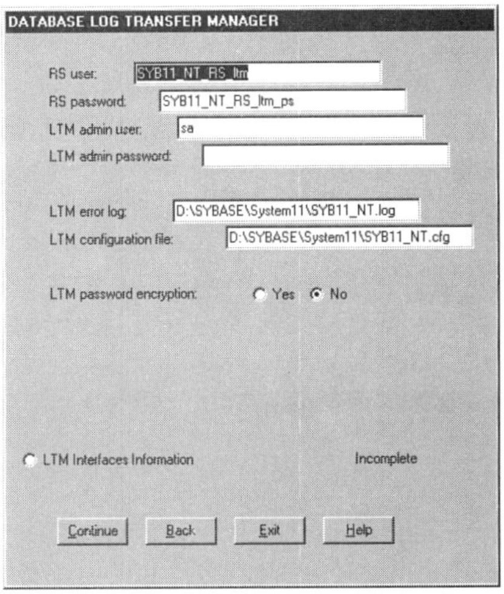

FIG. 24.24

The DATABASE LOG
TRANSFER MANAGER
dialog box lists all the
different users and
logins required to
access data on the
database and then
saves it in the RSSD to
be then replicated to
other servers.

DATABASE LOG TRANSFER MANAGER

RS user: SYB11_NT_RS_ltm
RS password: SYB11_NT_RS_ltm_ps
LTM admin user: sa
LTM admin password:

LTM error log: D:\SYBASE\System11\SYB11_NT.log
LTM configuration file: D:\SYBASE\System11\SYB11_NT.cfg

LTM password encryption: ○ Yes ⦿ No

○ LTM Interfaces Information   Incomplete

Continue   Back   Exit   Help

40. Enter the name and password that the LTM will use when attempting to connect to the
    Replication Server in the RS user and RS password fields.

41. Enter the name and password that will be used to administer the LTM in the LTM admin
    user and LTM admin password fields.

42. Modify the names of the error log and configuration files so that they are distinct from
    the Replication Server and the regular System XI data server. (You can normally append
    _LTM to the names of these two files to distinguish them.)

43. Turn on LTM password encryption so that a casual observer of the LTM does not have
    access to other users' password information.

44. Click the LTM Interfaces information option to configure the interfaces required for the
    LTM. (The configuration of these interfaces is identical to Steps 14 through 17.)

That was certainly a long set of arduous steps to get the basics of the Replication Server configured. Before continuing and actually creating the files and databases, you should have a NEW
REPLICATION SERVER dialog box that looks like the one in Figure 24.25.

If everything's in order, you will need to make sure that the Sybase System XI Data Server is
up and running before clicking Continue; otherwise, you will not be able to create the databases and devices that you specified earlier and you will receive errors.

Click Continue to perform all the steps in a script now. The RS_INIT program will verify if you
want to execute the Replication Server tasks now, to which you should answer Yes. While the
installation of the Replication Server is progressing, you will see a status dialog box indicating
the tasks that are being performed (see Fig. 24.26).

FIG. 24.25

The NEW REPLICATION SERVER dialog box shows that all steps have been completed.

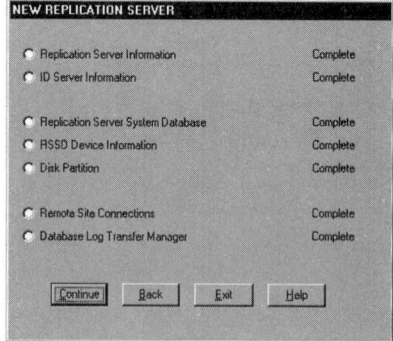

FIG. 24.26

The Setup dialog box shows you the tasks that are being executed to create the Replication Server. The Replication Server creation will take some time, so be patient!

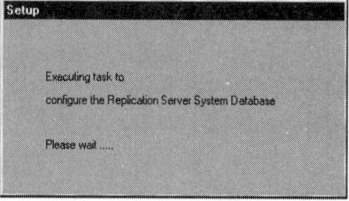

Confirming that Replication Server Has Started

By now, you should have hopefully gotten the Server side of the Replication System set up and working. There's really not a lot to see going on at any point in time that you can see, but to make sure that everything's up and running, you can start the Task Manager under Windows NT to see the active processes on the server. There are a couple of different ways to start the Task Manager:

- To start the Task Manager on Windows NT 3.51, type **Ctrl+Esc**.
- To start the Task Manager on Windows NT 4.0 with the keyboard, type **Ctrl+Shift+Esc**.
- To start the Task Manager on Windows NT 4.0 with the mouse, right-click the taskbar, and choose Task Manager from the context menu that is displayed.

In the Task Manager, you can see the currently active processes by clicking the Processes tab. In Figure 24.27, you can see that the top three tasks (sorted by memory used) are sqlsrvr.exe (the System XI Database Server), repsrvr.exe (the Replication Server), and LTM.EXE (the Log Transfer Manager).

Using Task Manager is an easy way to determine what processes are currently running on your server. Another way to determine whether Sybase products have been started is to use the Sybase Services Manager. The Sybase Services Manager will tell you whether any of the Sybase products have been started.

▶ **See** "Starting Sybase Using the Services Manager," **p. 48**

FIG. 24.27

The Task Manager under Windows NT 4.0 is much more detailed than the Task Manager in Windows NT 3.5x. It shows you all the processes that are currently running and how much CPU and Memory the processes are using.

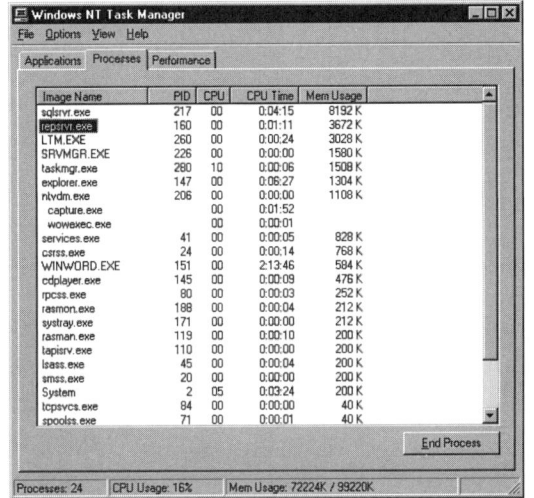

However, you should be aware of a *very* significant limitation or bug in the Sybase Services Manager product: It does not and cannot inform you of Sybase products that were started by another process other than itself. What this means is that if you start the Replication Server by running it from the command line, Sybase Services Manager will *not* think that the Replication Server has been started, and will give you the option of starting it again!

 On UNIX, you can use the command showserver to determine what Sybase products are currently running.

Adding a Database to the Replication System

In this section, you see how to enable a database to be replicated by the Replication Server. To add a Database to the Replication System, you use the Sybase utility program Replication Server Configuration (RS_INIT). Adding a database to the replication system is not that difficult; there are just quite a few steps involved:

1. Run RS_INIT and select the options to configure the Replication Server.

2. Select Add a Database to the replication system from the CONFIGURE REPLICATION SYSTEM dialog box shown in Figure 24.10, and click Continue. This will display the ADD DATABASE TO REPLICATION SYSTEM dialog box shown in Figure 24.28.

Part
IV

Ch
24

FIG. 24.28

The ADD DATABASE TO REPLICATION SYSTEM dialog box is like the NEW REPLICATION SERVER dialog box. It shows you the steps that you need to complete, and you click each item and then click Continue to complete that step.

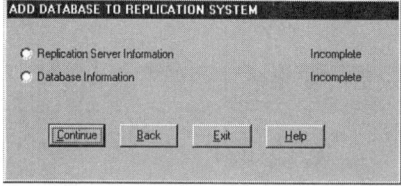

3. Click Replication Server Information and then click Continue to start configuring the information about the Replication Server that will be used for this database. This will display the REPLICATION SERVER NAME dialog box (see Fig. 24.29).

FIG. 24.29

Use the REPLICATION SERVER NAME dialog box to specify the name of the Replication Server that will be managing this database.

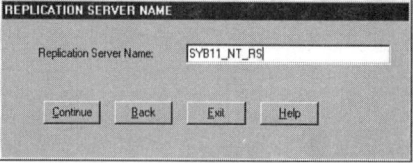

4. Enter the name of the Replication Server that was created earlier and click Continue to display the REPLICATION SERVER INFORMATION dialog box (see Fig. 24.30).

FIG. 24.30

The REPLICATION SERVER INFORMATION dialog box lets you specify the RS Administrator's password information. Note that the Interfaces information has already been completed in the prior part of the installation of Replication Server.

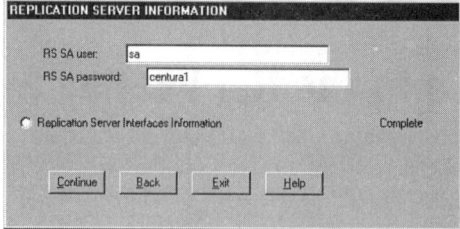

5. Enter the password for the RS SA, and click Continue. The Replication Server Configuration utility will attempt to connect to the Replication Server and will validate that the password you entered is correct. You will get a set of error messages indicating an invalid password if you do not enter the correct password. After validating your

password, you will be returned to the ADD DATABASE TO REPLICATION SYSTEM
dialog box.

 TIP Unless you have specifically changed the SA user's password in a previous use of the Replication
Server, the password will initially be NULL or blank.

6. Select the Database Information option and then click Continue to display the DATA-
   BASE INFORMATION dialog box (see Fig. 24.31).

FIG. 24.31

The DATABASE
INFORMATION dialog
box is where you
specify the details of
the database being
replicated.

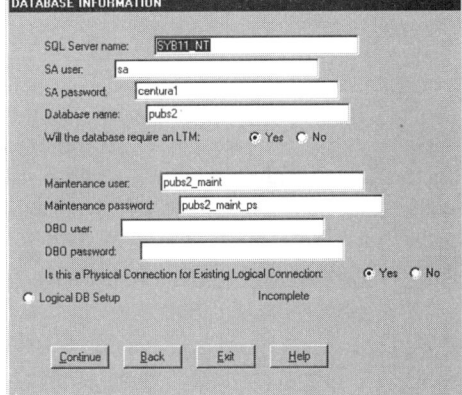

7. Enter the name of the SQL Server that you are going to connect to.

8. Enter the System Administrator (sa) password, and the database that is going to be
   replicated.

9. If this is the primary database, select Yes to requiring an LTM.

10. Alter the default user and passwords for the Maintenance user if necessary, and enter a
    specific DBO if you want. If you don't enter a DBO, then the sa account will be used.

11. If you want to take advantage of the Warm Standby option of Replication Server that
    writes transactions to the non-database transaction log in the event of a system down
    condition, choose the Yes to Is this a Physical Connection for Existing Logical Connec-
    tion option. Selecting Yes will cause the additional option Logical DB Setup to be
    displayed.

12. Click Logical DB Setup and click Continue to display the LOGICAL CONNECTION
    INFORMATION dialog box (see Fig. 24.32).

13. Enter the name of the Logical Database Server that will be used.

14. Enter the details about the Logical Database and Active Database name and passwords
    as necessary.

15. Select Yes to Initialize standby using dump and load to have the Replication Server
    create the Standby database by dumping (backing up) from the active database and
    loading it (restoring the backup). If you select No, the Standby database will be created
    by using the BCP utility (which will be considerably slower).

FIG. 24.32

The LOGICAL CONNEC-
TION INFORMATION
dialog box has two
views. If you enter
`active` in the top field,
you will see only the top
three fields in the dialog
box. Entering `standby`
in the top field will
display the additional
information fields at the
bottom of the dialog
box.

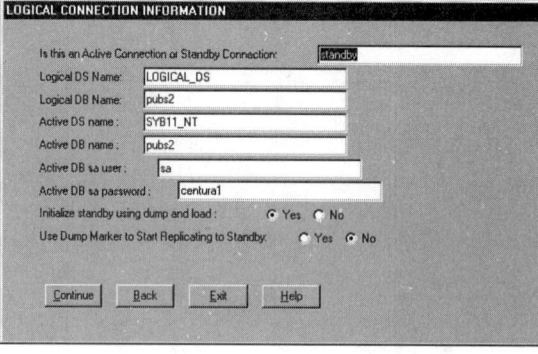

16. Select Yes to Use Dump Marker to Start Replicating to Standby if you anticipate transactions that will occur in the Active database while the Standby database is being initialized/built. If you are able to suspend activity in the Active database while the Standby database is built, you can select No.

17. Click Continue to return to the DATABASE INFORMATION dialog box (refer to Fig. 24.31).

18. Click Continue to return to the ADD DATABASE TO REPLICATION SYSTEM dialog box. You should notice that an option has been added to the dialog box: Database Log Transfer Manager (see Fig. 24.33).

FIG. 24.33

If you select that the
database requires an
LTM, the new option
(currently selected),
Database Log Transfer
Manager, is added to
the ADD DATABASE TO
REPLICATION SYSTEM
dialog box for you to
configure.

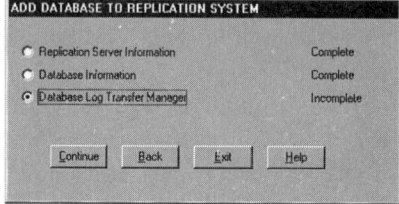

19. Select the Database Log Transfer Manager option and click Continue to display the LTM NAME dialog box. The LTM NAME dialog box and the following DATABASE LOG TRANSFER MANAGER dialog box are the same as the one used earlier in the setup process when creating an LTM for the RSSD (refer to Fig. 24.23). Follow the steps (38 through 43) described in the section "Setting up and Configuring the Primary or Publishing Server," for completing these two dialog boxes with the appropriate information.

After all these steps, you should be returned to the ADD DATABASE TO REPLICATION SYSTEM dialog box with each of the three options set to Complete. If so, click Continue to have the RS_INIT program actually go and perform the tasks you have just defined.

CAUTION

Make sure that you have recently dumped the transaction log in the database that you are adding to the Replication System; otherwise, you may run out of logs while the Replication System is installed. If you run out of log space while the installation of the Replication procedures is going on, you will need to restart the installation by clicking Continue in the ADD DATABASE TO REPLICATION SYSTEM dialog box.

After completing the addition of the database to the Replication System, you will be returned to the main CONFIGURE REPLICATION SERVER dialog box. If you want to add another database to the Replication System, you can do so now; otherwise, click Exit to shut down the RS_INIT program.

N O T E After adding a database to the Replication System, the Replication Server will start a copy of the LTM to manage data transfer from the logs of the database to any subscribers of the data. Take care that you don't run out of memory on the server because each LTM takes anywhere from 1M to 3M of RAM! ▥

Using Replication Server's Commands

Now that Replication Server has been installed and configured, it's time to actually start using it! The process of configuring and using Sybase's Replication Server to move data around the network is based on six core steps:

- Creating a Route between the two or more Replication Servers
- Creating users that can log in to the Replication Servers to perform the moving of data
- Creating a replication definition for a table or set of tables
- Setting a table or set of tables to be replicated
- Granting permissions to the maintenance user in the subscriber databases to perform replication operations
- Subscribing to the replicate data

In this section, you see how to set up each of these six steps as well as become acquainted with some basic administrative commands in the Replication Server API.

N O T E To interact with the Replication Server, you need to run ISQL. ISQL is probably the only tool that doesn't make assumptions about the type of Sybase Server that it is connecting to and therefore can connect to any sort of open server and execute any command that you want. Because Replication Server is an open server, you can connect to it with any application that can connect to a Sybase SQL Server. However, many of these applications (such as RapidSQL, for instance) attempt to do things like Use *Database_name* prior to executing a command that causes errors in the open server. Your best bet, by far, is to use ISQL from the command line and bypass any incompatibility problems that may arise. ▥

▶ **See** "Understanding Sybase Open Servers," **p. 434**

The principle of replication requires that you install a Replication Server to publish the data (i.e., pull it out of a primary database) and at least one Replication Server to subscribe to the replicated data and then apply it to the secondary database. The process of installing a subscribing database is identical to the process of installing a Primary Publishing Replication Server, with the exception that you don't need an LTM because all you are doing is applying replicate data, and you're not sending your own data anywhere.

Creating Routes in Replication Server

A Route is a communications bridge between two Replication Servers. The Replication Server model requires that there be a Replication Server at both the Publishing and the Subscribing ends of the network. These Replication Servers talk to each other across Routes. A Route is a logical way of identifying the remote server that is subscribing to the primary server's data. You use the `Create Route` command in the Replication Server to route between two different replication servers. The syntax for `Create Route` is as follows:

```
Create Route to Dest_Replication_Server
    {Set Next Site Thru_Replication_Server |
    Set Username User_Name
    Set Password Password}
```

The values for the command are as follows:

- `Dest_Replication_Server`—This is the name of the receiving Replication Server that you are routing to.

- `set next site Thru_Replication_Server`—If you are creating an indirect route through a pass-through Replication Server, enter it here.

- `User_Name`—Enter the name of the user that you want to login to the remote Replication Server with.

- `Password`—Enter the password of the user identified in `User_Name`.

For example, if you wanted to create a route from the primary Replication Server *SYB11_NT_RS* and a secondary Replication Server *SYB11_NT2_RS*, you would perform the following steps:

1. First, login to the SYB11_NT_RS Replication Server using ISQL:
   ```
   isql -Usa -SSYB11_NT_RS
   ```

2. Then, execute the appropriate `Create Route` command:
   ```
   Create Route to SYB11_NT2_RS
      Set Username SYB11_NT2_RS_rsi
      Set Password SYB11_NT2_RS_rsi_ps
   Go
   ```

N O T E If you have not yet defined SYB11_NT2_RS in the interfaces file as a valid server that can be reached from the current Replication Server, you will receive an error during the `Create Route` phase because the Replication Server cannot guarantee that the destination server exists or that you will be able to contact it. ▨

Creating a Replication Login to the Primary SQL Server

After establishing a Route to communicate between the two Replication Servers, it is necessary to create a login to the primary database on the primary SQL Server that will have the appropriate permissions to do database replication functionality. It is recommended that you name this user with a consistent name through all your Replication Systems for ease of identification. A good name is *repsysuser*.

The user needs to have the ability to Select from the primary tables that you want to work with. For example, if you were replicating between *SYB11_NT_RS* and *SYB11_NT2_RS* the table *publishers* in the *pubs2* database, you would execute a similar script to this one after first connecting to the Sybase System XI SQL Server that is hosting the *pubs2* database:

```
sp_addlogin repsysuser, repsysuser_pw
Go

Use pubs2
Go

sp_adduser repsysuser
Go

Grant Select on publishers to repsysuser
Go
```

This simple script adds the login *repsysuser* to the server and then adds it as a valid user of the *pubs2* database and then grants Select permission on the *publishers* table.

Creating Replication Server Users

The Replication Servers also need to know what user to use when moving the data between the two Replication Servers. To achieve this, you need to use the Replication Server command Create User. The syntax for Create User is as follows:

```
Create User User_Name
Set Password Password
```

User_Name and Password are the user name and password that you created earlier as the primary user in the primary database (repsysuser). After creating the user, you also need to grant the permission to create objects in the Replication Server database to that user. The command to grant the permission is as follows:

```
Grant Create Object to User_Name
```

For example, to add the repsysuser to the Primary Replication Server you would execute:

```
Create User repsysuser
Set Password repsysuser_pw
Go

Grant Create Object to repsysuser
Go
```

You would perform the same steps on the subscribing or secondary Replication Server.

Part
IV
Ch
24

Creating a Replication Definition

After creating users that can login and access the data, you need to tell the primary Replication Server what data you want to replicate. The command to create a definition for replication is `Create Replication Definition`. The syntax for the Replication Server command `Create Replication Definition` is as follows:

```
Create Replication Definition Replication_Def_Name
With Primary at Primary_Data_Server.Database_Name
[With All Tables Named 'Table_Name']
( Column_Name1 Datatype1, Column_Name2 Datatype2 ... )
[Primary Key( Column_Name1, Column_Name2 ... )]
[Searchable Columns( Column_Name1, Column_Name2 ... )]
[Send Standby{ All | Replication Definition } Columns]
[Replicate{ All | Minimal } Columns]
[Replicate_If_Changed{ Column_Name1, Column_Name2 ... ]
[Always_Replicate{ Column_Name1, Column_Name2 ... ]
```

The values for the `Create Replication Definition` command are as follows:

- *Replication_Def_Name*—This is the name of the replication definition that you are creating. The name must conform to standard Sybase naming conventions.

- *Primary_Data_Server.Database_Name*—This is the server and database that you are replicating from. You must make sure that you have defined an interface to the *Primary_Data_Server* and that it is available on the network to the Replication Server.

 TIP If you are using a `warm standby` Replication System that involves using a logical data server, then you should use the logical data server's name in place of the actual physical data server's name. This way, Sybase Replication Server can connect to either the real data server or to the standby file in the case or event of failure in the primary data server.

- *Table_Name*—This is the name of the table that you are replicating to the subscribing servers. This clause may be omitted from the `Create Replication Definition` statement if you use the table name as the name of the definition.

- *Column_Name1 Datatype1...*—This is the column structure of the table that is being replicated and should correspond to the table definition of the table in the System XI SQL Server.

- `Primary Key`—Use the `Primary Key` clause to specify the columns in the table that make up the `Primary Key` of the table.

- `Searchable Columns`—This clause is used to define which columns will be searchable in the replicated data. When a subscriber needs to do a `Where` clause-based search of replicated data, these are the only columns that can be queried.

- `Send Standby`—This clause is provided for use with a `Warm Standby` application. If you are in `Warm Standby` mode because of system down or network inactivity and you specify `Replication Definition Columns`, then the Replication Server will place only the columns defined in the Replication Definition to the `Standby` file. This can reduce the amount of data stored in the `Standby` file and is often used. If you don't specify this clause, the default is to log *all* columns in the base table to the `Standby` file.

- Replicate Minimal Columns—Use this clause if you want to move only the data in the columns that have been affected by a SQL operation. Otherwise, Replication Server will send every column to the subscribing Replication Servers. Using Replicate Minimal Columns can substantially reduce the amount of network traffic if the application you are writing does not make many changes to many columns in each logical transaction.

- Replicate_If_Changed—This is a new option for System XI-based Replication. Replicate_If_Changed is designed for Text and Image columns that are in a table that is being replicated. Replication Server will check that the column has actually been modified before attempting to send the data across the network.

- Always_Replicate—This option specifies that Replication Server should always copy Text or Image columns whenever a row is required to be replicated, regardless of whether their values have changed or not.

For example, to create a replicate definition for the *publishers* table, you would execute the following:

```
Create Replication Definition RepDef_Publishers
With Primary At SYB11_NT.pubs2
With All Tables Named 'publishers'
(
     pub_id  Char(4)     Not Null,
     pub_name Varchar(40)    Null,
     city   Varchar(20)    Null,
     state  Char(2)      Null
)
Primary Key( pub_id )
Searchable Columns( pub_name, city, state )
Go
```

N O T E You must login to the publishing Replication Server as the repsysuser that was created earlier to create the replication definition.

Enabling Replication for a Particular Table

To enable or disable Replication on a particular table, you use the system-stored procedure sp_setreptable. The syntax for the use of sp_setreptable is as follows:

```
sp_setreptable Table_Name, {True | False}
```

So, to enable the replication of the *publishers* table in the *pubs2* database, you would execute:

```
sp_setreptable publishers, True
Go
```

Granting Permissions to the Maintenance Login

Replication Server relies on the maintenance user defined at the time of creation of the Replication Server to have the ability to perform any operations on replicated tables at the subscribing server. What this means is that you have to grant all permissions on a replicated table to the maintenance user at the target or subscribing server.

N O T E It is assumed that the replicate or subscribing server has already been created with a table schema identical to that of the primary or publishing server. ▨

For example, in the SYB11_NT2 data server, you would need to grant permissions on the *publishers* table in the *pubs2* database; otherwise, the SYB11_NT2_RS Replication Server would not be able to perform the replication operations on the replicate table. An example of the syntax required for the appropriate Grant statements is as follows:

```
Use pubs2
Go

Grant Select, Insert, Update, Delete
On publishers to pubs2_maint
Go
```

Subscribing to the Replication Data

The final step in configuring a simple replication system is to get the subscribing Replication Server to move the replicated data to its Data Server that it is managing. The command to subscribe to data is the Replication Server command Create Subscription. The syntax for Create Subscription is as follows:

```
Create Subscription Subscription_Name
For Table_Name
With Replicate At Secondary_Data_Server.Database_Name
[Where Column_Name { < | <= | = | >= | > | & } Value ...
[Without Holdlock | Incrementally]]
```

The values for the Create Subscription command are as follows:

- ▪ *Subscription_Name*—This is the name of the subscription that you are creating. The name must be unique on the Replication Server and must conform to standard Sybase naming conventions.

- ▪ *Table_Name*—This is the name of the table that is being replicated.

- ▪ *Secondary_Data_Server.Database_Name*—This is the name of the server and database that the *Table_Name* resides in for replicating to. This *Secondary_Data_Server* must be defined in the interfaces file or you will get an error during the creation of the subscription.

- ▪ Where *Column_Name* ...—Use this clause to apply range criteria to the replication if necessary. If you don't specify this clause, then all data is replicated to the replicate table. The only columns that can be used for evaluation are those that are specified in the Searchable Columns clause of the Create Replication Definition statement.

- ▪ Without Holdlock—This command instructs Replication Server to request the data from the primary Replication Server without holding a lock on the data, thus allowing other Replication Servers to concurrently read the data if more than one server was subscribing to the same data.

■ Incrementally—This command instructs the Secondary Replication Server to hold a lock on the data in the primary Replication Server that is being replicated until it has completed replicating. This will stop concurrent access to the data in the primary Replication Server.

N O T E Note that when data is being subscribed, the data is moved in units of 10 rows. What this means is that if you are holding locks on the data, then at a minimum you will be locking not just one row in the Primary Replication Server, but anywhere from 10 to a multiple of 10 rows until the replication process has been completed. ■

For example, to subscribe all the records in the *publishers* table, you would execute the following:

```
Create Subscription Sub_Publishers
For publishers
With Replicate At SYB11_NT2.pubs2
Go
```

N O T E You must log into the subscribing Replication Server as the repsysuser that was created earlier to create the subscription. ■

Using the Replication Server Admin Command

The Admin command has a number of options in the Replication Server API and is used to monitor and manage the status of the Replication Server. The Admin command is a little bit like DBCC in that depending on the command being used, it has different parameters required for it. Some of the basic Admin commands that you should become familiar with as a DBA of a Replication Server are as follows:

■ Admin Disk_Space—This command displays the disk space utilized on the disks being used by the Replication Server.

■ Admin Health—This command returns the health of the Replication Server and informs you if any threads or processes have become infected.

■ Admin Pid—Use this command to return the process id of the task that is running the Replication Server. You may need the process id if you need to kill the Replication Server task under UNIX.

■ Admin RSSD_Name—This command returns the name of the RSSD databases for each of the SQL Servers that are being managed by the active Replication Server.

■ Admin Show_Connections—Use this command to display all the active connections to the Replication Server and to display the status of those connections.

■ Admin Version—This command returns the version of the Replication Server.

There are a number of other Admin commands that are documented more completely in the *Replication Server Commands Reference* from Sybase.

Alternatives to Replication Server

There are several different ways to achieve different levels of replication in your network that don't require the use of Replication Server. In this section, you see some alternatives that you have to perform data moving/replication in your environment that don't require the use of Sybase's Replication Server. These options include:

- Using operating system mirroring or server clustering
- Using backups and restores
- Writing your own replication system

You might wonder why you wouldn't want to use Replication Server. Well, there are a number of different situations where you may find different considerations or problems that can't be adequately addressed by Replication Server's model of data replication. For example, if you need to replicate the full database schema including all objects or multiple databases and their devices and so on to different servers on your network, you may find it difficult (if not impossible) to perform a level of replication satisfactory with Replication Server. Because Replication Server uses the LTM to pick up operations that need to be sent to other servers, it is difficult for such things as non-logged operations (e.g., Truncate) to be sent to other servers.

Operating System-Based Server Clusters for System Fault Tolerance

Using the operating system, or in some cases a combination of hardware and the operating system, to manage replication at the operating system level is the ultimate form of replication—and it also has the biggest price tag! The way this works is that at the operating system level, you define two or more physically separate servers/computers as a logical cluster of devices. If any of the computers fails for whatever reason, then the other computers will take over the responsibility of managing the clients and they will have access to an absolute mirror copy of everything on the box.

The costs involved in this scenario are significant. Why? Because you need to maintain two or more servers of equal capability and have them constantly in communication with one another. Usually this functionality is available only in the higher-end boxes from hardware vendors, such as HP, Digital, and Sun.

On HP-UX (HP's version of UNIX), for example, you can purchase an option to the operating system called MC/Service Guard. MC/Service Guard is enabled by fiber-optic cables between two or more HP9000 UNIX boxes that are used to transfer data between the systems that are working together as a logical *Enterprise Cluster*. In the event of a failure on a primary box (a server that has users currently connected), MC/Service Guard will switch over to a secondary box in the cluster and will move all user connections to the alternate TCP/IP address seamlessly without disturbing any of the users.

The beauty of MC/Service Guard is that the process and the selection of backup or alternate resources is completely automated and requires no user intervention. The whole switch-over process takes normally just a few seconds between the time that the error/failure is detected and the time that all users have been migrated to the backup server. For a detailed technical discussion of how MC/Service Guard works and what it can do for you, go to one of HP's many Web sites at **http://www.dmo.hp.com/cgi-bin/fe.pl/gsy/3c1.html**.

Similar products to MC/Service Guard are available from other hardware vendors, and here are a couple of Web sites for them for you to review:

- Digital: DECSafe and TruCluster— **http://www.unix.digital.com/cluster/**
- Sun: SPARCcluster—**http://www.sun.com/products-n-solutions/hw/servers/ product/HA/wp/ha.solstice.wp.html**
- IBM: High Availability Cluster Multi-Processing for AIX Version 4.2 —**http:// www.austin.ibm.com/software/Apps/hacmp.html**

If you are running extremely mission-critical systems that cannot support any downtime, then I recommend that you review these operating system-level replication strategies for your corporation or organization.

Using Backups to Move Data

A simple (and sometimes overlooked) option for performing basic replication is to use database backups (dumps) to move data between servers. Using backups is really not a bad choice for simple replication that doesn't need to be extremely timely, and is often the most efficient and cost-effective way of managing the replication process.

For example, say you have a production system that is being utilized throughout the day as a real-time transaction processing environment. During the day, you also have a competing demand from decision-makers in your environment to have a reporting database that they can analyze with complex reporting models to determine the performance of the company. In this world, you really want to have two separate databases so that if an errant query is run by a decision-maker, the database isn't locked for long periods of time—which would cause problems for the OLTP (Online Transaction Processing) system.

You could use Replication Server to move data between the two systems, but this may be overkill. In many companies and organizations, day-old data is more than adequate for this sort of analysis. In order to retrieve day-old data, all you need to do is to make a backup at the end of the business day and restore it to the other database for the analysts to access. This way, you have separation in your data between the OLTP requirements and the OLAP (Online Analytical Processing) requirements of your systems.

▶ **See** "Performing a Local Backup," **p. 496**

For better performance, provided you have enough disk space on the server, you can perform the backup straight to disk and then restore from the disk to the second database. This will yield substantial performance gains and will make it easier to automate the process because there's no external media that somebody can forget to place in the tape drive.

N O T E If you move a database between two different servers by using a backup and restore, then you will need to drop all the users and re-add them on the second server. This process of managing the logins and users can be quite a pain and needs to be carefully planned. Each login that is added to a server is assigned a unique server user ID (`suid`). This `suid` is assigned to the user when you perform `sp_adduser` to add the user as a valid login to the particular database that you are working with.

So even if you have the same logins added on two servers, there's no guarantee that the `suid`s will match for the same login between the two servers. The work-around is to drop all the users from the database immediately after restoring it and then re-add them all with `sp_adduser`. If you don't perform this drop and re-add, you will end up receiving error 916 from the database when you login—`this user is not a valid user or owner of objects in the database`.

If you have concerns about the logins existing on the second server, you could write a script that goes through the *sysusers* table in the restored database and performs the following steps:

1. Drop any objects that are owned by the user account. You need to do this so that you can drop the login.

2. Drop the user from the database.

3. Drop the login from the server. Note that if you get an error saying that the login doesn't exist, you should ignore it and just keep going.

4. Add the login to the server and set the password equal to the login name, or to some pre-defined value, so that the user will know how to login to the system.

5. Add the user to the database. This will ensure that you have the correct `suid` assigned to the user in the database and will eliminate any possibility for an error 916 note. ∎

Writing Your Own Application-Based Replication

There are times when Replication Server and backups just don't address all your needs. You may have some kind of custom application that has really unusual data replication requirements that you just cannot manage with Replication Server. It is not uncommon for developers to write some private replication schemes to solve these problems in house without the need for Replication Server. A common occurrence is to solve the problem of moving data between different application systems that may or may not have been on different types of relational database systems.

For example, say you have a large central system that runs perfectly well on a Sybase database in the main office. Now, you need to distribute a portion of the data to remote laptop-based users for field work. This sort of solution isn't easy to provide with Sybase because the only way to run System XI on a laptop is to have a really powerful laptop with a lot of memory— something that's not very practical if you have lots of remote users because the cost will be too high. An alternative might be to use another local database, such as Centura's SQLBase or Sybase's own SQL Anywhere. You can find out more information about SQL Anywhere in Appendix B, "Sybase's Baby Brother: SQL Anywhere."

This sort of replication requires a custom solution that's very difficult to accomplish using Replication Server, especially when it involves another type of relational database-management system. Some possible replication schemes that you might want to consider are described here.

Using E-mail to Replicate Data   E-mail is a perfect store-and-forward data-distribution scheme. By packaging up data in some kind of proprietary transaction file format, you can then distribute it to all the remote subscribers of the data and then, whenever they connect to the e-mail system, they can choose to receive the latest information from the system. You can write file import and export programs pretty simply in most 4GLs and then send the data to clients and receive it on the server rather easily.

If you wanted to automate the process further, you can write MAPI or VIM applications that send custom-mail attachments to move the data. Then, it is a case of writing an application that polls through MAPI or VIM to receive these custom-mail messages and then reads the data and performs whatever operations are required on the local or central server.

Part

IV

Ch

24

Using Files to Replicate Data   By far, the simplest approach to replication is to write data to a text file and then send the file across the network or put it on a floppy disk and load it on the other computer systems. This is an easy thing to do and the only issues that are involved are optimizing the reading and writing processes to minimize the amount of time required to move the data. The following are some tips for writing file read and write systems:

- Devise a file-format that you can use portably across systems. For example, have the header of the file describe the data coming in the file.

- Write file-processing engines to read and write files based on definitions that can either be supplied in a database table or in the file being read.

- In some cases, when loading the data, it may be quicker to drop and re-create the table than it is to `Delete` all the data—not all RDBMs support the `Truncate` command to delete all the data in a table without logging.

- Consider formatting and exporting the data from a stored procedure. That way, you can put any front-end application in front of the data to write the files. By having a flexible way of plugging in any front-end application, you can have the ability to write the fastest performing front-end program in any language you prefer and know that all you need to do is to take the formatted stored-procedure output and place it in a file.

Using a Direct Connection to Replicate Data   Replication of data can also be performed programmatically in front-end client/server code. All you need to do is have the ability in your client/server programming language to connect to multiple databases (possibly of different vendors) at the same time. The replication works like this:

1. Select the source table that needs to be replicated by opening a cursor on the data in the primary database.

2. Start reading the data from the source table, record by record.

3. Perform any custom processing of the source table data, if necessary.

4. Perform an `Insert` on a second connection to the alternate database to `Insert` the data on the remote database.

The only reason that you would want to write your own *Direct Connection* replication would be if you needed to perform custom processing of the data on its way through the system. Most server-to-server-based replication schemes (such as Sybase's Replication Server and Centura's Ranger products) will provide better performance than you can write in a client-based replication program. However, the commercial products typically lack the flexibility to perform custom data processing as the data is sent through the network.

From Here...

In this chapter, you learned how to install and configure Sybase's Replication Server. It wasn't a particularly easy process, but you—hopefully—got it installed OK. Using Replication Server once it's installed is generally pretty painless; however, you have to accept that once you add replication to a system, no matter how simple the core system is, you have introduced a substantial layer of additional complexity. This complexity is manageable and workable, but you must recognize that your duties as a DBA are going to increase.

You need to be proactive in monitoring the replication process to make sure that you are managing any performance bottlenecks and that the system is performing optimally. In the event that a failure occurs, rebuilding the Replication System will require some work. You owe it to yourself to carefully document your setup once you get it up and running so that in the event of a failure, the rebuilding process is at least a manageable one. If you have no idea of passwords and users, then you will find it very difficult to re-create the Replication System environment and may have to rebuild things from scratch—which could result in data loss.

I suggest that you look over the following chapters for some additional guidance on managing your System XI server and its databases:

- Chapter 19, "Managing Data Availability," provides guidance on performing backups and restores to maintain database integrity in the event of a media failure and to perform simplistic replication.

- Chapter 22, "Managing and Monitoring Performance," shows you how to monitor the way your server is performing to determine when a good time is available to perform backups and restores.

- Chapter 23, "Using Sybase's Configuration Options," helps you tune the server with the many different configuration options available to you.

Appendixes

Suggestions for Naming Conventions

What's in a name? Well, it turns out that naming objects, variables, stored procedures, and so on is a pretty contentious issue. Most people seem to have their own ideas about what makes a good name, so please approach this topic with some caution if you try to implement my suggestions in an environment that already has some standards in place.

Consider the following issues when naming objects in a database and in application programming:

- **Consistency**—It is important that when you start naming objects in the database that you apply the same rules throughout the development of the system. An inconsistent naming convention is as bad as none at all.

- **Simplicity**—When naming objects in the database, make sure that your rules are simple and easy to implement.

- **Brevity**—There's a tendency among some database designers to use long names for columns and tables simply because there are 32 characters available. Don't fall into this trap! Your programmers and application developers will resent you if they have to enter long names when a simplified form could have been used.

- **Sensibleness**—If you're naming something, don't come up with an irrational name. For example, if a table contains such data as that of a customer information file, don't name the table just "Information." Use words and names that *sensibly* describe the data that is being managed. ■

Creating a Dictionary

Before embarking on a database naming convention scheme, a lot of people neglect to create a dictionary of common terms to serve as the foundation for future naming of objects and tables. A great way of creating the dictionary is to get all the application designers and developers together in one room to brainstorm all the commonly used elements in the system. Once you've got a list of these items, then you want to come up with an agreed name and a description for people to review later.

In Table A.1, you can see a sample dictionary that I created from looking at one of the projects I was working on. It is used to name objects that get created in the database from now on. By using this same sort of model, you will find it really easy to define your database going forward.

Table A.1   A Sample Database Dictionary

Object	Suggested Name	Description
Account	Acct	A customer account
Bank	Bk	Anything related to a bank
Branch	Br	Anything related to a branch of a bank
Charge	Chg	A charge applied to a customer's account

Object	Suggested Name	Description
Date	Dt	Any date-based reference in the system
Deposit	Dp	Any deposit-related activity in the system
Effective Date	Effective_Dt	The posting date or date at which a transaction has meaning in the system
Loan	Ln	Any loan-related activity in the system
Transaction	Tr	A posted or pending transaction

Understanding Stropping, Underscores, and Case

One of the most important decisions that you can make early in the development of a system is the way that you capitalize words that are used to identify and name objects. This is a pretty divisive issue because just about everyone has ideas on whether you should capitalize the first letters of nouns in object names, use underscores to separate those nouns, or to use case to help standardize the object names. In this section, you'll see some suggestions that seem to make sense on most of the projects that I've worked on.

Using Case to Clearly Identify an Object

There are several different opinions on what is the best approach to declaring a name in terms of case. Is it better to name a table CUSTOMERDATA, CUSTOMER_DATA, Customer_Data, CustomerData, or some variation of these suggestions? I believe that you want to have a simple goal for the actual name: It must be as understandable as possible given the constraints of Sybase itself.

One thing is certain: If you *are* going to use different cases in your object names, you should make it a requirement to install a case-insensitive database. If you don't, you will have to rely on your application programmers to make sure that they correctly refer to objects without getting the case wrong.

▶ **See** "Understanding Sort Orders," **p. 632**

▶ **See** "Understanding Character Sets," **p. 631**

Once you have come up with a name for an object in English (or the language of your choice), such as "Customer Data," it then is a responsibility of the database administrator (or in some places, the application designer) to convert this into a name that is acceptable to the database.

Using Underscores

Many information systems shops that used to be mainframe-based prefer all capitals because that's all the mainframe used to be able to understand, so the value of the name would be something like CUSTOMERDATA. However, some of these environments were limited to eight-character names, so it ended up something like CUSTDATA—which wasn't particularly readable or understandable.

I highly recommend that you at least separate words with underscores for readability, and that wherever possible, you don't constrain yourself to eight characters. So, in this case, the name of the table would be CUSTOMER_DATA.

Using Stropping

Stropping is the process of changing the case of names in a table. The stropping process works by capitalizing the first letter of each word. For example, CUSTOMERDATA might become CustomerData.

> **CAUTION**
>
> I strongly caution you *not* to use object names that require the use of Quoted Identifiers. These are very difficult to manage from many client programming languages, such as SQLWindows, PowerBuilder, and Visual Basic. Instead, choose names that are defined by standard ASCII characters.

Suggested Object Prefixes

When it comes to naming database objects, there's a school of thought that says it's a good idea to prefix each object with a prefix type. The reason you might want to do this is that in a large database or complex application, it can make it easier to understand the structure of the database and/or the application if you can easily read a SQL statement and know what sort of object is being referred to.

Table A.2 is a list of possible prefixes for database objects. I have found that they are particularly useful for large projects that have a lot of developers. I highly recommend their use.

Table A.2 Suggestions for Object Prefixes

Object Type	Suggested Prefixes
Alternate Index	AK_, Ak_, Aidx_
Default	DEF_, Def_
Primary Index	PK_, Pk_, Pidx_
Rule	RULE_, Rule_, RL_, Rl_
Stored Procedure	PROC_, Proc_, <company_name>sp (e.g., Phoenix Stored Procedure = psp_)

Object Type	Suggested Prefixes
Table	`TB_`, `Tb_`, or nothing
Trigger	`TRG_`, `Trig_`, `TR_`, `Tr_`
View	`VW_`, `Vw_`, `View_`

Part

V

App

A

Naming Variables in Transact-SQL

One issue that is often overlooked when naming objects in the database is the naming of the variables and parameters used with stored procedures and Transact-SQL. First and foremost, you should try as much as possible to name the variable the same as the column or object in the database. Therefore, if you have a column named `Processing_Time`, you should try to name the variable `@Processing_Time`.

T I P It is often easier to work with stored procedure variables that are not separated by underscores, so a column named `System_Dt` becomes `@SystemDt` in a procedure.

Unlike table columns, it is far easier to make a mistake in a stored procedure if you don't clearly delineate the datatype of a variable that you are working with. In Table A.3, you can see a suggested list of prefixes that you may want to use to help make your code easier to work with.

Table A.3   Suggested Variable and Parameter Prefixes for Transact-SQL

Prefix	Description
dt	`Date` or `DateTime` datatypes
n	Numeric datatypes (`Number`, `Decimal`, `Float`, `Integer`, and so on)
p	Parameter (prefixes the actual datatype)
r	`Receive` or `Output` parameter (prefixes the datatype)
s	String datatypes (`Char`, `Varchar`)

For example, consider the following code:

```
Create Proc psp_test_variables
    @Param1   Datetime,
    @Param2   Varchar(20) output
As
Declare   @Var1   Decimal(14,2),
          @Var2   Char(10)
...
```

You could change it to read something like this:

```
Create Proc psp_test_variables
     @pdtParam1  Datetime,
     @rsParam2   Varchar(20) output
As
Declare  @nVar1  Decimal(14,2),
         @sVar2  Char(10)
...
```

Naming Objects in Application Programming Languages

Naming objects and variables in application programs follows the same basic rules as those in Transact-SQL. You want to make sure that the closest possible relationship exists between the variable or object in your application language and the object that it represents in the database. Some languages have limitations and requirements that make this naming difficult, but you will get the best results if you try to stay as close as possible to the name of the database object.

If you do name objects in your application programs the same as in the database, you will find it much easier to correlate and identify which database object is being referred to when "walking" through an application.

Understanding Names You Can't Use

Sybase has a list of reserved words that cannot be used when creating an object. You can, of course, use these words in combination with other words as a single name; it's just that you can't employ these reserved words on their own except when used in their correct Transact-SQL context.

Note that although these system reserved words can be entered in upper- or lowercase, they are still reserved. For example, you cannot name a table EXEC, Exec, or exec. The following is a list of the reserved words in Sybase System XI:

add	double	mirror	rowcount
all	dummy	mirrorexit	rows
alter	dump	national	rule
and	else	noholdlock	save
any	end	nonclustered	schema
arith_overflow	endtran	not	select
as	errlvl	null	set
asc	ordata	numeric_transacton	setuser
at	errorexit	of	shared
authorization	escape	off	shutdown

avg	except	offsets	some
begin	exec	on	statistics
between	execute	once	stripe
break	exists	online	sum
browse	exit	only	syb_identity
bulk	fetch	open	syb_restree
by	fillfactor	option	table
cascade	for	or	temp
char_convert	foreign	order	temporary
check	from	over	textsize
checkpoint	goto	nopartition	to
close	grant	perm	tran
clustered	group	permanent	transaction
commit	having	plan	trigger
compute	holdlock	precision	truncate
confirm	identity_insert	prepare	tsequal
constraint	if	primary	union
continue	in	print	unique
control row	index	privileges	unpartition
convert	insert	proc	update
count	intersect	procedure	use
create	into	processexit	user
currenterr	is	public	user_option
cursor	isolation	raiserror	using
database	key	read	values
dbcc	kill	readtext	varying
deallocate	level	reconfigure	view
declare	like	references	waitfor
default	line	replace	where
delete	load	return	while
desc	max	revoke	with
disk	max_rows_ per_page	role	work
distinct	min	rollback	writetext

As a rule, I've found that it is very difficult to write a credible specification for naming conventions early in a project because you just don't know enough about what it is you are working on. This is a decision that you will have to live with for quite some time, so take your time and be thoughtful about the process. Let the standards evolve, and make sure that you surround yourself with flexible developers who won't mind too much if you have to adapt or change the conventions as the project progresses. ●

Sybase's Baby Brother: SQL Anywhere

It's often wondered, What's Sybase doing to address the small or mobile computing market? The answer was to buy some new technology. Sybase's core product, SQL Server, was just never really scaled down to the low-end desktop and mobile computing environments like other databases, such as Microsoft's Access, Centura's SQLBase, and Borland's Paradox. Fortunately, however, Watcom's database Watcom-SQL was on the block after Powersoft bought Watcom; Sybase, in turn, bought Powersoft.

So, with some great technology on hand in the corporate technology coffers, Sybase spent about a year (following the acquisition of Powersoft) developing and re-engineering the Watcom-SQL product, and produced Sybase SQL Anywhere at the end of 1995. SQL Anywhere is an evolutionary product. Built on the base of Watcom-SQL, Sybase added a layer of Transact-SQL compatibility to make the database a truly worthy addition to the Sybase product line.

The purpose of SQL Anywhere is to provide a technological entry point for the small application developer (and the remote computing systems) that can be scaled to the enterprise by crossing over into Sybase's core products, such as System XI, when the developer has outgrown SQL Anywhere. In this sense, SQL Anywhere provides the capability to scale from a single user to many thousands on a high-end UNIX box. ■

Understanding the Small Footprint of SQL Anywhere

One of the key goals of a database that's going to add to Sybase's existing product line is that it be light on memory and thus a good candidate for remote or mobile computing (as well as for small workgroups). SQL Anywhere is an excellent example of producing a high-quality and feature-rich database that sports a very small memory footprint—as low as 1M, depending on the operating system.

SQL Anywhere in its current incarnation (version 5.0) runs on multiple operating systems: Windows 3.x, Windows NT 3.x and Windows NT 4.x, Windows 95, OS/2 2.x or higher, Novell NetWare, and MS-DOS 3.3 or higher. With that range of operating system support, you are bound to find it in use in many small workgroups and mobile environments. This is its key strength and the main area that Sybase is targeting for SQL Anywhere.

Despite this limited memory use, Sybase has added the support for a wide range of network communications protocols that can be used on the client to talk to the database:

- NetBIOS
- TCP/IP
- Novell NetWare IPX

What this means is that with a very limited amount of resources, either on the client (remote user) or on the server, you can get a functional database that works just like Sybase's SQL Server product. The feature richness of Sybase's SQL Anywhere is hard to overestimate. It has a number of capabilities that are important and useful (some of which aren't supported in SQL Server), as follows:

- Stored procedures
- Triggers
- External stored procedures (callable external DLLs)
- Built-in referential and entity integrity, including cascading updates and deletes
- Dynamic, multiple database support
- Transact-SQL and ANSI SQL support
- ODBC Version 2.5, Level 2 driver
- Full transaction processing and recovery with a checkpoint log and a forward transaction log
- Replication through SQL Remote

- Sybase Replication Agent support for Sybase Replication Server
- Integration with Sybase Clients through an Open Server Gateway
- SQL Central (GUI database administration tool)
- Bi-directional, scrollable, updatable cursors
- Easy data import/export with other formats
- High-performance, self-tuning, cost-based query optimizer
- Online backup
- Updatable multi-table views
- Binary large object (BLOB) support
- Multinational character set support, including MBCS
- Industry-standard embedded SQL interface
- Row-level locking

A very interesting point of note is that several key features listed above are not supported in the Sybase System XI product, much to the dismay of many users. Many big customers with hundreds and thousands of users have awaited Sybase's support of row-level locking for many years. In addition, SQL Anywhere's bi-directional cursor support (or true result set processing) enables you to write advanced database browsing applications that can go forward and backward through the table data while retaining a context (or pointer) to the individual row.

Using Transact-SQL in SQL Anywhere

Probably the most important addition to the Watcom-SQL product was the capability to use Transact-SQL in SQL Anywhere. Why is this important? Because it means that instantly (with minor modifications), thousands of existing applications written for Sybase SQL Server XI have the capability to be ported to a different database that allows for a portable and remotely distributable application.

Transact-SQL support in SQL Anywhere is excellent. There's very little that can't be done in SQL Anywhere. One of the excellent features of SQL Anywhere is its comprehensive documentation that is supplied in the online help that describes how to work with Transact-SQL on SQL Anywhere to maximize the portability of your application across SQL Anywhere and Sybase SQL Server XI.

N O T E   A quite reasonable limitation of SQL Anywhere is that you can't write stored procedures in a mixture of languages. For example, you can't begin a stored procedure using Transact-SQL and then switch over to get a feature from Watcom-SQL. You must stay within the confines of either interpreter and cannot wander randomly between them.

The level of Transact-SQL support is inherent in SQL Central, too. For example, in Figure B.1, you can see that SQL Central even goes to the extent of indicating the language that the procedure was compiled in.

FIG. B.1

Double-click any of the procedures in the right pane of the SQL Central explorer to launch a script editor.

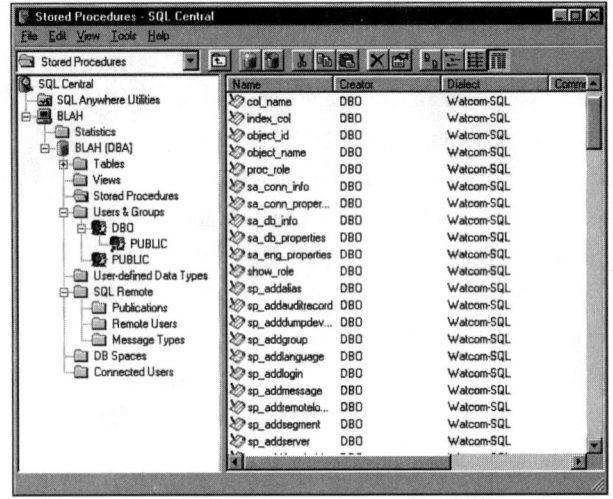

If you right-click any of the procedures, you get the opportunity to extract the SQL in either language, and it's translated if necessary. In Figure B.2, you can see the stored procedure col_name having been extracted in Transact-SQL.

FIG. B.2

The SQL Central procedure editor is a great utility because it supports syntax highlighting, making it easy to identify different parts of the SQL statement and the procedure being worked on.

```
alter procedure DBO.col_name(@object_id integer,
@column_id integer,@database_id integer=null)
as
begin
  declare @cname char(128)
  select "name" into @cname
    from DBO.syscolumns
    where id=@object_id
    and colid=@column_id
  if sqlcode<>0
    return(null)
  return(@cname)
end
```

The same procedure is shown extracted in Watcom-SQL in Figure B.3.

Working with Replication

What good would a remote database be if you couldn't get any data into it? SQL Anywhere's remote replication functionality is very good. Not only does it have its own replication between SQL Anywhere databases, called SQL Remote, it also can act as an agent to Sybase System XI's Replication Server.

FIG. B.3

The Watcom-SQL interpretation of the simple system procedure col_name demonstrates the differences between the two languages.

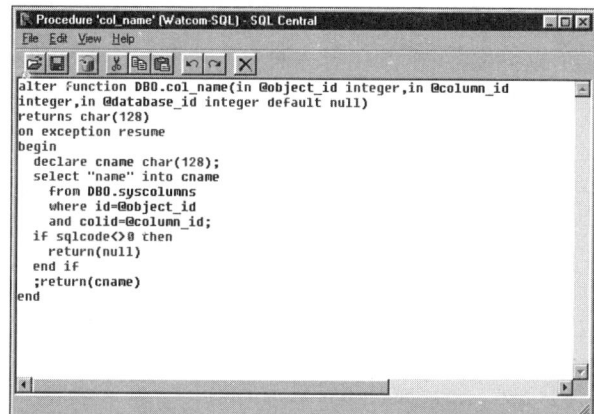

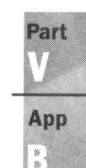

SQL Remote is a message-driven replication engine that is designed to transport data over several different protocols, including the following:

- **File**—This is a proprietary file format used for transferring data between servers.
- **MAPI and VIM**—These are popular e-mail standards from Microsoft and Lotus, respectively. Using mail as a transport protocol is highly effective when performing large amounts of remote data distribution to non-live connections.
- **SMTP**—This is an industry-standard protocol that is normally used to send network messages between network hardware. It also serves as a good live-link messaging protocol between SQL Anywhere databases.

The advantage of asynchronous message-based replication is that it doesn't require dedicated network connections to ensure data transfer. SQL Anywhere is very effective at transmitting data via e-mail, and this proves to be an excellent option when you need to send data across the Internet or through other public networks.

Using SQL Central

Easily one of the best relational database management tools, SQL Central (supplied with SQL Anywhere) makes all database operations a breeze. For example, creating a database is as simple as following a wizard. No longer do you have to remember the real SQL statements needed to create the database; you are guided through the process from start to finish.

SQL Central has (among other things) an excellent statistical management facility called the Performance Monitor. It looks a lot like the Windows NT performance monitor and has the same user interface characteristics of enabling you to monitor any of a bunch of statistics. In Figure B.4, you can see a sample of the available statistics in the right pane of the SQL Central explorer.

FIG. B.4

The variety of statistical options that you can monitor in SQL Anywhere makes it easy for you to gauge how well the server is performing and to understand what areas of the database server can be improved.

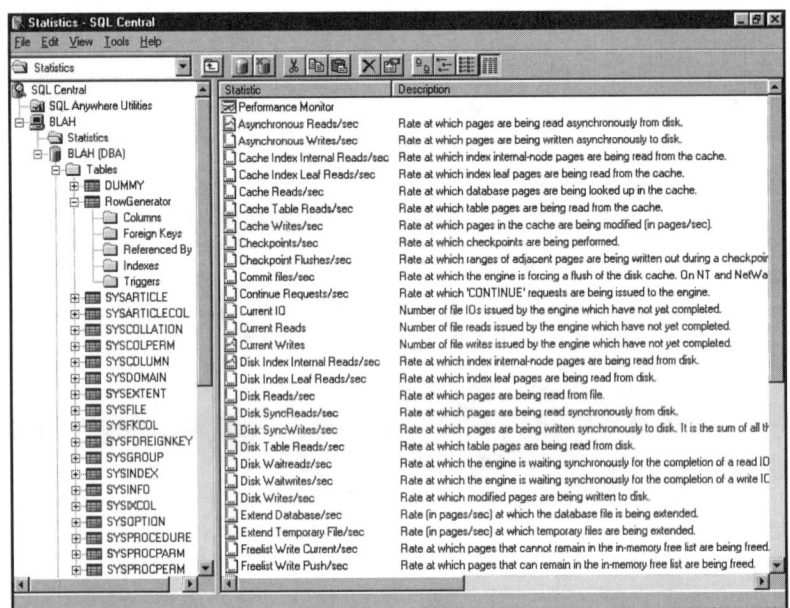

Using Interactive SQL

Unlike its big brother, System XI, SQL Anywhere is not ashamed of its database interactivity program, ISQL. SQL Anywhere's ISQL product is actually usable! It offers a great editor and shows the results of the query plan and the data after the execution of each statement. In Figure B.5, you can see the results of selecting from the system catalog table *sysoptions,* which is similar to the *sysconfigures* table in System XI in that it stores the currently selected options and/or configurations of the server.

FIG. B.5

The SQL Anywhere ISQL is a fully functional database interaction program that enables you to perform all the SQL statements you would need and enables you to see the results from those statements in a single resizable window.

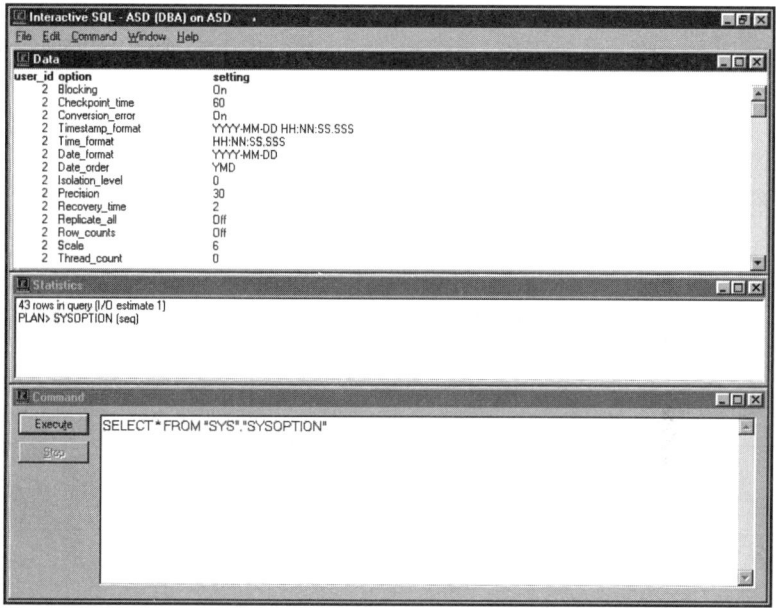

Understanding What SQL Anywhere Isn't

SQL Anywhere is not designed to compete with Sybase's core product, and as such, I doubt it will ever be ported to UNIX—that said, stranger things have happened! If you are developing a full-scale application, you should be aware of the following considerations before embarking on a project with SQL Anywhere:

- SQL Anywhere's support for client-side programming is realistically limited to ODBC. This is a fairly significant omission for a programming interface, and is something to consider if you are going to work with Sybase (using DBLibrary or Client Library) and then have to switch to SQL Anywhere's ODBC support. SQL Anywhere does have a client API called the WSQL HLI; however, none of the major client/server vendors (such as Centura, Visual Basic, and Powersoft) have adopted it, and instead are supporting ODBC.

- SQL Anywhere is unlikely to support anything over about 80 users. Sybase documents a limit of about 100 users, but in reality, you would want to stay below that for adequate performance.

- SQL Anywhere is not designed for large databases greater than a few gigabytes. Despite the printed limitations of one terabyte, performance will start to suffer with a database of over a few gigabytes in size.

That is not to say that SQL Anywhere won't be a good choice for you; it's just that you should be aware of the issues prior to starting development. Despite these limitations, SQL Anywhere remains one of the two top choices for a remote database or small workgroup solution—the other is Centura's SQLBase.

The Bottom Line

Sybase's SQL Anywhere product is a great database for the small-scale application that needs to have the capability of being portable (it can run effectively on laptops) and distributable. Sybase has gone to great pains to make the Transact-SQL implementation as complete as possible, and it's just a matter of time until they're identical. SQL Anywhere's strong replication functionality and its capability to be installed and managed by unsophisticated users make it an ideal choice for the remote sales officer who needs to keep up with the central inventory database and yet still be flexible enough to work alone.

If you are planning to use Sybase System XI for your main database and are looking for a compatible product that is cheap, easy to install, and highly efficient on low-end hardware, SQL Anywhere is a product that you should look into.

Are you still unsure if you really, really want to use SQL Anywhere? Well, you can try it before you buy it. Using your Web browser, go to **http://www.watcom.com/sql/eval/sqleval.html**, and complete the online evaluation form and then start the download. ●

Suggested Reading

The purpose of this appendix is to document various books that I've found helpful when working with relational databases and Sybase, and when dealing with general programming issues. This collection of books comes from a variety of publishers, and despite the emphasis on the Que series, it is really an unbiased guide to the *best of the best*. ■

Internet Sources

The list of books available relating to Sybase, SQL, and client/server development is constantly changing. On the Internet, there are two great resources that you should keep in mind:

- **http://www.sybase.com/inc/sypress/sy-list.html**—This lists all of the books that have a specific interest in Sybase or SQL.

- **http://www.mcp.com/**—This is Macmillan Computer Publishing's one place to search all of its imprints, including Que, Sams, and Ziff Davis.

Sybase System XI Books

The following are the Sybase books that I most often refer to:

Rankins, Garbus, Solomon, and McEwan: *Sybase System 11 Unleashed* (Sams: ISBN 0-672-309069-2)

Garbus, Solomon, and Tretter: *Sybase DBA Survival Guide* (Sams: ISBN 0-672-30651-4)

Worden: *Sybase Developer's Guide* (Sams: ISBN 0-672-30467-8)

Phillips, O'Neil, and Brain: *Sybase System XI Performance Tuning Strategies* (Prentice Hall: ISBN 0-134-94865-3)

Client/Server Application Programming Books

The following are all of the generally good books on SQL and client/server programming:

Celko: *Instant SQL Programming* (Wrox Press: ISBN 1-874-4165-0)

Rozenshtein: *Optimizing Transact-SQL: Advanced Programming Techniques* (SQL Forum Press: ISBN 0-964-98120-3)

Holmes-Kinsella: *Special Edition Using Gupta SQLWindows 5* (Que: ISBN 0-7897-0189-8)

Matcho: *Special Edition Using Delphi 2* (Que: ISBN 0-7897-0591-5)

Goren, Schmelzer, and Smith: *Visual Basic 4 Enterprise Development* (Que: ISBN 0-7897-0099-9)

Gill and Rao, edited by *Client/Server* magazine: *The Official Client/Server Computing Guide to Data Warehousing* (Que: ISBN 0-7897-0714-4)

Wood: *Special Edition Using PowerBuilder 5* (Que: ISBN 0-7897-0754-3)

Knowing Where to Go
for More Help

There's always a concern when jumping onto a new technology with being able to find enough peer support for the product. If you are a new user of Sybase products, such as System XI, you are largely shielded from this problem thanks to an excellent array of online and offline media through which you can get help and information. ∎

Sybase's electronic support is generally excellent, but is especially good for paid customers with technical support agreements. I highly recommend that you purchase support from Sybase so that you can get on the phone, if necessary, to talk to a human and get immediate support.

The most well-known electronic places to look for help are as follows:

- CompuServe: **GO SYBASE**
- The World Wide Web: **http://www.sybase.com**
- The World Wide Web: **http://www.powersoft.com**

> **CAUTION**
>
> Sybase's electronic forums are public places that are designed to promote communication among users. Sybase monitors and often adds good supporting answers to many questions. You must realize that they are *not* official support channels, with the exception of the new Web bug tracking system (Support Plus) available at **http://www-es1.sybase.com/plusgw.html**. If your system goes down, call the local Sybase representative in your country for immediate support. *Do not* rely on an electronic forum to get your answer if the situation is critical.

Using CompuServe

Sybase's CompuServe support network is excellent. I highly recommend going to CompuServe as your first choice for support. Local CompuServe access is available in most countries and is a relatively inexpensive service. Working with CompuServe is typically done using the WinCIM product, which CompuServe supplies free of charge to all of its users.

> **N O T E**   The following instructions assume you have already successfully installed WinCIM on your computer. If you have not installed WinCIM, please consult the documentation supplied by CompuServe for instructions on how to install and test WinCIM.

To use WinCIM to access Sybase's forum, follow these steps:

1. Launch WinCIM from the CompuServe group in Windows to start the WinCIM program (see Fig. D.1).
2. Choose Services, Go and enter **Sybase** in the Service field of the Go dialog box (see Fig. D.2). Choose OK.
3. After connecting to CompuServe, you are presented with the Sybase forum main menu. Click the Sybase OpenLine button, which is shown in Figure D.3, to access Sybase's main support and user forum.

FIG. D.1

After launching WinCIM, you are typically presented with the Favorite Places window from which you can go to different forums.

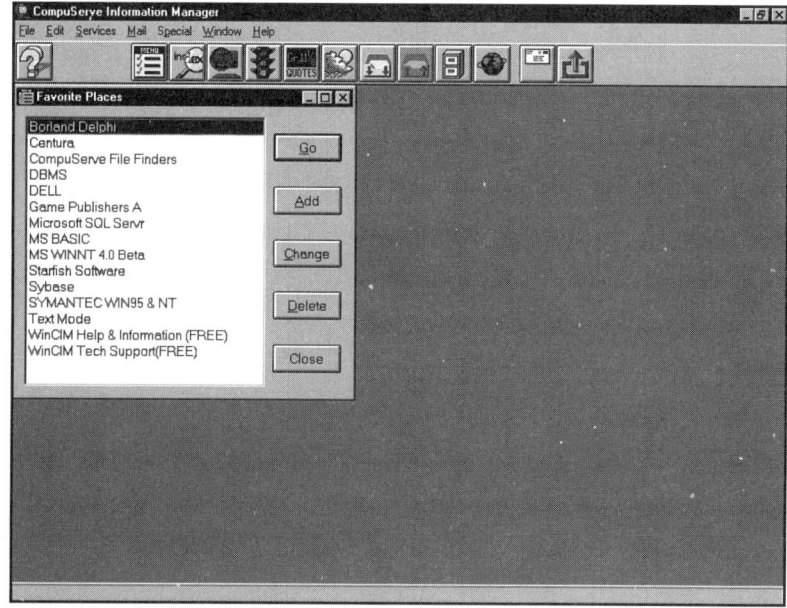

FIG. D.2

The Go dialog box enables you to access a service or forum. Clicking OK causes WinCIM to log in to the CompuServe network (if you aren't already connected) and enter the forum.

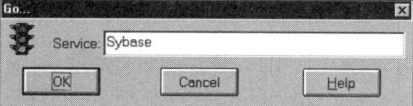

Once you are in the Sybase OpenLine forum—which, by the way, is the best place to go for general questions—find the appropriate section in the forum that you want to work with. To do so, choose Messages, Browse messages to bring up a list of sections available in the forum (see Fig. D.4), and then double-click any of the sections to see the list of messages. The forum sections are described in Table D.1.

FIG. D.3

The Sybase window in WinCIM enables you to connect to different Sybase-sponsored forums, including OpenLine (for general support) and PrivateLine (premier support for paying customers).It also links to the Powersoft and SQL Anywhere forums.

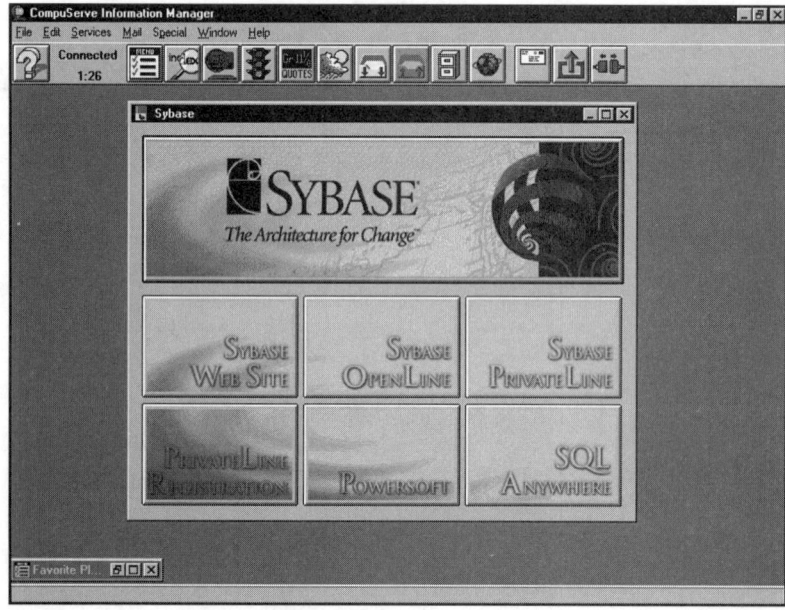

FIG. D.4

Sybase's CompuServe support has a number of different sections that enable you to have detailed and specific conversations (or threads) with different Sybase users and the Sybase staff.

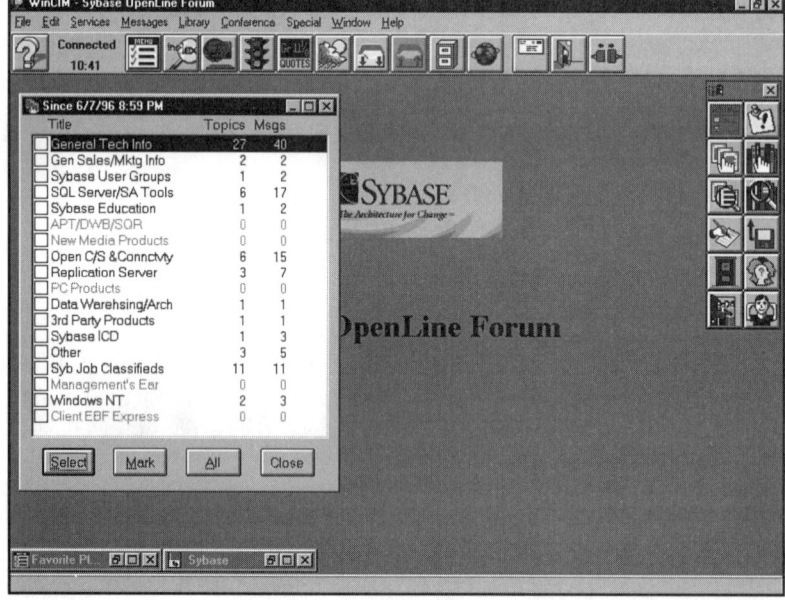

Table D.1 Sybase's CompuServe Forum Sections

Section Name	Description
General Tech Info	This is the most broadly used section and is generally a good place to post questions that are about issues of a technical nature. It is a great place to ask for tips on how to use Sybase more efficiently and effectively.
Gen Sales/Mktg Info	This is Sybase's primary vehicle for sales announcements and product launches. Check in here to ask questions about such issues as platform pricing.
Sybase User Groups	This is the ideal place to go to look for information about the regional user groups.
SQL Server/SA Tools	This is useful for asking questions about the server itself and how you interact with it through Sybase's administrative tools, such as Sybase SQL Server Manager and ISQL.
Sybase Education	This section discusses training seminars and courses that you can take to further your education and understanding of Sybase.
APT/DWB/SQR	If you use Sybase's SQR Report Writing tool, use this forum to ask questions.
New Media Products	This is a very low activity section and is only of much use if you are taking advantage of Sybase's software specifically designed for TV servers (i.e., Silicon Graphics servers).
Open C/S & Connctvty	If you have questions about connecting to Sybase using development tools, such as PowerBuilder, Visual Basic, SQLWindows, and C/C++, use this section to find out more about Client Library and DBLibrary.
Replication Server	If you are working in a large distributed environment and have questions about, or need help with, working with Sybase's high-end replication solution, use this forum.
PC Products	This is another low-intensity forum with very little activity—not much point to it!
Data Warehsing/Arch	This is an up and coming forum that is going to be of use to a large number of users who are developing data warehousing solutions.
3rd Party Products	This is an excellent place to look for help on the many different third-party products that are available for use with Sybase.

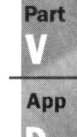

Part
V

App
D

continues

Table D.1 Continued

Section Name	Description
Sybase ICD	Sybase's InformationCONNECT Division (formerly the MDI Decisionware group) is here, and this is where you can get answers to high-end connectivity issues, including those about the gateways to the mainframe products.
Other	Well, what else can you say? This is for everything that doesn't fit in another section.
Syb Job Classifieds	Are you in the market to move to a different job? This is a great resource for opportunities for Sybase work.
Management's Ear	Want to be a grump? Drop a line to this section, and the management of Sybase will listen (you hope) and work to help you out.
Windows NT	This is a special section reserved for all the users of Sybase on Windows NT.
Client EBF Express	Are you sick of GPFs in Client Library? Send a message to the sysop of this forum to get access to this section, and download the latest patches and EBFs directly from Sybase.

N O T E Sybase's PrivateLine forum is available to all customers who pay for support from Sybase. To gain access, click the PrivateLine Registration button on the Sybase window (see Fig. D.3) and enter the information about your support contract. After doing so, you will be able to enter the PrivateLine forum. To be honest, there's not a whole lot more in the PrivateLine forum to read. The only difference is that you are guaranteed a response from a Sybase representative, which can be quite useful if you want to get the *official* policy on a particular issue. ■

Getting to Sybase on the Web

Sybase's presence on the Internet is really quite good. Their main Web page is accessible via all standard HTML-based browsers at **http://www.sybase.com**. Figure D.5 shows Sybase's home page on the Web (as of June 1996), as viewed through Microsoft's Internet Explorer 3.0.

On the Web, you can find a lot of good information. However, the Web sites are not quite as statically defined or organized as the CompuServe forum, so it is a little harder to navigate. Sybase's forum at **http://www.sybase.com** is mostly devoted to the Sybase line of products, including Sybase System XI, Sybase IQ, and Sybase MPP. For information about Sybase's developer tools, such as PowerBuilder 5.0, Watcom C++, Optima++, and S-Designor, go to Sybase's Powersoft division Web page at **http://www.powersoft.com**.

FIG. D.5
The Web is an excellent medium for displaying documentation and other static information, but CompuServe is still better for thread-based communication.

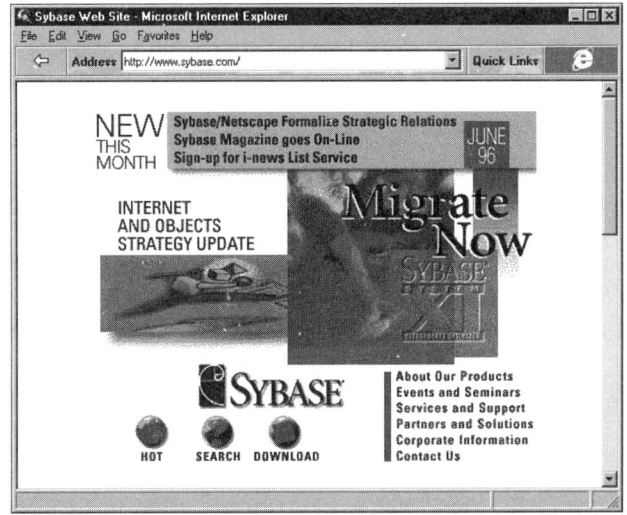

The following are some of the Sybase sites that you will probably want to check out:

- **http://www.sybase.com/Whatsnew/**—See this for an update of all the latest events at Sybase.

- **http://www.sybase.com/products/download.html**—Here you'll find a lot of demo versions of Sybase software that can be downloaded, including SQL Anywhere, web.sql, Visual Components, and Powersoft's S-Designor.

- **http://www-es1.sybase.com/**—This is a truly innovative online support offering. From here, you can log new cases with tech support and get updated information about the progress of your cases.

- **http://www.sybase.com/products/**—This page has a summary of *all of Sybase's products,* plus links to detailed white papers and other technical descriptions of the products.

- **http://www.sybase.com/Partners/**—Are you looking for products developed with, or developed to enhance, Sybase's tools and database servers? Go to this page to get access to Sybase's comprehensive partners database.

Part
V

App
D

Sybase Newsgroups

There's another way to contact Sybase users on the Internet—through the Sybase newsgroups. Newsgroups are a bit like CompuServe in that they attempt to logically group discussions based on threads of information between a lot of different people.

The best thing about newsgroups is that they are free (with the exception that you may have to pay for Internet access) and typically have a greater international participation, which means that you get a different perspective on questions asked and answered there.

Accessing a newsgroup requires two things:

- Access to the Internet, either through a dial-up connection or through a T1 or equivalent network-based connection.
- A news reader.

Assuming that you are on the Net, you need to choose a news reader. A good news reader is available free from Microsoft as part of their Internet Mail and News products. To use Internet News to connect to Sybase's newsgroup, perform the following steps:

1. Launch Internet News from the Start menu of Windows 95 or Windows NT, and Internet News will take you to the last newsgroup that you were active in (see Fig. D.6).

FIG. D.6

The Internet News user interface splits the main window into three sections: The icon bar on the left provides a simple way to run the common tasks, the upper part of the right side shows the threads, while the lower pane is a preview of the selected thread's content.

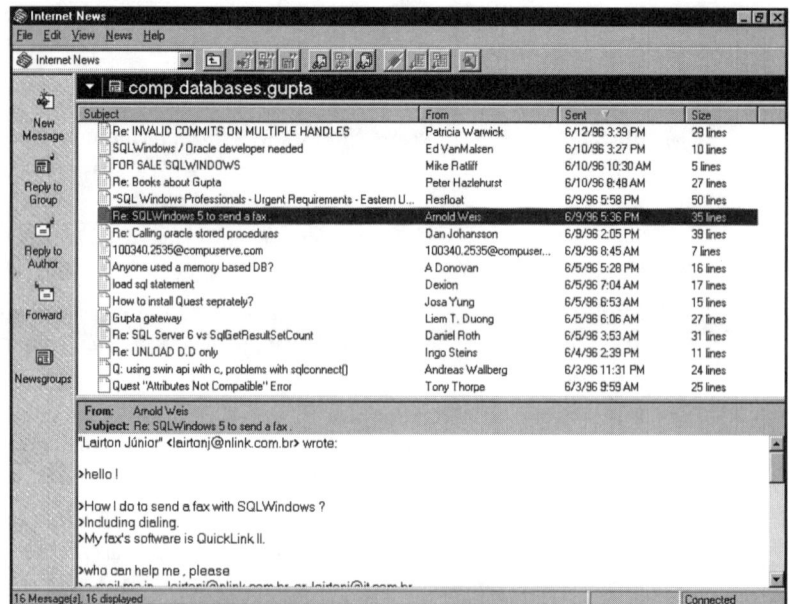

2. Choose <u>N</u>ews, Ne<u>w</u>sgroups, and enter **Sybase** in the field labeled Dis<u>p</u>lay Newsgroups Which Contain (see Fig. D.7).
3. Double-click the Sybase newsgroup and choose OK to continue.
4. Click the top of the newsgroup pane, and select the newly subscribed group (**comp.databases.sybase**) from the list to activate the group (see Fig. D.8). This should then display the threads that are available in the Sybase newsgroup.

FIG. D.7

The Newsgroups dialog box lists the available news servers on the left and the supported newsgroups that are searchable on the right.

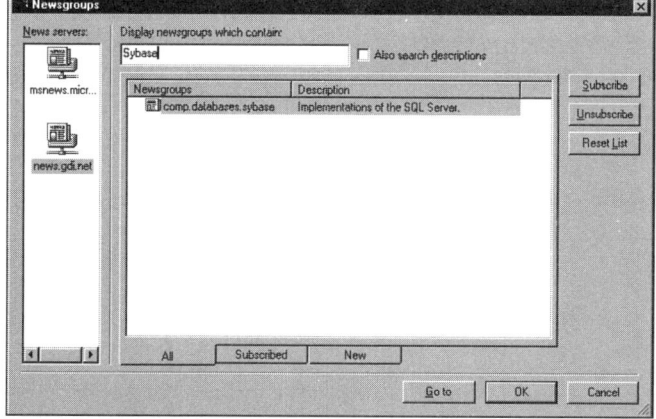

FIG. D.8

The Internet News new user interface takes a little getting used to, but is actually quite intuitive once you use it for a while. It's the new style that Microsoft will be adopting in all its products.

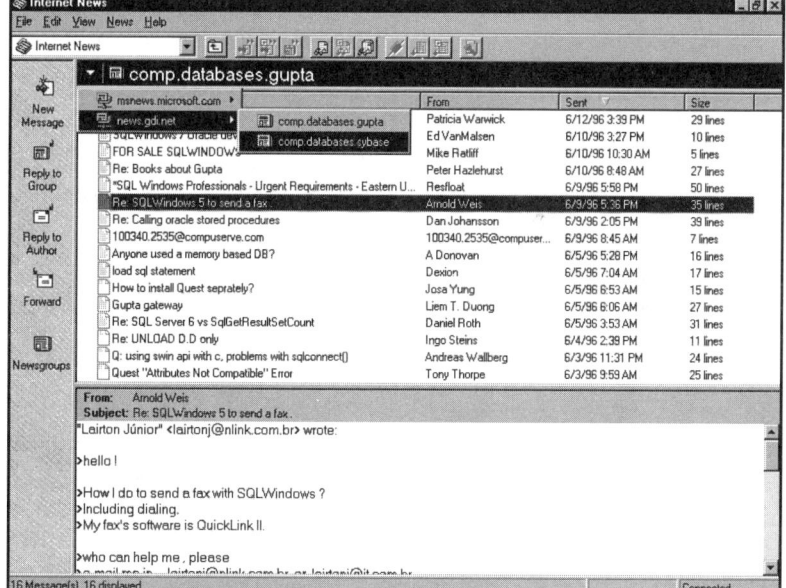

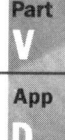

> **CAUTION**
>
> Newsgroups are never monitored for language content. It is quite common for someone to get "fired up" and flame someone with some rather off-color remarks. If you don't mind the risk of occasionally seeing some unpleasant commentary, then the newsgroup world is for you. If you have a problem with the seeming chaos of the newsgroups, use CompuServe as your communications method.

Sybase User Groups

Sybase has a very well organized (and company-sponsored) user group called ISUG (the International Sybase User's Group). Membership comes with a number of benefits, such as

- A free copy of Sybase SQL Anywhere;
- A subscription to the quarterly technical publication, the *Sybase Server;*
- A CompuServe packet with CD-ROM and "Sybase OpenLine" brochure;
- The Sybase's Answerbase CD-ROM with white papers and online answers to the most frequently asked technical questions;
- The *Sybase Education* catalogue of classes and "Self-Study Training Series" brochure (with discounts to ISUG members);
- Sybase education vouchers (six total) for a 20 percent discount on any of the Sybase CSP certification exams (DBA and IFD), available through Drake Prometric and Powersoft (three total) education vouchers;
- A free copy of *SYBASE SQL Server Troubleshooting Guide;*
- A free copy of *SYBASE SQL Server Error Messages* book;
- ISUG "Spring and Fall Enhancements" voting ballots and full reports;
- The *ISUG Membership Directory;*
- The "Sybase SQL Server XI Systems Table Diagram" foldout poster.

I highly recommend joining the user group and participating in the membership opportunities that it gives you. ISUG is a great community of developers and database administrators that will help you get access to information not normally available as an independent developer.

i.News—Sybase's Electronic Mailing Lists

i.News is Sybase's recently introduced news service, which is automatically distributed via electronic mail. E-mail distributed news update services are a very convenient way to have the latest information dropped off right at your "door" without any effort on your part. Sybase's e-mail services are slightly slanted toward marketing, but do serve a good role in keeping you informed of the latest information available on Sybase's product releases.

To subscribe to a mailing list, use your Web browser and go to **http://www.sybase.com/ programs/i.news**. At this site, you will be given the opportunity to subscribe to the following news services:

- **Sybase and Powersoft Web Site Update List**—This is a notification message that will inform you of any changes that occur at either of the Sybase or Powersoft Web sites. (inews-sybase-web-update and inews-powersoft-web-update)
- **Sybase, Powersoft, and Sybase, Inc. Corporate Press Release List**—These three news services deliver directly to your e-mail account all the latest press releases relating to the Sybase and Powersoft product lines and corporate Sybase information. (inews-sybase-press, inews-powersoft-press, and inews-inc-press)

- **System 11**—Get all the latest and greatest information on the Sybase System XI product line, including SQL Server, SQL Anywhere, Sybase IQ, and Sybase MPP. (inews-system11)

- **Enterprise CONNECT**—This is for information regarding Sybase's middleware technologies that connect you to different hardware and software solutions. You'll also receive information on such items as Open Client, Open Server, and Sybase's new Web enabling software web.sql. (inews-entconnect)

- **Data Warehouse**—This is a list service that gives you tips and tricks on how to be a successful data warehouse creator and manager. (inews-datawarehouse)

- **Internet**—This is a list service that brings you up-to-date with Sybase's offerings in the Internet arena that fall under the brand name web.works. This list service will give you solutions and information on hooking your database to the Internet and to your local intranet. (inews-web-works)

Summarizing the Areas of Sybase Support

There are a number of different avenues that you can take to get up-to-date information on the Sybase product line, including Sybase's electronic programs on CompuServe and the World Wide Web. If you need to ask a question on a particular topic, you have several ways of getting that question out into the public domain: CompuServe, the Web, and the Sybase-sponsored newsgroups.

Ultimately, it is really up to you to choose a service and mechanism for getting your questions answered. There are many options available; it's just a case of picking one and becoming familiar with it. ●

Part

V

App

D

Redundant Array of Inexpensive Disks (RAID)

*R*AID, which utilizes multiple physical devices for data storage, currently has six different implementations. The levels of RAID are continuously evolving as different companies seek to store data in more ingenious ways that give better performance and yet maintain good integrity. The levels (from 0–5) documented here represent the most commonly implemented RAID architectures that are generally accepted in the industry today. It is quite possible that other RAID levels exist, and they will no doubt be added to the common body of architecture as their marketplace acceptance encourages other users to try them. ■

RAID Level 0

RAID Level 0 is basic *data striping* across multiple physical devices. The striping refers to the fact that multiple drives are allocated for data as a group. The data is then placed across the drives evenly so that each drive has a portion of the data. Striping provides better performance than using single drives because multiple I/O threads from the operating system are allocated to servicing each drive. In addition, multiple physical reads and writes can occur simultaneously on the separate physical devices.

RAID Level 0 does not provide any fault tolerance and is purely a performance enhancement.

RAID Level 1

RAID Level 1 is *device mirroring*. As discussed in Chapter 5, "Understanding Databases, Devices, and Transaction Logs," mirroring provides an absolute duplication of the data on any physical device—on the mirror device. Mirroring can (depending on physical implementation) improve read performance if both drives are read in parallel and data is returned to the operating system in a single stream composed of the parallel reads. Mirroring generally imposes a slight performance cost when writing because two writes are done instead of one.

Mirroring is fault tolerant and media failure is generally handled by an automatic and complete switch over to the mirror device.

RAID Level 2

RAID Level 2 is an error-correcting algorithm that employs striping across multiple physical devices. It is more advanced than Level 0 because it uses error-correcting *parity* data that is striped across the devices, and copes with media failure on any particular device in the stripe set. However, the parity data consumes several disks and is quite inefficient as a storage mechanism.

RAID Level 2 is generally not used because it does not offer significant performance benefits over a straight mirroring implementation (Level 1).

RAID Level 3

RAID Level 3 is a different implementation of the striped, parity algorithm. It differs from Level 2 by utilizing only a single device in the stripe set for storing the parity data.

RAID Level 3 offers some performance benefits to reads and writes.

RAID Level 4

RAID Level 4 is the same as Level 3, except that it implements a larger block or segment storage size. This means that the basic unit that is being striped is large in size and generally gets better performance due to the more advanced modern physical devices that are able to read and write bigger blocks of data in a single I/O operation. RAID Level 4 stores the parity information on a separate device from the user data that is striped across multiple physical devices.

RAID Level 4 is an inefficient algorithm and is generally not used.

RAID Level 5

RAID Level 5 is currently the most commonly implemented RAID level. It is a striped implementation that stores parity information on the same striped drives. When an individual device fails, this enables the other devices in the stripe set to contain enough information to recover and keep processing. The parity information for any particular device is always stored on another device in the stripe set, ensuring that if media failure occurs on a particular device, its parity data is not affected.

RAID Level 5 uses the same large block algorithm as Level 4, although it is more efficient. Level 5 offers performance gains to reads and writes until media failure occurs. When media failure occurs, reads suffer because the information on the failed device must be constructed from the parity data stored on the other devices. ●

Part

V

App

E

Index

Licensing Agreement

Before using any of the software on this disc, you need to install the software you plan to use. If you have problems with this CD-ROM, please contact Macmillan Technical Support at (317) 581-3833. We can be reached by e-mail at **support@mcp.com** or by CompuServe at **GO QUEBOOKS**.

Read This before Opening Software

By opening this package, you are agreeing to be bound by the following:

This software is copyrighted and all rights are reserved by the publisher and its licensers. You are licensed to use this software on a single computer. You may copy the software for backup or archival purposes only. Making copies of the software for any other purpose is a violation of United States copyright laws. THIS SOFTWARE IS SOLD AS IS, WITHOUT WARRANTY OF ANY KIND, EITHER EXPRESSED OR IMPLIED, INCLUDING BUT NOT LIMITED TO THE IMPLIED WARRANTIES OF MERCHANTABILITY AND FITNESS FOR A PARTICULAR PURPOSE. Neither the publisher nor its dealers and distributors nor its licensers assume any liability for any alleged or actual damages arising from the use of this software. (Some states do not allow exclusion of implied warranties, so the exclusion may not apply to you.)

The entire contents of this disc and the compilation of the software are copyrighted and protected by United States copyright laws. The individual programs on the disc are copyrighted by the authors or owners of each program. Each program has its own use permissions and limitations. To use each program, you must follow the individual requirements and restrictions detailed for each. Do not use a program if you do not agree to follow its licensing agreement.